Relief in Greek, Roman, and Late Antique Art

The artistic category of relief has long dominated scholarly discussions of ancient Greco-Roman art for good reason: images in relief pervaded ancient visual culture from the rise of the Greek city-state through to the Christian era. They are witnessed in public and private contexts; terra-cotta, bronze, and stone media; techniques as varied as incision, modeling, or *repoussé*; and scales from the miniature to the monumental. Precisely because of the ubiquity and fluidity of ancient relief, the category as such has not been given full consideration in its own right, and many questions have remained under-theorized. Boasting an international cast of contributors, this volume addresses key questions about relief across the geographic and temporal scope of the ancient world, including how relief was conceptualized within antiquity, what role materials and techniques played in its creation, and what the relations were between relief media and their effects on viewers.

NATHANIEL B. JONES is Associate Professor of Art History and Archaeology at Washington University in St. Louis. He has written on painting, collecting practices, and visual narratives in Greco-Roman antiquity, and is the author of *Painting, Ethics, and Aesthetics in Rome* (2019).

MILETTE GAIFMAN is the Andrew Downey Orrick Professor of Classics and History of Art at Yale University. She is the author of *Aniconism in Greek Antiquity* (2012) and *The Art of Libation in Classical Athens* (2018), and served as the coeditor in chief of *The Art Bulletin* in 2020–2.

JAŚ ELSNER is Professor of Late Antique Art at the University of Oxford and Humfry Payne Senior Research fellow at Corpus Christi College, as well as being Visiting Professor of Art and Religion at the University of Chicago. He has worked on Greek and Roman art of all periods, and especially on sculpture and reliefs.

YALE CLASSICAL STUDIES

VOLUME XL

RELIEF IN GREEK, ROMAN, AND LATE ANTIQUE ART

EDITED FOR THE DEPARTMENT OF CLASSICS BY

NATHANIEL B. JONES
Washington University in St. Louis

MILETTE GAIFMAN
Yale University

JAŚ ELSNER
University of Oxford

CAMBRIDGE
UNIVERSITY PRESS

CAMBRIDGE
UNIVERSITY PRESS

Shaftesbury Road, Cambridge CB2 8EA, United Kingdom

One Liberty Plaza, 20th Floor, New York, NY 10006, USA

477 Williamstown Road, Port Melbourne, VIC 3207, Australia

314–321, 3rd Floor, Plot 3, Splendor Forum, Jasola District Centre,
New Delhi – 110025, India

103 Penang Road, #05–06/07, Visioncrest Commercial, Singapore 238467

Cambridge University Press is part of Cambridge University Press & Assessment,
a department of the University of Cambridge.

We share the University's mission to contribute to society through the pursuit of
education, learning and research at the highest international levels of excellence.

www.cambridge.org
Information on this title: www.cambridge.org/9781009505765

DOI: 10.1017/9781009505789

When citing this work, please include a reference to the DOI 10.1017/9781009505789

First published 2025

Printed in the United Kingdom by CPI Group Ltd, Croydon CR0 4YY

A catalogue record for this publication is available from the British Library

A Cataloging-in-Publication data record for this book is available from the Library of Congress

ISBN 978-1-009-50576-5 Hardback

To Sara, David, and Silvia

Contents

Figures

Contributors

Nicola Barham is Assistant Professor of Ancient Art in the Department of Art History at the University of Michigan and Assistant Curator at the Kelsey Museum of Archaeology. Her work focuses on the emic aesthetic conceptualization of ancient visual works (particularly where these ancient approaches to the visual subvert our received hierarchies of classical art). She has a special interest in the overlooked biographies of visual works from the ancient Middle East. Professor Barham has received grants for her research from the Center for Advanced Study in the Visual Arts, the Mellon Foundation, the Getty Foundation, and the American Council of Learned Societies.

Nikolaus Dietrich is Professor of Classical Archaeology at Heidelberg, and was previously based at the Humboldt University of Berlin. His research primarily investigates Greco-Roman art, especially vase painting and sculpture, and occasionally Roman wall painting and sarcophagi. Special interests include spatiality in/of images, ornament, material writing, object-oriented approaches to images, and questions of methodology. He is the author of *Bild ohne Raum? Bäume und Felsen in der attischen Vasenmalerei des 6. und 5. Jahrhunderts v. Chr.* (2010), and *Das Attribut als Problem: Eine bildwissenschaftliche Untersuchung zur griechischen Kunst* (2018), coauthor (with J. Fouquet and C. Reinhardt) of *Schreiben auf statuarischen Monumenten* (2020), and coeditor (with M. Squire) of *Ornament and Figure in Graeco-Roman Art: Rethinking Visual Ontologies in Classical Antiquity* (2018), and (together with J. Fouquet) of *Image, Text, Stone: Intermedial Perspectives on Graeco-Roman Sculpture* (2022).

Jaś Elsner is Professor of Late Antique Art and Humfry Payne Senior Research Fellow at Corpus Christi College Oxford, as well as being Visiting Professor of Art and Religion at the University of Chicago. He has worked on Greek and Roman art of all periods, and especially on sculpture and reliefs.

Seth Estrin is Assistant Professor in the Department of History of Art and Architecture at Harvard University, where he specializes in the art, archaeology, and visual culture of ancient Greece. He is the author of *Grief Made Marble: Funerary Sculpture in Classical Athens* (2023) and articles on Archaic funerary sculpture which have appeared in *Classical Antiquity* and *The Art Bulletin*.

Milette Gaifman is the Andrew Downey Orrick Professor of Classics and History of Art at Yale University. A scholar of ancient art and archaeology, her research interests include the interaction between visual culture and religion, the reception of Greek art in later periods, and the historiography of the academic disciplines of art history and classics. She is the author of *Aniconism in Greek Antiquity* (2012) and *The Art of Libation in Classical Athens* (2018) as well as coeditor of "Exploring Aniconism," thematic issue of *Religion* 47 (2017), and "The Embodied Object in Classical Antiquity," special issue of *Art History* (June 2018). She also served as the coeditor in chief of *The Art Bulletin* in 2020–2.

Guy Hedreen, the Amos Lawrence Professor of Art, Williams College, writes and teaches about ancient Greek art and culture and their modern interpretation. He has published three books: *Silens in Attic Black-Figure Vase-Painting: Myth and Performance* (1992), *Capturing Troy: The Narrative Functions of Landscape in Archaic and Early Classical Greek Art* (2001), and *The Image of the Artist: Art, Poetry, and Subjectivity* (2016). He is also the editor of the anthology *Material World: The Intersection of Art, Science, and Nature in Ancient Literature and Its Renaissance Reception* (2021). He is currently completing a book entitled *Unnatural History: Interspecies Beings in Greek Art and Intellectual Culture* and coediting the anthology *Phenomenology and the Painted Vase*.

Ashley Elizabeth Jones is Associate Professor of Art History at the University of Florida. Her research focuses on the art of the late antique Roman world, broadly conceived, and investigates questions of representation, materiality, the power of images, and the domain of the wearable. She is the author of *Lord, Protect the Wearer: The Imperial Portrait and Numismatic Jewelry, 220–650*, forthcoming with Brill. Her research has been supported by the Center for Advanced Study in the Visual Arts and the Kunsthistorisches Institut, Florence.

Nathaniel B. Jones is Associate Professor of Art History and Archaeology at Washington University in St. Louis. He has written on painting, collecting practices, and visual narratives in Greco-Roman antiquity and is the author of *Painting, Ethics, and Aesthetics in Rome*, published by Cambridge University Press in 2019.

Carolyn M. Laferrière is the associate curator of ancient Mediterranean art at the Princeton University Art Museum. She is the author of *Divine Music in Archaic and Classical Greek Art: Seeing the Songs of the Gods* (2024), and the associate editor for *Greek and Roman Musical Studies*.

Caspar Meyer is Professor of Classical Archaeology and Material Culture at the Bard Graduate Center in New York. His research focuses on the cultural dynamics of craft production in the Greek city-states of the Aegean and among the mobile pastoralists of Eurasia. Another area of his interest is the history of the instruments and media which archaeologists have developed to aid the transformation of artifacts into written explanations. He previously taught at Birkbeck College, University of London, and held research fellowships at the Getty Research Institute in Los Angeles and the Centre Louis Gernet in Paris. He is editor of *West 86th: A Journal of Decorative Arts, Design History, and Material Culture*.

Chris Pellettieri is a stone carver specializing in freehand sculpture, decorative design, portraiture, casting, and lettering. He started his career as a stonemason in an apprenticeship program at the Cathedral of St. John the Divine in New York City's Upper West Side and later trained in Italian techniques of sculpture and casting, including pointing method and portraiture, at Artida Atelier in New York. For the past thirty years, he has run a successful stone-carving business doing commissions for public and private clients. His work can be found in the collections of the Museum of Arts and Design and the American Folk Art Museum. He recently founded the Pellettieri Stonecarvers' Academy, a nonprofit organization dedicated to offering training in traditional carving techniques and promoting awareness and appreciation of stone carving.

Verity J. Platt is Professor of Classics and History of Art at Cornell University, where she also cocurates the university's cast collection. She is the author of *Facing the Gods: Epiphany and Representation in Graeco-Roman Art, Literature and Religion* (2011) and *Epistemic Objects: Making and Mediating Classical Art and Text* (forthcoming), as well as several essays on Pliny the Elder's *Natural History*.

Jennifer Trimble is Associate Professor of Classics at Stanford University, with interests in Roman portraiture, gender, the visual culture of Roman slavery, comparative urbanism, and ancient mapping. Trimble was codirector of the IRC-Oxford-Stanford excavations in the Roman Forum, which focused on interactions of commercial, religious, and monumental space. She codirected Stanford's Digital Forma Urbis Romae Project, a collaboration between computer scientists and archaeologists to help reassemble a fragmentary ancient map of the city of Rome. Her book *Women and Visual Replication in Roman Imperial Art and Culture* (2011) explored the role of visual sameness in constructing public identity and in articulating empire and place. Her current book project, *Seeing Roman Slaves*, is about the intersections of Roman visual culture and Roman slavery. In 2020–2, Trimble served as editor in chief of the *Journal of Roman Archaeology*.

Acknowledgments

Many of the chapters in this volume grew out of papers given at a gathering of the New Antiquity group at Yale University in May 2019. We are grateful to those who co-organized that occasion, Richard Neer, Verity Platt, and Michael Squire, and to the participants who made it a stimulating and memorable event: Benjamin Anderson, Nathan Arrington, Nicola Barham, Patrick Crowley, Francesco de Angelis, Nikolaus Dietrich, Seth Estrin, Carolyn Laferrière, Caspar Meyer, Richard Teverson, and Jennifer Trimble, as well as to Guy Hedreen and Ashley Jones, who generously added their contributions while the volume was in development. Participants in the event enjoyed the hospitality of the Yale Center for British Art and the Yale University Art Gallery, which facilitated an eye-opening session in its collections. Our conversations benefited from the attendance of members of the Yale community, especially Lisa Brody, Susan Matheson, and the late Jerome J. Pollitt and Diana E. E. Kleiner.

Producing this volume would not have been possible without the generous help of Kirk Freudenburg, Emily Greenwood, and Chris Kraus, current and former chairs of Yale University's Department of Classics, which cosponsored the event and supported this publication. We also extend our gratitude to Tim Barringer, former chair of the Department of the History of Art at Yale, which also cosponsored the event.

Many thanks to the anonymous readers for their insightful comments, and to Michael Sharp and Katie Idle at Cambridge University Press for facilitating the publication of this work.

We are indebted to Nick Geller, who assisted us in all editorial matters, improved earlier versions, and made the final submission to the Press a breeze.

This volume brings into sharp relief the new ways in which the field of ancient art is constantly evolving. It is a pleasure to have the opportunity to share these insights with the broad readership of Yale Classical Studies.

Abbreviations

AB = Austin, C. and Bastianini, G. *Posidippi Pellaei quae supersunt omnia.* Milan: LED.

ABL = Haspels, C. H. E. (1936). *Attic Black-Figure Lekythoi.* Paris: Boccard.

ABV = Beazley, J. D. (1956). *Attic Black-Figure Vase-Painters.* Oxford: Clarendon Press.

*ARV*² = Beazley, J. D. (1963). *Attic Red-Figure Vase-Painters.* 2nd ed. Oxford: Clarendon Press.

BAPD = Beazley Archive Pottery Database (www.carc.ox.ac.uk/carc/pottery).

CIL = Mommsen, T., et al., eds. (1893–). *Corpus Inscriptionum Latinarum.* Berlin: Königlich Preussische Akademie der Wissenschaften zu Berlin.

DNO = Kansteiner, S., et al., eds. (2014). *Der neue Overbeck: Die antiken Schriftquellen zu den bildenden Künsten der Griechen.* 5 vols. Berlin: De Gruyter.

IG I² = von Gaertringen, F. H., ed. (1924). *Inscriptiones Graecae.* Vol. 1, *Inscriptiones Atticae Euclidis anno anteriores.* 2nd ed. Berlin: De Gruyter.

IG I³ = Lewis, D., and Jeffery, L., eds. (1981–94). *Inscriptiones Graecae.* Vol. 1, *Inscriptiones Atticae Euclidis anno anteriores.* 3rd ed. Berlin: De Gruyter.

IG II² = Kirchner, J., ed. (1913–40). *Inscriptiones Graecae.* Vols. 2–3, *Inscriptiones Atticae Euclidis anno posteriores.* 2nd ed. Berlin: De Gruyter.

IG XI.2 = Durrbach, F. ed. (1912). *Inscriptiones Graecae.* Vol. 11, *Inscriptiones Deli.* Pt. 2, Nos. 105–289. Berlin: De Gruyter.

Inscriptions de Délos = Durrbach, F., ed. (1923–37). *Inscriptions de Délos.* Paris: Librairie Ancienne Honore Champion.

LSJ = Liddell, H. G., and Scott, R. (1925–40). *Greek–English Lexicon.* 9th ed., rev. H. Stuart Jones. Oxford: Clarendon Press.

Lewis and Short = Lewis, C. T., and Short, C. (1879). *A Latin Dictionary.* Oxford: Clarendon Press.

LTUR = Steinby, M. ed. (1993–2000). *Lexicon Topographicum Urbis Romae.* 6 vols. Rome. Quasar.

NIV = (2011). Holy Bible, New International Version. Palmer Lake, CO: Biblica.

OED = (1884–). *Oxford English Dictionary*. Oxford: Oxford University Press.

OLD = (1968–82). *Oxford Latin Dictionary*. Oxford: Oxford University Press.

PGM = Preisendanz, K., and Henrich, A., eds. (1974). *Papyri graecae magicae: Die griechischen Zauberpapyri*. 2nd ed. Stuttgart: Teubner.

PPM = Caratelli, G. P., and Baldassare I., eds. (1990–2003). *Pompei: Pitture e mosaici*, 11 vols. Rome: Istituto della Enciclopedia Italiana.

RIC X = Carson, R. A. G., Kent, J. P. C., and Burnett, A. M., eds. (1994). *Roman Imperial Coinage*. Vol. 10. London: Spink.

SEG = (1983–2023). *Supplementum Epigraphicum Graecum*. Leiden: Brill.

SVF = von Arnim, H. (1903–). *Stoicorum Veterum Fragmenta*. Leipzig: Teubner.

W.-I. = Winnington-Ingram, R. P. (1936). *Mode in Ancient Greek Music*. Cambridge: Cambridge University Press.

West = West, M. L. (1989–92). *Iambi et elegi Graeci ante Alexandrum cantati*. Oxford: Oxford University Press.

Introduction

NATHANIEL B. JONES, MILETTE GAIFMAN, AND JAŚ ELSNER

Witnessed in iconic examples of high-prestige art such as the Parthenon Frieze, the Gemma Augustea, or the Arch of Constantine, ancient relief cut across all kinds of contexts, media, techniques, and scales. It could appear in private households, on public architecture, or within funerary spaces, executed in terra-cotta, bronze, or stone, made by incision, modeling, or repoussé, from the miniature to the monumental. As the chapters in this volume attest, images in relief pervaded practically every aspect of ancient visual culture from the rise of the Greek city-state through to the Christian era.

Yet, in today's everyday language, when we use the word "relief," we are much less likely to be referring to an artistic phenomenon than to a fiscal or bodily one: Medicines offer relief from headache or indigestion, and state-run programs offer relief from student debt. Both uses depend on a fundamental sense of lifting a burden up and away; in the case of the body, the act of lifting is a powerful and deep-seated metaphor. A sense of alleviation from distress is already built into the Latin term *relevare*,[1] with the same idea attested in English by the late fourteenth century.[2] This sense of relief has both physical and psychological connotations: It can indicate the cessation of not only corporeal pain but anxiety or other pent-up emotions. In the various versions of the so-called relief theories of humor espoused by figures as varied as Herbert Spencer, John Dewey, and Sigmund Freud, what causes laughter is the release of nervous energy that has built up in the body through anger, anxiety, expectation, or the unconscious repression of other emotions.[3] The physiological bases of these theories have long been discredited, but in their metaphorical application of the idea of relief, they correspond to ways of thinking and talking about the body that many people today might still recognize.

This is all to say, although "relief" is an extremely familiar term, one that frequently appears in everyday conversation, even its most common uses are slippery, inevitably sliding among discourses and carrying both literal

[1] *OLD*, s.v. relevo, 2–3. [2] *OED*, s.v. relief, n.2.2.
[3] For discussion, see esp. Morreall 2009; cf. Spencer 1860; Dewey 1894; Freud 1974.

and metaphorical meanings. The situation is no different in the more specialized arena of the visual arts. Both a literal and metaphorical sense of lifting up and away from a flat surface is already present in the earliest uses of the term "relief" in Italian artistic treatises of the late fourteenth and fifteenth centuries.[4] In Cenino Cenini's handbook of art, written around 1400, the term *rilievo* serves a dual function. It means firstly the application of gesso to a surface in order to create a physical protrusion, what we would now call a genuine relief sculpture, and secondly an optical effect in painting, the use of light and shadows to create virtual volumes that seem *as though* they were raised from a surface but that are in fact two-dimensional.[5]

Relief in early modern Italy, at least the kind discussed in contemporary art writing, is thus both sculptural and pictorial. Lorenzo Ghiberti referred to his own Gates of Paradise panels, which he was commissioned to design in 1425, as narratives (*istorie*) in low relief (*pochissimo rilievo*); these same objects offer remarkable variation in the physical and pictorial depth of relief, with figures set within persuasive and all-encompassing environments and particularly complex early experiments in perspectival construction.[6] In his treatise on painting, Leon Batista Alberti would especially emphasize the metaphorical sense of *rilievo* as a virtual lifting up from a surface.[7] The idea of *rilievo* plays a fundamentally intermedial and intermediary role in *paragone* debates throughout the early modern period, oscillating between the real presence of sculpture and the as-if worlds of painting.[8] Within this critical art discourse, relief is an inherently unfixed and unstable concept, vacillating on the one hand between painting and sculpture in the round, and on the other between the brute facts of physical reality and the virtuality of fiction. In other words, one may say that relief offered the Renaissance artist and art theorist the opportunity to have his cake and eat it too. Arguably, what distinguishes relief in this sense is as much a matter of phenomenological effect as it is one of technique, material, facture, or style.[9]

[4] On this, see in particular the work of Christopher Lakey in Lakey 2018: esp. 151–70; cf. Freedman 1989; Ostrow 2004.

[5] Lakey 2018: 160–2, citing Cennini 2003: 151 for the former sense of the term and Cennini 2003: 67–8 for the latter.

[6] Lakey 2018: 166–8, citing Ghiberti 1998: 94–5.

[7] Henrike Lange described this as the "relief effect"; see Lange 2020a, 2020b, 2023. See also Lakey 2018: 168–9; cf. Alberti 1950.

[8] On this issue, see esp. Steven Ostrow's argument in Ostrow 2004.

[9] This is the argument put forth by David Summers; see Summers 2003: 448–52.

We raise these points here both to highlight the difficulty in pinning down any one sense of the term "relief" and to acknowledge that it is a historically contingent concept. We wish to acknowledge, moreover, that the current idea of *rilievo*/relief is rooted in specific historical circumstances and is concerned with specific types of art making; it privileges the kinds of relief sculpture most highly esteemed in Italian Renaissance art-theoretical discourse – namely carved marble and cast metal – especially relief engaged in architecture that featured figures standing out against an essentially flat, planar ground that is at once pictorial and physical. By contrast, the same relief techniques applied to objects that offer less of a figure–ground relationship, and that are often more engaged with the living human body, such as tableware or jewelry, tend to fall out of the discourse of the high arts of the early modern period. Yet it seems hard to deny that the raised figures on a metal vessel such as the Derveni krater, discussed at further length later in this introduction, are executed as much in relief as those on Ghiberti's Gates of Paradise.

Here ancient concepts may help us fill in the gaps left by modern ones. No comprehensive idea of relief – whether understood as mode(s) of artistic production or as effect of surface elaboration – existed in Greco-Roman antiquity. And no single term could cover the creation of carved marble or precious stones, cast bronze or silver, hand modeled or mold-made terracotta, or coins struck in dies. Instead, as Verity Platt's contribution to this volume (Chapter 1) highlights, what we find are complementary and interlocking ideas, including the typology of making in molds or taking impressions, the craft of chasing in metal or working in terra-cotta, and the optics of virtual space and surface texture, both metaphorical and real. Antiquity provides us with a constellation of concepts that circle around and highlight the diversity of techniques, media, and optics that relief adumbrates.

When we now think of ancient relief, however, we are likely to gravitate toward monumental, architecturally engaged stone sculpture. There are clear historiographic reasons for this affinity.[10] As art history developed as a formal academic discipline in modern institutional and university settings, the idea of relief became a particularly important one in the study of ancient art, in no small part because both Greek temples and Roman state monuments yielded high-quality reliefs, giving scholars a corpus of

[10] Koortbojian 2023, which elucidates in detail the historiography of the treatment of space in ancient relief from the mid nineteenth to the mid twentieth centuries, appeared only as this book was going into production. It promises to serve as an invaluable resource on the topic, and we refer readers there for in-depth treatment of many of the authors discussed in this introduction.

undoubted "originals" to evaluate and compare. The arrival in London of the sculptures from the Temple of Apollo at Bassai and, most famously, the Parthenon sculptures in the early nineteenth century had a well-known effect on both contemporary tastes and art theory.[11] Similarly, the first appearance in Berlin in 1879 of the monumental architecture and vast frieze of the Great Altar at Pergamon coincided with, and indeed partially sparked, a moment of remarkable fertility in art-historical canonization and theorization.[12] Particularly striking about this moment is the fact that an ancient monument would wield such influence far outside the group of scholars specializing in the art of antiquity. For not only classical archaeologists like Alexander Conze and Heinrich Brunn but also artists like Adolf Hildebrand and historians of later periods of art such as Heinrich Wölfflin, the Pergamon reliefs provided a jumping-off point for substantial disciplinary reevaluations. Such reevaluations were permissible, as Alina Payne points out, because the Pergamon sculptures were so obviously different from the established canon of Greek art, while being indisputably masterpieces of ancient carving.[13]

For Conze and Brunn, the emotive, expressive themes and the optically adept, "painterly" style of the Altar's gigantomachy frieze prompted them to rethink both the restrictions on content and the insistence on medium specificity that had been inherited from eighteenth-century figures like Johann Joachim Winckelmann and Gotthold Ephraim Lessing.[14] Beyond the field of ancient archaeology, Hildebrand would argue that a relief-like visual effect (which, as Nikolaus Dietrich demonstrates in Chapter 5 of this volume, is also implicitly photographic) could be a model for sculpture more generally.[15] Wölfflin would carry the idea of the "painterliness" of reliefs like those from Pergamon into the early modern period as a defining feature of the Baroque, one as applicable, ultimately, to architecture as to any other artistic form.[16] The Pergamon marbles not only allowed scholars to expand upon the purpose of relief sculpture in architectural settings and to debate the variously "painterly," "sculptural," and "architectonic" functions of relief; they provoked a rethinking of period styles, such as Classical/Hellenistic or Renaissance/Baroque, and of the critical judgments typically associated with those styles.[17]

[11] St. Clair 1998; cf. Marvin 2008: 133–7.

[12] On this issue, see esp. the important contributions of Alina Payne in Payne 2008, 2011; cf. Marchand 1996: 92–103; Gossman 2006; Koortbojian 2023.

[13] Payne 2008. [14] Conze 1882; Brunn 1884.

[15] Hildebrand 1893, 1994; cf. Barasch 1998: 133–42; Rankin and Schneider 2020: esp. 306–10, with bibliography.

[16] Wölfflin 1888, 1915. [17] Payne 2008, 2011.

Around the same time, relief was also playing a key role in attempts to define and redeem Roman and late antique art, especially prominently in the work of Franz Wickhoff and Alois Riegl, but also in the work of scholars who are less well known among Anglophone archaeologists and ancient art historians, such as Adolph Philippi and Edmond Courbaud.[18] For Wickhoff and Riegl, the attempt to determine what constituted Roman art, and what it had contributed to the history of European art writ large, hinged especially on what was unique about monumental Roman relief sculpture. For Wickhoff, both the impressionistic illusionism of Roman relief and its habit of driving narrative time forward by repeating figures within a single composition provided the historical matrix out of which Christian art would develop. For Riegl, reliefs such as those on the Arch of Constantine in Rome offered the opportunity to think through broad, epochal shifts in what he called *Kunstwollen*, or artistic volition, from a primarily tactile, or haptic, mode to a primarily optical one.[19] The story of Roman art, for Riegl, both performs a kind of Hegelian process of dematerialization and sets the stage for the optical experiments of Renaissance and modern art. We should note here that despite the prominence of monumental relief, intermediality was key to both projects. Wickhoff's reliefs are compared not only to manuscript illumination but to Baroque painting, while Riegl's theory of *Kunstwollen* expressly adumbrated not only the other figurative arts but architecture and decorative art as well.[20] In this sense, the status of relief as an intermediary medium seems to have been a key aspect of its importance to both authors.[21] This is all to say, for scholars of both Greek and Roman art around the turn of the twentieth century, while relief was at the core of the art-historical systems they were building, it seems to have played almost as important a role for its connections to what it was not – whether sculpture, painting, architecture, or the body – as for what it was.

Yet for all the undoubted significance of relief sculpture in this formative phase of the disciplines of classical archaeology and art history, many

18 Philippi 1872; Wickhoff and Hartel 1895; Courbaud 1899; Riegl 1901. For discussion of the broader historiographic tradition, see Brendel 1953; Koeppel 1982; Koortbojian 2023.

19 For modern accounts of *Kunstwollen*, see Olin 1992: 71–2, 129–53; Iversen 1993: 6–16, 71–3, 76–83, 96–112; Elsner 2006.

20 As Wood 2004 discusses, Riegl examined metalwork not only in the last chapter of the 1901 publication of *Spätrömische Kunstindustrie* but also in a second volume posthumously published in 1923.

21 The mediating function of Roman relief is visible in any number of other arenas, including the discussions that continue to the present day over the role of painting in the development of Roman historical commemoration, stretching from Philippi 1872 and Courbaud 1899 to e.g. Holliday 2002 and Hölscher 2004.

broader questions of relief as such have remained surprisingly undertheorized. For instance, how was relief conceptualized within antiquity itself? What are the consequences of the choice of materials and techniques in the creation of imagery in relief? How do various types of relief compare with respect to their visual impact? Ancient texts and artifacts speak to the pertinence of these issues in our current conceptualization of relief.

*

Take for instance the brilliantly provocative apology for painting, written at some point in the early third century CE, in which the Athenian sophist and historian Philostratus justifies the versatility of the medium he extols by contrasting it with a range of kinds of plastic art:

> Now, there are many forms of *plastike*: molding itself, mimesis in bronze, those who carve white or Parian stone, ivory, and by Zeus sculptural engraving. Painting, however, is composed from colours, yet it does not accomplish only this, but it also displays more ingenuity from this singular quality than the other kind of craftsmanship does from many.[22]

Like all such rhetorical justifications, this can be turned on its head. While painting – almost always tied to the flat surface, even in wall and ceiling decorations as well as in panels – needs all the ingenuity of trompe l'oeil and other spatial trickery in its use of colors, *plastike* offers an extraordinary range of media that themselves elicit multiplicities of techniques and methods to render visual images effective. By molding, Philostratus means fashioning objects from a mass of stucco or clay; by mimesis in bronze (and he might have named many other metals), he means both the hammering of metal and its casting (very different ways of proceeding with radically different effects); by the carving of stone and ivory (he might have added wood), he implies forms of sculpture that remove elements from the starting material block to bring a work of art to life – very different in the fine miniature of ivory from the grand scale of marble; and by engraving, he means all kinds of incision work, including the extraordinarily fine cutting

[22] Philostr. *Imag.* 1.Proem.2. Translated by M. Squire and J. Elsner. Philostratus' terminology of ζωγραφία and πλαστική as an antithetical pair (translatable as "painting" and "plastic art") underlies a vast strand of conceptual writing in the theory of art in its formative modern moment in the early twentieth century – including Heinrich Wölfflin's "malerisch" and "plastisch," which are so central to the concepts of his *Principles of Art History* (where "plastisch" is a synonym for "linear" at Wölfflin 1915: 20) and Erwin Panofsky's habilitation thesis of 1920, lost thereafter and only rediscovered in 2012, translated into English in 2020 (see e.g. Panofsky 2020: ix for the use of "malerisch" as "pictorial" in contrast to "plastisch" as "three-dimensional"), as well as in his famous essay "On the Relationship of Art History and Art Theory" (see e.g. Panofsky 1998, 2:1041–2, 1048, 1051).

of gems and tablets on a minuscule scale, perhaps with a magnifying glass. The fact that Philostratus chooses his examples with care to indicate different types and ways of creating relief signals a clear awareness and conceptualization within the Greco-Roman world of the diversity of options for the facture of three-dimensional rather than flat art. It is that range that gives life, variety, and immense "ingenuity" when we speak of imagery in relief more specifically.

In a passage from his *Life of Apollonius*, the same Philostratus extols a series of bronze panels showing the deeds of Alexander and Porus that are nailed into the walls of a temple in Taxila on the edge of ancient India:

> On them, in brass, silver, gold and dark bronze, there are depicted elephants, horses, soldiers, helmets and shields, with spears, javelins and swords all in iron. Just as they say of a famous painting, for example one by Zeuxis, Polygnotus or Euphranor that artists like shadow, verisimilitude and perspective, the same effects, so they say, are visible here, and the materials blended like colours.[23]

Here, in virtuoso contradiction of the argument in the *Imagines*, the multiplicity of metallic materials, each with its own hue, is compared with and indeed made to rival the coloristic and imitative effects of the best painting by a clutch of the most famous painters of the fifth and fourth centuries BCE. While both the paintings of the *Imagines* and the metal tablets of the *Life of Apollonius* are almost certainly fictions, the point is that the plastic workings of relief are both immensely diverse and – depending on the position you choose to adopt – as effective as the finest naturalistic paintings in their workings and impact.

The breadth and vivacity of imagery in relief is witnessed in a trio of large vessels that deploy relief in very diverse media and temporal moments within antiquity, but across a three-dimensional curving surface rather than the more typically flat plane. These containers, whose presence in their viewer's space is voluminous and effectively sculptural, highlight the place of relief between the two-dimensional ground of flatness and the volumetric force of three dimensions. Our objects come from different periods in the art history of the Greek and Roman worlds – one from the dawn of Archaic art in the early seventh century BCE, one from the last moments of Classical art in the fourth century BCE, and one from the early Roman Empire in the first century CE. In each case, the technical methods required and chosen to produce the object's final form in part determines

[23] Philostr. *VA* 2.20.2. Translated by C. P. Jones 2005, 177.

the ways relief is used to create its visual argument and definition. One of the effects of looking at vessels – objects designed to be containers and to respond directly (whether in actuality or through imagination) to the embodied handling of viewers – is that there is potential play between the voluminous form of the object, containing space as well as consisting in space, and the relief decoration on its body.[24]

In 1961, a large pithos of gritty clay with a fine slip covering, measuring 1.339 m in height and 0.733 m in maximum diameter, was excavated in Mykonos (Fig. I.1).[25] Decorated in low-relief figures on the front but not on the back or the lower third, this amphora was probably intended for display against a wall, and when it was found, it had certainly acquired a funerary function in that it contained bones.[26] The reliefs were freely modeled (not made from molds) in rather finer clay than that of the core and applied to the surface of the vessel while it was leather-hard. Much of the modeling appears to have been done after the clay for the reliefs was applied onto the pot, with the use of blades, points, stamps, punches, and other tools. Some figures were outlined by incision into the vessel's surface, and others were not.[27] The object belongs to a rich Archaic tradition of such pithoi, and particularly a class known as the Tenian-Boeotian group since many examples have been found in Tenos (near Mykonos) and Boeotia, though they were clearly made across the Cyclades and on the mainland.[28] It is one of the largest and finest of these vessels, dating probably to the second quarter of the seventh century BCE.[29]

The pot has been of galvanizing interest because its imagery shows one of the earliest representations of the Trojan Horse, in pride of place at the neck of the pithos at the front and larger than any other of its images, and then a series of war scenes presumably depicting episodes from the sack of Troy in a range of smaller pictorial panels (often described as "metopes") arranged in three tiers separated by bands of three incised lines. Our interest here is not in issues of narrativity or the relation of visual to literary narratives, as most frequently addressed in the scholarship, except insofar as they relate to relief.[30] But it is worth noting that the "metope" model of discrete scenes adopts an episodic strategy of storytelling that eschews both continuous narrative and any

[24] On some of the issues, see Wolf 2016, 2019; Brittenham 2019.

[25] Archaeological Museum of Mykonos, 2240. See Ervin 1963, with dimensions at 38–9.

[26] Ervin 1963: 41. Not all pithoi appear to have been used for burial, and it is conceivable that this was a secondary use for the Mykonos pithos; see esp. Ebbinghaus 2005: 52–9.

[27] See Ervin 1963: 41–5.

[28] See Schäfer 1957: 67–90; Ervin Caskey 1976: 28–9.

[29] Ervin Caskey 1976: 28–9.

[30] See e.g. Osborne 1998: 53–7; Snodgrass 1998: 88–90; Stansbury-O'Donnell 1999: 139–42; Ebbinghaus 2005: 59–68; Giuliani 2013: 57–70.

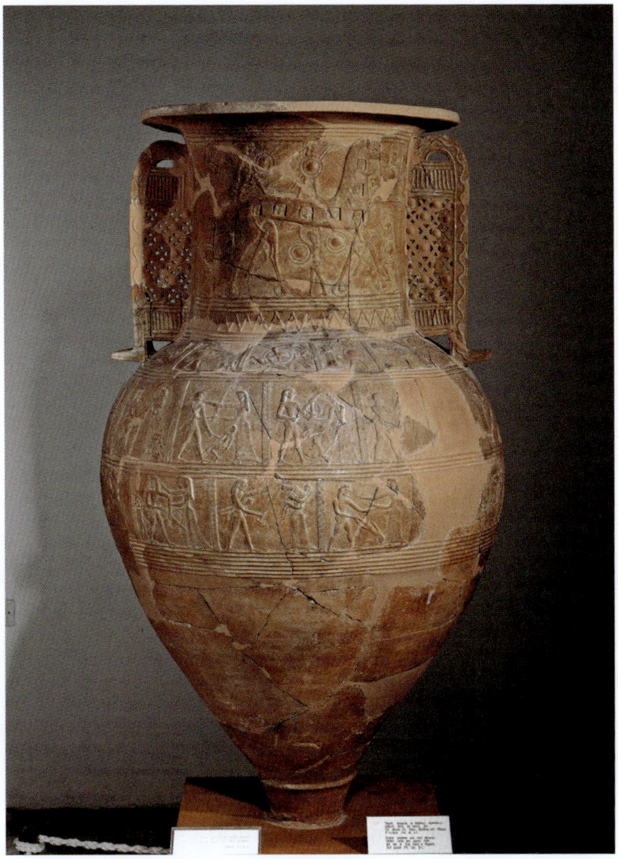

Fig. I.1 Relief pithos from Mykonos, second quarter of the seventh century BCE. Archaeological Museum of Mykonos, 2240 (White Images/Scala/Art Resource, NY).

expansive single conflation of the depicted themes. Likewise, despite the voluminous nature of the relief jar, as a kind of shaped egg tapered at the bottom and cut off at the top, the images insist on a horizontal groundline, responding to the needs of an embodied viewer whose feet are on the ground observing the pithos' surface.

The pot's most striking scene is the wonderful depiction on the neck of the Trojan Horse on wheels. On the horse's body, there are seven windows, cut out of the thickness of the clay used to make the body and so emphasizing its nature as applied relief. Within each of these a warrior's head faces forward in profile, while four – at the top of the horse's neck, at its foreleg, and its fore-belly, as well as at its rear – are handing down weapons (respectively, a plumed helmet, a sword, a shield, and a sword). Seven warriors are depicted outside the horse – whether the same seven at a later moment, having descended from their hiding place, or different ones, we cannot tell – but scholars largely agree that they are likely to be Greeks who are part of the attacking party rather than Trojans in resistance.[31] The emphasis on a container of men, the horse, is a brilliantly self-reflective commentary on the vessel's own function as a container – whether of the remains of a dead person by intent or of other materials and then later reused for a burial. Moreover, the hollow horse whose entire purpose was concealment fails to hide its occupants; its relief layering with cut-out windows over heads, as well as arms that reach out through the windows over its body, applies a further layer or relief to the relief and figures the jar's three-dimensional complexity of containment and concealment in the two dimensions of its narrative imagery. If the intended purpose of the object was funerary, that imagery is itself a story about the bringing of disaster and death.

The magnificent clay handles that sit alongside the Trojan Horse panel at the vessel's top are just under 10 cm thick and nearly 120 cm across their width. While their nonfigural ornament of relief lines, circles, and a wavy patterning at the outer curving edge resonates against much of the relief decoration of both figures and frames in the rest of the pot, the choice to make pierced windows through their thick clay – semicircles at the top, right-angled triangles at the base, and a range of small triangles in the form of Maltese crosses within the handles' main body – plays directly against the windows in the body of the Trojan Horse. The three-dimensional curving form of the vase's neck juts out as a kind of columnar relief in its own right against the handles' flatness, which sets out the plane of the pot's diameter line. The windows in the horse open onto the images of men contained within, by contrast with the windows of the handles that offer only empty space. This comparison emphasizes the fullness of three-dimensionality and what it can contain against the emptiness behind the flat plane constituted by the handles.

While much more extensive discussion is possible – notably of the "metopes" with their scenes of the slaughter of warriors, women, and children, of the places where depicted figures transgress the elaborate ornamental articulation of the framing borders of their scenes, or of the varieties of sizes (or miniaturizations) in play in the three tiers of narrative decoration – suffice it here to dwell only on one further feature. The "metope" model of framed windows showing traumatic scenes in the main body of the

[31] See e.g. Ebbinghaus 2005: 59; Giuliani 2013: 61.

jar is itself a kind of elaboration of the cut-out window strategy of depiction developed for the horse on the neck. Most strikingly the horse has seven windows, of which five make a horizontal line along its body. The horizontal line of "metope" panels in the upper tier on the curve of the pithos as it approaches the neck has five surviving windows out of what were probably originally seven, while each of the two lower tiers has seven windows, effectively replicating in each band the windowing of the horse.[32] Each panel on the body of the vessel acts out the slaughter that lies in potential in the warrior figures whose heads glare forward in windows of the Trojan Horse, and the seven fully armed standing fighters outside it. The windowing of the horse is itself fundamentally dependent on the vessel's commitment to relief decoration – allowing the use of levels and layers of overlapping relief to evoke insiderness and a hollow interiority that serves as a container. The "metopes" of the amphora's belly extend the decorative conceit of windows over what is in reality a container whose interior did in fact hold bones, evoking a figural play with the actions depicted on the belly and their theme of violent death. Relief is fundamental to the artistry and aesthetics of the Mykonos pithos, and specifically relief in relation to the voluminous three-dimensional structure on which the decoration is placed, to the invocation of a flat plane by the vessel's handles, and to the empty piercing of the handles' cut-through ornamentation.

In 1962, in the late fourth- and early third-century BCE burial ground of Derveni near Thessaloniki in ancient Macedonia, a great metal krater was excavated from an undisturbed grave known as Cist Tomb B (Fig. I.2).[33] Made of gold-colored bronze, the krater is 90.5 cm high (including the handles, which rise above the rim) and 51.5 cm at its greatest diameter.[34] It was discovered fallen on its side from a specially fashioned base (a block with a ring cut into it where the krater's foot sat) that stood 36 cm high. Tomb B is dated, on the basis of the range of other grave goods within it, to between 320 and 300 BCE,[35] while the date of the krater's manufacture is likely around 370 BCE.[36] It was inscribed in silver inlay in the egg-frieze around the lip to read ΑΣΤΙΟΥΝΕΙΟΣ ΑΝΑΞΑΓΟΡΑΙΟΙ ΕΣ ΛΑΡΙΣΑΣ, which means "of Astioun, son of Anaxagoras from Larissa."[37] There is discussion as to whether this man was the person intended to have his cremated remains interred in the krater, or whether the vessel had an original

[32] For numbers, see Ervin 1963: 47–54.

[33] See Barr-Sharrar 2008: 18–28 on the find. It is now in the Archaeological Museum of Thessaloniki (B1).

[34] Barr-Sharrar 2008: 31. [35] Barr-Sharrar 2008: 27. [36] Barr-Sharrar 2008: 44.

[37] *SEG* 24.571, with Bousquet 1966 and Barr-Sharrar 2008: 43–4.

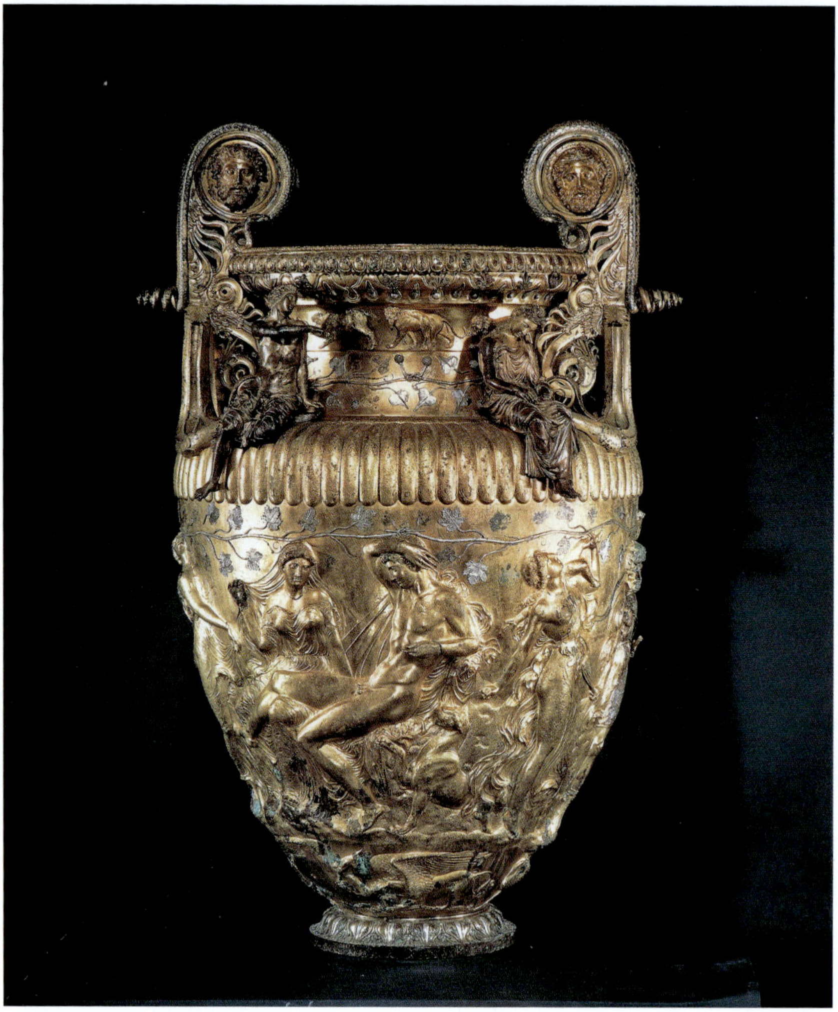

Fig. I.2 Bronze krater from Derveni, fourth century BCE. Archaeological Museum of Thessaloniki, B1 (DEA Picture Library/De Agostini/Getty Images).

function other than funerary;[38] but in any case, when it was found, the Derveni krater contained nearly 2 kg of well-burnt bones belonging to a man of between thirty-five and fifty years of age and a probably younger woman.[39] Thus the question of function in the case of the Derveni krater is exactly the same as with the Mykonos pithos, with a likely funerary intent as at least a secondary if not primary purpose and the certainty that it was indeed used, ultimately, for burial.

38 On functions, see Barr-Sharrar 2008: 180–2.

39 Musgrave 1990: esp. 316–21.

Like the Mykonos pithos, the mouth, neck, and body of the Derveni krater were not cast but raised from the raw material (metal in this case rather than clay and by hammering) in some places to a thickness of less than 1 mm.[40] The reliefs which then extensively decorated this core were created in a variety of ways. The great Dionysiac friezes of the main body as well as the animal figures at the very bottom were created by hammering with a variety of tools, both on the interior and exterior walls of the vessel in the repoussé technique, some of these figures raised to a depth of almost 2 cm. These were then elaborated with various overlays of bronze, silver, and gold (for instance, in the fine silver vines running below the neck frieze and above the Dionysiac scenes of the belly) and with specific soldered additions (such as the cast bronze hands of Dionysus or the sheet of copper added to the cape of Silenus),[41] as well as numerous surface treatments, such as the stippling of landscape features. The animal frieze of the neck, also rendered in repoussé, was not hammered from the object, but its elements were fashioned independently and fastened to the krater with solder in appliqué.[42] Major cast elements were then added to the object – notably the handles, which are complex combinations of separately made elements, including discretely made repoussé disks depicting the frontal masks of deities, with embossed surfaces, in the volutes.[43] Most striking of all are the four solid cast bronze statuettes of semi-reclining Bacchic figures, including Dionysus himself, a sleeping Maenad, an ecstatic Maenad, and Silenus lounging in the pose of the Barberini Faun but leaning on a sack of wine to his left.[44]

Although still adhering to a horizontal ground aligned to the embodied viewer's own posture, the spectacular Classical naturalism of this lavish object, potentially but not certainly made in Athens, strains to make a single thematic scene out of its Dionysiac imagery.[45] The flowing movement of its repoussé figures, whose very low-relief draperies billow about them as their own bodies undulate in and out of the curving surface of the krater's belly, demonstrates an extraordinary plasticity and fluidity of medium in relation to iconography. That plasticity is in part the result of the technique of hammering a bronze block into the thin walls of a vessel and then of hammering so many of its images as bulges out of those walls in the repoussé technique. But the cast elements – especially the entirely three-dimensional bronze figurines, who acquire relief status only by virtue

[40] Barr-Sharrar 2008: 76, 102. [41] Much more detailed discussion in Barr-Sharrar 2008: 102–5.
[42] Barr-Sharrar 2008: 36–8, 163–6. [43] Barr-Sharrar 2008: 29–42, 166–8.
[44] Barr-Sharrar 2008: 168–75.
[45] The argument for Athens is made by Barr-Sharrar 2008: 178–9.

of being soldered onto the curving ground between the lip, neck, and shoulder of the vessel – effectively thrust it toward three dimensions. Not only are they fully worked on all sides, but they eschew the hollowness of the imagery around the belly of the krater for a fully substantial and heavy materiality. Likewise, the rims of the handles turn into serpents – their tails spiraling outward at the base, their heads rising just below the volutes at the top, perhaps threatening to strike at anyone who tried to get into the krater's interior. Whereas the pithos' neck and handles proclaimed its narrative and decorative propositions (Trojan Horse and windows, whether entirely pierced or penetrative of an interior), the krater's two-dimensional repoussé base in Bacchic myth builds to a mounting three-dimensional neck and lip as the Dionysiac characters burst fully formed onto the great urn's exterior.

While the Mykonos pithos affirmed a relief space between the flat and the three-dimensional, using its handles to determine the nonvoluminous ground of the plane against which its form (including its form as relief sculpture) emerges, the Derveni krater plays between low and high relief, between repoussé, appliqué, and cast three-dimensionality to entirely different aesthetic ends. While the iconography of the Mykonos vase is effectively a lament for the kinds of heroism that result in death, the imagery of the Derveni krater looks to the Dionysiac afterlife, a world of bliss beyond the earthly, and makes little of death.[46] There is no evidence of colored glaze on the pithos, although it may still have been colored with temporary pigment, but effectively neither of these objects seeks to make it effects through the "ingenuity" of multiple colors, as Philostratus puts it. Rather, they use the ways relief plays against particular kinds of material surface – with some careful uses of silver, copper, and gold in specific contexts in the krater, often as part of a given technical foray, such as the engraved and then infilled letter forms of the inscription.

Our third example is a much more venerable discovery, excavated in the remains of the villa of the emperor Antoninus Pius at Monte Cagnolo in Lanuvium, just southeast of Rome, by the British artist, dealer, and archaeologist Gavin Hamilton in the year 1773 and sold after substantial restoration to the collector Charles Townley in 1774 (Fig. I.3).[47] This vast marble vase, 1.06 m in height, was carved out of a single block of stone with separate foot attached at the bottom. By contrast with the appliqué model

[46] Although the Maenad carrying a child over her shoulder by its left leg looks likely to be about to kill it in her ecstasy. See Barr-Sharrar 2008: 123–8.

[47] Smith 1904: 393–4, no. 2500; Cook 1985: 18–19; Neudecker 1988: 162, no. 21.11; Grassinger 1991: 169–72, no. 12; www.britishmuseum.org/collection/object/G_1805-0703-218. The object is part of the Townley Collection in the British Museum (1805,0703.218).

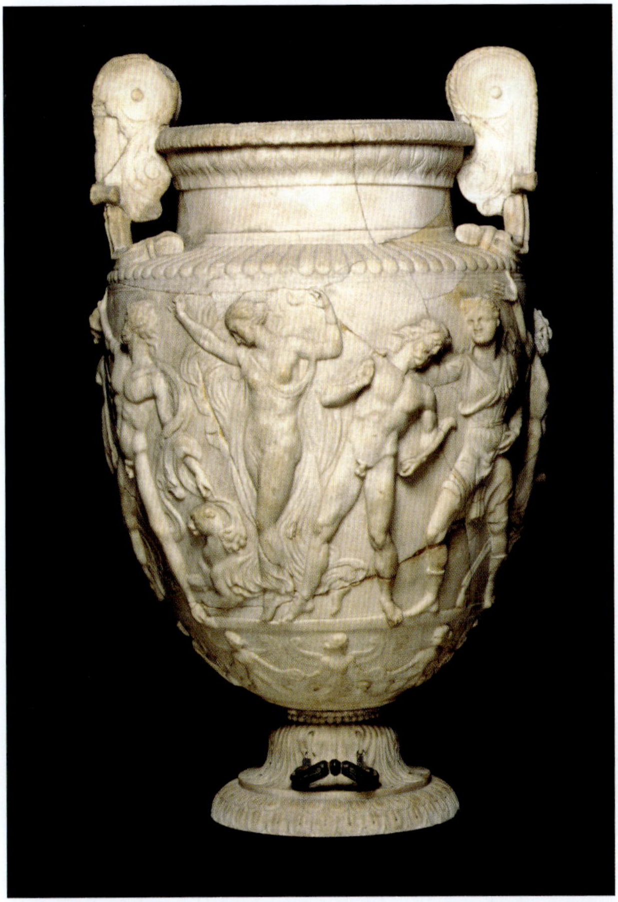

Fig. I.3 Townley vase from Monte Cagnolo, late first or early second century CE. London, British Museum, 1805,0703.218 (© The Trustees of the British Museum. All rights reserved).

of molded manufacture of reliefs in clay, as well as the hammering and casting of bronze, in this case sculptors had to realize the shape, its interior space, and its fine embellishments, such as the handles, by excavating stone from the block before realizing the fine relief of its sculpture from the ornament on the neck, lip, and handles to the figural decoration on its belly. The figures, a Bacchic procession encircling the main body and moving from right to left, include Dionysus and Ariadne, as well as a number of Maenads and Satyrs and a fine image of Pan carrying a vase of different shape to the Townley krater but nonetheless riffing on its form. These figures are carved in a diagonal plane so that their lower bodies are in low relief as the vase tapers in toward the foot but emerge from the background into high relief with heads and arms extending from the background just below the shoulder of the vessel. Draperies in very low relief play on the background against the much higher-set figures, as on the Derveni krater. A magnificent Roman work of the late first or early second century CE, the Townley vase (like the other major marble vases in its high elite class) borrows its imagery and iconography from a rich repertoire of Attic and Hellenistic precedents, confecting the fantasy of Dionysiac bliss on the body of an object whose form evokes the storage and drinking of wine.[48]

This object was probably not funerary but rather part of a parade of sculpture displayed in the lavish context of a top-end imperial villa. On the other hand, its imagery and execution are hardly unrelated to the extensive culture of relief sarcophagi of both Attic and Roman origin that depict Dionysiac processions and were used for the burial of many in the Roman elite from the early second century.[49] Indeed, the urn form of the vase, as much as it calls to mind a krater for holding wine, also evokes a typical kind of repository for ashes in the Roman world, of a sort made in the same material but at much smaller scale.[50] In part, the game here is that the iconography of figural Dionysiac processions is reserved for sarcophagi destined for the inhumation of bodies, rather than for cinerary urns, but is transferred at monumental scale to a kind of object that – if used for burial, as this was not – would have contained cremated bones. Quite apart from its free play with earlier styles and iconographic forms, this piece plays on the kinds of functions of earlier works that looked something like it. Moreover, it imitates in marble the cast forms of bronze in its handles,[51] while evoking (in a spectacularly realized but entirely different technique) both the appliqué and repoussé artistry of vases in other media. The uses of relief in the Townley vase are part of the learned but playful knowingness of this kind of high elite object – fashioning in different media and scales (that is, in monumental marble) the kind of form and iconography typically created in metal or clay. They speak of imperial appropriations, ownership of all media to the extent of substituting one with the other, of eclecticism and excess.

The Townley vase's knowingness and elite appropriation of aspects of other media indicate the ways that relief both was a way of making kinds of

[48] For a sophisticated account of the phenomenon, see Touchette 1995: 81, no. 46; Hölscher 2004.

[49] An excellent corpus is Matz 1968–75.

[50] See Sinn 1987: e.g. 94, no. 14; 96, no. 20; 188–9, no. 407, as well as the depicted relief imagery in 96, no. 21; 99–100, nos. 32–3; 101–2, nos. 40, 42; 109, nos. 71–2; 143, no. 202; 152, no. 243; 153, no. 245; 187–8, no. 403; 193, no. 427.

[51] See Smith 1904: 394. Though note that large parts of the handles are Hamilton's restorations.

visual statements in the ancient world and had become by the Roman imperial period a means of appropriating and commenting on those statements. The three pieces we have examined here offer a clear view of how objects could exploit relief imagery in the context of a given regime of representation to make claims or comments on their functions, their aspirations, and the visual tradition in which they stand. The Mykonos pithos uses its windowing facture to comment on their own function as container, as well as an iconography of slaughter to reflect on the human remains therein. The Derveni krater, in a regime of rampant naturalism at a golden age of large-scale bronze manufacture, uses the move from repoussé relief to three-dimensional figurines rendered as super high reliefs via appliqué to evoke Bacchic bliss in the afterlife within the regime of increasing lifelikeness in representation.[52] The Townley vase riffs across these kinds of precursors with rampant abandon, some substantial art-historical understanding, and sculptural command, while using a radically different medium with changed functions.

*

Objects like these three vessels expand our sense of the technical, thematic, and visual possibilities of relief offered by the monumental, architecturally engaged examples with which we began. As the chapters that follow demonstrate, many further aspects of ancient relief production offer themselves for exploration. What the chapters also show – whether discussing the interplay of surface decoration and bodily substitution of Archaic Greek grave stelai or the chain of replication in the striking of late antique coins and medallions from officially sanctioned imperial dies and subsequent imitation of those objects by nonofficial means – is relief's fundamental in-betweenness, its ability to act in the place of some other impetus and to fulfill such a wide range of functions. This is to say, in investigating the intricacies of ancient relief, in often quite detailed technical and lexical terms, the chapters also investigate how it functions *as*: as body, as medium, as process, as light effect, as movement, as replication, as fiction, as attestation of familial relation, or as point of connection to the numinous or the divine, to name just a few. Relief, in this sense, is both object of study in its own right and conduit to something else. It is the in-betweenness of relief, as much as its diversity of forms and functions, which makes a generalized theory of relief such a daunting and intellectually stimulating prospect. But it is also that same in-betweenness, we would suggest, that offers a through-line both for the chapters presented here and the phenomenon more broadly.

52 For the rise and development of bronze, see Mattusch 1988, 1996.

The chapters in this volume do not (and cannot) address the full breadth of issues raised by ancient relief as either theoretical subject or empirical phenomenon. But they point to both the complexity of the topic and to its transcultural and transhistorical ramifications, which reach practically every domain of visual culture. Of persistent interest precisely because it is never fully one thing or another, relief is an act of negotiation as much as it is an artistic technique or an optical effect. It negotiates among the integrity and smoothness of the notional surface out of which it seems to "emerge" (a surface which, we must emphasize, need not be a flat one), the visual and tactile texture of the elaboration of that surface and the actual material extension of the surface in space. Relief likewise negotiates among not just the two-dimensionality associated with painting and the three-dimensionality of sculpture but the singular dimension of the line. And it negotiates among monumental, figurative architectural sculpture, the humbler domains of pottery and other forms of terra-cotta production, and the luxury arts of gem-cutting and chasing and molding in precious metals.

Verity Platt (Chapter 1) opens the volume by approaching the topic of classical relief through an examination of ancient terminology, concepts, and mentalities. It proceeds from the premise that there was no single word, in Greek or Latin usage, which could function in the way that "relief" does in both everyday English and scholarly literature. Instead, a constellation of related concepts helped antiquity articulate relief across media and artistic technique, and further lent it a peculiarly indeterminate ontological status. Platt opens with the observation that the most common word in Greek for relief, *typos*, was also employed for an impression or stamp, what today we would still call a type. Platt further observes that the typology of molding and casting is especially connected to the act of carving through engraved gems used as seal-stones for the creation of reliefs. The chapter discusses a wide selection of evidence for ancient thinking about relief, ranging from Homer to Pliny and beyond. It emphasizes that what we might think of as phenomenological effect is as critical to ancient relief terminology as material support and process; hence, the relief effect of painting overlaps considerably with discussions of the figure–ground relationship in sculptural relief. Ultimately, Platt proposes, the constellation of thinking about relief diagrams an ontology of relationality, with as much to teach us about models of perception and cognition as about artistic creation.

For Caspar Meyer and Chris Pellettieri (Chapter 2), relief offers the opportunity to rethink the relationship between vision and meaning in ancient art-historical analysis. When viewed in a certain proximity, at a certain level of detail, autoptic analysis has typically threatened to rob art history of its ability to extract meaning from the visual arts. A single chisel mark, much less a more microscopic trace, may be enormously informative from the perspective of a history of technology or the construction of a chronological stemma, but it has typically seemed to lie outside the arena in which most European and American art history is able to locate interpretive meaning. This chapter works against that tendency by seeking to connect a technical, procedural understanding of the carving of Greek stelai with a deeper exploration of the frames of their creation and perception. Meyer and Pellettieri focus with particular acuity on the production of lines and planes that permitted a stele to act as a surface in the first place, both for figural relief and inscribed text, and thus as a literal and metaphorical ground for the production of meaning. The "immanent plane" of representation, they articulate, has become a basic given in modern representational acts, but in Archaic Greece it was an object of creation in its own right, one that could not be taken for granted and that required remarkable skill and creativity to produce. Ultimately, by attempting to think about monuments through the combination of stone, tool, and gesture, they argue, we both rescue the creative act from mere material determinism or historical teleology and open up new points of access to the connections between making and meaning.

Seth Estrin (Chapter 3) likewise takes on the topic of Archaic funerary sculpture, investigating in particular the question of the body. He reexamines the similarities and differences between the two primary forms of Archaic funerary sculpture, the freestanding statues known as kouroi, and the stelai decorated with relief, showing that rather than discrete, independent categories of artistic production, each blurs into the other. Rather than bodies fully in the round, Estrin shows, kouroi can in some senses be understood as quadrifacial high reliefs. And rather than mere surface elaborations, in turn, relief stelai often emphasize their bodily imposition in space. This blurring of boundaries is particularly important because recent scholarship has tended to see in the distinction between kouros and stele not just a question of artistic genre but one of representation itself and has frequently contrasted the copresence of kouroi in real space with the planar virtuality of the stelai. Yet despite the undeniable differences between them, Estrin argues, kouroi and relief stelai evince related forms of visualization, and – engaged as both inevitably were in complex, multipart monuments – they bespeak a common set of affective purposes that highlight not only the representational challenges but also the ethical implications of funerary commemoration.

In Chapter 4, Guy Hedreen examines relief in connection to Athenian vase painting. Already an intermediary form, where the pictoriality of painting and drawing stretch across and deliberately play with the three-dimensional shapes of the vessels themselves, Attic vase painting also features substantial experimentation with relief. As Hedreen explores, the phenomena of added clay relief and the raised relief-line are prominent in Archaic and Classical Attic painting, the latter especially in the red-figure technique, where it plays a complementary role to the incised line of black-figure painting by demarcating contours and adding physical and visual texture. These relief techniques are, on the one hand, sculptural, genuine physical protrusions from the surface of the vase. But they are also deeply pictorial, a way to influence the reflection of light off the vase by modulating the angle of incidence so as to create shining highlights and other optical effects. This play between the sculptural and the pictorial is also evident in the case of relief-mask kantharoi, which Hedreen argues develop not from sculpture, nor from genuine ritual masks, but from painted precursors. The dually sculptural and pictorial aspect of relief on Attic vases, Hedreen shows, has typically been suppressed in their photographic publication, which tends to employ certain lighting conditions and points of view that emphasize above all the graphic aspects of both the vase and its decorations, but when taken seriously, it helps us better understand not only important technical aspects of artistic production but even conceptions of pictoriality itself.

Nikolaus Dietrich (Chapter 5) also explores the borders between statuary in the round and relief sculpture, but does so by different means: through the lens of photography. Beginning with the observation that the role of photography in everyday scholarly practice is typically downplayed by students of ancient sculpture, Dietrich examines how the photograph converts the three-dimensional sculpture into a kind of relief, and how that conversion can either subvert or reinforce the compositional principles of the sculpture itself. Beginning already in the nineteenth century, the photographic reproductions employed in the scholarly study of Greek sculpture, he highlights, tend to exhibit a relief bias by choosing just a few angles onto a given statue and isolating it as much as possible from any surrounding context. Such acts of framing, on the one hand, are a legacy of neoclassical approaches to sculpture that sought for the best view of a given statue; they also accord closely with the late nineteenth-century prescriptions of the sculptor Adolf Hildebrand, who thought all statues should be essentially relief-like in their compositions. But they are not entirely modern fictions, however, and Dietrich also demonstrates that many Greek statues from the late Classical period onward were deliberately designed to encourage specific, privileged points of view.

Carolyn Laferrière (Chapter 6) takes us to Rome in the first centuries BCE and CE, where she examines the rhythmic and spatial compositions of so-called Neo-Attic reliefs. Sculpted marble objects of relatively modest size, seemingly designed for domestic display, these reliefs were designated as Neo-Attic insofar as they evoke the style and subject matter of Classical Athenian sculpture. But as Laferrière shows, they are much more than exercises in art-historical reference. Instead, such reliefs ally a multiplicity of temporal orientations – achieved through both the historical reference of figural style and the ambiguity of their narrative settings – with a deliberately uncanny spacelessness enacted in low relief. Although these objects often feature landscape elements, such as stones and trees, and their intricate patterns of overlapping indicate complex arrangements of pictorial depth, they rarely resolve into clear depth intervals from a plane, and the figures themselves – human, divine, and otherwise – only barely emerge from the background. The result, Laferrière argues, is that the reliefs evoke a sense of the past for their Roman audience that is at once historically specific (and specifically Greek) and at the same time lays outside the sequence of chronological time entirely.

Nathaniel B. Jones (Chapter 7) once again takes up the question of the intermediality of relief, this time through the examination of the remediation between ancient relief and painting, particularly in late Republican and early Imperial Rome. A concept developed in late twentieth-century media studies, remediation helps elucidate the degree to which one medium can contain, represent, and reflect on another medium through a dialectical process of acknowledging and denying its presence. Thus, as relief strives to be more like painting and vice versa, we find a series of reflections on the tensions between two and three dimensions, real and pictorial space, the haptic and the optic, form and color, and illusion and fiction. The chapter focuses in particular on the representation of relief sculpture within Roman murals, which, like other experiments in meta-pictoriality, permitted Roman painters to explore the boundaries of their capabilities by offering both a material limit of pictorialization and providing a host of ways in which the pictorial could seek to outflank the material. It concludes by reflecting on how the in-betweenness of relief, its ability to traffic in both real presence and virtuality, is in some ways analogous to the structure of fiction itself.

Jennifer Trimble (Chapter 8) takes us back to the production of carved marble reliefs, especially in early Imperial Rome. She examines the background of such reliefs, ostensibly a neutral, even negative zone, but in fact one of the final areas of the object to be carved. Rather than a stable plane of projection from which figures emerge, Trimble argues, from the perspective of a stone carver the background of a relief is in fact anchored by those figures, who typically come into existence first. This shift in focus turns the typical negation of the background on its head, revealing it to be a site of creative and dynamic fluidity. Trimble first takes us through the steps of the carving process before turning our attention to the specific example of a marble calyx krater used as a garden fountain in Villa A at Oplontis. A freestanding, volumetrically composed object carved from Pentelic marble, the krater features a host of relief decoration, including six nude, armed males dancing across its body. The background against which those figures dance, moreover, is not a flat surface but a precisely curved one that both imitates an emergent pictorial plane and follows the contour of the carefully considered geometric proportions of the body of a vessel. Achieving the appropriate symmetry and rhythm of that background, Trimble shows, would have been one of the prime challenges for the sculptural workshop. The fact that the final object playfully evokes a number of other media, including vessels in clay and metal, which would have been made according to very different protocols, and that similar marble kraters were depicted in the wall paintings at Oplontis, only serves to further foreground the significance of relief's background.

Nicola Barham (Chapter 9) examines the varieties of relief evident in Palmyrene funerary portraiture. Widely known but often not well archaeologically documented, Palmyrene funerary sculpture embodies relief's intermediateness, moving between shallow incision and sculpture in the round, between individualized portraiture and group identity. It likewise mediates between local, Parthian, and Mediterranean points of reference, both in style of execution and cultural signifiers like clothing, jewelry, and inscription. Indeed, Barham suggests that the primary purpose of Palmyrene tombs was to communicate the significance of the families they housed and commemorated to the surrounding empires. The fact that the portrait sculptures were used as loculus slabs, and were thus literally placed in between the represented dead and the living who mourned them, only further emphasizes their inherent mediateness. Beginning with a single relief portrait now in the Kelsey Museum of Archaeology in Ann Arbor, and then moving to a consideration of an ensemble of portraits in a corporate tomb, Barham shows how Palmyrene funerary sculpture in its original settings was capable of exploiting and subverting the norms of multiple artistic traditions, genres of portraiture, and affordances of relief in order to produce specific visual and commemorative effects.

Ashley Elizabeth Jones (Chapter 10) closes the volume by bringing us forward into late antiquity, to a relief phenomenon unique to the period between the third and seventh centuries CE: numismatic and nummiform gold jewelry. Her chapter examines coins and coin-like objects embellished with relief decoration and set into frameworks designed to be worn on the body. The objects she discusses elucidate not only the power of relief as personal adornment but also its role in a complex web of amuletic thinking in which aid, or indeed relief, was sought for the body of the wearer from a divine power, as attested by numerous inscriptions throughout the corpus she examines. Particularly important to this phenomenon, Jones elucidates, was a chain of typological associations. Literal typologies regulated the production of coins and struck medallions, which were produced from officially sanctioned dies in the imperial mint, but unofficial versions could be made from molds taken from the struck objects or through the direct impression of gold leaf. Metaphorical typologies have an important role to play, as well, as the relief imagery, along with the source of authority to which the jewelry appeals, moves between imperial and Christian. Ultimately, Jones demonstrates, the use of gold, the images themselves, and the invocations for aid connect these objects to a broad network of protective amulets and talismans throughout the ancient and late antique Mediterranean.

*

The chapters in this volume are marked by the diversity not only of their subject matter but of their approach as well. They cross chronological and geographic borders, from early Archaic Greece to late antique Rome, from Syria to Spain. They also range from the philological analysis of the lexicography of relief, to the formal analysis of its visual effect, to the technical analysis of its creation. In bringing these targeted contributions together, our aim as authors and editors has been to open up further space for deeper thinking about the multifaceted ontology of relief, its intermediate nature, multiple manifestations, varied processes of facture, impact on the eye, and complex construction of meanings, both in antiquity and in its later inheritances. So much of the long history of Greco-Roman art has been enabled and shaped by the artifactual interventions of the very production of relief that still invite further analysis and theorization. The place of incising or molding the surface is so obvious and so central in the histories of ancient artistic practice as to have been too long ignored as a key determinant for how visual culture articulated its themes. And in the sculptural arts, relief is the essence of so much image making and pictorial storytelling – across a tradition reaching continuously to modernity and well beyond the Greco-Roman world through Eurasia and Africa. A close consideration of relief brings to the fore how techniques of artistic making act with and against the given materials in aid of the purpose and content of the work being produced. Deepening our understanding of Greek, Roman, and late antique relief has much to teach us about the very nature of the art of antiquity and beyond.

References

Alberti, L. B. (1950). *Della pittura*. Ed. L. Mallè. Florence: Sansoni.

Barasch, M. (1998). *Theories of Modern Art. Vol. 2: From Impressionism to Kandinsky*. New York: New York University Press.

Barr-Sharrar, B. (2008). *The Derveni Krater: Masterpiece of Classical Greek Metalwork*. Princeton, NJ: American School of Classical Studies at Athens.

Bousquet, J. (1966). "L'inscription du cratère de Derveni." *Bulletin de Correspondance Hellénique* 90.1: 281–2.

Brendel, O. J. (1953). "Prolegomena to a Book on Roman Art." *Memoirs of the American Academy in Rome* 21: 7–73.

Brittenham, C., ed. (2019). *Vessels: The Object as Container*. Oxford: Oxford University Press.

Brunn, H. (1884). "Über die kunstgeschichtliche Stellung der Pergamenischen Gigantomachie." *Jahrbuch der königlichen preussischen Kunstsammlungen* 5: 231–92.

Cennini, C. (2003). *Il libro dell'arte*. Ed. F. Frezzato. Vicenza: Pozza.

Conze, A. (1882). "Uber das Relief bei den Griechen." *Sitzungsberichte der koniglichen preussischen Akademie der Wissenschaften zu Berlin* 26: 563–77.

Cook, B. F. (1985). *The Townley Marbles*. London: British Museum.

Courbaud, E. (1899). *Le bas-relief Romain à représentations historiques: Étude archéologique, historique et littéraire*. Bibliothèque des Écoles françaises d'Athènes et de Rome 81. Paris: Fontemoing.

Dewey, J. (1894). "The Theory of Emotion: (1) Emotional Attitudes." *Psychological Review* 1.6: 553–69.

Ebbinghaus, S. (2005). "The Protector of the City, or Art of Storage in Early Greece." *Journal of Hellenic Studies* 125: 51–72.

Elsner, J. (2006) "From Empirical Evidence to the Big Picture: Some Reflections on Riegl's Concept of *Kunstwollen*." *Critical Inquiry* 32.4: 741–66.

Ervin, M. (1963). "A Relief Pithos from Mykonos." *Archaiologikon Deltion* 18: 37–75.

Ervin Caskey, M. (1976). "Notes on the Relief Pithoi of the Tenian-Boiotian Group." *American Journal of Archaeology* 80.1: 19–41.

Freedman, L. (1989). "*Rilievo* as an Artistic Term in Renaissance Italy." *Rinascimento* 29: 217–47.

Freud, S. (1974). *Jokes and Their Relation to the Unconscious*. Trans. J. Strachey. New York: Penguin.

Ghiberti, L. (1998). *I commentarii: Biblioteca nazionale centrale di Firenze, II, I, 333*. Ed. L. Bartoli. Florence: Giunti.

Giuliani, L. (2013). *Image and Myth: A History of Pictorial Narration in Greek Art*. Trans. J. O'Donnell. Chicago, IL: University of Chicago Press.

Gossman, L. (2006). "Imperial Icon: The Pergamon Altar in Willhelminian Germany." *Journal of Modern History* 78.3: 551–87.

Grassinger, D. (1991). *Römische Marmorkratere*. Mainz: von Zabern.

Hildebrand, A. (1893). *Das Problem der Form in den bildenden Künst*. Strasbourg: Heitz.

(1994). "The Problem of Form in the Fine Arts." In F. Mallgrave and E. Ikonomou, trans., *Empathy, Form, and Space: Problems in German Aesthetics, 1873–1893*. Santa Monica, CA: Getty Center for the History of Art and the Humanities, 227–80.

Holliday, P. J. (2002). *The Origins of Roman Historical Commemoration in the Visual Arts*. Cambridge: Cambridge University Press.

Hölscher, T. (2004). *The Language of Images in Roman Art*. Trans. A. Snodgrass and A. M. Künzl-Snodgrass. Cambridge: Cambridge University Press.

Iversen, M. (1993). *Alois Riegl: Art History and Theory*. Cambridge, MA: MIT Press.

Jones, C. P. (2005). *Philostratus: Apollonius of Tyana. Vol. 1: Life of Apollonius of Tyana, Books 1–4*. Loeb Classical Library 16. Cambridge, MA: Harvard University Press.

Koeppel, G. (1982). "The Grand Pictorial Tradition of Roman Historical Representation during the Early Empire." *Aufstieg und Niedergang der römischen Welt* 2.12.1: 507–35.

Koortbojian, M. (2023). *The Representation of Space in Graeco-Roman Art: Relief Sculpture, Problems of Form, and Modern Historiography*. Berlin: De Gruyter.

Lakey, C. R. (2018). *Sculptural Seeing: Relief, Optics, and the Rise of Perspective in Medieval Italy*. New Haven, CT: Yale University Press.

Lange, H. C. (2020a). "Cimabue's True Crosses in Arezzo and Florence." In S. Elm and C. Ocker, eds., *Material Christianity: Western Religion and the Agency of Things*. Cham: Springer, 29–67.

(2020b). "Relief Effects in Donatello and Mantegna." In A. R. Bloch and D. M. Zolli, eds., *The Art of Sculpture in Fifteenth Century Italy*. Cambridge: Cambridge University Press, 327–43.

(2023). *Giotto's Arena Chapel and the Triumph of Humility*. Cambridge: Cambridge University Press.

Marchand, S. L. (1996). *Down from Olympus: Archaeology and Philhellenism in Germany, 1750–1970*. Princeton, NJ: Princeton University Press.

Marvin, M. (2008). *The Language of the Muses: The Dialogue between Roman and Greek Sculpture*. Los Angeles: J. Paul Getty Museum.

Mattusch, C. C. (1988). *Greek Bronze Statuary: From the Beginnings through the Fifth Century B.C.* Ithaca, NY: Cornell University Press.

(1996). *Classical Bronzes: The Art and Craft of Greek and Roman Statuary*. Ithaca, NY: Cornell University Press.

Matz, F. (1968–75). *Die dionysischen Sarkophage*. 4 vols. Antiken Sarkophagreliefs 4.2.1–4. Berlin: Mann.

Morreall, J. (2009). *Comic Relief: A Comprehensive Philosophy of Humor*. Malden, MA: Blackwell.

Musgrave, J. (1990). "The Cremated Remains from Tombs II and III at Nea Mihaniona and Tomb Beta at Derveni." *Annual of the British School at Athens* 85: 301–25.

Neudecker, R. (1988). *Die Skulpturenausstattung römischer Villen in Italien*. Mainz: von Zabern.

Olin, M. (1992). *Forms of Representation in Alois Riegl's Theory of Art*. University Park: Pennsylvania State University Press.

Osborne, R. (1998). *Archaic and Classical Art*. Oxford: Oxford University Press.

Ostrow, S. F. (2004). "Playing with the Paragone: The Reliefs of Pietro Bernini; For Rudolf Preimesberger." *Zeitschrift für Kunsgeschichte* 67.3: 329–64.

Panofsky, E. (1998). *Deutschsprachige Aufsätze*. 2 vols. Berlin: Akademie.

(2020). *Michelangelo's Principles of Design, Particularly in Relation to Those of Raphael*. Ed. G. Panofsky-Soergel and trans. J. Spooner. Princeton, NJ: Princeton University Press.

Payne, A. (2008). "Portable Ruins: The Pergamon Altar, Heinrich Wölfflin, and German Art History at the Fin de siècle." *RES: Anthropology and Aesthetics* 53–4: 168–89.

(2011). "On Sculptural Relief, *Malerisch*, the Autonomy of Artistic Media and the Beginnings of Baroque Studies." In H. Hills, ed., *Rethinking the Baroque*. London: Ashgate, 39–64.

Philippi, A. (1872). "Über die römischen Triumphalreliefe und ihre Stellung in der Kunstgeschichte." *Abhandlungen der philosophisch-historischen Klasse der Königlichen Sachsischen Gesellschaft der Wissenschaften* 6: 247–305.

Rankin, E., and Schneider, R. M. (2020). *From Memory to Marble: The Historical Frieze of the Vortrekker Monument. Vol. 1. The Frieze*. Berlin: De Gruyter.

Riegl, A. (1901). *Die spätrömische Kunstindustrie nach den Funden in Österreich-Ungarn: Im Zusammenhange mit der Gesammtentwicklung der bildenden Künste bei den Mittelmeervölkern*. Vol. 1. Vienna: Österreichische Staatsdruckerei.

(1923). *Die spätrömische Kunstindustrie nach den Funden in Österreich-Ungarn: Im Zusammenhange mit der Gesammtentwicklung der bildenden Künste bei den Mittelmeervölkern. Vol. 2, Kunstgewerbe des frühen Mittelalters*. Vienna: Österreichische Staatsdruckerei.

Schäfer, J. (1957). *Studien zu den griechischen Reliefpithoi des 8–6 Jahrhunderts v. Chr aus Kreta, Rhodos, Tenos und Boioten*. Kallmunz: Lassleben.

Sinn, F. (1987). *Stadtrömische Marmorurnen*. Mainz: von Zabern.

Smith, A. H. (1904). *A Catalogue of Sculpture in the Department of Greek and Roman Antiquities, British Museum*. Vol. 3. London: British Museum.

Snodgrass, A. (1998). *Homer and the Artists*. Cambridge: Cambridge University Press.

Spencer, H. (1860). "The Physiology of Laughter." *Macmillan's Magazine* 1 (March): 395–402.

St. Clair, W. (1998). *Lord Elgin and the Marbles*. Oxford: Oxford University Press.

Stansbury-O'Donnell, M. (1999). *Pictorial Narrative in Ancient Greek Art*. Cambridge: Cambridge University Press.

Summers, D. (2003). *Real Spaces: World Art History and the Rise of Western Modernism*. New York: Phaidon.

Touchette, L.-A. (1995). *The Dancing Maenad Reliefs: Continuity and Change in Roman Copies*. London: University of London, Institute of Classical Studies.

Wickhoff, F., and von Hartel, W. (1895). *Die Wiener Genesis*. Vol. 2. Jahrbuch des kunsthistorischen Sammlungen des allerhöchsten Kaiserhauses 16. Vienna: Tempsky.

Wolf, G. (2016). "Image, Object, Art: Talking to a Chinese Jar on Two Human Feet." *Representations* 133 (2016): 152–9.

(2019). *Der Vase und der Schemel: Ding, Bild oder eine Kunstgeschichte der Gefäße*. Dortmund: Kettler.

Wölfflin, H. (1888). *Renaissance und Barock: Eine Untersuchung über Wesen und Entstehung des Barockstils in Italien*. Munich: Bruckmann.

(1915). *Kunstgeschichtliche Grundbegriffe: Das Problem der Stilentwicklung in der neueren Kunst*. Munich: Bruckmann.

Wood, C. S. (2004). "Riegl's *Mache*." *RES: Anthropology and Aesthetics* 46: 154–72.

1 | Ancient Relief

Terminology, Medium, Ontology

VERITY J. PLATT

What is classical relief? This chapter attempts to crack open the question by exploring the terminology that is applied to relief-work in Greek and Roman texts. It starts from the fact that the most commonly used term for relief in ancient Greek (*typos*) also applies to the "impression" created by an engraved gem when it is stamped into a receptive medium such as wax or clay.[1] Intaglios are, in effect, devices for the production of miniature reliefs. As such, they feature prominently in the Greek philosophical tradition, where the act of sealing provides a metaphor for the storage of memories and the acquisition of knowledge through sense-perception.[2] Despite their different approaches to epistemology, Plato, Aristotle, and the Stoics all explore the idea that cognitive impressions are "stamped" onto the *psychē* as if creating reliefs within the waxlike "receiving device" of the mind.[3] As part of a large toolbox of ancient technologies for the production and replication of images, the acts of sealing, stamping, and impressing overlap in fascinating ways with those of casting, molding, and chasing or embossing – and thus with the creation of sculptural form across artistic mediums, including precious stones, bronze, plaster, terra-cotta, glass, and metal plate. The art of *glyptikē* (carving or engraving) is thus connected at a fundamental level to the arts of *plastikē* (molding or modeling) and *toreutikē* (literally, "piercing" or "punching"). But what is it that these different art forms actually share, given that their use of materials, scale, and techniques varies so widely? And how do relief forms in more malleable materials relate to sculptural reliefs created through carving – to the freestanding stelai or architectural friezes and metopes that most obviously come to mind when we think of "reliefs"? Can "relief" ever be spoken of as a single category? Is it a "medium" in itself? If so, what exactly does it "mediate"? And how does the notion of artistic medium (which art history tends to use in relation to *materials*) relate to the

[1] On the range of meanings associated with *typos* and its cognates, see Lippold 1925; von Blumenthal 1928; Roux 1961; Pollitt 1974: 272–93 (with extensive bibliography) together with Platt, in press, and my discussion in this chapter.

[2] See Platt 2006, 2020, in press.

[3] For example, Pl. *Tht.* 191d; Arist. *De an.* 424a19 (= 2.12); Diog. Laert. 7.45–6 (*Life of Zeno*) (= *SVF* 2, 53). For discussion, see esp. Ioppolo 1990; Long 2006; Ierodiakonou 2007.

more theoretical concept of "media" as tools or channels for the storage and transmission of information?[4]

This chapter tries to get at these questions by sketching out some of the terminology of relief in Greek and Latin, paying special attention to medium and technique, in the hopes that we might develop a few working principles, or points of reference, that might inform this volume as a whole. Words, as we know, are never straightforward guides to material culture, and reliefs are complex artifacts that arguably defy the constraints of language. Nevertheless, terminology can be revealing of cultural attitudes to and conceptualizations of the visual in ways that can both surprise and productively estrange.

Historiography

Textbook references or Google Images searches might suggest that most of us assume we have a pretty good idea of what we mean by the English term "relief." We think most immediately of marble, of figures "sandwiched" between a stable ground (usually comprised of the same medium) and a more open frontal plane; of a recession in space that is "cut away" around the figures as the carver works back into the slab; of figures that are compressed within a representational field that combines "real" and "illusionistic" space, constituting a complex blend of the sculptural and the pictorial (or the material and the virtual, as the medieval art historian Christopher Lakey discusses in his book *Sculptural Seeing*).[5] We are familiar with the various degrees of relief that such slabs might employ, from "high" relief that is almost fully in the round to the "shallow" or "low" relief styles of archaizing pieces, such as an example now in the Yale University Art Gallery (Fig. 1.1), where the diaphanous swallow-tailed folds of the processing deities merge almost imperceptibly into the relief's ground through a technique closer to engraving.[6] Indeed, we have a highly

[4] On the distinction between artistic "mediums" and the more technological concept of media of storage and transmission, see Shechtman 2020. On the ancient origins of the medium as concept (esp. in Aristotle's concept of the "in between," in e.g. *De an.* 2.11, 423b.), see Mersch 2002; Jäger 2004; Alloa 2012; Krämer 2015: 30–4; Alloa 2020. On media in antiquity and antiquity in theories of media, see Michelakis 2020.

[5] On the formal and phenomenological aspects of relief, see esp. Neer 2010: 183–214; Davis 2017; Lakey 2018; Squire 2018; Estrin 2023. The notion of "virtual volume" is developed in relation to relief sculpture by David Summers (2003: 448–50) in his influential *Real Spaces*.

[6] On Fig. 1.1, see Vermeule 1981: 195, no. 161; Zagdoun 1989: 87–90. On the Archaistic style (which was especially popular in Augustan relief sculpture), see Fullerton 1990.

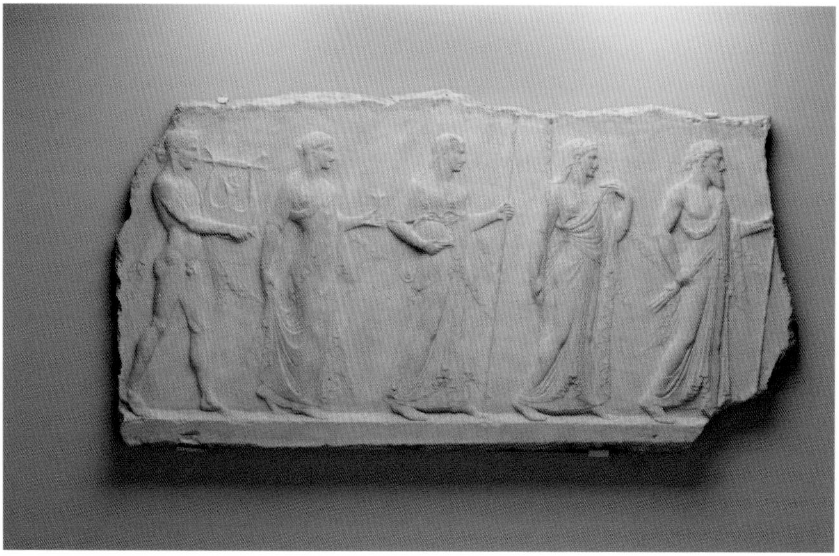

Fig. 1.1 Archaistic relief showing five divinities: Zeus, Hera, Athena, Aphrodite, and Apollo, 25 BCE–14 CE. Marble. New Haven, CT, Yale University Art Gallery, 1965.132 (open access).

developed vocabulary for such effects derived from Renaissance art writing: A specific term for the technique itself (*rilievo*) and its various degrees of modeling were developed by Lorenzo Ghiberti and Leonardo da Vinci and codified by Giorgio Vasari – *alto, mezzo, basso, stiacciato, cavo* (high, medium, low, "flattened," and hollow or "counter-relief," like intaglio); we also have "sunken" relief, associated most often with Egyptian sculpture and, in the Greco-Roman world, carved inscriptions.[7]

If we subject this system to any interpretative rigor, however, we immediately run into some very interesting problems. First, the term *rilievo*, which emerges in the early Renaissance writings of Cennino Cennini and Leon Battista Alberti, is applied to *painting* and the painter's ability to fashion a three-dimensional object on a flat ground through techniques of shading and modeling.[8] Painters may have been *inspired* by relief (as Lakey argues, based on sculptural workings out of "virtual volume" in the Middle Ages, which were informed by a familiarity with ancient optics).[9] But the *language* of *rilievo* emerges as part of a specific discourse about the illusionistic rendering of light and volume in two dimensions. As Steven

[7] On the Renaissance Italian terminology of relief, see Rogers 1974; Freedman 1989; Ostrow 2004; Lakey 2018: 151–70.

[8] Cennini 1932: 5; Leon Battista Alberti 1972: 69, 89.

[9] Lakey 2018.

Ostrow points out, *rilievo* was "a labile term" even in the sixteenth century.[10] In the Renaissance *paragone* of the arts, relief was more often spoken of in terms of what it was not: Leonardo da Vinci observed that *basso rilievo* "fails as both sculpture and painting," though he considered it more intellectually challenging than sculpture in the round, due to its use of perspective and foreshortening.[11] For Vincenzio Borghini, it was an imperfect hybrid, despite its noble pedigree, lacking the best of both painting and three-dimensional sculpture.[12] This sense that relief hovers between mediums, partaking fully of neither, takes us straight up to Alois Riegl, who described it as "Halbform," claiming in his 1899 *Historical Grammar of the Visual Arts* that "The art of form is freestanding sculpture, wherein objects are rendered in three dimensions as tactile surfaces. The art of surface is painting, wherein objects are portrayed in two dimensions as optical surfaces. Relief stands directly between these."[13] In the historiography of art, relief is often defined according to what it fails fully to be: It is condemned to hover somewhere between the "both ... and" and the "neither ... nor." Moreover, the historiographical tradition in which concepts of relief have been formulated assumes that relief-work is both monomedial and monochrome: Attempts to distinguish and then reconcile the relationship between sculpture and painting fall flat as soon as one takes into account that much ancient relief-work would also have been painted – as the recent Tetrarchic finds from Nicomedia so dramatically demonstrate (Fig. 1.2).[14] The addition of pigments (as well as in some cases metal accessories) would not only have complicated distinctions between artistic mediums but also introduced diverse materials that each brought their own cultural associations and aesthetic effects.

10 Ostrow 2004: 332.

11 Da Vinci 1956: I 42, II, fol. 25; I 43, II, fol. 22r–v:

> The sculptor says that low relief is a form of painting. This may be in part conceded as far as drawing is concerned, because it participates in perspective. As far as light and shade are concerned low relief fails both as sculpture and painting, because the shadows correspond to the low nature of the relief, as for example in the shadows of foreshortened objects, which will not exhibit the depth of those in painting or in sculpture in the round. Rather the art of low relief is a mixture of painting and sculpture. . . . Low relief entails considerably more intellectual considerations than sculpture in the round, and it approaches painting with respect to its intellectual considerations, because it is indebted to perspective.

12 See Vincenzio Borghini, *Selva di notizie* (1564) in Barocchi 1971: 658–60; see also Freedman 1989: 238–9; Ostrow 2004: 336–7.

13 Riegl 2004: 400.

14 On the polychrome reliefs from Nicomedia (in the Çukurbağr district of modern İzmit), see Ağtürk 2018; Abbe and Ağtürk 2019.

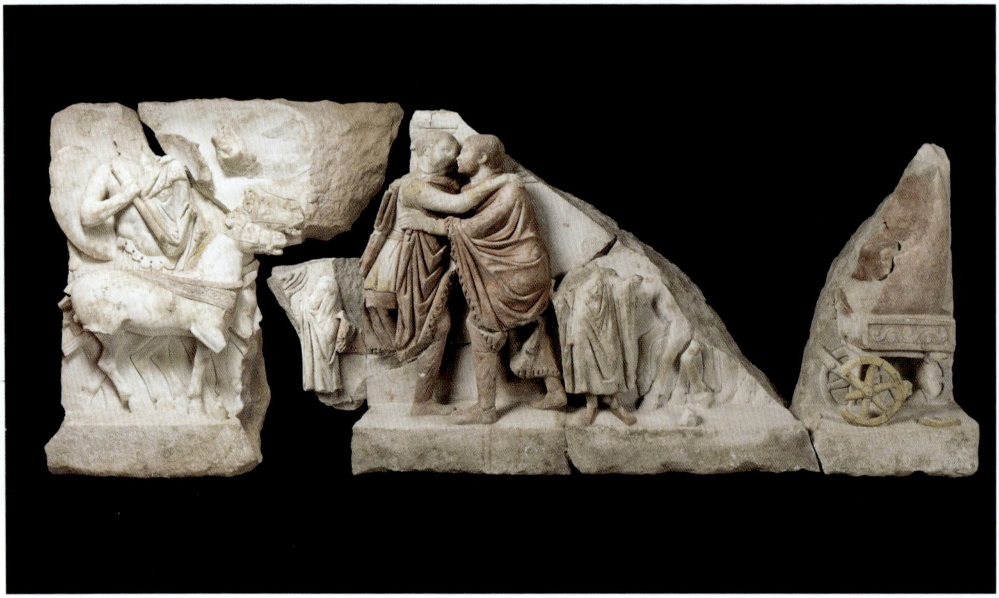

Fig. 1.2 Relief block with embracing emperors from Nicomedia, late third century CE. Marble. Kocaeli Archaeology Museum, TÜBİTAK 115K242 (© Nicomedia–Çukurbağ Archaeological Project [TÜBİTAK 115K242]/Kocaeli Archaeology Museum).

Second, the term *rilievo* comes from the Latin *relevare*, "to lift up," and refers primarily to the sense that pictorial forms are "raised" from their ground: This may well express the visual impression that relief forms "project" from the pictorial field (giving us the term "raised work"). At the same time, it runs counter to the strategies by which relief is most often achieved, which are about cutting *into* or *away* (in the case of hard materials) or pushing *in* or *out* (in the case of those that are molded; here French terms for metalwork such as *repoussé* [literally, "pushed up"] or "chased" [from the French *chasser*, "to drive out"] are more closely tied to technique). "Relief" does not, then, apply in any straightforward way to sculptural technique but rather raises complex questions about the perception of depth – questions that are particular to the medium and context-specific concerns of Renaissance artists and viewers.

This brings us, most importantly, to my third point: that the Latin term *relevare* and cognates such as *relevatio* associated with raising or lifting are never (to my knowledge) applied to relief-work in antiquity itself but are emphatically postclassical (and extremely rare).[15] Thus, like so many of the terms we employ for ancient art (such as "landscape" or "still life"), "relief"

[15] See e.g. Lewis and Short, s.v. relevatio, II, "A lightening, alleviation, relief (postclass. and very rare)."

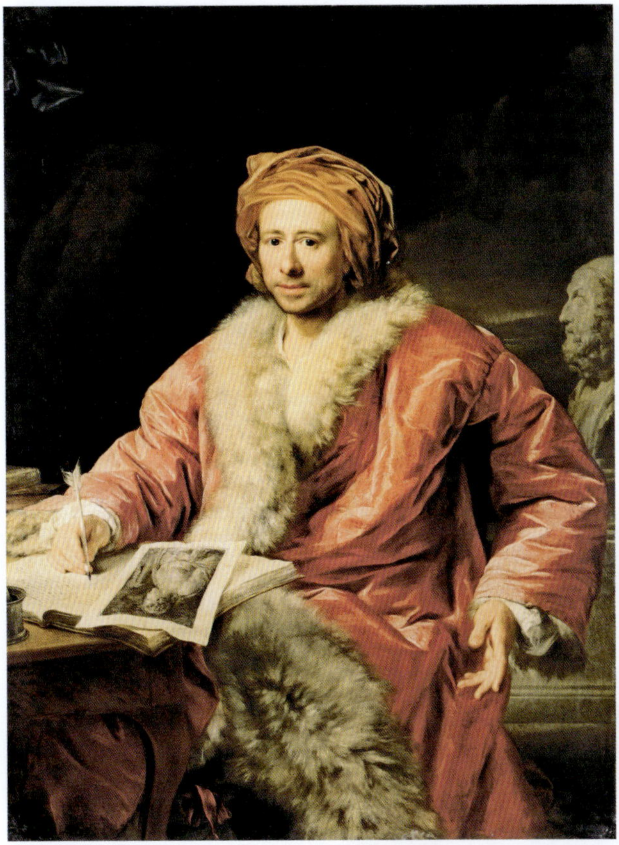

Fig. 1.3 Anton von Maron (1733–1808), *Portrait of Johann Joachim Winckelmann*, 1768. Schloss Weimar, G 70 (Wikimedia Commons).

(from *rilievo*) does not help us to access ancient terminology at all but rather allows us to maintain the fantasy that there was an equivalent concept.[16]

From Johann Joachim Winckelmann's *Albani Antinous* (Fig. 1.3) to Sigmund Freud's *Gradiva* (Fig. 1.4) by way of the Parthenon frieze, Greco-Roman marble reliefs could be said to be constitutive of the antique (and in their stucco form even more constitutive of the neoclassical).[17] Yet despite their ubiquity – and their critical role within our histories of classical

[16] For parallel terminological problems associated with "still life" (associated with *xenia* paintings in antiquity), see e.g. Squire 2017.

[17] On Winckelmann's interest in Antinous and role of the Albani relief in his history of ancient sculpture (as well as Anton von Maron's 1768 portrait), see Vout 2006. The Roman relief in the Vatican Museums that features in Wilhelm Jensen's 1903 novella *Gradiva* is famously discussed in Sigmund Freud's 1907 essay "Delusions and Dreams in Jensen's *Gradiva*" (Freud 1959: 7–95; see also Freud and Jensen 1917); Freud's plaster cast of the relief is still on display in his London home (3713); see Gay 1993; Armstrong 2006; Mayer 2012.

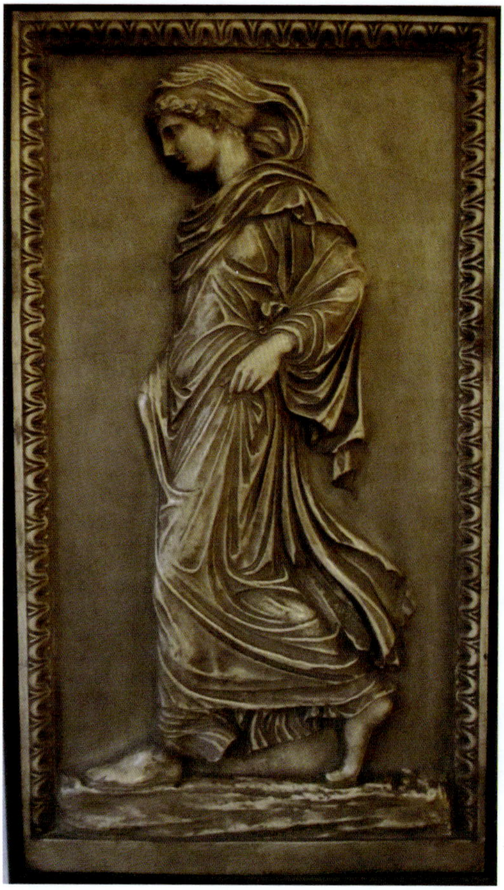

Fig. 1.4 Plaster cast of *Gradiva*, Freud Museum, London. (Wikimedia Commons).

art – reliefs are barely mentioned in our primary sources. Most strikingly, there is no single, unifying term to refer to "reliefs" (as objects) or "relief-work" (as a specific technique). This makes it maddeningly difficult to search for ancient references, even in these days of digital databases such as the *Thesaurus Linguae Graecae*. One can go to the obvious literary sources, such as Vitruvius' *On Architecture*, Pliny the Elder's *Natural History* (*HN*), or Pausanias' *Description of Greece*, but one soon discovers that not only is there no unifying term in those texts but also that reliefs themselves (certainly of the marble variety) are rarely mentioned within the literary record. When Pausanias overlooked the Parthenon frieze in his account of the Athenian Acropolis, this was entirely in keeping with a broader tradition of paying little attention to architectural relief at all.

When reliefs *are* mentioned, however, the language employed is extremely interesting; it reveals the following points, to which I shall keep returning in this chapter:

1. There is no single ancient term for relief; rather, there are clusters of terms that highlight different aspects of medium, facture, visual effect, texture, or value.
2. Terms applied to relief-work continually overlap between mediums and categories.
3. This is primarily because relief-work is characterized by a multiplicity of mediums and techniques; architectural relief is far less prominent in the ancient discourse of relief-work than it is in post-Renaissance receptions of the classical.
4. Because of this more pluralistic approach, relief should not be understood as a single phenomenon in antiquity but as a diverse and unstable category.
5. Relief is also marked by a particular *ontological* indeterminacy, which is often expressed through the vocabulary employed.

Etiology

Given the inherent pluralism of ancient terminology for relief, where might one start? There is no obvious way of imposing structure on what is a highly unruly mass of information. We could proceed chronologically from Homer, where the shield of Achilles is, crucially, an example of relief in the form of *toreutikē* – that is, chased and engraved metalwork.[18] We might observe that this technique, in particular, is the primary object of ekphrasis within the epic tradition. This establishes a fascinating relationship between relief as a visual strategy that mediates between two and three dimensions and ekphrasis as a rhetorical strategy that mediates between the visual and the verbal. In later discourse, both relief-work and ekphrastic description are discussed in terms

[18] Hom. *Il.* 18.478–608. On the material and technological language employed in the ekphrasis, see Francis 2009; Squire 2013 (with extensive bibliography); most recently, see Thein 2021. The Homeric poet does not employ terms specifically associated with "relief," but more general verbs of making such as *teuxō*, *poiein*, and *en . . . tithemi* ("put in/on"). In later texts, *toreutikē* applies to the working of surfaces through carving, chasing, and engraving and is applied to gold, silver, bronze, ivory, and gems. Pollitt (1974: 206) defines *toreutikē* as "the art of working the surface of an object with borer (*toros*), punch, hammer, drill, and so forth, that is, the art of 'chasing.' It applied equally to the working of the surface of a bronze statue, cauldron, or ring, to a stone gem, and to the working of ivory, wood, and other materials." Although for Pollitt there is "no sharp distinction between *toreutikē* and 'sculpture,'" he applies it to the "decorative arts," as distinct from statues and architectural reliefs.

of "impressions," or *phantasiai*, upon the *psychē*.[19] Meanwhile, relief in the so-called minor arts (such as metal plate, carved wood, and engraved gems) continues to dominate canonical ekphrastic texts from Theocritus' cup through Vergil's shield of Aeneas and golden gates of Daedalus to the engraved amethyst of Heliodorus' *Aethiopica*.[20] That is a topic for another chapter, though it is worth observing how little attention scholarship on ekphrasis has paid to the prominence of relief forms in epic ekphrases as opposed to their pictorialism, especially given that the relief impression provides the dominant metaphor for the cognitive effects of descriptive *enargeia*. Strabo, for example, claims that Homer's description of Zeus in Book 1 of the *Iliad* stirs the imagination to "visualize an impression [*typon*] of some mighty being" (ἀναζωγραφεῖν μέγαν τινὰ τύπον).[21] If, for a lyric poet like Simonides, painting is silent poetry, then for Homer and his successors, epic is arguably relief that speaks.

While Homer offers an originary literary site for thinking through relief-work on embossed metal plate, his equivalent in the historiography of art is Pliny the Elder. Conveniently, *HN* also gives us an origin myth for ancient relief sculpture (which I will come to later in this chapter), an etiological ground zero that highlights the problems just raised – the confusing nature of relevant terminology, as well as the instability and indeterminacy of relief as an artistic category.[22] Look to Pliny's sections on sculpture in Books 34 and 36, however, and one will find very limited discussion of relief.[23] One might take it as programmatic that in his celebration of Pheidias in Book 36 (on stones, *lapides*), Pliny describes the chased gold reliefs on the Athena Parthenos' helmet, shield, and base as "small matters" (*parva*) that inadvertently reveal the *magnificentia* of the whole.[24] As forms of *toreutikē* (described in the Latin as *caelatum*), these place Pheidias within

[19] On the role of *phantasia* in the language of ekphrasis, see especially Goldhill 1994: 207–10; Elsner 1995: 26–8; Dubel 1997; Manieri 1998; Thein 2002; Webb 2009: 87–130; Bates 2021. On reliefs as "impressions," see Platt, in press, and my discussion in this chapter.

[20] Theoc. *Id.* 1.27–60; Verg. *Aen.* 8.626–78, 6.14–33; Heliod. *Aeth.* 5.13–14.

[21] Strabo, *Geography* 8.3.30, referring to Hom. *Il.* 1.528 and its influence on Pheidias' chryselephantine statue of Zeus at Olympia. Note that Strabo mixes his metaphors here, employing the language of painting in his use of *anazōgraphein* as well as that of the impression; on this tendency in ekphrastic epigrams of the same period, see Platt 2018a, in press.

[22] Plin. *HN* 35.151, discussed later in this chapter.

[23] On the "art-historical" sections of *HN* in Books 33–7, which are all too often discussed in isolation from the rest of the text, see (from a vast and growing bibliography) Naas 2002; Carey 2003; Tanner 2006: 235–46; most recently, see Platt 2018a, 2018b; Anguissola and Grüner 2020; Darab 2020; Anguissola 2021.

[24] Plin. *HN* 36.18–19. The most thorough examination of evidence for the Athena Parthenos is Lapatin 2001: 61–95 (with further bibliography). On discussions of the Parthenos in literary sources, see *DNO*, s.v. Phidias no. 10, vol. 2, nos. 889–935, 171–214; Lapatin 1996, 2001: 154–92.

a grand tradition that goes back to both Homer's shield and Hesiod's Pandora, but in the context of Pliny's histories of bronze and marble sculpture, it is fully three-dimensional form that dominates.[25] Book 36 makes passing reference to the sculptors of the Mausoleum of Halicarnassus (36.30–1), again using the term *caelavit* (which can mean both "chased" and, by extension, "carved"); to the reliefs of the Temple of Artemis at Ephesus (*caelatae*, 36.95); and to the use of plaster stucco "for molded figures and garlands," where he uses the term *sigillum*, equivalent to the Greek *typos*, or "impression" (*sigillis aedificiorum et coronis*, 36.183), which we also find in the term given to the molded ceramic tableware known as *terra sigillata*, or "stamped earth."[26] The variety of terms used here – and the transfer of *caelare*, an equivalent to the Greek *toreuein*, from metalwork to carving in stone – demonstrates just how confusing and somewhat underdetermined the language of relief can be.

One of the reasons why relief has only a scattered presence across *HN* is because it is not an artistic *medium* in the traditional sense: It is not associated with a specific category of *matter* but rather pops up within Pliny's materially oriented taxonomy as and when relief techniques are deployed *across* various mediums.[27] It may thus come as a surprise to those who associate relief primarily with marble that Pliny actually mentions it most prominently in Book 35, which we commonly identify as the "Book on Painting." Actually, Book 35 is focused on earths (*terrae*) and therefore pigments and also includes clay and thus work in terra-cotta. At 35.151, Pliny introduces us to the "Corinthian potter's daughter," who famously established the medium of painting – and thus an enduring fantasy of the indexical image – by drawing the silhouetted outline of her departing lover on a wall (*in pariete lineis circumscripsit*).[28]

On Pliny's use of the phrase *magnificentiam ... in parvis* and his focus on the statue's relief elements, see Platt 2021.

[25] On the relief scene of Pandora on the base of the Athena Parthenos and its relationship to Hes. *Theog*. 560–612 and *Op*. 53–105, see Leipen 1971: 24–7 (with proposals for reconstructions), Schuhardt 1975; Loraux 1993: 114–15; Hurwit 1995, 2004: 151–3; Connelly 1996: 72–6; Lapatin 2001: 67; Platt 2011: 111–13.

[26] On techniques employed in the production of *terra sigillata*, see Van Oyen 2016. Pliny also refers to the carving (*inscalptae*) of a lizard and frog into the columns of temples enclosed by the Porticoes of Octavia as symbols of the Greek names of their patrons, Sauras and Batrachus (*HN* 36.42), and to carved bases and capitals of the columns in the Temple of Artemis at Ephesus (*columnis spirae subditae et capitula addita*, *HN* 36.179).

[27] On Pliny's focus on matter and materiality in *HN*, see Platt 2016, 2018a, 2018b, in press; Anguissola 2021; and esp. the diverse essays focused on Pliny's references to different materials in Anguissola and Grüner 2020.

[28] On Pliny's anecdote of the Corinthian potter Butades and his daughter, see e.g. Bettini 1999: 7–17; Naas 2012, with *DNO*, nos. 186–8 on sources for Butades. On its later European reception (memorably encapsulated in Joseph Wright of Derby's *The Corinthian Maid*, 1782–4, now in the

> Enough and more than enough has now been said about painting. It may be suitable to append to these remarks something about *plastice*. It was through the service of that same earth [*terra*] that modeling portraits from clay [*fingere ex argilla similitudine*] was first invented by Butades, a potter of Sicyon, at Corinth. He did this owing to his daughter, who was in love with a young man; and she, when he was going abroad, drew in outline on the wall the shadow of his face thrown by a lamp. Her father pressed clay on this and made a relief [*inpressa argilla typum fecit*], which he hardened by exposure to fire with the rest of his pottery, and it is said that this likeness was preserved in the Shrine of the Nymphs until the destruction of Corinth by Mummius. Some authorities state that the plastic art was first invented by Rhoecus and Theodorus at Samos, long before the expulsion of the Bacchiadae from Corinth, but that when Damaratus, who in Etruria became the father of Tarquin king of the Roman people, was banished from the same city, he was accompanied by the *fictores* Euchir, Diopus, and Eugrammus, and they introduced *plastice* to Italy. The method of adding red earth to the material or else modeling [*fingere*] out of red chalk was an invention of Butades, and he first placed masks as fronts to the outer gutter-tiles on roofs; these at the first stage he called *prostypa*, but afterward he likewise made *ectypa*. It was from these that the ornaments on the pediments of temples originated. Because of Butades modelers get their Greek name of *plastae*.[29]

For Pliny, the Corinthian maid's invention of two-dimensional drawing/painting is swiftly developed by her father, Butades, who then "pressed clay on this and made an image, which he hardened by exposure to fire with the rest of his pottery," so inventing portrait sculpture. The Latin reads *inpressa argilla typum fecit* ("with impressed clay he made a *typos*"), employing the Greek term for "impression," which is usually translated here as "relief." As the object was then dedicated in a local shrine to the Nymphs, perhaps we are to imagine

National Gallery of Art, Washington, DC, inv. 1983.1.46), see Rosenblum 1957; Stoichita 1997: 14–20; Muecke 1999; King 2004; Güthenke 2010. On the anecdote's role within a deep media history of the image and recursive "technologies of the self," see Macho 2013; Vauday 2017; on its relationship to contemporary strategies of remembrance in the visual arts, see Saltzman 2006.

29 Translation (with some adaptations) from Rackham 1938. *De pictura satis superque. contexuisse his et plasticen conveniat. eiusdem opere terrae fingere ex argilla similitudines Butades Sicyonius figulus primus invenit Corinthi filiae opera, quae capta amore iuvenis, abeunte illo peregre, umbram ex facie eius ad lucernam in pariete lineis circumscripsit, quibus pater eius inpressa argilla typum fecit et cum ceteris fictilibus induratum igni proposuit, eumque servatum in Nymphaeo, donec Mummius Corinthum everterit, tradunt. sunt qui in Samo primos omnium plasticen invenisse Rhoecum et Theodorum tradant multo ante Bacchiadas Corintho pulsos, Damaratum vero ex eadem urbe profugum, qui in Etruria Tarquinium regem populi Romani genuit, comitatos fictores Euchira, Diopum, Eugrammum; ab iis Italiae traditam plasticen. Butadis inventum est rubricam addere aut ex rubra creta fingere, primusque personas tegularum extremis imbricibus inposuit, quae inter initia prostypa vocavit; postea idem ectypa fecit. hinc et fastigia templorum orta. propter hunc plastae appellati.*

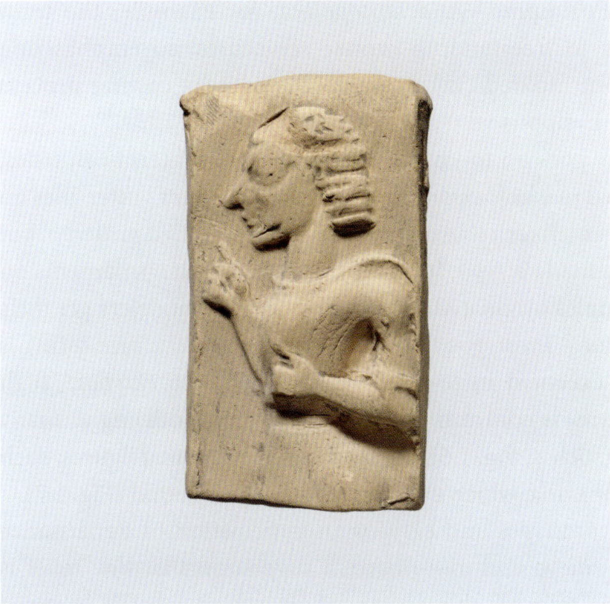

Fig. 1.5 Fragment of a plaque depicting the upper body of a youth, seventh century BCE, from Praisos, Crete. 7.6 × 4.1 cm. New York, Metropolitan Museum of Art, 53.5.15 (Creative Commons Zero [CC0]).

a votive *pinax*, such as an early Archaic terra-cotta relief of a youth in profile from Crete (Fig. 1.5).[30] In temple inventories such as those from Epidaurus, votive *pinakes* are repeatedly referred to as *typoi* (as Jerome Pollitt reminds us in his invaluable entry on the term *typos* in *The Ancient View of Greek Art*).[31]

Can we, however, assume so readily that Pliny is referring to relief, as opposed to sculpture in the round? Pliny lists Butades and his Corinthian associates alongside Rhoecus and Theodorus of Samos as developers of the art of *plastikē*, or "modeling," which eventually, he tells us, traveled from Corinth to Etruscan Italy.[32] But the term *plastikē* primarily refers to the nature of clay itself, and the process of molding form from a pliable material: Pertaining to both terra-cotta sculpture and the preliminary stages of bronze casting (which begins with a clay core), it is a reference to the properties of the medium employed rather than relative degrees of

[30] On Fig. 1.5, see Karoglou 2016: 7, no. 3.

[31] See e.g. Pollitt 1974: 276, no. 38 (*IG* II^2 1534, lines 35, 64, 87–8, sanctuary of Asclepius inventory, 276–275 BCE); 277, no. 40 (*IG* II–III^2 839, lines 18, 56–7, dedication to the Heros Iatros, 221–220 BCE).

[32] On Theodorus and Rhoecus of Samos, see *DNO*, nos. 267–93, 294–7, with Squire 2011: 283–302, 367–70, 383–4.

dimensionality. In Posidippus' *Andriantopoiika*, for example, the term *typos* seems to refer to freestanding bronze sculptures, so emphasizing their production from molded clay through the lost wax casting process by sculptors such as Lysippus who are also described as *plastae*.[33]

Nevertheless, Pliny goes on to give us two further useful terms: Butades, he tells us, "first placed masks [*personae*] as fronts to the outer gutter-tiles on roofs [i.e. terra-cotta antefixes]; these at the first stage he called *prostypa*, but afterward he likewise made *ectypa*. It was from these that the ornaments on the pediments of temples originated. Because of Butades modelers get their Greek name of *plastae*." *Prostypos* (which is actually quite a rare term) is often translated as "executed in low relief," in contrast to *ektypos*, "high relief."[34] Pliny, it seems, is contrasting the relatively flat modeling of many terra-cotta antefixes (such as Fig. 1.6) with Etruscan pedimental figures, such as those from Pyrgi or Luna, which are almost fully in the round (Fig. 1.7).[35] Do we have here in *prostypos* and *ektypos* an anticipation of Renaissance terms such as *basso-rilievo* and *alto-rilievo*, a suggestion that low relief is "pressed forward" or "toward" the viewer, whereas high relief is "pressed out" more fully? We should be careful not to assume such easy parallels. *Prostypoein* literally means "to mold to" something, carrying the sense of impressing a material "upon" or "against" a surface; it thus means "to mold to the shape of," as for Galen the lungs "mold to" the cavity of the thorax (προστετυπῶσθαι . . . τῷ θώρακι), echoing how for Aristotle the viscera of snakes take the form of their bodies "as if in a mold" (κάθαπερ ἐν τύπῳ).[36] It does not specifically imply the visual appearance of *low* relief but rather suggests the process of shaping through molding – a technique that would be especially appropriate for terra-cotta antefixes produced in replica series. Indeed, a quick survey of Greek and Italian antefixes demonstrates that they could range from very shallow relief right through to fully modeled almost three-dimensional forms – especially those that are closer to theatrical

[33] Posidippus AB 62, line 5, referring to the "hard *typoi* of the sculptor of Didyma" (οἱ Διδυμίδου σκληροὶ τύποι): see Seidensticker 2015: 250–4 for the text and commentary, with further discussion in Sens 2005: 207–9; Stewart 2005: 185–90; Adornato 2007: 15–18; Prioux and Santin 2017; Platt, in press.

[34] See e.g. *LSJ*, s.v. πρόστυπος.

[35] On Greek architectural terra-cottas (and the influence of the Corinthian system in particular), see Winter 1993. On Fig. 1.6, see Richter 1953: 30, pl. 19e. On Fig. 1.7, see Colonna 1996, 2000, 2006.

[36] See *LSJ*, s.v. προστυπόω, citing Galen 2.700 Kühn (*De anatomicis administrationibus* 9, προστετυπῶσθαι τὸν πνεύμονα κατὰ τοῦτο τῷ θώρακι); Arist. *Part. an.* 676b9 (Pollitt 1974: 275, no. 27). Compare the notion expressed by Dio Chrysostom (Pollitt 1974: 280, no. 63) that "Workmen give clay whatever form they wish by pressing it in molds, philosophers do the same with myths" (60.9, καὶ γὰρ ἐκεῖνοι τύπον τινὰ παρέχοντες, ὁποῖον ἂν πηλὸν εἰς τοῦτον ἐμβάλωσιν, ὅμοιον τῷ τύπῳ τὸ εἶδος ἀποτελοῦσιν).

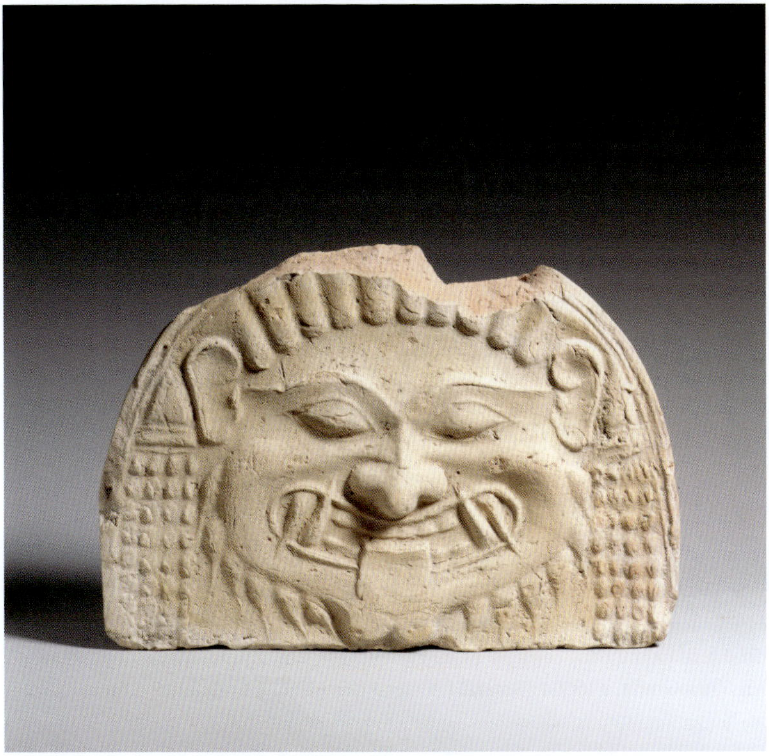

Fig. 1.6 Terra-cotta gorgoneion antefix, said to be from Taranto, ca. 580–570 BCE. Height: 17.1 cm; width: 24.4 cm. New York, Metropolitan Museum of Art, 10.210.44 (Creative Commons Zero [CC0]).

masks; meanwhile, several inscriptions from Delos refer to wooden molds for roof tiles as *typoi*.[37] The important point about Pliny's *prostypa*, I would argue, is that as architectural moldings placed along roof gutters, they are conceived and produced as sets.

Could it be, as some have suggested, that Pliny is thinking of *prostypa* as molds and *ectypa* as impressions taken from them? We can certainly find examples of such a usage in later Greek texts, such as when Lucian refers to pitch placed on the bronze statue of Hermes Agoraios in Athens by sculptors who wish to make molds from it, using the term ἐκτυπούμενος.[38] But this seems unlikely in Pliny's case, given that in Book 37, he refers to engraved gems which are deemed "suitable for the cutting of *ectypae*."[39] Here, *ectypa*

[37] For example, Pollitt 1974: 277, nos. 45, 46; *Inscriptions de Délos* (Compte des Hiéropes) 406.44 (ca. 190 BCE), 442B.72 (179 BCE), 444.12 (177 BCE), 457.22 (174 BCE).

[38] Pollitt 1974: 280, no. 66 (μιμηλῆ τέχνῃ σφραγῖδα χαλκοῦ πᾶσαν ἐκτυπούμενος).

[39] Plin. *HN* 37.173: "[Mormorion stones are] gems which are eminently suitable for cameo-engraving [*gemmae, quae ad ectypas scalpturas aptantur*]."

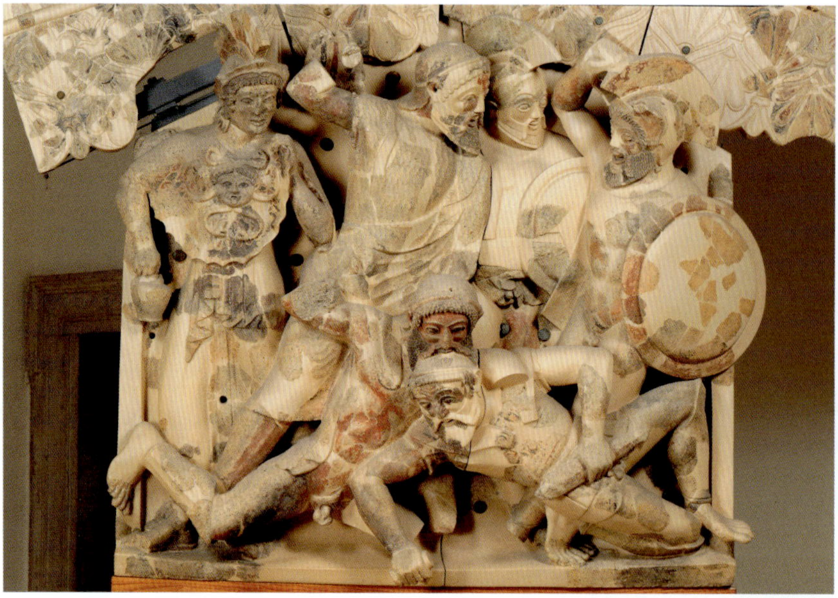

Fig. 1.7 Pedimental relief from Temple A at Pyrgi, Etruria, depicting the *Seven against Thebes*, first half of the fifth century BCE. Height: 146 cm. Rome, Museo Nazionale Etrusco di Villa Giulia, 146094 (Scala/Ministero per i Beni e le Attività culturali/Art Resource, NY).

seems to refer to the image carved within the gem itself (whether in intaglio or cameo) rather than the impressions it might form in wax or clay (though these can, of course, be implied). In earlier Greek texts, *ektypos* seems to be applied to relief effects across various media: It is used by Diodorus Siculus to refer to goat-stag *protomai* projecting from the gold cornice on Alexander's funeral carriage (18.26–7);[40] the verb *ektypoō* is also applied to the modeling of relief figures on statue bases (by Xenophon) and to stone stelai (by Plato).[41]

[40] Pollitt 1974: 278, no. 52; Diod. Sic. 18.26–7 (on Alexander's funeral carriage): "Beneath the roof all along the work was a rectangular cornice of gold, from which projected heads of goat-stags in high relief [ἔχων τραγελάφων προτομὰς ἐκτύπους]."

[41] Pollitt 1974: 275, no. 24; Xen. *Eq. mag.* 1: "True, there is already a treatise on horsemanship by Simon, who also dedicated the bronze horse in the Eleusinium at Athens and recorded his own feats in relief on the pedestal [ἐν τῷ βάθρῳ τὰ ἑαυτοῦ ἔργα ἐξετύπωσεν]." Pollitt 1974: 274, no. 21; Pl. *Symp.* 193a (Aristophanes' speech):

> Formerly, as I have said, we were one; but now for our sins we are all dispersed by God, as the Arcadians were by the Lacedaemonians; and we may well be afraid that if we are disorderly towards Heaven we may once more be cloven asunder and may go about in the shape of those outline-carvings on the tombs, with our noses sawn down the middle, and may thus become like tokens of split dice [ὥσπερ οἱ ἐν ταῖς στήλαις καταγραφὴν ἐκτετυπωμένοι, διαπεπρισμένοι κατὰ τὰς ῥῖνας, γεγονότες ὥσπερ λίσπαι].

The prefix *ek-*, when applied to materials, often seems to carry the association of "out of," as in the material "out of which things are made," as well as the notion of being "pressed out of" a mold. The image on an engraved gem is thus carved "out of" (yet is still bound to) the precious stone itself, just as Ionian reliefs referred to by Herodotus are described as *typoi* that are "carved out of" the living rock (ἐγγέγλυπται).[42] A terra-cotta *ektypon*, by extension, is "pressed out of" clay: It suggests an image that is molded or stamped (from *typoō*) and that *emerges from* its ground, thus projecting into the viewer's field of vision. In this sense, it complements the Latin verb *eminere*, "to stand out," and therefore "to project" or "extend from" a surface. Seneca thus describes a gemstone engraved with a portrait of Tiberius (*habens ectypa et eminente gemma*). This puts its drunken wearer at risk when he nearly wears it to go to the bathroom, thereby inadvertently insulting the emperor.[43] *Eminens*, here, seems to suggest a relief portrait (for which we would use the term "cameo," such as the Tiberian example in Fig. 1.8) rather than a seal cut in intaglio (such as that in Fig. 1.9), though it draws attention to the problem of how to understand engraved gems as a category of "relief."[44] While being appreciated as precious objects in their own right (as Posidippus' *Lithika* make clear), intaglios are also understood as molds for the production of reliefs: They are in effect the *archetypa* – the "originary molds" – from which

42 Hdt. 2.106: "Also there are in Ionia two figures [τύποι] of this man carven in rock, one on the road from Ephesus to Phocaea, and the other on that from Sardis to Smyrna. In both places there is a man of a height of four cubits and a half cut in relief [ἑκατέρωθι δὲ ἀνὴρ ἐγγέγλυπται μέγαθος πέμπτης σπιθαμῆς], with a spear in his right hand and a bow in his left, and the rest of his equipment answering thereto; for it is both Egyptian and Ethiopian; and right across the breast from one shoulder to the other there is carven a writing in the Egyptian sacred character, saying: 'I myself won this land with the might of my shoulders.' There is nothing here to show who he is and whence he comes, but it is shown elsewhere. Some of those who have seen these figures [εἰκόνα] guess them to be Memnon, but they are far indeed from the truth." Translation from Godley 1920.

43 Sen. *Ben.* 3.26: "Paulus, a praetorian, while dining on a certain festive occasion, was wearing a ring with a conspicuous stone on which the portrait of Tiberius Caesar was engraved in relief [*imaginem Tib. Caesaris habens ectypa et eminente gemma*]. I should be acting in very silly fashion if I tried, at this point, to find a polite way of saying that he took in his hands a chamber-pot – an action that was noticed simultaneously by Maro, one of the notorious informers of that time, and by a slave of the victim for whom the trap was being set, who drew off the ring from the finger of his drunken master. And, when Maro called the company to witness that the emperor's portrait had been brought in contact with something foul, and was drawing up the indictment, the slave showed that the ring was on his own hand. Whoever calls such a man a slave, will also call Maro a boon companion!" Translation from Basore 1935; for discussion, see Altman 1938.

44 On Fig. 1.8, see Platz-Horster 2008; Knudsen 2016, with previous bibliography. On Fig. 1.9, see von Bothmer et al. 1995: 18; Milleker et al. 2000: 59, 206; Picón 2009: 20–1, fig. 29.

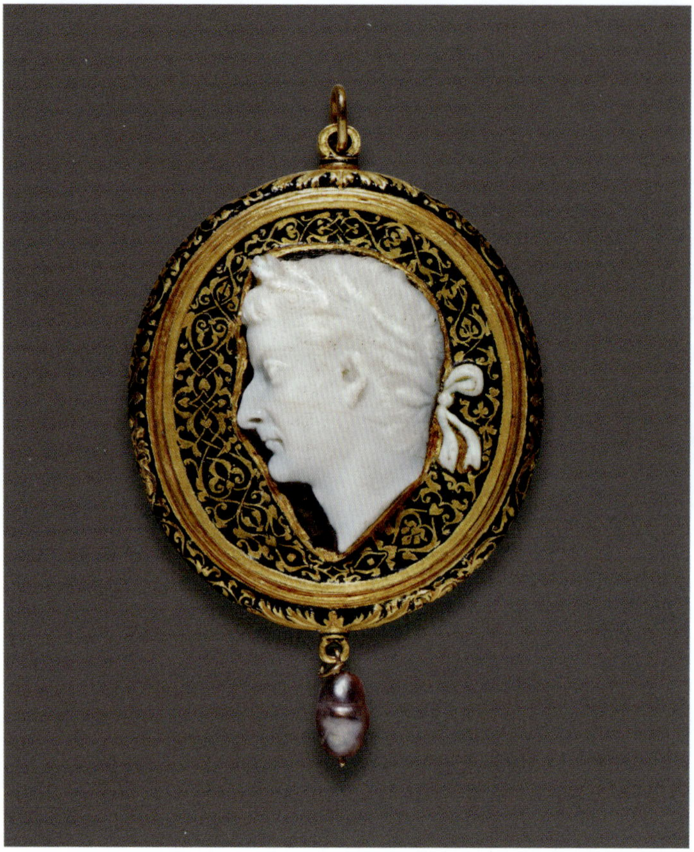

Fig. 1.8 Cameo with portrait bust of Tiberius, 14–37 CE, set into a mount dated 1525–50. Sardonyx, gold, enamel, and pearl, 8 × 4.8 × 1 cm. Art Institute of Chicago, 1992.297 (Creative Commons Zero [CC0]).

typoi are produced in the form of positive impressions.[45] At the same time, the term *ekmageion* (from *ekmassō*, "mold") is applied by Plato to the wax block that serves as his model for the mind's capacity to receive and hold memories in the *Theaetetus* and to the "molding stuff for everything" (ἐκμαγεῖον γὰρ . . . παντί) with which he explains the impression of Forms upon the world of Becoming in the *Timaeus*.[46] In all these contexts, the function of *ek-* seems to convey a particular kind of relationship between figure and ground – one in which relief effects can be impressed inward or projected outward (can be "negative" or "positive," "low," or "high"), in which they can be transferred

[45] On ancient use of the term *archetypon* (which seems to have emerged in the first century BCE), see Platt, in press.

[46] Pl. *Tht.* 191d–e; *Ti.* 50b–c; see (from a vast bibliography) Bostock 1988: 169–90; Burnyeat 1990; Harte 2010; Ambuel 2015: 148–73.

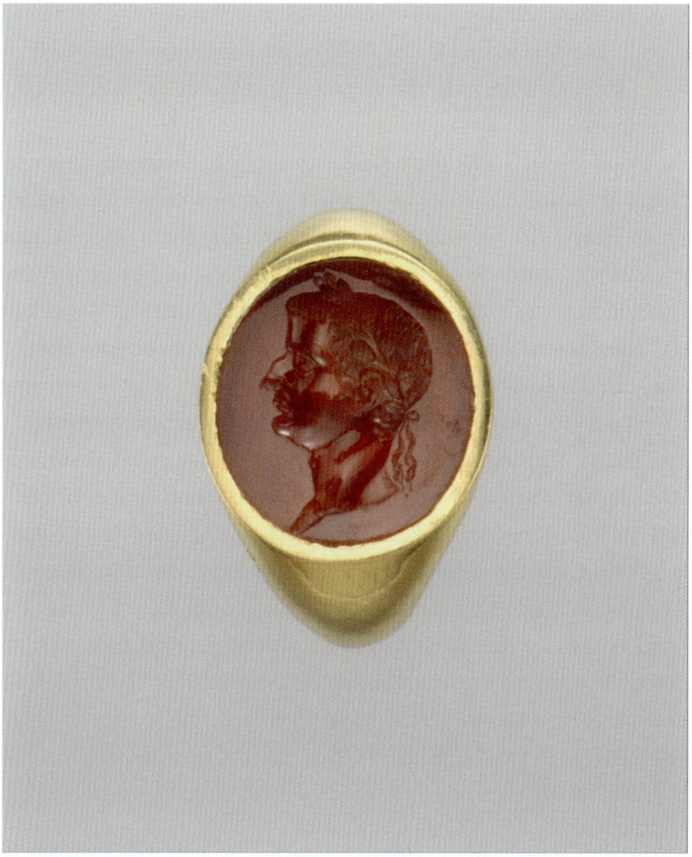

Fig. 1.9 Gold ring with carnelian intaglio portrait of Tiberius, 13–37 CE. Overall: 2.1 cm. New York, Metropolitan Museum of Art, 1994.230.7 (Creative Commons Zero [CC0]).

from one medium to another through the mechanism of stamping, but in which all are fundamentally bound to the material substrate from which they are formed.

In Pausanias' *Description of Greece*, the relationship between figure and ground actually becomes the means by which reliefs can be identified, here using the preposition *epi-*, "upon". For he repeatedly refers to them using the term *epeirgasmenos*, from *epergomai*, "to work upon" or "cultivate on": This is applied to figures on the helmet and base of the Athena Parthenos (as well as the bases of other cult statues), to the cedar wood carvings on the chest of Cypselus, to funerary and votive stelai, and to *pinakes* set into temple walls.[47]

[47] Paus. 1.24.6–7: "On the middle of her helmet is placed a likeness [εἰκών] of the Sphinx – the tale of the Sphinx I will give when I come to my description of Boeotia – and on either side of the

Pausanias uses it so consistently that it acquires the status of a *terminus technicus* – one that, like terms found in Pliny, is not concerned with style or representation so much as with material support and technical process (the idea of "working upon").[48]

Elsewhere in Book 35 of *HN*, Pliny uses the term *eminere* to describe illusionistic effects in painting, such as Apelles' portrait of Alexander, in which his fingers "have the appearance of projecting from the surface [*digiti eminere videntur*] and the thunderbolt seems to stand out from the picture [*extra tabulam esse*]"; likewise, Nicias makes "painting stand out from the panels" (*eminerent e tabulis picturae*).[49] This usage echoes that of Vitruvius, who applied it to Second Style fresco painting, in which columns and pediments seem to project into space (*eminentes proiecturas*).[50] Painting, in this sense, imitates the sense of volume that relief produces through its particular conjuring of both material and virtual space. In both cases, the visual impression of projection is tied to the idea that forms emerge *from* a ground. In the case of the *ektypon*, however, this is to be understood as both a virtual and a material phenomenon: Relief forms are *pushed out of* and comprise *the same substance as* the ground from which they are produced. We might compare a reference made by Quintilian to the art of metal-chasing (*toreutikē*/*caelatura*), which, as we have seen, overlaps considerably with the language of the *typos*. Commenting on the value of rough drafts in the composition of speeches, Quintilian states that

helmet are griffins in relief [ἐπειργασμένοι]. . . . On the pedestal is the birth of Pandora in relief [ἔστι δὲ τῷ βάθρῳ τοῦ ἀγάλματος ἐπειργασμένη Πανδώρας γένεσις]"; 5.2.14: "Beside Pyrrhus is a little man holding flutes, carved in relief upon a slab [ἐκτετυπωμένος ἐπὶ στήλῃ]"; 5.17.5: "There is also a chest made of cedar, with figures on it, some of ivory, some of gold, others carved out of the cedar-wood itself [ζῴδια δὲ ἐλέφαντος ἐπ᾽ αὐτῆς, τὰ δὲ χρυσοῦ, τὰ δὲ καὶ ἐξ αὐτῆς ἐστὶν εἰργασμένα τῆς κέδρου]"; 7.17.8: "A little before the city of Dyme there is, on the right of the road, the grave of Sostratus. . . . Even today there is a slab [στήλη] on the top of the mound, with a figure of Heracles in relief [Ἡρακλῆς ἐπειργασμένος]"; 8.37.1: "As you go to the temple there is a portico on the right, with reliefs of white marble on the wall [λίθου λευκοῦ τύποι πεποιημένοι]. On the first relief are wrought [ἐπειργασμέναι] Fates and Zeus surnamed Guide of Fate, and on the second Heracles wresting a tripod from Apollo."

48 On Pausanias' consistent use of specific terms for artifacts, see e.g. his use of *xoanon* and *agalma* in relation to sacred images, discussed by Donohue 1988: 140–9; Platt 2011: 91–9.

49 Plin. *HN* 35.92; see also 35.151: "[Apelles] also painted Alexander the Great holding a thunderbolt, in the temple of Artemis at Ephesus, for a fee of twenty talents in gold. The fingers have the appearance of projecting from the surface [*digiti eminere videntur*] and the thunderbolt seems to stand out from the picture [*extra tabulam esse*]."

50 Vitr. *De arch.* 7.5.2, a passage that is most often read in relation to both Vitruvius' comments on *scaenographia* in the Greek theater and the development of Second Style fresco paintings featuring perspectival scenes; see e.g. Rouveret 1989: 65–127; Tybout 1989; Stinson 2011. Note that this formulation of painting-as-relief is significantly different from discussions of painting as *rilievo* in later Renaissance texts, which are more concerned with the illusionistic modeling effects generated by light, shade, and perspective.

"The more correct method is . . . to exercise care from the very beginning, and to form the work from the outset in such a manner that it merely requires to be chased into shape, not fashioned anew [*ut caelandum, non ex integro fabricandum sit*]": The relief image is, as it were, already integral to its object but has to be "pushed" or "hollowed" into its final form rather than applied to a flat surface.[51]

In Pliny's Butades passage, then, ***ec**typa* do not seem to be *contrasted* with ***pros**typa* but rather are described as a progression from one kind of technique to another, most obviously from a replica series of antefixes to more complex pedimental sculpture. These *fastigia templorum* (if this is what *ectypa* refers to) tend to be individually modeled, complex compositions that may still be fixed to their ground but are closer to freestanding sculpture than to architectural moldings. Relief, in Pliny's narrative, thus emerges from painting as line, develops as architectural ornament, and then blossoms as more fully modeled architectural sculpture. Crucially, this all happens within a medium (clay) with very specific affordances: It is widely available, it is malleable, it can be stamped from molds, and it can be modeled freehand as high relief or sculpture in the round. It thus lends itself to both the serially produced and the unique, crossing between (and indeed challenging) the categories of architecture and sculpture, ornament and figure, quotidian craft and highly skilled artistry.[52]

Ontology

In the context of *HN*, the emergence of painting and sculpture from such modest origins (and the absence of marble from this narrative) is part of Pliny's broader ethical and political agenda: The humble medium of clay, as a category of *terra*, is capable of producing forms that are aligned with the logic of *Natura* herself, just as, in his account of Greek painting, the throwing of Protogenes' sponge famously creates an impression of foam that "produces Nature" in his depiction of a drooling dog.[53] Both the Butades and Protogenes anecdotes offer an alternative ontology of the image to that of *mimēsis* – a form of "truth" (*verum*) rather than "truthlikeness" (*verisimile*), which bypasses Platonic concerns about the deceptive illusionism of representation in order to celebrate the replicative potential

[51] Quint. *Inst.* 10.3.18. [52] See Hopkins 2024.

[53] On Pliny's investment in the materiality and integrity of artistic mediums, see note 27. On the sponge of Protogenes anecdote (*HN* 35.102–3), see especially Darab 2012, 2014a: 216–18, 2014b: 284–90, 2020: 70–8; Thein 2015; Falaschi 2018; Platt 2016: 74–6, 2018a, 2018b, in press.

of matter itself.[54] Here, painting and relief are not presented as an inferior imitations of reality but as contiguous with it, the artist playing the role not of transformative genius, but of Nature's unwitting agent. This is underlined by the indexical "truth" of Butades' first sculptural creation: It is no accident that the first relief is identified as a *typos* – an "impression" – for it follows the traced profile of its absent subject in such a way that it is "molded" to it, converting line into volume. Nor is it an accident that Butades goes on to make antefixes in the form of molded masks (*personae*), for these resonate with the wax *imagines* of Republican Roman ancestors on which Pliny places so much weight at the beginning of Book 35.[55] Indeed, his history of *plastikē* moves immediately from Butades to Lysistratus of Sicyon, brother of Lysippus, and the invention of three-dimensional wax and plaster casting techniques taken directly from the human body, in the service of sculptural realism in portraiture.[56] Here, as elsewhere in his histories of art, Pliny is deeply preoccupied with modes of image making formulated around the concepts of the impression and the trace: Relief *as typos* thus plays an important role in his broader ontology of the image.

[54] Plin. *HN* 35.103, on Protogenes: "vexed and tormented, as he wanted his picture to contain the truth and not merely a near-truth" (*anxio animi cruciatu, cum in pictura verum esse, non verisimile vellet*).

[55] Plin. *HN* 35.6: "In the halls of our ancestors, portraits were the objects to be displayed to be looked at, not statues by foreign artists, nor bronzes nor marbles, but wax models of faces were set out each on a separate side-board, to furnish likenesses [*imagines*] to be carried in procession at a funeral in the clan, occasions on which every member of the family that had ever existed was always present" (*Apud maiores in atriis haec erant, quae spectarentur; non signa externorum artificum nec aera aut marmora: expressi cera vultus singulis disponebantur armariis, ut essent imagines, quae comitarentur gentilicia funera, semperque defuncto aliquo totus aderat familiae eius qui umquam fuerat populus*). On this much-discussed passage, see esp. Bažant 1991; Flower 1996; Blöme 2001; Pollini 2012; on associated funerary practices, including wax and plaster masks from Roman tombs, see also Drerup 1980; Dasen 2010; Pointon 2014; Crowley 2016.

[56] Plin. *HN* 35.153: "The first person who modelled a likeness in plaster of a human being from the living face itself, and established the method of pouring wax into this plaster mould and then making final corrections on the wax cast, was Lysistratus of Sicyon, the brother of Lysippus of whom we have spoken. Indeed he introduced the practice of giving likenesses, the object aimed at previously having been to make as handsome a face as possible. The same artist also invented taking casts from statues, and this method advanced to such an extent that no figures or statues were made without a clay model" (*Hominis autem imaginem gypso e facie ipsa primus omnium expressit ceraque in eam formam gypsi infusa emendare instituit Lysistratus Sicyonius, frater Lysippi, de quo diximus. hic et similitudines reddere instituit; ante eum quam pulcherrimas facere studebant. idem et de signis effigies exprimere invenit, crevitque res in tantum, ut nulla signa statuaeve sine argilla fierent*). Again, this passage is fundamental to the history of Greco-Roman bronze sculpture: see e.g. Stewart 1990: 80, 293 (T 133); Mattusch 1996: 71–2; Konstam and Hoffman 2004; Dillon 2006 (downplaying the naturalistic precision of Greek portraiture); Pollini 2012: 33–9 (arguing that the Roman tradition of *imagines* was directly influenced by the Greek practice of casting directly from the body).

The concept of the impression suggests a close causal relationship between an image and its mold. In semiotic terms, this indexical formulation is quite distinct from the notion of representation as imitation (or, in its Peircean formulation, as an "icon").[57] As Lakey observes, relief does not present itself as "a surface through which we see"; in contrast to the Albertian model of painting, it is not "a window" onto a represented world but asserts a spatial and material contiguity between the phenomenal world of the viewer and that of the molded object, despite the fact that relief surfaces seldom present themselves as fully rounded bodies (indeed, in Plato's *Symposium*, the ἐκτετυπωμένοι [or "stamped out forms"] of funerary stelai are described as "sawn down the middle."[58] It is thus noteworthy that linguistic parallels between relief effects in sculpture and painting in the Roman tradition are expressed through the language of *eminens*, that which "projects out of" the pictorial plane, rather than an illusionistic recession of space.

Notably, notions of "likeness" and *mimēsis* are not prominent within the terminology that Pliny and his fellow Romans apply to relief-work. Instead, we tend to find terms suggestive of texture and surface. At the opening to Book 35, Pliny explicitly condemns his fellow Romans' use of marble panels for facing walls instead of plaster. This expensive revetment is described as *interrasum*, "scraped here and there," producing "vermiculated surfaces" (literally, "worm-eaten crusts," *vermiculatae crustae*) that form "the figures of objects and animals."[59] Here, the notion of *opus vermiculatum* (which we associate today with the "wormlike" appearance of outlines laid in mosaic tesserae) is applied to relief in order to convey the texture of an undulating surface, adding a particularly Plinian note of moral censure (he goes on to condemn the painting of marble surfaces as a particularly egregious violation of the integrity of matter).[60] Elsewhere, the notion of a hard surface, or *crusta*, is applied to

[57] On the difference between "index" and "icon" in Peircean semiotics, see Peirce 1982–2009, 2:56, with Short 2007: 215–23.

[58] Lakey 2018. On the Plato passage, see note 41.

[59] Plin. *HN* 35.1: "But at the present time [painting] has been entirely ousted by marbles, and indeed finally also by gold, and not only to the point that whole party-walls are covered – we have also marble engraved with designs and embossed marble slabs carved in wriggling lines to represent objects and animals [*verum et interraso marmore vermiculatisque ad effigies rerum et animalium crustis*]."

[60] On the painting of marble, see Plin. *HN* 35.3: "We are no longer content with panels nor with surfaces displaying broadly a range of mountains in a bedchamber; we have begun even to paint on the masonry" (*non placent iam abaci nec spatia montes in cubiculo dilatantia: coepimus et lapidem pingere*); cf. 37.1, on the "unnatural" practice of engraving precious gems such as emeralds.

relief in a rather more neutral manner. At 35.154, Pliny applies it to "Tuscanic work" (presumably early terra-cotta reliefs) that were "cut out of the walls" (*crustas parietum excisas*), then framed and preserved when the ancient shrine of Ceres in the Circus Maximus was restored.[61] This notion of relief as a hard, figured surface that forms the outer "crust" of its material ground is thus applied to both marble and clay. It also features in discussions of metal plate: Cicero refers to the plundering of silverware (*argentum caelatum*) by Verres, commenting that *crustae aut emblematae* were torn from precious vessels belonging to the Haluntines, who were afterward left with "plain silver" (*argento puro*).[62] In his discussion of metals in Book 33 of *HN* (on metals), Pliny refers to Teucer, a famed practitioner of *caelatura*, as a *crustiarius*.[63]

In that *crusta* suggests a certain kind of rough surface texture (one that is also characteristic of rinds, shells, and bark), it parallels a term employed by Pliny, Vergil, and Vitruvius that has a particularly haptic quality – that is, *asperitas* – "unevenness," "roughness," and, more generally, "textural contrast."[64] For Vergil, this pertains quite literally to the texture of embossed metal plate: In Book 9 of the *Aeneid*, we encounter bowls (*cymbia*) "wrought in silver and rough with *signis*" (*argento perfecta atque aspera signis*); note the terminology of "stamping" or molding" that is suggested by *signum*, often treated as a Latin equivalent to the Greek *typos*, and usually translated here as "reliefs."[65] Though few of us are fortunate enough to experience the sensation of holding Roman silver vessels in our hands, cups in high relief such as those recovered from

61 Plin. *HN* 35.154 (on the Shrine of Ceres by the Circus Maximus): "Varro states that before this shrine was built everything in the temples was Tuscanic work; and that when this shrine was undergoing restoration, the embossed work of the walls was cut out and enclosed in framed panels; and that the figures also were taken from the pediment and dispersed" (*ante hanc aedem Tuscanica omnia in aedibus fuisse auctor est Varro, et ex hac, cum reficeretur, crustas parietum excisas tabulis marginatis inclusas esse, item signa ex fastigiis dispersa*).

62 Cic. *Verr.* 2.4.52: "Vessels [*vasa*] were brought out without their cases; others were wrenched out of the hands of women; many people's doors were broken open, and their locks forced. . . . Do not suppose then that any one produced his carved plate [*argentum caelatum*] out of his house for another man to steal, without the greatest distress. Everything is brought down to the shore. The Cibyratic brothers are summoned; they condemn some articles; whatever they approve of has its figures in relief or its embossed emblems [*crustae aut emblemata*] torn off. And so the Haluntines, having had all their ornaments wrenched off, returned home with the plain silver [*argento puro*]." Translation from Yonge 1903.

63 Plin. *HN* 33.157: "Teucer the artist in embossed work attained celebrity" (*habuit et Teucer crustarius famam*).

64 *OLD*, s.v. *asperitas*.

65 Verg. *Aen.* 9.263–4: *bina dabo argento perfecta atque aspera signis / pocula, devicta genitor quae cepit Arisba* ("A pair of goblets I will give, wrought in silver and rough with chasing, that he took when Arisba was vanquished").

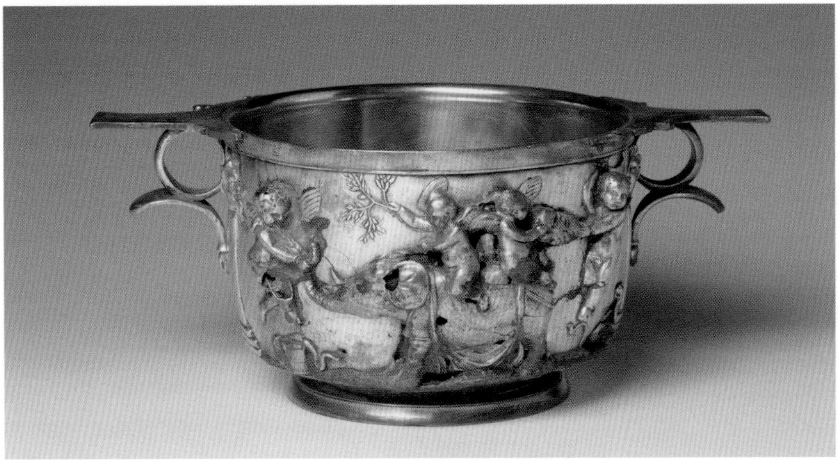

Fig. 1.10 Roman silver *skyphos* depicting Dionysiac scenes, one of a pair discovered at the Villa della Pisanella, Boscoreale. 25–50 CE. Height: 9.3 cm; width: 21.5 cm; diameter: 13.3 cm. Paris, Musée du Louvre, MNC 1964 (photograph by Hervé Lewandowski, © RMN-Grand Palais [Musée du Louvre]/Art Resource, NY).

Bosocreale give a sense of the intense textural contrasts that must have defined such haptic encounters (Fig. 1.10).[66] Pliny picks up the term *asperitas* in his critique of the Roman obsession with precious metal plate in Book 33, where he condemns "the demand ... for embossed ware [*anaglypta*] and rough surfaces [*asperitatem*], where the metal has been cut out along the lines of the figures."[67] John Bostock and Henry Thomas Riley commented that the "obscurity" of this passage "seems to set translation at defiance" (as so many passages of Pliny do!).[68] Are *anaglypta* (from the Greek αναγλυφειν, literally, "to carve upward") here to be understood in contrast to the roughness of figures that are "cut out" – perhaps *repoussé* as distinct from something like filigree? Or is it that the process through which figures are outlined in relief and then "carved upward" (or actually pushed out) from their ground produces a roughness of texture? And how does this discussion of carving and

[66] On Fig. 1.10, see Ricci 1988: 58, no. 13. On touching ancient art, see Gaifman 2018 (on the handling of Greek vases) and, more generally, Platt and Squire 2017.

[67] Plin. *HN* 33.139–40: "Fashions in silver plate undergo marvellous variations owing to the vagaries of human taste, no kind of workmanship remaining long in favor. At one time Furnian plate is in demand, at another Clodian, at another Gratian – for we make even the factories feel at home at our tables – At another time the demand is for embossed plate and rough surfaces, where the metal has been cut out along the lines of the figures [*nunc anaglypta asperitatemque excisa circa liniarum picturas quaerimus*]."

[68] Bostock and Riley 1855–7, 6:132n30, referring back to comments by Emile Littré.

cutting relate to the medium of silver, as opposed to hard materials such as stone and precious gems (where the language of glyptics is far more at home)?

To make matters more confusing, when *asperitas* is employed by Vitruvius, it is in reference to trompe l'oeil painted architecture and the illusionistic effects of *skēnographia*, when he describes the theater of Apaturius at Tralles as "charm[ing] the eyes of all on account of its roughness [*propter asperitatem*]."[69] Elsewhere, he applies the phrase to the satisfying intercolumniations of Hermogenes' peripteral temple designs – that is, to the sense of rhythmic contrast generated by the alternating presence and absence of columnar forms in architectural colonnades.[70] In each case, the *textural* contrast that is elsewhere used to describe the feel of embossed metal vessels in the hand is applied to the *visual* effects of high-contrast painting and architecture, as if the phenomenological impact of such projections and recessions upon the eye were akin to the haptic experience of relief, whether in two-dimensional painting or three-dimensional space. This accords quite neatly, of course, with the logic of intromission and the crucial role played by touch within ancient models of sense-perception.[71]

[69] Vitr., *De arch.* 7.5: "At Tralles, Apaturius of Alabanda had invented scenery of fine technique for the tiny theatre which they call the Small Assembly. In this he showed columns, statues, or centaurs supporting the architraves, the orbed roofs of domes, the projecting angles of pediments [*fastigiorum prominentes versuras*], cornices having lions' heads which provided outlets for the rain from the roofs. Besides, the story above the scenery had domes, porticoes, half pediments, and every kind of roof, with varied pictorial ornament. When, therefore, the appearance of such a stage, by its high relief [*propter asperitatem*] charmed the eyes of all." Translation from Granger 1934. On the relationship to Second Style fresco painting here, see note 50. For discussion, see Lakey 2018: 156, suggesting that Vitruvius asserts "A constitutive relationship between the *virtuality of space* and *objects located therein* produced in scenography (or perspective) and material relief: the roughness of a surface formed by projecting mass provided a model for the illusion of three-dimensionality, or plasticity, on the plane of projection" (emphasis in original).

[70] Vitr. *De arch.* 3.8–9: "[Hermogenes] made an opening for the ambulatory round the cella in a striking fashion, and in no respect detracted from the appearance. Thus without letting us miss the superfluous parts, he preserved the impressiveness of the whole work by his arrangement. For the columns round the temple were so devised that the view of them was impressive, because of the high relief given to the intercolumniations [*ut aspectus propter asperitatem intercolumniorum habeat auctoritatem*]."

[71] On the difference between "intromissionist" and "extramissionist" or "emissionist" models of sight in antiquity, see Lindberg 1976: 1–17; Rakoczy 1996: 19–37; Nightingale 2016; Rudolph 2016; Squire 2016b: 16–17, with Tanner 2016 on the implications for Greek painting. On the application of haptic models of sense-perception to all the senses, particularly by the pre-Socratics, see Purves 2017b, with Porter 2010: 416 (on Democritus) and Steiner Goldner 2017 (on Aristotle).

Relationality

It is through the sensory associations of terms such as *asperitas* that we might begin to uncover some of the logic underlying the material, conceptual, and linguistic diversity of relief that I have traced in this chapter. The idea of an undulating surface that is molded or projects from its ground, thereby impressing itself upon the sensorium of its viewers, echoes precisely the language of sense-perception and cognition that we find within the Greek philosophical tradition. We need not understand this in a merely metaphorical sense, as in the forms of haptic viewing advanced by early twentieth-century art historians such as Bernard Berenson or Riegl.[72] Rather, it is grounded in both embodied practices of handling objects and materialist models of knowledge acquisition, in which the literalism of the "impression" is repeatedly renegotiated. While the history of art associates relief-work primarily with architectural sculpture, it is clear from an analysis of ancient terminology that the governing art forms for thinking through what relief might be come from gems, terra-cotta moldings, and embossed metalwork. Seal stones and silver cups are small objects designed to be worn on or manipulated by the body, so that the close work of viewing goes hand in hand with intimate acts of touching or drinking, of slipping on and off the finger, pressing into wax, cupping in the hands, or bringing up to the mouth.

I shall not rehearse here the use of *entypōsis* (or "making impressions") and the metaphor of the seal ring stamped into wax by Plato, Aristotle, and the Stoics.[73] But it is worth remembering that the *ekmageion* – the "wax tablet in the mind" – that operates as a medium for the storage of memory and the reception of *phantasiai* ("sense-impressions") in Greek philosophy is itself understood as a ground for relief. Indeed, the quality of its surface, its degree of malleability, and the clarity of the percepts that were imprinted within it provided a rich set of physical and conceptual parameters through which to explore the receptive capacities of the *psychē* and the cognitive value of sense-perception. The Stoic Cleanthes, for example, referred explicitly to the "recession and elevation" (εἰσοχήν τε καὶ ἐξοχήν) of *typōsis*, conceiving the process of sense-perception not as the projection of flat "images" or "reflections" but as the shaping of relief surfaces in thoroughly haptic terms.[74]

[72] Berenson 1896; Riegl 2004; for discussion, see Platt and Squire 2017 (with further bibliography).

[73] See note 3; the significance of these concepts for the visual arts is explored more extensively in Platt, in press.

[74] Sextus Empiricus, *Against the Professors* 7.228–9 (= *SVF* 1, 484), in the context of the Stoic dispute over the literalism of the metaphor: "For whereas Cleanthes understood 'impression' as involving eminence and depression, just as does the impression made in wax by signet-rings,

Relief, then, may lack a specific name in antiquity; it may characterize materials, techniques, and classes of artifact that occupy a lower position in the various aesthetic hierarchies imposed upon classical art (aligning as it does with architectural ornament, terra-cottas, and the so-called minor arts of metal plate and glyptics). But it also reveals itself to be fundamental to the ways in which Greek thinkers conceived of the relationship between the world and the human mind. The world itself is experienced phenomenologically *as relief*, and it impresses itself upon the *psychē* as relief. As Riegl claimed, relief is both optic and haptic, but not because it fails to fully occupy either category – not because it is merely *Halbform* (for all Aristophanes' protestations in Plato's *Symposium*). Rather, relief serves as a metaphor for knowledge acquisition by means of perception because it is associated, like the Platonic *ekmageion*, with processes of transmission and emergence, or Becoming.

First, the language of *typos* (in Greek) and *signum* or *sigillum* (in Latin) explicitly relates relief-work to practices of stamping and molding that are associated with the transfer of form from one medium to another – whether from seal ring to wax or from clay or plaster mold to terra-cotta antefix, figured vessel, or stuccoed panel. Second, the inseparable relationship between figure and ground that governs the operations of relief generates forms that may project into the viewer's space but are also bound to their material substrates. As a visual and material phenomenon, relief may inhabit the realm of the "both . . . and" and the "neither . . . nor," yet this is not because of *insufficiency*. Rather, it is because relief is fundamentally *processual* and *relational*. As a metaphor, relief lends itself to materialist epistemologies so effectively because it inhabits the realm of Becoming: It is never about pure Form (in the Platonic sense) precisely because relief so emphatically inheres within and emerges from matter. Because they are not fully three-dimensional, however, relief forms simultaneously occupy both "real" and "virtual" space (as David Summers has argued).[75] This generates an ontological ambiguity that parallels the ambiguous status of the human *psychē* as both embodied matter and transcendent soul: Mind and relief are both places where the physical and metaphysical converge; they are, in Aristotelian terms, "hylomorphic."[76]

Chrysippus regarded such a thing as absurd" (Κλεάνθης μὲν γὰρ ἤκουσε τὴν τύπωσιν κατὰ εἰσοχήν τε καὶ ἐξοχήν, ὥσπερ καὶ τὴν διὰ τῶν δακτυλίων γινομένην τοῦ κηροῦ τύπωσιν, Χρύσιππος δὲ ἄτοπον ἡγεῖτο τὸ τοιοῦτο). For discussion, see Ioppolo 1990: 434.

[75] See note 5.

[76] For a helpful account of Aristotle's approach to the soul, and the doctrine of hylomorphism in particular, see Caston 2006, with a more thorough account in Caston 2005.

This capacity to exist simultaneously in two and three dimensions (or on two ontological planes) helps to explain a peculiar problem in the terminology of Greek art, which is ably set out in Pollitt's essay on the significance of the term *typos*.[77] For as he shows, *typos* can not only mean "impression" and, by extension, "relief" (or even simply "image") but can also mean model, sketch, or plan – an "impression," perhaps, in the sense of a "general idea." Scholars are especially puzzled by a reference to *typoi* commissioned from the celebrated sculptor Timotheus in the inscribed building accounts from the sanctuary of Asclepius at Epidaurus: Were these pedimental figures for the temple? Reliefs for some other building? Or models (more commonly called *paradeigmata*) of the architectural sculptures designed to be copied by other craftsmen – demonstrations, as Pollitt suggests, of the process by which sculptors "translated their preliminary conceptions into final form"?[78] Though the jury seems to be leaning in the direction of "relief," the very fact that it is so difficult to determine what precisely is meant tells us something important about the operations of Greek relief itself.

It is notable, then, that for Plato, the terms *typos* and *paradeigma* provide metaphors derived from craft for conceptualizing mental operations that bridge the ontological chasm enforced by dualism.[79] They are cast as mental concepts "molded" by philosophers as models to aid their followers in the cultivation of wisdom or matrices within the *psychē* that can "agree and harmonize" with one's physical form (*eidos*).[80] As such, *typoi* and *paradeigmata* manage to mediate between the realms of the "Intelligible" (*noēton*) and the "Perceptible" (*horaton*) in ways that parallel relief-work's ability to reconcile the virtual and the material.[81] That relief offers a means of reifying such ontological slippage helps to explain, perhaps, its peculiar power in the context of funerary art (an association foreshadowed by the originary relief of Butades, which traces the form of a lover departing for war). Or, to return to Freud's Gradiva, it explains how amongst the many

77 Pollitt 1974.

78 Pollitt 1974: 284–92, discussing *IG* II^2, 1534, lines 35, 64, 87–8 (with previous bibliography); see also Stewart 1990: 36.

79 For the close relationship between *typos* and *paradeigma* in Plato, see e.g. *Leg.* 876e, where lawmakers giving instructions to judges state "τύπους of penalties" (i.e. general principles that it would be wrong to transgress) and provide them with παραδείγματα (i.e. particular examples to emulate), with Pollitt 1974: 288, no. 6. For further discussion, see Allen 2010: 38–44.

80 Pl. *Resp.* 3.402d: "'Then,' said I, 'when there is a coincidence of a beautiful disposition in the soul [ἔν τε τῇ ψυχῇ] and corresponding and harmonious beauties of the same type [τοῦ αὐτοῦ … τύπου] in the bodily form [ἐν τῷ εἴδει] – is not this the fairest spectacle for one who is capable of its contemplation?'"

81 On the "Divided Line" (Pl. *Resp.* 509d–511e), see Smith 1981, 1996; Allen 2010: 38–44.

antiquities with which he was intimately acquainted, it was a relief figure (and the novel it inspired) that helped him to formulate the relationship between dreams, desire, and the unconscious (not to mention the pathologies of archaeologists!). Penelope Curtis argues that the power of sculpture lies in its ability to serve as a threshold, to "hover between one state and another."[82] In that relief is always poised on the brink of becoming something other than it is, despite its material fixity, it arguably offers not a dilution of sculpture but an intensification of its medial operations. Perhaps this is why the ancient terminology of relief forces us to focus so intensely upon prefixes. Rather than the volumetric adjectives of the Renaissance – the language of *alto, mezzo, basso, stiacciato* – the language of ancient relief is one of prepositions: *pros, ek, ana, en, epi.* These emphasize above all its relational operations as a kind of "super-medium" – one that not only forged associations between innumerable materials and techniques within ancient art but which also provided potent models for conceptualizing the relationship between mind, body, and the world itself.

References

Abbe, M. B., and Ağtürk, T. S. (2019). "The New Corpus of Painted Imperial Roman Marble Reliefs from Nicomedia: A Preliminary Report on Polychromy." *Techne* 48: 100–9.

Adornato, G. (2007). "Sguardi letterari e giudizi d'arte. Lisippo e gli artisti dell' aletheia." In F. De Angelis, ed., *Lo sguardo archeologicao: I normalisti per Paul Zanker.* Pisa: Edizioni della Normale, 3–18.

Ağtürk, T. S. (2018). "A New Tetrarchic Relief from Nicomedia: Embracing Emperors." *American Journal of Archaeology* 122.3: 411–26.

Alberti, L. B. (1972). *On Painting and On Sculpture: The Latin Texts of* De Pictura *and* De Statua. Ed. and trans. Cecil Grayson. London: Phaidon.

Allen, D. S. (2010). *Why Plato Wrote: Blackwell Bristol Lectures on Greece, Rome and the Classical Tradition.* Chichester: Wiley-Blackwell.

Alloa, E. (2012). "Metaxy oder: Warum es keine immateriellen Medien gibt?" In G. Koch, K. Maar, and F. McGovern, eds., *Imaginäre Medialität – Immaterielle Medien.* Munich: Fink, 13–34.

(2020). "*Metaxy*: Aristotle on Mediacy." In Michelakis 2020: 147–66.

Altman, M. (1938). "Ruler Cult in Seneca." *Classical Philology* 33.2: 198–204.

Ambuel, D. (2015). *Turtles All the Way Down: On Plato's Theaetetus, a Commentary and Translation.* Sankt Augustin: Akademie.

[82] Curtis 2017: vi.

Anguissola, A. (2021). *Pliny the Elder and the Matter of Memory: An Encyclopaedic Workshop*. London: Routledge.
Anguissola, A., and Grüner, A. eds. (2020). *The Nature of Art: Pliny the Elder on Materials*. Berlin: Brepols.
Armstrong, R. H. (2006). *A Compulsion for Antiquity: Freud and the Ancient World*. Ithaca, NY: Cornell University Press.
Barocchi, P. (1971). *Scritti d'arte del Cinquecento: Vol. 1, Generalia: Arti e scienze; Le arti*. Milan: Einaudi.
Basore, J. W., trans. (1935). *Seneca: Moral Essays: Vol. 3, De Beneficiis*. Loeb Classical Library 310. Cambridge, MA: Harvard University Press.
Bates, A. (2021). "Philostratus Visualises the Philosophical: *Imagines* 2.23, Hercules *Furens* and the Cataleptic Impression." *American Journal of Philology* 142.1: 137–75.
Bažant, J. (1991). "Roman Deathmasks Once Again." *AION: Sezione di archeologia e storia antica* 13: 209–18.
Berenson, B. (1896). *Florentine Painters of the Renaissance*. New York: Putnam.
Bettini, M. (1999). *The Portrait of the Lover*. Berkeley: University of California Press.
Blöme, P. (2001). "Die *imagines maiorum*: Ein Problemfall römischer und neuzeitlicher Ästhetik." In G. Brehm, ed., *Homo Pictor*. Munich: Sauer, 305–22.
Bostock, D. (1988). *Plato's Theaetetus*. Oxford: Clarendon Press.
Bostock, J., and Riley, H. T. (1855–7). *The Natural History of Pliny: Translated, with Copious Notes and Illustrations*. 6 vols. London: Henry G. Bohn.
Burnyeat, M. (1990). *The* Theaetetus *of Plato, with Translation of Plato's* Theaetetus *by M. J. Levett, Revised by Myles Burnyeat*. Indianapolis, IN: Hackett.
Carey, S. (2003). *Pliny's Catalogue of Culture: Art and Empire in the Natural History*. Oxford: Oxford University Press.
Caston, V. (2005). "The Spirit and the Letter: Aristotle on Perception." In R. Salles, ed., *Metaphysics, Soul, and Ethics: Themes from the Work of Richard Sorabji*. Oxford: Clarendon Press, 245–320.
(2006). "Aristotle's Psychology." In M. L. Gill and P. Pellegrin, eds., *The Blackwell Companion to Ancient Philosophy*. Chichester: Wiley-Blackwell, 316–46.
Cennini, C. (1932). *Il libro dell'arte*. Ed. Daniel V. Thompson. New Haven, CT: Yale University Press.
Colonna, G. (1996). *L'altorilievo di Pyrgi: Dei ed eroi greci in Etruria*. Rome: Bretschneider.
(2000). "Il santuario di Pyrgi dalle origini mitistoriche agli altorilievi frontonali dei Sette e di Leucotea." *Scienze dell'antichità: Storia, archeologia, antropologia* 10: 251–336.
(2006). "Sacred Architecture and the Religion of the Etruscans." In N. Thomson de Grummond and E. Simon, eds., *The Religion of the Etruscans*. Austin: University of Texas Press, 132–68.

Connelly, J. B. (1996). "Parthenon and *Parthenoi*: A Mythological Interpretation of the Parthenon Frieze." *American Journal of Archaeology* 100.1: 53–80.

Crowley, P. R. (2016). "Roman Death Masks and the Metaphoric of the Negative." *Grey Room* 64: 64–103.

Curtis, P. (2017). *Sculpture Vertical, Horizontal, Closed, Open*. London: Paul Mellon Centre.

da Vinci, L. (1956). *Treatise on Painting*. Trans. A. P. McMahon. Princeton, NJ: Princeton University Press.

Darab, A. (2012). "Ialysus: The Lack of Description." *Acta Classica Universitatis Scientiarum Debreceniensis* 48: 75–89.

(2014a). "Natura, Ars, Historia: Anecdotic History of Art in Pliny the Elder's *Naturalis Historia*. Part 1, Natura and Ars: The Place of Art History in the *Naturalis Historia*." *Hermes* 142.2: 206–24.

(2014b). "Natura, Ars, Historia: Anecdotic History of Art in Pliny the Elder's *Naturalis Historia*. Part 2." *Hermes* 142.3: 279–97.

(2020). *The Anecdotal Narration and Encyclopedic Thought of Pliny the Elder's* Naturalis Historia. Newcastle upon Tyne: Cambridge Scholars.

Dasen, V. (2010). "Wax and Plaster Memories: Children in Elite and Non-elite Strategies." In V. Dasen and T. Späth, eds., *Children, Memory, and Family Identity in Roman Culture*. Oxford: Oxford University Press, 109–46.

Davis, W. (2017). *Visuality and Virtuality: Images and Pictures from Prehistory to Perspective*. Princeton, NJ: Princeton University Press.

Dillon, S. (2006). *Ancient Greek Portrait Sculpture: Contexts, Subjects, and Styles*. Cambridge: Cambridge University Press.

Donohue, A. A. (1988). *Xoana and the Origins of Greek Sculpture*. Atlanta, GA: Scholars Press.

Drerup, H. (1980). "Totenmaske und Ahnenbild bei den Römern." *Mitteilungen des Deutschen Archäologischen Instituts: Römische Abteilung* 87: 81–129.

Dubel, S. (1997). "*Ekphrasis* et *enargeia*: La déscription antique comme parcours." In C. Lévy and L. Pernot, eds., *Dire l'évidence: Philosophie et rhétorique antiques*. Paris: Harmattan, 249–64.

Elsner, J. (1995). *Art and the Roman Viewer: The Transformation of Art from the Pagan World to Christianity*. Cambridge: Cambridge University Press.

Estrin, S. (2023). *Grief Made Marble: Funerary Sculpture in Classical Athens*. New Haven, CT: Yale University Press.

Falaschi, E. (2018). "More Than Words: Restaging Protogenes' *Ialysus*; The Many Lives of an Artwork between Greece and Rome." In G. Adornato, I. B. Romano, G. Cirucci, and A. Poggio, eds., *Restaging Greek Artworks in Roman Times*. Milan: LED, 173–90.

Flower, H. (1996). *Ancestor Masks and Aristocratic Power in Roman Culture*. Oxford: Clarendon Press.

Francis, J. A. (2009). "Metal Maidens, Achilles' Shield and Pandora: The Beginnings of 'Ekphrasis.'" *American Journal of Philology* 130.1: 1–23.

Freedman, L. (1989). "'Rilievo' as an Artistic Term in Renaissance Art Theory." *Rinascimento* 29: 217–47.

Freud, S. (1959). *The Standard Edition of the Complete Psychological Works of Sigmund Freud: Vol. 9, Jensen's Gradiva and Other Works (1906–1908).* Trans. J. Strachey. London: Hogarth Press.

Freud, S., and Jensen, W. (1917). *Delusion and Dream: An Interpretation in the Light of Psychoanalysis of* Gradiva, *a Novel, by Wilhelm Jensen, Which Is Here Translated.* Trans. H. M. Downey. New York: Moffat.

Fullerton, M. D. (1990). *The Archaistic Style in Roman Statuary.* Leiden: Brill.

Gaifman, M. (2018). "The Greek Libation Bowl as Embodied Object." In M. Gaifman, V. J. Platt, and M. J. Squire, eds., "The Embodied Object in Classical Antiquity," special issue, *Art History* 41.3: 444–65.

Gay, P. (1993). *Sigmund Freud and Art: His Personal Collection of Antiquities.* London: Thames and Hudson.

Godley, A. D., trans. (1920). *Herodotus: The Persian Wars: Vol. 1, Books 1–7.* Loeb Classical Library 117. Cambridge, MA: Cambridge University Press.

Goldhill, S. (1994). "The Naïve and Knowing Eye: Ecphrasis and the Culture of Viewing in the Hellenistic World." In S. Goldhill and R. Osborne, eds., *Art and Text in Greek Culture.* Cambridge: Cambridge University Press, 197–223.

Granger, F., trans. (1934). *Vitruvius: On Architecture: Vol. 2, Books 6–10.* Loeb Classical Library 280. Cambridge, MA: Harvard University Press.

Güthenke, C. (2010). "The Potter's Daughter's Sons: German Classical Scholarship and the Language of Love circa 1800." *Representations* 109.1: 122–47.

Gutzwiller, K., ed. (2005). *The New Posidippus: A Hellenistic Poetry Book.* Oxford: Oxford University Press.

Harte, V. (2010). "The Receptacle and the Primary Bodies: Something from Nothing?" In R. D. Mohr and B. M. Sattler, eds., *One Book, The Whole Universe: Plato's* Timaeus *Today.* Las Vegas, NV: Parmenides, 131–40.

Hopkins, J. N. (2024). *Unbound from Rome: Art and Craft in a Fluid Landscape, ca. 650–250 BCE.* New Haven, CT: Yale University Press.

Hurwit, J. M. (1995). "Beautiful Evil: Pandora and the Athena Parthenos." *American Journal of Archaeology* 99.2: 171–86.

(2004). *The Acropolis in the Age of Perikles.* Cambridge: Cambridge University Press.

Ierodiakonou, K. (2007). "The Stoics and the Skeptics on Memory." In M. M. Sassi, ed., *Tracce nella mente: Teorie della memoria da Platone ai moderni.* Pisa: Edizioni della Normale, 47–65.

Ioppolo, A.-M. (1990). "Presentation and Assent: A Physical and Cognitive Problem in Early Stoicism." *Classical Quarterly* 40.2: 433–49.

Jäger, L. (2004). "Störung und Transparenz: Skizze zur performativen Logik des Medialen." In S. Krämer, ed., *Performativität und Medialität.* Munich: Fink, 35–74.

Karoglou, K. (2016). "The Collection of Greek Terracotta Figurines at the Metropolitan Museum of Art." *Les carnets de l'ACoSt* 14. https://doi.org/10.4000/acost.798.

King, S. (2004). "Amelia Opie's 'Maid of Corinth' and the Origins of Art." *Eighteenth-Century Studies* 37.4: 629–51.

Knudsen, S. E. (2016). "Cat. 137 Fragment of a Cameo Portraying Emperor Tiberius: Curatorial Entry." In K. A. Raff, ed., *Roman Art at the Art Institute of Chicago*. Chicago, IL: Art Institute of Chicago. https://publications.artic.edu/roman/reader/romanart/section/1946.

Konstam, N., and Hoffman, H. (2004). "Casting the Riace Bronzes (2): A Sculptor's Discovery." *Oxford Journal of Archaeology* 23.4: 397–402.

Krämer, S. (2015). *Medium, Messenger, Transmission: An Approach to Media Philosophy*. Amsterdam: Aarhus University Press.

Lakey, C. (2018). *Sculptural Seeing: Relief, Optics, and the Rise of Perspective in Medieval Italy*. New Haven, CT: Yale University Press.

Lapatin, K. D. S. (1996). 'The Ancient Reception of Pheidias' *Athena Parthenos*: The Physical Evidence in Context." In L. Hardwick and S. Ireland, eds., *The January Conference 1996: The Reception of Classical Texts and Images*. Milton Keynes: Open University, 1–20.

(2001). *Chryselephantine Statuary in the Ancient Mediterranean World*. Oxford: Oxford University Press.

Leipen, N. (1971). *Athena Parthenos: A Reconstruction*. Toronto: Royal Ontario Museum.

Lindberg, D. C. (1976). *Theories of Vision from Al-Kindi to Kepler*. Chicago, IL: University of Chicago Press.

Lippold, G. (1925). "ΤΥΠΟΣ." *Jahrbuch des Deutschen archäologischen Instituts* 40: 206–9.

Long, A. A. (2006). "Zeno's Epistemology and Plato's *Theaetetus*." In A. A. Long, ed., *From Epicurus to Epictetus: Studies in Hellenistic and Roman Philosophy*. Oxford: Oxford University Press, 223–35.

Loraux, N. (1993). *The Children of Athena: Athenian Ideas about Citizenship and the Division between the Sexes*. Trans. C. Levine. Princeton, NJ: Princeton University Press.

Macho, T. (2013). "Second-Order Animals: Cultural Techniques of Identity and Identification." *Theory, Culture and Society* 30.6: 30–47.

Manieri, A. (1998). *L'immagine poetica nella teoria degli antichi: Phantasia ed enargeia*. Pisa: Istituti editoriali e poligrafici internazionali.

Mattusch, C. C. (1996). *Classical Bronzes: The Art and Craft of Greek and Roman Statuary*. Ithaca, NY: Cornell University Press.

Mayer, A. (2012). "Gradiva's Gait: Tracing the Figure of a Walking Woman." *Critical Inquiry* 38.3: 554–78.

Mersch, D. (2002). "Wort, Bild, Ton, Zahl: Eine Einleitung in die Medienphilosophie." In T. Georgen, ed., *Kunst und Medium: Vol. 3, Gestalt und Diskurs*. Kiel: Muthesius Kunsthochschule, 131–254.

Michelakis, P., ed. (2020). *Classics and Media Theory*. Oxford: Oxford University Press.

Milleker, E. J., et al. (2000). *The Year One: Art of the Ancient World East and West*. New York: Metropolitan Museum of Art.

Muecke, F. (1999). "'Taught by Love': The Origin of Painting Again." *Art Bulletin* 81.2: 297–302.

Naas, V. (2002). *Le projet encyclopédique de Pline l'Ancien*. Rome: École française de Rome.

(2012). "La jeune fille de Corinthe: De l'anecdote à l'invention de l'art." In S. Alexandre, N. Philippe, and C. Ribeyrol, eds., *Inventer la peinture grecque antique*. Lyon: École normale supérieure, 71–93.

Neer, R. (2010). *The Emergence of the Classical Style in Greek Sculpture*. Chicago, IL: University of Chicago.

Nightingale, A. (2016). "Sight and the Philosophy of Vision in Classical Greece: Democritus, Plato and Aristotle." In Squire 2016a: 54–67.

Ostrow, S. F. (2004). "Playing with the Paragone: The Reliefs of Pietro Bernini; For Rudolf Preimesberger." *Zeitschrift für Kunstgeschichte* 67.3: 329–64.

Peirce, C. A. S. (1982–2009). *The Writings of Charles S. Peirce: A Chronological Edition*. Ed. Peirce Edition Project. 8 vols. Bloomington: Indiana University Press.

Picón, C. A. (2009). "Glass and Gold of the Hellenistic and Early Roman World." In J. R. Houghton et al., eds., *Philippe de Montebello and the Metropolitan Museum of Art, 1977–2008*. New York: Metropolitan Museum of Art, 20–1.

Platt, V. J. (2006). "Making an Impression: Replication and the Ontology of the Graeco-Roman Seal Stone." In J. Trimble and J. Elsner, eds., "Replication in Ancient Art: Greece, Rome, and Beyond," special issue, *Art History* 29.2: 235–57.

(2011). *Facing the Gods: Epiphany and Representation in Graeco-Roman Art, Literature and Religion*. Cambridge: Cambridge University Press.

(2016). "The Matter of Classical Art History." *Daedalus* 145.2: 69–78.

(2018a). "Ecology, Ethics and Aesthetics in Pliny the Elder's *Natural History*." In C. P. Heuer and R. Zorach, eds., *Ecologies, Agents, Terrains*. New Haven, CT: Yale University Press, 219–42.

(2018b). "Of Sponges and Stones: Matter and Ornament in Roman Painting." In N. Dietrich and M. Squire, eds., *Ornament and Figure in Graeco-Roman Art: Rethinking Visual Ontologies in Classical Antiquity*. Berlin: De Gruyter, 241–78.

(2020). "The Seal of Polycrates: A Discourse on Discourse Channel Conditions." In Michelakis 2020: 53–76.

(2021). "Bodies, Bases and Borders: Framing the Divine in Greco-Roman Antiquity." In J. Elsner and R. Wood, eds., *Imagining the Divine: Exploring Art in Religions of Late Antiquity across Eurasia*. London: British Museum, 19–39.

(In press). *Epistemic Objects: Making and Mediating Classical Art and Text.* Oxford: Oxford University Press.

Platt, V. J., and Squire, M. J. (2017). "Getting to Grips with Classical Art: Rethinking the Haptics of Graeco-Roman Visual Culture." In Purves 2017a: 74–104.

Platz-Horster, G. (2008). "Zwei römische Kaiserkameen der Sammlung Alsdorf in Chicago." In G. Platz-Horster, ed., *Mythos und Macht: Erhabene Bilder in Edelstein.* Berlin: Antikensammlung Staatliche Museen, 22–8, 85–6, figs. 1–3.

Pointon, M. (2014). "Casts, Imprints, and the Deathliness of Things: Artifacts at the Edge." *Art Bulletin* 96.2: 170–95.

Pollini, J. (2012). *From Republic to Empire: Rhetoric, Religion, and Power in the Visual Culture of Ancient Rome.* Norman: University of Oklahoma Press.

Pollitt, J. J. (1974), "Τύπος (*Typos*)." In J. J. Pollitt, *The Ancient View of Greek Art: Criticism, History, and Terminology.* New Haven, CT: Yale University Press, 272–93.

Porter, J. I. (2010). *The Origins of Aesthetic Thought in Ancient Greece: Matter, Sensation and Experience.* Cambridge: Cambridge University Press.

Prioux, É., and Santin, E. (2017). "Mimesis et filiation artistique: La question du style de Lysippe et de ses disciples dans l'épigramme 62 A.-B de Posidippe et chez Pline l'Ancien (*NH* 34, 66)." *Aitia* 7.1. https://doi.org/10.4000/aitia.1737.

Purves, A., ed. (2017a). *Touch and the Ancient Senses.* London: Routledge.

(2017b). "Introduction: What and Where Is Touch?" In Purves 2017a: 1–20.

Rackham, H., trans. (1938). *Pliny: Natural History. Vol. 1, Books 1–2.* Loeb Classical Library 330. Cambridge, MA: Harvard University Press.

Rakoczy, T. (1996). *Böser Blick, Macht des Auges und Neid der Götter: Eine Untersuchung zur Kraft des Blickes in der griechischen Literatur.* Tubingen: Narr.

Ricci, F. M. (1988). *Il tesoro di Boscoreale: Una collezione di argenti da mensa tra cultura ellenistica e mondo romano; Pitture, suppellettili, oggetti vari della "Pisanella."* Milan: Ricci.

Richter, G. M. A. (1953). *The Metropolitan Museum of Art: Handbook of the Greek Collection.* Cambridge, MA: Harvard University Press.

Riegl, A. (2004). *Historical Grammar of the Visual Arts.* Trans. J. E. Jung. New York: Zone.

Rogers, L. R. (1974). *Relief Sculpture.* Oxford: Oxford University Press.

Rosenblum, R. (1957). "The Origin of Painting: A Problem in the Iconography of Romantic Classicism." *Art Bulletin* 39.4: 279–90.

Rouveret, A. (1989). *Histoire et imaginaire de la peinture ancienne (Ve siècle av. J.C.–1er siècle ap. J.-C.).* Rome: École française de Rome.

Roux, G. (1961). "Le sens de ΤΥΠΟΣ." *Revue des études anciennes* 63.1–2: 5–14.

Rudolph, K. (2016). "Sight and the Presocratics: Approaches to Visual Perception in Early Greek Philosophy." In Squire 2016a: 36–53.

Saltzman, L. (2006). *Making Memory Matter: Strategies of Remembrance in Contemporary Art*. Chicago, IL: University of Chicago Press.
Schuhardt, W.-H. (1975). "Zur Basis der Athena Parthenos." In Institut für Klassische Archäologie der Universität München, ed., *Wandlungen: Studien zur antiken und neueren Kunst; Ernst Homann-Wedeking gewidmet*. Waldsassen: Stiftland, 120–30.
Seidensticker, B. (2015). "Andriantopoiika." In B. Seidensticker, A. Stähli, and A. Wessels, eds., *Der Neue Poseidipp: Text – Übersetzung – Kommentar*. Darmstadt: Wissenschaftliche Buchgesellschaft, 247–82.
Sens, A. (2005). "The Art of Poetry and the Poetry of Art: The Unity and Poetics of Posidippus' Statue-Poems." In Gutzwiller 2005: 206–25.
Shechtman, A. (2020). "The Medium Concept." *Representations* 150.1: 61–90.
Short, T. L. (2007). *Peirce's Theory of Signs*. Cambridge: Cambridge University Press.
Smith, N. D. (1981). "The Objects of *Dianoia* in Plato's Divided Line." *Apeiron* 15.2: 129–37.
(1996). "Plato's Divided Line." *Ancient Philosophy* 16.1: 25–46.
Squire, M. J. (2011). *The* Iliad *in a Nutshell: Visualizing Epic on the* Tabulae Iliacae. Oxford: Oxford University Press.
(2013). "Ekphrasis at the Forge and the Forging of Ekphrasis: The 'Shield of Achilles' in Graeco-Roman Word and Image." *Word and Image* 29.2: 157–91.
(ed.) (2016a). *Sight and the Ancient Senses*. London: Routledge.
(2016b). "Introductory Reflections: Making Sense of Ancient Sight." In Squire 2016a: 1–35.
(2017). "Framing the Roman 'Still Life': Campanian Wall-Painting and the Frames of Mural Make-Believe." In V. J. Platt and M. J. Squire, eds., *The Frame in Classical Art: A Cultural History*. Cambridge: Cambridge University Press, 188–253.
(2018). "Embodying the Dead on Classical Attic Grave-Stelai." In M. Gaifman, V. J. Platt, and M. J. Squire, eds., "The Embodied Object in Classical Antiquity," special issue, *Art History* 41.3: 518–45.
Steiner Goldner, R. (2017). "Aristotle and the Priority of Touch." In Purves 2017a: 50–63.
Stewart, A. (1990). *Greek Sculpture: An Exploration*. 2 vols. New Haven, CT: Yale University Press.
(2005). "Posidippus and the Truth in Sculpture." In Gutzwiller 2005: 183–205.
Stinson, P. (2011). "Perspective Systems in Roman Second Style Wall Painting." *American Journal of Archaeology* 115.3: 403–26.
Stoichita, V. I. (1997). *A Brief History of the Shadow*. London: Reaktion.
Summers, D. (2003). *Real Spaces: World Art History and the Rise of Western Modernism*. New York: Phaidon.

Tanner, J. (2006). *The Invention of Art History in Ancient Greece: Religion, Society and Artistic Rationalisation*. Cambridge: Cambridge University Press.

(2016). "Sight and Painting: Optical Theory and Pictorial Poetics in Classical Greek Art." In Squire 2016a: 107–22.

Thein, K. (2002). "Gods and Painters: Philostratus the Elder, Stoic Φαντασία and the Strategy of Describing." *Ramus* 31.1–2: 136–45.

(2015). "The Poetics of Mind and Matter: Some Remarks on Ancient Images and Imagination." *Eirene: Studia Graeca et Latina* 51.1–2: 303–34.

(2021). *Ecphrastic Shields in Graeco-Roman Literature: The World's Forge*. London: Routledge.

Tybout, R. A. (1989). *Aedificiorum figurae: Untersuchungen zu den Architekturdarstellungen des frühen zweiten Stils*. Leiden: Brill.

Van Oyen, A. (2016). *How Things Make History: The Roman Empire and Its Terra Sigillata Pottery*. Amsterdam: Amsterdam University Press.

Vauday, P. (2017). *The Invention of the Visible: The Image in Light of the Arts*. Trans. J. Bly. London: Rowman and Littlefield.

Vermeule, C. (1981). *Greek and Roman Sculpture in America: Masterpieces in Public Collections in the United States and Canada*. Berkeley: University of California Press.

von Blumenthal, A. (1928). "ΤΥΠΟΣ and ΠΑΡΑΔΕΙΓΜΑ." *Hermes* 63: 391–414.

von Bothmer, D., et al. (1995). "Recent Acquisitions: A Selection, 1994–1995." *Bulletin of the Metropolitan Museum of Art* 53.2: 6–19.

Vout, C. (2006). "Winckelmann and Antinous." *Cambridge Classical Journal* 52: 139–62.

Webb, R. (2009). *Ekphrasis, Imagination and Persuasion in Ancient Rhetorical Theory and Practice*. Farnham: Routledge.

Winter, N. A. (1993). *Greek Architectural Terracottas: From the Prehistoric to the End of the Archaic Period*. Oxford: Oxford University Press.

Yonge, C. D., trans. (1903). *The Orations of Marcus Tullius Cicero*. London: Bell.

Zagdoun, M.-A. (1989). *La sculpture archaïsante dans l'art hellénistique et dans l'art romain du Haut-Empire*. Paris: Boccard.

2 Thinking through Marble

Early Attic Stelai as Lithic Technology

CASPAR MEYER WITH CHRIS PELLETTIERI

How an object is looked at conditions what can be known about it. If new ways of knowing begin with new ways of looking, live encounters with objects should be of intense interest in art history and archaeology. In reality, the particulars of how investigators contact their materials are rarely examined – let alone recognized – as a potential area of discussion. Of course, university curricula make plentiful provisions for practical exercises in study collections equipped with an array of replicas, models, and originals. In some prestigious institutions, such collections rival the holdings of major public museums. Visitors are encouraged to handle objects, peruse open-access storage, or wheel around large items on movable bases. Despite these accommodations attending to the act of looking, *what* is looked at is invariably more important than *how* one looks. Students are taught to identify specific features that allow objects to be subsumed into established typologies and narratives, often centered on connoisseurship or stylistic evolution. But the cultivation of viewing habits as such tends to proceed through the tacit transfer of norms that resemble the practice-based pedagogies of apprenticeships more than anything we normally associate with university instruction.

The foremost factor in ocular examinations of artifacts is, without doubt, the relationship between proximity and the possibility of meaning. How near should we move to a work of art to understand it? At what point does the saturation of visible detail begin to obscure the object's overarching historical connections? The criterion of proximity is especially urgent in the study of stone reliefs. If examined from a sufficiently distant vantage point, most reliefs can be approached as purely visual phenomena, akin to flat pictures or dematerialized images.[1] Only when one draws close enough are questions about the relief's figural composition and iconography complicated by

The principal author is grateful to Milette Gaifman and the New Antiquity group for the invitation to take part in their 2019 meeting at Yale University. A previous version of this chapter was presented in a seminar series at the Department of Classics, University of Oslo. I thank Boris Maslov and the participants for the fruitful discussion that ensued. I am also deeply indebted to Edward Jones (Balliol College, Oxford) and Kate Morton (British Museum) for their help in producing appropriate illustrations.

1 Among the few recent studies of Greek reliefs that pivot their investigative framework explicitly around the objects' three-dimensional qualities are Neer 2010: 183–214; Estrin 2016; Squire 2018.

questions about its qualities as a three-dimensional object – namely a medium or composite covered all over with intersecting traces of its facture, finish, and fragmentation. The closer one concentrates on these traces, the more difficult it becomes to accommodate the object in established models of historical explanation. It goes without saying that in the face of such perplexing detail, most specialists prefer to keep their distance. Looking at objects as if they were images streamlines the tasks of identification and classification.[2]

The implications of observational proximity for the writing of historical accounts have been raised in relation to other types of material. James Elkins, for instance, grapples with the problems of looking too closely in the wake of writing his book *What Painting Is.* As critics point out, his project of adopting the language of alchemy to explore new ways of understanding painting entails the substitution of myopic, mark-by-mark descriptions of surfaces for historical accounts of seeing art. His response to the excessive "opticality" of art historical analysis runs, as he realizes, into similar difficulties as the works written by scholars who turn to phenomenological philosophy to discuss pictures as embodied experiences. Philosophy provides interesting theories of sensory relations and materiality, but its usefulness all too often collapses in close-up encounters with actual examples, when materials begin to collide with abstractions.[3] Beyond a certain level of detail, as Elkins concludes, art history and its cognate fields still lack the means of reconciling the very specific particulars of crafted objects with historical explanations of the changing ways of making and perceiving them.

To examine Greek stone reliefs up close is simultaneously easier and much more difficult than pursuing this aim for modern paintings. Ancient sculpture of all formats is today almost completely denuded of its applied coloration. So little is known about the original painted and inserted details that the plain forms of the remaining stone or metal fragments are habitually mistaken for the works' essences.[4] The loss of coatings is conceivably an advantage if techniques of sculpting stone are the motivation for close looking. In contrast to modeling in clay or casting metal, stone carving is a subtractive and irreversible process.[5] A detached flake of stone cannot be reattached and leaves

[2] As other contributions in this volume highlight, photography has been instrumental in conditioning certain favored viewpoints of sculptural works, often of the kind that bring out formal connections with items previously gleaned in illustrated texts. The mediatory power of the printed photograph can establish canonical perspectives, affecting how a piece is remembered and even how the original is looked at in subsequent encounters. See the contribution by Nikolaus Dietrich in this volume (Chapter 5) and, previously, McCauley 2011; Klamm 2017; C. Meyer 2017.

[3] Elkins 1999, 2008, with parallel critiques from anthropology and archaeology spelled out in Ingold 2007.

[4] See now Stager 2022. [5] As stressed in Wootton, Russell, and Rockwell 2013: 1, 5.

a trace both of its own crystalline structure and of the tool-mediated action through which it was removed. The hardness of crystalline stones ensures, in turn, that toolmarks have the potential to remain detectable as indices of the object's genesis in manual dexterity. In practice, however, such traces are not always easy to spot. Greek sculptors tended to erase the imprints of the tools they used as the process of carving advanced through successive stages. The final stages of smoothing and polishing rarely left visible clues of how the stone was brought into shape. But even where unfinished pieces or out-of-view areas of finished works preserve such clues, the existing literature on ancient sculpture has shown little interest in connecting technological descriptions of stone carving with accounts of its historical conditions of creativity and perception.

The choice of whether one looks at a relief from afar or from up close is therefore methodological. To date, the major interpretative approaches to ancient sculpture have relied on looking from a safe distance, leaving a whole realm of potential information untapped. This chapter seeks to demonstrate the value of close examination by relating the mechanics of carving observable in the finished object to the interrelated ways of making and understanding that sustained marble carving as a generative strand of cultural production. The discussion concentrates on stelai from Archaic and early Classical Athens – more precisely, on the carved lines and planes that came to constitute stone slabs as a standard material support for inscribed texts, sculpted figurations, or combinations thereof. I will employ the term "stele" in a technical sense, by giving the methods involved in making the objects center stage, and in a nontechnical sense, by disregarding the customary typological distinctions between grave and votive reliefs and documentary stelai.[6] By the Classical period, the sanctuaries and civic spaces of Athens were crowded with oblong stone slabs, normally higher than they were wide, that marked boundaries or commemorated deceased individuals, votive dedications, and military victories.[7] In the course of the fifth century BCE, stelai bearing public decrees, religious regulations, and lists of honorands, payments, or inventories began to proliferate in an

[6] Ancient usage prioritizes functional rather than morphological criteria; see *LSJ*, s.v. στήλη: block of stone used as a prop or buttress to a wall; block or slab used as a memorial, monument: gravestone; monument inscribed with record of victories, dedications, votes of thanks, treaties, laws, decrees, etc.; post placed on mortgaged ground, as a record of the fact; boundary-post or turning-post at the end of the racecourse.

[7] The genesis of inscribed stelai is an established topic. For recent treatments, see e.g. Davies 2005; E. Meyer 2016. Major collections of Athenian inscribed and sculpted stelai include Raubitschek and Jeffery 1949; Payne 1951: pls. 126–30; Hausmann 1960: 10–32 (votive inscriptions and reliefs), Richter 1961; Jeffery 1962 (gravestones); and Lalonde, Langdon, and Walbank 1991: 5–51 (horoi).

expanding range of locations.[8] Although the production of these monuments relies on similar technological skills and infrastructures, modern scholarship tends to allocate their study to separate disciplines and even separate subgenres of text and image. In disregarding these conventional categories, my goal is to shift attention to the genealogy of artisanal operations supporting the production of stelai as structurally self-sufficient units for monumental signaling. Such a shift is needed both to see the monuments afresh in the present and to understand how they performed their work in the past. Stelai only achieved their intended task, as we will see, if their viewers were able to read words and recognize figural representations on the carved surfaces without being distracted by the presence of the material support – that is, if the stones receded from consciousness in the process of being looked at.

The transparency of the stele is certainly deceptive, as any experienced mason or sculptor will confirm. The work of creating "neutral" surfaces is anything but trivial, involving the labor-intensive and wasteful processes of squaring, roughing out, and smoothing regular stone slabs from an unforgiving medium, not to mention the carving of words and figures on its surfaces. The quarrying and transport of marble must also be taken into account, including the deliberations required to identify an appropriately sized block, free of cracks and impurities, as well as the sheer physical effort of extracting it from the bedrock. But even a perfectly cuboid monolith provides only one external precondition for its perception as an appropriate surface for writing and relief carving. In Athens, as I hope to show, the rise of the stele as a preferred locus for inscription and figuration went hand in hand with the practice of reserving separate areas of marble surfaces for chiseling grooves and for sculpting three-dimensional forms. Linear incisions are widely recognized as characteristic of Archaic sculpture, marking, for instance, anatomical features, dress folds, nonfigural decoration, and letters applied directly onto sculpted bodies.[9] If such lines receive any comment in academic literature, they are described in a negative light, as manifestations of the period's awkward preoccupations with conceptual patterning that would soon be overcome by Classical naturalism.

[8] On locations, see esp. Liddel 2003. For major collections of relevant material, see Conze 1893; Dinsmoor 1913, 1921; Meritt, McGregor, and Wade-Gery 1939–53; M. Meyer 1989; Clairmont 1993–5; Harris 1995; Lawton 1995; Bergemann 1997; Hildebrandt 2006; and Osborne and Rhodes 2017.

[9] On the inclination in literature on Archaic sculpture to confuse the linear rendering of anatomy and dress with conceptual abstraction, see esp. Schneider 1999: 9–15, 242–3; Dietrich 2011, 2017. On the Archaic practice of applying inscriptions directly onto sculpted bodies, see Lorenz 2010; Dietrich 2020.

A closer look at linear carvings on stone opens opportunities for an alternative account of morphological change, one that draws on the monuments' internal constitution as opposed to propositions about how Athenian sculpture might relate to Athenian ways of seeing the world. To realize such an account, we will explore lines and planes as mutually dependent phenomena, creating varying ontological conditions for telling things with stone. To begin, I highlight the contradiction between human creativity and material determinism in previous literature on Greek sculpture and the opportunities that enactive notions of knowledge present for evaluating ancient craft in cross-disciplinary debates about human technicity. The two subsequent sections discuss how grooves were carved into planes and what different technological choices might reveal about the epistemic affordances of linear marks in figures and letters. To conclude, I will relate the finished carvings back to their origin in quarry-bedded blocks to bring out the broader arc of cultural knowledge involved in accommodating natural fissures in stone into spatial projections of urban design.

My research for this study is much indebted to my collaborator, Chris Pellettieri, a stone carver specializing in freehand sculpture, decorative design, portraiture, casting, and lettering for public and private use.[10] Pellettieri originally trained as a stonemason in an apprenticeship program at the Cathedral of St. John the Divine – a colossal, still unfinished Gothic revival structure in New York City. He generously agreed to discuss relevant pieces during a visit to the Metropolitan Museum of Art and experimental reconstructions of carving techniques in his workspace in the Bronx. Although Pellettieri's preferred medium is limestone rather than marble, his experience with stone as a material for building as well as sculpting enriched this project immeasurably. It encouraged me to look beyond the studio practices foregrounded in previous collaborations between art historians and sculptors and connect descriptions of carving techniques with knowledge of its material, what it means to "think through stone."[11]

Stelai as Lithic Technology

It would be misleading to claim that academic specialists do not closely examine their objects of investigation or are summarily naive about their

[10] He is also the founder of the Pellettieri Stone Carvers' Academy, a nonprofit organization promoting awareness and appreciation of stone carving and providing training in traditional techniques (see www.stonecarversacademy.com).

[11] The potential of such collaborations is discussed in Russell and Wootton 2017: 254–5.

methodological predispositions. The study of Greek and Roman sculpture has always involved meticulous scrutiny of surfaces. The issue that interests me is less some deficit in attention than a shift in intellectual focus, which a change in viewpoint can signal. Experts who view carved stone up close tend to be interested in questions of conservation or authenticity, whose resolution is considered at best preliminary to the more serious aims of historical interpretation. Even more pronounced is the positional shift in studies of sculptural technique. Such studies have a long and venerable tradition, beginning with occasional observations by Johann Joachim Winckelmann and other eighteenth-century connoisseurs through the first systematic survey of the tools and methods of sculptural production by Comte de Clarac.[12] With the formation of disciplines, studies written in this vein came to stand in increasing and largely unacknowledged tension with historicist trends in the humanities, so much so that investigation of stone carving is today seen as a separate field. Although textbooks on Greek sculpture often feature a chapter devoted to tools and techniques, insights from its examinations rarely find mention in the substance of discussions on style, artistic personalities, or visual culture. The goal of this section is to examine this impasse in the light of previous scholarship and to relate salient problems in the study of our particular material to theoretically grounded interrogations of skilled activity.

As is clear from Comte de Clarac's parallel treatment of ancient and modern studio practices, the original motivation for technological studies was to measure the abilities of contemporary European sculptors against those of their Greek predecessors. This interest in comparison is still alive in the debates surrounding both the introduction of pointing methods to transfer preliminary designs done in clay or plaster into stone with the aid of measuring frames, calipers, and plumb lines and the harnessing of the associated procedures for the "mass production" of copies from the late Hellenistic period.[13] The compelling evidence for such assistive technologies from traces of measuring points on works of the early Classical period

[12] Comte de Clarac 1841: 1–193, discussed in Boschung 2014 and in the online edition of Comte de Clarac's work on https://arachne.uni-koeln.de/drupal/?q=node/113.

[13] The details of the debate are of little concern in the present context. Earlier interpretations of preserved measuring points as evidence for the use of pointing machines in antiquity have been firmly rejected by, among others, Boschung and Pfanner 1990: 137; Rockwell 1993: 122. As shown by Palagia (2003, 2006: 262–70), such measuring points do demonstrate, however, that the practice of transferring designs by means of plumb lines and caliper-assisted pointing goes back to the fifth century BCE, if not earlier. Possibly the earliest examples of measuring points have been identified on the metopes from the temple of Zeus at Olympia; see Ashmole and Yalouris 1967: pls. 69, 90, 144, 147, 161. Pointing without pointing machines is also known in early modern workshops, as documented (and usefully illustrated) by Honour 1972.

upended the long-held assumption that Greek sculptors were, in essence, freehand carvers who realized their designs directly in stone.[14] The recognition that marble carvers of the "best" period had already relied on such devices encouraged modern scholars to draw a strict distinction between the conceptual work of the master who innovates original designs and the "mechanized" task of execution, likely delegated to assistants.

Such tool-supported division of labor probably had little currency in earlier workshops. For all we know, Archaic sculptors really were the proficient free carvers romanticized by European aesthetes. Perhaps they relied solely on charcoal guidelines sketched out on the stone blocks, which were then given form by chiseling off layers of stone progressively from multiple sides, normally beginning this process in the quarry and ending it at the statue's intended place of installation. The evidence that those outlines might adhere to proportional grid systems inspired by Egyptian practice has not affected the basic premise about Archaic sculpture that what we see in its forms are expressions of both the maker's personality and historical conditions.[15] Just how one might best peel apart the different facets of this identity is a different matter. Since the nineteenth-century discovery of the first specimens of Archaic sculpture, archaeologists have proposed many different taxonomies to assign meaning to material morphology. Stylistic examination has suggested a variety of more or less plausible classifications, ranging from chronological, regional, ethnic, or racial divisions all the way to individual "hands." With the premillennial spread of constructionist paradigms from the social sciences, however, the assumptions upon which these taxonomies rested have unraveled. The stylistic criteria that were once thought to present indices of hardwired facts are now more likely viewed as self-conscious proclamations of collective character on behalf of those who commissioned Archaic sculptural projects.[16]

In hindsight the idea that a crafted object can reveal its maker's cultural identity through rule-bound classification was always precarious. It involves a giant leap from *our* pragmatic categorizations to assumptions about how ancient actors might have perceived and assigned meaning to those very same traits. Whichever way we approach it, in its current form the study of Greek sculpture subordinates the work of hands to the

[14] As envisaged by Casson 1933; Blümel 1943: 16–17; Adam 1966: 1, 6–7.

[15] Guralnick 1976; Davis 1981; Donohue 2005: 20–154; cf. Carter and Steinberg 2010.

[16] For interpretations of regional style in Archaic sculpture as a conscious assertion of the patron's cultural identity as opposed to a reflex of the artist's personality or ethnicity, see Viviers 1992; Müller and Prost 2002; Duplouy 2006: 217–49. New interpretations of the Severe Style as visual avowals of Hellenic superiority (notably by Stewart 2008: 599–610) are also fully consistent with this trend.

intentions of the mind, be it because these hands are thought to externalize preexisting inner templates or to implement the outlines of a master's superior designs. The study of technology is sidelined, regardless of its achievements.

One undisputed strength, however, is its success in identifying toolmarks on surviving sculpture with the type of implement. For demonstrations of close autopsy, one need not look any further than Olga Palagia's detection, for instance, of the early use of the claw chisel in Archaic sculpture "at the back of the hair of the Attic Pomegranate Kore" or the introduction of the drill in the fifth century BCE for such detailed work as "cut[ting] tear ducts or mark[ing] the corners of the mouth as on the heads of Akropolis Museum 699 and Kerameikos Museum P 1455."[17] Recent studies have also made great advances in working out how and for what purpose different tools were put to use.[18] Despite the general agreement that the range of implements employed in antiquity was very similar to that found in modern workshops (prior to the introduction of electric power tools), we should not expect that the particulars of carving, beyond the general progression from the general to the specific, followed a standardized method.

The process would normally begin with the blocking out of forms using punches or point chisels, then continue with the initial phases of modeling with claw or tooth chisels, before moving on to defining figural details more closely with flat and bull-nose chisels. The use of the drill could occur at a variety of stages to remove larger volumes of stone or accentuate details on modeled surfaces. In a subsequent step, the working traces would be removed more or less thoroughly with rasps and abrasives to create smooth or polished surfaces ready for applying paint and colorless protective coatings of wax and oil. In between those stages, however, processes could be repeated if the shaping of forms called for the removal of excess stone to create recesses after the preliminary planes had been created. The recursive creation and removal of surfaces would have been pronounced in modeling the variable levels of depth of relief sculpture, from the protruding parts through the intervening planes to its backplate. For the late

[17] Palagia 2006: 252, 255–6, commenting on an early sixth-century BCE kore (Athens, Acropolis Museum, 593), as well as the early Classical heads of an ephebe or Athena (Athens, Acropolis Museum, 699) and of a warrior from near the Dipylon Gate (Athens, Kerameikos Museum, P 1455).

[18] See esp. results of the extended collaborative project "Art of Making" (www.artofmaking.ac.uk) presented in Wootton, Russell, and Rockwell 2013. Although focusing on stone carving in the Roman period, the project's centering of practical craft experiences from resource procurement to project completion provided decisive inspiration for the present study.

Hellenistic and Roman periods, from which a greater number of unfinished pieces remain extant, we have plentiful evidence that carvers could switch back and forth between rough shaping with the point and finer work with flat or bull-nose chisels. Furthermore, preferences in tool selection could be idiosyncratic. In the well-known workshop at Aphrodisias, for instance, the use of the claw chisel appears to have gone against "house rules." The unfinished pieces from the site show none of the telltale marks of this implement, although traces of its utilization are commonplace on works produced elsewhere in the city.[19]

Such finely scaled differences in craft processes have to date not mattered as much as they should. This indifference is understandable to some extent. After all, why should we expect the choices of some nameless craftsperson to contribute anything substantive to the questions that really matter to historians, especially if the effects of those choices were not intended to be visible in the finished product? As I will make clear, the toolmarks we are concentrating on need to be distinguished from the stylistic traits that scholars prioritize in classifying their material, not least because Archaic sculptors wanted those traits to be visible from afar. The relative disinterest in the minutiae of making is also in keeping with the prevailing conceptions of sculpture as manifestations of disembodied and reproducible visual culture. If the art of stone carving is solely conceived as a means to an end, then craftspeople's particular decisions are indeed functionally equivalent and interchangeable, as long as they result in an image that suits whatever purpose we think it might have had. But this heuristic circularity between method and goal – that is, between how classical archaeologists look at ancient sculpture and what they want to know about it – should make us think again. Equifinality in technological choice ought not to be mistaken for equivalence, especially in the waning Anthropocene.

The functional understanding of stone carving is at odds with approaches to technology in other branches of archaeology. The past twenty years have seen a surge of interest in technological practice as a central interpretative juncture between material and cognitive dimensions of culture.[20] Among the theoretical directions that have come to converge in this field is a shared awareness, first, that multiple technological possibilities are available to achieve a particular goal in a particular

19 Van Voorhis 2012: 43, with the material from the workshop now fully published in Van Voorhis 2018.

20 For historiographical reviews, see e.g. Lemonnier 1992; Schlanger 1994; Killick 2004; Dobres 2010.

setting and, second, that the selection of a workable solution comes down to social values no less than purely practical considerations. Technological choices are examined as cultural choices governed by beliefs and traditions as much as functional criteria, material constraints, or any notions of rational efficiency.[21] In this way, the expertise invested in the making of material culture transpires as a formative component of its broader historical contexts of display, circulation, and use. Empirical evidence of this expertise comes from the object's mode of crafting; but unlike the object's style and typology, the technological choices constituting this evidence can be difficult to recognize given that they were rarely meant to be visible in the finished product. They are also difficult to interpret through established archaeological categorization, for they attest to the complex interplay of workshop organization, training, formal intentions, and the material properties of locally sourced or imported materials.[22] With regard to the carved stelai that interest us here, one could hold that what they denote as finished images or texts is only the most explicit aspect of what their process of carving contributes to implicit frameworks of understanding.

The interest in craft in anthropology and prehistoric archaeology has led to a broader shift from theories prioritizing the consumption, exchange, and agency of material culture to approaches that stress the far-flung ramifications of technological actions, from the level of individual gestures and intentions all the way to the social and ecological impact of procuring raw materials. Technology is envisaged as a sprawling web of connections in which the skill of making objects is inseparable from the knowledge and sensory dispositions required to put them to cultural use. Accounts that operate on such diverging scales of analysis are difficult to achieve even under the best of circumstances. In studying Attic sculpture as a technology, we are in a comparably privileged position thanks to the volume of documented material that can be brought into play and the potential methodological models available in other disciplines. If examples from related fields have had little impact so far, one reason is likely the aforementioned deceptive resemblance between ancient and modern working methods. If a preserved toolmark is easily associated with an implement whose form and function is still familiar to us, why should its use warrant closer examination? By omitting such scrutiny, however, we risk writing accounts about a revered strand of Greek creative genius that collides with what Greeks themselves tell us about the work of chisels.

[21] On technological choice, see esp. Sillar and Tite 2000.

[22] The issues surrounding the visibility and social meaning of technical choices (in sub-Saharan pottery production) are particularly well explained by Gosselain 2000.

Reliefs Cannot Be Drawn

Before we try to reconnect traces of ancient tooling with ancient makers, let us turn to an example: a marble stele in the Louvre featuring a finial of the double volute–palmette type and the outlines of a youth in right-facing profile, with his left leg stepping forward and a mantle over his left shoulder (Figs. 2.1a–b).[23] The stele is one of a larger group of Archaic works that show their subject in incised outlines. This method of rendering remained a viable option in different regional traditions from the late seventh century to the second half of the sixth century BCE. It coexisted with, and was indeed preceded by, relief carving in the customary sense, with its visual elements modeled in continuous forms and protruding from the ground.[24] It is unclear what factors might have motivated the use of incisions. One could think of a number of conditions of display and lighting in which sharp outlines combined with a painted surface could create attractive visual effects. The method certainly had nothing to do with primitive artistry or lack of ability, as our example underlines.

Incised stelai provide a productive case study in our context for two main reasons. First, since the incised lines were regularly left unpolished even in otherwise finished pieces, the interior faces of the grooves tend to preserve tool traces and, hence, evidence of the kind of choices we are interested in. Second, the use of linear marks to suggest the presence of bodies blurs conventional boundaries in art history between two-dimensional drawing and three-dimensional sculpture. In other words, such incised stelai compel us to confront our established interpretative frameworks that prioritize the graphic effect of the finished work over the skills and procedures involved in its making.

Generally speaking, linear marks of appreciable depth can be created by three methods of free carving. Such grooves need to be distinguishable from the surface scratches that serve as guidelines for the application of

[23] Charbonneaux 1940; Richter 1944: 109–12, 1961: 41, no. 57, figs. 138–40; Rumpf 1953: 74, pl. 22.1.

[24] The earliest known Greek relief carving (normally dated to the second half of the seventh century BCE) shows its figural representation projecting outward from a lightly recessed background. See the grave stele no. 760 from Paroikia, showing a woman seated on a chair, in Paros Museum, published in Mauragani 2000: 157–8, figs. 2–3; Nolte 2006: 38–9, no. 35, pl. 20. For Archaic Greek incised stelai, see e.g. Lempese 1976 (four limestone reliefs in Heraklion Museum, Crete, dated to the second half of the seventh century BCE); Kourayos and Detoratou 2005–6 (votive relief from sanctuary of Asklepios in Paroikia, Paros, second half seventh century BCE); Richter 1961: 21, no. 24 (upper part of stele shaft in Berlin showing figure of a youth, 575–570 BCE, identified as Hymettian marble); Steinhauer 2001: 262, no. 348 (grave stele from Troizen showing hoplite, sixth century BCE).

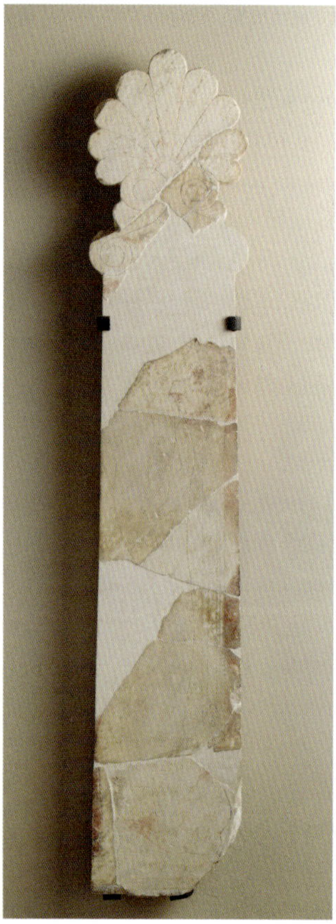

Fig. 2.1a Shaft of a stele with incised youth and a palmette finial, 520–510 BCE. Parian marble, remains of red and black paint still visible on the palmette and the stele, 216 × 32–37 × 7–9.5 cm. Paris, Musée du Louvre, MND 1863 (Photograph by Tony Querrec. © RMN-Grand Palais/Art Resource, NY).

paint and not create clearly visible shadows.[25] The most straightforward technique involved closely spaced strokes made by a vertically held pointed chisel. This method is known from a few early inscriptions from Attica.[26] It never became a standard choice, however, not least because repeated, vertical chisel blows risk uncontrolled chipping or fracturing inside the rock. Composed almost entirely of mineral calcite, both marble and limestone are relatively soft and brittle. Depending on the grain size and

[25] See e.g. the stele of Lyseas from Velanideza in Athens, National Archaeological Museum, 30; Richter 1961: 48, 170, no. 70, figs. 158–60, 215; Jeffery 1962: 141, no. 53. For Classical examples, see esp. the Boeotian black limestone stelai showing figures in lightly incised or dotted lines, now in the Thebes Archaeological Museum; Aravantinos 2010: 282–7. On scratched guidelines on Archaic sculptures in general, see Brinkmann 2003: 35–6.

[26] Duncan 1961: 185.

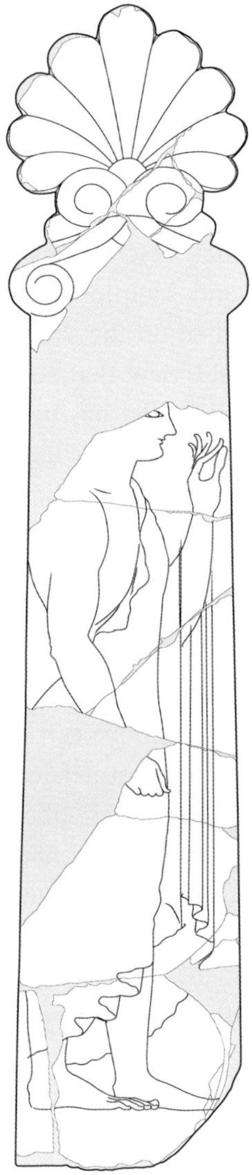

Fig. 2.1b Outline drawing of the incised figure on the stele (drawing by Kate Morton).

direction of the crystallographic structure, sharp blows with the edge or point of a tool can cause internal shattering of larger crystals in the marble, an effect called bruising or stunning by sculptors.[27] Such strokes are normally only used during the initial steps of shaping in order to remove large chips from stone blocks with a point.

27 Higgins and Pritchett 1965: 367–8, examining earlier assumptions that sculpting and letter cutting regularly entailed perpendicular tool action.

A more common technique for making linear marks used a drill or gouge to create a series of small adjacent holes that are then connected into a continuous groove by knocking through the remaining stone with a chisel. The method relies on the honeycombing principle used to remove larger chunks of stone.[28] The characteristic preparatory holes are still visible in the figure of a youth depicted in outline on a fragmentary stele shaft of Hymettian marble in Berlin and on several Archaic inscriptions.[29]

A third technique, widely used by letter carvers and sculptors, was employed by the maker of the stele in the Louvre. It relied on the skilled handling of flat chisels of various widths. The long-held view that such chisels were held almost vertically when struck with the mallet has been dispelled by Sheila Adam and by Charles G. Higgins and William K. Pritchett, who stress the importance of the oblique stroke.[30] Oblique cutting motions that drive the edge of the chisel into the stone are more economical and minimize the risk of accidental spalling or bruising.[31] Marble reacts better if the tools are applied at varying angles, causing abrasion, incision, scratching, and flaking. Such oblique chisel strokes result in grooves with arched or V-shaped cross-sectional profiles. Depending on the gradient of the chisel, the slopes of the groove can be more or less steep. In rounded grooves, the slopes can be asymmetrical, with the outer ones cut first at a steeper angle and the inner ones subsequently pared down from the interior edge (Fig. 2.2). Whatever the shape of the incised groove, it is easier and safer to start with a steep slope, struck with the full chisel length, before the opposite slope is cut. If the slopes are cut down to form a wider incision with flatter angles, the chisel can be guided in the direction of the line, scraping the slopes with its square corner pointing toward the center of the groove (Fig. 2.3).

Modern carvers are still well versed in the processes of incising lines in order to carve inscriptions. Pellettieri told me that he avoids retracing the interior of the grooves of letters after incising them. Although such retooling might lend the incisions more regular outlines, it tends to blunt the

[28] See Palagia 2006: 257.

[29] Berlin, Staatliche Museen, A2; Blümel 1940: 8, pl. 9; Richter 1944: 41, fig. 58; 1961: 21, no. 24. For inscriptions, see e.g. *SEG* 10.452a, 433 (*IG* I[2] 981); Richter 1961: 157–65, nos. 35, 37.

[30] Higgins and Pritchett 1965: 367–8; Adam 1966: 27–8.

[31] For epigraphers this insight meant that the width of the chisel's indentation could no longer be depended upon as a diagnostic feature in identifying the hands of individual letter cutters who were associated with a distinctive set of tools. In any case, since ancient craftspeople were unacquainted with tempered steel, their tools had to be resharpened repeatedly during the carving, changing shape in the process. A flat chisel could, in effect, become a bull-nose chisel. Duncan (1961: 181) identified resharpening in well-preserved inscribed stelai every twelve lines or so.

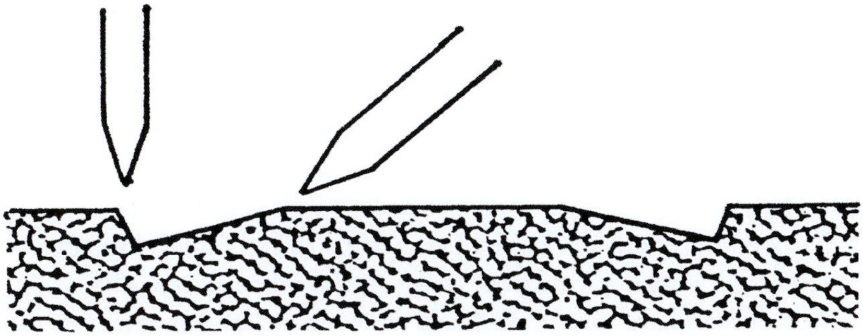

Fig. 2.2 Schematic cross-section of a rounded groove cut with flat chisels. The drawing shows the approximate angles at which the tools must have been held to produce the inner and outer slopes. From Higgins and Pritchett 1965: 369, fig. 1.

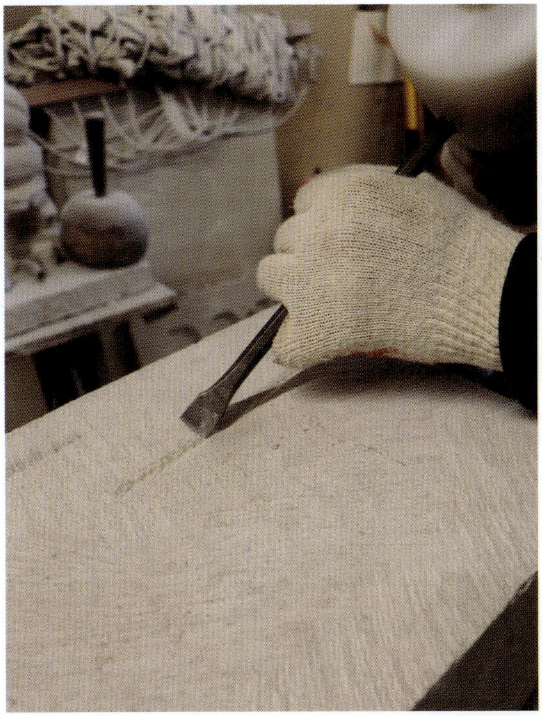

Fig. 2.3 Chris Pellettieri creating a linear incision with a flat chisel held at an oblique angle, carving into the limestone with the corner of the tool (photograph by author).

edges of the grooves and make them appear less sharp in the finished product. Ancient carvers might have had a similar rationale in mind to judge by the toolmarks left visible inside the carved grooves. Such toolmarks would, in any case, be concealed by shade once the inscriptions were displayed in raking daylight and the grooves painted with dark hues (in antiquity, inscriptions were typically colored with red ochre, cinnabar, or blue frit).

The incised stele in the Louvre is a work of consummate excellence in craft. The obverse plane is carefully finished with a flat chisel. The sides show oblique striations, while the back is evenly stippled and framed by a narrow, chiseled margin that produces a sharp finish at the edges. The incised outlines of the figure vary in thickness from less than 0.5 millimeters to 3 millimeters. In the principal edition of the piece, Jean Charbonneaux interprets the subtle gradations as an attempt to convey pictorial depth and corporeal presence. His description dwells on the accentuated, writhing incisions of the boy's facial features and left hand, where he recognizes a "real effect of perspective."[32] His eye was clearly predisposed by graphic conventions that date back to neoclassical drawings and engravings. In their well-known adaptations of Greek painted vases, Wilhelm Tischbein and John Flaxman rely on such calligraphic juxtapositions of thin and thick "shadow" lines to suggest incident light in the strictly bichrome, linear profile views of the depicted figures (Figs. 2.4a–b).[33] Charbonneaux's evaluation of the stele as if it were a drawing is also evident in his admiration for the unbroken line running from the left shoulder along the front of the body to the (missing) toe of the left foot, interrupted only by the overlapping tip of the figure's right thumb. Seemingly oblivious to its origins in chisel strokes, he attributes the virtuoso flowing line to a generic "tool" whose "resumption is difficult to detect."[34]

This interpretation of the stele through the principles of modern drawing fails to account for how the variable thickness and texture of the incisions were actually deployed. If pictorial depth had been a consistent concern, we would expect more detail in the carving of the fabric folds across the youth's body. The outlines of the mantle show that the garment was slung diagonally over the chest to the left shoulder, with its loose end falling over the boy's left arm. As Charbonneaux points out, the three wide drop folds at the lower edge correspond to two subtle undulations at the upper left shoulder, close to where the chest meets the wavy border of the mantle. While the garment's draping at the two ends of the mantle is therefore logically connected, the intervening area shows no diagonal

[32] Charbonneaux 1940: 57.

[33] Tischbein's renderings after the antique were in many ways a foundational moment for modern graphic practices; see e.g. Busch 2001: 31; C. Meyer 2023a.

[34] Charbonneaux 1940: 57.

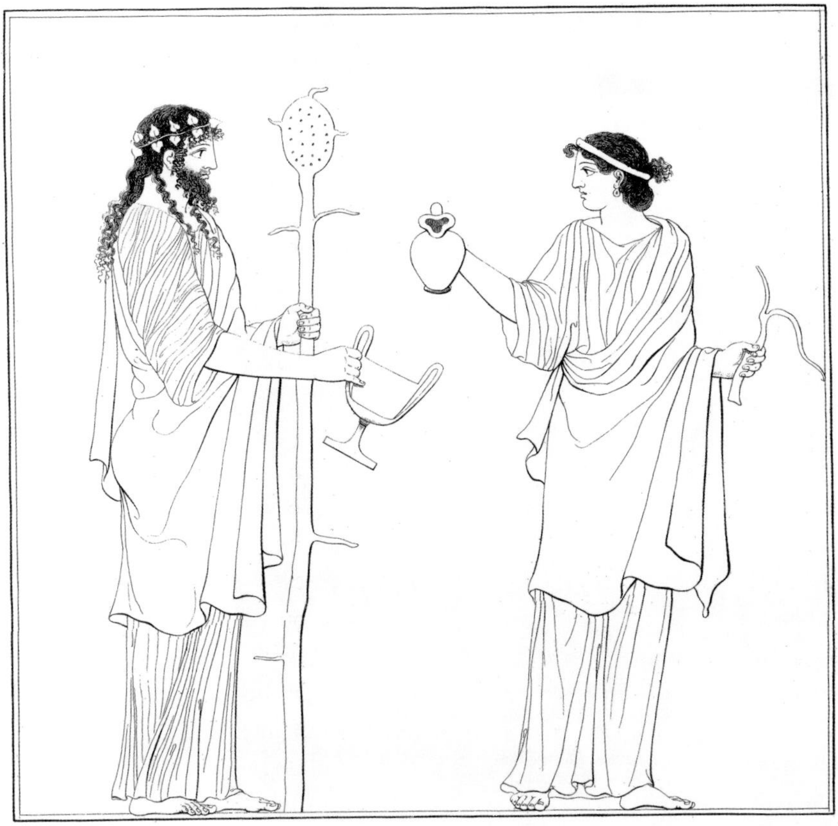

Fig. 2.4a Copper engraving of Dionysos and woman pouring wine from an Athenian red-figure belly amphora. From Hamilton and Tischbein 1791–5, vol. 2: plate 23.

creases or pipe folds running across the body. To the viewer accustomed to the spatial effects of modern drawing, this lack of naturalistic plasticity is puzzling. Charbonneaux argues that the folds must have been painted on the marble in a manner resembling the pictorial schema of mantles shown in contemporary vase painting (Fig. 2.5). The presumed loss of these painted details allows him to maintain that the incised lines of the stele should be viewed as inverse "equivalents" of lines painted on vases.[35]

This confusion of chiseled grooves for drawn or painted lines might seem inconsequential if the stele is understood as an essentially graphic

[35] Charbonneaux 1940: 63–4. Although the stele shows no traces of paint on the youth's body, the dress folds posited by Charbonneaux have become a truism perpetuated, for instance, in the description of Richter 1961: 41. Charbonneaux and Richter compared the style of the stele to the work of Euphronios and Psiax, respectively (and, accordingly, they date the piece to 510–505 and 520–510 BCE).

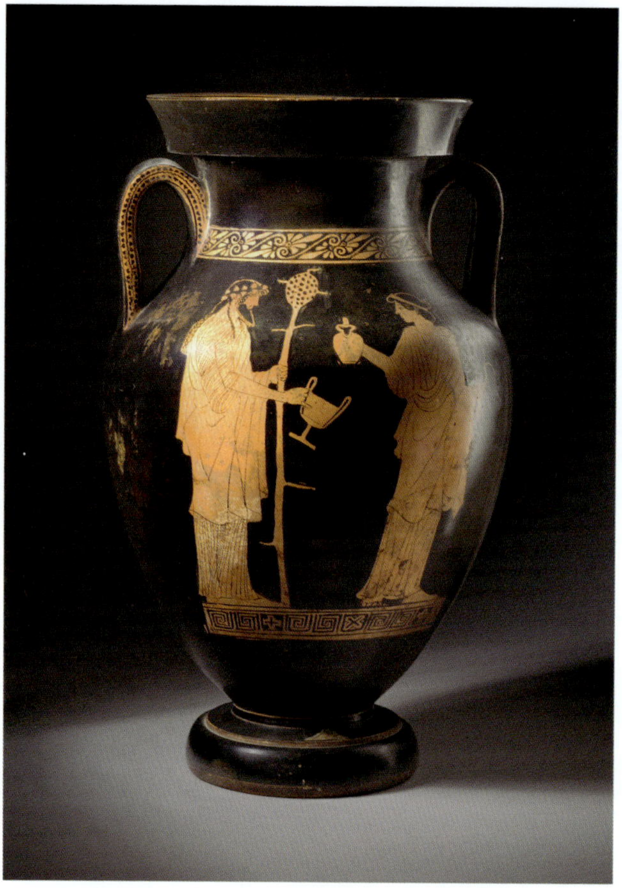

Fig. 2.4b Athenian red-figure belly amphora, attributed to the Deepdene Painter, 475–450 BCE. Height: 47 cm. Los Angeles, County Museum of Art, 50.8.21 (Digital image Museum Associates/LACMA. Licensed by Art Resource, NY).

creation, achieved by moving a point over a surface to produce an uninterrupted trace. But in viewing it as such, we are prevented from examining how the making of the object is part of its meaning. The diverging implications of drawing and chiseling lines in our example are best explained by contrasting the pictorial conventions of the incised figure with those of modern contour drawing. Such contour lines are an ambiguous category in that the same toolmark can denote not only the real boundaries and edges of depicted objects or figures but also the shape outlines of rounded bodies and features that have no real edges. Known as "occluding contours," these shape outlines are pivotal in suggesting the presence of three-dimensional forms through two-dimensional lines. They are also key to understanding

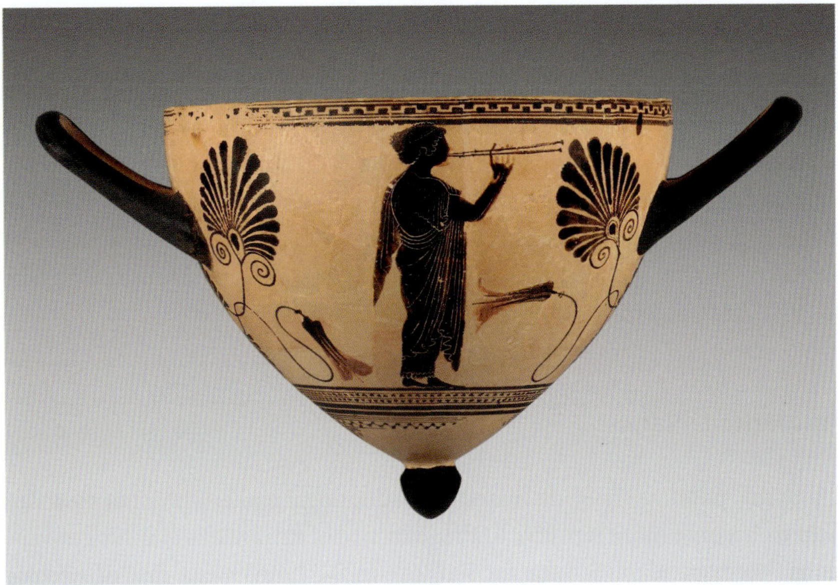

Fig. 2.5 Attic black-figure *mastos*, attributed to Psiax, 520–500 BCE. Height of vessel: 12.1 cm. Malibu, CA, J. Paul Getty Museum, 90.AE.122 (Getty's Open Content Program).

and producing drawings competently. Learning how to draw occluding contours is fundamental to any serious studio art course, tantamount to drawing itself, as some manuals seem to maintain.[36] It requires the draftsperson to *really* see what is in front of them without allowing the brain to intervene. This skill is acquired through concerted still-life drawing exercises involving the sketching of an object's contours with the eyes firmly fixed on it, resisting the temptation to look at the paper.

Charbonneaux interprets the outline figure on the stele, in effect, as a flawed contour drawing. While his proposed reconstruction of the figure's garment with painted folds would indeed produce an image that approximates the conventions of modern contour drawing, there is no evidence that the piece was painted in this manner. While the preserved incisions do show dress folds where the mantle falls over the figure's raised left arm, the carving suggests that the textural rather than spatial qualities of the depicted subject were of primary concern to the sculptor. The disposition of the grooves contrasts between boundaries of skin and boundaries of cloth, with thicker sinuous incisions delineating body parts

[36] See e.g. Sheehan 1994; Olivier 2020. On outlines and contour lines more generally, see Maynard 2005: 63–4, 77, 98–9.

and thinner ones with sharper turns conveying the qualities of the mantle's fine fabric. The sculptor seems to indicate haptic awareness of the depicted substances and not how they might have been seen at a particular moment in time. Furthermore, the deep grooves of the outline figure depend on a literal understanding of incision as a means to divide the continuous marble surface into foreground, background, and separate objects. In so doing, they bring out a cognitive overlap between the acts of depiction and substitution that is alien to the mimetic understanding of represented space in post-Archaic art.

Immanent Planes

Up to this point, we have discussed how adopting a maker's point of view can help us become more sensitive to the influence of extraneous graphic conventions. We have identified the incised stele in the Louvre as a case of Archaic realism that pairs pictorial abstraction with objective consistency in ways that confound expectations shaped by later manifestations of empirical naturalism. To explore the significance of technological choice, let us now turn our attention to the double-tiered volutes and palmette at the top of the stele.

As Charbonneaux notes, while the elements of this finial were carved with extraordinary care, the maker refrained from using a compass to draft the eyes of the volutes.[37] In fact, the sculptor appears to have avoided a strictly geometrical appearance by giving the upper pair of volutes an elliptical shape and placing the base and leaves of the palmette slightly off-center. In many other finials on stelai of the period, these same elements were carved with a view to strict symmetry, using a cutting compass to outline the volutes.[38] The central dot created by the tool's fixing device is often left visible on the polished surface as if to stress the use of mechanical aids in the carving process. The use of the compass to cut figural details visible in the finished work is a common feature in Archaic Greek sculpture. In addition to plant-derived motifs on finials and capitals, it was employed to outline irises on the eyeballs of humans, animals, and mythical creatures, as well as for patterns on dress or animal pelts (Figs. 2.6a–b).[39]

[37] Charbonneaux 1940: 56.

[38] In the Metropolitan Museum in New York, see e.g. intaglio-carved lyre-design capital with double volutes, (44.11.5; Richter 1944: 81–4; 1961: 31, no. 43) and the incised cavetto capital (17.230.6; Richter 1961: 19–21, no. 21).

[39] See Adam 1966: 82–3, for an extensive list of examples and the disuse of the cutting compass at the close of the Archaic period.

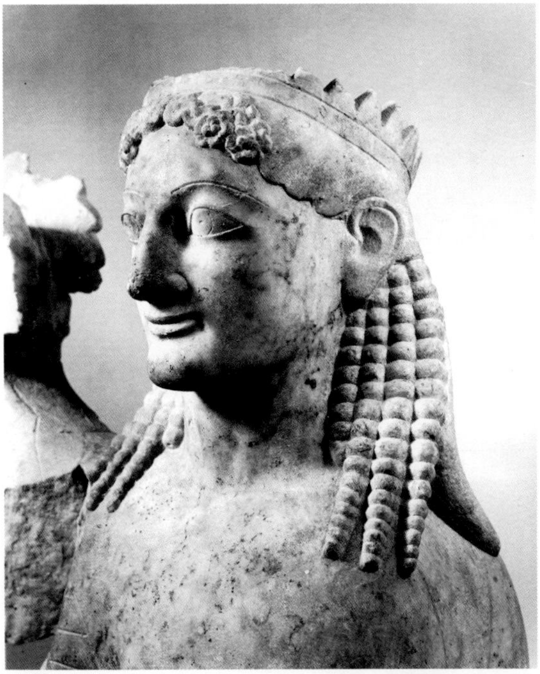

Fig. 2.6a Detail of a marble sphinx from a grave monument, from the bank of the Eridanos in the Sacred Gate area, 575–550 BCE. Height of sphinx: 63 cm. Athens, Kerameikos Museum, P 1050 (American School of Classical Studies at Athens, Archives, Alison Frantz Photographic Collection, AT 259).

Occasionally, compass-cut arcs could convey the feathered or scaly texture of a sphinx's breast.[40] The application of the tool is a technological choice because all of these features were habitually also carved freehand.

To understand this choice, we have to extend our purview to contemporary inscriptions, which attest to an interesting range of mechanical aids for cutting the circular letters omicron, phi, and theta. Antony Raubitschek posits three different implements on the basis of surviving toolmarks.[41] The most common one is the cutting compass, attested from the second quarter of the sixth century BCE. Early examples of its use include the Acropolis dedications of Rhonbos (the "Moschophoros") and of the Alcmaeonids.[42] A second method involved an instrument described as a tridental drill, with two shorter legs revolving around a slightly longer

[40] See e.g. the headless limestone sphinx in New York, Metropolitan Museum of Art 43.11.6; Richter 1961: 16–17, no. 14.

[41] Raubitschek 1951. On the use of these same tools in sculpture, see Casson 1933: 69–70 (incision compass), 118–21 (tridental drill), and 209–15 (tubular drill).

[42] Raubitschek and Jeffery 1949: 62–3, 338–40, nos. 59, 317.

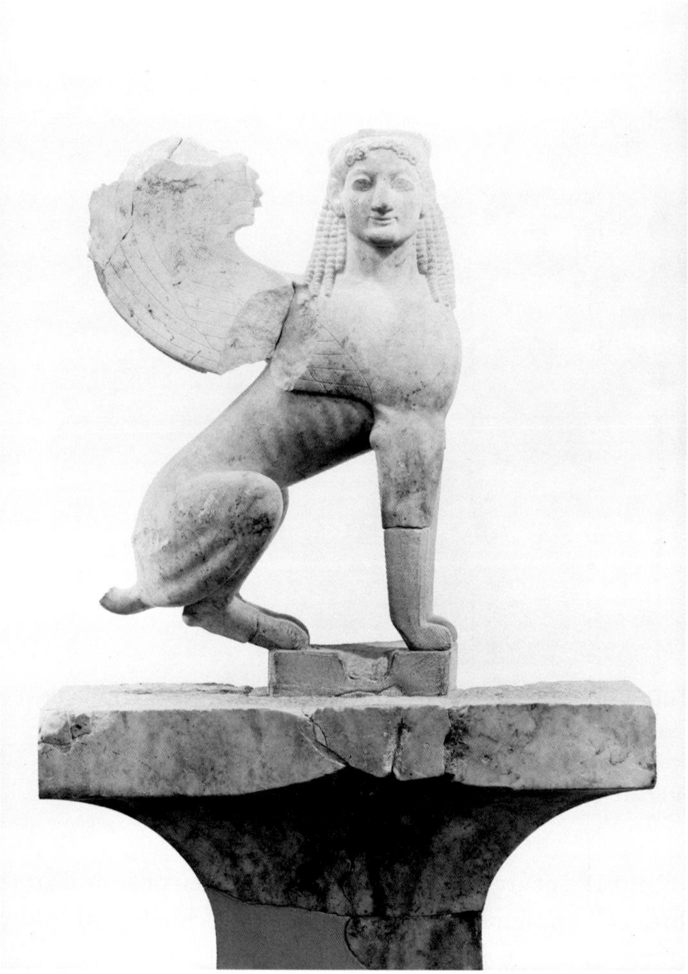

Fig. 2.6b Marble sphinx Kerameikos P 1050 on crowning capital of grave stele (D-DAI-ATH-Kerameikos 7258).

central spike. No surviving examples of this implement are known; its design is inferred from dotted omicrons with deep grooves and pronounced central indentations on inscriptions dating between the mid sixth and the first half of the fifth century BCE.[43] Finally, Raubitschek identifies a tubular drill, consisting of a hollow metal cylinder that was turned at high frequency around a fixed axis, probably a wooden core pressed against the surface of the stone. The cutting effect proper must have been achieved through an abrasive agent, such as ground emery or pumice,

[43] Among the Acropolis inscriptions, in chronological order, see Raubitschek and Jeffery 1949: 65, 365–7, 170–1, nos. 61, 331, 152.

reducing the need for vertical force. Such a tool would explain the perfectly circular letters with thick grooves visible on several well-known monuments of the early fifth century BCE, such as the first Marathon epigram, the Hekatompedon inscriptions, and the stele from the city Eleusinion.[44] Another telltale sign comes from the instances in which the cut letter is outlined by one or two lighter, slightly off-center circles that were incised by accident, as the engraver did not apply the central core with sufficient pressure, causing it to jolt sideways (Fig. 2.7).[45]

To the casual eye looking from afar, the differences resulting from these engraving methods might not seem striking, especially if the letter grooves were filled with paint. From the point of view of the letter cutter, however, the differences in tool action were significant, especially if we also include the method of producing circular letters with a point chisel. On the inscription on the base of the so-called Boy-and-Girl stele in the Metropolitan Museum of Art, the application of this method required at

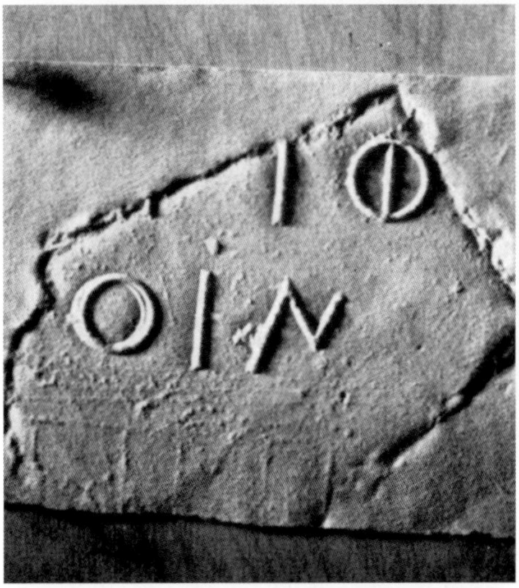

Fig. 2.7 Squeeze taken from a fragment of *IG* I^3 4 ll. 26–7 = *SEG* 10.5 (Hekatompedon inscription). Athens, Epigraphic Museum, EM 6794 (© Hellenic Ministry of Culture/ Hellenic Organization of Cultural Resources Development [H.O.C.RE.D.]).

[44] Marathon: *SEG* 10.404 (*IG* I^3 503/4); Hekatompedon: *SEG* 10.4, 5 (*IG* 1^3 4); Eleusinion: *SEG* 10.6 (*IG* I^3 6).

[45] This error can be seen in both the Marathon and Hekatompedon inscriptions, as detailed by Raubitschek 1951: 343.

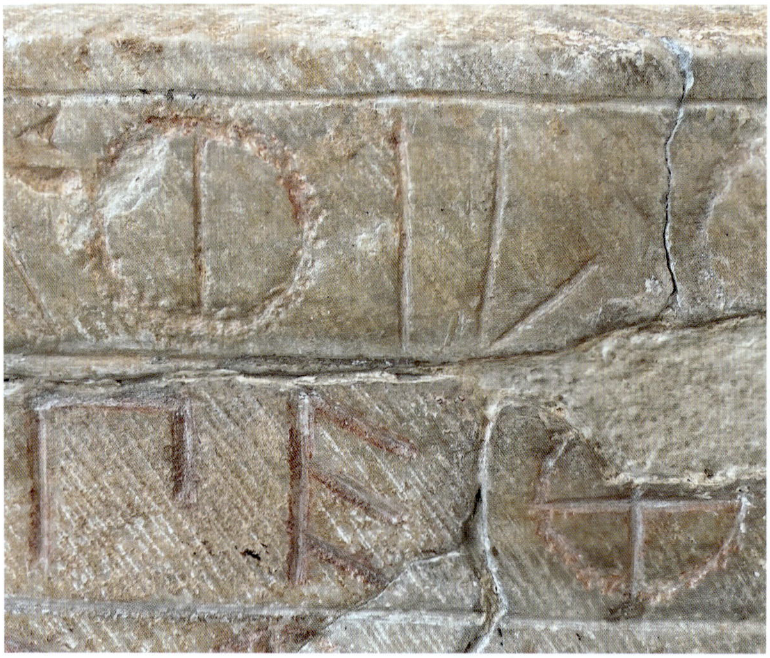

Fig. 2.8 Detail of the inscribed base of a marble stele, ca. 530 BCE. New York, Metropolitan Museum of Art, 11.185 (photograph by author).

least one hundred strokes to close the circle, with a point chisel held almost vertically (Fig. 2.8).[46] Whereas the creation of grooves through sculpting involves bimanual coordination between the percussive blows of the mallet with one hand and the adjustment of the chisel's position and angle with the other, the mechanical aids convert repetitive kinematic movements (pulling, twisting, turning, etc.) into determinate motions (scratching and grinding, in particular). In Greek descriptions of tool use, these biomechanical distinctions were important. As Ursula Duncan noticed long ago, Greek usage put greater emphasis on the type of gesture the stone carver performed than the type of tool used or the material to which it was applied.[47] Literary descriptions attest to a broad distinction between implements that carve or chip (κολαπτήρ, σμίλη, and ξοίς), bore through torsion (τρύπανον), hit through percussion (σφῦρα), or rounded off through rotation (τόρνος). Only for the *kolaptēr* can one claim that it designates a stonemason's chisel as opposed to any craftsperson's carving tool,

[46] New York, Metropolitan Museum of Art 11.185a–c, f, g; Richter 1961: 27, 159–65, no. 37 (*IG* I[3] 1241). On the restoration of the inscription, see now Estrin 2023: 45–8.

[47] Duncan 1961: 179–80.

employed on wood, metal, and leather, as well as stone. The *smilē*, by contrast, can be the knife of a shoemaker, a surgeon, a vinedresser – in fact, almost any implement for cutting or carving something, including stone.[48] Note that this limitation in vocabulary for naming tools typologically applies to the arcane diction of inscribed building contracts and dedications by craftspeople as much as literary texts in which one might expect little awareness of shop-floor vernacular.[49]

This diverse tool repertoire for creating grooves was almost entirely supplanted by the flat chisel in the course of the fifth century BCE.[50] To attribute the earlier heterogeneity of approaches to some presumed Archaic penchant for "experimentation" defers explanation without examining the conditions of artisanal innovation at the time.[51] It would also be difficult to maintain that one or the other method was more efficient or involved less risk. Even the tubular drill, which provided the most rigorous constraint of kinematic movement among all these tools, still required constant observation and adjustment by a skilled hand, as the accidental off-center incisions in the Hekatompedon inscription show. Even more problematic is the proposition that a particular method of letter cutting was selected to enhance the legibility of the resulting texts. Such an assumption posits a teleological ideal of textuality that precedes the genesis of inscriptional practices and implements. All the same, the contrast between the punched circular letters on the base of the so-called Boy-and-Girl stele and the circular letters created with mechanical devices does seem to speak to some deeper epistemic shift in the makers' understanding, akin to conceiving letters either as individually created objects (*this* omicron) or as interchangeable instantiations of a type of alphabetic grapheme (*an* omicron). It is tempting to connect this shift with the changing conceptions of writing witnessed in Greek literature. Early descriptions tend to conceive its mediatory power in relation to specific lettered surfaces rather than textual entities detachable from their materials. As Athena Kirk stresses, the reluctance to separate writing from its surface transpires especially from Herodotos' unwieldy descriptions of inscribed objects (including

[48] *LSJ*, s.v. σμίλη.

[49] See Prêtre 2014: 545–6, on Delos inventories *IG* XI.2 199A.86 and 224B.31, mentioning dedication of *kolaptēr*; Dworakowska 1979, on *kolaptēr*, *xois* (chisel), and *leistrion* (tool for smoothing) in the building contract from Lebadeia.

[50] Some rare examples of roughly punched-in circular letters still known from the Athenian epigraphic output during the empire are usually associated with careless workmanship. See e.g. the heading of the tribute quota list of 422/421 BCE (*IG* I^3 77) in Meritt 1939: 54–9, no. 20; Duncan 1961: 185.

[51] Snodgrass 1980: 217–18.

inscriptions in stone) as having "letters that say things" (γράμματα λέγοντα τάδε) or conveying "through letters" (διὰ γραμμάτων). The noun *epigraphē* (ἐπιγραφή), normally translated as "inscription," never occurs in his work and should, according to Kirk, strictly be taken to designate texts composed elsewhere before they were inscribed – that is, laws, decrees, epigrams, and curses – as opposed to dedicatory inscriptions, name labels, and other identifying marks.[52]

Herodotos' description of textual agency in terms of objects with letters conceived qua objects also resonates with the indeterminacy of letter orientations in early Greek inscriptions. This phenomenon is familiar from the so-called false boustrophedon inscriptions, in which the letters of one or several lines are rotated "upside down" (namely by 180 degrees) rather than mirror inverted. As Nikolaus Dietrich recently pointed out, whereas this flexible approach to lettering might look faulty to modern readers accustomed to the typographic regimes of printed text, to ancient eyes the variable orientations denoted not a disruption of legibility but a wide-open field for realizing the pictorial and calligraphic possibilities of text based on the artifactual individuality of its characters.[53] The same "thingness" of letters can also be recognized in the countless instances of letters being inscribed in retrograde or vice versa, where one would expect the contrary.[54] The direction of such letters might at most be considered irregular but certainly not "wrong."

From the perspective of the maker, the individual distinctiveness of letters as things was diminished through the technological shift discussed earlier in this chapter: from chiseled grooves to incisions created with the help of mechanical aids. The circular letters cut with such aids might look somewhat more regular and mutually interchangeable, but more importantly, they imply a shift in how the relationship between groove and ground was understood. The substitution of scratching for chiseling entails a transition from sculpting through indirect percussion (that is, percussion with mallet and chisel) to graphic work involving the marking of a surface by moving a sharp point or edge on an uninterrupted track.

[52] Kirk 2018: 30, 33–8. See e.g., Herodotos' description of Cheops' pyramid in *Histories* 2.125.6: σεσήμανται δὲ διὰ γραμμάτων αἰγυπτίων ἐν τῇ πυραμίδι ὅσα ἔς τε συρμαίην καὶ κρόμμυα καὶ σκόροδα ἀναισιμώθη τοῖσι ἐργαζομένοισι; trans. by Godley 1920–5, vol. 1: "And it was made known via Egyptian letters on the pyramid how much of radishes, onions, and garlic was consumed by the workmen."

[53] Dietrich 2020: 151–2, with reference to the well-known Nikandre inscription. On "false" boustrophedon, see Jeffery 1961: 49–50.

[54] See e.g. sigmas in the second and third lines of the boustrophedon inscription on the base of the grave monument of Chairedemos in New York, Metropolitan Museum of Art 16.174.6 (see Richter 1961: 156, no. 34).

The sculptor's creation of form through percussion comes close to what the Greeks originally understood under the term *rhythmos*. In early Greek literature (from the lyric poets through the tragedians and Attic prose), the meaning of *rhythmos* approximates notions of material form, shape, or pattern, thus differing from our modern usage of "rhythm" to designate the systematic repetition of sounds or visual phenomena without any reference to the bodily motions through which they come into being. Eugen Petersen defines its original meaning as "unbewegte Gestalt, die durch Bewegung entstand" (an unmoving form, created through motion) or the temporal palimpsest of the "rests" (ἠρεμίαι) that limit repetitive movements.[55] In an influential essay, Emile Benveniste connects the form-centered understanding of *rhythmos* with the atomistic theories of the Ionian philosophers, describing it as the momentary form "that is assumed by what is moving, mobile and fluid," whereas from Plato onward, *rhythmos* is rescripted as Form by associating movement with measure (μέτρον) and harmonious regulation through numerical relationships.[56] In the earlier understanding of *rhythmos* as a "way of flowing" (as opposed to rhythm as metric or arithmetic organization), sculpture and dance have in common the creation of form through the controlled constraints of the movement of limbs. Rhythm is also key to André Leroi-Gourhan's groundbreaking anthropological theory of technicity, exemplified in his studies of gestural agency in Paleolithic toolmaking. In his view, human bodies present a twofold framework for rhythmic integration, through movements of feet and hands, respectively. Whereas the treading motions of walking integrate the sensory awareness of time and place, manual rhythmicity enables the "capture and immobilization of volumes" through impact-making gestures.[57] The sculptor's ability to capture forms in stone originates, according to his account, not in some mental capacity to envisage designs ahead of their realization but in

[55] Petersen 1917: 12; see also the helpful synopsis of his arguments in Pollitt 1974: 220–5. The locus classicus is Archilochus fr. 66 (Bergk): γίγνωσκε δ'οἷος ῥυσμὸς ἀνθρώπους ἔχει, trans. in Gerber 1999: "Know what sort of *pattern* governs mankind" (emphasis mine). Petersen's etymological derivation of *rhythmos* from ἐρύω (draw, pull) and related words, as opposed to ῥέω (to flow) has not been accepted; see note 56.

[56] Benveniste 1971: 285–6. *Rhythmos*, in his view, derives etymologically from ῥεῖν (to flow), with the ending -(θ)μός designating the noun's abstract sense: "not the accomplishment of the notion, but the particular modality of its accomplishment as it is presented to the eye." An illustrative example is provided by ὄρχησις (act of dancing) and ὀρχηθμός (a particular dance taking place). On the epistemic legacy of the term *rhythmos*, see Wellmann 2017; Michon 2018–21; Barletta 2020; C. Meyer 2023b.

[57] Leroi-Gourhan 1993: 310: "In the human the treading motion that constitutes the rhythmic framework of walking is accompanied by rhythmic movements of the arm: whereas the former governs spatiotemporal integration and is the source of animation in the social sphere, the latter has to do with the individual's integration in what is not a time-and-space-creating but a form-

the zoological features of the sensate body that enable it to appropriate materials through tool-mediated gestures and to revise those gestures continuously in response to instruction, imitation, creative intuition, and the awareness of variations in the material.

Marking a stone's surface through scratching, by contrast, is a graphic operation in the original sense of the word. The Greek verb *graphein*, as is often noted, can comprise activities that we would distinguish as writing, drawing, and painting. What mattered in Greek usage was not the mode of signification through which the finished mark generated meaning but the manual process – the tracing of a point over a surface – through which it was created. Through the geometrical devices discussed previously, sculptors and letter cutters replaced *rhythm* as a creator of forms with *scraping* as a means to mark materials. Whether the momentum of the gesture was relayed through the twin points of a compass or the cutting edge of a drill is insubstantial in comparison to the shift from percussion to scratching. Neither should it matter whether the resulting marks look like dots or lines to us; strictly speaking, they are all three-dimensional forms, not ideal geometrical constructs. In relative terms, however, the perceptual differentiation of one-dimensional points and two-dimensional lines from three-dimensional forms becomes a concern in graphic actions in a way that is not the case in percussive sculpting, for the dot-like or linear quality of a graphic trace depends on its support in a way that the modeled forms of sculpture in relief and in the round do not.[58] Thanks to such planes, grooves in stone can be deployed in a manner suggesting the presence of three-dimensional spaces occupied by three-dimensional bodies or of two-dimensional lines that commend themselves to being read as a text rather than being looked at as individual *grammata*. Read in this manner, text can be imagined to have an existence beyond its given instantiation and to be separable from its material. The transformative quality of the immanent plane resides in its ability to modulate perceptions of a scratched or sculpted mark between different spatial registers. In so doing, the plane also recedes from awareness, allowing the viewer to recognize textual and pictorial representations without being distracted by speculations about the exact composition and facture of the support.

creating system. The rhythmicity of walking led eventually to the kilometer and the hour, while manual rhythmicity let to the capture and immobilization of volumes, a purely human construct." On Leroi-Gourhan's theory of human gestures and agentic dispositions, see Ingold 1999, 2013: 33–45; Noland 2009: 93–118. The influence of Leroi-Gourhan's teacher Marcel Mauss (2007: 147), who designated the human as the "rhythmic animal," is clear.

[58] On this point, see Maynard 2005: 62–3; Krämer 2015.

To the modern observer accustomed to an array of graphic surfaces and screens, it is exceedingly difficult to unthink the immanent plane as a prior given, such as a sheet of paper on which to sketch out preliminary designs before they are realized.[59] By addressing the presumption that Archaic practices of writing and image making transcended the material on which they were realized, we can also begin to examine the process of working stones into stelai as a cultural technique that gave rise to new ways of seeing and making sense of the marks on them. From the point of view of the ancient maker, we should indeed consider as a seminal moment in Greek art not the supposed conquest of three-dimensional representational space in the early Classical period but the recognition of a surface crafted in stone as a plane with immanent spatial properties. By the same token, the priority usually given in scholarship to sculpted bodies should yield more room to the contemplation of planes that can constitute scratched grooves as lines in the strong sense of an ideal two-dimensional construct.

How Marble Matters

However smooth and regular the surfaces of a finished stele might be, they cannot in themselves be taken as diagnostic of their perception as geometrical planes. Many other traditions of stone carving developed methods for producing even surfaces that had little implication for how the marks on them were made and understood. But just as two-dimensional surfaces do not exist in nature, the idea of the geometrical plane cannot be taken for granted. Rather, the plane is an artifact that comes into being – both as a thing and as a concept – through skilled engagement with materials. In this concluding section, I will highlight how changes in carving techniques corresponded to changes in how the primary stones for sculpture and construction were sourced in late Archaic Attica. We begin with an experimental reconstruction of the planar carving techniques required to shape a stone block into a stele and then work our way back in the production process to explore how the decisions taken in the final stages of sculpting and letter cutting relate to the stone's origin in a quarry bed, structured by its natural divisional planes.

[59] It goes without saying that papyrus was expensive and of limited size even in much later periods of Greek history. On the usefulness of sketches or scaled plans for ancient architects and stonemasons, see the discussions in Coulton 1977: 53; Haselberger 1985; Hahn 2001: 107–9; Capelle 2019.

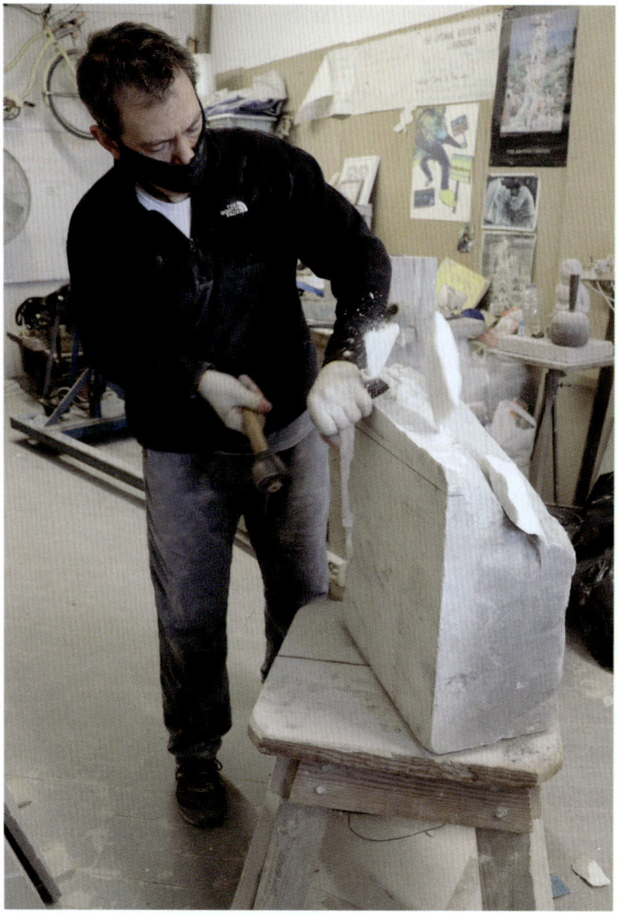

Fig. 2.9a Chris Pellettieri pitching off a quarried (Vermont) marble block along a pencil guideline (photograph by author).

The creation of flat surfaces is a staple of any stoneworker's procedural repertoire, be it a stonemason or sculptor. It is often the first task a novice is expected to tackle at the beginning of an apprenticeship. Pellettieri was asked to shape a plane on his very first day at the stone yard. The principles of carving were likely to have been the same in antiquity, even if details of tool use and working sequences differed. Pellettieri gave me a demonstration of how he shapes a block of marble. He begins by marking horizontal guidelines on the block (mechanically precut on five sides) with a pencil and mason's square. The mass of stone above this guideline is then removed with a heavy pitch, leaving just under a centimeter of marble between the break and the pencil line (as visible in Fig. 2.9a). The blunt edge of the tool can take off large chunks of stone but requires a preexisting surface to deliver a blow. Once an even edge has been created around the block, the protruding mass on the top is removed with a fairly heavy point chisel. Since the impact of the point creates bruising inside the marble, a protective skin must be left in place above the level of the plane marked by the guidelines. In a subsequent stage, the excess stone at the edge is cut down to the level of the guidelines with a sharp-edged flat chisel (Fig. 2.9b) and finished successively with a narrow tooth chisel and a flat chisel to create a horizontal margin, or draft line, around the intended surface (Fig. 2.9c). From that stage onward, the protective layer above the surface is pared down first with a finer-point chisel and then by alternating between tooth and flat chisels. The final smoothing of the plane involves low-angled strokes with a flat chisel (Fig. 2.9d) and intermittent checking of the surface level with a mason's square or straightedge (Fig. 2.9e).

In these modern working stages, the plane comes into existence through the chisel strokes that extend the penciled guidelines horizontally into a flat surface. This simplified description risks presenting the process as an application of human intention onto the natural raw material by way of a preset series of manual tasks. In reality, the process involves a fluid conversation between the gestures of the stoneworker and the variable tensions and densities inherent in the marble. In the block Pellettieri used in his demonstration, for instance, the energetic charge of the material made itself felt when he began to use the pitch to blow off chunks of stone

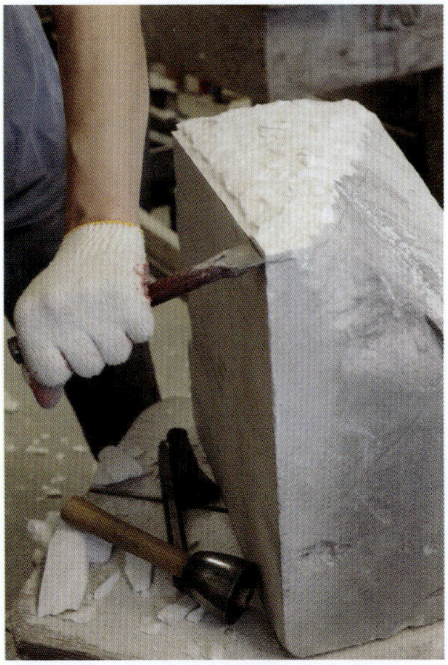

Fig. 2.9b Use of flat chisel to par down pitched edge to guideline (photograph by author).

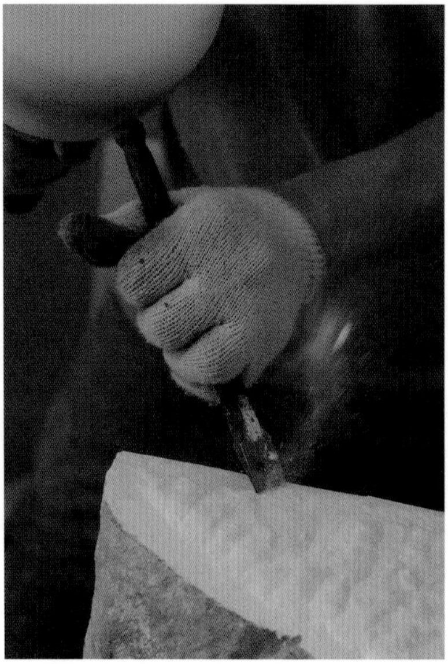

Fig. 2.9c Use of tooth chisel to create draft line (photograph by author).

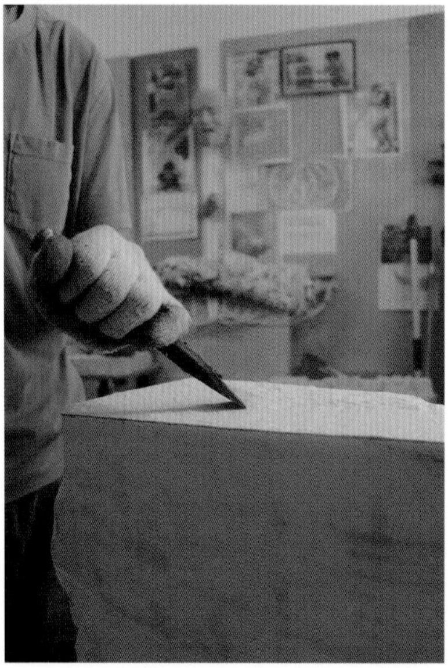

Fig. 2.9d Flat-chisel strokes are applied at a low angle to remove surface irregularities and level off a smooth surface (photograph by author).

from the top of the block. The marble's grain pulled the fracture lines of the chisel strokes downward, as he explained, threatening to spall concave hollows beyond the intended level of the working surface.

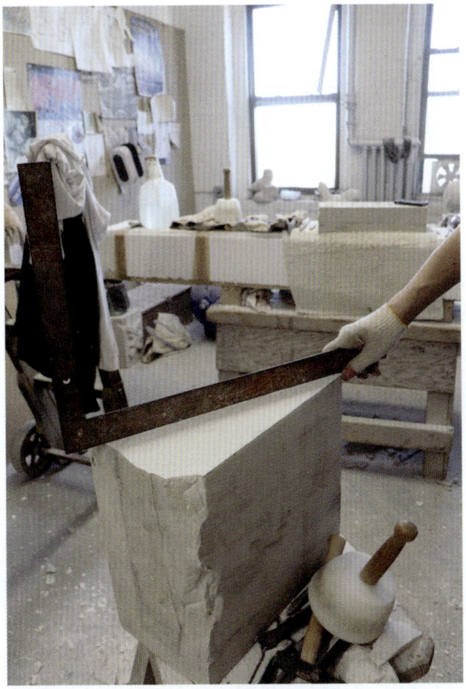

Fig. 2.9e The surface regularity is recurrently checked with a mason's square (photograph by author).

The conversation between gesture and material goes back even further in the operational chain involved in carving ancient stelai. To the quarry workers extracting the marble blocks from the parent rock, the tensile force in the material is visible as joins, fractures, veins, and foliations. In modern quarrying, the interior of a block's integrity is also sounded out by knocking the stone and assessing its resonance for potential disturbances. While natural fissures in the quarry face delimit the shape and size of the usable blocks that can be obtained, they can also facilitate its splitting from the parent rock in response to wedges and levers carefully positioned into sockets.[60] At every stage of the process, the quarry workers and marble carvers have to accommodate the proclivities of the material originating in

[60] On early quarrying methods on Mount Pentelikon, see esp. Korres 2000 and the general surveys in Nolte 2006: 209–15; Fant 2008; Hochscheid 2015: 119–21. The relationship between marble type (especially the geological and mechanical conditions of its quarry bed) and the shape of the finished sculpture is highlighted by Sturgeon 2006: 34, and in a forthcoming work on the Naxian quarries by Evan Levine and Rebecca Levitan (for a preliminary report, see www.ascsa.edu.gr/news/newsDetails/notes-from-naxos). For revealing examples from Greek marble architecture attesting how the petrological properties of marble affect the shape and use the products made from it, see e.g. Draganits 2009; Bernard and Pike 2015.

the geological recrystallization into metamorphic rock of the carbonate minerals in sedimentary limestone or dolomite.

Working with the internal properties of marble also involves measuring the distances between discontinuities visible on the quarry face and estimating through mental projection how they might continue inside the stone. Once the block is detached from the parent rock, the skill of reckoning internal structures from external marks turns into the practical task of transforming its irregular outlines into the geometric shapes from which sculptural and architectural planning proceed. The geometric properties of the various blocks and cylinders are latent in the crystalline composition of the quarried block and brought out by the quarry workers or masons by defining reference surfaces, centers, and margins through the use of a straightedge, mason's square, and calipers.

In the second half of the sixth century BCE, Athenian workshops acquired experience in the full gamut of marble technologies, from locating quarry-bedded blocks to finishing marble surfaces. Although the Attic quarries on Mount Hymettos and Pentelikon had been active for at least a generation, imported marbles from Naxos and Paros remained the preferred material for sculpture.[61] The great majority of architectural works were done in limestone from the Piraeus hills. Limestone was, by comparison, a homogeneous mass that could be readily cut into large shapes (monolithic column shafts, in some instances), but it lacked the permanence and radiance of marble. Its geological structure did not present the same intricate combinations of mechanical and geometrical challenges.[62] Only with the building works of the pre-Parthenon in the 480s BCE did Attic marble quarrying evolve into operations comparable in scale and complexity to those in the Cyclades and Ionia, with different teams coordinating their work simultaneously across multiple locations to produce shapes that could be fitted into the increasingly tight configurations of monumental construction and meaning that characterized Athens' urban fabric.[63] Developing skills in this new material was a matter of learning to seize the possibilities inherent to it and, in the process, continuously reimagining the possibilities of skill itself.

[61] On the switch from Cycladic to Pentelic marble in Athenian sculpture, see Sturgeon 2006; Lazzarini and Marconi 2014.

[62] This characteristic of limestone emerges clearly from the studies of Corinthian limestone quarrying by Hayward (2003, 2013). For more recent work on Archaic limestone sculpture and architecture from the Athenian Acropolis, see Klein 2015; Mertens and Conte 2019.

[63] On the separation and specialization of quarrying and sculpting in fifth-century BCE Athens, see Hochscheid 2015: 134–7.

The genealogy of the stele as a locus for pictorial and alphabetic marks unfolded in the same sprawling technoscape as that of the many other more eye-catching Athenian marble monuments. The account that I have tried to develop is by no means intended to supersede or criticize the previous investigations into the origins and typological development of Attic stelai. If anything, it is meant to complement their focus on finished monuments with one that looks into the material and technological requirements of their production, ranging from geological conditions to the muscle memory entrained over generations of craftspeople. Such a perspective is necessary if we accept that the knowledge involved in making objects is inevitably part of what makes them meaningful to their users. Yet such a perspective is also difficult because it decenters the epigraphic and pictorial features that have traditionally been seen as the very raison d'être for the marble supports and that have determined how and by whom the surviving material was studied.[64] Moreover, this perspective decenters the dominant research agendas in classical archaeology built around the core humanist ideals of autonomous understanding and creative freedom. If humanist premises are generally never far off in the study of classical art, in the study of stelai they surface in the priority accorded to social factors or individual makers as prime movers in the type's genesis, stressing either the determining context of city-state politics outgrowing the limits of face-to-face interaction or the innovations of named sculptors or anonymous "hands" identified through connoisseurial study.[65]

For material culture specialists, it is discouraging to think that the traces we study should hold in themselves no real explanatory force – that historical change always takes place in minds before it takes hold in things. The presumption is all the more frustrating if the actors who are thought to have motivated change are bound to remain names without biographies, hands without bodies. Foregrounding the properties of marble, as I have tried to show, goes a long way in reconnecting traces on marble with sensing bodies. To acknowledge these properties is to acknowledge that the planes that Athenian marble carvers released from their medium were in fact already incipiently present in its crystalline structure and that the interplay of forces involved in creating such planes set in motion a host of

[64] See notes 7 and 8.

[65] In a recent investigation into the origins of the Athenian documentary stele, E. Meyer (2016), for instance, stresses the role of the Hekatompedon Master in synthesizing the heterogeneous array of inscribed dedications on the Acropolis (stone objects that had previously served as racecourse posts, pillars, or metopes) into the new format: thin, tall, and purpose-made from the outset to bear text. Hurwit (2015: 3–10) posits Greek artists' signatures as direct indices of Greek artistic consciousness and the study of such signatures as an antidote to the allegedly corrosive impact of posthumanism in contemporary academia.

new forms and movements in an already dynamic landscape of pathways and connections. Considering marble carving as lithic technology requires a granular scale of examination, and this call for us to stop and look ever more closely may be justification enough.

References

Adam, S. (1966). *The Technique of Greek Sculpture in the Archaic and Classical Periods.* London: British School of Archaeology at Athens.

Aravantinos, V. (2010). *The Archaeological Museum of Thebes.* Athens: Olkos.

Ashmole, B., and Yalouris, N. (1967). *Olympia: The Sculptures of the Temple of Zeus.* London: Phaidon.

Barletta, V. (2020). *Rhythm: Form and Dispossession.* Chicago, IL: University of Chicago Press.

Benveniste, E. (1971). "The Notion of 'Rhythm' in Its Linguistic Expression." In E. Benveniste, *Problems in General Linguistics*, trans. M. E. Meek. Miami, FL: University of Miami Press, 281–313.

Bergemann, J. (1997). *Demos und Thanatos: Untersuchungen zum Wertsystem der Polis im Spiegel der attischen Grabreliefs des 4. Jahrhunderts v. Chr. und zur Funktion der gleichzeitigen Grabbauten.* Munich: Biering and Brinkmann.

Bernard, S. G., and Pike, S. (2015). "Isotopic Analysis of Marble from the Stoa of Attalos in the Athenian Agora and the Hellenistic Quarries of Mount Pentelikon." In P. Pensabene and E. Gasparini, eds., *Interdisciplinary Studies on Ancient Stone: Proceedings of the Tenth International Conference of ASMOSIA.* Vol. 10. Rome: Bretschneider, 451–60.

Blümel, C. (1940). *Staatliche Museen zu Berlin: Katalog der Sammlung antiker Skulpturen. Vol. 2.1: Griechische Skulpturen des sechsten und fünften Jahrhunderts v. Chr.* Berlin: Schoetz.

(1943). *Griechische Bildhauer an der Arbeit.* 3rd ed. Berlin: De Gruyter.

Boschung, D. (2014). "Comte de Clarac: Zur Geschichte der Skulpturenforschung." In P. Scheding and M. Remmy, eds., *Antike Plastik 5.0: 50 Jahre Forschungsarchiv für Antike Plastik in Köln; Ausstellung im Akademischen Kunstmuseum, Antikensammlung der Universität Bonn.* Berlin: Lit, 116–23.

Boschung, D., and Pfanner, M. (1990). "Les méthodes de travail des sculpteurs antiques et leur signification dans l'histoire de la culture." In M. Waelkens, ed., *Pierre éternelle du Nil au Rhin: Carrières et préfabrication.* Brussels: Crédit communal, 127–42.

Brinkmann, V. (2003). *Die Polychromie der archaischen und frühklassischen Skulptur.* Munich: Biering and Brinkmann.

Busch, W. (2001). "Die Neudefinition der Umrisszeichnung in Rom am Ende des 18. Jahrhunderts." In M. Stuffmann and W. Busch, eds., *Zeichnen in Rom, 1790–1830*. Cologne: König, 10–44.
Capelle, J. (2019). "Ancient Blueprints: New Prospects and Interpretations in Light of Recent Discoveries." In P. Sapirstein and D. Scahill, eds., *New Directions and Paradigms for the Study of Greek Architecture*. Leiden: Brill, 56–73.
Carter, J. B., and Steinberg, L. J. (2010). "Kouroi and Statistics." *American Journal of Archaeology* 114.1: 103–28.
Casson, S. (1933). *The Technique of Early Greek Sculpture*. Oxford: Clarendon Press.
Charbonneaux, J. (1940). "Stèle archaïque gravée du Musée du Louvre." *Monuments et mémoires de la Fondation Eugène Piot* 37: 46–72.
Clairmont, C. W. (1993–5). *Classical Attic Tombstones*. 7 vols. Kilchberg: Akanthus.
Comte de Clarac, C. O. F. J.-B. (1841). *Musée de sculpture antique et moderne ou descriptions historique et graphique du Louvre*. Vol. 1. Paris: Imprimerie Royale.
Conze, A. (1893). *Die attischen Grabreliefs*. Vol. 1. Berlin: Spemann.
Coulton, J. J. (1977). *Ancient Greek Architects at Work: Problems of Structure and Design*. Oxford: Oxbow.
Davies, J. K. (2005). "The Origins of the Inscribed Greek Stela." In P. Bienkowski, C. Mee, and E. Slater, eds., *Writing and Ancient Near Eastern Society: Papers in Honour of Alan R. Millard*. New York: T and T Clark, 283–300.
Davis, W. (1981). "Egypt, Samos, and the Archaic Style in Greek Sculpture." *Journal of Egyptian Archaeology* 67.1: 61–81.
Dietrich, N. (2011). "'Archaischer Realismus': Archaische Plastik als alternatives Konzept von Realismus im Bild." *Jahreshefte des Österreichischen Instituts in Wien* 80: 13–46.
(2017). "Framing Archaic Greek Sculpture: Figure, Ornament and Script." In M. Squire and V. Platt, eds., *The Frame in Classical Art: A Cultural History*. Cambridge: Cambridge University Press, 270–316.
(2020). "Überlegungen zum Layout griechischer Statueninschriften ausgehend von der Nikandre-Weihung." In N. Dietrich, J. Fouquet, and C. Reinhardt, eds., *Schreiben auf statuarischen Monumenten: Aspekte materialer Textkultur in archaischer und frühklassischer Zeit*. Berlin: De Gruyter, 147–93.
Dinsmoor, W. B. (1913). "Attic Building Accounts, I: The Parthenon; II: The Erechtheum; III: The Propylaea." *American Journal of Archaeology*, 2nd ser., vol. 17.1–3: 53–80, 242–65, 371–98.
(1921). "Attic Building Accounts, IV: The Statue of Athena Promachos; V: Supplementary Notes: Parthenon and Erechtheum." *American Journal of Archaeology*, 2nd ser., vol. 25.2–3: 118–29, 233–47.
Dobres, M.-A. (2010). "Archaeologies of Technology." *Cambridge Journal of Economics* 34.1: 103–14.
Donohue, A. A. (2005). *Greek Sculpture and the Problem of Description*. Cambridge: Cambridge University Press.

Draganits, E. (2009). "The Archaic Sanctuary on Despotiko Island (Cyclades): Geological Outline and Lithological Characterization of the Building Stones, with Their Possible Provenance." *Austrian Journal of Earth Sciences* 102.1: 91–101.

Duncan, U. K. (1961). "Notes on Lettering by Some Attic Masons in the Sixth and Fifth Centuries BC." *Annual of the British School at Athens* 56: 179–88.

Duplouy, A. (2006). *Le prestige des élites: Recherches sur les modes de reconnaissance sociale en Grèce entre les Xe et Ve siècles avant J.-C.* Paris: Belles lettres.

Dworakowska, A. (1979). "Notes on the Tools Mentioned in the Building Contract from Lebadeia: Kolapter, Xois, Leistrion." *Archeologia* 29: 16–23.

Elkins, J. (1999). *What Painting Is.* New York: Routledge.

(2008). "On Some Limits of Materiality in Art History." In S. Neuer and J. Gelshorn, eds., *Taktilität: Sinneserfahrung als Grenzerfahrung.* Special issue, *Magazin des Instituts für Theorie* 12: 25–30.

Estrin, S. (2016). "Cold Comfort: Empathy and Memory in an Archaic Funerary Monument from Akraiphia." *Classical Antiquity* 35.2: 189–214.

(2023). "Archaic Sculpture and Archaisms of Gender: Rethinking the 'Brother and Sister Stele.'" *Art Bulletin* 105.3: 33–60.

Fant, J. C. (2008). "Quarrying and Stoneworking." In J. P. Oleson, ed., *The Oxford Handbook of Engineering and Technology in the Classical World.* Oxford: Oxford University Press, 121–35.

Gerber, D. E., ed. and trans. (1999). *Greek Iambic Poetry: From the Seventh to the Fifth Centuries BC; Archilochus, Semonides, Hipponax.* Cambridge, MA: Harvard University Press.

Godley, A. D., ed. and trans. (1920–5). *The Histories of Herodotus.* 4 vols. (Cambridge, MA: Harvard University Press).

Gosselain, O. P. (2000). "Materializing Identities: An African Perspective." *Journal of Archaeological Method and Theory* 7.3: 187–217.

Guralnick, E. (1976). "The Proportions of Some Archaic Greek Sculptured Figures: A Computer Analysis." *Computers and the Humanities* 10.3: 153–69.

Hahn, R. (2001). *Anaximander and the Architects: The Contributions of Egyptian and Greek Architectural Technologies to the Origins of Greek Philosophy* Albany: State University of New York Press.

Hamilton, W., and Tischbein, J. H. W. (1791–5). *Collection of Engravings by J. H. W. Tischbein from Ancient Vases, Mostly of Pure Greek Workmanship, Discovered in Sepulchres in the Kingdom of the Two Sicilies but Chiefly in the Neighbourhood of Naples.* 4 vols. Naples: Tischbein.

Harris, D. (1995). *The Treasures of the Parthenon and Erechtheion.* Oxford: Clarendon Press.

Haselberger, L. (1985). "The Construction Plans for the Temple of Apollo at Didyma." *Scientific American* 253.6: 126–33.

Hausmann, U. (1960). *Griechische Weihreliefs.* Berlin: De Gruyter.

Hayward, C. L. (2003). "Geology of Corinth: The Study of a Basic Resource." *Corinth* 20: 15–42.

(2013). "Corinthian Stone Exploitation and the Interpretation of Inscribed Building Accounts." In K. Kissas and W.-D. Niemeier, eds., *The Corinthia and the Northeast Peloponnese: Topography and History from Prehistoric Times until the End of Antiquity*. Athenaia 4. Munich: Hirmer, 63–78.

Higgins, C. G., and Pritchett, W. K. (1965). "Engraving Techniques in Attic Epigraphy." *American Journal of Archaeology* 69.4: 367–71.

Hildebrandt, F. (2006). *Die attischen Namenstelen Untersuchungen zu Stelen des 5. und 4. Jahrhunderts v. Chr.* Berlin: Frank and Timme.

Hochscheid, H. (2015). *Networks of Stone: Sculpture and Society in Archaic and Classical Athens*. Oxford: Peter Lang.

Honour, H. (1972). "Canova's Studio Practice I: The Early Years." *Burlington Magazine* 114.828: 146–59.

Hurwit, J. M. (2015). *Artists and Signatures in Ancient Greece*. Cambridge: Cambridge University Press.

Ingold, T. (1999). "'Tools for the Hand, Language for the Face': An Appreciation of Leroi-Gourhan's Gesture and Speech." *Studies in History and Philosophy of Science* 30.4: 411–53.

(2007). "Materials against Materiality." *Archaeological Dialogues* 14.1: 1–16.

(2013). *Making: Anthropology, Archaeology, Art and Architecture*. London: Routledge.

Jeffery, L. H. (1961). *The Local Scripts of Archaic Greece: A Study of the Origin of the Greek Alphabet and Its Development from the Eighth to the Fifth Centuries BC*. Oxford: Clarendon Press.

(1962). "The Inscribed Gravestones of Archaic Attica." *Annual of the British School at Athens* 57: 115–53.

Killick, D. (2004). "Social Constructionist Approaches to the Study of Technology." *World Archaeology* 36.4: 571–8.

Kirk, A. (2018). "What Is an ἐπιγραφή in Classical Greece?" In A. Petrovic, I. Petrovic, and E. Thomas, eds., *The Materiality of Text: Placement, Perception, and Presence of Inscribed Texts in Classical Antiquity*. Leiden: Brill, 29–47.

Klamm, S. (2017). "'Pictorial Silhouettes' and Their Surroundings: Antique Sculpture and Archaeological Photography." In S. Hamill and M. R. Luke, eds., *Photography and Sculpture: The Art Object in Reproduction*. Los Angeles, CA: Getty Research Institute, 50–66.

Klein, N. L. (2015). "The Architecture of the Athenian Acropolis before Pericles: The Life and Death of the Small Limestone Buildings." In K. F. Daly and L. A. Riccardi, eds., *Cities Called Athens: Studies Honoring John McK. Camp*, vol. 2. Lewisburg, PA: Bucknell University Press, 137–64.

Korres, M. (2000). *Stones of the Parthenon*. Los Angeles, CA: J. Paul Getty Museum.

Kourayos, Y., and Detoratou, S. (2005–6). "Κυβόλιθος, με παράσταση Απόλλωνα-Αρτέμιδος." *Eulimene* 6–7: 45–54.

Krämer, S. (2015). "Graphism and Flatness: The Line as Mediator between Time and Space, Intuition and Concept." In M. Faietti and G. Wolf, eds., *The Power of Line*. Munich: Hirmer, 10–17.

Lalonde, G. V., Langdon, M. K., and Walbank, M. B. (1991). *Inscriptions: Horoi, Poletai Records, Leases of Public Lands*. Athenian Agora 19. Princeton, NJ: American School of Classical Studies at Athens.

Lawton, C. L. (1995). *Attic Document Reliefs: Art and Politics in Ancient Athens*. Oxford: Clarendon Press.

Lazzarini, L., and Marconi, C. (2014). "A New Analysis of Major Greek Sculptures in the Metropolitan Museum: Petrological and Stylistic." *Metropolitan Museum Journal* 49: 117–40.

Lemonnier, P. (1992). *Elements for an Anthropology of Technology*. Ann Arbor: Museum of Anthropology, University of Michigan.

Lempese, A. (1976). *Οι στήλες του Πρινιά*. Athens: National Government Publication.

Leroi-Gourhan, A. (1993). *Gesture and Speech*. Cambridge, MA: MIT Press.

Liddel, P. (2003). "The Places of Publication of Athenian State Decrees from the 5th Century BC to the 3rd century AD." *Zeitschrift für Papyrologie und Epigraphik* 143: 79–93.

Lorenz, K. (2010). "'Dialectics at a Standstill': Archaic *Kouroi*-Cum-Epigram as *I-Box*." In M. Baumbach, A. Petrovic, and I. Petrovic, eds., *Archaic and Classical Greek Epigram*. Cambridge: Cambridge University Press, 131–48.

Mauragani, K. (2000). "Παρατηρήσεις στην Αρχαιότερη Ταφική Στήλη του Μουσείου Πάρου." In D. U. Schilardi, ed., *Paria Lithos: Parian Quarries, Marble and Workshops of Sculpture; Proceedings of the First International Conference on the Archaeology of Paros and the Cyclades, Paros, 2–5 October 1997*. Athens: Paros and Cyclades Institute of Archaeology, 155–61.

Mauss, M. (2007). *The Manual of Ethnography*. Trans. D. Lussier. New York: Berghahn.

Maynard, P. (2005). *Drawing Distinctions: The Varieties of Graphic Expression*. Ithaca, NY: Cornell University Press.

McCauley, E. A. (2011). "Fawning over Marbles: Robert and Gerardine Macpherson's *Vatican Sculptures* and the Role of Photographs in the Reception of the Antique." In S. Bann, ed., *Art and the Early Photographic Album*. Studies in the History of Art 77. New Haven, CT: Yale University Press, 91–122.

Meritt, B. D. (1939). "Greek Inscriptions (14–27)." *Hesperia* 8.1: 48–82.

Meritt, B. D., McGregor, M. F., and Wade-Gery, H. T. (1939–53). *The Athenian Tribute Lists*. 4 vols. Princeton, NJ: American School of Classical Studies at Athens.

Mertens, J. R., and Conte, L. (2019). "Watercolors of the Acropolis: Émile Gilliéron in Athens." *Metropolitan Museum of Art Bulletin* 76.4: 4–46.

Meyer, C. (2017). "All about the Body? The Matter of Temporality in the Study of Greek Sculpture." In A. Lichtenberger and R. Raja, eds., *The Diversity of Classical Archaeology*. Studies in Classical Archaeology 1. Turnhout: Brepols, 235–51.

(2023a). "Why Drawing Still Matters: Connecting Hands and Minds in the Study of Greek Vases." In C. Meyer and A. Petsalis-Diomidis, eds., *Drawing the Greek Vase*. Oxford: Oxford University Press, 24–56.

(2023b). "Rhythm and Possibility: Making Space for Ancient Futures." *Possibility Studies and Society* 1.1–2: 145–51.

Meyer, E. A. (2016). "Posts, Kurbeis, Metopes: The Origins of the Athenian 'Documentary' Stele." *Hesperia* 85.2: 323–83.

Meyer, M. (1989). *Die griechischen Urkundenreliefs*. Mitteilungen des Deutschen Archäologischen Instituts, Athenische Abteilung 13. Berlin: Mann.

Michon, P. (2018–21). *Elements of Rhythmology*. 4 vols. Paris: Rhuthmos.

Müller, C., and Prost, F. (2002). *Identités et cultures dans le monde méditerranéen antique*. Paris: Publications de la Sorbonne.

Neer, R. T. (2010). *The Emergence of the Classical Style in Greek Sculpture*. Chicago, IL: University of Chicago Press.

Noland, C. (2009). *Agency and Embodiment: Performing Gestures/Producing Culture*. Cambridge, MA: Harvard University Press.

Nolte, S. (2006). *Steinbruch – Werkstatt – Skulptur: Untersuchungen zu Aufbau und Organisation griechischer Bildhauerwerkstätten*. Beihefte zum Göttinger Forum für Altertumswissenschaft 18. Gottingen: Ruprecht.

Olivier, D. (2020). "To Learn to Draw, Start with Your Shoe." *New York Times*, July 25. www.nytimes.com/2020/07/25/at-home/coronavirus-learn-to-draw.html.

Osborne, R., and Rhodes, P. J. (2017). *Greek Historical Inscriptions, 478–404 BC*. Oxford: Oxford University Press.

Palagia, O. (2003). "Did the Greeks Use a Pointing Machine?" *Bulletin archéologique du Comité des traveaux historiques et scientifiques: Antiquité, Archéologie classique* 30: 55–64.

(2006). "Marble Carving Techniques." In O. Palagia, ed., *Greek Sculpture: Function, Materials, and Techniques in the Archaic and Classical Periods*. Cambridge: Cambridge University Press, 243–79.

Payne, H. (1951). *Archaic Marble Sculpture from the Acropolis*. New York: William Morrow.

Petersen, E. (1917). *Rhythmus*. Berlin: Weidmannsche.

Pollitt, J. J. (1974). *The Ancient View of Greek Art: Criticism, History, and Terminology*. New Haven, CT: Yale University Press.

Prêtre, C. (2014). "L'offrande dans les inventaires de Délos: Objet rituel ou sacré?" *Revue de l'histoire des religions* 231.4: 539–57.

Raubitschek, A. E. (1951). “The Mechanical Engraving of Circular Letters.” *American Journal of Archaeology* 55.4: 343–4.

Raubitschek, A. E., and Jeffery, L. H. (1949). *Dedications from the Athenian Akropolis: A Catalogue of the Inscriptions of the Sixth and Fifth Centuries BC*. Cambridge, MA: Archaeological Institute of America.

Richter, G. M. A. (1944). *Archaic Attic Gravestones*. Cambridge, MA: Harvard University Press.

(1961). *The Archaic Gravestones of Attica*. London: Phaidon.

Rockwell, P. (1993). *The Art of Stoneworking: A Reference Guide*. Cambridge: Cambridge University Press.

Rumpf, A. (1953). *Malerei und Zeichnung der klassischen Antike*. Munich: Beck.

Russell, B., and Wootton, W. (2017). “Makers and Making: Classical Art in Action.” In A. Lichtenberger and R. Raja, eds., *The Diversity of Classical Archaeology*. Studies in Classical Archaeology 1. Turnhout: Brepols, 253–70.

Schlanger, N. (1994). “Mindful Technology: Unleashing the *Chaîne opératoire* for an Archaeology of Mind.” In C. Renfrew and E. Zubrow, eds., *The Ancient Mind: Elements of Cognitive Archaeology*. Cambridge: Cambridge University Press, 143–51.

Schneider, E. (1999). *Untersuchungen zum Körperbild attischer Kuroi*. Moehnesee: Bibliopolis.

Sheehan, S. (1994). “Two Types of Line Drawings.” *American Artist* 58.625: 10.

Sillar, B., and Tite, M. S. (2000). “The Challenge of ‘Technological Choices’ for Materials Science Approaches in Archaeology.” *Archaeometry* 42.1: 2–20.

Snodgrass, A. M. (1980). *Archaic Greece: The Age of Experiment*. Berkeley: University of California Press.

Squire, M. (2018). “Embodying the Dead on Classical Attic Grave-Stelai.” In M. Gaifman, V. Platt, and M. Squire, eds., “The Embodied Object in Classical Antiquity.” Special issue, *Art History* 41.3: 518–45.

Stager, J. (2022). *Seeing Color in Classical Art: Theory, Practice, and Reception, from Antiquity to the Present*. Cambridge: Cambridge University Press.

Steinhauer, G. (2001). *The Archaeological Museum of Piraeus*. Athens: Olkos.

Stewart, A. (2008). “The Persian and Carthaginian Invasions of 480 BCE and the Beginning of the Classical Style. Part 2: The Finds from Other Sites in Athens, Attica, Elsewhere in Greece, and on Sicily. Part 3: The Severe Style: Motivations and Meaning.” *American Journal of Archaeology* 112.4: 581–615.

Sturgeon, M. (2006). “Sixth-Century Athens and the Cyclades.” In O. Palagia, ed., *Archaic and Classical Greek Sculpture: Functions, Materials and Techniques*. Cambridge: Cambridge University Press, 32–76.

Van Voorhis, J. (2012). “The Working and Re-working of Marble Sculpture at the Sculptor’s Workshop at Aphrodisias.” In B. Poulsen and T. M. Kristensen, eds., *Ateliers and Artisans in Roman Art and Archaeology*. *Journal of Roman Archaeology*, supplement 92. Portsmouth, RI: Journal of Roman Archaeology, 38–54.

(2018). *The Sculptor's Workshop at Aphrodisias.* Aphrodisias 10. Wiesbaden: Reichert.

Viviers, D. (1992). *Recherches sur les ateliers de sculpteurs et la cité d'Athènes à l'époque archaïque: Endoios, Philergos, Aristoklès.* Brussels: Académie royale de Belgique.

Wellmann, J. (2017). *The Form of Becoming: Embryology and the Epistemology of Rhythm, 1760–1830.* Trans. K. Sturge. Brooklyn, NY: Zone.

Wootton, W., Russell, B., and Rockwell, P. (2013). "Stoneworking Techniques and Processes (Version 1.0)." The Art of Making in Antiquity: Stoneworking in the Roman World. www.artofmaking.ac.uk/content/essays/3-stoneworking-techniques-and-processes-w-wootton-b-russell-p-rockwell.

3 The Body in Relief in Archaic Funerary Sculpture

SETH ESTRIN

Toeing the Line

On a funerary stele erected sometime toward the middle of the sixth century BCE, something sticks out (Fig. 3.1).[1] It is not the tall, slender form of a spear-bearer, his body mutilated when the marble block was later built into the Themistoklean wall in the Athenian Kerameikos.[2] Nor is it the Gorgon below his feet, the element that has given the stele its modern name. What sticks out, above all, is a single toe – a big toe on an otherwise somewhat undersized left foot (Fig. 3.2). The toe stretches all the way to the banded frame of the stele, but it does not stop there. For in the presence of this toe, the border has seemingly recoiled, leaving an opening with edges carefully finished at right angles both above and below. Presented with this opening, or perhaps causing it, the toe plunges through, fully penetrating the boundaries of the frame. When we move to the side, we see quite plainly the hole it has created – a hole that would have stood out all the more when the monument still preserved painted details (recorded when it was excavated) consisting of bands of alternating colors at the outer edges of its side faces that were, like the frame itself, interrupted by the hole.[3] This hole, I suggest, is no accidental hole, no product of poor planning on the sculptor's part, as it has often been interpreted.[4] Rather, it is a hole that quite deliberately threatens to unravel the stele's representational logic.[5]

In challenging the authority of the frame that surrounds it, the toe on the Gorgon stele simultaneously challenges received notions of what constitutes relief sculpture. In histories of the funerary sculpture of Archaic Attica, my focus in this chapter, relief sculptures like the Gorgon stele are set in opposition to another type of sculpted monument that could also

[1] Athens, National Archaeological Museum, 2687; Noack 1907: 514–17; Richter 1961: 22, no. 27; Kaltsas 2002: 51, no. 50; Despinis and Kaltsas 2014: 382–5, no. 1.1.354 (entry by M. Salta).

[2] See Keesling 1999: 515–16.

[3] For the polychromy, see Noack 1907: 515, fig. 26.

[4] Poor planning: Despinis and Kaltsas 2014: 383.

[5] On frames and representational logic in ancient art, an excellent introduction is Platt and Squire 2017. The contribution by Dietrich (2017) on framing the Archaic body is especially pertinent. See also Squire 2018 on frames and Attic funerary monuments, though the focus is primarily Classical.

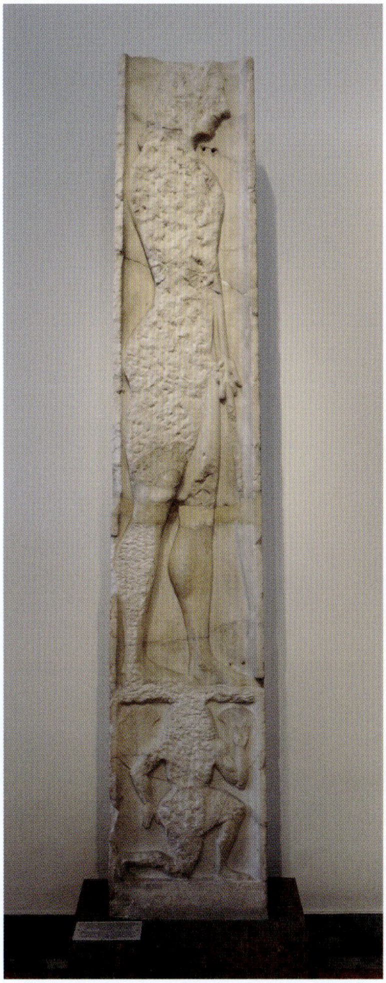

Fig. 3.1 Funerary stele of a youth (Gorgon stele), from the Kerameikos, Athens, ca. 560–550 BCE. Height: 2.40 m. Athens, National Archaeological Museum, 2687 (photograph by author).

function as a grave marker in the same period: the freestanding statue carved in the round.[6] A direct comparison of the figure on the Gorgon stele

[6] In most accounts of Archaic sculpture, discussions of freestanding and relief funerary monuments are broken up either into different volumes (e.g. Richter 1960 on kouroi and Richter 1961 on stelai) or into different sections of the same publication (e.g. Ridgway 1993 with sculptures in the round at 217–19 and those in relief at 230–43; Karanastassis 2002 with kouroi at 172–80 and stelai at 208–12). Note that for the purposes of this chapter, I focus on the classic comparison between the kouros and his male counterpart in relief on monuments like the Gorgon stele. Further consideration of other funerary sculptures carved in the round – not only the kouros' female counterpart, the kore, but equestrian and seated statues (for recent overview

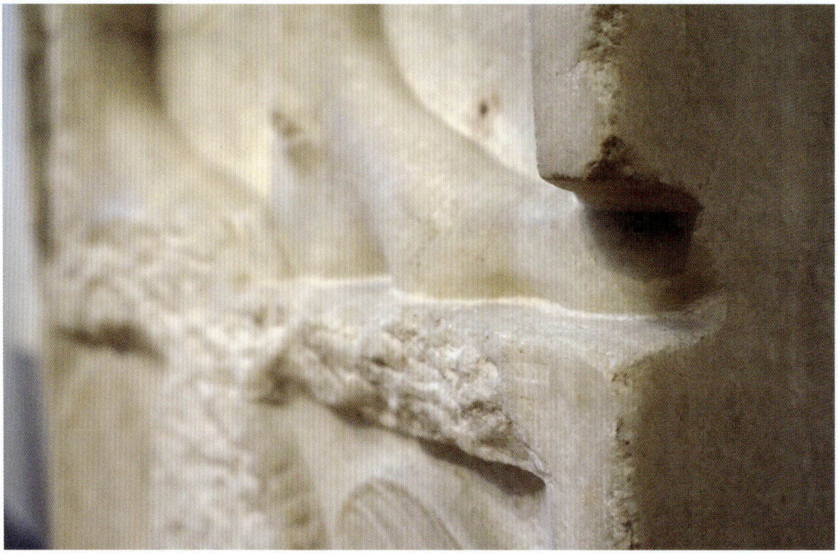

Fig. 3.2 Detail of Gorgon stele (see Fig. 3.1) (photograph by author).

with his counterpart in the round – a statue type known as a kouros, here illustrated by a contemporary example from Volomandra (Fig. 3.3) that is extremely close in proportions and carving to the figure on the Gorgon stele – makes clear the continuities between them.[7] Both are carved of fine Parian marble finished with paint, appearing in approximately the same scale, with the same degree of nudity, the same physique, the same hairstyle, and the same posture.

The contemporary usage of both types of monuments has traditionally been explained as a meeting of two different artistic traditions. As a statue type, the kouros is considered to have been adopted from Egyptian prototypes in the late seventh century – simultaneously, it seems, as votive dedications in sanctuaries and as funerary monuments at grave sites.[8] Though the kouros was increasingly modified and adapted by Greek sculptors over the course of the Archaic period, it retains its characteristic nudity and stiff posture until its gradual disappearance in the early fifth

of which, see Walter-Karydi 2015: 51–100) – would, I believe, only strengthen the arguments presented here.

[7] Volomandra kouros: Athens, National Archaeological Museum 1906 (Kaltsas 2002: 50, no. 47). For the comparison, see Harrison 1956: 30–1.

[8] What is perhaps the earliest example of a funerary kouros, the so-called Dipylon Head (Athens, National Archaeological Museum 3372; Kaltsas 2002: 38, no. 13) dates from the late seventh century. On the chronology of the earliest kouroi, see Vorster 2002: 120–5. On the cultural origins of the kouros, see recently Martin 2017: 43–9, 53–9.

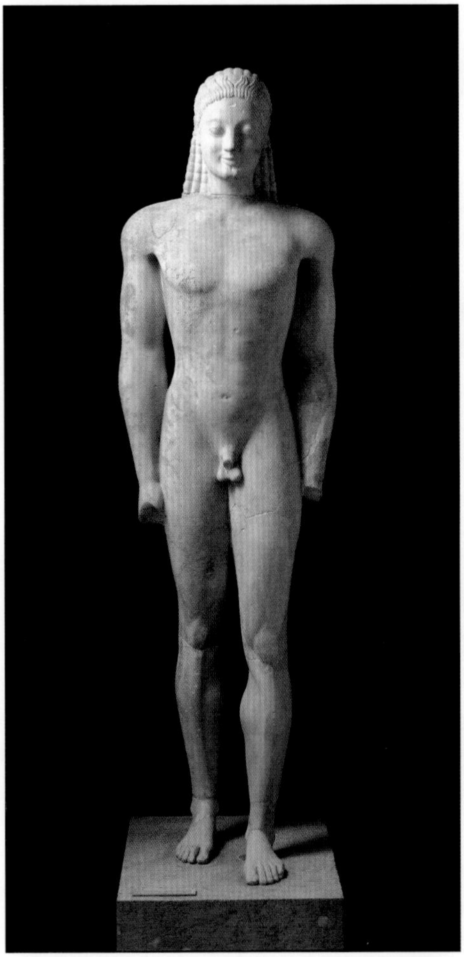

Fig. 3.3 Funerary kouros, from Volomandra, Attica, ca. 560 BCE. Height: 1.78 m. Athens, National Archaeological Museum, 1906 (Getty Images).

century. The relief figure first appears at the Attic grave site a few decades after the kouros, in the second quarter of the sixth century, making the Gorgon stele among the earliest surviving examples.[9] Yet carved out of a marble stele, it is a merely a new embellishment of a much older monument type, as stone stelai had been used to mark burials long before the appearance of the first monumental sculptures in the round. The

[9] Note that sphinxes crowning stelai, some perhaps figural, survive from slightly earlier. One of the earliest sphinxes that is unambiguously funerary in function, as indicated by its inscription, dates from ca. 580–75 BCE (New York, Metropolitan Museum of Art, 24.97.87; Richter 1961: 10, no. 1). See Walter-Karydi 2015 for recent overviews of Geometric (17–48) and Archaic (51–100) funerary monuments.

appearance of figures like that on the Gorgon stele are thought to be derived from kouroi, so that the stele essentially depicts a kouros in profile, his form flattened into the confines of a preexisting monument type.[10]

In recent decades, this distinction has been increasingly perceived as a question not only of sculptural form but of representation: Where the kouros presents a body that stands on its own two feet, that occupies the same space as our own, the relief sculpture presents a body projected against a surface plane and inscribed within a frame, visible from only one angle rather than in the round. Relief figures, that is to say, are seen as representing the body in a fundamentally different manner than free-standing statues.[11] Where the kouros, it is argued, presents the body to us directly, as a corporeal copresence in our own space, the relief stele holds it back from us within a secondary, virtual space, one discontinuous with our own. The distinction has often been elaborated in correlation with perceived differences in iconography. By operating in its own virtual space, apart from the beholder, the relief body is both liberated from the limiting conditions of marble sculpture and is capable of adopting more complex poses – raised or outstretched arms, more widely spaced feet, even crouched positions – that are impossible to achieve in free-standing marble, or could even stand alongside a second figure.[12] So too is the relief figure liberated from the conventional nudity of kouroi, and figures in relief often sport garments and attributes that suggest specific occupations or social positions, such as an athlete, a soldier, or a symposiast. Juxtaposed with the kouros' alleged anonymity, such distinctions have acquired interpretive weight, presenting the deceased in a social guise rather than through an abstract sculptural ideal that the kouros is often said to represent. In some interpretations, these differences have been assigned ideological or political significance, with the relief figure understood as a more democratic alternative to the

[10] See Richter 1961: 2: "The youths represented on the shafts are the counterparts in relief of the statues of the Archaic kouroi. . . . Their anatomical development closely follows that of the kouroi, and a comparison between the two enables one to assign probable dates also to the reliefs." See also Richter 1961: 14, where she hypothetically reconstructs the earliest sculpted stele from Attica as a profile representation of one of the earliest kouroi.

[11] On distinctions between the kouros and his relief counterpart, see, among others, D'Onofrio 1985; Stewart 1986; Osborne 1988: 8–9; Neer 2010: 186–7; Squire 2018: 526. Studies focused on the function of these monuments in the funerary context tend to treat them more synthetically (e.g. Himmelmann 1999: 12–19).

[12] Most famously, the so-called Brother and Sister stele (divided between New York, Metropolitan Museum of Art, 11.185a–d, f, g, x, Staatliche Museen zu Berlin, Sk 1531, and Athens, National Archaeological Museum, 4518; see Richter 1961: 27–9, no. 37, 1974; Estrin 2023b).

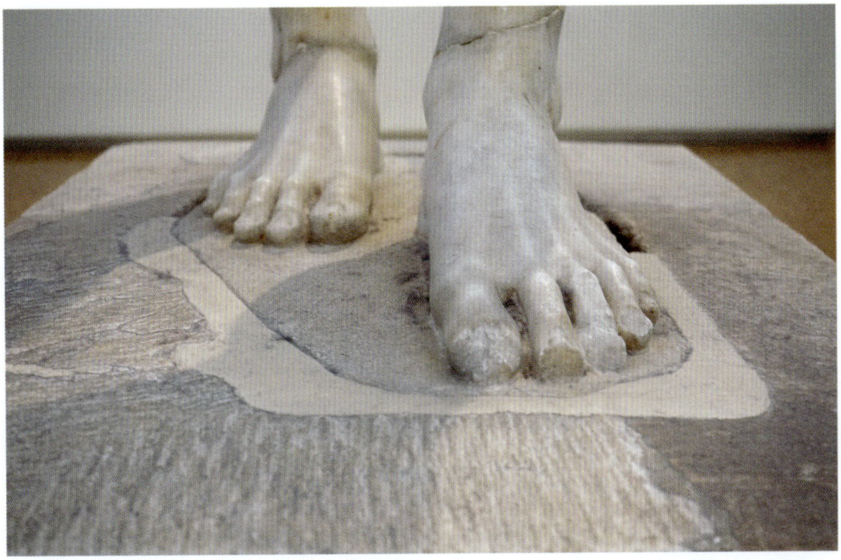

Fig. 3.4 Detail of feet, plinth, and base of the funerary kouros of Aristodikos, from Attica, ca. 500 BCE. Height (of full kouros without base): 1.96 m. Athens, National Archaeological Museum, 3938 (photograph by author).

aristocratic kouros, even though both types of monuments were erected by the same families in the same contexts.[13]

Yet if we follow the lead of our toe – if we admit into our discussion elements that cross the line between sculpture in relief and in the round – we might end up turning this narrative on its head. Consider the kouros. Is it really "freestanding," or is this merely a sculptural conceit? Like the relief body, the kouros too emerges from a flat surface of stone: the plinth on which it stands, from which it is materially inseparable (Fig. 3.4). This plinth is inserted flush into a socket in the separately carved base, as if the human figure merely stands atop it. Yet the kouros' entire stance – his upright, vertical torso, his arms close to the trunk, his feet separated yet implausibly flat – is motivated by a need to keep the connection between body and plinth structurally sound. The result is a body that, as has often been noted, is inherently unstable. Some see it as walking, others as standing. Some see it as confrontational, others as aloof. Some see it as a vibrant corporeal presence bursting into life, others as a body barely liberated from the quadrifacial block of stone from which it was carved.[14]

[13] See esp. D'Onofrio 1985; Neer 2010: 186–7. For a critique, see Sourvinou-Inwood 1995: 217–77, esp. 227.

[14] On the carving of kouroi, see Stewart 1990: 34, 109–10; Sturgeon 2006: esp. 36–40; Neer 2010: 33–8. The Anavyssos kouros (Athens, National Archaeological Museum, 3851) has in

As the many scholarly debates it has occasioned make clear, the kouros offers a sculptural presence that allows and even solicits multiple visualizations, including some that are mutually exclusive to one another. If the kouros never succeeds to the stance of a real body, that is the price it pays for trying to stand on its own.

The relief body is bounded by a different but related set of material constraints. Supported by the secondary plane against which it is projected rather than by the plinth beneath its feet, the relief body can arrange its feet or extend its limbs in a more natural manner. Through relief, the sculptor of the Gorgon stele (see Fig. 3.1) could easily have resolved the ambivalence of the kouros' stance. Instead, the conditions of relief sculpture are used to exacerbate them even further. As with a kouros, the upper body is straight and vertical, its silhouette clearly delineated from and sharply turned against the concave background plane. Elements of the body are articulated so as to be maximally visible to us, with as little overlap as possible. The youth's left hand, for instance, is improbably placed in front of his thigh, its curled fingers oriented toward us, clutching a spear that obediently terminates right at the margin of the framed interior. Yet from the waist down, the body loses spatial consistency. As the legs – drastically elongated compared to the rest of the body – spread apart, the background plane deepens. In contrast to the flat-edged outline of the upper body, the legs are strongly undercut and rounded, the bulbous calf of the youth's right leg overflowing onto the banded frame. Most inconsistent are the feet. The toes of the right foot are all visible, yet they turn inward, plowing beneath the left (Fig. 3.5). This left foot, in turn, tends slightly in the opposite direction, toward us, though not quite far enough to avoid crashing through the border. The legs, in short, have different and conflicting relationships to the relief surface: The right and back sides of his body, including his right calf, are placed in front of the frame, while the left leg is placed behind, with the big toe excavating beneath the frame. These distinct orientations collide,

particular attracted a number of different, sometimes conflicted readings: Among many other discussions, see those of Osborne 1988: 6–9; Stewart 1997: 64–70; Elsner 2006; Lorenz 2010; Neer 2010: 21–30. For strong technical arguments in favor of the kouros as in movement, see Kleemann 1984 and 2008 (the latter for a funerary kouros from the Kerameikos). Movement in some cases was perhaps suggested by setting the kouros at a slightly oblique angle, as can be ascertained from the plinths and sockets on preserved bases, which are sometimes oriented away from a frontal perspective. The base of the kouros inscribed for Xenokles discussed later in this chapter is one such example (see Kissas 2000: 291n213, and confirmed by personal observation). The votive kouroi from Sounion are similarly famously twisted away from their bases (discussed in, among many others, Sturgeon 2006: 41; Neer 2010: 42).

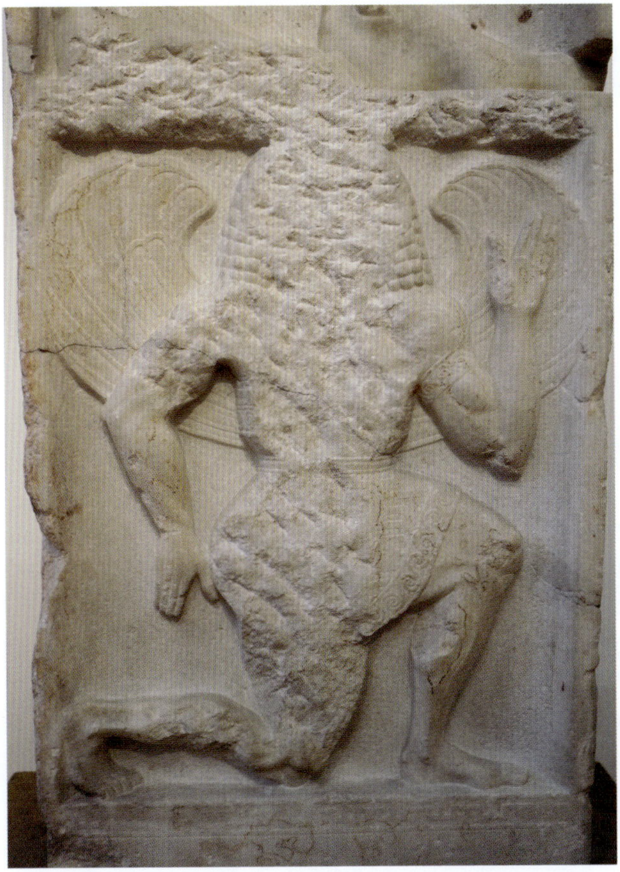

Fig. 3.5 Detail of Gorgon stele (see Fig. 3.1) (photograph by author).

without any resolution, where the feet meet, so that the left foot is somehow at once to the side of the right foot, in front of it, and on top of it. Taken as a whole, the figure might lead us to the same conflicted corporeal copresence as a kouros, but it does so by using effects that are calibrated through the carved surfaces of a stele, through effects that are specific to relief.

As this comparison suggests, attending to the continuities between kouros and its relief counterpart does not efface their differences. Instead, it allows us to account for them with greater precision, by exploring how contrastive sculptural techniques might open up related forms of visualization. In studies of Archaic funerary monuments, the term "relief" has come to be applied to any figure projected onto a stele, thereby constituting less a consistent sculptural technique in its own right than a catch-all category for almost everything that is not freestanding sculpture. Figures on stelai were not always strictly sculpted in relief: Some were only engraved into the flat surface of a monument, others were covered in a plaster surface that was then painted, while still others were rendered only in paint, and many monuments combine a range of different techniques even on a single figure.[15] When monuments are distinguished as either freestanding or in relief, the effects of such contrastive techniques are flattened. The left toe of the youth on the Gorgon stele, for instance, is hardly the only corporeal element of a relief figure on Archaic funerary stelai to challenge the frame and take on qualities usually associated with freestanding sculpture; numerous other monuments present similarly disruptive digits.[16] Yet such details are easy to marginalize – to discount even as mistakes – when the bodies they belong to are categorized as "relief." By contrast, to the extent that "relief" designates a body held apart from the space of the beholder, and "freestanding" a body that is spatially commensurate, all sculpted bodies on Archaic Attic funerary monuments, I argue, can be understood to contain elements of both.[17]

To argue for such continuity in visualization is precisely *not* to deny the formal difference between the body sculpted in relief and the body sculpted in the round. That these bodies occupy different spatial

[15] Engraved monuments: Paris, Louvre, MND 1863 (Richter 1961: 41, no. 57); Athens, National Archaeological Museum, 6688 (Despinis and Kaltsas 2014: 388–9, no. 1.1.357); Tancke 1993. Plastered monument: Athens, Kerameikos Museum, P 1133 (Richter 1961: 20–1, no. 23). Painted monuments: Athens, Kerameikos Museum, 747 (Richter 1961: 41–2, no. 58); New York, Metropolitan Museum of Art, 15.167 (Richter 1961: 44–5, no. 61). On polychromy, see Brinkmann 2007.

[16] Some further examples:

(1) On the stele of Aristion (Athens, National Archaeological Museum, 29; Richter 1961: 47, no. 67; Kaltsas 2002: 70, no. 100), the big toe of the left foot, the buttocks, and the right calf go over the banded edge of the monument.

(2) On a stele fragment showing a youth holding an aryballos (Athens, National Archaeological Museum, 5826; Kaltsas 2002: 53, no. 54), the extended thumb of the left hand pushes into the raised band.

(3) On the shaft of a stele showing a hoplite (Athens, National Archaeological Museum, 3071; Richter 1961: 33, no. 46; Kaltsas 2002: 64, no. 86), the toe of the left foot cuts through the band that borders the stele, as do the knuckles of the left hand, curled around a spear shaft.

(4) The spear held by a youth on another stele (Athens, National Archaeological Museum, 2825. Richter 1961: 23, no. 29) projects upward beyond the frame of the relief onto the flat, smooth surface of the blank stele, where it is lightly indicated in a technique that assimilates it with the decorative motifs of engraved lines that frame the relief.

[17] In thinking about the virtual possibilities of sculpture and the way relief in particular can allow different visualizations to succeed or fail, I am indebted to Summers 2003 (esp. 431–85) and Davis 2017 (on Greek relief sculpture, see esp. 229–63). In thinking about sculpture as "copresence," I have benefited from Getsy 2014.

relationships with the beholder is unquestionable, and the fact that Archaic sculptors employed such distinct carving techniques for monuments of the same function indicates that these differences were as palpable in antiquity as they are for the modern observer. Yet rather than see the virtual potential of a sculpted body – the degree to which a beholder might perceive it as analogous to a living one – as predetermined by its medium, I consider both relief and freestanding sculptures as capable of succeeding to the same range of visualizations depending on how they were framed at the grave site.[18]

Today, Archaic funerary monuments survive in isolated fragments, and many (like the Gorgon stele) were deliberately broken up in antiquity. As they enter museum collections or handbooks on Greek art, these fragments can be readily classified as freestanding or relief sculptures and are generally cataloged and displayed as such. Yet the monuments to which they originally belonged are more difficult to categorize. Many of them, including the Gorgon stele in its original appearance, were large, complex ensembles, consisting of multiple, joined blocks of stone, their surfaces treated in a myriad of different techniques and finishes. So too could kouroi, as we shall see, be embedded in large-scale ensembles, ones that framed the beholder's visualization of them sometimes through other decorative elements carved in relief. Monuments, moreover, were not necessarily seen in isolation but could be paired together or even joined together in a common base, so that their appearance only emerged in relation to that of another carved blocks of stone.[19] Seen in context as functional grave markers, the formal as well as iconographical distinctions that have often been perceived

[18] I follow Davis (2017) in using visual and virtual (or visualization and virtualization) as a complementary set of terms, the one referring to the beholder's experience of what they comprehend while looking at depicted space and the other to what they attribute to the construction of space in the depiction itself.

[19] See e.g. bases that supported a stele surrounded by columns, presumably topped with statues: Athens, Epigraphical Museum, 13290 (Kissas 2000: 67–8, no. A38); Athens, Kerameikos Museum, I 332 (Kissas 2000: 48–50, no. A16). Groups of sculptures discovered together in recent years further this picture, such as the cache of Archaic funerary monuments excavated in 2002 in the Kerameikos (see Niemeier 2002; Stroszeck 2014: 43–4) or the twin kouroi from Klenia, illegally excavated in 2010 and now in the Archaeological Museum of Ancient Corinth, where they are displayed together with their associated burials, which were excavated after the statues' recovery (see Kissas 2018). Other built features of the grave site, which I do not discuss here but which certainly inflected ancient appreciations of sculpted monuments, include mounds, tomb structures, and offering pits. For general discussion with earlier bibliography, see Vlachou 2012: 373–5. For a recent overview of excavations of the Kerameikos, where many Archaic funerary monuments were discovered and where much of our evidence for Archaic Attic funerary practices derive, see Stroszeck 2014, with 144–7 for an overview of the Archaic sculptural finds.

between the kouros and the relief figure – the one as anonymous and withdrawn, the other as specific and engaged – would have largely dissipated. Instead, as I explore in the remainder of this chapter through select case studies, different techniques of carving bodies in relief and in the round worked together to generate visualizations that are best understood as continuous.

A Leg Up

If the feet of the youth on the Gorgon stele appear capable of transcending the limitations of the frame that hems in his body, it is, in part, because he is directly set against another, more compliant body: that of the Gorgon below that gives the monument its modern name (see Fig. 3.5). Nestled in a panel much shallower than the one containing the youth, the Gorgon's pinwheel posture, her broad, frontal face, and her spread wings lend her figure a flat appearance, flush with the background. In contrast to the figure of the youth above, the Gorgon is inscribed precisely within the framed panel, her body extending right to the edge on all four sides, and her *Knielauf* posture allowing her feet to acknowledge not only the base of the panel but also the side band as impenetrable groundlines. Moreover, the meander patterning of the Gorgon's chiton, carved in an extremely low, almost engraved relief, replicates the meander pattern that frames the upper and lower bands surrounding the panel, assimilating her body further within the geometrical structure of the stele. The sculptor of the toe above, she seems to remind us, was certainly capable of respecting borders when he wanted to.

At the grave site, the contrast between the figure of the youth and that of the Gorgon on her namesake stele would be seen not simply as a question of carving but of the monument's more essential function as a grave marker. The Gorgon was renowned in antiquity for her ability to turn anyone she looked at into stone, and she appears frequently in Archaic art to disrupt the voyeuristic experience of looking at representational art, calling back at the beholder from within the space of representation.[20] By undercutting the youth, the figure of the Gorgon suggests the degree to which, at the grave site, a represented body only takes on a sense of presence within a network of other bodies. Most immediately, through her gaze and power to petrify, the Gorgon interpellates

[20] For a compelling account of the visual dynamics of encountering the Gorgon in early Greek art, see Mack 2002.

our own body as we stand and look at the monument, threatening to turn our own living body into one made of marble.[21] Yet by assimilating her body into the surface of the stele, she points us simultaneously to the corpse whose existence the monument serves to mark out, to the counterpart of the standing youth who is buried below. If the sculpted youth seems to overcome the confines of his surroundings, suggesting the possibility of a stone body entering into life, the Gorgon works from the other end, reminding us that the toe for all its apparent ability to break free of the confines of the stele is, ultimately, still that of a man who is dead.

Gorgons only rarely appear on Archaic funerary monuments.[22] Yet the function of this subsidiary panel to set off our perception of the figure above is typical of Archaic funerary monuments, which similarly often contrast the principal figure with other bodies rendered in smaller scale and different technique. The predella of the Gorgon stele is unusual in showing a mythological subject; on most stelai, in the same location we find depictions of elite male activities, especially equestrian figures. These are usually interpreted as semibiographical representations of the deceased or ones meant to ascribe to him a set of fictive heroic values.[23] Yet if we examine these scenes in context, we can better understand them as presenting a body that deliberately contrasts with the one above – a body that is more dynamic, more active, more socially engaged, and yet, through scale and technique, less visually present.

On some monuments, the figures above and below resemble one another. On a fragmentary stele now in New York, for instance, the full-scale legs of an armed hoplite solider are juxtaposed with another armed solider in the predella below (Fig. 3.6).[24] The man above is carved in relatively robust, if not quite high, relief, the carefully articulated toes of his right foot curling over the edge of the projecting groundline, while those of his left foot overlap and obscure the guilloche border that otherwise hems him in. The scene on the predella panel below, in contrast, is carved in an engraved technique, with the flat of the chisel used to dig out chamfered edges outlining the main figures. The distinction in scale and technique is matched by a distinction in iconography. The soldier above stands still, his spear firmly planted on the ground and aligned with the border, his left foot edging toward the stele's limits. The solider below, in contrast, adopts a similar stance but in a moment of action.

21 On interpellation in this context, see Mack 2002: 596.

22 The only other parallel example of a Gorgon in the predella is New York, Metropolitan Museum of Art, 55.11.4. On Gorgons on funerary monuments, see Woysch-Méautis 1982: 81–3.

23 For scenes on predellai, apart from individual entries in Richter 1961, see Sourvinou-Inwood 1995: 224–6; Keesling 1999: 536–41.

24 New York, Metropolitan Museum of Art, 38.11.13; Hall 1944; Richter 1944, 1961: 32–3, no. 45; Lazzarini and Marconi 2014: 125–7; Walter-Karydi 2015: 70.

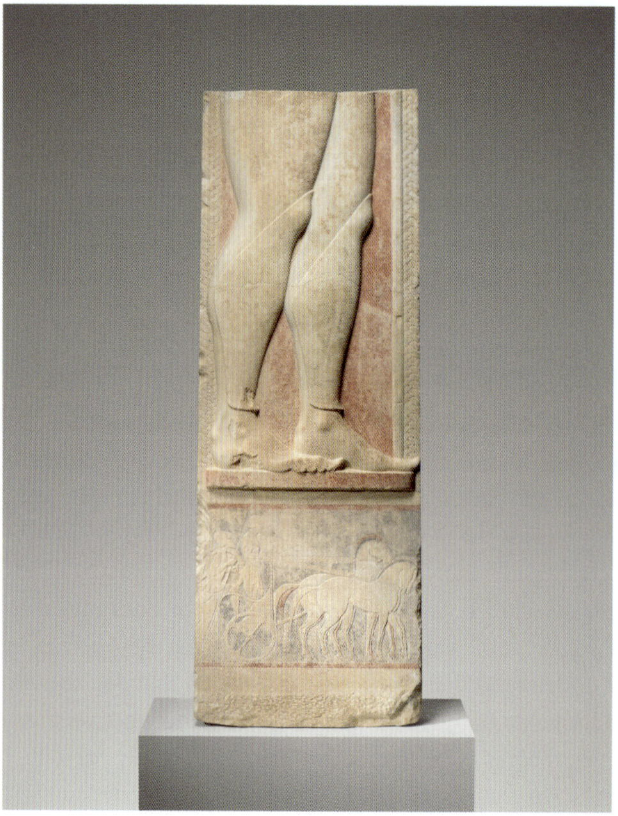

Fig. 3.6 Fragment of a funerary stele of a hoplite, Attic, ca. 525–515 BCE. Marble, height: 1.42 m. New York, Metropolitan Museum of Art, Fletcher Fund, 1938, 38.11.13 (Creative Commons Zero [CC0]).

Leaning forward and tilting his spear, he does not merely place his left foot forward but lifts his left leg off the ground to mount the chariot, propelling himself into a narrative that will only find its fulfillment elsewhere, outside of the visual confines of the stele.

On such a monument, the body of the deceased emerges through surfaces that are not only carved in different ways but are also suggestive of media beyond sculpture. The elaborate patterning of the double-guilloche border, delicately carved and once brightly colored, recalls similar borders found in Archaic metalwork, including those used to decorate armor.[25] Together with the greaves, originally painted a bright blue, it offsets the warrior's body as

[25] See e.g. the patterning around the belly of fifth-century amphora now in New York (Metropolitan Museum of Art, 2004.171a–b; Gaunt 2017: 215) or, closer to the stele, on the border of a shield strap fragment signed by Aristodamos of Argos, ca. 575 BCE (Malibu, J. Paul Getty Museum, 82.AC.11; Mattusch 2014: 60–1).

flesh encased in material surroundings.[26] The effect is that of a warrior whose body is simultaneously shaped by the armor he wears and emerges itself from a marble monument that takes on the decorative qualities of engraved metal.

In contrast, the predella – not only in its polychromy but in its scale, composition, placement, and even its carving technique – recalls contemporary ceramic funerary plaques painted in black-figure, with details engraved into the flat ceramic surface, that were likely originally affixed to tombs.[27] One such example (Fig. 3.7), produced in Athens around the same time as the stele, is pierced with holes for attachment to a tomb and is bordered with a painted double-guilloche similar to that on the stele but only on the right edge, suggesting the scene originally continued with one or more plaques to the left.[28] Like the stele itself, the plaque is divided into

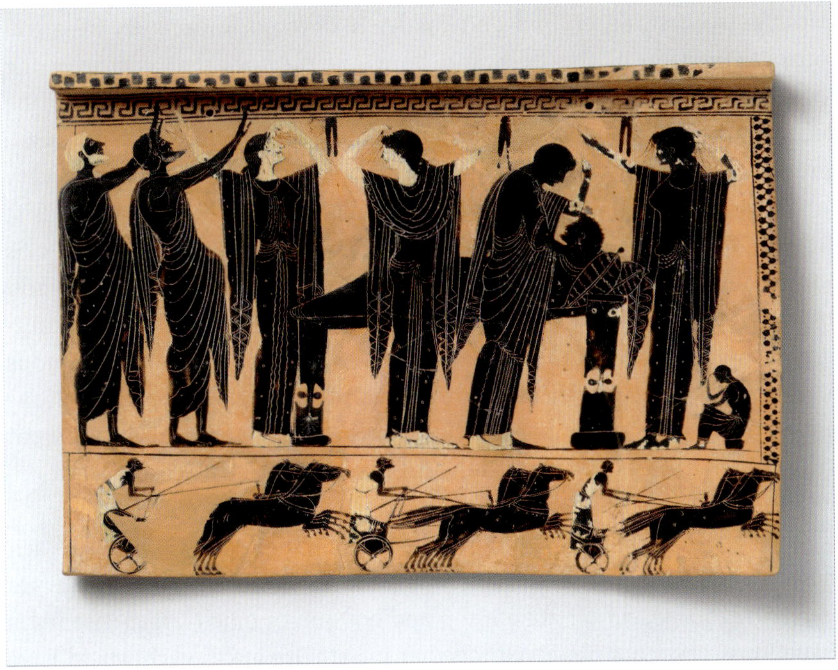

Fig. 3.7 Terra-cotta black-figure funerary plaque, Attic, ca. 520–510 BCE. Height: 26 cm. New York, Metropolitan Museum of Art, Rogers Fund, 1954, 54.11.5 (Creative Commons Zero [CC0]).

[26] On the polychromy of the stele, see Hall 1944.

[27] As Richter (1944: 324) notes, the polychromy is, in fact, closer to red-figure pottery, but surviving funerary plaques of the period tend to be black-figure. On ceramic funerary plaques, see Boardman 1955; Shapiro 1991; Mommsen 1997; Walter-Karydi 2015: 113–18; Williams and Rasmussen 2015; Bournias 2017.

[28] New York, Metropolitan Museum of Art, 54.11.5. On this example, see Shapiro 1991: 638–9.

two similarly proportioned zones, with a prothesis scene of mourners surrounding the corpse of a bearded man surmounting a scene of three charioteers below.[29] Though the scenes are discrete, their juxtaposition once again invites comparison, this time between the posture of the mourner and the posture of the charioteer. The three charioteers are not the same: The ones at left and center are bearded like the deceased, the one on the right clean-shaven. Conspicuously, while the right-hand charioteer fixes his eyes straight ahead, each of the two bearded charioteers cants his head upward (the one in the center more so than the one on the left) so that their eyes appear oriented toward the deceased above. As on the stele, the juxtaposition invites us to compare as much as contrast the effects of different bodily poses.

In potentially referencing such an object through its carving and polychromy, the predella on the Hoplite stele asserts its materiality, its status as something crafted and made. It does so, moreover, in direct contradistinction to the flesh and bones of the toes that curl over the edge just above it. Set against these surroundings, the body of the deceased warrior emerges as something radically different than metal, ceramic, or stone, something that strives to come into life in the very context where it remains most clearly dead, and something that strains at the material limits of carved stone itself. The deceased, as a result, is represented only in a discursive fashion, with the larger body above and the chariot scene below offering us two competing images that continuously play against one another, without resolving into an unambiguous presentation. The variegated surfaces and modes of representations speak to the essentially undialectical nature of the funerary monument itself, which can gesture toward the deceased only in a piecemeal fashion, without bringing him to life.

These effects would have been magnified when such a monument was seen in its original state. The preserved shafts of the Gorgon and Hoplite stelai are merely fragments, cut off at both top and bottom, of much larger ensembles that almost never are preserved together intact. Originally, each would have been topped with an elaborate finial, one that, judging by parallels from other monuments, would almost certainly have taken the form of a cavetto capital supporting a statue of a sphinx – another ferocious mythological creature, featuring the head of a woman atop the body of a lioness and the chest and wings of a bird of prey. Both the Gorgon stele and the Hoplite stele have been

[29] For the interpretation of chariot scenes on such plaques, see Woysch-Méautis 1982: 27–35; Shapiro 1991: 639–42.

tentatively linked with surviving sphinxes. The Gorgon stele has sometimes been associated with a fragmentary sphinx discovered at the foot of the same wall where the stele was found (a cast of this sphinx has been mounted atop a cast of the stele next to the original in the galleries of the National Archaeological Museum in Athens).[30] The Hoplite stele, meanwhile, has been associated with a sphinx, preserved together with its supporting capital, said to have been found in Vari and acquired by Museum of Fine Arts in Boston around the same time the fragment of the shaft arrived in New York (Fig. 3.8).[31] Whether or not these are the exact sphinxes that topped the Gorgon and Hoplite stelai seems impossible to prove based on available evidence.[32] Yet their pairings help us imagine the fascinatingly complex monuments of which our stelai would have originally been part – multimedia installations consisting of different forms of stone carving, different figures at different scales, different forms of representational practice.

By flaring upward or blossoming into volutes, capitals break away from the quadrifacial rigidity of the stele's shaft, their surfaces engraved and brightly painted with floral and geometric patterns or even, on one example from Lamptrai, a figural scene of a rider surrounded by mourners.[33] Though it lacks such figurative decoration, the Boston capital is among the most

[30] Athens, National Archaeological Museum, 2891; Noack 1907: 550–4; Richter 1961: 17, no. 16; Ridgway 1990: 590.

[31] Museum of Fine Arts, Boston, 40.576 (capital and sphinx); 40.724a–b (fragments of base). On capital and sphinx, see Richter 1961: 29, no. 38. On base fragments, see Clairmont 1974. As Clairmont notes, a third fragment of the inscription was evidently lost before the other two were acquired by the Museum of Fine Arts, Boston; an earlier photograph of it together with fragments of the sphinx is illustrated in Clairmont 1974: 224, fig. 1.

[32] The possible correlation of the elements in Boston with the stele in New York is noted by Richter 1961: 29: "One cannot help but wonder whether this finial once surmounted the warrior stele no. 45. The dimensions, as far as one can tell, would fit, the period is the same, and so is the preservation of the colors (including the relatively rare green). Furthermore, both pieces seem to have come to the antiquity market at about the same time, which might indicate that they were found together." See also Harrison 1965: 6 ("everything indicates" that they "belong together"); Clairmont 1974: 225 ("sphinx and capital in Boston, the stele in New York, and the inscribed fragments as the third element belong to one and the same memorial. This memorial must have been one of the most splendid Archaic Attic gravestones"). The uncertain provenance of the fragments does not help us determine whether they belonged together. While all fragments were acquired from the Brummer Gallery, they appear to have arrived there by different routes. Those now in Boston, which were "said to have been found in Vari, near Sounio, Greece," were acquired by Edward Zoumpoulakis in Athens in 1930 before they were sold to Brummer in 1940 (https://collections.mfa.org/objects/151019). The earliest record of the New York fragment, meanwhile, is that it was said to be from Attica and "purchased from Roussos in Paris" by Joseph Brummer in 1938 (www.metmuseum.org/art/collection/search/253566).

[33] Capital from Lamptrai: Athens, National Archaeological Museum, 41 (Richter 1961: 18–19, no. 20).

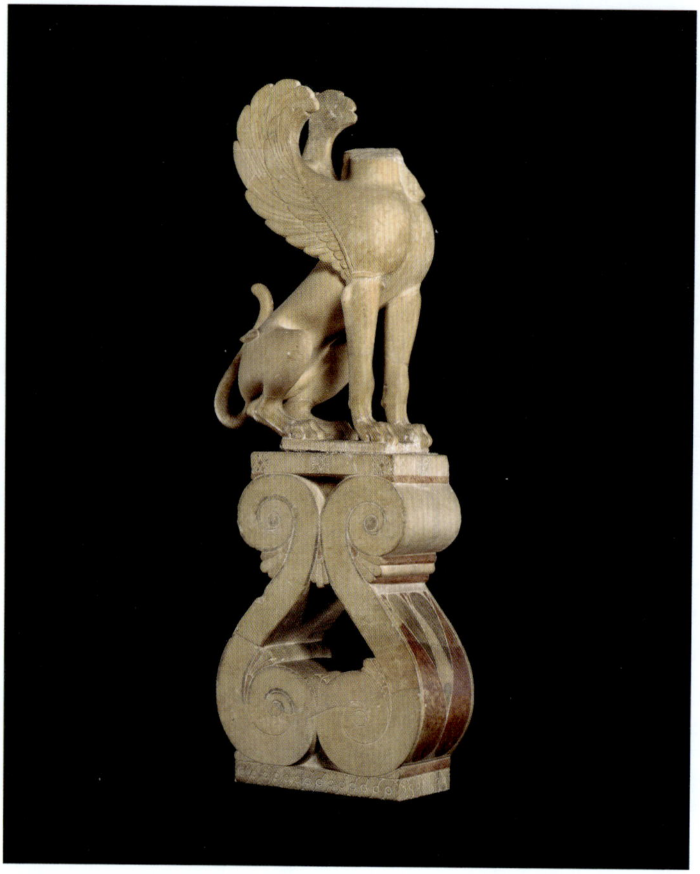

Fig. 3.8 Upper part of a funerary stele (sphinx and capital), from Attica (said to have been found in Vari, near Sounio), ca. 530 BCE. Height: 1.41 m. Museum of Fine Arts, Boston, 1931 and 1939 Purchase Funds, 40.576 (photograph © Museum of Fine Arts, Boston).

fanciful surviving stele capitals, consisting of a double-volute, daringly opened up in the middle and embellished with flowering palmettes between the interstices, set between an abacus and a base carved from the same block. All the outward surfaces are elaborately patterned with a variety of motifs, including a delicate guilloche around the base that recalls the more complex guilloche on the borders of the Hoplite stele, and the fields are filled with red and black paint.

Atop it sits a separately carved sphinx, one that embodies qualities both of freestanding and relief sculpture. In carving, she is like a kouros: Resting on all four paws, she gathers these together in close quarters in order to fit inside the limits of a continuous plinth, which is itself configured, in turn, to conform to the shape of a socket in the capital's upper surface, the two elements joined with molten lead. Like a body carved in relief – perhaps, indeed, like the warrior below – the sphinx is forced into a profile pose by the shape of the monument on which she rests, her extended wings even taking on the appearance of relief sculpture with their delicately carved feathers painted alternately green, red, black, and blue. And yet as a figure carved in the round, she is capable of overcoming the shape and limitations of the block below. Her hind legs and haunches greatly exceed the dimensions of the abacus under her. Her sinuous tail, which appears to impatiently flicker as it curls twice off the body before landing on her right haunch, doubles the arabesque of the volute below but liberates it from serving as an architectural support and brings it into life. Above all, it was the head of the sphinx, now broken, that would have most obviously defied the constraints to which her paws are subjected. Turning it sharply to the right, she would have faced directly outward, enacting a frontal stare that, like that of the Gorgon, was more commonly found on statues in the round than figures carved in relief.[34]

If the top of a relief stele opens up into twisting forms and an animated, conflicted sphinx body, the base into which it was set would have implicated another body: our own. Like the sphinx above it, each stele would itself have been sunk into a cutting on the upper surface of another block – a large, quadrifacial base, usually made of the same marble as the stele itself. Such bases are rarely preserved together with the stelai they once supported, but many survive on their own, with only their cuttings testifying to the large dimensions of the stele they once supported.[35] Such bases were not mere supports, but objects of visual interest in themselves. They could be painted or sculpted with scenes similar to those found on the predellai of stelai. More commonly, they could be inscribed with an epigram.[36] Rather than describe the deceased, epigrams inscribed on bases often comment directly on our movements and actions as we approach the monument, and as we read, they choreograph our physical and emotional responses to the sculpture before us.

[34] Compare the effect of the sphinx on the top of the so-called Brother and Sister stele; see Estrin 2023b: 43–5.

[35] For bases, see Kissas 2000; Kosmopoulou 2002; Dietrich, Fouquet, and Reinhardt 2020.

[36] Epigrams are collected in Hansen 1983. Sculpted monuments with epigrams are collected in Clairmont 1970, with additions in Clairmont 1974. The classic account of reading such epigrams is Svenbro 1993; more generally on reading inscribed Archaic epigram, see Day 2010. A recent introduction to the epigrams themselves can be found in González González 2019.

While the full range and significance of such inscriptions cannot be considered here, attending to them briefly helps give verbal precision and narrative structure to our visualizations of the sculpted figures that rise above them.[37] Inscriptions often explicitly juxtapose the representation of a body in the sculpture they support – its stillness, its permanence – with our own mobility and animation. In so doing, they give emotional and ethical weight to our very presence at the grave site. Like the Gorgon that apprehends the beholder with her gaze, epigrams often address the passerby directly, calling out to us in the second person as a "stranger" and asking us to halt in our paths and cathect before the monument.[38]

No trace of the base of the Gorgon stele survives. Yet if the Boston capital and sphinx do belong with the Hoplite stele, so too do three small fragments (one of them illustrated in Fig. 3.9) of an inscribed base that apparently come from the same monument.[39] Each fragment preserves only a few letters, but their arrangement over multiple lines indicates that the monument's base was inscribed with a poem of either three or four lines. Unfortunately, the fragments are too incomplete to reconstruct anything more than a few isolated words. Yet of what is left, two features

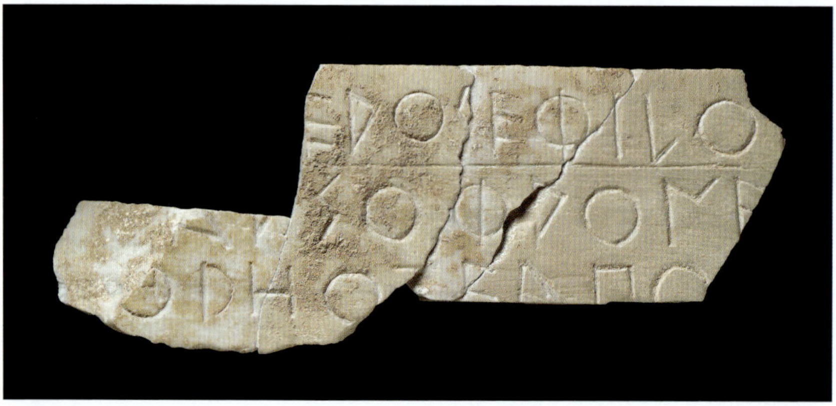

Fig. 3.9 Inscribed fragment of base, from Attica (said to have been found in Vari, near Sounio), ca. 530 BCE. Height: 10.8 cm. Museum of Fine Arts, Boston, 1931 and 1939 Purchase Funds, 40.724b (photograph © Museum of Fine Arts, Boston).

[37] For more detailed accounts of the visual effects of such inscriptions, see, among others, Sourvinou-Inwood 1995: 108–297; Lorenz 2010; Estrin 2016; Dietrich, Fouquet, and Reinhardt 2020.

[38] On epigrams that call out to the passerby directly, see Tueller 2010.

[39] *SEG* 26:56; Clairmont 1974; Peek 1976: 76–7 (offering a rather fanciful reconstruction of the epigram); Hansen 1983: 21–3, no. 30 (rejecting most of Peek's reconstruction).

stand out, both according with common formulas for funerary epitaphs found on more complete bases.

First, the inscription identifies the monument itself as a kind of object in its own right rather than simply as the deceased.[40] The letters εμα on one fragment almost certainly indicate that the monument presented itself, as did so many other funerary monuments, as a *sema* ("marker") or a *mnema* ("remembrance") of the deceased – as something through which a beholder might come to recognize or even remember the deceased, as some epitaphs explicitly demand.[41] Laden with a range of semantic significations, these terms as they are deployed in funerary epigram evoke the cognitive-affective demands made on the beholder who engages with the funerary monument more than they define a type or form of monument.

Second, the inscription identifies the deceased. Though no name can be reconstructed, the words "faithful" (πιστ[ὸς), "loved" (φίλον̣, visible in the first line of Fig. 3.9), and "wise" (σόφρον, visible in the second line) are almost certainly descriptors of the deceased. Such characteristics evoke the faculties not of a corpse who lies beneath the earth but of the living person he once was. They articulate the perspective of a family member who remembers the deceased and who erected the monument, one who, in many epigrams, is identified as a parent of the deceased.[42] In so doing, they enliven the generic, impersonal figure of the hoplite as a human being filled with the individual character of a named, remembered person.

Best Foot Forward

Precisely the same dynamics were staged in the case of a monument that took the form of a kouros. Kouroi, of course, were not crowned with capitals or sphinxes.[43] Yet like stelai, they were set into large stone bases, ones that often are indistinguishable from those used to support stelai except for the shape of the socket on their upper surface – an offset ovoid in the case of a kouros rather than a rectangle for a stele.[44] The quadrifacial structure of these bases

40 On this distinction, see esp. Sourvinou-Inwood 1995: 136–47.

41 On the significance of these terms in the funerary context, see Estrin 2023a: 12–14, with further bibliography.

42 See e.g. the epigram on the so-called Brother and Sister stele (note 11; Hansen 1983: 18–19, no. 25), which claims the monument was erected by the deceased's parents.

43 On decorative elements that might have emerged from the heads of some kouroi (as well as sphinxes atop stelai), see Ridgway 1990.

44 Note that votive statues, including kouroi, did not always have quadrifacial bases. For an early example, compare the base of the kouros dedicated by Euthykarides on Delos (Delos,

delineated specific sightlines or angles of viewing, guiding the movements of the beholder's body, while the upper surface served as a horizon from which a virtual form of a human body might emerge. As on the bases of stelai, the lateral faces of bases were often adorned with inscriptions, paintings, or relief images that articulate a primary face from which a beholder should engage with the monument, and the details of some freestanding sculptures are less finished on their sides (as determined by the orientation of a base) than they are from the front.[45] Even when sculpted in the round, that is to say, bodies were still visualized through the square blocks from which they emerged, from below if not from behind.

Notably, the language of inscriptions on bases for kouroi is identical to that on bases for stelai, including the nomination of the monument as either a *sema* or a *mnema* and the invocations to the passerby to look and engage emotionally. Monuments were defined at the grave site not by their formal type but by the cognitive-affective demands they made on their beholder, by the shared visualizations of sculpture they solicited.[46] Looking at funerary monuments through the language of their epigrams invites us to attend to continuities between formally different monuments, and an epigram on the base for a kouros could even endow it with the kind of attributes more likely to be depicted on stele. One base for a now-lost kouros, for instance, is inscribed with a poem stating that anyone "standing and looking at your marker (*sema*), Xenokles, will recognize the courage of a spear-bearer."[47] The inscription, in a sense, endows the kouros with the same kind of spear that is depicted in the hand of the men on the Gorgon and Hoplite stelai.

Perhaps the most direct way in which a base could alter our perception of a freestanding statue was by framing it with sculpture in relief. A series of bases for kouroi from the Kerameikos preserve sculpted decoration on three of their lateral faces, ones that correspond to the frontal and side viewpoints of the

Archaeological Museum, 728; Kosmopoulou 2002: 158–9, no. 3), which conforms in shape more or less to the shape of the statue's plinth.

45 See e.g. the equestrian monument of Xenophantos (Athens, Kerameikos Museum, P 6999; Eaverly 1995: 87–93). Though carved in the round, the monument was set upon a base (Athens, Kerameikos Museum, I 389; Kissas 2000: 55–6, no. A21) inscribed on its short end, indicating a primary viewing angle from this perspective, which is simultaneously confirmed by the detailed meander pattern painted only on those sections of the garment visible from this perspective. See Brinkmann 2007: 39–40.

46 Notably, when an inscription references a stele, it is in contradistinction to the monument's function as a *sema*; see Hansen 1983: 29–30, no. 42.

47 Athens, Kerameikos Museum, I 425; Hansen 1983: 14–15, no. 19. See also Kissas 2000: 39–40, no. A4; Robertson 2003; Walter-Karydi 2015: 92.

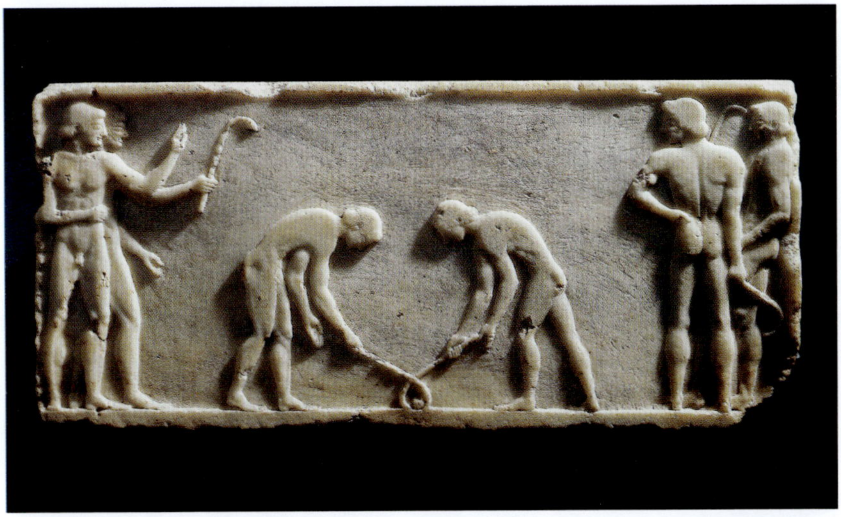

Fig. 3.10 Base of a funerary kouros ("Hockey player" base), from the Kerameikos, Athens, ca. 500 BCE. Height: 28 cm. Athens, National Archaeological Museum, 3477 (Getty Images).

kouros above, as can be ascertained from their cuttings.[48] Iconographically, the multifigure compositions carved into these faces are more elaborate versions of scenes found on the predellai of stelai, such as the Hoplite stele, with groups of men engaged in elite social activities. A fine example is the "Hockey Player" base (Fig. 3.10), found, like the Gorgon stele, built into the Themistoklean wall together with two other elaborate bases for kouroi.[49] On the front, two men are engaged in a ball game played with hooked sticks – the so-called hockey match that gives the base its modern name – while two pairs of men stand on either side, watching the game and holding sticks themselves (Fig. 3.11). The left (Fig. 3.12) and right sides of the base (Fig. 3.13) are both carved with the same scene but in reverse: that of a chariot procession, consisting of two armed men followed by a third who mounts the horse-drawn chariot.

Studies of this base have focused almost exclusively on its iconography, which scholars have speculatively interpreted as depicting honors performed

[48] Besides the example discussed in detail here, the two other sculpted bases for funerary kouroi are Athens, National Archaeological Museum, 3476, and Athens, Kerameikos Museum, 1002. Among many discussions of these bases, see Philadelpheus 1922a, 1922b; Dinsmoor 1923: Casson 1925; D'Onofrio 1986; Sourvinou-Inwood 1995: 255–8; Keesling 1999; Kosmopoulou 2002: 43–63; Walter-Karydi 2015: 70–2.

[49] Athens, National Archaeological Museum, 3477; Philadelpheus 1922a, 1922b; Dinsmoor 1923; Casson 1925: 164–9; Kissas 2000: 75, no. A45; Kaltsas 2002: 68, no. 96; Kosmopoulou 2002: 166–8, no. 9; Despinis and Kaltsas 2014: 461–6, no. 1.1.394 (entry by Kaltsas). On the "hockey" game itself, see Bentz 2004: 205–6.

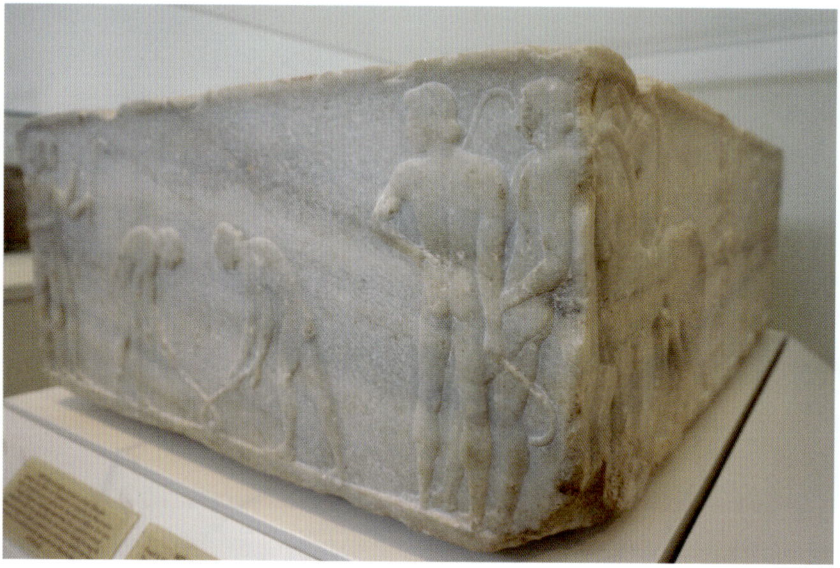

Fig. 3.11 Detail of "Hockey player" base (see Fig. 3.10), showing the meeting of front and right sides of the relief (photograph by author).

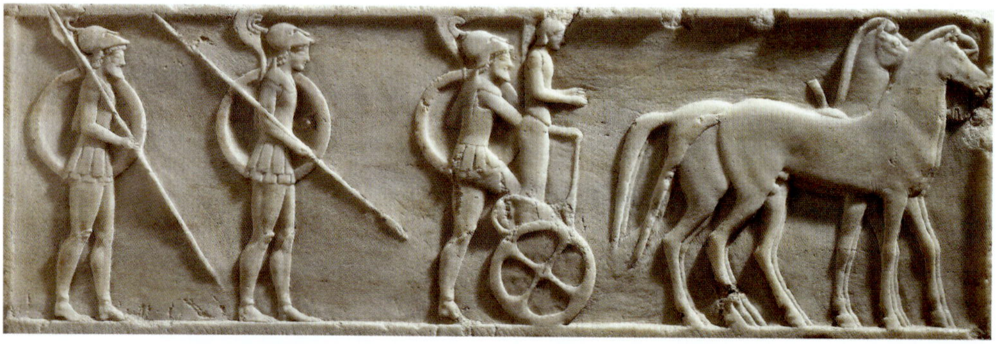

Fig 3.12 Left side of "Hockey player" base (see Fig. 3.10) (Getty Images).

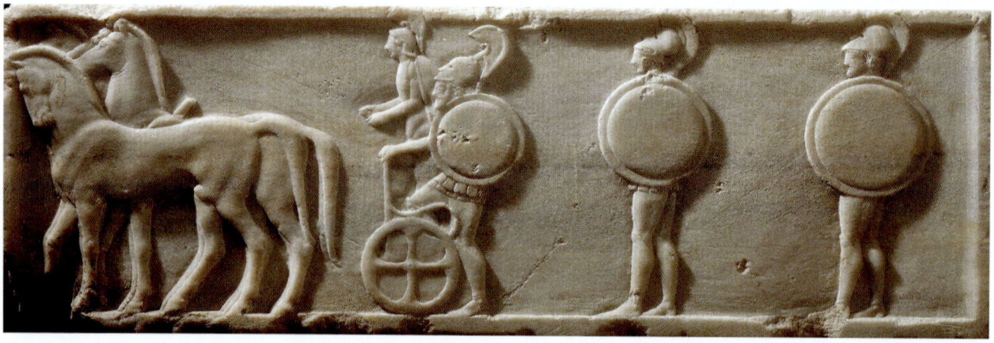

Fig. 3.13 Right side of "Hockey player" base (see Fig. 3.10) (Getty Images).

for the dead or as communicating the biography or social status of the deceased.[50] Yet the significance of these scenes only comes into focus when we see the relief base as simply one part of a large-scale ensemble of marble blocks – in particular, when we see it in conversation with the freestanding sculpture it supported.

We can reconstruct the appearance of this ensemble from two cuttings preserved on the upper and lower sides of the relief base. The irregular ovoid shape of the cutting on the top was for a kouros, its left foot advanced.[51] A cutting on the underside, while measuring about the same width as that for the kouros, is regular and square, configured, as William Dinsmoor first showed, so that the base could be set atop a rectangular stone pillar, one perhaps with similar dimensions to the block from which the kouros itself was carved.[52] The surviving block, as Dinsmoor noted, is not simply a statue base but the capital of a pedestal.[53] Indeed, when we reconstruct the monument even in hypothetical terms, it becomes clear that the surviving fragment is an intermediary between pillar and kouros – merely one element in a multitiered, multimedia monument.[54]

Considering this monument as a whole enables us to better appreciate the dynamic relationship between relief and freestanding sculptural elements. Even a rudimentary reconstruction of this monument (Fig. 3.14) reveals a remarkable yet previously unnoted feature of the base: The figures on all three sides are consistently oriented so as to dynamically amplify our visualization of the kouros above. The two lateral sides with armed soldiers and chariots are configured so as to show the same scene at exactly the same moment, where one soldier moves from slow march to the speeding chariot. The scene is not simply flipped on either side of the base, as if it were two depictions of the same event. Rather, the figures are

50 Kosmopoulou (2002: 52–5), synthesizing the earlier literature, argues that relief bases gave viewers additional information about the deceased, providing generic scenes that contributed to their social persona. On linking such scenes to the biography of the deceased, see esp. D'Onofrio 1986. Walter-Karydi (2015: 70) has rightfully cautioned that these scenes do not provide any biographical information, and instead argues they serve as praise for the dead.

51 Some scholars, most notably Jeffrey (1962: 127–8), have argued that the base might have supported a statue other than a kouros, though the arguments in favor remain much stronger; see D'Onofrio 1986: 176; Despinis and Kaltsas 2014: 462.

52 Dinsmoor 1923.

53 As Dinsmoor (1923: 24) states, "we are concerned, not with bases in the proper sense of the term, but with capitals of pedestals."

54 See similarly, but with somewhat different emphasis, Sourvinou-Inwood 1995: 258: "The scenes on the base, like the epitaphs, helped shape the way the grave statue and the deceased's social persona was perceived. The statue, the context, the base and the epitaph were all parts of one system, each acquiring its meanings also through its interaction with the others"; contra (as she notes) Osborne 1988: 6–7.

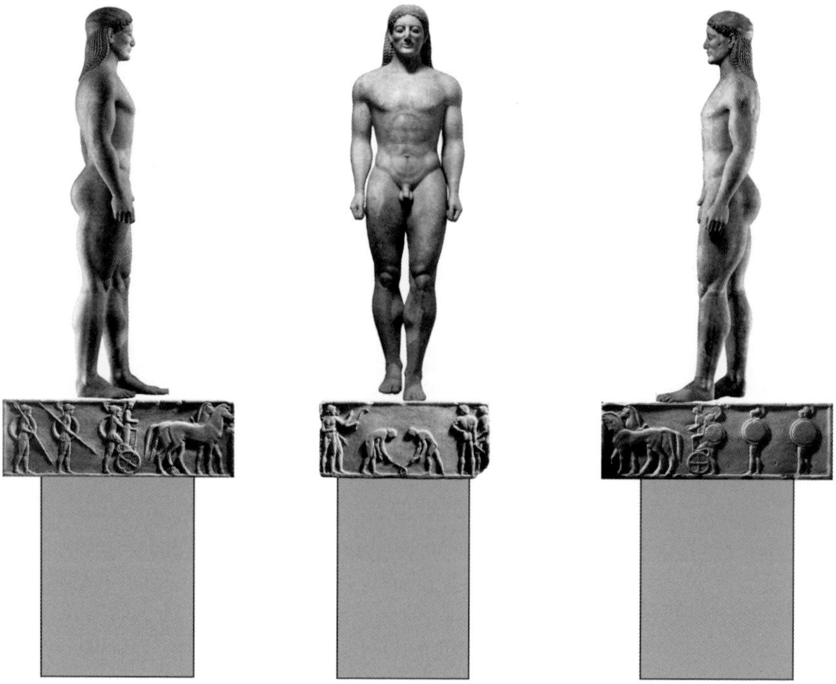

Fig. 3.14 Hypothetical reconstruction of a funerary monument based on W. B. Dinsmoor's drawing of the pedestal for the "Hockey player" base (see Fig. 3.10; Dinsmoor 1923: 23, fig. 1), photographs of the "Hockey player" base, and photographs of a funerary kouros from Anavyssos, Attica (Athens, National Archaeological Museum, 3851) (reconstruction by author).

shown from opposite angles, as if, on either side of the base, we were looking at the exact same bodies but from different sides.[55] Therefore, while on the left side of the base (see Fig. 3.12), the warriors' shields are seen from the inside, on the right side (see Fig. 3.13), they are seen from the outside, covering their bodies. Most significantly, on both sides, each soldier processes with his left foot forward, regardless of whether this foot is closest to the viewer. In so doing, they emulate the stance of the kouros above, who likewise advances left foot forward. When seen from both sides, in other words, the soldiers behave not like figures in relief, bound to their surface, but figures with their own independent spatiality – bodies which emerge, like that of the kouros above, from *within* the block.

Turning to the front of the base (see Fig. 3.10), the youths are shown in a variety of poses, their bodies arranged in contrastive pairs so as to show

[55] This mirroring is noted already by Della Seta 1922; see also Philadelpheus 1922a: 25; Casson 1925: 171.

off oppositional stances, twisting from frontal poses on the left, through profile poses in the center, to dorsal ones on the right. Once again, the virtualizing effects of three-dimensional sculpture are translated into relief. And once again, this effect is achieved by emulating the stance of the kouros, by depicting the figures with their left feet forward. The scene is bookended by pairs of figures, each consisting of one figure whose body is either frontal (on the left) or dorsal (on the right) – aligned, that is, with the surface of the block – and another figure whose body is in profile, turned away from the corner – aligned instead with the adjacent perpendicular face of the block, ostensibly outside the virtual space of the relief. These pairs, in effect, embody the very corners of the block, virtualizing its quadrifaciality through representations of bodies. Yet at the same time, the frontal and dorsal views of the body at the outer edges comment on the dynamic between the stance of the kouros above and our own oppositional stance as we look at the kouros who arises from the very same block of stone.

While their bodies are oriented in accordance with the shape of the block, the heads and limbs of these figures are all oriented toward the center of the composition, toward the game that occupies the central figures. The shallowness of relief collapses real and virtual spaces: the ball is placed not simply on the groundline but seemingly on the surface of the block itself, so much so that it is impossible to tell which player is closer to us, which stick overlaps the other. Situated right on the surface of the relief, the visual focus of both our world and the virtual world of the carved figures, the ball operates as a fulcrum between different kinds of space, one that serves to orient both the bodies depicted on the relief and our own body as we stand before it.

There is one more body that the relief surface orients: that of the kouros above, who strides forward left foot first, presenting us, once again, with a big left toe as the most proximate point of entry into his representational world (cf. Fig. 3.4). If the toe on the Gorgon stele seems to push beyond the confines of relief sculpture, this toe might be seen as doing something similar, pushing forward to the edge of the plinth from which it is materially inseparable, edging past the body it supports as if toward the ball depicted on the face of the base below. The upper surface of the base, the one hollowed out to support the plinth that enables the kouros to stand, is carved in a manner not all that different from its lateral surfaces. Like them, it constitutes a representational horizon that somehow makes another body present before ours, another world visible within our own.

References

Bentz, M. (2004). "Mannschaftssport." In R. Wünsche and M. Bentz, eds., *Lockender Lorbeer: Sport und Spiel in der Antike*. Munich: Staatliche Antikensammlungen, 205–12.

Boardman, John. (1955). "Painted Funerary Plaques and Some Remarks on Prothesis." *Annual of the British School at Athens* 50: 51–66.

Bournias, L. (2017). "A Newly Discovered Funerary *Pinax* from the Athenian Kerameikos." In V. Vlachou and A. Gadolou, eds., *ΤΕΡΨΙΣ: Studies in Mediterranean Archaeology in Honour of Nota Kourou*. Brussels: CReA-Patrimoine, 247–60.

Brinkmann, V. (2007). "The Coloring of Archaic and Early Classical Sculpture." In V. Brinkmann, R. Wünsche, U. Koch-Brinkmann et al., eds., *Gods in Color: Painted Sculpture of Classical Antiquity*. Munich: Biering and Brinkmann, 28–43.

Casson, S. (1925). "The New Athenian Statues Bases." *Journal of Hellenic Studies* 45.2: 164–79.

Clairmont, C. W. (1970). *Gravestone and Epigram: Greek Memorials from the Archaic and Classical Period*. Mainz: von Zabern.

(1974). "Gravestone and Epigram." *Archäologischer Anzeiger* 89: 223–32.

(1986). "Un 'programma' figurativo tardo arcaico (le basi ateniesi con 'Ballspielszenen' riconsiderate)." *Annali dell'Istituto universitario orientali di Napoli* 8: 175–93.

Davis, W. (2017). *Visuality and Virtuality: Images and Pictures from Prehistory to Perspective*. Princeton, NJ: Princeton University Press.

Day, J. W. (2010). *Archaic Greek Epigram and Dedication: Representation and Reperformance*. Cambridge: Cambridge University Press.

Della Seta, A. (1922). "Un'altra base ateniese con rilievi arcaici." *Dedalo* 3.2: 409–23.

Despinis, G., and Kaltsas N., eds. (2014).*Εθνικό αρχαιολογικό μουσείο: Κατάλογος γλυπτών. Vol. 1.1, Γλυπτά των αρχαϊκών χρόνων από τον 7ο αιώνα έως το 480 π.Χ.* Athens: Archaeological Receipts and Expropriations Fund.

Dietrich, N. (2017). "Framing Archaic Greek Sculpture: Figure, Ornament, and Script." In Platt and Squire 2017: 270–316.

Dietrich, N., Fouquet J., and Reinhardt C. (2020). *Schreiben auf statuarischen Monumenten: Aspekte materialer Textkultur in archaischer und frühklassischer Zeit*. Berlin: De Gruyter.

Dinsmoor, W. B. (1923). "A Note on the New Bases at Athens." *American Journal of Archaeology* 27.1: 23–4.

D'Onofrio, A. M. (1985). "Kouroi e stele: Iconografia e ideologia del monumento funerario arcaico in Attica." *Annali dell'Istituto universitario orientali di Napoli* 7: 201–4.

Eaverly, M. A. (1995). *Archaic Greek Equestrian Sculpture*. Ann Arbor: University of Michigan Press.

Elsner, J. (2006). "Reflections on the 'Greek Revolution' in Art: From Changes in Viewing to the Transformation of Subjectivity." In S. Goldhill and R. Osborne, eds., *Rethinking Revolutions through Ancient Greece*. Cambridge: Cambridge University Press, 68–95.

Estrin, S. (2016). "Cold Comfort: Empathy and Memory in an Archaic Funerary Monument from Akraiphia." *Classical Antiquity* 35.2: 189–214.

(2023a). *Grief Made Marble: Funerary Sculpture in Classical Athens*. New Haven, CT: Yale University Press.

(2023b). "Archaic Sculpture and Archaisms of Gender: Rethinking the 'Brother and Sister Stele.'" *Art Bulletin* 105.3: 33–60.

Gaunt, J. (2017). "Toward the Derveni Krater: On the Rarity of Large Bronze Vessels of the Archaic and Classical Periods Bearing Large Figural Registers." In J. Daehner, K. Lapatin, and A. Spinelli, eds., *Artistry in Bronze: The Greeks and Their Legacy. XIXth International Congress on Ancient Bronzes*. Los Angeles, CA: J. Paul Getty Museum and Getty Conservation Institute, 214–23.

Getsy, D. J. (2014). "Acts of Stillness: Statues, Performativity, and Passive Resistance." *Criticism* 56.1: 1–20.

González González, M. (2019). *Funerary Epigrams of Ancient Greece: Reflections on Literature, Society and Religion*. London: Bloomsbury.

Hall, L. F. (1944). "Notes on the Colors Preserved on the Archaic Attic Gravestones in the Metropolitan Museum." *American Journal of Archaeology* 48.4: 334–6.

Hansen, P. A. (1983). *Carmina Epigraphica Graeca*. Berlin: De Gruyter.

Harrison, E. B. (1956). "Archaic Gravestones from the Athenian Agora." *Hesperia* 25.1: 25–45.

(1965). *Archaic and Archaistic Sculpture*. Athenian Agora 11. Princeton, NJ: American School of Classical Studies at Athens.

Himmelmann, N. (1999). *Attische Grabreliefs*. Opladen: Westdeutscher.

Jeffrey, L. H. (1962). "The Inscribed Gravestones of Archaic Attica." *Annual of the British School at Athens* 57: 115–53.

Kaltsas, N. (2002). *Sculpture in the National Archaeological Museum*. Trans. D. Hardy. Los Angeles, CA: J. Paul Getty Museum.

Karanastassis, P. (2002). "Hocharchaische Plastik." In P. C. Bol, ed., *Die Geschichte der antiken Bildhauerkunst. Vol. 1, Frühgriechische Plastik*. Mainz: von Zabern, 171–221.

Keesling, C. (1999). "Endoios's Painting from the Themistoklean Wall: A Reconstruction." *Hesperia* 68.4: 509–48.

Kissas, K. (2000). *Die attischen Statuen- und Stelenbasen archaischer Zeit*. Bonn: Habelt.

(2018). "Die Kouroi von Tenea: Die Entdeckung der Nekropole von Klenia." *Antike Welt* 49.1: 45–54.

Kleemann, I. (1984). *Frühe Bewegung: Untersuchungen zur archaischen Form bis zum Aufkommen der Ponderation in der griechischen Kunst.* Mainz: von Zabern.

(2008). "Zum Kuros Athen, NM 71 vom Kerameikos und den mitgefundenen Fragmenten." *Jahrbuch des Deutschen Archäologischen Instituts* 123: 1–49.

Kosmopoulou, A. (2002). *The Iconography of Sculptured Statue Bases in the Archaic and Classical Periods.* Madison: University of Wisconsin Press.

Lazzarini, L., and Marconi, C. (2014). "A New Analysis of Major Greek Sculptures in the Metropolitan Museum: Petrological and Stylistic." *Metropolitan Museum Journal* 49: 117–40.

Lorenz, K. (2010). "'Dialectics at a Standstill': Archaic *Kouroi*-cum-Epigram as *I-Box.*" In M. Baumbach, A. Petrovic, and I. Petrovic, eds., *Archaic and Classical Greek Epigram.* Cambridge: Cambridge University Press, 131–48.

Mack, R. (2002). "Facing Down Medusa (An Aetiology of the Gaze)." *Art History* 25.5: 571–604.

Martin, S. R. (2017). *The Art of Contact: Comparative Approaches to Greek and Phoenician Art.* Philadelphia: University of Pennsylvania Press.

Mattusch, C. C. (2014). *Enduring Bronze: Ancient Art, Modern Views.* Los Angeles, CA: J. Paul Getty Museum.

Mommsen, H. (1997). *Exekias. Vol. 1, Die Grabtafeln.* Mainz: von Zabern.

Neer, R. (2010). *The Emergence of the Classical Style in Greek Sculpture.* Chicago, IL: University of Chicago Press.

Niemeier, W.-D. (2002). *Der Kuros von Heiligen Tor: Überraschende Neufunde archaischer Skulptur im Kerameikos in Athen.* Mainz: von Zabern.

Noack, F. (1907). "Die Mauern Athens: Ausgrabungen und Untersuchungen II." *Mitteilungen des Deutschen Archäologischen Instituts, Athenische Abteilung* 32: 473–566.

Osborne, R. G. (1988). "Death Revisited, Death Revised: The Death of the Artist in Archaic and Classical Greece." *Art History* 11.1: 1–16.

Peek, W. (1976). "Archaische Epigramme." *Zeitschrift für Papyrologie und Epigraphik* 23: 75–81.

Philadelpheus, A. (1922a). "Bases archaïques trouvées dans le mur de Thémistocle à Athènes." *Bulletin de correspondance hellénique* 46: 1–35.

(1922b). "Three Statue Bases Recently Discovered at Athens." *Journal of Hellenic Studies* 42.1: 104–6.

Platt, V., and Squire, M., eds. (2017). *The Frame in Classical Art: A Cultural History.* Cambridge: Cambridge University Press.

Richter, G. M. A. (1944). "Polychromy in Greek Sculpture with Special Reference to the Archaic Attic Gravestones in the Metropolitan Museum." *American Journal of Archaeology* 48.4: 321–33.

(1960). *Kouroi: Archaic Greek Youths.* London: Phaidon.

(1961). *The Archaic Gravestones of Attica.* London: Phaidon.

(1974). "The Story of the Megakles' Stele in New York." In A. F. Mansel, ed., *Mélanges Mansel*, Vol. 1. Ankara: Türk Tarih Kurumu Basimevi, 1–5.
Ridgway, B. S. (1990). "Birds, 'Meniskoi,' and Head Attributes in Archaic Greece." *American Journal of Archaeology* 94: 583–612.
(1993). *The Archaic Style in Greek Sculpture*. 2nd ed. Chicago, IL: Ares.
Robertson, G. I. C. (2003). "The *Andreia* of Xenocles: *Kouros*, *kallos* and *kleos*." In R. M. Rosen and I. Sluiter, eds., *Andreia: Studies in Manliness and Courage in Classical Antiquity*. Leiden: Brill, 59–78.
Shapiro, H. A. (1991). "The Iconography of Mourning in Athenian Art." *American Journal of Archaeology* 95: 629–56.
Sourvinou-Inwood, C. (1995). *"Reading" Greek Death: To the End of the Classical Period*. Oxford: Oxford University Press.
Squire, M. (2018). "Embodying the Dead on Classical Attic Grave-Stelai." *Art History* 41.3: 518–45.
Stewart, A. F. (1986). "When Is a Kouros Not an Apollo? The 'Tenea Apollo' Revisited." In M. A. Del Chiaro and W. R. Biers, eds., *Corinthiaca: Studies in Honor of Darrell A. Amyx*. Columbia: University of Missouri Press, 54–70.
(1990). *Greek Sculpture: An Exploration*. New Haven, CT: Yale University Press.
(1997). *Art, Desire, and the Body in Ancient Greece*. Cambridge: Cambridge University Press.
Stroszeck, J. (2014). *Der Kerameikos in Athen: Geschichte, Bauten und Denkmäler im archäologischen Park*. Moehnesee: Bibliopolis.
Sturgeon, M. C. (2006). "Archaic Athens and the Cyclades." In O. Palagia, ed., *Greek Sculpture: Function, Materials, and Techniques in the Archaic and Classical Periods*. Cambridge: Cambridge University Press, 32–76.
Summers, D. (2003). *Real Spaces: World Art History and the Rise of Western Modernism*. London: Phaidon.
Svenbro, J. (1993). *Phrasikleia: An Anthropology of Reading in Ancient Greece. Myth and Poetics*. Trans. J. Lloyd. Ithaca, NY: Cornell University Press.
Tancke, K. (1993). "Eine archaische Ritzstele vom Kerameikos." *Mitteilungen des Deutschen Archäologischen Instituts, Athenische Abteilung* 108: 49–58.
Tueller, M. (2010). "The Passer-By in Archaic and Classical Epigram." In M. Baumbach, A. Petrovic, and I. Petrovic, eds., *Archaic and Classical Greek Epigram*. Cambridge: Cambridge University Press, 42–60.
Vlachou, V. (2012). "Death and Burial in the Greek World." In *Thesaurus Cultus et Rituum Antiquorum*, Vol. 8. Los Angeles, CA: Getty Publications, 363–84.
Vorster, C. (2002). "Früharchaische Plastik." In P. C. Bol., ed., *Die Geschichte der antiken Bildhauerkunst. Vol. 1, Frühgriechische Plastik*. Mainz: von Zabern, 97–132.
Walter-Karydi, E. (2015). *Die Athener und ihre Gräber (1000–300 v. Chr.)*. Image and Context 14. Berlin: De Gruyter.

Williams, D., and Rasmussen, B. B. (2015). "A Funerary Plaque from Athens." In B. B. Rasmussen, ed., *The Past in the Present*. Copenhagen: National Museum of Denmark, 123–44.

Woysch-Méautis, D. (1982). *La représentation des animaux et des êtres fabuleux sur les monuments funéraires grecs: De l'époque archaïque à la fin du IVe siècle av. J.-C.* Lausanne: Bibliothèque historique vaudoise.

4 Relief in Athenian Vase Painting

Reflectivity, Presence, and Pictorial Space

GUY HEDREEN

At a special exhibition at the National Archaeological Museum in Athens, a fragment of a late fifth-century Athenian red-figure kylix caught my eye (Fig. 4.1).[1] A female figure, identified by name as Timokratē, is seated alone on a couch. She is buttoning or unbuttoning her chiton. The couch and footstool are drawn from a striking three-quarter point of view. But the eye-catching feature for me was the light reflected from the vase painting. Almost every line oriented horizontally reflected white light. Lines that one knew to be jet black in hue appeared bright white. In my photo, one can see this along Timokratē's forearm. Moreover, if I moved my head a little to the right or left, the hue of the line switched from white to black or black to white. The fragment appeared to shimmer whenever my eye was in motion.

What was the cause of those light effects? Most of the black lines on the cup are not flat but slightly raised in relief. These so-called relief lines are produced with the same chemical compound as the shiny black glaze forming the background around the reserved clay figure and objects, but the material used for the relief lines is less dilute.[2] Imagine a viscous, shiny, black paint squeezed out of a tube, which retains something of the three-dimensional curvature of the circular opening of the tube even after it is dry. Flat black glaze lines are familiar from black-figure vase painting in the outline technique. Relief lines occur occasionally in black-figure to define the borders of ornament, such as palmettes. In the earliest red-figure vase

For the invitation to participate in this project and for extensive discussion of early drafts of this chapter, I thank Milette Gaifman, Jaś Elsner, and Nate Jones. I thank Ann Steiner and Mary Ann Eaverly for reading earlier drafts, as well. Following the guidelines of the *American Journal of Archaeology* (www.ajaonline.org/submissions/antiquities-policy), I have identified those vases without known, pre-1974 provenances as [unprov.].

[1] Athens, National Archaeological Museum, 20185, found at the Olympieion and accessioned in 1980. The fragment does not appear to be in BAPD but is published in Lagogianni-Georgakarakos 2018: 104, fig. 14. I thank George Kavvadias for that information.

[2] I use the term "glaze" instead of "gloss," following Chaviara and Aloupi-Siotis 2015. For the technical details, see Noble 1965: 56–8. Much of the scholarly writing on relief line has focused on the question of how it was created and applied – whether through a kind of pastry tube or the use of a very fine brush or the use of a human hair: see Noble 1960; Seiterle 1976; Boardman 2001: 285–6. Particularly informative is the recent study of Artal-Isbrand and Klausmeyer 2013.

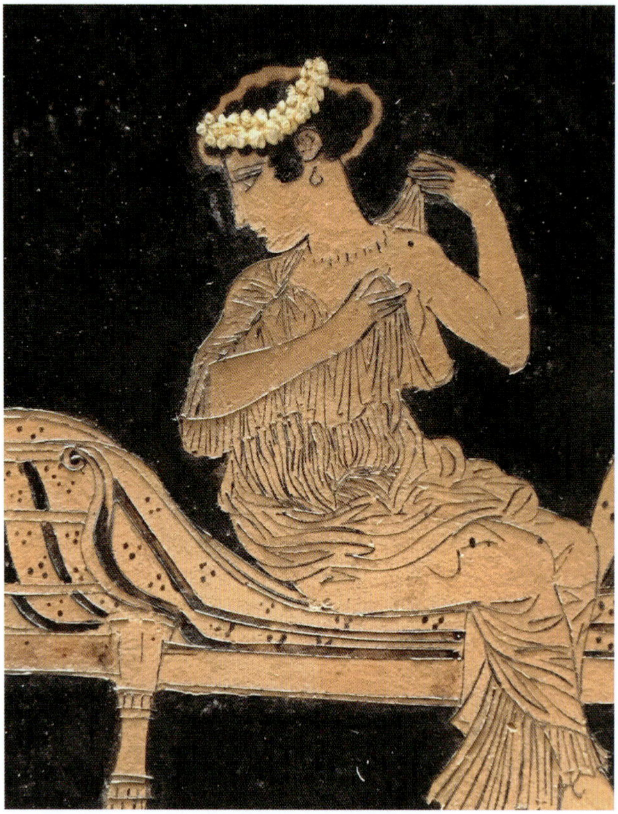

Fig. 4.1 Athenian red-figure kylix, fifth century BCE. Athens, National Archaeological Museum, 20185, found at the Olympieion and accessioned in 1980; see Lagogianni-Georgakarakos 2018: 104, fig. 14 (photograph by author).

painting, the flat black glaze line was used to define the contours of figures, but the resulting border between the figure and ground was not as emphatic as it was in the black-figure technique, in which sharp incised lines emphasize the borders between orange clay and glossy black. In the new red-figure technique, the black relief line was quickly repurposed to function similar to incision, expressing linear contours and many internal lines with, as John D. Beazley mysteriously put it, "masculine precision and power."[3]

In the exhibition, the fragment was lit from above by a single, strong source of light (see Fig. 4.1). The direction of the light was nearly parallel to the painted surface of the cup. As a result, every raised, rounded relief line flashed white whenever it was oriented so as to reflect the light to my

[3] Beazley 1961: 53.

eye.[4] Upstairs, in the permanent galleries of Athenian vases at the National Archaeological Museum, there are many dozens of red-figure vases with relief lines or added-clay relief. But very few of those vases afford the visitor the same visual experience as the one just described. The illumination of the vases in the permanent galleries is diffuse. The flat light allows one to appreciate the course of the drawn lines, their combinations into compositional patterns, and their representational value, but not their reflectivity or the changeability of their color. The appreciation of vases in antiquity was augmented, however, by perspectives not available to most of us today because ancient viewers were not limited in their inspection of the vases to permanent museum installations and fixed lighting. Far more often, if not most of the time, a vase was a mobile object. It was possible to turn the vase in the hand, look at it from one direction and then another, or examine it outdoors in the bright sun or indoors by the light of a single flickering lamp.[5] This point was noticed by John Boardman, who is among the few to have written about the reflectivity of relief line: "in the hand [vases] can be shifted to reflect light from different angles, and the whole image gains life. This is particularly effective when attempting to see and appreciate the sparkling relief-line of early red figure."[6]

My iPhone photo of the fragment in Athens (see Fig. 4.1) captures some of the reflections off the relief lines, but in doing so, my photo fails to meet the expectations surrounding the photography of ancient vases. "Too often a vase is poorly photographed . . . obscuring the vase drawing by misplaced highlights."[7] To eliminate those highlights, Joseph Noble recommended photographing vases in a darkened room illuminated by four or more lights with scrims between the lights and the vase.[8] Not many ancient homes, needless to say, were lit in such a way. Two of his other recommendations are worthy of note. One is that the photographer should use a lens with a long focal length, so that the camera can be placed at a distance of at least six times the height of the vase. The other is the use of a special camera designed to take a friezelike photograph of the entire circumference of a vase, "in effect unroll[ing] the drawing on the vase." Long before the invention of photography, as far back as the earliest modern scholarly publications, illustrations of Greek vases transformed the curvilinear surface decorations into flat

[4] Adding to the light effects would have been the woman's crown, which is formed out of clay affixed on top of the surface of the vase and then, originally, mostly likely leafed in glittering gold. I discuss this form of relief in the body of this chapter.

[5] For some of the phenomological aspects of lamplight, see Bielfeldt 2014.

[6] Boardman 2001: 188. Compare von Bothmer 1966: 205: "Lines that stand out in relief and catch the light, much as the printing on engraved letterheads or calling cards."

[7] Noble 1965: 100. [8] Noble 1965: 101n11.

pictures.[9] Those illustrations as well as Noble's recommendations transform potting, drawing, and painting of vases into two-dimensional media. The recommendations privilege the linear design of pottery and vase painting over other qualities, such as dynamic light effects.

Relief beyond Relief Line

In this chapter, I use the term "relief" to describe features on a vase that physically rise above the painted surface. These features include not only relief lines but also several other raised clay pictorial elements.[10] Those elements include raised clay dots and other shapes to indicate curly hair, gilded raised clay representations of metal objects, and mold-made raised relief masks of Dionysos or a satyr. There are other sculptural elements on painted Athenian vases, including the mold-made faces of the so-called head vases and the mold-made bodies of crocodiles and other types of figures in animal rhyta. But the relief features of vase painting examined in this chapter stand apart from the more fully sculptural head vases and animal rhyta because the relief features, I will argue, are developed and used pictorially – that is, to extend the range of visual effects possible for painting on vases.

It has been suggested in the past that relief features of vase painting, such as hair or masks, are emulations of representations in stone sculptural relief or metalwork. The impulse to see relief features as "foreign" to vase painting perhaps reflects modern assumptions about what is germane to painting as a two-dimensional medium. We are all familiar with Clement Greenberg's ideas about modernist painting: "To achieve autonomy, painting has had above all to divest itself of everything it might share with sculpture."[11] I will argue that potters and painters developed relief techniques for their pictorial effects, but also that the effects call into question how rigorously policed the distinctions between painting and other media really were in antiquity.

First, I will examine the use of added-clay relief for the representation of the hair of special figures in black- and red-figure vase painting. In the case of relief hair, it is perhaps easier to see than in the case of relief line how the goal of the technique was at least as much to encourage light effects as it was to develop mimetic precision. Second, I will examine the relatively little-known class of relief mask kantharoi. In this group of vases, relief was not employed to enhance reflectivity or light effects. Rather, relief afforded the potter and

[9] See Marconi 2017: 118–22.

[10] For further thoughts on relief line, see Hedreen 2022. In this chapter, I address other forms of relief.

[11] Greenberg 1995: 88.

painter the opportunity to translate a venerable two-dimensional pictorial formula for the frontal face of Dionysos or a satyr, the so-called mask eye cup, into a partially three-dimensional form. It is not a coincidence that the pictorial formula chosen for three-dimensional embodiment, the mask of Dionysos or a satyr, itself affords perhaps the most intense visual encounter in Athenian vase painting. The purpose of translating that formula into three dimensions, I will argue, was to further intensify the visual presence of the god and his follower for the viewer. Third, a particularly interesting interpretation of relief in vase painting in earlier scholarship is that it contributed to the development of a conception or experience of pictorial space. In the earlier history of writing on pictorial space, such as that of Adolf Hildebrand and Aloïs Riegl, relief played a perhaps surprisingly important role. I will argue, however, that in vase painting, relief serves primarily to make one more attuned to material surfaces, not less.

Added-Clay Relief Hair

A frequent occurrence in Athenian red-figure vase painting from around 525 until 480 BCE or so is the depiction of the hair of gods, heroes, and occasionally even unheroic mortals by means of raised and rounded dots painted glossy black. The most important and imaginative study of that phenomenon was written by Beth Cohen. For many years, scholars believed that the relief hair was created by the concentrated application of relief line and therefore an innovation of red-figure vase painters. Cohen persuasively demonstrated, however, that the relief was in fact created out of clay pressed onto the surface of the leather-hard clay vase, which was then glazed.[12] Added-clay relief thus had a different genealogy from relief line, which originated as a modification of the glaze used by the vase painter.

Indeed, Cohen argued that the idea of clay relief was introduced from outside of the potters' quarter altogether. Among the very early examples of the added-clay technique is the red-figure side of a bilingual amphora in London of around 520 BCE (Fig. 4.2): Here black-glazed raised relief-dots are used for Herakles' hair and beard, and even for the hair of his squire Iolaos.[13] In her comprehensive study of bilingual vases (i.e. black-figure and red-figure on the same pot), Cohen argued that the painter of the

[12] See Cohen 2006: 106–7.

[13] London, British Museum, B193 (1839,1109.2); *ARV*^{2} 4,8; Andokides Painter, BAPD 200008. Good photos can be found on the British Museum website: www.britishmuseum.org/collec

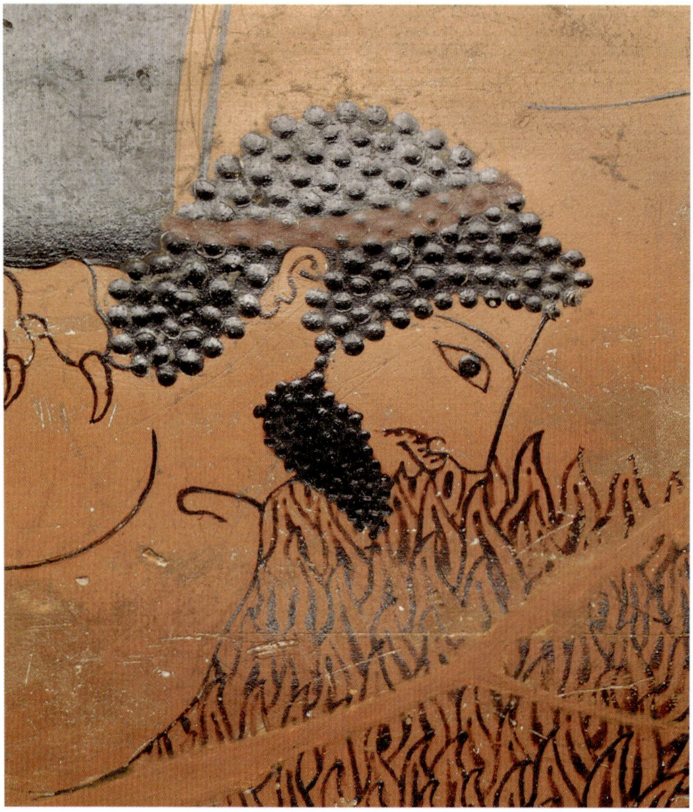

Fig. 4.2 Athenian bilingual amphora, ca. 520 BCE. Andokides Painter. London, British Museum, B193 (1839,1109.2); see *ARV*² 4,8; BAPD 200008 (© The Trustees of the British Museum).

London red-figure scene – who Beazley called the Andokides Painter, who is often credited with the invention of the red-figure technique, and who Cohen believed was responsible for the application of the added clay – did not begin his career painting vases in the older black-figure technique. She observed that the style of the Andokides Painter is especially close to that of the relief sculptures of the Siphnian Treasury, and she suggested that the Andokides Painter worked on relief sculpture, applying color, prior to taking up painting red-figure vases at Athens.[14] Athenian red-figure, in this scenario, is a translation of certain conventions of relief sculpture, such as light-colored figures against a dark ground and relief modeling into vase

tion/object/G_1839–1109-2. See also Berlin, Antikenmuseen, F2159; *ARV*² 3,1; Andokides Painter, BAPD 200001, with a good photo of the hair in Mackay 2002: pl. 55b.

[14] Cohen 1977: 111–15. For the chronological relationship between the work of the Andokides Painter and the Siphnian Treasury, see now Rotroff 2009: 255.

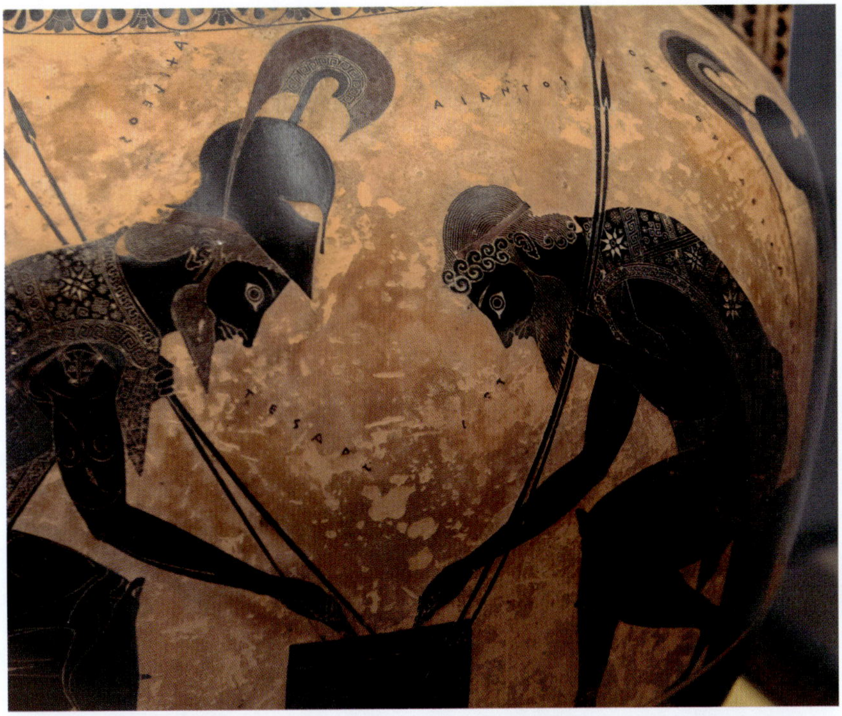

Fig. 4.3 Athenian black-figure amphora signed by Exekias, ca. 540–530 BCE. Vatican City, Museo Gregoriano Etrusco Vaticano, 344 (16757); see *ABV* 145,13; BAPD 310395 (photograph by Egisto Sani [flic.kr/p/2kfKLft]; used by permission).

painting.[15] Cohen acknowledged that added-clay relief was used for hair on an earlier black-figure vase of around 530 BCE, the well-known amphora in the Vatican Museums (Fig. 4.3), signed by Exekias as painter and potter. On the obverse, the forelocks of Ajax are rendered with black-glazed added-clay relief in the shape of spiraliform curls, the outlines of each raised curl traced with an incised line. The back-locks of the hero's hair end in incised curls with a raised clay dot in the center of each curl.[16] On the reverse of the Vatican amphora (Fig. 4.4), the long hair of Leda is represented via black-glazed raised relief.[17] Cohen discounted the significance of the comparison for the understanding of where the Andokides Painter picked up the technique of added-clay relief because the spiraliform added-clay hair of

15 Cohen 1977: 111, 2004: 61–62. Knauer (1965: 23) also considered the possibility that the added-clay relief was inspired by the Siphnian Treasury. Compare Boardman 1975: 14.

16 Vatican City, Museo Gregoriano Etrusco Vaticano, 344 (16757); *ABV* 145,13; BAPD 310395. For Ajax, see the detail in Mackay 2010: color pl. 1; see also Mackay 2002: pl. 54d.

17 For a good photo, see Mackay 2002: pl. 54e.

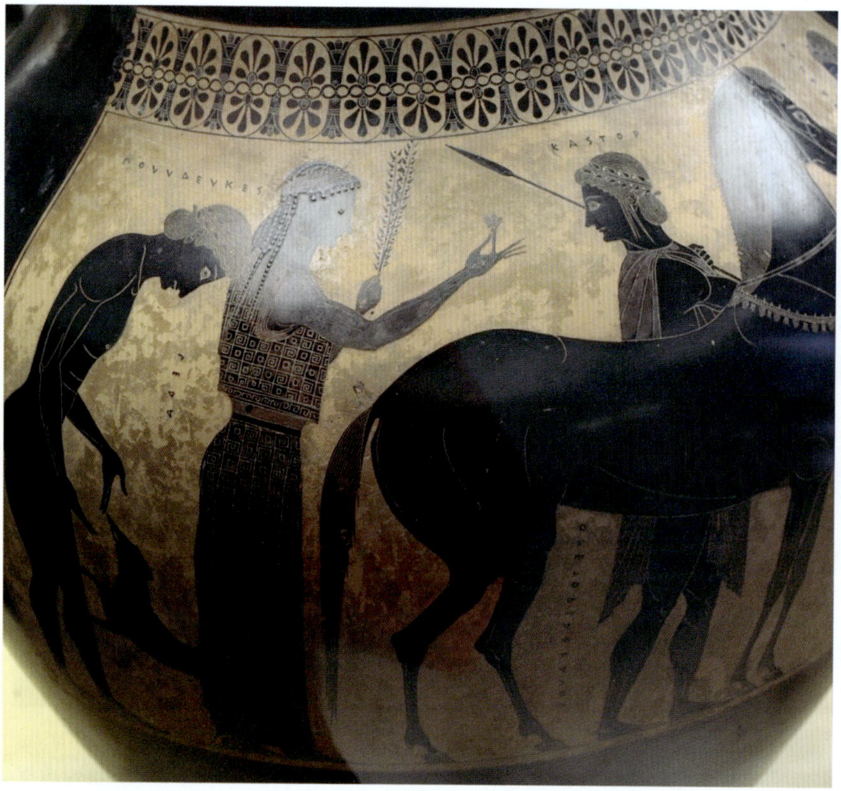

Fig. 4.4 Athenian black-figure amphora signed by Exekias, ca. 540–530 BCE. Vatican City, Museo Gregoriano Etrusco Vaticano, 344 (16757); see *ABV* 145,13; BAPD 310395 (photograph by author).

Ajax or ropy relief hair of Leda differed so significantly in form from the rounded dots of the Andokides Painter.[18]

The vase painting of Exekias, however, contains a wider range of added-clay relief techniques for the rendering of hair than just the incised relief curls of Ajax. On one side of a neck-amphora in London, two light-armed fighters have black-glazed raised, rounded clay dots for hair.[19] Those hairstyles provide an exact and precise parallel for the black-glazed relief hair of Herakles on the earliest red-figure vases (see Fig. 4.2). Moreover, on a black-figure fragment attributed to the artist called by Beazley the Lysippides Painter, the hair of Herakles, rendered in raised relief spirals with incised contours, corresponds very closely to the incised spiraliform

18 Cohen 1977: 111n20.

19 London, British Museum, B209 (1849,0518.10); *ABV* 144,8; Exekias, BAPD 310390. See Mackay 2010: 202, 211, pl. 51b.

relief forelocks of Exekias' Ajax (see Fig. 4.3).[20] The close similarities are most likely not a coincidence because the Lysippides Painter emulated the art of Exekias in many other ways.[21]

The link between the hair of Ajax and the hair of Herakles on those two black-figure vase paintings suggests an alternative genealogy for the technique of added-clay relief: Rather than entering red-figure vase painting from outside of the potters' quarter, from the field of relief sculpture via the Andokides Painter, the technique originated with the potter-painter Exekias and was learned from him by his pupil, the Lysippides Painter. The technique entered the red-figure vase painting of the Andokides Painter, in turn, in emulation of its use in the black-figure work of the Lysippides Painter, since those two artists are believed to have worked together closely to decorate several bilingual vases, if the Andokides Painter did not learn it directly from Exekias himself.[22]

Why does the origin of added-clay relief matter? The hypothesis that relief entered vase painting from an artistic medium outside the potters' quarter coincides with modern conceptions of painting and sculpture. Those two media are regularly distinguished primarily through their dimensionality, with painting being understood to be "flat," and sculpture, "in the round." From that point of view, it is harder to see how added-clay relief might have developed wholly within the practices of potting and painting vases, and how the technique served pictorial purposes.

A Pictorial Interpretation of Added-Clay Relief

Let us begin again with the amphora in the Vatican (see Fig. 4.3) and reconsider the function of added-clay relief within the work. One can advance sculptural parallels for the relief hair on this vase, as Anne Mackay has pointed out, but it is not clear what significance, if any, those sculptural parallels have. A close parallel for the relief hair of Ajax occurs on a carved stone relief in New York; for the relief hair of Leda, there is a less-than-perfect parallel on the so-called Peplos Kore. In describing the

[20] The present whereabouts of the fragment by the Lysippides Painter are unknown to me; see BAPD 4480 [unprov.], with excellent photo in Mackay 2002: pl. 55a.

[21] On this point, Boardman 1974: 105; Cohen 1977: 9–104; Robertson 1992: 10.

[22] This alternative genealogy was considered by Cohen 2006: 116n7. Perhaps needless to say, if the Lysippides Painter and Andokides Painter were the same artist, a possibility considered by Beazley and other scholars, then the derivation of added-clay relief from Exekias becomes even more likely. For the one-artist theory, see Beazley 1986: 69n2bis; Robertson 1992: 10–12; Boardman 2001: 81–2.

use of added-clay relief for hair as "*seemingly* in reminiscence of archaic sculptural effects" (my emphasis), Mackay was right to doubt the significance of the parallels between the media of vase painting and stone sculpture in this instance.[23]

First of all, the particular spiraliform style of the relief hair of Ajax is closely paralleled not only by the hair on the carved stone relief in New York but also by the hair of Ajax on another, earlier painted vase attributed to Exekias himself, the well-known vase in Boulogne depicting Ajax preparing to take his own life.[24] Like the figure of Ajax on the Vatican amphora, the hero in Boulogne has corkscrew-curls, but here they are articulated exclusively through incision and not through clay relief. Rather than an imitation of stone sculpture, the relief curls on the Vatican vase alternatively can be interpreted as imitations or translations of a two-dimensional painted Aiacian hairstyle into a three-dimensional painted relief representation of the same basic design.

The second point is that the painting of the Vatican vase does not thematize a relationship between painting and sculpture in any systematic way. It limits the use of raised relief to hair, whereas relief is used for so many other features of the body in carved stone. There is in fact a depiction of an object in raised relief on the Vatican amphora – the device on the shield of Achilles, an en face silen, shown in profile, which extends beyond the curved surface of the shield. The brushed-up forelocks, prominent brow, and snub nose of the silen are unambiguously depicted as if the shield device were rendered in raised, presumably metal relief. As a means of suggesting that it is possible to encompass the three-dimensional medium of relief within the two-dimensional medium of painting, the shield device is effective because it is unambiguously a *representation* of relief. Moreover, it is an imitation of metal relief that does not utilize added clay to achieve its goal. The comparison suggests that the relief hair of Ajax and Leda has some function besides imitation of sculptural relief.

The primary function of the relief hair on this vase is, Mackay suggests, to "catch the light with glancing reflections . . . and so momentarily attract the viewer's gaze." Ajax is endowed with such an "eye-magnet," as she called it, lest attention go exclusively to the more dominant figure of Achilles; the plain black hair of Leda, typical of female figures in black-figure, needed some visual complication to compete for attention with the

[23] New York, Metropolitan Museum of Art, 11.185; Athens, New Archaeological Museum, Acropolis 679; Boardman 1978: figs. 232 and 115, respectively. See Mackay 2010: 350.

[24] Boulogne, Musée Communale, 558; *ABV* 145,18; BAPD 310400. For the relative dating, see Mackey 2010: 359.

elaborately incised hair of the men and the horse.[25] Added-clay relief coiffures have both nonmimetic as well as mimetic functions within this vase painting. They represent the particular hairstyles of distant mythological figures. But they also provide visual contrast to the incised glaze and reserved clay all around them, thereby attracting the viewer's attention.[26]

How, more specifically, does added-clay relief achieve this effect of visual attraction? In raking light, each curl of Ajax's hair contains within itself a full range of tonalities, from the brightest gleaming white to a light-absorbing dark. As one's eye or the vase moves in relation to a source of light, the bright white and inky black move across the surface of the curls, as if the forms were alive. On this vase (see Figs. 4.3–4), black-glazed relief is not the only formal feature to facilitate light effects. The extraordinary amount of incised detail lavished on the hair and beards of many figures and on the intricately decorated capes of the Trojan War heroes also dazzles the eye in its complexity. Like relief curls, the lavish incised detail on this vase is dynamic in the sense of being chameleonlike in changing light: The play of light across solid black glaze silhouette incised with pattern results in the black flashing white and incised lines switching from light to dark in tonality.[27] But there is a difference: The light effects created by multiple rows of incision are distributed more broadly across the surface of the vase than those caused by glossy relief; by comparison, the flashes of light across the glazed relief curls of Ajax are like fireworks.

The earliest instances of added-clay relief in red-figure vase painting, considered as evidence of the reception and interpretation of the technique developed by the black-figure artist Exekias, confirm the role it played in expanding the range of visual contrasts possible for painting on vases. On the early amphora attributed to the Andokides Painter (see Fig. 4.2), the well-preserved black blobs of Herakles' hair are beautifully set off by the flame-like tufts of the lion's mane: Rows of alternating bright white and shadowy black round forms versus alternating orange and brown elongated wavy lines.[28] In the next generation, on the famous Antaios krater of Euphronios (Fig. 4.5), the contrast between the jet-black hair of Herakles, framed by glossy black raised-relief-dotted fore- and back-locks, and the

25 Mackay 2010: 350.

26 Compare the analyses of the simultaneously figurative and abstract roles played by ornament in archaic sculpture described in Dietrich 2017: 279, 2018: 169.

27 Compare Orvieto, Museo Civico, Faina 2747; *ABV* 144,10; Exekias, BAPD 310392; Mackay 2010: color pl. 2.

28 Compare Basel, Antikenmuseum und Sammlung Ludwig, BS 491; ARV^2 3,4; BAPD 200004, with good illustrations in Cohen 2006: 118–19, for another juxtaposition of clay relief and painted patterns.

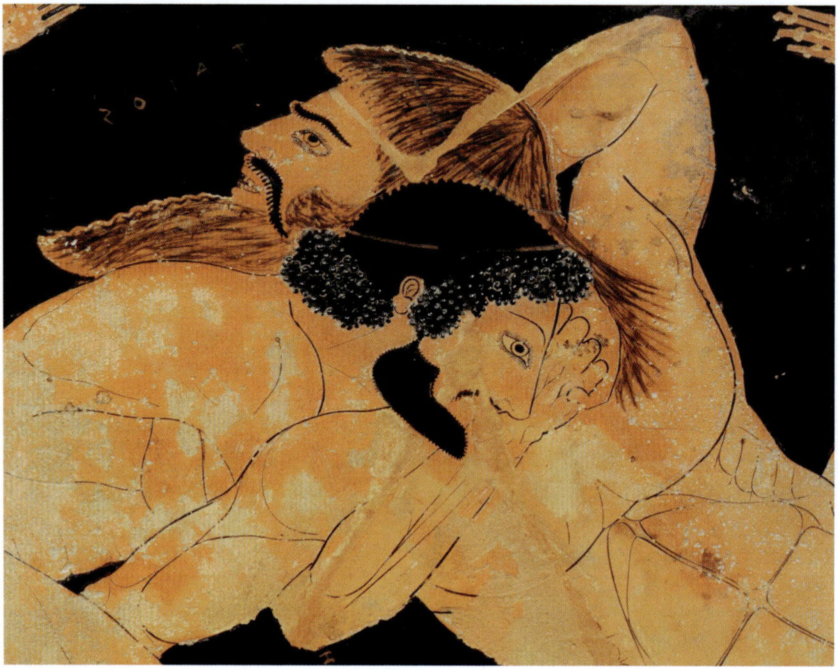

Fig. 4.5 Athenian red-figure calyx-krater signed by Euphronios, ca. 510 BCE. Paris, Musée du Louvre, G103; see *ARV*² 14,2; BAPD 200064 (Erich Lessing/Art Resource, NY).

tawny, feathery, brushy beard and hair of Antaios could hardly be more obvious or obviously intentional.[29]

On a cup from the Acropolis (Figs. 4.6–7), Euphronios has expanded the range of uses of added-clay relief: in addition to black-glazed bumps for the forelocks of Zeus, one can also see unglazed added-clay globules on the forelocks of Hera. It is widely assumed that this unglazed clay relief would have been gilded because at least three other objects depicted on this cup were of unglazed added-clay relief, and those objects – bracelets and phiale – were presumably gilded to suggest that they are metal.[30] It is notable that the objects in addition to hair that are singled out in their representation through the use of added clay and gilding, beginning with Euphronios and extending well into the fifth century, are objects made of metal. The proliferation of highly reflective, gilded relief features in vase

[29] Paris, Louvre, G103; *ARV*² 14,2; BAPD 200064. Compare Neer 2002: 46.

[30] Athens, National Archaeological Museum, Acropolis 176 (NM 15214); *ARV*² 17,18; BAPD 200081.

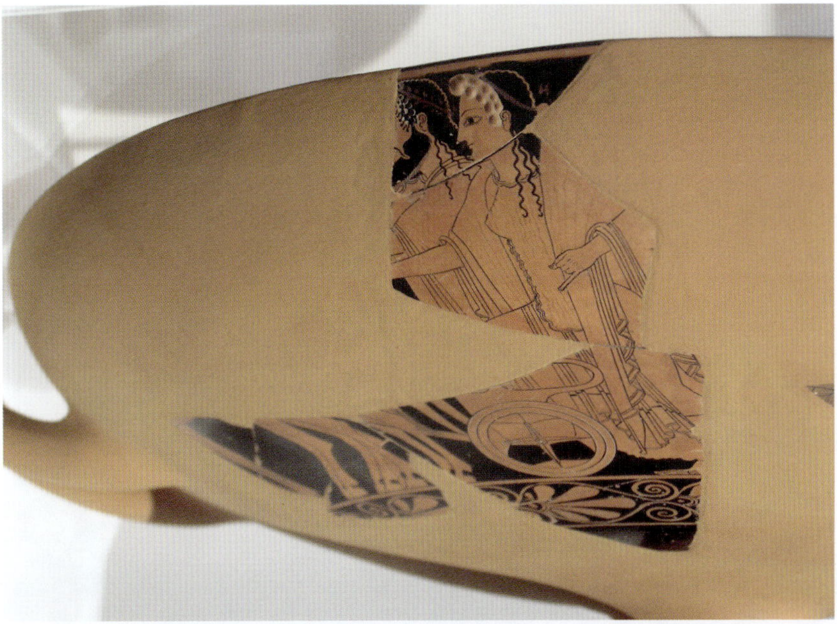

Fig. 4.6 Athenian red-figure cup probably signed by Euphronios, ca. 510 BCE. Athens, National Archaeological Museum, Acropolis 176 (NM 15214); see *ARV*[2] 17,18; BAPD 200081 (National Archaeological Museum, Athens, photograph by Irini Miari. © Hellenic Ministry of Culture/Hellenic Organization of Cultural Resources Development [H.O.C.RE.D.]).

painting suggests that light effects were perhaps the most desirable features of relief in this medium.

While gilded clay relief was often used in fifth-century BCE vase painting for mimetic representation of shiny metal objects such as a phiale, it is worth noting that on the Vatican amphora (see Figs. 4.3–4), added-clay relief is not used to depict the relief decoration on the shield of Achilles, even though that decoration was meant to be understood as metal. On this vase, black-glazed relief generates an effect similar to the light effects of metal relief but seems intended to complement the light effects created by the materials of vase painting, the black glaze, and the incision. That is what I mean when I describe my interpretation as "pictorial."

Mold-Made Relief Masks: The Intensification of the Pictorial

Let us turn to a more ambitious form of relief vase painting – relief mask kantharoi (e.g. Fig. 4.8). Here too the use of relief has been interpreted as

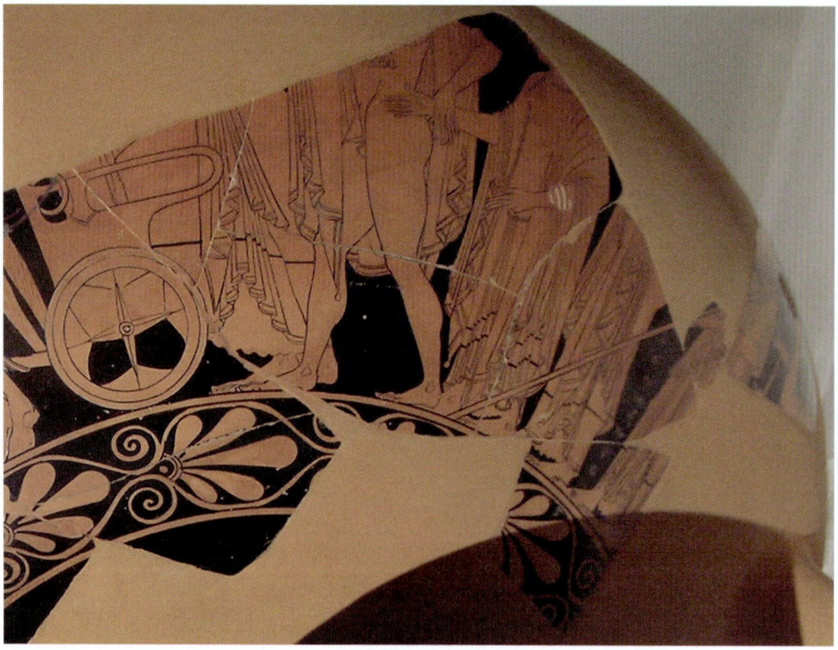

Fig. 4.7 Athenian red-figure cup probably signed by Euphronios, ca. 510 BCE. Athens, National Archaeological Museum, Acropolis 176 (NM 15214); see *ARV*[2] 17,18; BAPD 200081 (National Archaeological Museum, Athens, photograph by Irini Miari. © Hellenic Ministry of Culture/Hellenic Organization of Cultural Resources Development [H.O.C.RE.D.]).

primarily mimetic in the sense of imitative of another medium, such as metal relief or painted wood. Underappreciated is the manner in which the relief mask kantharoi engage creatively with earlier vase painting. Like Exekias' remodeling of the flat-painted representation of the curly hair of Ajax into an enhanced, three-dimensional representation (see Fig. 4.3), so too the relief mask kantharoi, I argue, are remodeling a traditional black-figure decorative scheme into three dimensions. Of particular importance for the interpretation of this innovation is the content of the original black-figure decorative scheme: It is the frontal mask of Dionysos or a satyr, two motifs in vase painting, that visually most elicit a response from the viewer. I will argue that the function of the clay masks attached to the kantharoi is to increase the intensity of that engagement of the viewer by making the masks palpably present.

Marion True attributed to the potter Euphronios a series of kantharoi with attached, mold-made masks of Dionysos or a satyr in relief. The vases unfortunately have no securely established provenance. One fairly

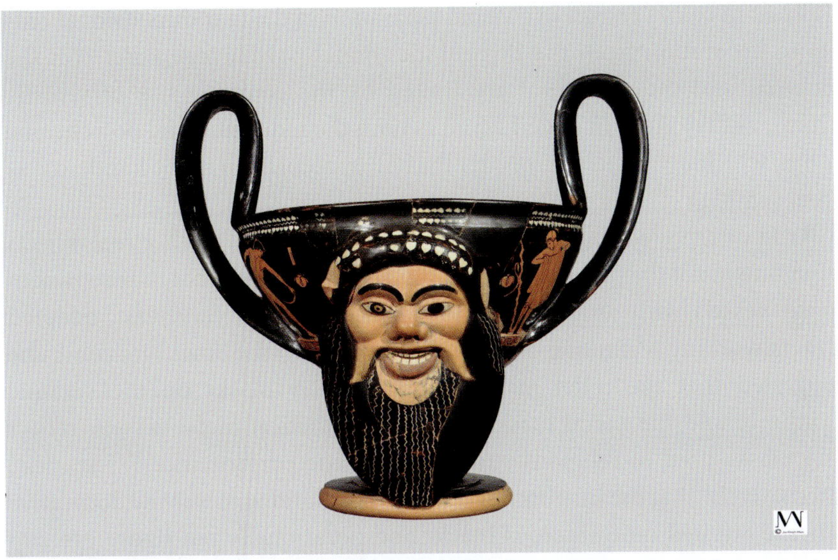

Fig. 4.8 Athenian red-figure mask kantharos attributed to the Foundry Painter, ca. 490–480 BCE. Naples, Museo Archeologico Nazionale, 248775; see BAPD 28753 [unprov.] (Ministero della Cultura – Museo Archeologico Nazionale di Napoli – photograph by Giorgio Albano).

complete example now exists in Naples (see Fig. 4.8), as well as fragments of two smaller examples and a very large one in Malibu.[31] The vases are ordinary, wheel-made kantharoi, to which have been attached, in the center of each exterior side, a bearded face of either Dionysos or a satyr in high relief. While the top of the face is attached high up on the side of the bowl, the full beard extends all the way down to the toe of the foot, to which it is affixed. Although the painted decoration to the left and right of the masks is in the red-figure technique, the relief masks themselves are colorfully decorated with several untraditional pigments: pink-orange for the faces; the lips, dark red; chins and other details, beige-orange; eyes and ivy crown, white – all colors not used within traditional red-figure decoration. The black-glazed beards are a throwback to black-figure vase painting, as they are incised with wavy lines, like the beards of Exekias (see Fig. 4.3). The

[31] Formerly Malibu, Getty Villa, 85.AE.263, now Naples, Museo Archeologico Nazionale, 248775; Foundry Painter, BAPD 28753 [unprov.]. See Cohen 2006: 274–5, which includes a side view. The more fragmentary examples include Malibu, Getty Villa, 81.AE.195.A [unprov.] and 81. AE.195.B [unprov.] (those vases do not appear to be in BAPD, although the inventory number shows up under BAPD 24385, discussed later in this chapter). For some of the issues around the lack of provenance, see Gill 2020: 58. The fullest description of all of the mask kantharoi is True 1986: 141–62.

contrast in colors results in a visual separation of the two-dimensional red-figure decoration from the three-dimensional polychrome relief. Yet the pictorial and the sculptural are united by the common use of visually prominent ivy vines in added white in both the red-figure and polychrome zones, which invites us to consider the entire decoration of the kantharos as an ensemble.

True interpreted the mask kantharoi as imitations of other real objects from outside of the potters' quarter. First, she suggested that they represent metal vessels with attached metal masks or, at the very least, adapted a metalworking technique of affixing appliques to the bowl.[32] Second, she suggested that the relief masks, both the clay masks on the ceramic kantharoi and the metal masks on the hypothetical metal vessels, reflect real masks used in religious ritual or dramatic performance.[33] I suggest, alternatively, that the inspiration for the mask kantharoi was the decorative scheme attested on numerous black- and occasionally red-figure eye-cup paintings, dating from around 530 to nearly 480 BCE (e.g. Fig. 4.9).[34] Like the kantharoi, this type of cup features a mask of Dionysos or a satyr in the center of each exterior side of the vessel, only in this case, it is a mask painted in the outline technique. Although it has been suggested that the outline-painted masks are also imitations of masks used in ritual, it is harder to sustain the hypothesis in this case. The outline technique was the subject of considerable experimentation within Athenian black-figure vase painting at the time when the mask eye cup was invented, and the motif of a painted outline mask was already familiar from earlier sixth-century vase paintings of the gorgoneion.[35] The outline-painted masks of Dionysos or silen can be understood as abstractions or translations of the frontal faces of the god or his follower that are also well attested in earlier black-figure vase painting, such as the well-known image of Dionysos en face on the François vase – abstractions in the sense of isolation of the face

[32] True 1986: 163–6.

[33] True 1986: 173–8, with further references. The use of masks of Dionysos in ritual is widely thought to be attested historically by the so-called Lenaia vases. As Peirce (1998) has argued, however, the "Lenaia" imagery is better interpreted as an artificially constructed inversion of pictorial representations of men engaging in komastic drinking, dancing, and sacrifice than as faithful representations of actual ritual. I believe that the images are best understood as depicting imaginary Dionysiac ritual set in the distant past: see Hedreen 2014. For the possible relationship of the eye cups to dramatic masks, see Ferrari 1986: 19.

[34] Oxford, Asmolean Museum, 1974.344; manner of the Lysippides Painter, BAPD 396. For a red-figure example, see Florence, Museo Archeologico Etrusco, AB1 plus 1B5; *ARV*[2] 160; AMA Group, BAPD 200056. On cups with mask between eyes, see Bell 1977; Ferrari 1986: 16–19.

[35] On the relationship between outline drawing and the invention of the red-figure technique, see Mertens 1987: 171–2; Williams 1991: 103–4.

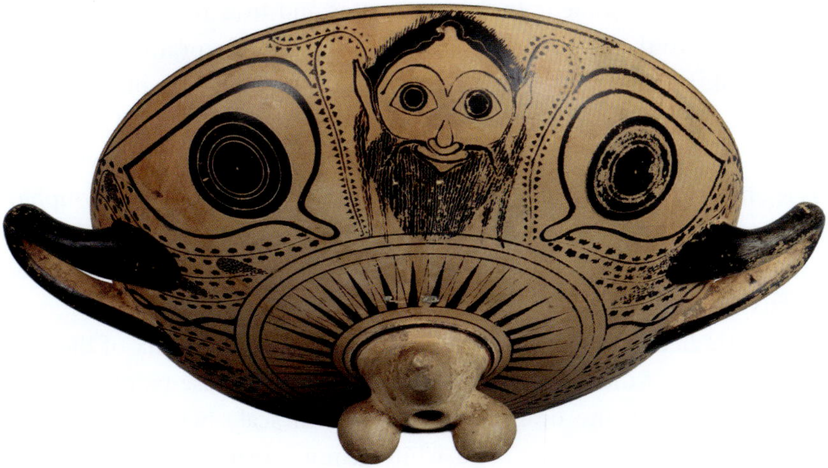

Fig. 4.9 Athenian black-figure mask eye cup attributed to the Lysippides Painter, ca. 520 BCE. Oxford, Ashmolean Museum, 1974.344; see BAPD 396 (© Ashmolean Museum).

from the rest of the body, and translations in the sense of flipping the material for the representation of the face from black glaze to reserved clay. In short, the outline-painted masks (see e.g. Fig. 4.9) do not necessarily depend on anything outside of vase painting.[36] The relief kantharoi (see Fig. 4.8) can be understood, in turn, as translations of earlier *painted* mask eye cups into hybrid painted-and-relief vessels. The kantharoi are playing with pictorial conventions.

Of particular interest in this respect are fragments of the larger and more elaborately decorated kantharos with attached, mold-made relief masks of Dionysos on each side.[37] On these relief masks, along the perimeter of the god's hair, there is one row of ivy leaves in reserve of a large ivy crown. On the body of the kantharos, the other row of ivy leaves is depicted in red-figure, which means that the leaves are also reserved. Thus, the ivy crown is only complete, or whole, when the mask is affixed to the vase. This remarkable means of unifying the two-dimensional vase painting and three-dimensional clay relief is a powerful incentive to think holistically about the component parts of the vase rather than separating them according to modern ideas of media into painting and relief. But there is more: Unlike the red-figure decoration of the smaller mask kantharoi (see e.g.

[36] That claim I have argued for in greater detail in Hedreen 2017: esp. 165.

[37] Malibu, Getty Villa, 81.AE.215; BAPD 24385 [unprov.]. For the attribution of the red-figure decoration (perhaps the Magnoncourt Painter), see Williams 2008: 169.

Fig. 4.8), which is athletic in subject matter and thus not directly related thematically to the Dionysiac masks, the red-figure decoration of the very large mask kantharos is entirely Dionysiac. On each side of the vase is a dancing silen to the left of the mask and a nymph to the right. The painted figures move or look toward the relief masks: The satyr on the reverse lifts his leg high into the air, as if stepping around the mask, and the nymph on the obverse reaches over the top of the mask to her companion. By these actions, the two-dimensional painted figures incorporate the three-dimensional relief mask into their own pictorial world.

It contradicts one's expectations of pictorial unity to think of the relief masks as part of the representational content of the vase painting on the kantharos, due to the dramatic differences in scale between mask and painted Dionysiac figures. Yet a white-ground, black-figure lekythos in Palermo, which is probably slightly earlier than the very large mask kantharos, suggests just this interpretation. On the lekythos, a large painted mask of Dionysos fills the entire height of the figure frieze. It is surrounded by two pairs of a satyr and a nymph much smaller in scale. Like their red-figure counterparts on the large mask kantharos, the black-figure satyrs and nymphs plainly engage with the mask as if it were part of their visual experience, despite the significant difference in scale.[38]

To summarize, there are considerable similarities between the large and small relief mask kantharoi (see Fig. 4.8), the outline mask eye cups (see Fig. 4.9), and the lekythos in Palermo: The lower edge of the god's beard rests on the bottom of the vase or the pictorial field; beards are black-glazed with vertical wavy incisions indicating individual hairs; the moustache extends over the beard; and the god wears a prominent ivy wreath. The similarities suggest that the potter of the relief mask kantharoi has reworked a traditional two-dimensional vase painting scheme into three dimensions. Part of the fun of the mask kantharoi would have been the recognition of an audacious act of translation of an unusual painted scheme into an even more unusual, hybrid painted/molded design.

At the same time, the two motifs translated into three dimensions by the use of clay relief – the mask of Dionysos and the mask of the satyr – engage more directly or insistently with the viewer than almost any other motif in Athenian vase painting. It is hard not to see the embodiment of the faces of

[38] Palermo, Museo Archeologico Regionale, 2023; *ABL* 206,3; Gela Painter, BAPD 11021. Williams (1991: 111) suggested that the superimposition of nymphs above the silens on this lekythos is an attempt to depict space and distance, but another vase painting suggests that the nymphs are actually dancing on the shoulders of the satyrs: Cambridge, Fitzwilliam Museum, G48 (GR 27.1864), *ABV* 259,7; manner of the Lysippides Painter, BAPD 302249.

Dionysos and the satyr in the modeling of clay as a means of intensifying the sense of presence of the god and demigod for the viewer. Here too as in the case of added-clay relief hair, the function of relief is not, or not merely, to imitate some object in the world that particularly invites relief treatment but rather to create special visual effects – and a special visual experience – for the viewer.

Added-Clay Relief and "Pictorial Space"

In her study of added-clay relief, Cohen did observe that the raised black dots for curly hair are "eye-catching foci." She offered a bold interpretation of that effect, which differs from the one I am offering here. About the black-glazed raised relief hair on the fragmentary krater signed by Euphronios and now in Cerveteri, she wrote:

> [Raised black dots] not only describe texture, but also cast real shadows before the invention of painted ones and, thereby, augment the vase-painting's two dimensional layers of suggested depth. Thus, beyond any initial associations with relief sculpture, details in added clay appear to have played a role in the avant-garde exploration of pictorial space that characterized Athenian red-figure vase painting beginning in the late sixth century.[39]

On Euphronios' cup on the Acropolis (see Figs. 4.6–7), the jewelry and metal vessels formed by gilded added-clay relief "literally embodied luxurious objects . . . before their three-dimensionality and their reflective surfaces could both be suggested entirely through paint." The familiar painted foreshortenings receding fictitiously into depth were augmented, she suggested, by the actual projection of relief features into the foreground – that is, into viewer's space.[40] This is an original and sophisticated interpretation, but it has the effect of loosening attention to the surface and materiality of the vase itself for the sake of an illusory perceptual experience of space.

The relationship between pictorial representation and the human experience of space has been explored many times in art history. In several influential texts, relief played key roles in the arguments. In the present volume focused on relief, it would be useful to consider several of the theories. One particularly influential text was Hildebrand's "Das Probleme

[39] Cohen 2004: 62. The vase discussed by Cohen is in the Museo Nazionale Cerite; BAPD 7501 [unprov.].

[40] Cohen 2004: 63.

der Form in der bildenden Kunst" (1893).[41] Hildebrand distinguished between two modes of perception, the kinesthetic and the "visual": At close range, we take in an object from multiple points of view, over a period of time, through kinesthetic movement of our eye. From far enough away, however, binocular vision effectively becomes monocular, perceptual experience becomes limited to a two-dimensional perceptual or retinal image, and any sense of an object's three-dimensional form is acquired solely "visually" from contrasts between light and dark in the two-dimensional perceptual image. Fundamental to that effect is being distant enough from an object that it begins to appear as a coherent, planar, surface image. Our imagination begins to apprehend the two-dimensional scene spatially by "advancing into depth": "All spatial relations . . . are *read off* from a single vantage point, so to speak, *from front to back*."[42] Hildebrand held that it is the function of art to make self-conscious this process by which we discern spatial form in flat perceptual images. For him, Classical Greek relief seemed to preserve the perceptual qualities of the "distant view" such as, planarity, *even close up*. This seems to have validated for him the belief that this is the way people experience the world visually; it is not just a mode of perception special to art.[43] Hildebrand might have appreciated an interpretation of added-clay relief on painted vases that saw it as a means of conveying a three-dimensional form within a two-dimensional medium. But the manner in which Athenian vases were most likely experienced corresponds much more closely to his kinesthetic mode of perception and seems poorly designed to promote the "distant view."

Cohen's phrase "exploration of pictorial space" suggests that the vase painters were engaged in a systematic attempt to create a convincing illusion of three-dimensional space within a two-dimensional medium. The primary evidence of such an interest, however, is the practice of foreshortening in late Archaic vase painting, and objects depicted in foreshortening, by themselves, are not the same thing as a coherent spatial illusion. That point was made in "Die Perspective als 'symbolische Form,'" an important 1927 study of pictorial space by Erwin Panofsky:

[41] Quotations are after the Mallgrave translation in Hildebrand 1994. Wölfflin (2013: 54, 58, 2015: 159–60) incorporated Hildebrand's findings into his understanding of sculpture and how it ought to be photographed, as well as into his influential interpretive categories of plane and recession. On Hildebrand, see also Gombrich 1961: 16–17.

[42] Hildebrand 1994: 243, emphasis in original.

[43] Podro 1982: 111: "We might be inclined to say that he had projected onto ordinary perception the problem of the representation of form in painting and relief. But this was precisely what the perceptual psychologists of the nineteenth century had already done."

> We shall speak of a fully "perspectival" view of space not when mere isolated objects, such as houses or furniture, are represented in "foreshortening," but rather only when the entire picture has been transformed . . . into a "window," and when we are meant to believe we are looking through this window into a space. The material surface upon which the individual figures or objects are drawn or painted or carved is thus negated, and instead reinterpreted as a mere "picture plane." Upon this plane is projected the spatial continuum which is seen through it and which is understood to contain all the various individual objects.[44]

It was part of Panofsky's purpose to show that ancient Greek and Roman artists did not depict objects according to a fully perspectival view of space because, in antiquity, "that feeling for space which was seeking expression in the plastic arts simply did not demand a systematic space."[45] By systematic space, Panofsky meant a spatial continuum in the sense of "infinite, unchanging and homogenous . . . in short, a purely mathematical space,"[46] which no ancient spatial theory explicitly articulated.

If the foreshortenings in vase painting cannot be understood as part of a systematic or mathematical conception of space, then to what sort of space do they relate? Riegl argued in *Spätrömische Kunst-Industrie* of 1901 – to which "Die Perspective als 'symbolische Form'" may be understood to be in part a response – that foreshortenings in ancient art articulated a kind of "cubic" space around an object: "Antiquity . . . recognizes space as an enclosed individual (cubic) shape and not yet as infinite free space."[47] Related to this claim about the phenomenology of space is a corollary, namely that in art prior to Constantine, objects are understood always in relation to the material plane of the representation.[48] The priority of planarity in art is grounded in several ideas. First, like Hildebrand, Riegl argued that the eye by itself creates not a three-dimensional form but a two-dimensional surface image in the act of perception; it is the sense of touch that assures us of the three-dimensionality of the world's objects. Second, he asserted that the earliest humans found chaotic the visual experience of the world. In response, they desired above all the isolation and clarification of individual objects. That was achieved in art by approximating the tactile experience of reality in two-dimensional representations. Such surface representation – for example, the ubiquitous low relief in Egyptian art – was

44 Panofsky 1991: 27. 45 Panofsky 1991: 43. 46 Panofsky 1991: 28–9.

47 Riegl 1985: 13. *Spätrömische Kunst-Industrie* is now supplemented by the analyses contained in the posthumously published *Historische Grammatik der bildenden Künst* (composed between 1897 and 1899). My translations are after Riegl 1985 and Riegl 2004, respectively.

48 Riegl 1985: 12.

designed to be seen close up and even touched with the fingers. Shadows were avoided because shadows suggest three-dimensionality and free space is "chaotic." In painting or relief sculpture, the gap between represented figures and objects is no less objective: "This ground is not space (not even an ideal one) such as in modern art, but tactile matter appearing as absolute plane without depth."[49]

How does "cubic" space emerge within such a resolutely antispatial conception of ancient art? There is, Riegl suggested, a contradiction built into surface or planar representation: "How can material individuality be recognized within the plane, if it does not emerge from the plane at least a little?" In relief, any emergence from the plane results in shadow, and that, in turn, provided an impetus for stylistic development within ancient art.[50] "With these shadows an element not exclusively tactile, but purely optical, which was usually suppressed by the Egyptians, now [i.e. in Greek art] found legitimate acceptance among the visual arts."[51] Shadows began to suggest the existence of "cubic space" around individual objects. That explanatory model is comparable to the notion of "thematization" in the theory of pictorial representation of Richard Wollheim – the "process by which the agent abstracts some hitherto unconsidered, hence unintentional, aspect of what he is doing . . . and makes the thought of this feature contribute to guiding his future activity."[52] Riegl might have appreciated the manner in which raised clay relief creates highlights and shadows in vase painting, and in this way creates a small amount of space around, say, the head of Herakles (see Fig. 4.2). But he would not speak of it in terms of an exploration of pictorial space in general terms, for that, he believed, was inconceivable in antiquity.

In the most recent book-length study of space in Athenian vase painting, Nikolaus Dietrich argued in favor of an even more circumscribed and limited applicability of the concept of space. The "space" of any vase painting is coterminous with the pictorial field itself. "The concept of a fictional pictorial space . . . does not apply to Attic vase-painting."[53]

49 For the argument just summarized, see Riegl 2004: 395, 401, 402–3; cf. Riegl 1985: 59.

50 Riegl 2004: 24; see also Riegl 1985: 24.

51 Riegl 1985: 62. The explanatory mechanism of internal contradiction recurs throughout Riegl's texts; see Riegl 1985: 22, 60, 2004: 411. These passages have a bearing on the interpretation of a well-known, highly problematic term within the writing of Riegl, *Kunstwollen*. See e.g. Binstock's discussion of *Kunstwollen* in Riegl 2004: 14: "The principle at stake is . . . grounded in art's evolving formal or visual elements or language . . . the art wants what it wants." There is a considerable body of writing on the meaning of this term in the works of Riegl: See also Pächt 1963: 189; Panofsky 1981; Elsner 2006.

52 Wollheim 1987: 20.

53 Dietrich 2010: 552.

Landscape elements such as rocks and trees do not constitute a virtual, pictorial space in which the depicted figures might be seen to live or act. All elements of the natural world exist on the same level as the figures, which is to say, the picture field. As he memorably put it, describing the grape and ivy vines that fill many vase paintings of Dionysos and his followers, "you have to image the branches as creepers growing on the vase wall."[54] From that point of view, the added-clay relief hair or metallic vessels depicted in Athenian vase painting cannot be understood as contributing to the creation of an illusion of pictorial space or depth because such an illusion was outside of the conceptual possibilities for vase painting.

Before leaving behind the question of how represented figures and viewers relate spatially, let us consider briefly the relief mask kantharoi (see Fig. 4.8). One of the ways in which those vases seem to heighten the feeling of presence of the faces of Dionysos and the satyr is by extending them in a very literal way further into the space of the viewer. They are physically closer, more palpable, more full-bodied than their prototypical outline-painted masks (see Fig. 4.9). Of course, the ceramic god and demigod cannot literally see us or interact with us.[55] But thanks to the use of relief, it feels even more like they can.

Conclusions

Relief features in vase painting have received relatively little attention in scholarship. That is due perhaps to presumptions about what is and what is not proper to painting. Exekias is admired as a painter for the nobility of his figures, the originality of his pictorial narrative technique, the elegance of his compositions, and the precision of his linear detail. Adding clay relief to the surfaces of his paintings is not usually numbered among his achievements. When relief features of vase painting become a subject of scholarship, it is the origin or inspiration for the development of the technique that is of interest. Perhaps because scholarly writing on vase painting for a long time focused more attention on the point of view of the artist than on that of the viewer, the striking visual effects of relief on vases has received much less attention. I have argued that relief generates or affords two effects: first, black-glazed or gilded added clay (see Figs. 4.2–7) generates variegated reflections, or sparks, of light

[54] Dietrich 2010: esp. 97, 220 (quotation).

[55] On this point, see Wollheim 1987: 102, and chap. 3 generally.

whenever the vase moves in relation to the viewer and a source of illumination. In this respect, glazed or gilded added clay creates light effects similar to those generated by relief line (see Fig. 4.1). Second, mold-made clay masks attached to kantharoi (see Fig. 4.8) made it possible to intensify the sense of presence of the already "in your face" painted masks of Dionysos or a satyr on eye cups (see Fig. 4.9) and other vases. Both effects are well attested as something of value in Greek culture generally. In early Greek literature are numerous descriptions of the visual effects of objects of art and other technologies. In those passages, reflections of light and the relationship between reflectivity and movement are prominent. The passages bring together three things: Certain materials have the ability to reflect the light, those reflections only occur when the objects are in motion, and the effect of the reflections on a beholder is wonder. The passages have been well analyzed by Richard Neer and Jasper Gaunt.[56] Turning to the sense of palpable presence of Dionysos and the satyr, it hardly needs to be said that making the god and his henchmen present at Athens was a goal of many ritual practices, one of which was, of course, the wearing of masks of the satyrs and occasionally even the god in dramatic performances.[57] There is more to be said about precisely what sort of experience is offered by the relief mask kantharoi. Has Dionysus or his satyr entered the space of the symposium? Or does the vase invite the symposiast to see himself or his friends as satyrs or even the god?[58] In either case, relief is utilized here to intensify the presence of the painted figure.

References

Artal-Isbrand, P., and Klausmeyer, P. (2013). "Evaluation of the Relief Line and the Contour Line on Greek Red-Figure Vases Using Reflectance Transformation Imaging and Three-Dimensional Laser Scanning Confocal Microscopy." *Studies in Conservation* 58.4: 338–59.

Beazley, J. D. (1961). "An Amphora by the Berlin Painter." *Antike Kunst* 4.2: 49–67.

(1986). *The Development of Attic Black-Figure*. Ed. D. von Bothmer and M. B. Moore. Berkeley: University of California Press.

[56] Neer 2010: 73–88; Gaunt 2014: esp. 353.

[57] This is a large topic, with an extensive bibliography. See Hedreen 1992; Easterling 1997; Hedreen 2007, with further references.

[58] See Hedreen 2017.

Bell, E. E. (1977). "Two Krokotos Mask Cups at San Simeon." *California Studies in Classical Antiquity* 10: 1–15.
Bielfeldt, R. (2014). "The Lure and Lore of Light: Roman Lamps in the Harvard Art Museums." In S. Ebbinghaus, ed., *Ancient Bronzes through a Modern Lens: Introductory Essays on the Study of Ancient Mediterranean and Near Eastern Bronzes*. Cambridge, MA: Harvard Art Museums, 171–91.
Boardman, J. (1974). *Athenian Black Figure Vases*. London: Thames and Hudson.
(1975). *Athenian Red Figure Vases: The Archaic Period*. London: Thames and Hudson.
(1978). *Greek Sculpture: The Archaic Period*. London: Thames and Hudson.
(2001). *The History of Greek Vases: Potters, Painters and Pictures*. London: Thames and Hudson.
Chaviara, A., and Aloupi-Siotis, E. (2015). "The Story of a Soil That Became a Glaze: Chemical and Microscopic Fingerprints on the Attic Vases." *Journal of Archaeological Sciences: Reports* 7: 510–18.
Cohen, B. (1977). "Attic Bilingual Vases and Their Painters." PhD dissertation, New York University.
(2004). "Bubbles = Baubles, Bangles and Beads: Added Clay in Athenian Vase Painting and Its Significance." In C. Marconi, ed., *Greek Vases: Images, Contexts and Controversies. Proceedings of the Conference Sponsored by the Center for the Ancient Mediterranean at Columbia University, 23–24 March 2002*. Leiden: Brill, 57–71.
(2006). *The Colors of Clay: Special Techniques in Athenian Vases*. Los Angeles, CA: J. Paul Getty Museum.
Dietrich, N. (2010). *Figur ohne Raum? Bäume und Felsen in der Attischen Vasenmalerei des 6. und 5. Jahrhunderts V. Chr.* Berlin: De Gruyter.
(2017). "Framing Archaic Greek Sculpture: Figure, Ornament and Script." In V. Platt and M. Squire, eds., *The Frame in Classical Art: A Cultural History*. Cambridge: Cambridge University Press, 270–316.
(2018). "Order and Contingency in Archaic Greek Ornament and Figure." In N. Dietrich and M. Squire, eds., *Ornament and Figure in Graeco-Roman Art: Rethinking Visual Ontologies in Classical Antiquity*. Berlin: De Gruyter, 167–201.
Easterling, P. E. (1997). "A Show for Dionysus." In P. E Easterling, ed., *The Cambridge Companion to Greek Tragedy*. Cambridge: Cambridge University Press, 36–53.
Elsner, J. (2006). "From Empirical Evidence to the Big Picture: Some Reflections on Riegl's Concept of *Kunstwollen*." *Critical Inquiry* 32.4: 741–66.
Ferrari, G. (1986). "Eye-Cup." *Revue Archeologique*, n.s., vol. 1: 5–20.
Gaunt, J. (2014). "Story and Status: The François Vase and the Krater from Vix." In A. Avramidou and D. Demetriou, eds., *Approaching the Ancient Artifact: Representation, Narrative, and Function*. Berlin: De Gruyter, 349–61.

Gill, D. W. J. (2020). "Context Matters: The Fragmentary Gifts of Werner Nussberger." *Journal of Art Crime* 24: 57–60.

Gombrich, E. (1961). *Art and Illusion: A Study in the Psychology of Pictorial Representation*. 2nd ed. New York: Pantheon.

Greenberg, C. (1995). "Modernist Painting." In J. O'Brian, ed., *Clement Greenberg: The Collected Essays and Criticism*, vol. 4, *Modernism with a Vengeance, 1957–1969*. Chicago, IL: University of Chicago Press, 85–93.

Hedreen, G. (1992). *Silens in Attic Black-Figure Vase-Painting: Myth and Performance*. Ann Arbor: University of Michigan Press.

(2007). "Myths of Ritual in Athenian Vase-Paintings of Silens." In E. Csapo and M. C. Miller, eds., *The Origins of Theatre in Ancient Greece and Beyond: From Ritual to Drama*. Cambridge: Cambridge University Press, 150–95.

(2014). "The Artificial Sculptural Image of Dionysos in Athenian Vase Painting and the Mythological Discourse of Early Greek Life." In A. Avramidou and D. Demetriou, eds., *Approaching the Ancient Artifact: Representation, Narrative, and Function*. Berlin: De Gruyter, 267–80.

(2017). "Unframing the Representation: The Frontal Face in Athenian Vase-Painting." In V. Platt and M. Squire, eds., *The Frame in Classical Art: A Cultural History*. Cambridge: Cambridge University Press, 154–87.

(2022). "Relief Line in Athenian Red-Figure Vase-Painting: Reflectivity and Light-Effects." In R. Morais, R. M. Sobral Centeno, and D. Ferreia, eds., *Myths, Gods and Heroes: Greek Vases in Portugal*. Porto: Santa Maria da Feira, 242–52.

Hildebrand, A. (1994). "The Problem of Form in the Fine Arts." In H. F. Mallgrave and E. Ikonomou, trans., *Empathy, Form, and Space: Problems in German Aesthetics*. Santa Monica, CA: Getty Center for the History of Art and the Humanities, 227–79.

Knauer, E. R. (1965). *Die Berliner Andokides-Vase*. Stuttgart: Reclam.

Lagogianni-Georgakarakos, M., ed. (2018). *The Countless Aspects of Beauty in Ancient Art*. Athens: National Archaeological Museum.

Mackay, E. A. (2002). "The Hairstyle of Herakles." In A. J. Clark and J. Gaunt, eds., *Essays in Honor of Dietrich von Bothmer*. Amsterdam: Allard Pierson Series, 203–10.

(2010). *Tradition and Originality: A Study of Exekias*. BAR International Series 2092. Oxford: Archaeopress.

Marconi, C. (2017). "The Frames of Greek Painted Pottery." In V. Platt and M. Squire, eds., *The Frame in Classical Art: A Cultural History*. Cambridge: Cambridge University Press, 117–53.

Mertens, J. R. (1987). "The Amasis Painter: Artist and Tradition." In *Papers on the Amasis Painter and His World*. Malibu, CA: J. Paul Getty Museum, 168–83.

Neer, R. T. (2002). *Style and Politics in Athenian Vase-Painting: The Craft of Democracy, ca. 530–460 B.C.E.* Cambridge: Cambridge University Press.

(2010). *The Emergence of the Classical Style in Greek Sculpture*. Chicago, IL: University of Chicago Press.

Noble, J. V. (1960). "The Technique of Attic Vase-Painting." *American Journal of Archaeology* 64.4: 307–18.

(1965). *The Techniques of Painted Attic Pottery*. New York: Metropolitan Museum of Art.

Pächt, O. (1963). "Art Historians and Art Critics – VI: Alois Riegl." *Burlington Magazine* 722: 188–93.

Panofsky, E. (1981). "The Concept of Artistic Volition." Trans. K. J. Northcott and J. Snyder. *Critical Inquiry* 8.1: 17–33.

(1991). *Perspective as Symbolic Form*. Trans. C. Wood. New York: Zone.

Peirce, S. (1998). "Visual Language and Concepts of Cult on the 'Lenaia Vases.'" *Classical Antiquity* 17.1: 59–95.

Podro, M. (1982). *The Critical Historians of Art*. New Haven, CT: Yale University Press.

Riegl, A. (1985). *Late Roman Art Industry*. Trans. R. Winkes. Rome: Bretschneider.

(2004). *Historical Grammar of the Visual Arts*. Trans. J. E. Jung. New York: Zone.

Robertson, M. (1992). *The Art of Vase-Painting in Classical Athens*. Cambridge: Cambridge University Press.

Rotroff, S. I. (2009). "Early Red-Figure in Context." In J. H. Oakley and O. Palagia, eds., *Athenian Potters and Painters*, vol. 2. Oxford: Oxbow, 250–60.

Seiterle, G. (1976). "Die Zeichentechnik in der rotfigurigen Vasenmalerei: Die Rätsel der Relieflinien." *Antike Welt* 7.2: 2–10.

True, M. (1986). "Pre-Sotadean Red-Figure Statuette Vases and Related Vases with Relief Decoration." PhD dissertation, Harvard University.

von Bothmer, D. (1966). "Andokides the Potter and Andokides the Painter." *Metropolitan Museum of Art Bulletin* 24: 201–12.

Williams, D. (1991). "The Invention of the Red-Figure Technique and the Race between Vase-Painting and Free Painting." In T. Rasmussen and N. Spivey, eds., *Looking at Greek Vases*. Cambridge: Cambridge University Press, 103–18.

(2008). "Some Thoughts on the Potters and Painters of Plastic Vases before Sotades." In K. Lapatin, ed., *Papers on Special Techniques in Athenian Vases*. Los Angeles, CA: J. Paul Getty Museum, 161–72.

Wölfflin, H. (2013). "How One Should Photograph Sculpture." Trans. G. A. Johnson. *Art History* 36.1: 52–71.

(2015). *Principles of Art History: The Problem of the Development of Style in Early Modern Art*. Trans. J. Blower. Los Angeles, CA: Getty Research Institute.

Wollheim, R. (1987). *Painting as an Art*. Princeton, NJ: Princeton University Press.

5 | Sculpture, Relief, and the Surrounding Space

Sculpture *versus* Relief, Sculpture *as* Relief

NIKOLAUS DIETRICH

Most people would characterize sculpture in the round as an artistic medium distinct from painting or relief by virtue of its three-dimensionality. We base our scholarly discourse concerning Greek sculpture, however, mostly on material illustrations of statues that are two-dimensional – namely photographs – rather than on the direct experience of the three-dimensional statues themselves. By its photographic reproduction, sculpture becomes assimilated to the medium of relief, standing in between two-dimensionality and three-dimensionality. In this chapter, I shall analyze what might be called the relief bias inherent in the photographic depiction of sculpture. At the same time, I would like to show how this relief bias reaches further back in the history of modern engagement with Greek sculpture – namely to a neoclassical vision of sculpture – and, finally, I will suggest that such a relief bias may be justified in some cases.

Seeing Sculpture through the Photographic Lens

Looking at sculpture through the two-dimensional medium of photography seems to be an awkward thing to do, especially if three-dimensionality counts as sculpture's defining characteristic. We may nevertheless justify this scholarly practice by taking photography as a merely auxiliary means of illustration, which is needed in those cases where autopsy of the statue itself may not be possible. In this way, the direct experience of sculpture through autopsy keeps its place of honor as the most valid way of viewing sculpture. As a matter of fact, phrases such as "only autopsy will allow us to make a judgment on this question" are often heard among scholars of Greek sculpture, which testifies to the need felt by archaeologists to emphasize, within their methodologies, the importance of direct engagement with the materiality of their objects of interest, even though autopsy tends to play a rather infrequent role in everyday scholarly practice.[1] Instead of openly

[1] The high valuation of autopsy within the production of knowledge on ancient art reaches far back in the modern era. See Oy-Marra 2020, with further references in n. 52.

admitting this basic fact, classical archaeology over the past century has generally preferred to downplay the heuristic weight of photography.[2] But we do find positive statements on the uses of photography, especially in the decades around 1900, when photography still had to assert itself against older media of illustration, such as etchings or drawings. These positive statements generally emphasize rather technical aspects, such as the accuracy of detail achieved by photography.[3] The argument commonly goes like this: Although autopsy is always to be preferred, with photography we still lose less information than with any other medium of illustration. Or even more simply: Photography is a deficient medium of illustration, but it is the lesser of two evils.

We do not find much in the way of a straightforward, positive evaluation of the uses of photography within notoriously conservative German classical archaeology of the earlier part of the twentieth century. But we need not wait for the self-reflexive engagement with photography of present-day scholarship, either. Rather, the modernist theoretician Walter Benjamin already gives such a straightforward positive evaluation in his short history of photography published in 1931.[4] There, he claims that looking at art as photography is a much more promising endeavor than the seemingly avant-garde habit of looking at photography as an art. This claim might seem provocative and was probably intended to be so. But, in fact, Benjamin is only describing a practice that had already been well established in German

[2] While the use of photographs in daily scholarly practice in one's own time has rarely been commented in the past century, there is a large bibliography on early photography in archaeology. See in general e.g. Schubert and Grunauer-von Hoerschelmann 1978; Gimon 1980; Collet 1996; Shanks 1997; Lindner 1999; Brinkmann 2001; Alexandridis and Heilmeyer 2004; Hübner 2004; Lyons and Papadopoulos 2005; Klamm 2007, 2010, 2017a; Kopf 2007; Marcoci 2010: 41; Bohrer 2011a, 2011b: 36–41; Dally 2017; Filser 2017, 2018; Hamill and Luke 2017; Bärnighausen et al. 2020. Scholarly interest was especially focused on early topographical archaeology. When it comes to the photography of objects, ancient sculpture is the prime topic of interest. The notable rise in the number of publications from the past two decades has coincided with the spread of digital pictorial media. Arguably, this new reshaping of the medial foundation of our disciplines, as well as its still unclear trajectory, makes it all the more attractive to look at the past medial revolution of photography, whose future we do know.

[3] The enthusiastic appraisal of photography given by Adolf Michaelis in his monograph on the achievements of nineteenth-century archaeology is an excellent illustration of this point. He does not write about any intrinsic artistic value of photography but about its objectivity and wealth of detail: Michaelis 1906: 258–9. See on this the remarks in Dally 2017: 4–6. Similar aspects of photography are highlighted by another keen proponent of this technique of reproduction in archaeology: Adolf Furtwängler (1893). See Dally 2017: 42–7. On the early debates on the value of photography as compared to traditional media of illustration, see Kopf 2007: 154–5.

[4] Benjamin 1977: 381. Benjamin 2015 provides English translations of his texts on photography. As far as my limited knowledge allows, Benjamin's short remarks on art as photography does not seem to play any significant role in the very large scholarly literature on his theory of photography. Emerling 2012: 44–5 touches upon this point, but rather allusively.

academia – namely the widespread use of photographic reproductions in art-historical research.

In institutes of classical archaeology across Germany, the funds that would formerly have been spent on the enlargement of a study collection of originals and plaster casts were in Benjamin's day invested more and more in the construction of large photographic collections.[5] In the study of Greek sculpture and especially the practice of *Kopienkritik*, or copy-criticism, the systematic documentation of statues through photographs was key.[6] Only photographic reproductions of sculpture in a more or less standardized form would allow scholars to trace out minute similarities and differences in individual motifs across a body of sculptures, and thus to attempt to reconstruct the Greek models that the practitioners of *Kopienkritik* believed lay behind every series of typologically related Roman statues. The specific requirements of specialized sculpture research, *Skulpturforschung*, may have been one reason why photography had its breakthrough with ancient sculpture at a considerably earlier time than with vase painting, in which the traditional medium of drawing had a much longer life in twentieth-century scholarship.[7] The founding book of *Kopienkritik*, Adolf Furtwängler's *Meisterwerke der griechischen Plastik* published in 1893, counted among the early examples of an archaeological publication to privilege photography over the traditional media of illustration – etching or drawing – while John D. Beazley still made extensive use of drawings for his attributions in the middle of the twentieth century.

Whether or not we agree with Benjamin's claim that looking through the photographic lens benefits our understanding of sculpture, there can be no doubt that this is essentially what scholars of Greek sculpture have done for

[5] For the institute at Heidelberg (founded in 1866), the bulk of its large collection of plaster casts and originals was acquired in the decades around 1900. From the 1920s onward, the limited financial resources of the university were concentrated on the enlargement of the library and the photo collection instead. For a minute history of the institute and its changing acquisition policies, see Zenzen 2016 (esp. 73, with specific reference to the funds allocated to photographs and books in 1927). The Winckelmann-Institute at Berlin shows a similar pattern. Its megalomaniac plaster cast collection (which occupies major parts of the university's main building [Unter den Linden 6] before World War II; see Stürmer and von Wrede 1998) ceased to be a financial priority rather soon after its inauguration as a museum in 1921, when funds were allocated to the enlargement of the photographic collection instead (Stürmer and von Wrede 1998: 31).

[6] On the use of photography in combination with plaster casts as the first systematic attempt to gain secure knowledge of Greek sculpture through *Kopienkritik* – namely Furtwängler's *Meisterwerke der griechischen Plastik* from 1893 – see Klamm 2010: 54–60, 2017a: 347–55; Dally 2017: 43–7.

[7] See Dietrich 2023. On drawing in engagement with Greek vases, see most recently Meyer and Petsalis-Diomidis 2023.

more than a century of modern scholarship. Our vision of Greek sculpture is basically a photographic one, and only occasionally is this photographic vision supplemented by autopsy of single statues or their plaster casts. Many classical archaeologists would like to put it the other way round, by saying that photography supplements autopsy as the only valid experience of sculpture. But this is clearly a fiction. Indeed, when imagining the famous bronze statue of Zeus from the Artemision, our mental image of this statue is much more likely to resemble the standard photographic view, as we find it in textbooks on Greek sculpture (Fig. 5.1), than it is the actual experience of the statue in the National Archaeological Museum in Athens.[8] A profile view of this statue is generally thought to provide the best and most complete account of its main formal characteristics – that is, to best represent the three-dimensional statue within the two dimensions of photography. In this case, it seems difficult to deny that photography brings sculpture closer to the medium of relief. In this view, all the elements of the plastic body appear to lie in the same flat pictorial plane, just as the sculpted bodies of a marble relief necessarily all lie within the thickness of the marble slab out of which the relief is carved. And the parallel between such a photographic vision of sculpture and relief may be even more finely attuned, since not only do all body parts of the Artemision Zeus lie in the same plane, but the god's direction of movement and his gaze also remain within that plane. If we were to imagine an enemy against whom Zeus launches his thunderbolt, that figure would perforce also lie in this same plane.

The directions of action and gazes do not always remain within the relief plane, of course. In early Renaissance reliefs from Florence, for example, we find more or less the same perspectival construction of space, which had newly developed in painting and which was neatly transposed to the medium of relief, as is famously showcased by the relief panels of the pulpits in San Lorenzo by Donatello (Fig. 5.2). Here, only the physical relief remains within a flat plane, while the pictorial space in which the action takes place transcends the dimensions of the relief plane. There is thus no commensurability between the physical space of the relief plane and the pictorial space of the depiction. Archaic and Classical Greek relief sculpture, however, typically retains this commensurability, allowing the figures on the relief to act basically within the same relief plane out of which they had been physically carved. This holds true at least until the Hellenistic period, when the oblique orientations of bodies and

[8] Athens, National Archaeological Museum, Br. 15161, ca. 470–460 BCE. The photograph given of this statue in Peter C. Bol's (2004: fig. 20d) large handbook of ancient sculpture would be an example of such a standard profile view. On the statue, see recently e.g. Neer 2010: 86–8; Dietrich 2018: 79–81, with further bibliography in n. 68.

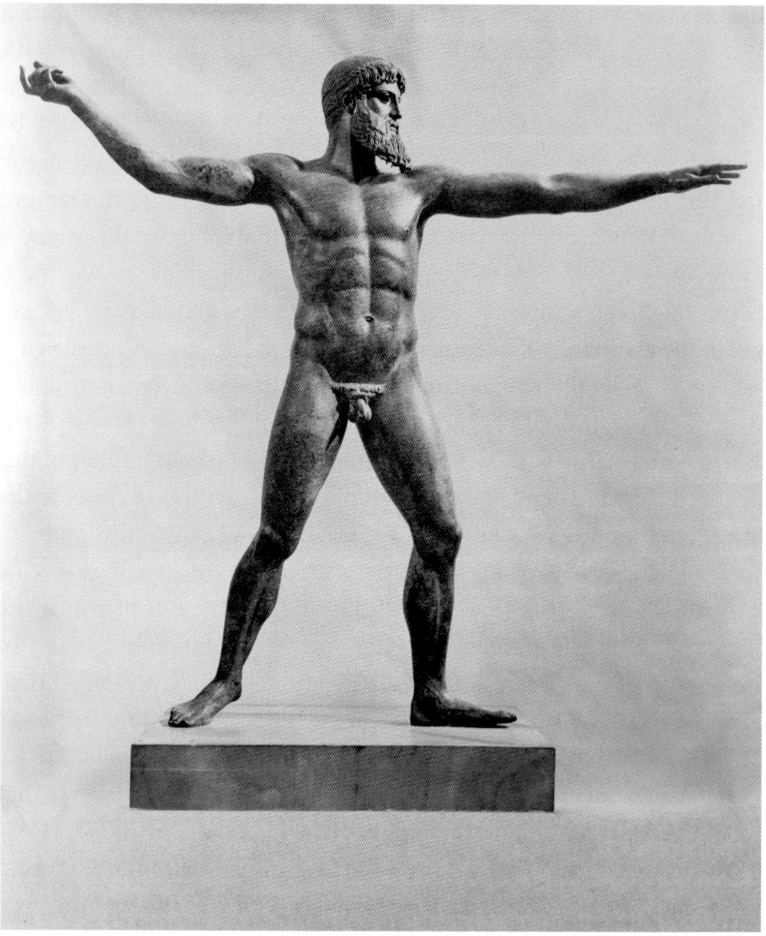

Fig. 5.1 Artemision Zeus, ca. 460 BCE, in a relief-like photographic profile view. Athens, National Archaeological Museum, Metalwork Collection, X 15161 (Deutsches Archäologisches Institut Rom, photograph D-DAI-ROM 55.75 R. © Hellenic Ministry of Culture/Hellenic Organization of Cultural Resources Development [H.O.C.RE.D.]).

directions of movements and gazes that break the frame of their relief plane all become important components of relief carving.[9]

The correspondence between the relief's material frame as physically defined by the thickness of the carved marble slab and the conformity of

[9] The gigantomachy frieze of the Great Altar of Zeus at Pergamon is the most obvious example here (for a full visual documentation of the frieze, see Winnefeld 1910; a recent compelling discussion is e.g. Lorenz 2013). However, late fourth-century BCE Attic grave reliefs already occasionally show figures in dramatic action, in such a way as to break the frame of the aedicula (see e.g. the grave relief of Aristonautes: Athens, National Archaeological Museum, 738; Kaltsas 2002: 204, fig. 410).

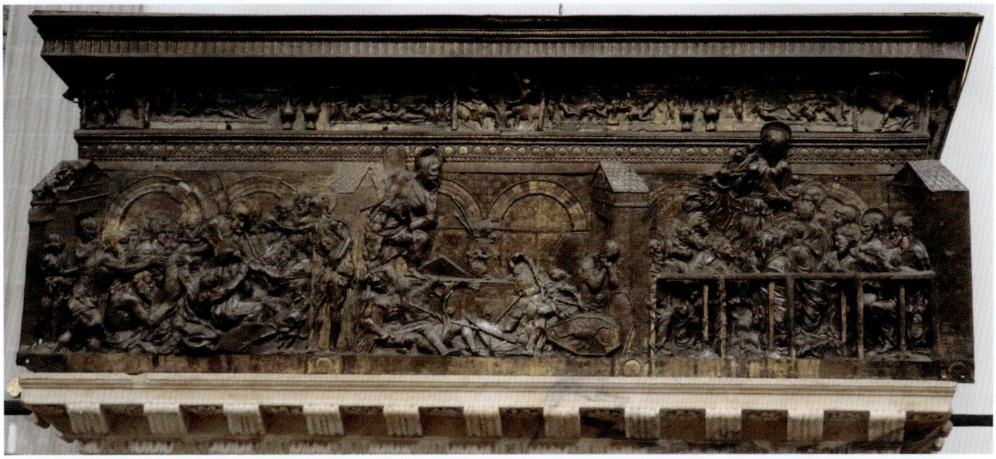

Fig. 5.2 Relief panel with scenes of the life of Christ from the pulpits of San Lorenzo (Florence) by Donatello, 1460–5 (photograph by Henk Bekker [Flickr], CC BY-NC-SA 2.0, changed by author).

the relief's pictorial space to the same relief plane, however, is followed consistently in Archaic and early Classical relief sculpture. This can be showcased by the north frieze of the Siphnian Treasury at Delphi.[10] On the gigantomachy section shown in Fig. 5.3, whatever the individual figures may do – engage in direct combat with an enemy, shoot arrows, run away – they do without ever extending beyond the relief plane. Individual body parts, such as the chest, often appear frontally, but all movements and gazes are oriented to the sides, keeping within the relief plane. We do find several frontal faces – and thereby frontal gazes – in this late Archaic gigantomachy. But they all concern particular figures or situations for which a frontal posture is acceptable by way of exception, and just as on contemporary Attic vases, frontal faces are given to wild animals, such as felines or gorgons, or to figures on the verge of death.[11]

However, the tourist who seeks to record his or her real experience of the Artemision Zeus in the museum by taking a picture might well adopt a perspective on the statue that is very different from the relief-like profile view which is preferred by scholars of Greek art. Specifically, they might choose a more frontal angle, in which the god's aggression is

[10] On the friezes of the Siphnian Treasury, see e.g. Brinkmann 1994 (with good illustrations). Recent discussions include Neer 2001; Dietrich, Fouquet, and Reinhardt 2020: 171–3.

[11] On the intrinsic logic of frontality in Archaic and early Classical vase painting, see Frontisi-Ducroux 1995: esp. 77–80. See also Korshak 1987.

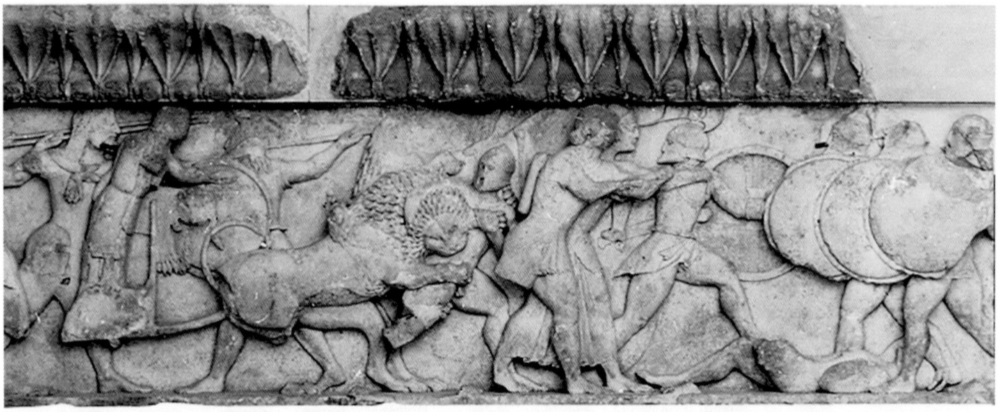

Fig. 5.3 Portion of the north frieze of the Siphnian Treasury at Delphi, 525 BCE, with a gigantomachy (Photograph by École française d'Athènes [G. Réveillac]. © Hellenic Ministry of Culture/Hellenic Organization of Cultural Resources Development [H.O.C.RE.D.]).

oriented toward the viewer and not toward some invisible enemy within a notional picture plane. As a matter of fact, although the profile view in which the figures act within a virtual pictorial plane dominates illustrations of the Artemision Zeus in academic publications, it is nevertheless the frontal view (Fig. 5.4) that occurs most frequently on the largest platform for the nonspecialist: Google Images. In such frontal photographic views, the Artemision Zeus loses all resemblance to a relief. It is hence not photography as such but a certain manner of photographing sculpture that transforms sculpture into relief. This manner tends to objectivize the statue and reduce the illusion of the figure's action on its surrounding real space – and with it the figure's agency as an interlocutor with the viewer. Such an act of objectification furthers a certain kind of research agenda, and, therefore, it is no wonder that *Skulpturforschung* favors the profile view on the Artemision Zeus, while the tourist who seeks a lively experience of this statue would mostly favor the frontal view.[12]

[12] The differences that I pointed out here between photographs of Artemision Zeus found in scholarly literature and nonspecialists' photographs of the same statue bear many points of contact (albeit with different evaluations!) with the remarks made already in the late nineteenth century by Heinrich Wölfflin in his normative claims about adequate sculpture photography. See Billeter 1997: 409–17, esp. 409 (reprint of the short articles Wölfflin 1896, 1897, and 1914, all published in the *Zeitschrift für bildende Kunst*; for an English translation by Geraldine A. Johnson, see Wölfflin 2013). Koortbojian 2023, 117–130 ("fronts and sides"), dealing the frontal vs. the profile view of late Archaic and early Classical statues (including the Artemision Zeus: fig. 3.33–3.34), is directly relevant to the above discussion. Unfortunately, it appeared too late to be properly taken into account.

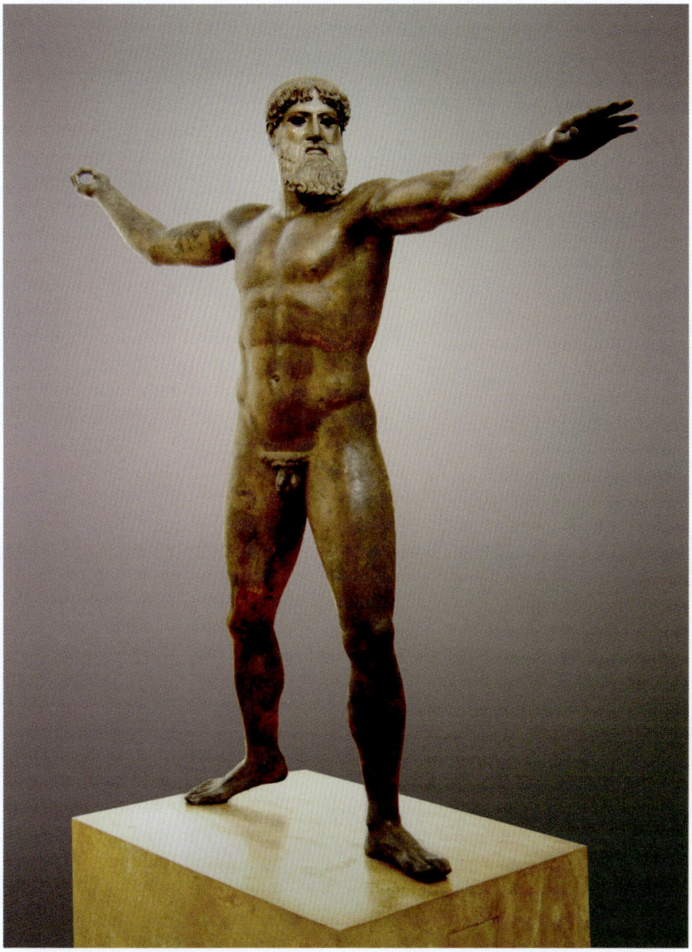

Fig. 5.4 Artemision Zeus, ca. 460 BCE, in a frontal photographic view. Athens, National Archaeological Museum, Metalwork Collection, X 15161. © CC BY-SA 3.0; photograph by Ricardo André Frantz (Wikipedia). © Hellenic Ministry of Culture/ Hellenic Organization of Cultural Resources Development [H.O.C.RE.D.].

Viewing Sculpture before the Age of Photography

Early modern engravings of sculpture, when compared to modern scholarly photographs, often make very different choices concerning their perspectives onto – and the mise-en-scène of – the statue. Even a rapid survey of Renaissance and Baroque engravings of antique statues makes clear that oblique views (Fig. 5.5), backside views (Fig. 5.6a–d), and views from underneath (Fig. 5.7) are surprisingly common. One would not have placed the real three-dimensional Laocoön obliquely in his niche in the Belvedere

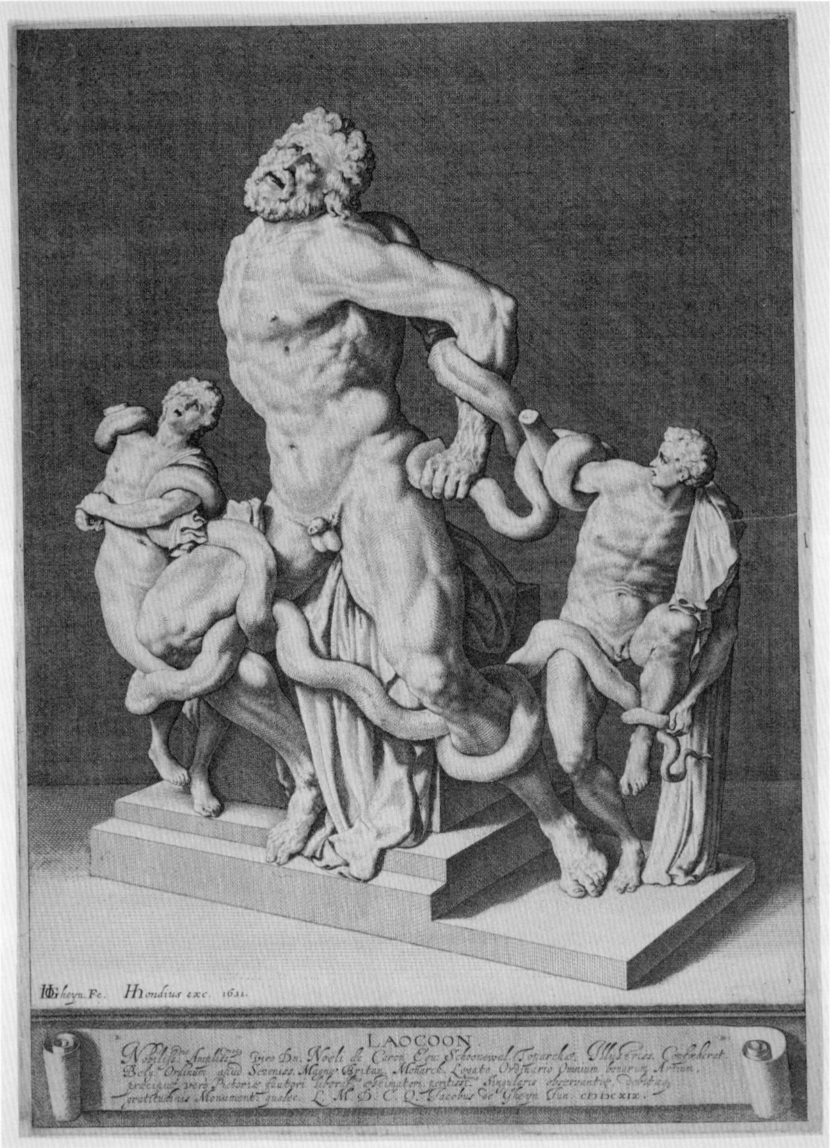

Fig. 5.5 Print of an etching of the Laocoön in oblique view by Jacques de Gheyn III (1619). London, British Museum, 1917,1208.499 (© The Trustees of the British Museum. All rights reserved).

Court, for example, since this most relief-like of all ancient sculptural groups obviously calls for a viewer that stands directly in front of it. In the two-dimensional medium of the engraving, however, an oblique depiction of the Laocoön, which thereby deviates slightly from the perspective of

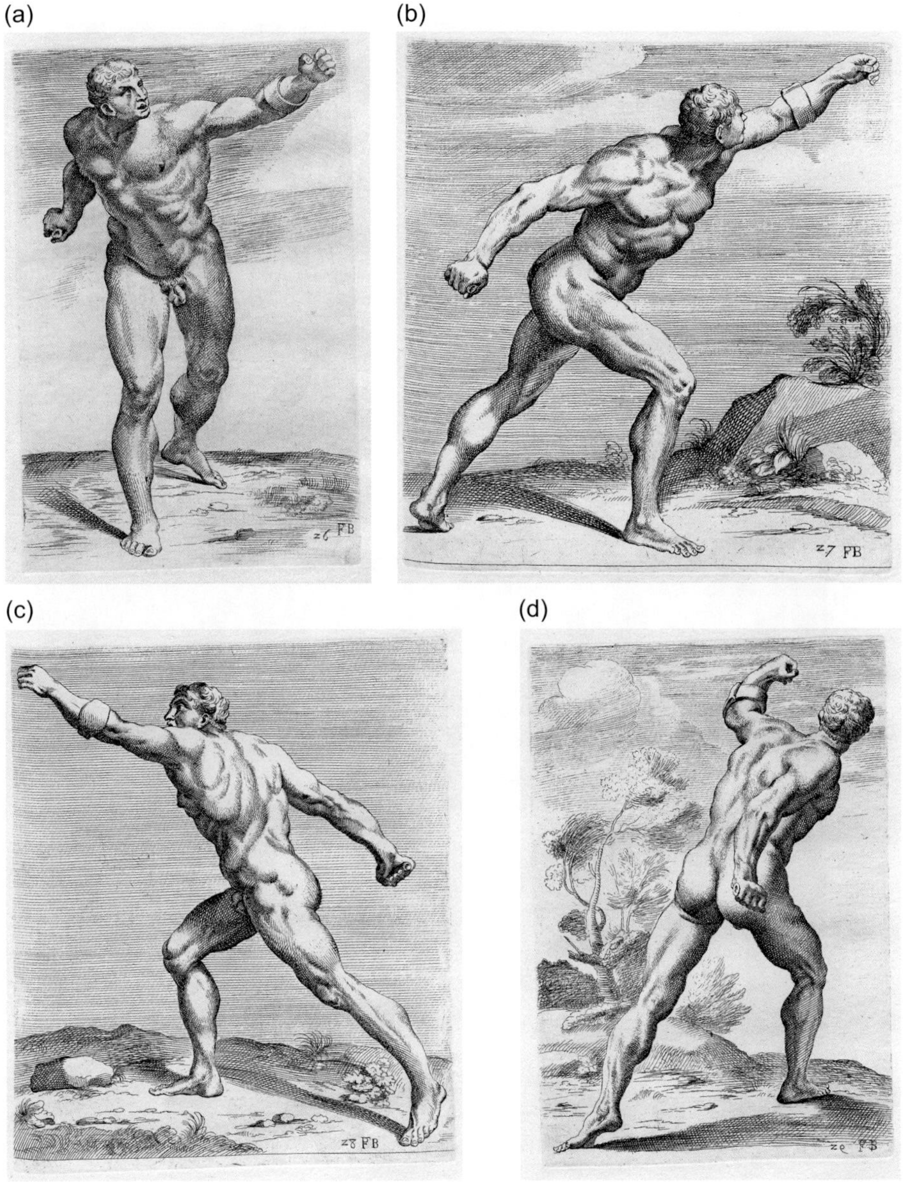

Fig. 5.6a–d A series of engravings of the Borghese warrior by F. Perrier. From Perrier 1653: plates 34–7 (© Universitätsbibliothek Heidelberg/80 B 392 RES).

an "ideal viewer," *was* an option – an option that highlighted the three-dimensional quality of this large marble sculpture. In general, while relief-like views onto sculpture dominate early photography of sculpture for scholarly use, we find a much greater plurality of perspectives on ancient sculpture among Renaissance and Baroque engravings.

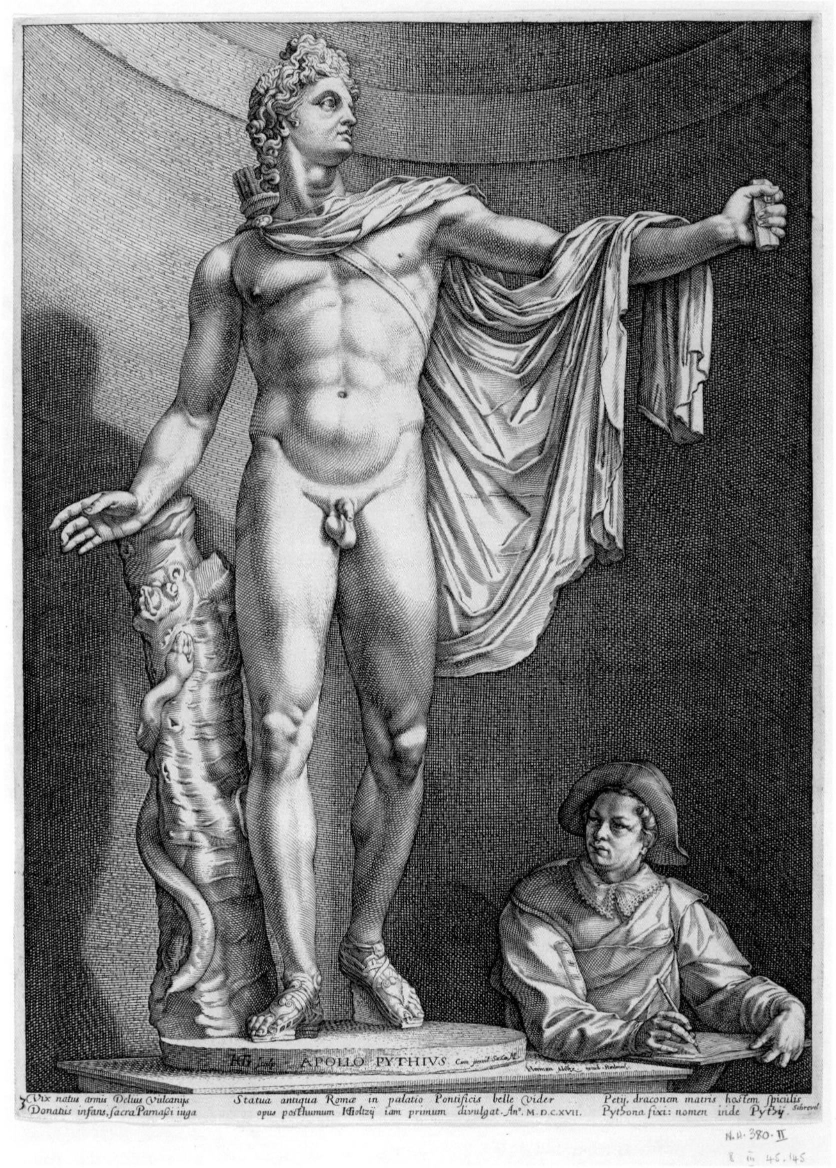

Fig. 5.7 Engraving of the Belvedere Apollo by Hendrick Goltzius, printed 1617. London, British Museum, 1854,0513.106 (© The Trustees of the British Museum. All rights reserved).

But there is another interesting difference, too. Early photography of sculpture makes a considerable effort to present the ancient statue or its fragments against a neutral black or white background, either by means of a curtain that hides all other elements which would otherwise enter the photograph or by cutting out the sculpture in postproduction and printing it against a completely neutral and, we might say, nonpictorial backdrop.[13] The ancient statues are thus isolated as much as possible, appearing without any setting at all. By contrast, premodern engravings of ancient sculpture prefer to present the statues within a setting. However, this does not involve "putting ancient sculpture back into its original context," as scholars since the generation of Andrew Stewart and Tonio Hölscher have asked us to do. In fact, there is no attempt at reconstructing an "original" context.[14] What we find on such premodern engravings is rather context tout court, no matter whether it is an imaginary natural context, as with the four views of the Borghese gladiator included in François Perrier's *Segmenta nobiliarum signorum et statuarum* from 1638 (see Fig. 5.6a–d),[15] or the built context of a pedestal.[16] As massive three-dimensional objects, these statues dominate a space and may even act out into this space, although their spatial surroundings are the implicit viewer's "real" space more than the figure's pictorial space.[17] The bulkier they appear in the space they occupy, the more impressive they seem.

One might be inclined to ascribe this to the Baroque style of these engravings. However, we find the same principle in later neoclassical engravings, such

[13] A drawing by Friedrich Adler from 1877 documents the complex installations built for photographing the finds from the great excavation at Olympia, which created a kind of photographer's "field studio" isolating the photographed sculpture from their context (see Klamm 2017a: 15–17, with fig. 2). The general practice of photographing sculpture on a dark background lasted at least until the 1920s, when it started to face criticism. See Kopf 2007: 158–63. The publication of the great German excavations at Olympia well illustrates this practice. The lavish plates of the volume devoted to images in clay and stone present the sculptures in photographs on a plain white and sometimes black ground. See Curtius and Adler 1894 (freely available online through the Heidelberg University Library: https://digi.ub.uni-heidelberg.de/diglit/curtiusadler1894). On the process of recontextualizing the insulation of the sculptural finds from Olympia from the excavation through multiple steps until their final photographic publication, see Klamm 2017a: 295–316.

[14] A good example of a sculpture put back into a supposedly original context would be Alma-Tadema's painting *An Audience at Agrippa's* from 1876, roughly contemporary to early photography, with the Prima Porta Augustus appearing in the middle-ground (Kilmarnock, Dick Institute, FA/A03; see https://commons.wikimedia.org/wiki/File:Lawrence_Alma-Tadema_-_An_Audience_at_Agrippa%27s.jpg).

[15] Perrier 1638: pls. 26–9. A 1653 reedition of Perrier's successful book has been digitalized by the Universitätsbibliothek Heidelberg; see https://digi.ub.uni-heidelberg.de/diglit/perrier1653. On Perrier's *Segmenta*, see recently Di Cosmo (2013) and esp. Laveissière (2011), who provides a systematic presentation of the *Segmenta* and its reeditions, as well as a full catalogue of the depicted statues (with bibliographies), which juxtaposes each of Perrier's etchings with modern photographs taken from similar perspectives (for the Borghese gladiator, 134–41; for further bibliography on Perrier's etchings of the statue, 136).

[16] Both may well be combined, as e.g. in the case of the Laocoön in Perrier 1638: pl. 1, in which the statue is set up on its pedestal but is standing not in its niche in the Belvedere Court but in an imaginary rocky landscape.

[17] Züchner (1959: 35) already came to similar conclusions in his comparative evaluation of drawing and photography. On the paragone of drawing and photography as media for the depiction of sculpture in archaeology, see the concise remarks in Kopf 2007: 154–5.

as those found in the lavish eighteenth-century publications of the finds from Pompeii and Herculaneum, the *Antiquità di Ercolano*, which is probably the closest one might come in the eighteenth century to a modern publication of archaeological discoveries.[18] Even if the famous Doryphoros herm from the Villa dei Papiri appears here in a comparatively reduced setting, there is always at least *something* that the depicted objects stand on and cast their shadow over, if even no more than a simple table (Fig. 5.8). No matter whether we talk of pathetic Baroque or a more restrained neoclassical style, there seems to be a common rule. Statues on engravings stand *somewhere*, while statues in early scholarly photography stand *nowhere*.[19] With photographs in mind such as the Belvedere Apollo, which is set on a plain, black ground in Brunn-Bruckmann's photographic corpus of Greek sculpture (Fig. 5.9), one might even ask whether they stand at all or rather float as weightless astronauts in empty space.[20] This difference between the "somewhere" of sculpture as engraving and the "nowhere" of sculpture as photography echoes the manner in which engravings highlight three-dimensionality through the oblique positioning of sculpture, as well as the reduction of three-dimensionality in relief-like photographic views of statues in early photographic compendia, such as the Brunn-Bruckmann series. In sculpture-as-engraving, it is the three-dimensional object that counts most, whereas in sculpture-as-photography, it is the two-dimensional view of that object that dominates.

Subjecting Sculpture to a View before Photography

The described transition from the three-dimensional to the relief-like two-dimensional view of sculpture has so far been presented as a technological

18 On the Doryphoros herm from the Villa dei Papiri in the *Antichità di Ercolano* (identified there as a portrait of Augustus[!]), see *Antichità* 1767: 157–63 (freely available online through the Heidelberg University Library: https://doi.org/10.11588/diglit.3709).

19 See Klamm (2017a: 300), who talks of the "Ortlosigkeit," or placelessness, of photographed sculpture. See also Hamill and Luke 2017: 2: "The photograph divorces the sculptural object from any temporal or spatial context" (referring to the photograph of the Belvedere Apollo from Brunn-Bruckmann's compendium shown here in Fig. 5.9).

20 This very large photographic compendium of Greek and Roman sculpture was started in 1888 in collaboration of the publisher Friedrich Bruckmann and the archaeologist Heinrich Brunn (Brunn, Bruckmann, and Arndt 1888–1900) and later continued and expanded by the archaeologist Paul Arndt, reissued in various editions until 1947. On this essential tool for archaeological *Skulpturforschung*, on which Furtwängler largely relies in his *Meisterwerke* (1893), and whose photographs meet the criticism of Wölfflin, see Hamill and Luke 2017: 2n7; Klamm 2017a: 342–7, 2017b: 50–1. On the Bruckmann Verlag as an important player on the German market for photography of artworks, see Klamm 2008. On the rise and the uses of such photographic compendia in late nineteenth-century archaeology, see Dally 2017: 46–7.

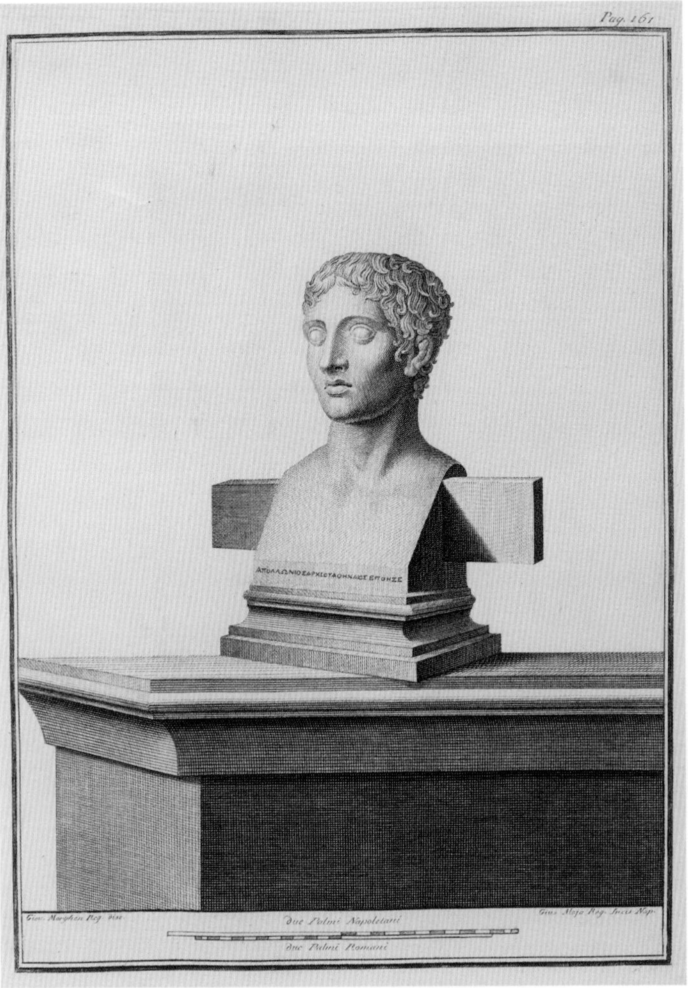

Fig. 5.8 The Doryphoros herm from the Villa dei Papiri at Herculaneum. From *Antichità* 1767: 161 (© Universitätsbibliothek Heidelberg/C 3594 Gross RES::5).

history of evolving apparatus of depiction. However, in the wake of Neo-Classicism, we find elements that point to this newly relief-like vision of ancient sculpture even before the invention of photography. The canvas *Three Persons Viewing the Gladiator by Candlelight* (1765) by the English painter Joseph Wright of Derby provides a good starting point for a "prehistory" of the "photographic" view of sculpture (Fig. 5.10).[21] In this painting, the three men

[21] On this painting, see most recently Craske 2020: 90–107. Looking at and drawing (ancient) sculpture is a recurrent theme in the oeuvre of Joseph Wright of Derby. In his painting *An Academy by Lamplight* (1769), we see the same emphasis put on the artificial (and thereby fully controlled) lighting of the sculpture within a dark room (New Haven, CT, Yale Center for British Art, 1973.1.66;

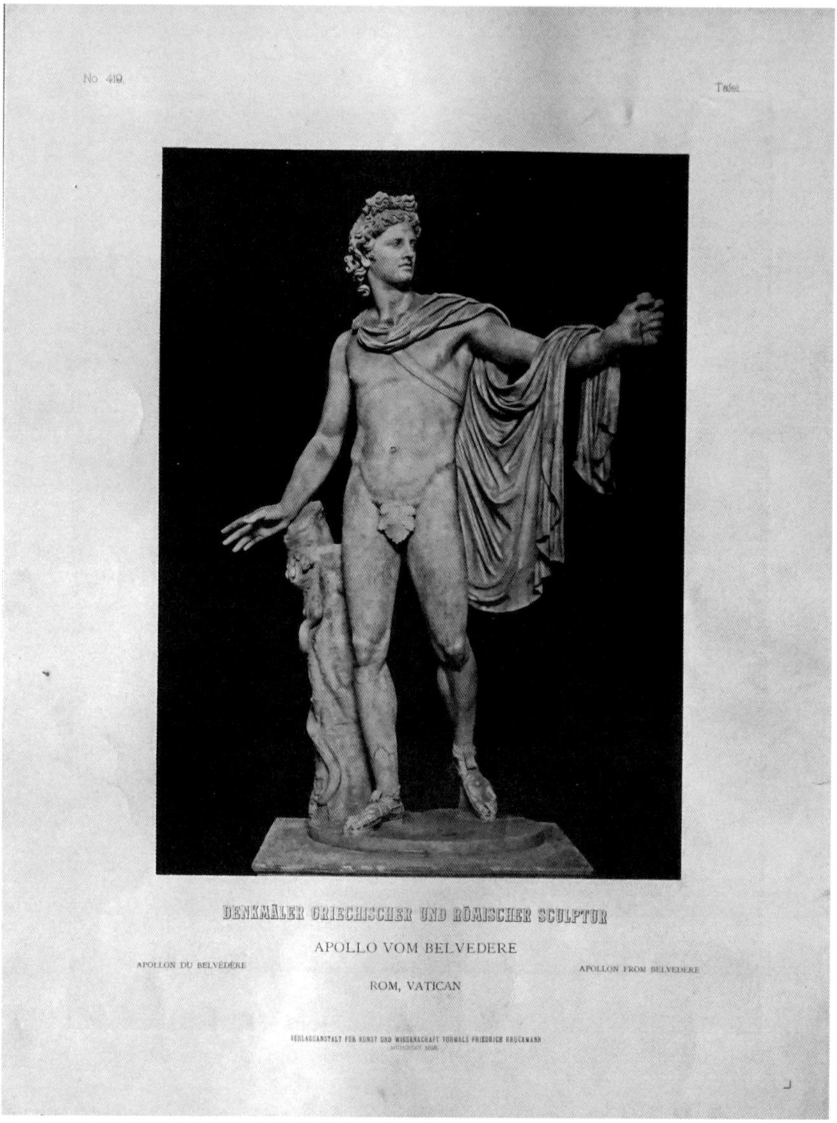

Fig. 5.9 Photographic view of the Belvedere Apollo. From Brunn, Bruckmann, and Arndt 1888–1900: pl. 419 (photograph by author).

appear to be looking for a specific view onto the statue, rather than examining the statue as a three-dimensional object. By adjusting his angle of vision and the

see Graciano 2013–4; Craske 2020: 99, fig. 55). In the painting *The Antique School of the Royal Academy at New Somerset House* ascribed to Johann Zoffany from 1780–3, which shows a drawing session, the same two components – the mobility of the statues and the control of the sources of light – create a proto-photographic viewing *dispositif* (London, Royal Academy of Arts, 03/846; see Geyer 2012: 101 and pl. 9).

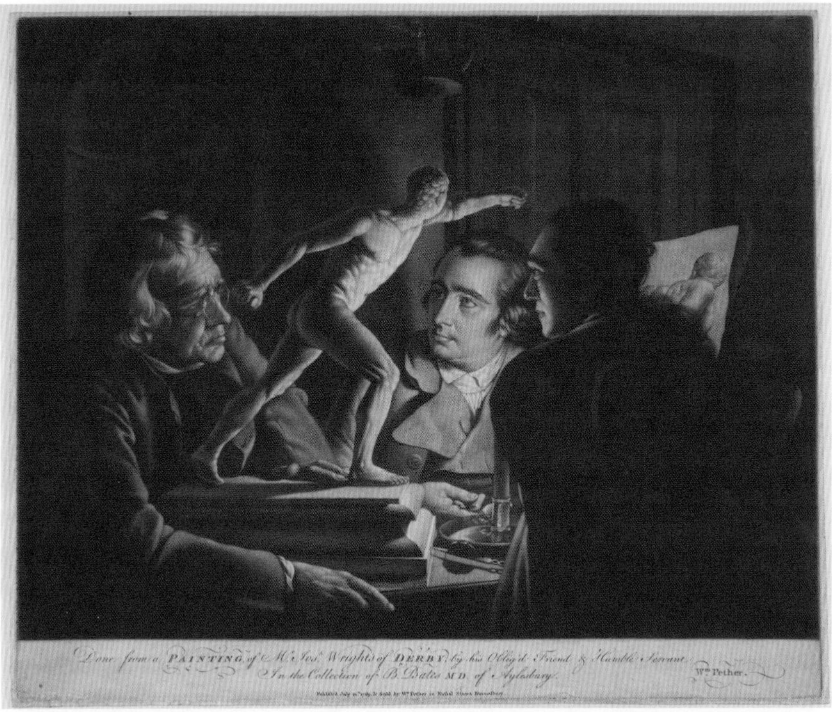

Fig. 5.10 William Pether after Joseph Wright of Derby, *Three Persons Viewing the Gladiator by Candlelight*, 1769. Mezzotint. New York, Metropolitan Museum of Art, Harris Brisbane Dick Fund, 53.600.564 (Creative Commons Zero [CC0]).

source of light – a candle – the man on the left tries to make his view of the statuette replica of the Borghese gladiator coincide with the drawing of the same statue on the right. The artificial light shines directly on the statuette and isolates the figure from its physical surroundings, while the rest of the room retreat into the shadows – an effect that parallels the practice of cutting out the statue from its background in the printing of early photography of sculpture.

What the gentlemen on this canvas do – searching for the right view of the statue by moving their gazes and their source of light – is exactly what Johann Wolfgang Goethe did, according to his own autobiographical account, when he had his first opportunity to see in three dimensions those praised masterpieces of ancient sculpture which he had read about in Johann Joachim Winckelmann and Gotthold Ephraim Lessing, but which he had previously known from engravings only, while visiting the world-class collection of plaster casts in the newly installed *Antikensaal* in Mannheim in 1767.[22] As he writes:

> Die herrlichsten Statuen des Altertums nicht allein an den Wänden gereiht, sondern auch innerhalb der ganzen Fläche durch einander aufgestellt; ein Wald von Statuen, durch den man sich durchwinden, eine große ideale Volksgesellschaft, zwischen der man sich durchdrängen mußte. Alle diese herrlichen Gebilde konnten durch Auf- und Zuziehen der Vorhänge in das vorteilhafteste Licht gestellt werden; überdies waren sie auf ihren Postamenten beweglich und nach Belieben zu wenden und zu drehen.[23]

By moving the curtains of this *Antikensaal*, Goethe is able to play with the light, just like the gentlemen with their candle in Wright's painting. However, in order to obtain the right viewing angle, Goethe had a more technical means at his disposal than the three gentlemen – namely the turning bases on which the plaster casts were mounted. Instead of moving himself around the statue, the statue is moved on its turning pedestal according to his will, subduing it in a very concrete sense to his gaze. This plaster cast collection might have provided him with his first experience of ancient masterpieces of sculpture in three dimensions, but what Goethe the art lover and proto-scholar of Greek sculpture is actually looking for are not the three-dimensional statues themselves but very specific perspectives on them. Control of both light and the viewing angle happen to be the two most important components of early photography of sculpture, and what Goethe does in the Mannheim *Antikensaal* is in a sense directly comparable to that practice.[24]

[22] On the *Antikensaal* in Mannheim in the context of plaster cast collections in eighteenth-century Germany, see Hofmann 1982: 312–43 (mainly a collection of sources); Socha 2006; Schreiter 2014: 56–60; Suchezky 2019: 152–7.

[23] Goethe 1986: 546 (eleventh book). Translated in Goethe 1908: 49: "The noblest statues of antiquity were not only ranged along the walls, but also stood in groups all about the room, forming a forest of statues, through which one had to thread one's way; a great ideal popular assembly, through which one was obliged to force a passage. All these noble forms could be placed in the most advantageous light by drawing or pulling back the curtains, and beside this, were moveable on their pedestals, and could be turned round at pleasure."

[24] In the invoice written in 1792 by the craftsman who made a turning base for the Capitoline Venus on the behalf of Ennio Quirino Visconti, curator of the Capitoline Museum, the aim of this technical device is described in a similar way: "Per uso de Studenti si possa voltare secondo i Lumi, e le vedute necessarie per ben copiarla" (for the use of students one can turn it according to the light, and the views necessary to copy it well). See Arata 2009: 144. Alexander Heinemann provided the reference to this interesting document in his answer to my comment to the editorial of the internet blog *Das Rollpodest*: https://rollpodest.hypotheses.org/225.

Turning pedestals are also occasionally mentioned in the context of Renaissance collections of ancient sculpture in Italy.[25] The Idolino, for example, was mounted on such a base in 1533 soon after its discovery. We also know of turning bases for a Pan-and-Daphnis group and a Leda-and-the-Swan group, which were both placed in niches as highlights within the sixteenth-century sculpture garden of Cardinal Cesi in Rome.[26] In this case, the turning base is situated in a context of tricky mechanics of which the Renaissance seems to have been particularly fond.[27] Given the subjects chosen for this display, there is an obvious erotic dimension, too. But the great period of turning bases, for both the display of plaster casts and original sculpture, lay in the second half of the eighteenth and early nineteenth centuries, where it featured not in the context of luxurious palaces and gardens but rather the serious study of art and the first public museums.[28] What, after all, should the art lover do in front of a statue if not look for the "best" possible view? Moving the statue instead of moving around the statue testifies to a fundamentally new approach to sculpture. This search for the "best" view used to be the engraver's task – but from this period on, engravers shared this task with the public.

But what is the "best" view of a statue? Orienting oneself according to the choices made by engravers may be a good start, and this is precisely what the gentlemen on the canvas in Fig. 5.10 are doing. Turning bases provide the technical means for obtaining a particular view. But theory is also needed in order to find criteria for deciding on what the "best" view might be, a task that was increasingly professionalized in the twentieth century. In their search for the ideal viewing angles of statues, scholars of

[25] See Geyer 2012: 99–101. Next to Geyer 2012 as a study on the display of ancient statues (and their plaster casts) on rotating bases, see Penny 2008: 463–5, for short but interesting remarks on turning bases within an essay on the evolution of bases in the modern age.

[26] See Leibundgut 1999.

[27] On turning bases for the display of statues and plaster casts in the eighteenth and nineteenth centuries, see Geyer 2012: 101–8. Interestingly, the author was unable to find any examples of turning bases from the seventeenth century. Hence, we ought not to see the neoclassical turning bases in continuity with the few known Renaissance examples. Nicholas Penny (2008: 464) credits the introduction of electric light in museums in the later nineteenth century, solving all problems of enlightening statues, with explaining the fall of turning bases into disuse.

[28] Penny (2008: 463–4) makes the interesting remark that turning bases, before they were used for the display of sculpture in the eighteenth and nineteenth centuries, had their place in the sculptor's studio as a working device. Using them for the museum display of statues would therefore amount to the art-loving public's adopting of a vision formerly reserved for the "professionals" of sculpture.

Greek sculpture sometimes undertook a kind of experimental archaeology by using reproductive plaster casts and photographs in parallel with one another. In his history of Greek sculpture, the East German scholar Ludger Alscher published an extensive series of photographic images of individual statues, each of which was taken from a slightly different angle.[29] The turning bases had by then disappeared from public museums, since they obviously no longer fulfilled the viewing expectations of the general public. Among professionals of *Skulpturforschung*, the principle of the turning base survived for a much longer period, just as photography continued to be the predominant medium of illustration in scholarship on sculpture.[30]

In the context of this search for the "best" view, an influential essay on sculpture by the Munich sculptor Hildebrand published in 1893 makes a series of most interesting statements.[31] Hildebrand's basic idea is that sculpture should be relief-like.[32] That is, the composition should be designed in such a way as to allow within one specific view of the statue a complete and aesthetically convincing appraisal of its three-dimensional form. The experience of the three-dimensional statue should be included in one view only, making all other potential angles of view superfluous or even disturbing. In order to further explain his idea, Hildebrand proposes imagining that the

[29] See Alscher 1961: pl. 1a–b (Kouros of Tenea and Kritios Boy). See the comments in Klamm 2017b: 60–2. A similar combined use of plaster casts and photography is made by Ernst Buschor in his attempt to reconstruct the statue group of the Tyrant-slayers (see Buschor 1940). The implicit working hypothesis of any search for the perfect view of a statue is that statues were indeed designed for specific views.

[30] Turning bases are also still very much valued and present in academic plaster cast collections in Germany today. Accordingly, a recent blog initiated by the academic collections of Greek and Roman originals and plaster casts from the Universities of Freiburg, Heidelberg, and Tübingen chose to call themselves *Das Rollpodest* ("the mobile base"). See the programmatic editorial written by the curators Polly Lohmann (Heidelberg), Jens-Arne Dickmann (Freiburg), and Alexander Heinemann (Tübingen), which is directly relevant to the present subject (https://rollpodest.hypotheses.org/225).

[31] Hildebrand 1893 (made available online by the Universitätsbibliothek Heidelberg: https://digi.ub.uni-heidelberg.de/diglit/hildebrand1893), with an English translation in Mallgrave and Ikonomou 1994: 227–79. On Hildebrand's art theory and its connection with scholarly engagement with sculpture photography, see Dobbe 2007: 34–46; Melius 2017; with Classical sculpture, see Neer 2010: 183–6, with further bibliography in n. 2, and Koortbojian 2023, 61–88.

[32] Hildebrand 1893: 63–82 ("Die Reliefauffassung"). This "relief-conception" of sculpture would have been predominant among the Greeks: "Diese so entwickelte allgemeine künstlerische Vorstellungsweise ist aber nichts Anderes als die in der griechischen Kunst herrschende Reliefvorstellung" (Hildebrand 1893: 66). Translation in Mallgrave and Ikonomou 1994: 252: "This artistic method of representation, developed here in a very general way, is none other than the idea of relief that prevailed in Greek art."

statue has been placed between two parallel glass panels.[33] This is quite a direct way of stating that three-dimensional sculpture should stay within a strict relief plane and face the viewer. Although Hildebrand does not mention it directly, it seems clear that his concept is very close to principles of early photography of sculpture which were being developed at precisely that time.

Hildebrand makes another most interesting comment in this context. He complains about the fact that sculptors in his own lifetime often receive state commissions that make his ideal of good sculpture impossible to realize.[34] Indeed, at this time of exploding urbanism, newly designed public places have a strong tendency to be endowed with a central statuary monument that memorializes and puts on display an important person for the nation. But if a statue is positioned within an open space, there is no way to prevent people from viewing the statue from all possible angles rather than from the perfect angle in which the statue would appear in relief-like composition. Instead of worrying about sculpture's potential loss of three-dimensionality through its submission to a limited set of "correct" views, as we would probably do today, Hildebrand has the exact opposite worry – namely how to eradicate all these "wrong" views from the experience of viewing the sculpture! This concept of sculpture falls clearly under the paradigm of sculpture *as* photography; the statue should exist only in its correct and fully controlled view.[35]

[33] See Hildebrand 1893: 64–6.

[34] Hildebrand 1893: 98–101; e.g. 99: "Unter Plastik denkt sich der moderne Mensch nur noch runde Figuren, die in der Mitte eines Platzes stehen. Diese unglücklichen Monumente sind fast die einzige Bühne, auf der der Bildhauer seine Phantasie ausleben darf." Translation in Mallgrave and Ikonomou 1994: 266–7: "Modern man thinks of sculpture only as a figure in the round set up in the middle of a square. These unhappy monuments are almost the only stage upon which the sculptor may exercise his imagination."

[35] Hildebrand is very explicit in his criticism. How can his ideal of sculptural art be realized, he asks, "wenn die Plastik nur als Rundplastik im leeren Raum, auf der Mitte eines Platzes vorkommen darf, da wo sie nie stehen sollte, weil alle Richtungen gleichwertig sind, es kein vornen und hinten gibt, und die Situation der Bildwirkung der Plastik möglichst entgegenarbeitet; der Beschauer kreist um das Standbild herum und hat vier Ansichten zu schlucken, was nur bei sehr wenigen Statuen ein Vorteil ist und immer nur bei nackten Figuren ein Genuss sein kann" (Hildebrand 1893: 100). Translation in Mallgrave and Ikonomou 1994: 268: "when a figure in the round must stand isolated in empty space, in the middle of a square – exactly where it should never be placed because all directions are of equal value and there is no front or back. The location works against the sculptural effect. The observer must walk around the statue and digest at least four views. This is advantageous with only very few statues, and it can only ever be a pleasure where the form is a nude." Sculpture in the round ("Rundplastik") is clearly a negatively connoted term, just as the viewer's movement around the statue is something to be avoided.

Among the Greeks, Hildebrand continues, sculptors had many more opportunities to put into practice his ideal of relief-like sculpture.[36] This statement might seem surprising because statues positioned within open spaces were absolutely standard in Greco-Roman antiquity. If Hildebrand thought that relief-like sculpture was predominant among the Greeks, this was probably because architectural sculpture, such as temple friezes, metopes, or pediments, had become the paradigmatic examples of Greek sculpture, rivaling and even surpassing the freestanding Roman statues on which earlier thinking on Greek sculpture had been based since Winckelmann. This was especially true in Germany since excavations had begun at Olympia, which provided far fewer examples of freestanding sculpture than had been hoped for, but which compensated for this with the spectacular architectural sculpture from the temple of Zeus.

With Heinrich Wölfflin's groundbreaking essays on how one should photograph sculpture, the search for the "best" (or in Wölfflin's words: the "correct") view of a statue eventually entered a more narrowly scholarly debate.[37] Published just a few years after Hildebrand's *Problem der Form*,

[36] Hildebrand 1893: 98–100. His praise of the past, however, is not focused on the ancient Greeks but includes Roman and Christian art, as well: "Wenn wir in unserer Zeit so häufig die Beobachtung machen, dass Vorstellungen eines Vorgangs, anstatt in Reliefdarstellung ihren natürlichen Ausdruck zu finden, barbarischer Weise als Rundplastik zur Darstellung kommen, so hängt das zum Teil damit zusammen, dass zu Reliefdarstellungen fast gar keine Gelegenheit mehr gegeben ist. Denken wir an die vielen Denkmäler, an Kirchenwände oder andere Bauten sich anlehnend, an die Tempel, Triumphbögen etc., wie sie frühere Zeiten zeigen, so ist diese Plastik viel reicher als die freistehende Rundplastik" (Hildebrand 1893: 98). Translation in Mallgrave and Ikonomou 1994: 266: "If today we so often find that ideas of action are barbarously rendered in the round instead of having their natural expression in the form of a relief, then this is in part because there are almost no opportunities to make reliefs. If we recall the many monuments of earlier times that were attached to the walls of churches and other edifices, such as temples, triumphal arches, and so on, we find a greater wealth of such works than of standing figures."

[37] Wölfflin 1896, 1897, and 1914, reprinted in Billeter 1997: 409–17; for an English translation by Geraldine A. Johnson, see Wölfflin 2013. On Wölfflin's approach to the problem of the viewpoint, see Johnson 2013: 27–31. More generally, Johnson 2013 is highly relevant to the subject matter of the present chapter, although dealing with Renaissance sculpture and its depiction before and after photography. Villinger (1997: 64–6) notes that critical reflection of photography as a medium of depiction in the still nascent discipline of art history began considerably later than the use of photography in scholarly practice. In the first half-century before Wölfflin's essays, the new medium was rather plainly welcome for its alleged objectivity and the help that it could provide for the positivist project of collecting all available sources for art historical knowledge. Only later did the paragone between photography and drawing begin for the depiction and documentation of sculpture in the field of art-history (see Dobbe 2007: 39–44, followed by a discussion of the paragone between photography and sculpture centered on Wölfflin, 44–58; Kopf 2007: 154–5). Wölfflin's first discussion of how to photograph sculpture with its highly prescriptive tone would later be followed by similar discussions in classical archaeology, often with significantly different results. See e.g. Langlotz 1929 and 1979

these essays are heavily (and openly) influenced by his "relief-conception" of sculpture.[38] While a photographic view of sculpture already underlies Hildebrand's "relief-conception," though without ever being mentioned as such, in Wölfflin the question of the viewpoint is now explicitly tackled through the photographic lens. In the following decades, the question of the "best" viewpoint, which might well count as the very embodiment of a subjective matter of taste, gained the status of an objective matter that needed to be clarified in a well-argued form for every statue, in much the same way as questions of date or origin.[39] Additionally, the stylistic development of Greek sculpture began to be studied according to the changing ways by which statues present themselves to their viewers. The best example here is perhaps Gerhard Krahmer's model of style epochs in Hellenistic sculpture. In two highly influential articles, he traced through the identification of single (or multiple!) "correct" views of statues a development from early Hellenistic multi-perspectival sculpture to late Hellenistic "single-perspectival" statues, which were best seen from one specific viewpoint.[40]

Relief-Like Sculpture in Ancient Greece

Despite what has been said so far about the "photographic bias" of sculpture scholarship, it would nevertheless be an oversimplification to regard the "relief-conception" of Greek sculpture solely as a result of modern photography. Greek pedimental groups often correspond very closely to Hildebrand's idea of relief-like sculpture.[41] For rather obvious technical

(commented upon in Klamm 2017a: esp. 51–2) and Züchner 1959 (commented upon in Kopf 2007: 154–5). In focusing more on the need to standardize sculpture photography than on the question of the proper rendition of three-dimensional statues in two-dimensional photography, Fittschen 1974 (on how to photograph Roman portraits) mentions an aspect that seems intellectually less compelling but whose impact on what kind of sculpture photography is to be found in scholarly literature might be even greater.

[38] See Hamill and Luke 2017: 2–4.

[39] The inclusion of the (decision regarding the) *Hauptansicht*, the principal point of view, in a thorough publication of a work of sculpture, at least in German classical archaeology, is reflected in the standard set of photographic views that would ideally be provided. The publication of the Roman portraits from the Capitoline and other communal museums in Rome by Fittschen and Zanker is one general example. Next to four orthogonal views (from the front, the back, and either side), one *Hauptansicht* is provided for the "better" portraits, as far as possible (see e.g. Fittschen, Zanker, and Cain 2010, the latest volume of this series that set the standard for Roman portrait publications).

[40] Krahmer 1923–4, 1927.

[41] Correspondences between Hildebrand's ideals and actual monuments of Greek sculpture may, of course, also be recognized for their reliefs themselves. Neer (2010: 200) notes, for instance, a perfect match between Hildebrand's ideals and the famous High Classical "Cat stele."

reasons, pedimental groups could be perfectly fit in between two imaginary glass panels. But the figures' conformity to the material frame of the pediment triangle goes beyond technical necessity. Both on the west pediment at Olympia and on the pediments of Aegina, all figures except the central divinity appear in profile, move and act within the relief plane, and do not break through this imaginary frame.[42] Post neoclassical perspectives that look at three-dimensional sculpture as if through the photographer's lens are therefore not a completely modern fiction. Greek sculpture of the Archaic and Classical periods could very well conform to the "relief-conception," especially when we are speaking of architectural sculpture whose main purpose was to adorn monumental buildings.

The phenomenon of relief-like sculpture in ancient Greece, however, extends even beyond architectural sculpture. We witness an interesting reversal in the late Classical period, when Greek reliefs became more and more three-dimensional and Greek freestanding sculpture more and more relief-like. At the same time as reliefs from the fourth century BCE onward assimilated themselves to fully three-dimensional sculpture – both by giving greater bodily substance to figures that were now carved in greater depth and by breaking through the relief's material frame with actions and gazes directed outside the relief plane[43] – sculpture in the round tended to become more relief-like. Indeed, statues such as the Belvedere Apollo (see Figs. 5.7, 5.9), which is commonly thought to depend on a late fourth-century prototype, display the body limbs within a (nonexistent) relief plane.[44] In this case, moreover, the directions of movement and gaze also remain within the imaginary relief plane. The figure's whole composition is thus oriented toward one specific viewing angle to which the statue presents itself. More generally, late Classical statues tend to become *einansichtig*, or "single-perspectival," in Krahmer's terminology. Although we might

[42] Any even schematic reconstruction drawing of these pediment groups may show this point. See e.g. Neer 2010: 93, fig. 49 (Olympia, after Herrmann 1972), 95, figs. 51–2 (Aegina, after Ohly 1976).

[43] The dense series of Classical Attic grave reliefs from the mid fifth to the late fourth century BCE is best at exemplifying this development (see the style chronology of Attic grave reliefs in Diepolder 1931), starting with flat reliefs in the late fifth century, which are comparable to the Parthenon frieze (see e.g. the stele of Hegeso: Athens, National Archaeological Museum, 3624, ca. 420 BCE; Diepolder 1931: pl. 20), and ending with very high reliefs, such as the stele of Aristonautes (Athens, National Archaeological Museum, 738, ca. 340–330 BCE; Squire 2018: 540, fig. 21), or even with fully three-dimensional statues set into the frame of a "real" aedicula architecture, as in the case of the Kallithea monument (Athens, Piraeus Museum, 2413–2529, ca. 330 BC; on this monument and more broadly on embodying the deceased on Attic grave stelai, see Squire 2018).

[44] On this fundamental change in the compositional design of statuary in the fourth century BCE, see Borbein 1973.

credit modern photography with transforming sixth- and fifth-century sculpture into relief, such intentional *Einansichtigkeit* shows that the ancient sculptors themselves sought the same effect in later periods.

The privileging of a single viewing angle often goes hand in hand with the relative neglect of a statue's backside. This is famously exemplified by the late fourth-century BCE Greek marble original of the Hermes by Praxiteles in Olympia, which features a coarse surface on the figure's back.[45] Unfinished, coarse surfaces on the backside of statues would also become very common in Greek marble sculpture of the Hellenistic age. It seems as if such statues consciously conformed to a photographic view long before the invention of photography as a mechanical means of producing such a view.

There is, however, a fundamental difference between the relief-likeness of sculpture as produced by the medium of photography and the relief-likeness which is inherent to the statue itself, as articulated by its composition or its different grades of surface finish on front and back. In sculpture experienced through photographic reproduction, a statue is virtually identical to a limited set of photographic views, which show the statue from perspectives particularly pleasing to the eye, while all other possible views are virtually nonexistent. In fact, it is very hard to find published photographs of the coarse backsides of Hellenistic or Roman marble statues.[46] Yet for ancient viewers of such statues, it was often perfectly possible to experience such statues from the "wrong" side.[47] Indeed, they apparently

[45] The marks of different sculpting tools visible on the figure's back are recorded e.g. in Antonsson 1937: 25, fig. 1.

[46] In order to see the rough backsides of many Hellenistic marble statues, autopsy in the museum is therefore required. See, however, the thorough photographic documentation of the marble sculptures from Pergamon on the large object database Arachne of the Deutsches Archäologisches Institut and the Arbeitsstelle für Digitale Archäologie of the archaeological institute at Cologne University (https://arachne.uni-koeln.de). Photographs of rough backsides of several marble sculptures of mostly seated figures from the Altar Terrace at Pergamon are found in Hofter 2015. After a detailed discussion of these figures and their "unfinished" backsides, Hofter follows the usual path of archaeological *Skulpturforschung* by looking for a conceivable setting of these statues that would make their backsides virtually invisible for ancient viewers. His tentative suggestion of a diorama-like setting with landscape elements which provides a background that would mask the "unfinished" backsides of the seated figures seems, however, rather adventurous (see Hofter 2015: 153–4).

[47] This fundamental point has already been noted by Wölfflin in his second essay (Wölfflin 1897). Indeed, in seeing the statue itself (and not its photograph), he even defines the process of moving from unsatisfactory perspectives into the perfect viewing angle in front of the statue itself as a particularity of sculpture: a pleasure that painting cannot provide. "Angesichts der Originale aber wird man finden, dass es ein besonderer Genuss ist, von den minderwertigen Ansichten zu den vollkommenen überzugehen, und man wird nicht müde, das Experiment wiederholend, aus den unzulänglichen Erscheinungsweisen das gereinigte Bild hervorgehen zu lassen, das ruhig und klar dasteht und im wahren Sinne al seine Befreiung empfunden wird. Das ist eine Freude, die die Malerei uns nicht geben kann," Billeter 1997: 412. Translated in Wölfflin

did not all stand in niches, as *Skulpturforschung* of previous generations implicitly assumed, but could also be erected as freestanding statues in open spaces, such as in the case of the numerous marble statues of female draped figures on the terrace of the Great Altar of Pergamon.[48] Many of these statues have coarse, or at least strongly simplified, surfaces on their backside.[49] Statues of this kind, if set up as freestanding figures in an open space, would influence people's movement within that space to their own benefit. Such a monument would divide a formerly homogenous and neutral space into sectors toward which the statue turns its coarse backside and other sectors toward which it presents its more decorous front, ultimately emphasizing the relatively small viewing angle addressed by the statue's front. The statue's *Einansichtigkeit* invites viewers to occupy this angle of perfect vision, while they pass through busy urban spaces where honorary statues tend to be erected. This angle of perfect vision *onto* the statue mostly coincides with the statue's own area of vision (if we may for a moment ascribe to the statue itself the faculty of seeing). Stepping into this area of vision therefore creates a face-to-face encounter and an exchange of gazes between the honorific statue and her/his viewer, as if a client were entering her/his patron's atrium.

This is exactly the effect that the relief-decoration of Archaic and Classical grave monuments and monumental architecture had often tried to produce. Both Archaic and Classical Attic grave stelai concentrate their decorative splendor on the stele's front side, whereas the lateral sides are

2013: 59: "When coming face to face with the original, however, one will find a particular relish in moving from the inferior views to the completely convincing [view], and one does not tire, when repeating the experiment, of allowing from inadequate appearances the purified image to emerge, which stands calm and clear and in the true sense is felt to be a liberation. This is a pleasure that painting cannot give us."

48 Generally speaking, statuary ensembles arranged in monumental facades of the *scaenae frons* type are an Imperial phenomenon. Within typical spatial arrangements of honorific statuary in the Hellenistic period, statues would rather stand in long rows in front of stoai or alongside processional ways, such as in the case of the agora of Priene, the Dromos at Delos, or in the sanctuary of Olympia. In these cases, the statues would "shine" onto the important spaces (*epiphanestatoi topoi*: see Bielfeldt 2012) in front of them, but their backsides would nevertheless stay perfectly visible – e.g. from the inside of the stoai in front of which they stand. On the setting of honorific statuary in the Hellenistic period, see esp. Ma 2013.

49 The numerous female marble statues from the Altar Terrace have not been found in situ but in later reuse. We therefore cannot go any further than to say that we are dealing with *freestanding* sculpture. Early attempts to position these statues in the intercolumnia of the Altar itself – in such a way as to make their backsides invisible – have been rejected for good reason. See Hofter 2011. Even though the details of the statues' spatial arrangement on the Altar Terrace remains unfortunately unclear, common sense advises us to imagine the setting of statues in a way to highlight their frontsides rather than their rough backsides. At the same time, the backsides of these freestanding statues can hardly have been completely invisible within that open space.

normally left undecorated and much less carefully flattened.[50] Even the sphinx that is often found on top of Archaic stelai always seems to turn its head to a frontal posture.[51] More than in any other type of sculptural monument, these grave monuments present themselves to static viewers who stand directly in front of them. But no other type of monument so consistently deals with a moving public, since grave monuments tend to be positioned next to busy roads. By their frontal design, these grave monuments hence ask a moving public to stand still and turn into static viewers – and this is exactly what many grave epigrams do which address the passerby and prompt her/him to stand still and mourn.[52] The one-sidedness of Archaic and Classical Attic grave reliefs thereby narrows the ideal viewing angle in order to turn the moving passerby into a static viewer and produce a more intense face-to-face moment between the living and the dead.

Similar things may be said for Archaic and Classical architectural sculpture: Thanks to the specific compositional features of sculptural temple decoration, visitors are often invited to move around the temple and engage in a frontal contact with the temple and its awe-inspiring divine inhabitants. The best example for this is, of course, the Parthenon frieze, in which the galloping horses accompany the visitor on her/his way to the temple's entrance side, as Robin Osborne has shown.[53] But the pediments of Olympia function similarly.[54] On the temple's backside, we see violent movement depicted in a centrifugal composition, which moves from the center to the sides and at the same time strictly remains within the relief plane. Even the central figure of Apollo orients his arm and his gaze to the side. Conversely, on the temple's entrance side, the pedimental group's composition is absolutely static. It is a centripetal composition with the figures on the sides oriented to the center and the central figures shown frontally and oriented toward the outside, above all the figure of Zeus himself. Hence, whereas the backside pediment invites movement, the frontside pediment invites static viewing and a direct encounter with the

[50] As for coarse backsides of Hellenistic marble statues, very few published photographs show the less carefully flattened lateral sides of the grave steles. See, however, the lateral side of the fragment preserved in Berlin of the New York Brother-and-Sister stele: Antikensammlung, SK 1531; Dietrich 2022: 420–1, fig. 19.4.

[51] The turn of the head to the side is at least the criterion by which archaeologists approach uncontextualized Archaic sphinxes on the question of whether to understand them as grave sphinxes (looking to the side) or as votive sphinxes (looking ahead).

[52] On Archaic Attic grave monuments and their inscriptions, see now the comprehensive study by Corinna Reinhardt in Dietrich, Fouquet, and Reinhardt 2020: 31–102 (with earlier literature).

[53] Osborne 1987. See also Osborne 2000: 231–5.

[54] See Neer 2010: 93, with reconstruction drawings of the two pedimental groups (fig. 49).

god, which prepares the visitor for the yet more overwhelming confrontation of the Phidian chryselephantine Zeus inside.

Conclusion

To conclude, we may say that both Archaic and Classical grave monuments and temple decoration produce the kind of static viewing situations that we might initially be tempted to blame on the photographic view of sculpture. In the later Classical and Hellenistic eras, freestanding sculpture also often shows a strong preference for a single and specific viewing angle. Looking at sculpture through the photographer's lens – as Walter Benjamin explicitly prompts us to do, standing at the end of a long tradition of viewing sculpture "photographically," one that has a "prehistory" in neoclassical engagement with ancient sculpture – has shown how ill-suited the two-dimensional medium of photography is for a proper appraisal of ancient Greek three-dimensional sculpture, but it has also helped us detect some surprising similarities with the effects of Greek sculptural mise-en-scène. However, no matter how close the photographic understanding of sculpture might occasionally come to ancient experiences, there is still a fundamental difference. In sculpture as photography, all other views are nonexistent; for the material statue itself, all possible views are in play, no matter how *einansichtig* that statue might be. Put otherwise, sculpture *as* photography addresses the viewer. The statue erected in a public space addresses the passerby. Conversely, the relief-like design of sculpture, after increasing in popularity from the late Classical period onward and seemingly anticipating the effects of photography, still addresses the passerby but within a strategy that aims at transforming her/him into a static viewer.

References

Alexandridis, A., and Heilmeyer, W.-D. (2004). *Archäologie der Photographie: Bilder aus der Photothek der Antikensammlung Berlin*. Mainz: von Zabern.

Alscher, L. (1961). *Griechische Plastik*. Vol. 2.1, *Archaik und die Wandlung zur Klassik*. Berlin: Deutscher Verlag der Wissenschaften.

Antichità (1767). *Delle antichità di Ercolano*. Vol. 5/*De' bronzi di Ercolano e contorni incisi con qualche spiegazione*. Vol. 1, *Busti*. Naples: Regia Stamperia.

Antonsson, O. (1937). "The Praxiteles Marble Group in Olympia." PhD dissertation, Uppsala University.

Arata, F. P. (2009). "Il Museo Capitolino sotto il pontificato di Pio VI Braschi (1775–1799): Acquisti, restauri e calchi di antichità." *Bullettino della Commissione Archeologica Comunale di Roma* 110: 111–52.

Bärnighausen, J., Caraffa, C., Klamm, S., Schneider, F., and Wodtke, P., eds. (2020). *Foto-Objekte: Forschen in archäologischen, ethnologischen und kunsthistorischen Archiven*. Bielefeld: Kerber.

Benjamin, W. (1977). "Kleine Geschichte der Photographie." In R. Tiedemann and H. Schweppenhäuser, eds., *Gesammelte Schriften*, vol. 2, *Aufsätze, Essays, Vorträge*. Frankfurt: Suhrkamp, 368–85.

(2015). *On Photography*. Ed. and trans. E. Leslie. London: Reaktion.

Bielfeldt, R. (2012). "Polis Made Manifest: The Physiognomy of the Public in the Hellenistic City with a Case Study on the Agora in Priene." In C. Kuhn, ed., *Politische Kommunikation und öffentliche Meinung in der antiken Welt*. Stuttgart: Steiner, 87–122.

Billeter, E., ed. (1997). *Skulptur im Licht der Fotografie: Von Bayard bis Mapplethorpe*. Bern: Benteli.

Bohrer, F. N. (2011a). *Photography and Archaeology*. London: Reaktion.

(2011b). "Archaeology, Photography, Sculpture: Correspondences and Mediations in the Nineteenth Century and Beyond." In P. J. Bonaventura and A. Jones, eds., *Sculpture and Archaeology*. Farnham: Ashgate, 31–44.

Bol, P. C., ed. (2004). *Geschichte der antiken Bildhauerkunst*. Vol. 2, *Klassische Plastik*. Frankfurt: von Zabern.

Borbein, A. H. (1973). "Die griechische Statue des 4. Jahrhunderts v. Chr.: Formanalytische Untersuchungen zur Kunst der Nachklassik." *Jahrbuch des deutschen archäologischen Instituts* 88: 43–212.

Brinkmann, V. (1994). *Beobachtungen zum formalen Aufbau und zum Sinngehalt der Friese des Siphnierschatzhauses*. Studien zur antiken Malerei und Farbgebung 1. Munich: Biering and Brinkmann.

(2001). "Die Fotografie in der Archäologie." In S. Altekamp, M. R. Hofter, and M. Krumme, eds., *Posthumanistische klassische Archäologie: Historizität und Wissenschaftlichkeit von Interessen und Methoden; Kolloquium Berlin 1999*. Munich: Hirmer, 403–11.

Brunn, H., Bruckmann, F., and Arndt, P. (1888–1900). *Denkmäler griechischer und römischer Sculptur*. Vol. 1. Munich: Bruckmann.

Buschor, E. (1940). *Die Tyrannen-Mörder*. Sitzungsberichte der Bayerischen Akademie der Wissenschaften, Philosophisch-Historische Abteilung 5. Munich: Bayerische Akademie der Wissenschaften.

Collet, P. (1996). "La photographie et l'archéologie: Des chemins inverses." *Bulletin de correspondance hellénique* 120.1: 325–44.

Craske, M. (2020). *Joseph Wright of Derby: Painter of Darkness*. New Haven, CT: Yale University Press.

Curtius, E., and Adler, F. (1894). *Olympia: Die Ergebnisse der von dem Deutschen Reich veranstalteten Ausgrabung*. Vol. 3, *Die Bildwerke von Olympia in Stein und Thon*. Berlin: Asher.

Dally, O. (2017). *Zur Archäologie der Fotografie: Ein Beitrag zu Abbildungspraktiken der zweiten Hälfte des 19. und des frühen 20. Jahrhunderts*. Berlin: De Gruyter.

Di Cosmo, L. (2013). "Un nuovo canone per la 'bella maniera': I *Segmenta* di François Perrier." In L. Di Cosmo and L. Fatticcioni, eds., *Le componenti del Classicismo secentesco: Lo statuto della scultura antica; Atti del convegno internazionale; Pisa, Scuola Normale Superiore, 15–16 settembre 2011*. Rome: Ginevra Bentivoglio EditoriA, 133–58.

Diepolder, H. (1931). *Die attischen Grabreliefs des 5. Und 4. Jahrhunderts v. Chr.* Berlin: Keller.

Dietrich, N. (2018). *Das Attribut als Problem: Eine bildwissenschaftliche Untersuchung zur griechischen Kunst*. Berlin: De Gruyter.

(2022). "Archaic Grave Monuments: Body or Stele?" In J. Barringer and F. Lissarrague, eds., *Images at the Crossroads: Media and Meaning in Greek Art*. Edinburgh: Edinburgh University Press, 421–44.

(2023). "Drawing vs. Photography: On the Gains and Losses of Technical Innovation." In Meyer and Petsalis-Diomidis 2023: 246–75.

Dietrich, N., Fouquet, J., and Reinhardt, C. (2020). *Schreiben auf statuarischen Monumenten: Aspekte materialer Textkultur in archaischer und frühklassischer Zeit*. Materiale Textkulturen 29. Berlin: De Gruyter.

Dobbe, M. (2007). *Fotografie als theoretisches Objekt: Bildwissenschaft, Medienästhetik, Kunstgeschichte*. Munich: Fink.

Emerling, J. (2012). *Photography: History and Theory*. London: Routledge.

Filser, W. (2017). "Illustrated Travel Journals in the Nineteenth Century/Bilder-Reisen im 19. Jahrhundert." In W. Filser and R. Reisen, eds., *Asia Minor Reprise: Contemporary Photographs Revisiting the Sites of Nineteenth-Century Archaeological Views in Anatolia/Historische Abbildungspraxis und zeitgenössischer Standpunkt; Eine fotografische Erkundung der antiken Stätten Kleinasiens*. Tübingen: Wasmuth, 7–21.

(2018). "Magda und Max Ohnefalsch-Richter als Photographen und der Einsatz der frühen Photographie in der Archäologie: Mit einem Anhang zu einem Photofund im Winckelmann-Institut." In S. G. Schmid and S. G. Horacek, eds., *"I Don't Know What I Am to Myself, It Is So Very Difficult to Explain": Max Ohnefalsch-Richter (1850–1917) und die Archäologie Zyperns*. Berlin: Logos, 143–84.

Fittschen, K. (1974). "Über das Photographieren römischer Porträts." *Archäologischer Anzeiger* 89.3: 484–94.

Fittschen, K., Zanker, P., and Cain, P. (2010). *Katalog der römischen Porträts in den Capitolinischen Museen und den anderen kommunalen Sammlungen der Stadt Rom*. Vol. 2., *Die männlichen Privatporträts*. Berlin: De Gruyter.

Frontisi-Ducroux, F. (1995). *Du masque au visage: Aspects de l'identité en Grèce ancienne.* Paris: Flammarion.

Furtwängler, A. (1893). *Meisterwerke der griechischen Plastik: Kunstgeschichtliche Untersuchungen.* Leipzig: Giesecke and Devrient.

Geyer, C. M. (2012). "Bewegliche Sockel für antike Statuen und deren Abgüsse: Ausdruck neuer Erkenntnisinteressen und ästhetischer Bedürfnisse." In C. Schreiter, ed., *Gipsabgüsse und antike Skulpturen: Präsentation und Kontext.* Berlin: Reimer, 95–114.

Gimon, G. (1980). "La photographie ancienne et l'archéologie." *Revue archéologique*, n.s., vol. 1: 134–6.

Goethe, J. W. (1908). *Poetry and Truth: From My Own Life.* Trans. M. Steele Smith. London: Bell.

(1986). *Sämtliche Werke, Briefe, Tagebücher und Gespräche.* Vol. 14, *Aus meinem Leben: Dichtung und Wahrheit.* Ed. K.-D. Müller. Frankfurt: Deutscher Klassiker.

Graciano, A. (2013–4). "Observation, Imitation and Emulation in *An Academy by Lamplight* by Joseph Wright of Derby (1734–97)." *British Art Journal* 14.3: 36–41.

Hamill, S., and Luke, M. R., eds. (2017). *Photography and Sculpture: The Art Object in Reproduction.* Los Angeles, CA: Getty Research Institute.

Herrmann, H. V. (1972). *Olympia: Heiligtum und Wettkampfstätte.* Munich: Hirmer.

Hildebrand, A. (1893). *Das Problem der Form in der bildenden Kunst.* Strasbourg: Heitz.

Hofmann, E. (1982). "Peter Anton von Verschaffelt: Hofbildhauer des Kurfürsten Carl Theodor in Mannheim." PhD dissertation, Heidelberg University.

Hofter, M. R. (2011). "Die Altarterrasse als 'sakraler Ort': Überlegungen zur Skulpturenausstattung des Altarplatzes." In R. Grüßinger and A. Scholl, eds., *Pergamon – Panorama der antiken Metropole: Begleitbuch zur Ausstellung.* Petersberg: Imhof, 219–23.

(2015). "Technische Beobachtungen zu freistehenden Skulpturen der Altarterrasse von Pergamon." In R. Grüßinger, U. Kästner, and A. Scholl, eds., *Pergamon als Zentrum der hellenistischen Kunst: Bedeutung, Eigenheiten & Ausstrahlung; Internationales Kolloquium Berlin, 26–28 September 2012.* Petersberg: Imhof, 144–55.

Hübner, G. (2004). "Zu den Anfängen der Photographie in der deutschsprachigen Klassischen Archäologie: Ihre Anwendung während der ersten zwei Jahrzehnte der Pergamongrabung." *Istanbuler Mitteilungen* 54: 83–111.

Johnson, G. A. (2013). "'(Un)richtige Aufnahme': Renaissance Sculpture and the Visual Historiography of Art History." *Art History* 36.1: 12–51.

Kaltsas, N., ed. (2002). *Sculpture in the National Archaeological Museum, Athens.* Los Angeles, CA: J. Paul Getty Museum.

Klamm, S. (2007). "Bilder im Wandel: Der Berliner Archäologe Reinhard Kekulé von Stradonitz und die Konkurrenz von Zeichnung und Fotografie." *Jahrbuch der Berliner Museen* 49: 115–26.

(2008). "Bruckmann Verlag, Friedrich (1814–1898): German Fine Art Publisher." In J. Hannavy, ed., *Encyclopedia of Nineteenth-Century Photography*. New York: Routledge, 225–7.

(2010). "Neue Originale: Medienpluralität in der Klassischen Archäologie des 19. Jahrhunderts." In T. Bartsch, M. Becker, H. Bredekamp, and C. Schreiter, eds., *Das Originale der Kopie: Kopien als Produkte und Medien der Transformation von Antike*. Berlin: De Gruyter, 47–67.

(2017a). *Bilder des Vergangenen: Visualisierung in der Archäologie im 19. Jahrhundert – Fotografie, Zeichnung und Abguss*. Berlin: Mann.

(2017b). "'Pictorial Silhouettes' and Their Surroundings: Antique Sculpture and Archaeological Photography." In Hamill and Luke 2017: 50–66.

Koortbojian, M. (2023). *The Representation of Space in Graeco-Roman Art. Relief Sculpture, Problems of Form, and Modern Historiography*. Berlin/Boston: De Gruyter.

Kopf, B. (2007). "Skulptur im Bild: Visuelle Dokumentation und ihr Beitrag zur Entwicklung der archäologischen Wissenschaft." In I. Reichle, S. Siegel, and A. Spelten, eds., *Verwandte Bilder: Die Fragen der Bildwissenschaft*. Berlin: Kadmos, 149–67.

Korshak, Y. (1987). *Frontal Faces in Attic Vase Painting of the Archaic Period*. Chicago, IL: Ares.

Krahmer, G. (1923–4). "Stilphasen der hellenistischen Plastik." *Mitteilungen des Deutschen Archäologischen Instituts, Römische Abteilung* 38–9: 138–85.

(1927). *Die einansichtige Gruppe und die späthellenistische Kunst*. Gottingen: Nachrichten der Gesellschaft der Wissenschaften zu Göttingen, Philologisch-Historische Klasse.

Langlotz, E. (1929). "Review of J. Sieveking and C. Weickert, eds., Fünfzig Meisterwerke der Glyptothek König Ludwigs I. Paul Wolters zum 70. Geburtstag dargebracht (Munich: Obernetter, 1928)." *Gnomon* 5: 481–5.

(1979). "Über das Photographieren griechischer Skulpturen." *Jahrbuch des Deutschen Archäologischen Instituts* 94: 1–17.

Laveissière, S. (2011). "L'antique selon François Perrier: Les *Segmenta nobilium signorum* et leurs modèles." In M. Bayard and E. Fumagalli, eds., *Poussin et la construction de l'Antique*. Rome: Académie de France à Rome, 49–305.

Leibundgut, A. (1999). "Von der 'Lüsternheit des Auges': Gedanken zu den Gruppen Pan-Daphnis und 'Leda ignuda' im Antiquarium des Kardinals Federico Cesi in Rom." In P. C. Bol, ed., *Hellenistische Gruppen: Gedenkschrift für Andreas Linfert*. Mainz: von Zabern, 365–425.

Lindner, R. (1999). "Reinhard Kekulé von Stradonitz – Alexander Conze: Zum Diskurs der Fotografie in der klassischen Archäologie des 19. Jahrhunderts." *Fotogeschichte: Beiträge zur Geschichte und Ästhetik der Fotografie* 73: 7–16.

Lorenz, K. (2013). "Der Große Fries des Pergamon-Altars: Die narratologische Kategorie Metalepse und die Analyse von Erzählung in der Flächenkunst." In U. E. Eisen and P. von Möllendorff, eds., *Über die Grenze: Metalepse in Text- und Bildmedien des Altertums*. Narratologia 39. Berlin: De Gruyter, 119–47.

Lyons, C. L., and Papadopoulos, J. K., eds. (2005). *Antiquity & Photography: Early Views of Ancient Mediterranean Sites*. Los Angeles, CA: J. Paul Getty Museum.

Ma, J. (2013). *Statues and Cities: Honorific Portraits and Civic Identity in the Hellenistic World*. Oxford: Oxford University Press.

Mallgrave, H. F., and Ikonomou, E., eds. (1994). *Empathy, Form, and Space: Problems in German Aesthetics, 1873–1893*. Santa Monica, CA: Getty Center for the History of Art and the Humanities.

Marcoci, R. (2010). "The Original Copy: Photography of Sculpture from 1839 to Today." In R. Marcoci, ed., *The Original Copy: Photography of Sculpture from 1839 to Today*. New York: Museum of Modern Art, 12–19.

Melius, J. (2017). "Sculpture from Behind." In Hamill and Luke 2017: 67–80.

Meyer, C., and Petsalis-Diomidis, A., eds. (2023). *Picturing the Greek Vase: Classical Reception between Art and Science*. Oxford: Oxford University Press.

Michaelis, A. (1906). *Die archäologischen Entdeckungen des neunzehnten Jahrhunderts*. Leipzig: Seemann.

Neer, R. (2001). "Framing the Gift: The Politics of the Siphnian Treasury at Delphi." *Classical Antiquity* 20.2: 273–334.

(2010). *The Emergence of the Classical Style in Greek Sculpture*. Chicago, IL: University of Chicago Press.

Ohly, D. (1976). *Die Aegineten: Die Marmorskulpturen des Tempels der Aphaia auf Aegina*. Vol. 1, *Die Ostgiebelgruppe: Ein Katalog der Glyptothek München*. Munich: Beck.

Osborne, R. (1987). "The Viewing and Obscuring of the Parthenon Frieze." *Journal of Hellenic Studies* 107: 98–105.

(2000). "Archaic and Classical Greek Temple Sculpture and the Viewer." In N. K. Rutter and B. A. Sparkes, eds., *Word and Image in Ancient Greece*. Edinburgh: Edinburgh University Press, 228–46.

Oy-Marra, E. (2020). "Autopsie, Aufzeichnung und Bildkritik: Das Paradigma der Augenzeugenschaft und der Diskurs über den Aussagewert der Kopie bei Pietro Sante Bartoli, Giovan Pietro Bellori und Sebastiano Resta." In E. Oy-Marra and I. Schmiedel, eds., *Zeigen – Überzeugen – Beweisen: Methoden der Wissensproduktion in Kunstliteratur, Kennerschaft und Sammlungspraxis der Frühen Neuzeit*. Heidelberg: arthistoricum.net, 215–55.

Penny, N. (2008). "The Evolution of the Plinth, Pedestal, and Socle." In N. Penny and E. Schmidt, eds., *Collecting Sculpture in Early Modern Europe*. Studies in the History of Art 70. Washington, DC: National Gallery of Art, 461–81.

Perrier, F. (1638). *Segmenta nobilium signorum e statuarum: Quae temporis dentem invidium euasere Urbis aeternae ruinis erepta Typis aenis ab se commissa Perpetuae uenerationis monumentum*. Rome: De Rubeis.

(1653). *Segmenta nobilium signorum e statuarum: Quae temporis dentem invidium euasere Urbis aeternae ruinis erepta Typis aenis ab se commissa Perpetuae uenerationis monumentum.* Reedition. Rome: De Rubeis.

Schreiter, C. (2014). *Antike um jeden Preis. Gipsabgüsse und Kopien antiker Plastik am Ende des 18. Jahrhunderts.* Transformationen der Antike 29. Berlin: De Gruyter.

Schubert, F., and Grunauer-von Hoerschelmann, S. (1978). *Archäologie und Photographie: Fünfzig Beispiele zur Geschichte und Methode.* Mainz: von Zabern.

Shanks, M. (1997). "Photography and Archaeology." In B. L. Molyneaux, ed., *The Cultural Life of Images: Visual Representation in Archaeology.* London: Routledge, 73–107.

Socha, S. (2006). "Der Antikensaal in der Mannheimer Zeichnungsakademie." In B. Savoy, ed., *Tempel der Kunst: Die Geburt des öffentlichen Museums in Deutschland, 1701–1815.* Mainz: von Zabern, 243–57.

Squire, M. S. (2018). "Embodying the Dead on Classical Attic Grave-Stelai." In M. Gaifman, V. J. Platt, and M. S. Squire, eds., "The Embodied Object in Classical Antiquity," special issue, *Art History* 41.3: 518–45.

Stürmer, V., and von Wrede, H. (1998). *Ein Museum im Wartestand: Die Abgußsammlung antiker Bildwerke.* Winckelmann-Institut der Humboldt-Universität zu Berlin 3. Berlin: Arenhövel.

Suchezky, E. (2019). *Die Abguss-Sammlungen von Düsseldorf und Göttingen im 18. Jahrhundert: Zur Rezeption antiker Kunst zwischen Absolutismus und Aufklärung.* Berlin: De Gruyter.

Villinger, V. (1997). "Der Fotograf zwischen Kunstwerk und Kunstgeschichte: Aufnahmen von Skulpturen des Mittelalters und der frühen Neuzeit." In Billeter 1997: 59–69.

Winnefeld, H. (1910). *Altertümer von Pergamon.* Vol. 3.2, *Die Friese des Großen Altars.* Berlin: Reimer.

Wölfflin, H. (1896). "Wie man Skulpturen aufnehmen soll I." *Zeitschrift für bildende Kunst*, n.s., vol. 7: 224–8.

(1897). "Wie man Skulpturen aufnehmen soll II." *Zeitschrift für bildende Kunst*, n.s. vol. 8: 294–7.

(1914). "Wie man Skulpturen aufnehmen soll?" *Zeitschrift für bildende Kunst*, n. s. vol. 26: 237–44.

(2013). "How One Should Photograph Sculpture" (= Wölfflin 1896, 1897, and 1914). Trans. G. A. Johnson. *Art History* 36.1: 52–71.

Zenzen, N., ed. (2016). *Objekte erzählen Geschichte(n): 150 Jahre Institut für Klassische Archäologie; Eine Ausstellung im Universitätsmuseum Heidelberg, 26. Oktober 2016 bis 18. April 2017.* Heidelberg: Universität Heidelberg, Zentrum für Altertumswissenschaften, Institut für Klassische Archäologie.

Züchner, W. (1959). *Über die Abbildung.* Winckelmannsprogramm der Archäologischen Gesellschaft zu Berlin 115. Berlin: De Gruyter.

6 | Seeing the Past

Neo-Attic Reliefs as Sites of Temporal and Spatial Contact

CAROLYN M. LAFERRIÈRE

Neo-Attic reliefs created in the first centuries BCE and CE offer something of an art-historical enigma to their modern viewers. Primarily made for an elite Roman audience with deep interests in Greek language and culture, the distinctive reliefs invoke stylistic techniques from different periods of Greek art and creatively combine figural types taken from other, earlier objects.[1] The reliefs' stylistic and figural plurality aligns them with multiple points in the past, establishing an implicit timelessness within each scene. Further complicating the ambiguous temporality of the reliefs is the frequent representation of mythological subjects, such that the events they portray occur in a distant but indeterminate mythical past. Maenads, in particular, are commonly depicted on Neo-Attic reliefs (e.g. Fig. 6.1), but whether it is their intricately dancing bodies or the contorted movements and floating drapery of other divine and mythological figures, the scenes depicted on Neo-Attic reliefs generally appear as grounded not so much in a particular historic style, but rather as moving between the various temporal moments that they encapsulate.[2] At the same time, throughout the corpus there is also a pervading sense of spacelessness, established by the representation of figures, objects, and landscapes in shallow relief and by the distorted play with depth and space that occurs within many of the compositions. As a whole, therefore, Neo-Attic reliefs resist a clear depiction of either time or space, and instead blur together multiple times and multiple spaces for their viewers. As Alexander Nagel and Christopher S. Wood have suggested, "The ability of the work of art to hold incompatible models in suspension without deciding is the key to art's anachronic quality, its ability really to 'fetch' a past, create a past, perhaps even fetch the future."[3] In considering the significance of time and space for the composition and effect of Neo-Attic reliefs in the first centuries BCE and CE, this chapter argues that the varied

My thanks go to the editors for their careful reading, astute suggestions, patience, and guidance. I am also grateful to Cliff Robinson and R. R. R. Smith for reading an earlier draft and to the audiences at the University of Southern California and Princeton University for their comments and questions, all of which have improved this chapter.

[1] Fullerton 1998: 94. [2] Daremberg and Saglio 1873: 312–13; Dütschke 1878, no. 516.
[3] Nagel and Wood 2010: 18.

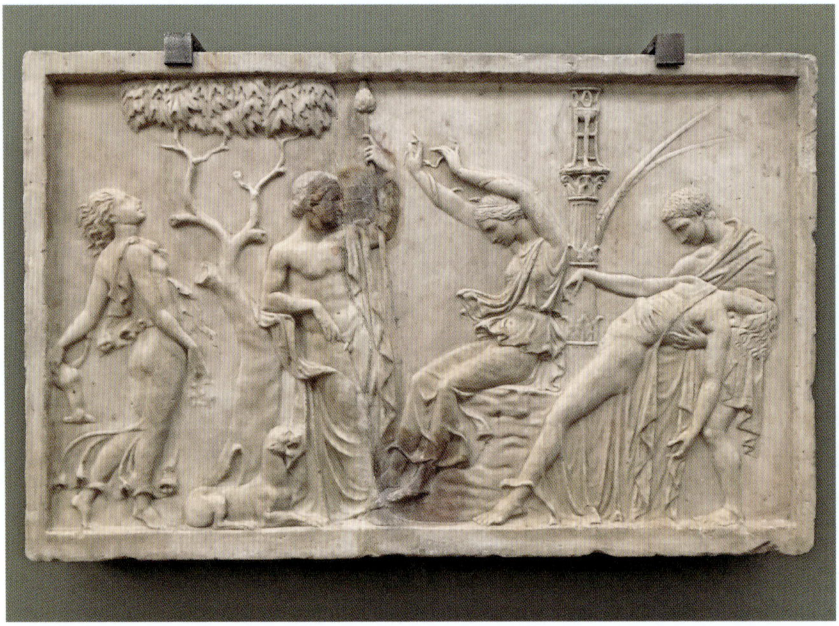

Fig. 6.1 Relief with Dionysian scene, first half of the first century CE. Fine-grained marble, 37 × 45 cm. Florence, Galleria della Statue e delle Pitture degli Uffizi, inv. 1914 n. 314 (by permission of the Ministry of Culture).

formal elements of Neo-Attic reliefs work in concert to "fetch a past" and its associated cultural values for their Roman viewing audience.[4]

The objects were first labeled as Neo-Attic by Heinrich Brunn and then by Friedrich Hauser, who used the term to describe reliefs from the late Hellenistic period that emulated the Archaic and Classical sculptures of Athens in their formal style and in their replication of specific figural forms.[5] Following J. J. Pollitt's discussion of the second phase of Neo-Attic sculpture, which spans the first centuries BCE and CE, we may further characterize this corpus of reliefs by their prevailing use of specific Archaizing features, such as gravity-defying zigzag folds for drapery, elongated bodies that move in impossible ways, and subjects that evoke ancient religious practices. In their styles of representation, Neo-Attic

[4] Compare Elsner and Squire 2016. For discussion of how Nagel and Wood's concept of substitutionality might be adapted to polytheistic antiquity, see also Jones 2019b: 179–229.

[5] Heinrich Brunn (1853: 559–70) referred to a small corpus of late Hellenistic sculptors as *neu-attische*, as compared to the *alt-attische* sculptors of Classical Athens, while Friedrich Hauser grouped together a larger corpus under the same name. Hauser, moreover, collected more than 150 examples of Neo-Attic reliefs and used the large corpus to isolate commonly reproduced figural types. See Hauser 1889; Fuchs 1959; Havelock 1964, 1965; Pollitt 1986: 164–84; Fullerton 1990, 1998, 2016: 489–99; Di Franco 2017.

reliefs are thus necessarily bound up with the past: for instance, on the relief above, the position of the dancer on the left replicates Classical images of dancing maenads,[6] the Archaizing style used to depict bodies and drapery loosely positions the scene as a continuation of earlier modes of representation, the plain frame suggests a relationship with the formal structure of fourth-century BCE votive reliefs,[7] and the inclusion of Delphic landscape markers positions the scene at the famous sanctuary, which functioned as a religious center of the Greek world. The mannered style used to create these scenes thus marks off the figures within it as existing in a distinct and separate space from the external world of the viewer, so that their clothing, bodies, and precise movements are presented as occurring in a place that is not our own. We might even, following Pollitt, suggest that Neo-Attic reliefs evoke a general sense of "nostalgia" for an idealized, remote past by frequently depicting gods and mythological figures alone among themselves, away from their human worshippers.[8] A less remarked upon feature of the reliefs is their shallowness – that is, the low relief in which they are carved, so that the figures and landscape elements seem barely to emerge from the blank background and, in turn, seem equally able to disappear back into it at any moment.[9] The images as a group are thus compelling examples of the self-conscious visual exploration of both time and space, presented through the technique of relief. In other words, not only do Neo-Attic reliefs point to multiple pasts, but they

6 The left maenad, Dionysos, and the two figures on the right all seem to have been derived from motifs seen elsewhere, whereas the seated maenad who raises her arms seems to be unique to this image. Perhaps the most frequently replicated scene of dancing maenads is Kallimachos' relief from the late fifth century BCE, which was reproduced in whole and in part, at various scales, and in different media throughout the Roman period. However, some of the figures also seem to echo those on Attic red-figure vases: The movement of drapery around torsos and legs recalls the scene on a kylix by Makron (Berlin, Antikensammlung, F 2290) or another by the Briseis Painter (London, British Museum, 1843,1103.54); the snakes that twist up another maenad's arms recalls similar scenes of maenads on a volute krater by the group of Polygnotos (Ferrara, Museo Nazionale di Spina, 2897) or even of Dionysos himself (London, British Museum, 1843,1103.54); and the maenad on the left, who holds a deer, recalls scenes of Dionysos and maenads also dancing with whole or partially torn deer (London, British Museum, 1836,0224.35 and 1867,0508.1126).

7 Issues of framing are particularly pronounced with relief sculpture, and we need only look to fourth-century BCE votive reliefs, such as those votives to Pan and the Nymphs that are surrounded by cave frames or the eyes that were set atop the frame on a votive for Amphiaraos at Oropos, to see that there existed in Greek visual culture a self-conscious interplay of landscape, relief, and frame. See esp. Hurwit 1977; Platt 2011: 44–7; Gaifman 2017; Platt and Squire 2017. On the phenomenological and ritual consequences of the visual manipulation of the frame, see Laferrière 2019.

8 Pollitt 1986: 175–8; Di Franco 2017: 63–101.

9 On the tension between two- and three-dimensions in relief, see Summers 2003: 15–60; Davis 2017: 229–63; Lakey 2018: 151–3.

also employ multiple points of reference to achieve a mode of representation that exists outside of space and beyond time. On the one hand, the prevailing choice of mythological or religious subject matter points to a deep, albeit indeterminate past that predates or even exists outside of human history. On the other hand, the deliberate use of the Archaizing style and creative replication of earlier forms reference and visualize specific moments in the human process of artistic facture. Following Nagel and Wood, we could even say that these reliefs, by virtue of their style, material, and composition, "hold multiple temporalities in suspension,"[10] ultimately offering their viewers an atemporal vision of a remote past that is nevertheless accessible through particular acts of looking, remembering, and experiencing.

For this relief's Roman viewers, who likely belonged to a wealthy, erudite elite familiar with Hellenic artistic and religious traditions, the play of styles, figural models, and compositions created a specific kind of viewing experience. After all, as Jaś Elsner and Michael Squire have shown, "it is only in a culture with an acute historical and aesthetic awareness of stylistic differences that free and widespread creative usage, replication, and play with different models is possible."[11] We might approach the scene from a number of perspectives: the portrait of the god and his followers in Euripides' *Bacchai*, the place of Dionysian ritual in Greek religion, and female choral dance, to name just a few.[12] Previous approaches to these reliefs have focused especially on isolating the models for the first-century BCE and CE adaptations.[13] Yet, in its reformulation of style and composition, as well as in its position somewhere between decoration and ritual object, the relief does not simply attempt to recreate previous scenes of Dionysian revelry. Rather, it engages in a dialectic between competing models of image production, as Nagel and Wood might describe it, where the tension between the two is continually negotiated by the object itself.[14] Drawing on recent work on the Roman practice of replication,[15] together with the inherent

[10] Nagel and Wood 2010: 26. [11] Elsner and Squire 2016: 204.

[12] On Dionysos' relationship with Apollo and Delphi, see Strauss Clay 1996. We see maenads already in Homer (*Il.* 22.461), and they are frequently depicted in the visual arts. For general discussions, see Lawler 1927; Henrichs 1978; McNally 1978; Bremmer 1984; Hedreen 1994; Peirce 1998.

[13] See e.g. Fuchs 1959. The finds from the Mahdia shipwreck present a distinct challenge to earlier attempts to organize the reliefs into any sort of chronology. See Cain 1985; Grassinger 1991; Fullerton 1998, 2016: 489–99; Hemingway 2016: 89–90.

[14] Nagel and Wood 2010: 7–20.

[15] On the Roman practice of replicating Greek objects, see, among others, Gazda 2002; Perry 2005; Trimble and Elsner 2006; Varner 2006; Marvin 2008, 168–247; Hallett 2012. Compare also Anguissola 2012; Hallett 2015; Jones 2019a, with previous bibliography.

creativity and deliberation with which the Romans visualized their relationship with the Greek past,[16] it seems more fruitful to put to one side, as Mark D. Fullerton suggests, "the very concept of [a] prototype."[17] Instead, we should understand Neo-Attic reliefs as having been created in a Roman aesthetic, in a Roman context, for a Roman viewing audience, albeit an audience that was intensely focused on the artistic and cultural achievements of the Greek past.[18] By self-consciously combining past works of art and thus collapsing multiple temporalities within a single frame, Neo-Attic reliefs invite us to consider the formal and material implications of relief as a medium or technique, the distinct creation and manipulation of space and time within the limits of each image's composition, and the effect that such temporal and spatial manipulations had on their Roman viewers.

A number of questions arise, therefore, with respect to what those elite Romans who purchased these reliefs for their villas or used them to decorate public buildings hoped to experience when looking at these reliefs.[19] Were the objects meant to function as decoration, to be looked at during moments of *otium* – that is, leisure and rest from politics or public service?[20] Or were they intended to connect their viewers with an idealized, though remote past, so that the Archaizing style and figural pastiches would link the cultural life of first-century BCE and CE Rome with Archaic and Classical Athens? Much work has been done on the Roman habit of emulating and replicating earlier Greek art, and although this was a complex and multivalent practice, if something general can be asserted, it is that Roman relationship to Greek originals was not limited to the repetition of so-called masterpieces.[21] Rather, a vast array of motivations lay behind it, including the political, cultural, and religious. Miranda Marvin persuasively argued that the Roman elite who surrounded themselves with works of art that drew upon the Greek past, such as our Neo-Attic reliefs, "were not merely passive recipients of cultural artifacts" but rather "actively engaged with them [so that] meaning is created at the point of reception."[22] Working between Marvin's "aesthetic of repetition" and Nagel and Wood's dialectic of substitutional and authorial image making, in what follows, I examine certain formal elements of Neo-Attic reliefs, such as their

[16] Hölscher 2005. [17] Fullerton 1998: 93.

[18] In this approach, I draw especially from Elsner's discussion of a "cultural memory bank" of earlier styles (2005: 275–6). See also Hölscher 2005; Varner 2006: 284, 288–99; Marvin 2008: 168–247; Elsner and Squire 2016.

[19] On the tension between displaying Greek or Greek-inspired art works in public and private contexts, see Jucker 1950; Becatti 1951; Pollitt 1978; Bravi 2012; Rutledge 2012; Gahtan and Pegazzano 2015.

[20] We see a similar discussion of *otium* as it is mentioned by Pliny the Younger in Leach 2003.

[21] Marvin 2008: 168–247. See note 15 for relevant scholarship. [22] Marvin 2008: 245.

shallow depth, their elongated and mannered movements, and their lack of narrative, mythological, or historical time, in order to think through how these reliefs interacted with and worked upon their first-century BCE and CE viewers. I take as my evidence a small selection of this large corpus, focusing in particular on scenes featuring gods and mythological figures. I argue that the visually constructed space of the reliefs suggests a temporality that at once acts as an index of past times, even as it also materializes a timelessness that remains ever available to its Roman viewing audience. Moreover, I posit that the particular Archaizing styles employed for these reliefs, where the figures' movements are at once dynamic and delicate, interconnected and individual, served not only to determine and reinforce the remoteness of the spaces in which they move but also to expand the limits of that space into the surrounding environment, so that this aesthetic of temporality, of simultaneous closeness and remoteness, ultimately offered the viewers an experience of contact with the otherwise stylized and inaccessible scenes.

Bodies in Relief

The shallow visual field and relatively sparse background of the Dionysian relief (Fig. 6.1) focus the viewer's attention on the movements of the depicted figures. Every outstretched arm or turned head stands out within the scene since, pictorially, each element seems to push up to and extend out from the surface of the background by virtue of its location in notional space. A number of actions stand out in particular: one figure holds a deer as she rotates into the scene, another holds up her arms as snakes twist and turn around them, Dionysos holds up his *thyrsos*, a panther screams, and a young man catches a third dancer, who seems so overcome by her performance that she falls to the ground. These are all actions that we might expect to find in a Dionysian scene, whether it was created in the Archaic or Classical periods or in the late Hellenistic or early Roman periods. To determine, however, how these actions interact with each other within the shallow space of the Neo-Attic relief and how, in turn, they engage with their audience, we might also characterize them as gestures, understood generally as actions undertaken by an individual when s/he moves to reach out to another person, object, or place.[23] Alex Purves has recently argued that gesture could also be more broadly conceived as a comprehensive "manner of carrying the body," so that we can isolate certain movements as significant markers within any given narrative.[24] By focusing

[23] Purves 2019: 5. [24] Purves 2019: 5.

upon these movements in the relief, a visuality of gesture emerges wherein bodies can be understood as moving in complex and interrelated patterns that come together to determine the meaning and significance of the scene for its viewing audience.

The expansive definition of gesture finds its parallel in the Greek term *schēma*, which can generally be understood as denoting a pose or posture.[25] Importantly, *schēma* offers us a helpful tool with which to determine how these shallow, stylized bodies relate to each other, their background, and their viewers. In the Classical period, the term was often used to describe the particular pose of a statue or to describe the movements of a body that are captured by an image, such as putting something down or picking something up.[26] It is also a term that is particularly used within descriptions of dance, where it denotes the endpoint of danced movement, the final pose a dancer takes before moving on to the next sequence.[27] Within this understanding of *schēma*, especially as it is discussed by Aristides Quintilianus, a dancer continuously moves between *schēmata*.[28] One dances, therefore, by linking a sequence of gestures, of *schēmata*. Drawing on Pollitt's discussion of *schēma*, moreover, we might even think of the term as a more colloquial counterpart to *rhythmos*, a technical term in both musical and visual theory.[29] Not only can *rhythmos* designate the form or shape of a figure, object, or composition, but in the fifth and fourth centuries BCE, it also took on a sense of repetition, so that it could also refer to the configuration or proportion of the component parts of a melody or of a pattern painted onto a vase or sculpted into stone.[30]

If we take *rhythmos* and *schēma* together as a methodological framework for our discussion of the relief, the two terms offer us a technical language with which to describe how a visual image might appear to set a body in motion. With respect to relief proper, this language becomes all the more important since the forms of the figures appear to move not only in relation

25 Catoni 2008; Purves 2019: 4–5.

26 Dem. *De falsa legatione* 251; Xen. *Mem.* 3.10.7; Pollitt 1986: 258.

27 Bocksberger 2017; Robinson 2021.

28 The movements that lead up to and determine the form of the poses are described as *peras* or *semeia*. For further discussion, see Robinson 2021: 307–10. For more on dance in Aristides Quintilianus, see *De musica* 73.28–74.6 W.-I.; Barker 1989: 475–6.

29 Pollitt 1974: 218–28 (*rhythmos*), 58–62 (*schēma*). On isolating *rhythmos* in a visual image, see Laferrière 2020, 2024.

30 The term *rhythmos* first appears among the lyric and elegiac poets of the seventh and sixth centuries BCE. The earliest attested usage is in a fragment of Archilochus (128 West), in which he implores his heart to recognize the changeable nature of life (οἷος ῥυσμὸς ἀνθρώπους ἔχει). It acquired a sense of patterning already by the beginning of the fifth century, when Aeschylus (*Cho.* 793–9) describes the regular beat of a horse's strides as *rhythmos*. See Pollitt 1974: 218–28.

to one another but to the background from which they emerge. Such language further clarifies the visual pattern and aesthetic effect the relief produces as forms arrange themselves in space, as figures reach out to each other, as they move alongside each other. We may see, then, how this relief offers much more nuance to our exploration of the visual effect their *schēmata* have on their viewers. Mythic bodies splay out across the image, each physically raised the same amount from the background plane, one captured mid-dance as she moves deeper into the image, another writhing on a stone as she holds out her arms, the twisting bodies of the snakes further enhancing her seated dance. The third maenad, who collapses, offers perhaps the most dramatic *schēma*, as she falls back, creating a dynamic diagonal with her body, even as her right arm reaches out, her limp hand delicately drawing our eye to her companion. She has been positioned in such a way that her outstretched arms and loose body enhance the visual rhythm created by the other figures. Even though their gestures echo the bodies of other maenads that Hauser identified in other Neo-Attic reliefs and in earlier Classical examples,[31] the visual effect is a unified display of related experiences of Dionysos' presence. The drapery also moves in similar ways, whether falling to the ground in zigzag folds or twirling around legs and bodies, suggesting that there has been a careful attempt to construct the scene in such a way that the *schēmata* or *rhythmoi* of the bodies work together to communicate the erratic energy associated with Dionysos. Although the maenads' hands and arms are occupied by other movements, it is above all the motion that each body undertakes that not only suggests their cohesiveness as a group but also demarcates the space in which they move as belonging to a divine world, where the sounds of divine music can so affect the body that it causes groups to move in a unified harmony.

Gesture, however, also articulates points of difference, both between the figures who move in the composition and between those stylized figures and the bodies of the viewers who encounter them. In this relief, it is above all with the central maenad that we see the visual consequences of a body that deviates from a typical *schēma*. The central figure demands particular visual attention by the strangeness of her position: although she sits on a rock, her body moves in an ecstatic dance, as if she stretches more than should be physically possible. Moreover, the drapery around her abdomen swings out in front of her, while the cloth around her legs extends behind, as if she has just rushed into place. The jarring *schēmata* of her body and her clothing are further enhanced by her outstretched arms, around which

[31] Hauser 1889: esp. nos. 28 and 29; Pollitt 1986: 169–72.

the bodies of snakes twist. The sinuous lines created by the snakes are repeated in the shapes that make up her hair, as well as the hair of her two companions. Such resonances not only establish a visual unity within the composition, but the particular way in which these repeating lines and inexplicably moving drapery come together in the central maenad marks her and the space of the relief in which they are depicted as distinct from the space of the viewer. Here, where the figures seem barely to have emerged from the stone background, the relief presents a glimpse into a place where bodies, collected from earlier works of art, are brought together to move in evidently impossible ways.

The attention given to the seated maenad's arms and hands is a common feature of Neo-Attic reliefs. Elsewhere, Hermes similarly encourages viewers to contemplate how his body might move across the surface of the relief (Fig. 6.2).[32] As with the maenads, he is pushed up to the frontal plane of the relief, seeming to spill out into real space, even as his shallow form barely emerges from the background. He is shown in profile, his intricately curled hair pulled back off his face, drapery falling in precise sharp points, while he holds up a *kerykeion*, the messenger staff topped by two intertwined snakes that he carries with him as he moves between worlds, with a single finger and thumb that barely seem to touch the object and yet effortlessly hold it aloft. The position of his left hand further accentuates the relief's spatial manipulation, as he is not shown grasping a physical, fleshy material body, but rather the left arm and hand are positioned as though only resting on his hip, the depth intervals and foreshortening rendering his actions ambiguous or, at the very least, confused. Even more, Hermes' fingers do not curl around the curve of his body, but instead are rigidly splayed out, suggesting that the god may not even be resting his hand on his hip, but instead holds out a bent arm. Space has thus been manipulated in the relief, so that the god is shown from multiple angles at once: his lower body is in profile, his torso is awkwardly shown on an oblique angle, drapery falls behind his body at yet another aspect, and his arm is uneasily positioned.

The Archaizing style employed in the image further places the god at a distance from his viewers: the relief depicts the god with a stylized body, neat zigzag folds of drapery, careful curls of hair, and contorted hand position, all of which are more reminiscent of the sixth century BCE than the first.[33] The image thus collapses the distance between the two points in time, offering instead a blended timescape for its viewers. The blank

[32] Picón et. al. 2007: 357, 486, no. 12; Zanker et al. 2019: 174–5, no. 68.

[33] For further discussion of the ability of the work of art to collapse stylistic temporalities, see Nagel and Wood 2010: 32.

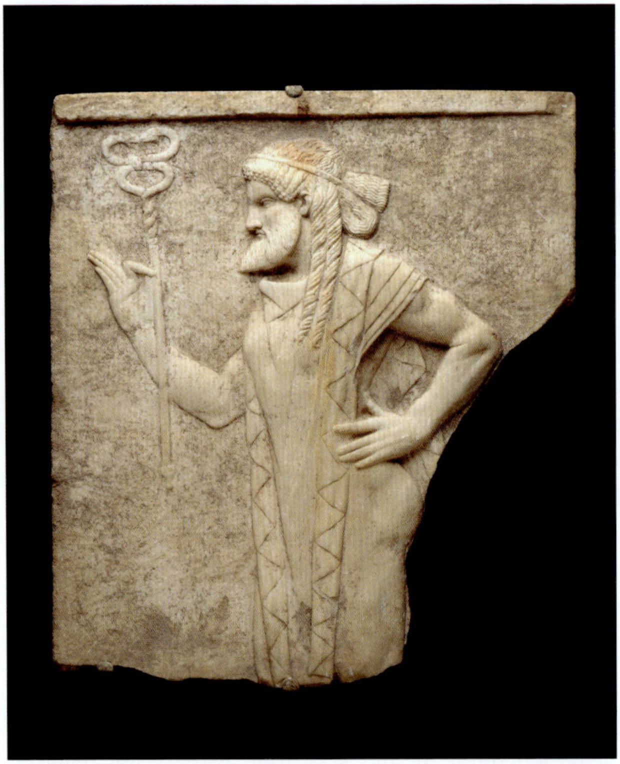

Fig. 6.2 Marble relief with Hermes, ca. 27 BCE–68 CE. Marble, 67.9 × 59.7 cm. New York, Metropolitan Museum of Art, Harris Brisbane Dick Fund, 1991, 1991.11.8 (Creative Commons Zero [CC0]).

background further amplifies the sense that the relief offers us a privileged, atemporal glimpse of the god as he emerges in shallow relief an expanse of color or, as we see now, of blank, white marble.[34] We might even start to think that the god stands in a distinctly divine space, where a hand can be delicately outstretched but nevertheless holds a heavy staff, where bodies seem almost fragile in their elongation, or where drapery can be rhythmic as it folds in repeating lines down the image, separately from any movement the body underneath may or may not take. As a whole, these *schēmata* visually mark off both the god's actions and the space in which he stands as divine, idealized, and remote from human experience. The external viewers of this image are thus continually relegated to the status of

[34] This would be true even if the background was painted at one point, possibly a solid blue as was conventional for many relief sculptures, especially on Archaic and Classical architecture. We see, for instance, traces of a blue background on a Neo-Attic terracotta relief in the Metropolitan Museum of Art (12.232.8a). For more on polychromy and Roman statues, see Abbe 2015, with earlier bibliography. On relief as emergence, see Lakey 2018: 151–3.

distant spectators, who may watch him as he contemplates his messenger's staff, but who lack access to him. At the same time, the collapsed temporality offered by the relief gives the illusion of availability, as if the Archaizing style offers a glimpse into another time that it invites its viewers to join.

The flattening of bodily movement and distortion of gestures is further exaggerated on another relief, where Apollo plays his *kithara*, a type of lyre reserved for virtuoso performances, and with his other hand balances a *phialē* into which Nike pours a libation (Fig. 6.3).[35] Although this particular kind of representation of Apollo displays a challenging feat of simultaneous music-making and ritual performance,[36] Nike's *schēmata* here are no less impressive and distinctive. She stands on tiptoes, as if she

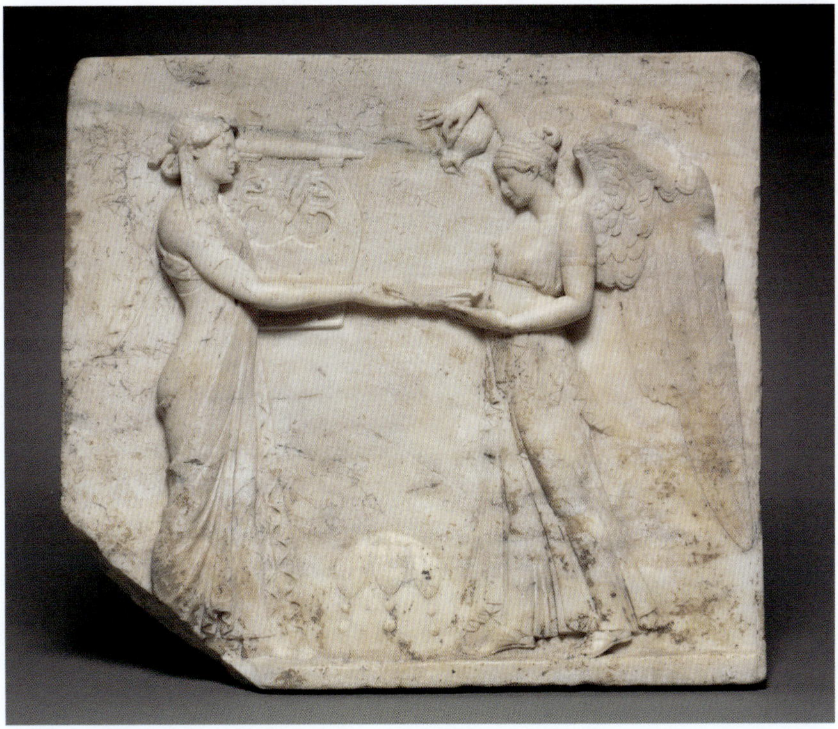

Fig. 6.3 Relief of Apollo with Nike, ca. 27 BCE–14 CE. Marble, 41.6 × 46.4 cm. Cleveland, Ohio, Cleveland Museum of Art, purchase from the J. H. Wade Fund, 1930.522 (Creative Commons Zero [CC0]).

[35] Di Franco 2017: 31.

[36] For more on gods pouring libations, see esp. Patton 2009, with previous bibliography; Gaifman 2018: 117–50. For more on gods playing music while pouring a libation, see Laferrière 2024: ch. 2.

has just flown into the scene but is also moments from leaving it. At the same time, she performs a ritual with Apollo, her hand raised above her head, delicately holding a jug she tips over to pour out its contents. The space in which the liquid falls is also elongated, much like the tall bodies of the gods themselves, so that the visual field within the relief draws attention to the simultaneity of the actions being performed. Set against a now empty background, a blank void of marble that was perhaps once a solid expanse of color, the delicate, fantastical gestures that are performed by the gods in this relief deny the presence of an external human world. Instead, in the three reliefs discussed thus far, the gods move, dance, play music, and perform rituals completely apart from their worshippers, who, upon looking at these scenes, necessarily intrude into these moments that occur in a separate, sacred, and mythological space reserved for the gods.

Space in Relief

The presence of an *omphalos* in the relief depicting Apollo and Nike suggests that the figures are located in Delphi, the sanctuary in northern Greece most associated with Apollo.[37] The central position of the *omphalos* here localizes the scene to a specific place and thus actively works against the blank background. As with the two figures, the dome-shaped stone and its decorated surface have been carved in shallow relief, so that, lacking any added paint to offset it against the rest of the scene, it barely seems to emerge from the marble. The entire scene, in fact, plays with depth: the *omphalos* lays almost flat against the relief's surface, as do the folds of Apollo's drapery that flow out behind him, his hand, and his instrument. Similarly, the far side of Nike's wings are little more than a mere outline scratched onto the background, while her drapery likewise recedes into the background. The bodies of the two gods project somewhat further, their outstretched arms in the deepest relief, so that the shadows they cast draw attention to the ritual they undertake. These overlapping points of depth come to a head, however, around the *omphalos*. As the gods' drapery descends in front of their bodies, it begins to fade into the background, cloth fusing with marble. At the same time, each divinity's leg reaches forward as they move toward each other, their similarly positioned feet beginning to encroach upon the stone dome. Even more, each god's toes encroach slightly upon the *omphalos* itself, introducing a startling

[37] On representations of depth and space in relief, see esp. Davis 2017: 229–63; Lakey 2018: 151–3.

indication of notional depth within an otherwise flattened space. Space thus seems to be inherently malleable here, so that the scene at once takes place at Delphi, a physical, tangible location visited by worshippers, and in a place where the gods reside, where space can be bent and collapsed, where materials blend into each other.

A stylized Delphic landscape also acts as the backdrop for the relief with which we began (Fig. 6.1), where maenads dance and fall while Dionysos watches. Here, the visual field has been fully enclosed by a frame which delineates the composition. The relationship of the figures to the frame, as well as to the frontal plane of the image, marks a distinct point of departure from the typical Classical votive relief which it evokes. Rather than surrounding a self-contained scene, the frame appears to cut across a larger sequence of actions and landscape features, representing to its viewers only a small portion of what actually occurs. In particular, the figures are depicted in such a way that suggests that their movements and actions continue beyond the frame, as if it has merely opened up a small window into their world. For instance, if we look at the maenad who dances on the left, although most of her own body is fully enclosed within the frame, the hand that holds the deer pushes up against the formal delineation of space, even as the body of the animal disappears behind the frame, lost to our sight. The same can be said of the background details that have been included, lending a sense of a landscape. The tree positions the scene outside, though without any more specific indication of location; just as with the animal on the left, the top of the tree projects beyond the image, suggesting a world that exists beyond our access. The *thyrsos* that Dionysos holds runs up against the upper frame of the image, its point disappearing behind the plain border. Further confusing the spatial relationship between figure and background, the entire scene is pushed right up against the frontal plane of the relief, so that figures confusingly overlap with each other within the shallow ledge upon which they move. The tree offers perhaps the most extreme manipulation of space, as it is set right up against the frontal plane of the image, flattening the ground within the relief, even as the panther and Dionysos are set in front of it, offering a striking allusion to depth, even as the upper portion of the tree illogically recedes far into the distance. Similarly, the rock upon which the maenad sits is also depicted as if it is at the relief's pictorial surface, even though it is paradoxically also situated behind the bodies of Dionysos and the falling figure, offering a conflated rendering of space within the relief's pictoriality. Adding to the complexity of the flat, layered space is the column with a tripod on top, which seems to be the farthest back from the frontal plane but is otherwise the same size and orientation as the other figures and elements in the composition. The visual play with space – where the image both suggests an internal, comprehensive landscape, even as it denies the presence of a logical, physical space – introduces the importance of considering how a viewer might have encountered and understood this depiction of space.[38] What this image thus seems to suggest is that the setting of this image is removed from the viewer's own space since it is enclosed within and behind the frame, even as the potentially performable danced *schēmata* exhibited by the maenads offer the possibility of human participation.[39]

Although we know little about the relief's original site of display, one likely context is within the elite world of senatorial and high status equestrian Romans, where it would have been used to decorate opulent domestic residences.[40] Cicero, for instance, asks Atticus to find some low reliefs that can be laid in the stucco near the entrance to his villa at Tusculum.[41] If we tentatively position this Neo-Attic relief within a domestic viewing space, it could have opened up a window into another time and another world, ultimately offering a privileged view into an another point in history. For the discerning viewer, familiar with the Hellenic visual tradition, the use of the mannerist Archaizing style positions the scene in another, earlier period, so that the relief acts as a material link between two points in time. The subject matter also evokes a sense of a distant past, more in line with the Homeric Hymns than the historical present, a time when maenads danced around Dionysos. In considering the legibility of this image for its Roman viewer, the inclusion of the tripod in the background would have also established a spatial link with the sanctuary of Apollo at Delphi, a site where Dionysos was present during the winter months and to where women would travel and dance ecstatically for the god of wine.[42] These Thyiades, as Pausanias calls them,[43] also appeared together with the god on the eastern pediment of the temple to Apollo, further affirming a concrete location.[44] In linking the time and space of the relief with the Roman domestic context in which it was displayed, the

[38] Mitchell 2002.

[39] Some have argued, ranging from Panofsky (1997) through to La Rocca (2008), that this kind of disjointed, nonhomogeneous space is how antiquity conceived of space in both real and pictorial terms. However, as I show throughout this chapter, the deliberate manipulation of both space and time in these reliefs suggests, at the very least, a self-conscious attitude toward important questions of representation and spatial composition.

[40] For an in-depth examination of one such lavishly decorated villa, see Wyler 2006. Compare among others, Platt 2009; Barham 2021.

[41] Cic. *Att.* 1.10.3.

[42] On the historical context of the Thyiades, see McInerney 1997: 270–5.

[43] Paus. 10.32.7; McInerney 1997, with earlier bibliography.

[44] Paus. 10.19.4.

scene offered its viewers the opportunity to experience a divine revel. Viewers could gain access to the world depicted in the scene by imagining that they too experience the power of Dionysos in their own bodies. In exploring the dynamic blurring and overlap between human and divine worlds, the relief thus pushes the boundaries of how visual space is conceived, depicted, and perceived. Here, the landscape is at once one particular sacred space that is ecstatic, dynamic, and exclusively reserved for the gods, and yet it also has made available a mythic rendition of the Delphic landscape, implicitly inviting all those who look upon the image to join in the revel.

Time in Relief

We have thus seen how some Neo-Attic reliefs make use of a blank background to suggest an absence or a flattening of space, while others deliberately evoke specific places through the inclusion of distinct landscape elements.[45] Throughout the Archaic and Classical periods, there were different approaches to addressing the space around the figures: objects were inserted to indicate the place in which the scene was meant to take place; structures such as stoas or caves could indicate where the backdrop could be imaginatively positioned; or it could remain blank, acting as a backdrop against which the actions unfold. What is so striking, however, about the Neo-Attic reliefs that we have encountered is that whether they depict a blank backdrop or a landscape, as a group they are concerned to flatten the visual field, to push the figures right up to the image's frontal surface, regardless of whether the figures are positioned within a distinct landscape or not. Such a denial of any sense of depth in the pictorial field thus reinforces that the figures depicted are representations, that they function at once as an image of the divine and as a decorative body that moves in elongated, elegant *schēmata*. Intimately related to these issues of spatiality is the importance of temporality. Time unfolds across these reliefs in a number of ways. On a basic level, each image displays its own internal sense of time, which governs the movement of figures across the visual field, neither capturing a single moment in time nor putting the sequence of actions into a temporally linear order that is immediately legible to the viewer. However, the Neo-Attic proclivity for combining distinct formal styles and figures introduces yet another sense of temporality within the scene, so that each image might evoke multiple points in the

[45] Compare Lakey 2018: 1–3.

past, both historic and mythic. Ultimately, these notions of time come together within the Neo-Attic reliefs, which, by virtue of their mode of fabrication as carved reliefs, create their own spaceless and timeless visual field. It is above all through the medium of relief, which is a three-dimensional object, even as, with the case of Neo-Attic reliefs, it approaches a two-dimensional image, that the Neo-Attic reliefs mediate between the image carved into stone and the external viewer, so that the visual and stylistic temporalities are put into tension with the viewer's own experience of looking at the relief over time.

A marble relief depicting a divine procession establishes and reinforces a particularly clear sense of time within its composition (Fig. 6.4).[46] On a large fragment of white marble, five figures walk along a shallow ledge, legs moving together in tandem, each figure isolated against the background. The identities of these figures are indicated by the objects they each hold. Leading the group is Zeus, identifiable by thunderbolt and staff. Following him is Hera, her veiling gesture a common feature of her representation, while Athena follows, wearing her aegis and holding a helmet and spear. A female figure holding out a blooming flower behind the warrior goddess is likely Aphrodite. Concluding the procession is Apollo, shown here as a youthful, nude musician playing the *kithara*, a performance lyre.

In depicting a procession, the image carved into the relief necessarily concerns itself with the passing of time. After all, the movement of figures through space is a temporal act, even if those figures are divine.[47] Here, the gods move together as a group, each taking a measured step forward. Another visual evocation of time occurs with the performing Apollo, who actively plays his instrument. The viewers are thus invited to imagine the sounds of that instrument, to understand that music floats through the image, in no small part because we see the effect the sounds of that music have had upon the bodies of the other gods, which have been coordinated in symmetrical *schēmata*.[48] In this sense, we should perhaps more correctly understand the gods' procession as a dance, a choral performance that unfolds through space and time. Together, the gods dance forward, moving collectively across the shallow space of the ledge. The figure of Aphrodite

[46] Vermeule 1981: 195, no. 61; Sauser 1987: 6; Zagdoun 1989: 87–8, 90–4, 97, 100. On the frequency with which the basic structure of the composition was replicated throughout the first centuries BCE and CE, see Fullerton 1998: 94–5.

[47] Offering a phenomenological approach to processions and addressing issues of time is Warford 2019.

[48] On various approaches to seeing musical performances, see Bundrick 2005; Porter 2010: 436–44; Yatromanolakis 2016; Laferrière 2020, 2024.

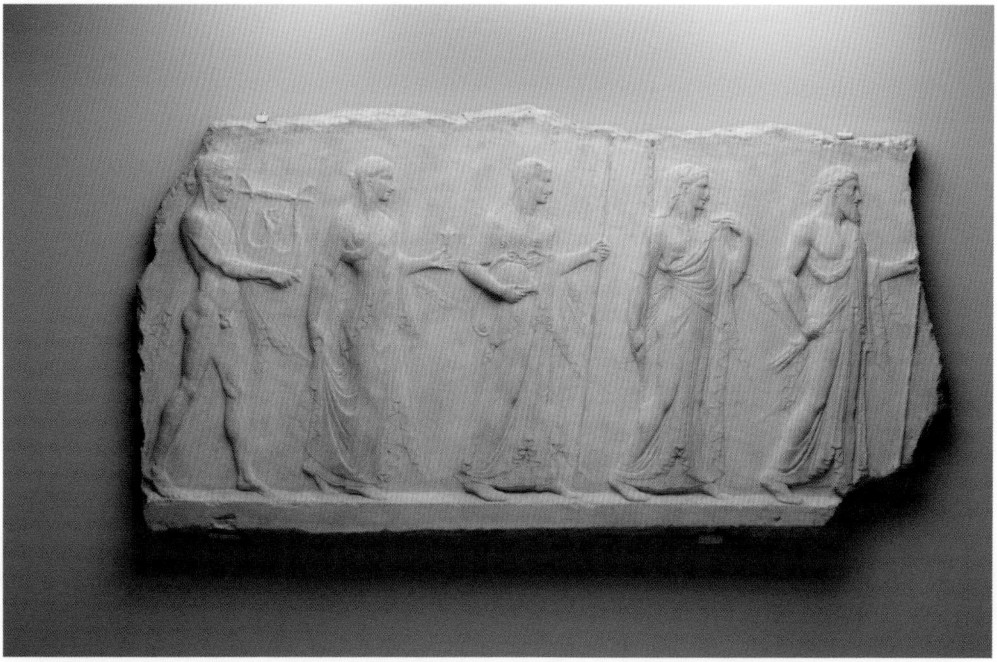

Fig. 6.4 Archaistic relief showing five divinities, ca. 25 BCE–14 CE. Marble (apparently Thasian), 70 × 130 × 5.5 cm. New Haven, CT, Yale University Art Gallery, Leonard C. Hanna Jr., Class of 1913 Fund, 1965.132 (open access).

deviates from the regular pattern of movements exhibited by her companions, reaching down to lift up her robes as she steps up on tiptoes, out of sync with her fellow gods who walk as a collective. Instead, seemingly caught up in Apollo's music, she performs a dance of her own making, even lifting up a flower in front of her, her careful pinch of its stem almost suggesting that its physical body and its smell are as delicate as her grasp.[49] Her gesture and pose, her *schēmata*, thus distinguish her from her companions, even as her participation in the shared dance establishes her as a member of the chorus.

In its depiction of dance, the relief explores how divine bodies move through space, however underdetermined that space may be, and how their movement occurs over time, making their representation here at once inherently ephemeral and permanently captured in stone.[50] It is above all with the figure of Aphrodite that we see the consequences of this

[49] On solo dancers, see esp. Olsen 2020.

[50] I do not mean to imply that it is possible, or even desirable, to attempt to reconstruct the type of music to which they move or the sequence of steps that any of the gods perform. Rather, I draw on Smith (2010a: 12–13), who argues that representations of dance communicate "the idea of

approach. If we hold, with Frederick Naerebout, that "dance is an *effective* medium of communication, because it is an *affective* [one]," these bodies offer us the opportunity to explore how divine *schēmata* could visually communicate important features of the gods' dance, as well as a collective experience of dance in which the viewers might imaginatively participate.[51] It is within this framework that the figure of Aphrodite is particularly significant, for she both belongs to the divine procession and is excluded from it, acting as a member of the chorus, even as she deviates from its rhythmic movements through her own dance. Such aberrations from the group's movements visually suggests that the goddess experiences a unique reaction to the music and responds to it in her own way, moving through space in a manner distinct from her companions, exploring her bodily response to the music in her own time. The goddess' hand has been positioned awkwardly, partially shown in profile as she holds a flower pinched between her index finger and thumb, while the rest of her fingers and palm of her hand are rotated in such a way to face the frontal plane of the relief. Within the image, this abstracted gesture is essential for determining the sequence of movements that link the gods together. Her three remaining fingers extend outward, almost touching the arm of Athena, who walks in front of her. Aphrodite's drapery even mimics the movement of her hand, and indeed the movement of Apollo's own drapery behind her, as it swings forward in front of her body to nearly touch the crest of Athena's helmet, connecting the source of music with chorus of dancers. Time and space have been brought together in awkward, irreconcilable tensions that nevertheless communicate the profound effect that Apollo's music could have on divine bodies and, by extension, on the bodies of the Roman viewers.

We might also think of the temporality of this relief in relation to the conflation of styles and their referents. In collapsing and fusing together chronological changes in the visual arts, the image offers multiple temporalities simultaneously to its viewers, evoking the Archaic and Classical periods of Greece for a Roman audience. In other words, this relief and the others we have discussed "*picture* history by pointing to a gap in the historical sequence of representational conventions," so that "pictorial

dance, not an actual one." For further discussion, see Naerebout 1997: 60–77, 112–13, 2017: 60; Smith 2010b, 2014: 231.

51 Naerebout 2006: 64 (emphasis in original). For more on dance's ability to communicate, see Naerebout 1997: 165–6, 234, 2015: 108; Smith 2010a: 8, 2016: 147, 2021. On the importance of considering the spectator in any discussion of dance and its significance, see Peponi 2015: 207.

form [acts] as an index of history."[52] The image thus offers material traces of time to its viewers, even as it denies us, as Nagel and Wood argue, the ability to isolate or to understand the specific time with which it is engaged. With respect to its subject matter, the gods featured are not only prominent within the Greek and Roman pantheon, but they have been depicted with typical iconography, and their staggered representation here is reminiscent of other Classical reliefs.[53] We need only think of the repeating rhythm of seated gods on the east side of the Parthenon frieze or the Siphnian Treasury, or even the careful pacing of bodies and horses in the friezes on the Athenian temple to Athena Nike.[54] In its composition, the image refers back to other specific examples, the most notable of which is the altar of the twelve gods in Athens. Indeed, one group of figures isolated by Hauser was a procession of gods, and their isolation in his study, even at the level of gesture, points to the frequency with which they were depicted.[55] The style with which bodies have been formed also fuses together temporal changes. As we have already seen with other Neo-Attic examples, here too are the figures rendered with a mannered, Archaizing style, which emerges in the exaggerated triangular falls of drapery, the delicate, precise gestures, and the hint of an Archaic smile.[56] In adopting a visual rhetoric appropriate to the sixth and fifth centuries BCE in Athens,[57] the relief evokes the religious landscape of the past and, in so doing, introduces the city of Athens, with all of its rituals, to those Romans who would have looked upon this image. The gods thus seem to emerge only passingly from the stone itself, appearing before the viewers and almost disappearing again as they move between the two times. Such a dialectic between past and present creates an aesthetic of timelessness, which paradoxically is bound up with the frequent replication of this image. Time thus becomes layered within the relief through such acts of replication, so that the present is visually and materially tied to the past. As such, in moving between the Archaic and Classical past and the contemporary present, as well as between the numerous examples that existed in the first centuries BCE and CE, the relief flattens the distance between Athens and Rome, so that the gods play music and dance between the two, fusing both times and both spaces before the viewer. The image thus evokes not one particular moment in time, but

52 Nagel and Wood 2010: 83 (emphasis in original).

53 Hauser 1889: esp. pl. 1; Sauser 1987: 4.

54 For more on the visuality of ancient reliefs, and in particular the Parthenon frieze, see Davis 2017: 229–63.

55 Hauser 1889: pl. 1. 56 Pollitt 1986: 178.

57 For more on cultures of visuality, see Davis 2010, 2017.

rather it presents the entirety of the Greek past to its Roman audience, ultimately offering them a material experience of the past.

Dancing through Relief

The ancient viewer's experience of the stylized and flattened scenes is fundamental to our understanding of how Neo-Attic reliefs functioned within their Roman context. As Elaine Gazda has shown, Roman residences, both elite and non-elite, would have been filled with sculpture in many forms, whether it was ancestor portraits in the atrium, portable sculptures in the dining areas, or reliefs set into the walls of porticoes.[58] We should thus imagine the Neo-Attic reliefs discussed here as having been possibly inset into the very structure of these residences, so that their viewers could have encountered them as part of a larger experience of moving through the home or its associated gardens. In considering how and where ancient viewers may have once seen Neo-Attic reliefs, together with the formal issues of how the figures display distinct *schēmata* and the reliefs' conflation of space and time, it remains to examine how certain reliefs encouraged their Roman audience not only to position themselves on a continuum with the Greek past but also to immerse themselves in the mythical scenes through their experience of looking at the image.

If we were to imagine that the Neo-Attic reliefs discussed in this chapter were inset into the walls of a villa, then viewers would have come across the images as they were walking through the domestic space, perhaps stopping to look more closely at one scene while passing others by quickly. In each case, however, the suspended temporalities held by the reliefs offered the viewers the opportunity to engage with the particular aesthetic connotations of cultural memory that were put on display.[59] At times, the reliefs could further blur their time and space with the viewer's own world through visual slips beyond the image and its frame. Such visual infringements on the frame are not uncommon in Greek art from the Archaic period onward,[60] and within the Neo-Attic style, there continue to be visually important attempts to play with the surface of the image, to push

[58] Gazda 2018: 374–5. Cf. e.g. Neudecker 1988; Mattusch 2005. See also the recent exhibition *Buried by Vesuvius: Treasures from the Villa dei Papiri*, Getty Villa, Malibu, CA, June 26–October 28, 2019.

[59] Elsner and Squire 2016: 181–2.

[60] On framing in ancient art, see Hurwit 1977; Platt and Squire 2017. For a more general discussion of the frame, see Derrida 1987.

on its formal limitations, and to expand the sacred space it depicts out into the external world. On another relief, which features a maenad that replicates one of Hauser's prototypes,[61] the dancing body is depicted in shallow relief, once again barely emerging from the background (Fig. 6.5).[62] She dances by herself, so that her animated drapery twists and turns, hinting at the energy behind her movements and the constant shifting *schēmata* with which she arranges her body. However, as she dances, one foot slips off the frontal ledge of the image, out of the relief.[63] She seems to take no notice of this startling aberration against the surface of the image, as if she slips effortlessly from one space to another.

Such an engagement with the relief's surface blurs the spatial and material distinction between the relief and the external world, so that the relief implicitly pushes its carved image into the world of the viewer.[64] Moving between image and external world, between the past and the present, the maenad's dance allows the relief to oscillate between the two, moving between the image and the viewer's space. As her slipping foot suspends and reinforces this tension, it continually reasserts the blurriness between the relief as an aesthetic object, where her garments twist and flow as a virtuoso artistic exercise, and the relief as an object of ritual, where the slippage between the world of the image and that of the human viewer has important theological consequences.[65] The tension between art and ritual is significant for our discussion of time and space in relief, for in moving from extremely shallow relief at the maenad's head to progressively deeper cuts into the stone until, finally, her foot expands beyond the frame, the maenad has been captured in a moment of becoming. Paused both mid-step and mid-manifestation, the maenad is at once an art object and an actual ritual dancer for the god. She thus embodies the tradition of depicting maenads in this particular mode, even as she continues to offer her viewers a unique experience of dance, inviting them to join her revel as the relief pushes her into the external world.

This tension between the space and time of the image with that of the viewer is particularly poignant with a marble vase, the so-called Borghese krater (Fig. 6.6a–b).[66] This marble vase renders in stone a calyx krater,

[61] Hauser 1889: no. 26, pl. 2.

[62] Richter 1954: 39–40, no. 58; Touchette 1995: 75–6, no. 27; Picón et al. 2007: 133, 433, no. 146; Zanker et al. 2019: 53, no. 10.

[63] On the potential theological consequences of such slips beyond the frame, see esp. Gaifman 2017.

[64] Derrida 1987: 52–68. [65] Nagel and Wood 2010: 7–19.

[66] Fuchs 1959: 108–18; Grassinger 1991: 181–3; Hamiaux 1998: 199–201, no. 17; Picón and Hemingway 2016: 285–7, no. 30.

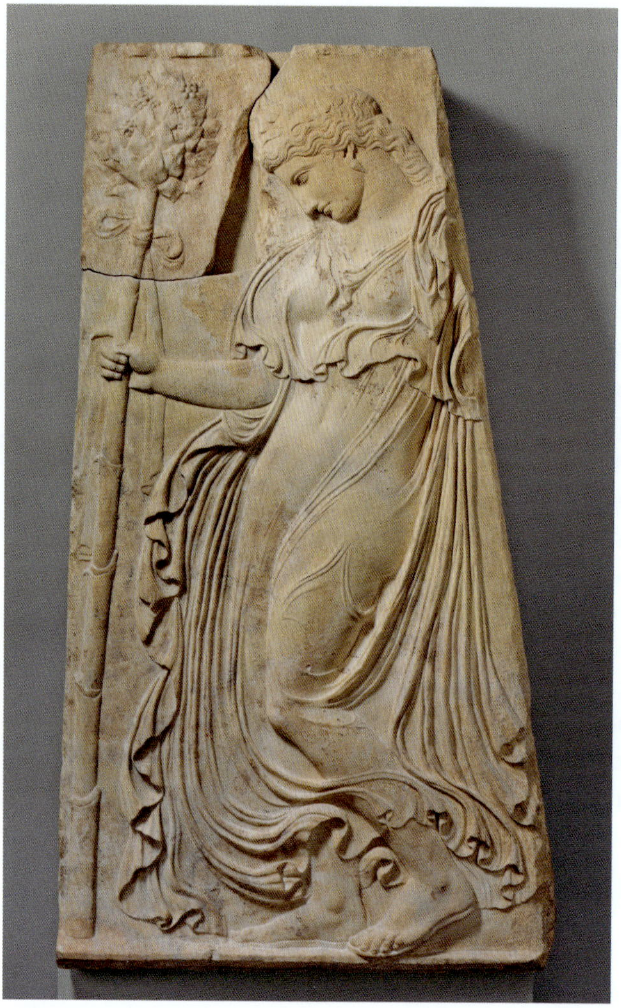

Fig. 6.5 Marble relief with dancing maenad, adaptation of work attributed to Kallimachos, ca. 27 BCE–14 CE. Height: 143 cm. New York, Metropolitan Museum of Art, Fletcher Fund, 1935, 35.11.3 (Creative Commons Zero [CC0]).

a shape commonly associated with the Athenian symposium.[67] With this object, our otherwise flat relief has now gained a new three-dimensional mass as it spreads out around the surface of the vase. At 170 cm high, the vase is an impressive and imposing physical presence. In antiquity, it likely would have decorated the gardens of an elite Roman villa, so that its ritual,

[67] For more on the role of krater within the Archaic and Classical Greek symposium, see esp. Lissarrague 1990. On the likely Attic provenance of this krater, see Hamiaux 1998: 199–201, no. 17.

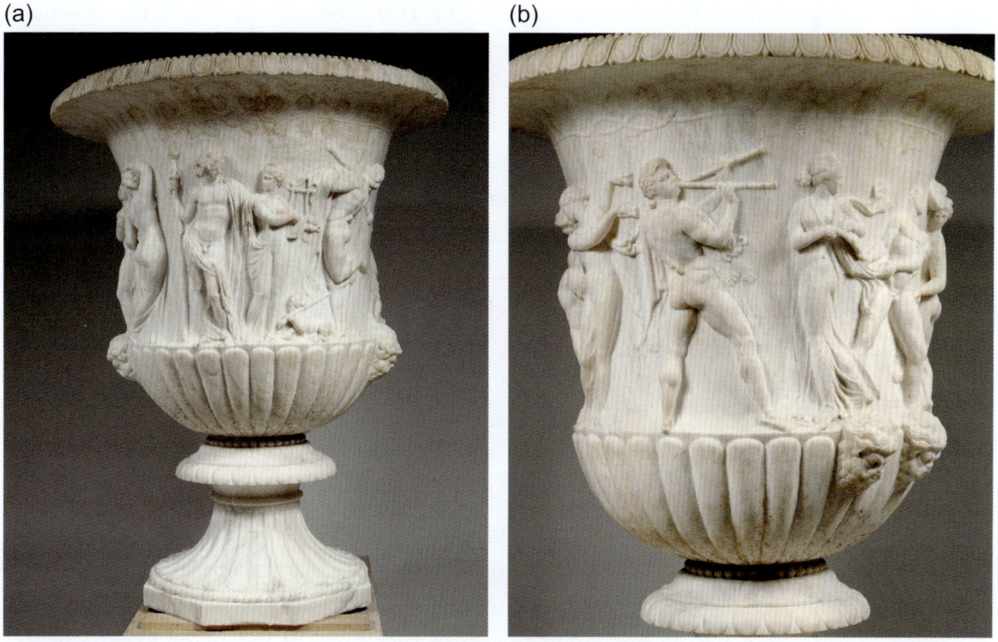

Fig. 6.6a–b Dionysian scene, Borghese krater, ca. 40–30 BCE, discovered in the Gardens of Sallust, Rome, ca. 1569. Marble, 170 × 91.4 cm. Paris, Musée du Louvre, MA 86 (© RMN-Grand Palais/Art Resource, NY).

sympotic context is exchanged for a domestic one, where it serves an atmospheric and decorative purpose.[68] But just as the Neo-Attic Archaizing style looks back to the past, bringing the style of Archaic ritual art into the first century BCE, so too does the choice to carve scenes in relief onto the sides of marble vases look back to the Classical period, where marble vases could be used to mark graves, ultimately serving as longer-lasting replacements for the ceramic vases that also performed the same function.[69] Its form also echoes large metal vases that were popular in the fourth century BCE, such as the Derveni krater, though this style of vase too could also be intended at some point in its life for a funerary context. In both style and form, then, this mixing bowl makes use of the past, evoking other temporalities even as it re-presents them for a different purpose, and ultimately resituates them from a sacred space of ritual and mourning to a site of leisure, erudition, and restorative distance from urban life.

In its transformation of context, the significance of the image carved upon the krater changes and adapts to its new site of viewing. The figures

[68] Cohon 1993: 319; Gazda 2018: 375, 379–80.

[69] The most comprehensive study on marble kraters is Grassinger 1991.

depicted on the vase participate in a Dionysian revel, where the maenads and satyrs play music, drink, and dance together, all under the influence of the god of wine, who stands prominently in the middle (see Fig. 6.6a). Complementing the elaborate figural scene are the three decorative bands of pattern that surround the vase, demarcating the various sections of its body, such as the lip and lower band with its geometric patterns, and the band of ivy or grape vines that encircle the top area of the entire scene. There are no handles, although the decorative faces that so frequently appear on metal vessels are included, as if materially hinting at the change in medium.

Although the image is fully contained within the bands of decorative patterns that encircle the vase, there are also visual slips between the ground of the relief and the external world. Similarly to the maenad's protruding foot in the previous relief, a female dancer has been startled by Silenus' fallen wine cup and quickly steps away, her toes protruding beyond the bottom ledge. Another maenad is caught up in her dance, so that her toes also slip over the slight edge, as does the heel of the satyr musician beside her. Even the god's toes push at the frontal plane of the relief, extending beyond the ledge to intrude slightly upon the external world. Though these figures are shown in higher relief than the previous examples I discussed, they nevertheless appear as though they too have been pushed closer to the pictorial surface of the image, so that the further they sink into their revel, the closer they come to breaking the frontal plane of the image and emerging out into the viewer's space. One satyr, who grabs at a dancing maenad, even tilts his head in such a way that makes it seem like he looks out of the image, at us, the external viewers, further breaking the frontal plane of the relief.[70]

Once again, we see attention given to the blurring of spaces, where the visual space in which the revel occurs is brought together with the human space in which the vase itself stands. For the Roman viewer, who may have been walking in a garden in which this vase once stood, the swirling image of dance and music implicitly invites its viewers to experience imaginatively both the vessel as an art object and the relief that has been carved into its sides. Moreover, through its form and arrangement of figures in relief around the vessel, the relief invites its viewer to move around the vase, to encircle the vessel in a manner akin to a choral dance that echoes the never-ending dance carved into the stone. Time is thus also shared between image

[70] In general, important work on frontal figures in ancient art has been carried out by Korshak 1987; Frontisi-Ducroux 1995; Mackay 2001; Mack 2002; Hedreen 2007, 2017. I also follow Schapiro's (1973: 37–48) argument that these frontal faces actively look at their viewers.

and world as the audience contemplates the sculpted figures, imagining how it might feel to move their bodies into sympathetic *schēmata*.[71] Pushing at the surface of the relief is a satyr who dances with particular abandon, foot kicked up behind him, head leaning back in song, creating a dynamic curve with his body. The satyr's body is twisted in such a way that his shoulders and torso protrude out of the scene, so that he seems almost to dance and move between the image and our space, in the physical space that the three-dimensional vase has claimed for itself. Bodies thus come together, both sculpted and human, to dance in a moment of visual and kinesthetic unity as they share the same expansive time and space that has been made available.

In many ways, the Archaizing reliefs discussed throughout this chapter represent a real attempt to access the past, to create a sense of the past through objects that collapse the distance between moments in time by using certain styles and repeating visual forms from earlier works of art. In attempting to recreate the visual effect and aesthetic of the Archaic and Classical periods, and in returning to these representational styles and depicting them again and again, in different combinations, the Neo-Attic reliefs of the first centuries BCE and CE point to a shared Roman fascination with the past. The visual repetition of these scenes, where figures interact in both familiar and new ways, renders these spaces accessible to the viewers by asking them to recall Archaic and Classical ritual practice, where the possibility of a divine encounter mediated through a visual representation was always possible. The implications of such aesthetically and ritually charged seeing is explored by another marble krater, on which dancing female bodies move (Fig. 6.7). Stepping around the surface of the vase, the figures offer us a now familiar sight as they dance, clack their *krotala*, and play the *aulos*, their drapery floating in impossible folds and patterns against the blank background.[72] Emerging on one side between the two groups of dancers is a votive relief, presenting an embedded scene within the carved image.

Three dancers fill the space of this embedded relief, too, as two hold hands and move together as a chorus, reaching out to their companion to

[71] Sklar 2001: 198–9n3. In her discussion of *choreia* in the Greek theater, Olsen (2021: 158–9) expands upon Sklar's work to suggest that dance, though "initially received visually by the audience, ancient and modern theories of kinesthetic empathy and proprioception would suggest that viewers can also have an embodied response to dance, a sensation of felt participation or inner mimicry." For a similar approach within the context of material culture, see Laferrière 2021.

[72] Grassinger 1991: 112–13, 136–44, 149, 174, 294–5, no. 17; Cohon 1993: 314–25; Touchette 1995: 81–2, no. 47.

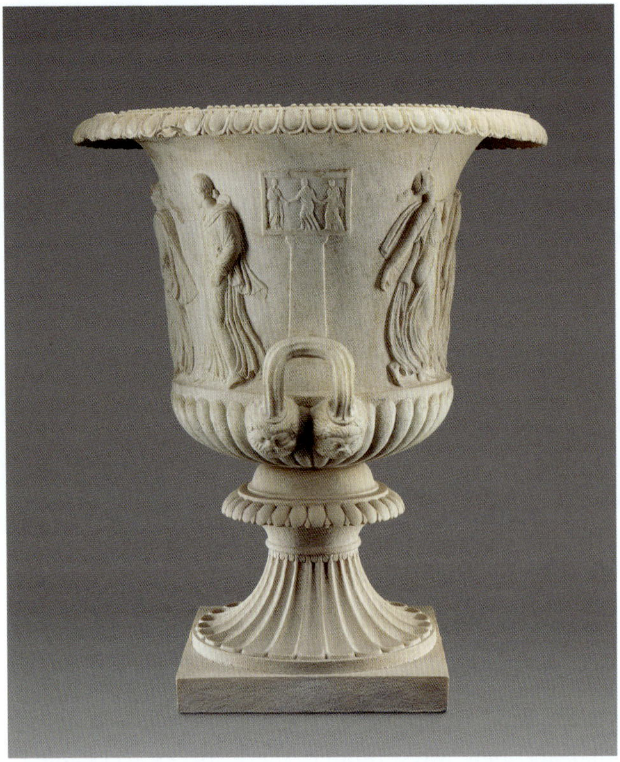

Fig. 6.7 Dionysian scene, calyx krater, 25 BCE–25 CE. Marble, 52 × 69 cm. Malibu, CA, J. Paul Getty Museum, Villa Collection, 82.AA.170 (Getty's Open Content Program).

draw her into their performance. The manner in which the votive is set up on a stele recalls how votives were displayed in Greek sanctuaries, especially in the fourth century BCE, when such offerings were a relatively frequent dedication. Its placement here lends a sense of specificity to this scene, as if the viewer were meant to understand that it should be situated within a sacred landscape. However, as with the larger scene in which this embedded relief is displayed, there is nothing in the image that would suggest that it takes place in any specific space. Instead, in an effort to empty itself of spatial or temporal specificity, the layered spaces and times presented in the relief offer a general, idealized, yet fundamentally remote presentation of Hellenism. In other words, the image reflects a self-conscious attempt at re-presenting the perceived religious life of the Greeks of the Classical period, but repackaged in such a way that is free from any specific place of use, any specific place of ritual. In this stylistic tension, this dialectic between two competing aesthetics of mannered, Archaizing representation and the theological representation of human and divine interaction, the distinct time and space created by and in these reliefs allowed them to become powerful sites of contact. In connecting their viewers with an idealized past that takes place in a generic space, the reliefs offered their elite Roman audience the opportunity not only to engage visually with the past temporalities of Archaic and Classical Greece but also to become immersed in them by sharing the same space as the stylized figures, who could easily slip from their timeless, even spaceless background to the Roman world in which they were displayed.

References

Abbe, M. B. (2015). "Polychromy." In E. A. Friedland, M. G. Sobocinski, and E. K. Gazda, eds., *The Oxford Handbook of Roman Sculpture*. Oxford: Oxford University Press, 173–89.

Anguissola, A. (2012). *"Difficillima imitatio": Immagine e lessico delle copie tra Grecia e Roma*. Rome: Bretschneider.

Barham, N. (2021). "Theorizing Image and Abstraction in Ancient Rome: The Case of the Villa Farnesina." *Art History* 44.1: 164–85.

Barker, A. (1989). *Greek Musical Writings*. Vol. 2, *Harmonic and Acoustic Theory*. Cambridge Readings in the Literature of Music. Cambridge: Cambridge University Press.

Becatti, G. (1951). *Arte e gusto negli scrittori latini*. Florence: Sansoni.

Bocksberger, S. M. (2017). "Dance as Silent Poetry, Poetry as Speaking Dance: The Poetics of *Orchesis*." In L. Gianvittorio, ed., *Choreutika: Performing and Theorising Dance in Ancient Greece*. Pisa: Serra, 159–77.

Bravi, A. (2012). *Ornamenta urbis: Opere d'arte greche negli spazi romani*. Bari: Edipuglia.

Bremmer, J. N. (1984). "Greek Maenadism Reconsidered." *Zeitschrift für Papyrologie und Epigraphik* 55: 267–86.

Brunn, H. (1853). *Geschichte der griechischen Künstler*. Vol. 1. Braunschweig: Schwetschke.

Bundrick, S. D. (2005). *Music and Image in Classical Athens*. Cambridge: Cambridge University Press.

Cain, H.-U. (1985). *Römische Marmorkandelaber*. Mainz: von Zabern.

Catoni, M. L. (2008). *La communicazione non verbale nella Grecia antica: Gli schemata nella danza, nell'arte, nella vita*. Turin: Boringhieri.

Cohon, R. (1993). "The Typology, History, and Authenticity of Roman Marble Craters." *Journal of Roman Archaeology* 6: 312–30.

Daremberg, C. V., and Saglio, E. (1873). *Dictionnaire des antiquités grecques et romaines, d'après les textes et les monuments*. Vol. 2. Paris: Hachette.

Davis, W. (2010). *A General Theory of Visual Culture*. Princeton, NJ: Princeton University Press.
(2017). *Visuality and Virtuality: Images and Pictures from Prehistory to Perspective*. Princeton, NJ: Princeton University Press.
Derrida, J. (1987). *The Truth in Painting*. Trans. G. Bennington and I. McLeod. Chicago, IL: University of Chicago Press.
Di Franco, L. (2017). *I rilievi "neoattici" della Campania: Produzione e circolazione degli ornamenta marmorei a soggetto mitologico*. Rome: Bretschneider.
Dütschke, H. (1878). *Antike Bildwerke in Oberitalien*. Vol. 3, *Die Antiken Marmorbildwerke Der Uffizien in Florenz*. Leipzig: Engelmann.
Elsner, J. (2005). "Classicism in Rome." In J. I. Porter, ed., *Classical Pasts: The Classical Traditions of Greece and Rome*. Princeton, NJ: Princeton University Press, 270–97.
Elsner, J., and Squire, M. (2016). "Sight and Memory: The Visual Art of Roman Mnemonics." In M. Squire, ed., *Sight and the Ancient Senses*. London: Routledge, 180–204.
Frontisi-Ducroux, F. (1995). *Du masque au visage: Aspects de l'identité en Grèce ancienne*. Paris: Flammarion.
Fuchs, W. (1959). *Die Vorbilder der Neuattischen Reliefs: Jahrbuch des deutschen archäologischen Instituts*, supplement 20. Berlin: De Gruyter.
Fullerton, M. D. (1990). *The Archaistic Style in Roman Statuary*. Leiden: Brill.
(1998). "Atticism, Classicism, and the Origins of Neo-Attic Sculpture." In O. Palagia and W. Coulson, eds., *Regional Schools in Hellenistic Sculpture*. Oxford: Oxbow, 93–9.
(2016). *Greek Sculpture*. Chichester: Wiley Blackwell.
Gahtan, M. W., and Pegazzano, D. (2015). *Museum Archetypes and Collecting in the Ancient World*. Leiden: Brill.
Gaifman, M. (2017). "Framing Divine Bodies in Greek Art." In V. Platt and M. Squire, eds., *The Frame in Classical Art: A Cultural History*. Cambridge: Cambridge University Press, 392–424.
(2018). *The Art of Libation in Classical Athens*. New Haven, CT: Yale University Press.
Gazda, E. K. (2002). *The Ancient Art of Emulation: Studies in Artistic Originality and Tradition from the Present to Classical Antiquity*. Ann Arbor: University of Michigan Press.
(2018). "Domestic Displays." In E. A. Friedland, M. G. Sobocinski, and E. K. Gazda, eds., *The Oxford Handbook of Roman Sculpture*. Oxford: Oxford University Press, 374–89.
Grassinger, D. (1991). *Römische Marmorkratere*. Mainz: von Zabern.
Hallett, C. H. (2012). "The Archaic Style in Sculpture in the Eyes of Ancient and Modern Viewers." In V. Coltman, ed., *Making Sense of Greek Art*. Exeter: University of Exeter Press, 70–100.

(2015). "Defining Roman Art." In B. E. Borg, ed., *A Companion to Roman Art.* Chichester: Wiley Blackwell, 11–33.

Hamiaux, M. (1998). *Les sculptures grecques.* Vol. 2, *La période hellénistique (IIIe–Ier siècle avant J.-C.).* Paris: Réunion des musées nationaux.

Hauser, F. (1889). *Die Neu-Attischen Reliefs.* Stuttgart: Wittwer.

Havelock, C. M. (1964). "Archaistic Reliefs of the Hellenistic Period." *American Journal of Archaeology* 68.1: 43–58.

(1965). "The Archaic as Survival versus the Archaistic as a New Style." *American Journal of Archaeology* 69.4: 331–40.

Hedreen, G. (1994). "Silens, Nymphs, and Maenads." *Journal of Hellenic Studies* 114: 47–69.

(2007). "Involved Spectatorship in Archaic Greek Art." *Art History* 30.2: 217–46.

(2017). "Unframing the Representation: The Frontal Face in Athenian Vase-Painting." In V. Platt and M. Squire, eds., *The Frame in Classical Art: A Cultural History.* Cambridge: Cambridge University Press, 154–87.

Hemingway, S. (2016). "Seafaring, Shipwrecks, and the Art Market in the Hellenistic Age." In Picón and Hemingway 2016: 85–91.

Henrichs, A. (1978). "Greek Maenadism from Olympias to Messalina." *Harvard Studies in Classical Philology* 82: 121–60.

Hölscher, T. (2005). "Greek Styles and Greek Art in Augustan Rome: Issues of the Present versus Records of the Past." In J. I. Porter, ed., *Classical Pasts: The Classical Traditions of Greece and Rome.* Princeton, NJ: Princeton University Press, 237–69.

Hurwit, J. M. (1977). "Image and Frame in Greek Art." *American Journal of Archaeology* 81.1: 1–30.

Jones, N. B. (2019a). "Truth from Fiction: Connoisseurship in Greco-Roman Antiquity." *RES: Anthropology and Aesthetics* 71–2: 229–40.

(2019b). *Painting, Ethics, and Aesthetics in Rome.* Cambridge: Cambridge University Press.

Jucker, H. (1950). *Vom Verhältnis der Römer zur bildenden Kunst der Griechen.* Frankfurt: Klostermann.

Korshak, Y. (1987). *Frontal Faces in Attic Vase Painting of the Archaic Period.* Chicago, IL: Ares.

La Rocca, E. (2008). *Lo spazio negato: La pittura di paesaggio nella cultura artistica greca e romana.* Milan: Mondadori Electa.

Laferrière, C. M. (2019). "Sacred Sounds: The Cult of Pan and the Nymphs in the Vari Cave." *Classical Antiquity* 38.2: 185–216.

(2020). "Painting with Music: Visualizing *Harmonia* on Archaic Representations of Apollo Kitharoidos." *Greek and Roman Musical Studies* 8.1: 63–90.

(2021). "Dancing with Greek Vases: Communicating through Sight, Movement, and Material." *Greek and Roman Musical Studies* 9.1: 85–114.

(2024). *Divine Music in Archaic and Classical Greek Art: Seeing the Songs of the Gods*. Cambridge: Cambridge University Press.

Lakey, C. R. (2018). *Sculptural Seeing: Relief, Optics, and the Rise of Perspective in Medieval Italy*. New Haven, CT: Yale University Press.

Lawler, L. B. (1927). "The Maenads: A Contribution to the Study of the Dance in Ancient Greece." *Memoirs of the American Academy in Rome* 6: 69–112.

Leach, E. W. (2003). "*Otium* as *Luxuria*: Economy of Status in the Younger Pliny's *Letters*." *Arethusa* 36.2: 147–65.

Lissarrague, F. (1990). *The Aesthetics of the Greek Banquet: Images of Wine and Ritual*. Princeton, NJ: Princeton University Press.

Mack, R. (2002). "Facing Down Medusa (an Aetiology of the Gaze)." *Art History* 25.5: 571–604.

Mackay, E. A. (2001). "The Frontal Face and 'You': Narrative Disjunction in Early Greek Poetry and Painting." *Acta Classica* 44: 5–34.

Marvin, M. (2008). *The Language of the Muses: The Dialogue between Greek and Roman Sculpture*. Los Angeles, CA: J. Paul Getty Museum.

Mattusch, C. C. (2005). *The Villa dei Papiri at Herculaneum: Life and Afterlife of a Sculpture Collection*. Los Angeles, CA: J. Paul Getty Museum.

McInerney, J. (1997). "Parnassus, Delphi, and the Thyiades." *Greek, Roman and Byzantine Studies* 38.3: 263–83.

McNally, S. (1978). "The Maenad in Early Greek Art." *Arethusa* 11.1–2: 101–35.

Mitchell, W. J. T. (2002). "Preface to the Second Edition." In W. J. T. Mitchell, ed., *Landscape and Power: Space, Place, and Landscape*, 2nd ed. Chicago, IL: University of Chicago Press, vii–xii.

Naerebout, F. G. (1997). *Attractive Performances: Ancient Greek Dance. Three Preliminary Studies*. Amsterdam: Gieben.

(2006). "Moving Events: Dance at Public Events in the Ancient Greek World. Thinking through Its Implications." In E. Stavrianopoulou, ed., *Ritual and Communication in the Graeco-Roman World, Kernos*, supplement 16. Liège: Centre international d'étude de la religion grecque antique, 37–67.

(2015). "Dance." In R. Raja and J. Rüpke, eds., *A Companion to the Archaeology of Religion in the Ancient World*. Chichester: Wiley Blackwell, 107–19.

(2017). "Moving in Unison: The Greek Chorus in Performance." In L. Gianvittorio, ed., *Choreutika: Performing and Theorising Dance in Ancient Greece*. Pisa: Serra, 39–66.

Nagel, A., and Wood, C. S. (2010). *Anachronic Renaissance*. New York: Zone.

Neudecker, R. (1988). *Die Skulpturenausstattung römischer Villen in Italien*. Mainz: von Zabern.

Olsen, S. (2021). "Narrating Neoptolemus: Dance and Death in Euripides' *Andromache*." In L. Gianvittorio and K. Schlapbach, eds., *Choreonarratives: Dancing Stories in Greek and Roman Antiquity and Beyond*. Leiden: Brill, 156–79.

(2020). *Solo Dance in Archaic and Classical Greek Literature: Representing the Unruly Body*. Cambridge: Cambridge University Press.

Panofsky, E. (1997). *Perspective as Symbolic Form*. Trans. C. S. Wood. New York: Zone.

Patton, K. C. (2009). *Religion of the Gods: Ritual, Paradox, and Reflexivity*. Oxford: Oxford University Press.

Peirce, S. (1998). "Visual Language and Concepts of Cult on the 'Lenaia Vases.'" *Classical Antiquity* 17.1: 59–95.

Peponi, A.-E. (2015). "Dance and Aesthetic Perception." In P. Destrée and P. Murray, eds., *A Companion to Ancient Aesthetics*. Malden, MA: Wiley Blackwell, 204–17.

Perry, E. (2005). *The Aesthetics of Emulation in the Visual Arts of Ancient Rome*. Cambridge: Cambridge University Press.

Picón, C. A., and Hemingway, S., eds. (2016). *Pergamon and the Hellenistic Kingdoms of the Ancient World*. New Haven, CT: Yale University Press.

Picón, C. A., Mertens, E., Milleker, C. S., et al. (2007). *Art of the Classical World in the Metropolitan Museum of Art: Greece, Cyprus, Etruria, Rome*. New York: Metropolitan Museum of Art.

Platt, V. (2009). "Where the Wild Things Are: Locating the Marvellous in Augustan Wall Painting." In P. Hardie, ed., *Paradox and the Marvellous in Augustan Literature and Culture*. Oxford: Oxford University Press, 41–74.

(2011). *Facing the Gods: Epiphany and Representation in Graeco-Roman Art, Literature and Religion*. Cambridge: Cambridge University Press.

Platt, V., and Squire, M. (2017). "Framing the Visual in Greek and Roman Antiquity: An Introduction." In V. Platt and M. Squire, eds., *The Frame in Classical Art: A Cultural History*. Cambridge: Cambridge University Press, 3–99.

Pollitt, J. J. (1974). *The Ancient View of Greek Art: Criticism, History, and Terminology*. New Haven, CT: Yale University Press.

(1978). "The Impact of Greek Art on Rome." *Transactions of the American Philological Association* 108: 155–74.

(1986). *Art in the Hellenistic Age*. Cambridge: Cambridge University Press.

Porter, J. I. (2010). *The Origins of Aesthetic Thought in Ancient Greece: Matter, Sensation, and Experience*. Cambridge: Cambridge University Press.

Purves, A. (2019). *Homer and the Poetics of Gesture*. Oxford: Oxford University Press.

Richter, G. M. A. (1954). *Catalogue of Greek Sculptures*. Cambridge, MA: Harvard University Press.

Robinson, C. A. (2021). "The Teacher of Dance: Rhythmic Systems and Dance Steps in Aristides Quintilianus' *De Musica*." *Greek and Roman Musical Studies* 9.2: 285–319.

Rutledge, S. (2012). *Ancient Rome as a Museum: Power, Identity, and the Culture of Collecting*. Oxford: Oxford University Press.

Sauser, J. S. R. (1987). "The Twelve Gods Relief in the Walters Art Gallery." *Journal of the Walters Art Gallery* 45: 2–18.
Schapiro, M. (1973). *Words and Pictures: On the Literal and the Symbolic in the Illustration of a Text*. The Hague: Mouton.
Sklar, D. (2001). *Dancing with the Virgin: Body and Faith in the Fiesta of Tortugas, New Mexico*. Berkeley: University of California Press.
Smith, T. J. (2010a). *Komast Dancers in Archaic Greek Art*. Oxford Monographs on Classical Archaeology. Oxford: Oxford University Press.
(2010b). "Reception or Deception? Approaching Greek Dance through Vase-Painting." In F. Macintosh, ed., *The Ancient Dancer in the Modern World: Responses to Greek and Roman Dance*. Oxford: Oxford University Press, 77–98.
(2014). "Guess Who's Coming to Dinner? Red-Figure Komasts and the Performance Culture of Athens." In J. Oakley, ed., *Athenian Potters and Painters*. Vol. 3. Oxford: Oxbow, 231–41.
(2016). "Instant Messaging: Dance, Text, and Visual Communication on Corinthian and Athenian Vases." In D. Yatromanolakis, ed., *Epigraphy of Art: Ancient Greek Vase-Inscriptions and Vase-Paintings*. Oxford: Archaeopress Archaeology, 145–64.
(2021). "Bodies in Motion: Dance, Gesture, and Ritual on Greek Vases." *Greek and Roman Musical Studies* 9.1: 49–84.
Strauss Clay, J. (1996). "Fusing the Boundaries: Apollo and Dionysos at Delphi." *Métis: Anthropologie des mondes grecs anciens* 11: 83–100.
Summers, D. (2003). *Real Spaces: World Art History and the Rise of Western Modernism*. New York: Phaidon.
Touchette, L.-A. (1995). *The Dancing Maenad Reliefs: Continuity and Change in Roman Copies*. Bulletin of the Institute of Classical Studies, supplement 62. London: Institute of Classical Studies.
Trimble, J., and Elsner, J. (2006). "Introduction: 'If You Need an Actual Statue . . . '" In J. Trimble and J. Elsner, eds., *Art and Replication: Greece, Rome and Beyond*." Special issue, *Art History* 29.2: 201–12.
Varner, E. R. (2006). "Reading Replications: Roman Rhetoric and Greek Quotations." In J. Trimble and J. Elsner, eds., *Art and Replication: Greece, Rome and Beyond*." Special issue, *Art History* 29.2: 280–303.
Vermeule, C. C. (1981). *Greek and Roman Sculpture in America: Masterpieces in Public Collections in the United States and Canada*. Berkeley: University of California Press.
Warford, E. (2019). "Performing Piety: A Phenomenological Approach to Athenian Processions." In W. Friese, S. Handeberg, and T. M. Kristensen, eds., *Ascending and Descending the Acropolis: Movement in Athenian Religion*. Aarhus: Aarhus University Press, 23–41.

Wyler, S. (2006). "Roman Replications of Greek Art at the Villa Della Farnesina." In J. Trimble and J. Elsner, eds., *Art and Replication: Greece, Rome and Beyond.*" Special issue, *Art History* 29.2: 213–32.

Yatromanolakis, D. (2016). "Soundscapes (and Two Speaking Lyres)." In D. Yatromanolakis, ed., *Epigraphy of Art: Ancient Greek Vase-Inscriptions and Vase-Paintings*. Oxford: Archaeopress Archaeology, 1–42.

Zagdoun, M.-A. (1989). *La sculpture archaïsante dans l'art hellénistique et dans l'art romain du Haut-Empire*. Paris: Diffusion de Boccard.

Zanker, P., Hemingway, S., Lightfoot, C. S., Mertens J. (2019). *Roman Art: A Guide through the Metropolitan Museum of Art's Collection*. New York: Scala.

7 | Remedial Relief

NATHANIEL B. JONES

Relief is a difficult thing to characterize. Is it a process, a product, or something else? The creation of relief can be either additive or subtractive, singular or multiple. Once realized, a relief exists somewhere between two and three dimensions, offering neither quite the full presence of three-dimensional sculpture nor the dematerialized visuality of painting, but tapping into aspects of both. For David Summers, this combination of the corporeal and the optical produces an intermediate "relief space," a specific kind of confrontation between work of art and human body in which the real begins to open itself up to the virtual.[1] Understood in this way, relief is above all a mode of experience, albeit one defined by ambiguity and multiplicity. Further complicating the study of relief in the ancient world, as Verity Platt's (Chapter 1) contribution to this volume shows, is the fact that neither Greek nor Latin possesses an equivalent word. There is, to be sure, a rich vocabulary of shaping, molding, and impressing, on the one hand, and of carving, sculpting, and inscribing, on the other. Numerous ancient writers discuss aspects of both the production and consumption of what we would call relief objects, but no one seems to have verbally articulated a concept equivalent to the modern term *relief*. This does not mean, however, that an implicit, working version of such a concept did not exist among the producers or consumers of ancient artworks. Antiquity did not have a single word for "art" as such, either, but it seems difficult to deny that the Greco-Roman world was filled with what we would today recognize as "art-like situations."[2]

In this vein, the current chapter seeks to examine ancient conceptions of relief through comparison with an apparently fixed reference point: painting, especially Roman wall painting of the first centuries BCE and CE. To do so, it looks to how painting and relief feed off and reverberate around each other, to the ways in which they overlap, and thus, ultimately, to the ways in which they also seek to distinguish themselves. That ancient painting and relief

[1] Summers 2003: 448–52; cf. esp. Davis 2017; Lakey 2018; and now Koortbojian 2023, which appeared as this book was entering production and whose arguments could not fully be taken into account.

[2] See e.g. Tanner 2006; Platt and Squire 2010. For the concept of the art-like situation, see Gell 1998: 13; cf. Polanyi 2009 on the significance of various modes of unspoken, or tacit, knowledge.

were intimately connected was recognized already in the nineteenth century. Writing in part in response to the arrival of the Pergamon Altar in Berlin in 1882, Alexander Conze proposed that Greek relief was something like a subgenre of painting, an opinion quoted verbatim some thirteen years later in Franz Wickhoff's seminal discussion of the stylistic development of Roman art.[3] The essentially pictorial quality of Roman relief sculpture, for Wickhoff, helped give rise to what he characterized as illusionism, an "impression of pulsating life," which is not a merely dry transcription of visual experience but a vivid evocation of the lived reality of the embodied viewer.[4] By the same token, the opposite proposal could be made, as well, that ancient painting was never fully painting in the sense that we tend to know it now – that is to say, a purely optical mode of expression, meant to be consumed by a disembodied vision. Something like this position was held by Erwin Panfosky, who viewed Greek and Roman painting as less genuinely pictorial than relief-like, interested above all in the representation of individual figures and in achieving the effect of projection and recession in depth intervals close to a picture plane, but not in the rationalized, mathematical exploration of deep space of Renaissance one-point perspective.[5]

This chapter seeks to understand the ways in which ancient painting and relief interact with and play off one another by investigating how they are remedial to one another. I do not mean this, at least not primarily, in its traditional curative sense, but rather in the sense that painting and relief remediate one another. Developed by Jay Bolter and Richard Grusin, the concept of remediation represents an attempt to systematize Marshall McLuhan's axiom that the content of one medium is always another

[3] Conze 1882: 574; Wickhoff and von Hartel 1895: 45. Eugénie Strong's translation of the passage runs as follows (Wickhoff 1900: 80–1):

> I will begin by quoting what Conze says on the relation between painting and sculpture in his treatise on Greek relief: "It appears more akin to painting than we were at first inclined to grant. As a fact, it is more correctly classified as a special kind of painting than as a branch of sculpture, and, at any rate, it is as reasonable to speak of the pictorial character of Greek reliefs as of the relief-like characteristics of ancient painting, which has so habitually been done. Above all, must we remember a truth universally conceded today, that in Greek art there was no such sharp division between sculpture as representation by form and painting as representation by colour, as we moderns have introduced both in our practice and in our theory."

For discussion of the transmedial role of the concept of the painterly, or *malerisch*, in German art-historical scholarship around the turn of the century, see Payne 2008, 2011; Koortbojian 2023.

[4] Wickhoff 1900 52–3; cf. Wickhoff and von Hartel 1895: 31.

[5] Panofsky 1991: esp. 42–3 (originally published 1927), following in broad strokes terms laid out in Alois Riegl's 1901 discussion of the gradual change in ancient art from a predominantly haptic to a predominantly optic aesthetic sensibility (*Kunstwollen*).

medium.[6] Remediation is a process by which one medium acknowledges other media within itself. It operates according to a recursive logic of what Bolter and Grusin term immediacy and hypermediacy. Immediacy offers a fast, direct mode of communication, which affects to deliver reality itself, as though the medium of that delivery were nonexistent. It elides the facticity of the mediating object by using "art to conceal art," so to speak.[7] Conversely, hypermediacy accentuates its own medial status by highlighting the artificiality of medium, the simple fact of its having been made. Rather than immediacy's illusionistic pretensions to transparency, hypermediacy tends toward communicative opacity. It thereby slows down the transmission of a message from sender to receiver and focuses our attention on the mechanisms of mediation – that is, on the various ways in which messages are constructed and delivered by external devices. As media are nested within one another, their immediate and hypermediate aspects are at some times accentuated and at others effaced.

Bolter and Grusin first articulated the concept of remediation as a way to understand how the "new" digital media of the 1990s grew out of, refashioned, and, ultimately, came to incorporate older media, such as print, radio, and television, through an alternating pattern of immediacy and hypermediacy. I would argue that this same oscillating, double logic characterizes relationships among ancient media, as well, especially that between painting and relief. What a comparison between relief and painting as media reveals is a consistent blurring of the boundaries between apparent opposites: two and three dimensions, real and pictorial space, the haptic and the optic, form and color, and illusion and fiction, as relief strives to be more like painting and vice versa. This dynamic, I further suggest, plays out especially productively in the representation of relief sculpture within Roman murals, which, like other experiments in metapictoriality, permitted Roman painters to explore the boundaries of their capabilities by both offering a material limit to pictorialization and providing a host of ways in which the pictorial could seek to outflank the material.[8]

[6] McLuhan 1964; Bolter and Grusin 1999; cf. Jennifer Trimble's (Chapter 8) contribution to this volume.

[7] Greenberg 1993: 86. As Verity Platt has pointed out to me, the categories of immediacy and hypermediacy echo in media-theoretical terms Michael Fried's 1980 concepts of absorption and theatricality in early modern European painting, which alternately ignore and acknowledge the beholder as participant in the fiction of a painting. For an ancient analogue to this play of all-encompassing illusion and self-aware fiction, see Newby 2009 on absorption and erudition in the *Imagines* of Philostratus. On classical studies and media theory, see Michelakis 2020.

[8] Cf. e.g. Jones 2019.

The conditions of production of ancient painting and relief, especially of the canonical works that fill our textbooks on Greek and Roman art, can appear to be extremely disparate – the humble world of the Athenian vase painter's workshop seems as far away from the sculptures of the Parthenon as that of the Pompeian muralist from the Ara Pacis Augustae. But we should not forget that Pliny returns to his assertion early in Book 35 of the *Natural History* that the origin of painting lay in tracing the outline of a person's shadow (35.15) near the end of the book, when he retells a version of the same story to explain the origin of modeling in relief (35.151):

> De pictura satis superque. contexuisse his et plasticen conveniat. eiusdem opere terrae fingere ex argilla similitudines Butades Sicyonius figulus primus invenit Corinthi filiae opera, quae capta amore iuvenis, abeunte illo peregre, umbram ex facie eius ad lucernam in pariete lineis circumscripsit, quibus pater eius inpressa argilla typum fecit et cum ceteris fictilibus induratum igni proposuit.
>
> Enough and more than enough has now been said about painting. It may be suitable to append to these remarks something about the plastic art. It was through the service of that same earth that modelling portraits from clay was first invented by Butades, a potter of Sicyon, at Corinth. He did this owing to his daughter, who was in love with a young man, and she, when he was going abroad, drew in outline on the wall the shadow of his face thrown by a lamp. Her father pressed clay on this and made a relief, which he hardened by exposure to fire with the rest of his pottery.[9]

A number of scholars have explored the dynamics of presence and absence, love and loss, visibility and occlusion, and the two- and three-dimensional in the story of Butades, and Platt's chapter in this volume examines in persuasive detail the significance of this passage for the concept of relief as impression.[10] Here, however, I would simply like to draw our attention to how intertwined the semantic fields of the graphic and the plastic, the haptic and the optic, and the material and the pictorial are in Pliny's account. A shadow is created when a material, three-dimensional thing, the head of the young man, intervenes between a light source and a surface (*umbram ex facie eius ad lucernam in pariete*). The shadow, a silhouette, is transformed into a human-made representation when Butades' daughter draws lines around it (*lineis circumscripsit*); the

9 Text and translation from the Loeb edition of Rackham 2003: 370–3.

10 Further on Butades, see e.g. Derrida 1993: 49–51; Stoichita 1997: 11–20; Bettini 1999: 7–9; Carey 2003: 132; Naas 2011; Koch 2013: 19–20, 131–2; *DNO*, nos. 186–8.

fact that Pliny indicates the drawing represents the youth's face and not merely a vaguely ovoid blob should lead us to think that what is produced is a profile portrait.

So far so good. The three-dimensional is transformed into the two-dimensional by basic laws of optics – the imposition of a body between a light source and a surface – and the essentially mechanical act of tracing. The result is an epistemologically trustworthy image, a true portrait, although a degree of abstraction will have occurred. But what happens next is more unusual. Butades makes a relief (*typum fecit*), reintroducing the three-dimensional by applying clay (*inpressit argilla*) and firing it. What are we to imagine that the finished product looked like? A raised outline of just the contour of a face seems unlikely; more probable is a low-relief profile portrait, complete with the articulation of the youth's face – eye, nostril, mouth, hair – something like what we would see in a coin portrait.[11] This seems to be the interpretation offered in the late second century CE by Athenagoras (*Leg. pro. Christ.* 17.3), who does not directly mention Butades by name but clearly recounts the same story as Pliny.[12] Not only does Athenagoras call the final product a relief (*typos*), he gives us some sense of how Butades might actually have made it, creating a raised form by filling in an outline drawing with potter's clay: ἀναγλύψας τὴν περιγραφὴν πηλῷ προσανεπλήρωσεν.

My point in mentioning this is to raise the idea that the physical, indexical relationship between living body and drawing created by Butades' daughter is resubsumed to an optical, imagistic relationship as the transformation from three to two dimensions is reverse engineered by the act of modeling clay. In other words, as relief remediates painting or drawing, it adds both a reality effect and a sense of referential uncertainty – both immediacy and hypermediacy. That this dynamic was of interest to Pliny is indicated by the fact that he almost immediately turns to portraits that are both hyperrealistic and true – portraits produced from molds (themselves a kind of relief) of the sitters' faces (*HN* 35.153).[13] Pliny asserts that this technique was invented in the fourth century BCE by Lysistratus, brother of Lysippos, before whom artists were less interested in accurate representations than in producing the most beautiful face possible (*ante*

[11] A subsequent anecdote about Butades in Pliny (*HN* 35.152) asserts that he was the first artist to create relief antefixes in the form of masks (*personas*) as temple decorations, which Pliny calls variously *prostypa* and *ectypa*. We should note that in this instance it is more likely that such objects were in fact frontal representations of faces rather than profile depictions. See *DNO*, no. 188.

[12] *DNO*, no. 187.

[13] *DNO*, nos. 2259–61; cf. Pollini 2007: esp. 249–52; Koch 2013: 39; Crowley 2016.

eum quam pulcherrimas facere studebant). Such earlier artists would perforce include Butades, who thus ends up as a kind of Ur-type for the artist who works in clay, the *fictor*, insofar as he not only shapes earth into form but creates inventions, fictions. This is a point to which we shall return at the end of the chapter.

How else does relief remediate painting? First, by being actually painted, imbued with color, *pictus*.[14] This color, which is so fundamental to the Latin idea of *pictura*, painting, is not as etymologically present in the Greek equivalents *graphe* or *zoographia*, which are much more closely related to the production of linear marks, including writing and other forms of incision.[15] But as is discussed at further length later in this chapter, Philostratus the Elder makes clear in the prologue to his *Imagines* that the use of color is the single defining feature of painting, and it seems uncontroversial to take it to be fundamental to painting as a medium. The color reconstructions occasionally projected onto the Ara Pacis Augustae, among the most public reconstitutions of polychrome Roman relief, are largely hypothetical, according to Paolo Liverani.[16] But we know that ancient sculptures, including reliefs, were painted, and strong visual evidence often remains.[17] To take just a few well-known examples, the so-called Alexander Sarcophagus from the royal cemetery at Sidon employs polychromy to accentuate the hair and clothing of the combatants and to articulate the tack of the horses, the decoration of armor and shields, and even flowing blood.[18] The recently published Tetrarchic reliefs from Nicomedia point to the intensity and ubiquity of polychromy on imperial state monuments, apparently for both expressive purposes and to accentuate visual clarity (Fig. 1.2).[19] At Rome itself, Gottfried Semper reported observing not only paint but even gilding on the Column of Trajan in the mid nineteenth century.[20]

But more than simply being colored, ancient reliefs, especially Roman ones, are also compositionally pictorial. From simple votive reliefs with sacro-idyllic landscape scenes to official, state-sponsored art, Roman reliefs depict figures within environments – comprehensible, encompassing places characterized as much by the natural as the human-made. They show objects that are far away from the viewer not just in physical terms,

[14] Cf. *OLD*, s.v. *pingo*, to color, employed both figuratively and literally.

[15] See *LSJ*, s.v. γραφή; ζωγραφία; cf. esp. Platt (in press).

[16] Liverani 2010: 296–300.

[17] Brinkmann et al. 2007; Panzanelli, Schmidt, and Lapatin 2008; Brinkmann, Primavesi, and Hollein 2010. On the significance of color in ancient art and beyond, see esp. Barry 2020; Stager 2022.

[18] See e.g. von Graeve 1970; Stewart 1993: 294–306, 422–3; Cohen 2010: 119–27.

[19] See e.g. Abbe and Ağtürk 2019; Ağtürk 2021.

[20] Semper 2004: 411–13.

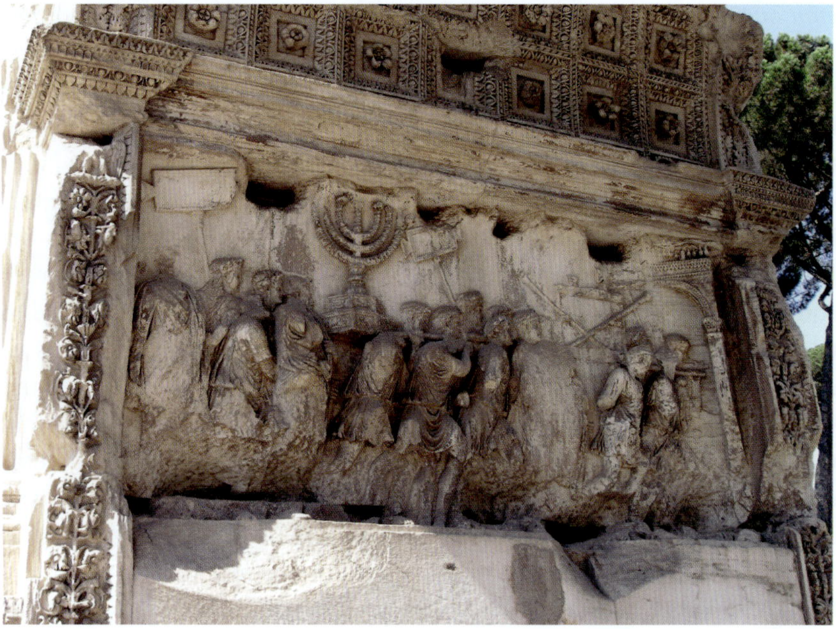

Fig. 7.1 Spoils panel, Arch of Titus, Rome, late first century CE (photograph by author).

through the actual protrusion from the back edge of the relief or through overlapping alone, but in optical ones, following the basic convention that what is higher up on a plane is necessarily farther away, and that what is farther away is perceived as smaller. And in certain cases, such as the spoils panel of the Arch of Titus, Roman reliefs play intensely with spatiality (Fig. 7.1).[21] The figures in the procession hoist a variety of objects above their heads – trumpets, *tabulae ansatae*, a *ferculum* laden with spoils and the candelabrum taken from the Temple in Jerusalem – thus setting them off against a background plane that could only read as space, even when originally painted. Accentuating this is the fact that at the rightmost end of the relief, the processional figures seem to turn slightly to the left, to pass underneath an arch (albeit one whose scale and relative position within the scene are not fully clarified), of which the relief shows only half. Wickhoff suggested that the other half must have been painted onto the background plane.[22] Given that all of the decoration that we would expect to find on top of an entire arch – the horses of two triumphal chariots, presumably those

[21] See e.g. Wickhoff and Hartel 1895; Wickhoff 1900; Lehmann-Hartleben 1934; Pfanner 1983; F. S. Kleiner 1990; D. E. E. Kleiner 1992: 183–91; Davies 2004: 19–24, 57–71.

[22] Wickhoff and Hartel 1895: 45; Wickhoff 1900: 80.

of Vespasian and Titus, as well as a central figure usually identified as Domitian – has been visibly sculpted, I am not sure how likely this supposition is.[23] But either way, the self-evident dematerialization of the surface of the relief imparts a strong sense that what is shown is just a smaller part of a much larger totality, the vast majority of which lies far beyond the actual plane of depiction at hand but whose accessibility is whispered by an apparent parallelism between the real world of the viewer and the fictional world of the artwork.

Just as relief remediates painting, of course, so too painting remediates relief, in both expected and unexpected senses. One place to start is to note that a significant corpus of what is commonly referred to as Roman mural painting is in fact relief. I am referring, of course, to the First Style of Roman wall painting, as well as its predecessors in the Hellenistic Mediterranean, which should be understood at least in part as an exercise in relief, a game not of pictorial virtuality but of the arrangement of projecting surfaces in real space organized in a pattern so as to produce an image (Fig. 7.2).[24] As we see in the *fauces* of the Samnite House at Herculaneum, the image that the surfaces produce is, obviously, that of a surface, a marble-clad wall, but the image is neither fully equal to the material that gives rise to it, nor is it a fully pictorial representation, the pigmentation of the plaster and articulation of veining and variegation of marble notwithstanding.[25] This ambiguity extends to the decor's interaction with the built space of the house. As Jaś Elsner has shown, the real and the virtual are closely intertwined in the raised columns and balustrade decorating the second story of the atrium of the Samnite House, where at least one wall (not pictured) actually opens out onto a view of the garden.[26] And it seems likely that Vitruvius is referring to something like the First Style in his discussion of early modes of wall painting, explicitly designated as *pictura*, in Book 7 of his treatise on architecture (*De arch.* 7.5.1–4).[27] Nevertheless, I would suggest that what the majority of First Style painting produces may be less a picture than a figure, a *figura*, of a wall, a plastic form that serves as bodily substitute as well as illusion.[28] Among such figurations, further, we should include the raised, relief-like stucco ceiling decorations that appear in a wide range of Roman interiors.[29] The plaster

23 Davies 2004: 24, fig. 14.

24 See, selectively, Bruno 1969; Laidlaw 1985; Bilde 1993; Rosenberg 2010; Barry 2020: esp. 80–103.

25 Laidlaw 1985: 304–7; Clarke 1991: 85–93; Croisille 2005: 43–6.

26 Elsner 1995: 70–4.

27 In general for Vitruvius' views on painting, see, selectively, Tybout 1989: 55–108; Grüner 2004: 218–84; Nichols 2017: 130–62.

28 See *OLD*, s.v. *figura*; Auerbach 1959.

29 See e.g. Mielsch 1975; Lipps 2018; Plant 2022.

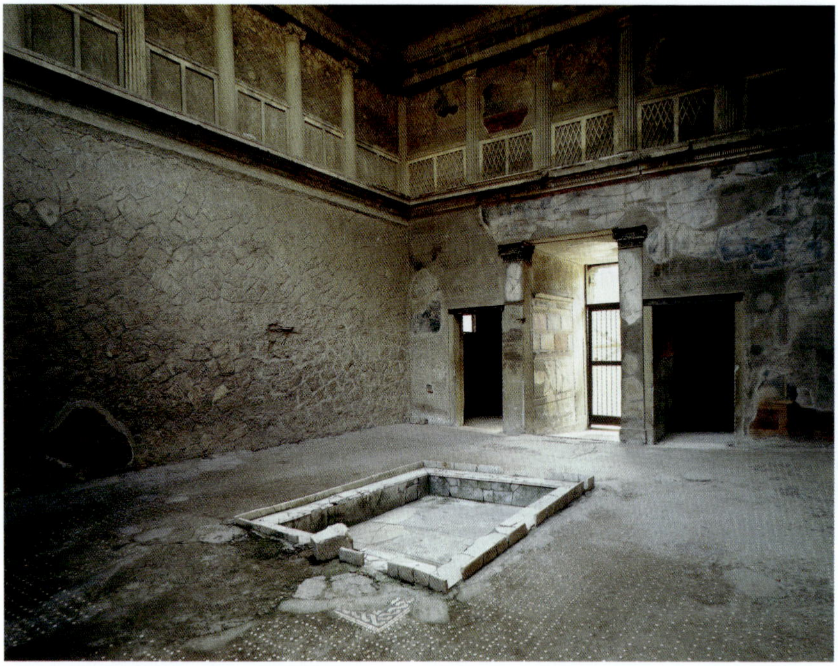

Fig. 7.2 First Style wall painting, fauces and atrium, Samnite House, Herculaneum, ca. 100 BCE (De Agostini/Getty Images).

from which First Style painting or ceiling stuccoes were formed may be set rather than fired, and these decorations may have been made using molds and other tools according to a highly systematized working pattern, but it is difficult to say that the basic process of production – the application of an earthen substance to a surface in a way that intrudes into real space – is fundamentally different than Pliny's account of Butades' discovery of plastic art.

In addition to such genuine three-dimensionality, paintings also produce the optical experience of relief. The decoration of Room II in the House of the Griffins in Rome, for example, creates the effect of protrusion from a surface – whether the podia extending from the dado in the painting or the *opus scutulatum* pattern on the floor (Fig. 7.3).[30] This sense of intrusion into the real space of the viewer is crucial to discourses of illusionism in the ancient world. As Vitruvius asserts, Agartharchus of Samos' exposition of scene decoration explained how: "from an uncertain thing certain images may represent the appearance of buildings in the paintings of stages, and things which are drawn upon straight and flat surfaces may sometimes seem to

[30] Rizzo 1936a: 9–13; Clarke 1991: 42–5.

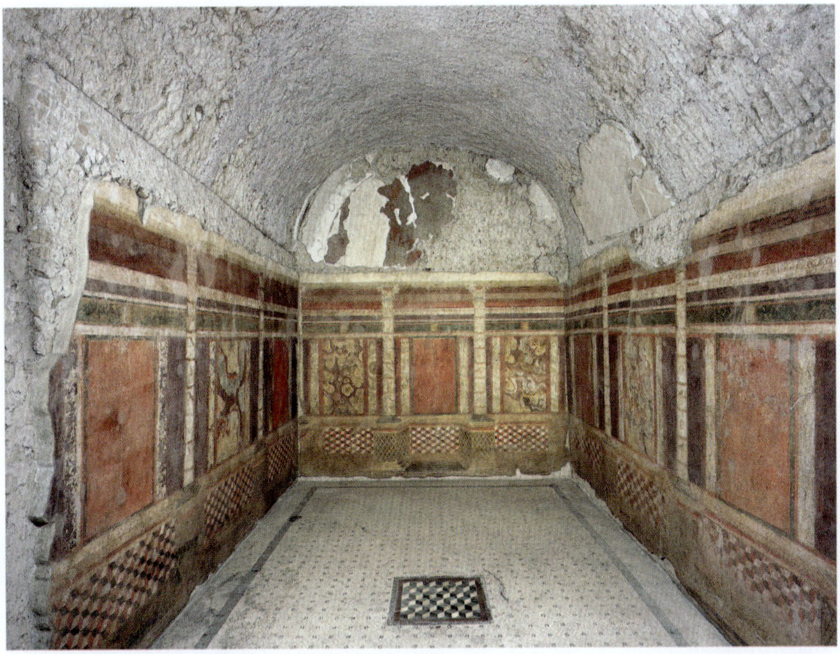

Fig. 7.3 Room II, House of the Griffins, Rome, Palatine Hill, ca. 100–80 BCE (Scala/Luciano Romano/Art Resource, NY).

recede, and sometimes to project" (*De arch.* 7.praef.11).[31] But there are other relief-like elements in painting, as well, which often employs the techniques of overlapping, foreshortening, highlight, shadow, and perspective not for the depiction of deep space, but for the sake of the play of contrast between depth intervals set close to the picture plane. These correspond to what Henrike Lange has called "relief-effects" in discussing trecento and quattrocento Italian art.[32] For Lange, who deliberately places herself in a tradition that goes back to nineteenth- and early twentieth-century discussions by figures like August Schmarsow and Adolf Hildebrand (treated in this volume by Nikolaus Dietrich [Chapter 5] in relation to the photography of sculpture and by Guy Hedreen [Chapter 4] in relationship to Attic vase painting), a relief-effect is the approximation of the experience of relief space in the medium of painting.[33] It depends upon stereoscopic, binocular vision, and especially the moving gaze,

[31] "De incerta re certae imagines aedificiorum in scaenarum picturis redderent speciem et, quae in directis planisque frontibus sint figurata, alia abscedentia, alia prominentia esse videantur." Text: Cam 2003: 5–7; cf. White 1987: 251; Stinson 2011: 406; *DNO*, nos. 1620–35.

[32] Lange 2020a, 2020b, 2023.

[33] Hildebrand 1893: esp. 63–82; Schmarsow 1899: esp. 142–217; Schmarsow 1905: esp. 295–309. Cf. Barasch 1998: 133–42; Etlin 1998; Koenderink and van Doorn 2006: esp. 140–2; Pinotti 2012; Basu 2016–17.

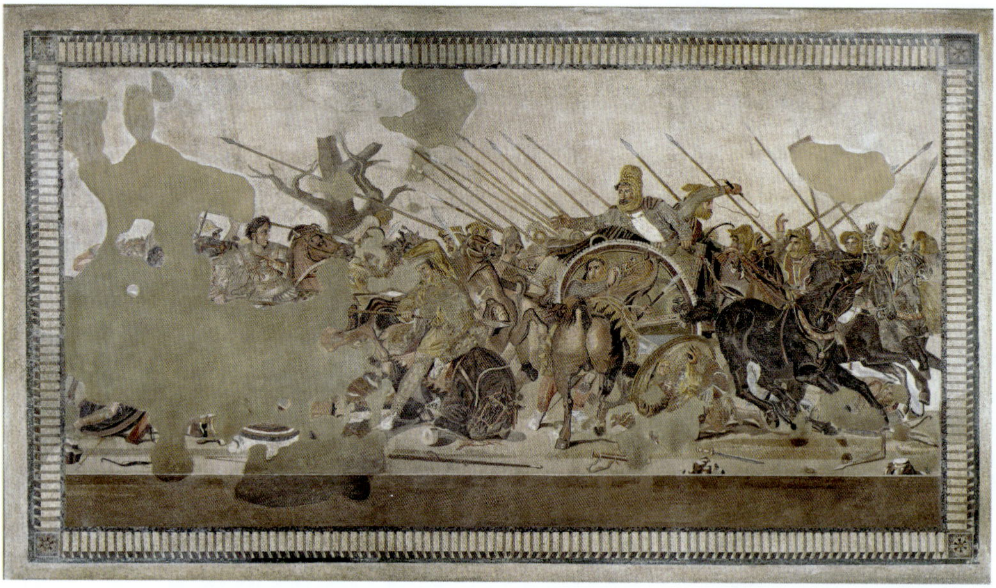

Fig. 7.4 Alexander Mosaic, House of the Faun, Pompeii, late second or early first century BCE (Leemage/Corbis/Getty Images).

which produces, in turn, the effect of motion. The scholarly investigation of relief-effect, Lange has argued, was at its most intense in the nineteenth century, when scholars had still been trained primarily through the study of casts.[34] The interactive relation between physical cast and living body of the viewer was soon replaced by the monocular, still vision of photography, however, and interest in relief-effects faded away.

This kind of animating, vibrant relief-effect is widely present in ancient painting and mosaic. It is characteristic of the Alexander Mosaic, with its energetic motion within an utterly ambiguous spatial setting, its limited depth intervals, which tend to push out rather than back into a pictorial plane, and its experimentation with representations of concavity and convexity and with the absorption and reflection of light (Fig. 7.4).[35] Thought of in terms of relief-effect rather than in the construction of a geometrically coherent space, the Alexander Mosaic practically pulsates. The vibrancy of this relief-effect may have been even more pronounced when the mosaic was experienced in situ, installed on the ground of the House of the Faun (VI.12.2–7).[36] A great deal of figural painting from

[34] Lange 2018.

[35] See e.g. Fuhrmann 1931; Stewart 1993: 130–50, 431; Cohen 1997; *DNO*, nos. 2740–1.

[36] See e.g. Moholt 2011; Crowley 2019: 114–32 for the experience of walking on Roman mosaics.

Rome and Campania shares many of these same characteristics – ambiguous settings, figures set close to the picture plane in pronounced but limited depth intervals, the strategic use of dark shadow and brilliant highlight to articulate conditions of visibility and invisibility and to bring the figures, relief-like, into the world of the viewer. In the great frieze of the Villa of the Mysteries, even though the modeling of the painted figures is less pronounced, the simple juxtaposition of their bodies against the bright red of the backing wall produces the effect of tipping them over into our space.[37] In all these cases, painting is remedial insofar as it aims to partake in the status of relief, at least as an optical effect. To do so, it deploys Bolter and Grusin's double logic in the immediacy of the dissolution of surface through techniques of illusion and in the hypermediacy of compositional principles, which follow from what we might call relief thinking, which both bring the figure out of the pictorial plane and, in their obvious stagedness, betray the fiction of such works.

Despite all of these acts of remediation, there are some basic, ineradicable differences between painting and relief. The simplest of these is also the most significant: Relief exists at least in part in the three dimensions of real space; it has physical as well as pictorial depth. The way in which the real and pictorial qualities of relief must be united by the active, ongoing participation of a viewer differs dramatically from the perception of painting, which, regardless of the painting's specific approach to the construction of pictorial space, perforce operates according to the organization of colors on a two-dimensional surface. In the proem to the *Imagines*, Philostratus the Elder points precisely to this distinction.[38] Painting is the superior art, for Philostratus, because it employs color alone, in two dimensions, and in so doing is not only able to reproduce optical experiences but to more effectively render emotion and to place its actions within environments:

> πλαστικῆς μὲν οὖν πολλὰ εἴδη – καὶ γὰρ αὐτὸ τὸ πλάττειν καὶ ἡ ἐν τῷ χαλκῷ μίμησις καὶ οἱ ξέοντες τὴν λυγδίνην ἢ τὴν Παρίαν λίθον καὶ ὁ ἐλέφας καὶ νὴ Δία ἡ γλυφικὴ πλαστική – ζωγραφία δὲ ξυμβέβληται μὲν ἐκ χρωμάτων, πράττει δὲ οὐ τοῦτο μόνον, ἀλλὰ καὶ πλείω σοφίζεται ἀπὸ τούτου ἑνὸς ὄντος ἢ ἀπὸ τῶν πολλῶν ἡ ἑτέρα τέχνη. σκιάν τε γὰρ ἀποφαίνει καὶ βλέμμα γινώσκει ἄλλο μὲν τοῦ μεμηνότος, ἄλλο δὲ τοῦ ἀλογοῦντος ἢ χαίροντος . . . θαλάμους τε καὶ οἰκίας καὶ ἄλση καὶ ὄρη καὶ πηγὰς καὶ τὸν αἰθέρα, ἐν ᾧ ταῦτα.

[37] Maiuri 1931; Brendel 1980; Sauron 1998; Gazda 2000.

[38] Maffei 1991; Primavesi and Giuliani 2012; Platt 2014: 220–1; cf. Dubel 2009.

> There are many forms of plastic art – plastic art proper, or modelling, and imitation in bronze, and the work of those who carve Lygdian or Parian marble, and ivory carving, and, by Zeus, the art of gem-cutting is also plastic art – while painting is imitation by the use of colors; and not only does it employ color, but this second form of art cleverly accomplishes more with this one means than the other form with its many means. For it both reproduces light and shade and also permits the observer to recognize the look, now of the man who is mad, now of the man who is sorrowing or rejoicing . . . chambers too and houses and groves and mountains and springs and the air that envelops them all.[39]

An aspect of these media Philostratus does not touch on, however, is their ability to contain and represent one another. One thing painting can do that relief cannot is to unambiguously represent other media within itself. To illustrate this point, we need only compare the London and Naples versions of the so-called Ikarios relief.[40] Each has the same depiction of a votive panel on a tall base, yet in what medium that panel was meant to be decorated has been left underdetermined. The London panel shows a chariot drawn by two horses, but it is indecipherable whether this is meant to be sculpted or painted decoration, nor is it clear whether the Naples version was originally painted or simply left blank. This is to say, the nature of relief simply forbids it from picturing painting. The clearest examples I know of reliefs of paintings are depictions of votive panels set in outdoor sanctuaries, but here the medium of painting is announced by format, as the panels have foldable wings – an object type known as a *pinax tethuromenos* which seems to be associated only with painting.[41]

The corpus of Roman painting, by contrast, contains a wide range of representations of architecture, freestanding sculpture, and other painting, as well as relief. Often these coexist in the same space, as in the Room of the Masks of the House of Augustus, where a metapictorial representation of a sacro-idyllic landscape is framed by the architecture of a temporary stage building articulated, in its turn, by masks and freestanding akroteria, as well as a frieze decorated in what appears to be relief and, in two coffers set behind the stage building, sculpted stone reliefs with palmettes and bearded faces.[42] In the atrium of Villa A at Oplontis, we find gilded bronze doors

[39] Text and translation from the Loeb edition of Fairbanks 1931: 2–5.

[40] London, British Museum, 1805,0703.123; Naples, Museo Archeologico Nazionale, 6713. See e.g. Moreno 1999; Ridgway 2002: 236–9, 256, no. 55; Jones 2019: 62–4.

[41] See e.g. an Augustan-era relief in the Vatican Apostolic Library, 6566; and a scene of Dionysiac sacrifice in Paris, Musée du Louvre Ma 50, acq. 1803, the latter recently illustrated in Beckman 2023: 65, fig. 8, with bibliography.

[42] Carettoni 1983a: 377–8, 1983b: 23–7; Leach 2004: 83–95; Iacopi 2008: 16–29.

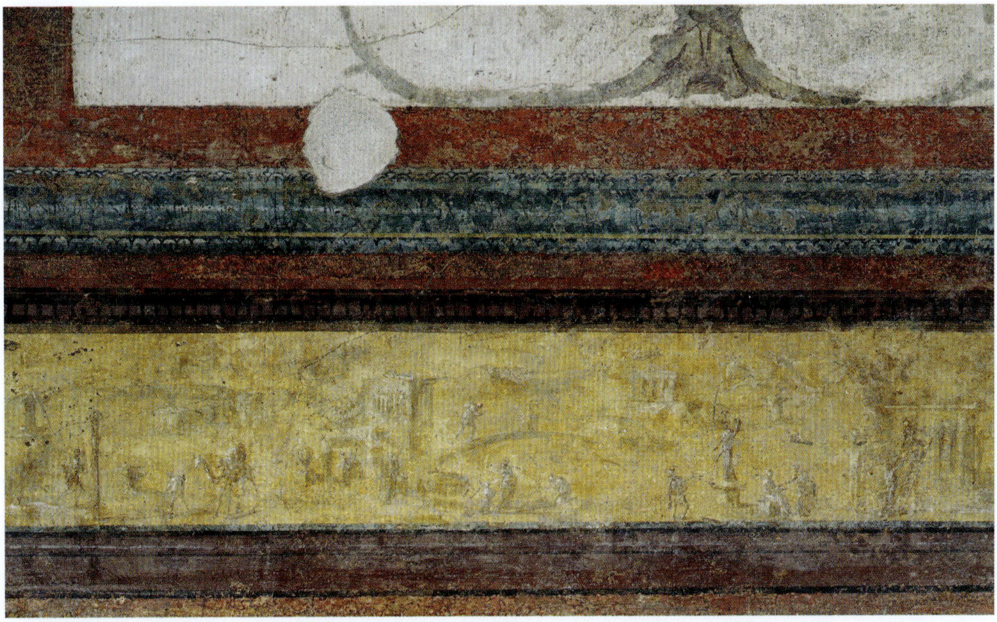

Fig. 7.5 Yellow frieze, House of Livia, Rome, late first century BCE (De Agostini/Getty Images).

with relief decorations of Victories, flanked by griffin protomes and shield portraits, which, however, the artists were at pains to make clear, were painted onto the continuously curving surface of the shield.[43] This is in contrast to the examples from the House of the Beautiful Impluvium at Pompeii (I.9.1), where the decorated shields extend outward in three dimensions into relief profiles of human faces.[44]

Despite their medium's ability to encapsulate other media, however, Roman painters seem to have particularly delighted in more ambiguous means of embedding representational forms within their murals. Such is the case in the right ala of the so-called House of Livia on the Palatine Hill in Rome (Fig. 7.5).[45] The decorative program of the room presents the viewer with a portico of white marble columns on a low green stage running in front of a backing wall of large white orthostats. Between the columns hangs a garland decorated with fruit and bucrania; in the intercolumniations of the upper register, ornate silver candelabra rest in front of

[43] See e.g. Cerutti and Richardson 1989; Clarke 1991: 113; Sauron 1994: 540–1, 2007, 55–66; Leach 2004: 81–5.

[44] *PPM*, 1.919–20.

[45] See, selectively, Rostovzteff 1911: 12–26; Rizzo 1936b: 41–50; Ling 1977: 7–10; Leach 1988: 263–7; La Rocca 2008: 38–41; Croisille 2010: 80–1.

illusionistic white revetment. Between the upper and lower registers of the backing wall is a yellow frieze upon which has been painted monochromatic landscape scenes. These scenes span the length of the frieze, interrupted only when it passes behind the columns of the portico. The frieze is, in some sense, a second-order fiction, a representation of a representation. But in what sense precisely is difficult to say: Such monochromatic paintings may represent reliefs worked in colored stone.[46] From the point of view of the fictive architecture of the room, which evokes a variety of precious stones, this makes perfect sense. But it is not necessarily the way the actual scenes are handled. Instead, we find painterly, even sketchy depictions of natural elements like rivers, trees, and stone formations, human-made structures like bridges, temples, and statues of deities, and people such as fishermen, herders, camels, worshippers, and travelers. We find, in other words, landscapes that are genuinely pictorial despite their monochromy. The figures cast shadows and, perhaps even more importantly, as Haritini Kotsidou has elucidated, the landscape is represented as an *inhabitable* space; these scenes show human, animal, and architectural figures dispersed amongst natural elements at such a scale so as to indicate that humanity and its products are, in fact, relatively smaller parts of a larger setting – actors whose physical presence is defined by their environment. Kotsidou has also identified the strategies by which the illusion of inhabitability has been effected: a high vantage point looking down onto the figures, atmospheric perspective, and the gradual reduction of size of the figures further back in the picture plane and, accordingly, farther away from the viewer's notional position.[47] What is more, there is no clear narrative thread, no set of identifiable mythological or historical activities which are occurring within the landscape. It is the setting itself, rather than any specific activities occurring within it, which seems to offer a guiding structural principle.

The dialectic of remediation is perhaps even clearer in a fragment of a wall taken from a villa near Portici (Fig. 7.6), which displays a vertically oriented green monochrome painting set within an illusionistically depicted architectural framework of a late Second Style decorative scheme.[48] As at the House of Livia, the monochromy of the green panel might lead us to associate it with relief sculpture, especially one executed in a precious, imported colored marble. But the scenes within the panel seem to deny that possibility. Even more painterly and impressionistic, the panel

[46] See e.g. Moormann 1988: 36–9; Eristov 2010. [47] Kotsidou 2007: 47–8.

[48] Moorman 1988: 226–7; Bragantini and Sampaolo 2009: 206–7, no. 75, with bibliography; Jones 2019: 152.

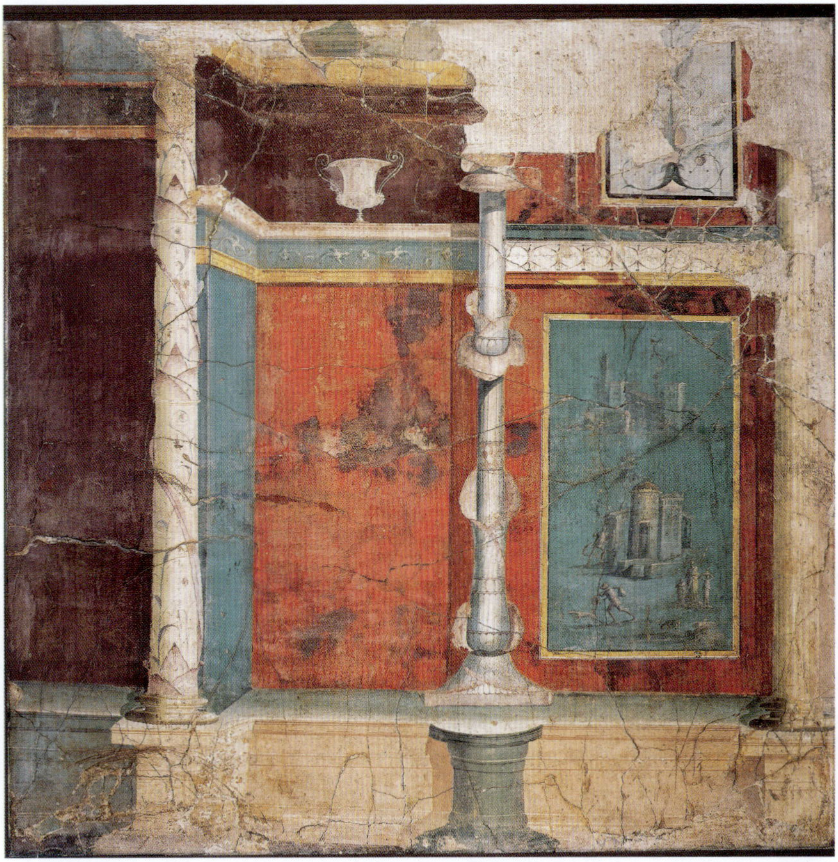

Fig. 7.6 Fresco with green monochrome landscape, villa at Portici, late first century BCE (Luigi Spina/Electa/Mondadori Portfolio/Getty Images).

contains no fewer than five groupings of figures, human, animal, architectural, and natural, each arrayed on independent, albeit ambiguously related, ground lines, and each illuminated as though by a light source streaming in from the upper right. The vertical orientation of the panel lends the sensation of depth in space, as what is placed higher on the wall seems to be farther away, and there is some diminution of the figures in the upper registers. Whether there is any narrative or thematic cohesion among the various vignettes, or even whether this is anything like a single landscape scene, however, cannot be determined. Once cued into the inconsistencies within the figural panel, moreover, we start to notice them in the framing composition as well. Orthogonal lines in the articulation of the stage and lower edges of the backing wall, for example, which would be easy to depict as parallel to one another or converging toward a common area, are shown as sharply divergent.[49] And though the architectural elements also seem to be illuminated by a light source coming from the upper right, just like the figures within the panel, they cast shadows in selective and often unrealistic ways. This is all to say that the oscillation of immediacy and hypermediacy in the painting is not limited to the figural scene alone but plays out even among apparently neutrally transparent representations.

Similar impulses are at play in a number of garden paintings in Pompeii. At the House of the Orchard (I.9.5), the dynamic of painting and relief is complicated by questions of style.[50] Within a representation of a domesticated garden punctuated by a variety of birds and framed by a kind of attenuated portico and hanging masks and garlands, we see marble panels painted in both Greco-Roman and Egyptianizing styles. The latter should remind us that the connection between painting and relief was much closer in the tradition of Pharaonic Egypt, where composition and coloring might be the same among extremely low reliefs, so-called sunken reliefs, and paintings.[51] The paradoxes of remediation are even more overt in a garden scene recovered from the House of the Golden Bracelet in Pompeii (VI.17.42), which is lush with flora, fauna, and representations of finely crafted art objects (Fig. 7.7).[52] At once deeply illusionistic and critically self-reflexive, the painting stages the dialectic of immediacy and hypermediacy in no small part through the play of represented and representing media. Polychrome panels rest on herms in the lower part of the wall. The stone frames of these panels and the fact that the scene as a whole is set outdoors might lead us to think that they are painted marble relief carvings. But while the frames themselves are consistently modulated in light and shadow from a light source to the upper left, and thus meant to be three-dimensional objects within the broader fiction of the wall, the shading of the figures within these scenes operates according to an independent logic and gives us no sense of protrusion in space. These may be paintings of paintings, in other words, as much as paintings of reliefs. The heads of the herms, moreover, which are fully three-dimensional and appear to be continuous with the stone of both the plinths

[49] On such convergence, see esp. Stinson 2011.

[50] *PPM*, 2.1–137, esp. 2.15–35; de Vos 1980: 15–21; Moormann 1988: 151; Elsner 2006: 278–84; Jones 2019: 214.

[51] The connections among relief, painting, and drawing in the Egyptian tradition were at times related to the story of Butades' invention of relief in nineteenth-century scholarship. See e.g. Münzer 1895: 511–12.

[52] *PPM*, 6.44–145, esp. 6.117–28; Moormann 1988: 202–3; Ciardiello 2006; Mattusch 2008: 172–3, no. 65; Bergmann 2014: esp. 264–6, 270–72; Jones 2019: 156–7.

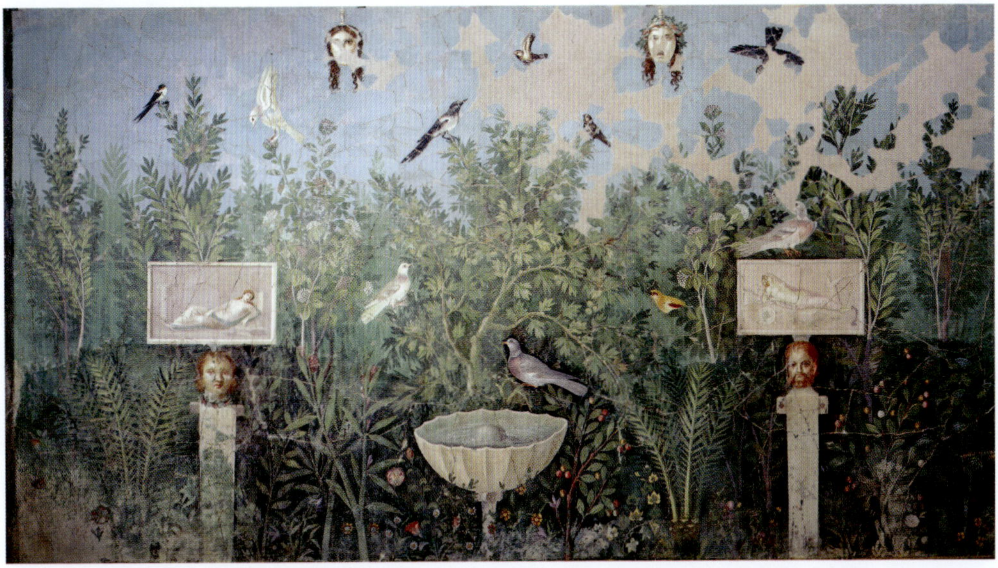

Fig. 7.7 Garden painting, House of the Golden Bracelet, Pompeii (VI.17.42), early first century CE (DEA/L. Pedicini/De Agostini/Getty Images).

below them and panels above, are painted to look uncannily alive. Their alert expressions and modulated flesh tones contrast with both the figures painted on the panels and the smoothly modeled and more overtly relief-like masks hanging above the scene, though they all share similarly flowing, carefully coiffed auburn hair. The contrast evokes Pliny's discussions of Butades and Lysistratus, and in so doing, it also invites comparisons between actual living bodies and mere representation as much as it does reflections on similarities and differences among media.

The painting from the House of the Golden Bracelet thus literalizes what I would view as the primary point of tension animating painting and relief's acts of remediation – namely, that the oscillating logic of immediacy and hypermediacy roughly maps on to the dueling impulses of all-encompassing illusion and self-disclosing fiction, between the desire to dissolve the boundaries separating viewer and object of representation and the desire to acknowledge that this is nothing more than make-believe. To return, briefly, to questions of terminology, while *illudo* means to fool or trick, and *illusio* ridicule or doublespeak, *fingo* carries a slightly different charge, as it can mean to shape, mold, or fashion, as well as to fake or pretend.[53] The *fictor*, accordingly, is thus more than just the worker in clay or the producer, like

[53] See *OLD*, s.v. *illudo* 1–2; *illusio*, *fingo* 1–3, 9.

Butades, of objects in relief.[54] They are also the paradigm for anyone who might wish to produce a fiction. Such a fiction inevitably draws attention to the differences as well as the similarities between a representing object and its object of representation. The mutual remediation of painting and relief hangs right along the border between the two.

To close, I would like to take a step back and suggest that much of this had already been alluded to in a fragment of the second-century BCE satirist Lucilius preserved by the early Christian writer Lactantius (*Div. Inst.* 1.22.13):[55]

> Terriculas Lamias, Fauni quas Pompiliique
> instituere Numae, tremit has, hic omnia ponit.
> Ut pueri infantes credunt signa omnia aena
> vivere et esse homines, sic isti somnia ficta
> vera putant, credunt signis cor inesse in aenis.
> Pergula pictorum, veri nil, omnia ficta.
>
> As for scarecrows and witches, which the fauns and Numa Pompiliuses established – he trembles at them, and thinks them all-important. Just as infant children believe that all bronze statues live and are men, so these ones think that fictitious dreams are true, and they believe that there is a heart inside bronze statues. These things are a painters' gallery: nothing real, all fictions.[56]

On the surface, the passage seems to mock superstition and credulity, comparing those who believe in mythical creatures with mere children who are unable to distinguish between works of art and living bodies. Yet the language Lucilius employs plays precisely on the relationship between illusion and fiction, and the passage consistently reinforces a recursive link between creation and dissimulation. The true and the untrue are set up as though they were opposites, and Lucilius positions himself on the side of the skeptic, but unverbalized in this apparent dichotomy is the fact that enormous care was put into making fictions such as statues look like their objects of representation. In the case of the experience of the divine, whether mediated by works of art or in dreams, the immediacy of this illusionistic quality was precisely part of its power.[57] Yet hypermediacy may rear its head once more, depending on how we read the fragment. In the

[54] *OLD*, s.v. *fictor*.
[55] In general on Lucilius, see Conte 1994: 112–18; cf. e.g. Gruen 1992: 272–318; Freudenburg 2001.
[56] Text from and translation adapted from the Loeb edition of Warmington 1938: 166–7. Lucretius 6.35–41 closely echoes Lucilius' language; O'Hara 1987. See also Jones 2019: 35–7.
[57] See e.g. Platt 2011.

version of the text above, we find reference to a *pergula pictorum*, a phrase attested in other contexts as a kind of display pavilion for paintings, a stage which puts forward the paintings themselves in relief, so to speak.[58] The fictions of which Lucilius speaks, in other words, may be represented within paintings, themselves framed and contained by a *pergula*. In at least one edition of Lucilius, *pictorum* is emended to *fictorum*, and if this is the correct editorial decision, we would remain in the realm of three-dimensional sculpture, and the play between truth (*vera*) and fiction (*ficta*) would be neatly transposed to the difference between life (*homines*) and art (*signa*).[59] But if we accept that Lucilius really did write *pictorum*, then the third term of painting interrupts such an easy dichotomy and we find ourselves within the recursive dialectic of remediation.[60]

We may wish to return at this point to the problem of characterizing relief with which we began. Is relief process, product, effect, or phenomenological encounter? Is it a matter of painting or sculpture? Without ever using one of relief's ancient – albeit always partial – cognates, Lucilius seems to expose not only the futility of the question but the advantage of embracing ambiguity. Lucilius' fictions oscillate from painting to sculpture as much as they do from the real to the merely make-believe. In this sense, like relief, they are always remedial, and to seek to pin either down too precisely may be to miss their power. In its equilibrium between painting and sculpture, neither fully real nor fully virtual, neither absolutely true nor patently false, relief mirrors the structure of fiction itself.

References

Abbe, M. B. and Ağtürk, T. S. (2019). "The New Corpus of Painted Imperial Roman Marble Reliefs from Nicomedia: A Preliminary Report on Polychromy." *Technè* 48: 100–9.

Ağtürk, T. S. (2021). *The Painted Tetrarchic Reliefs of Nicomedia: Uncovering the Colourful Life of Diocletian's Forgotten Capital*. Turnhout: Brepols.

Auerbach, E. (1959). "Figura." In E. Auerbach, ed., *Scenes from the Drama of European Literature*. New York: Meridian, 11–76.

Barasch, M. (1998). *Modern Theories of Art*. Vol. 2, *From Impressionism to Kandinsky*. New York: New York University Press.

Barry, F. (2020). *Painting in Stone: Architecture and the Poetics of Marble from Antiquity to the Enlightenment*. New Haven, CT: Yale University Press.

[58] Plin. *HN* 35.84; Ulp. *Dig*. 9.3.5.12. Cf. Rouveret 1989: 381–2. [59] Marx 1904: M484–9.
[60] In defense of *pictorum*, see e.g. Housman 1907: 152–3.

Basu, P. (2016–17). "Ornament and Empathy in August Schmarsow's Psychophysical History of Art." *RES: Anthropology and Aesthetics* 67–8: 94–110.

Beckmann, S. E. (2023). "The Naked Reader: Child Enslavement in the Villa of the Mysteries Fresco." *American Journal of Archaeology* 127: 55–83.

Bergmann, B. (2014). "The Concept of Boundary in the Roman Garden." In K. Coleman, ed., *Le jardin dans l'antiquité*. Vandoeuvres: Fondation Hardt pour l'étude de l'antiquité classique, 245–300.

Bettini, M. (1999). *The Portrait of the Lover*. Trans. L. Gibbs. Berkeley: University of California Press.

Bilde, P. G. (1993). "The International Style: Aspects of Pompeian First Style and Its Eastern Equivalents." In M. Nielsen, I. Nielsen, and P. G. Bilde, eds., *Aspects of Hellenism in Italy: Towards a Cultural Unity?* Copenhagen: Museum Tusculanum Press, 151–77.

Bolter, J. D., and Grusin, R. (1999). *Remediation: Understanding New Media*. Cambridge, MA: MIT Press.

Bragantini, I., and Sampaolo, V., eds. (2009). *La pittura pompeiana*. Verona: Electa.

Brendel, O. (1980). "The Great Frieze in the Villa of the Mysteries." In O. Brendel, ed., *The Visible Idea: Interpretations of Classical Art*. Washington, DC: Decatur House Press, 90–138.

Brinkmann, R., Wünsche, R. Koch-Brinkmann, U., et al., eds. (2007). *Gods in Color: Painted Sculpture of Classical Antiquity*. Munich: Biering and Brinkmann.

Brinkmann, V., Primavesi, O., and Hollein, M., eds. (2010). *Circumlitio: The Polychromy of Antique and Medieval Sculpture*. Frankfurt: Hirmer.

Bruno, V. J. (1969). "Antecedents of the Pompeian First Style." *American Journal of Archaeology* 73.3: 305–17.

Cam, M. T., ed. (2003). *Vitruve, De l'architecture: Livre VII*. Paris: Belles Lettres.

Carettoni, G. (1983a). "La decorazione pittorica della casa di Augusto sul Palatino." *Mitteilungen des Deutschen Archäologischen Instituts, Römische Abteilung* 90: 373–419.

(1983b). *Das Haus des Augustus auf dem Palatin*. Mainz: von Zabern.

Carey, S. (2003). *Pliny's Catalogue of Culture: Art and Empire in the Natural History*. Oxford: Oxford University Press.

Cerutti, S. M., and Richardson, L. (1989). "Vitruvius on Stage Architecture and Some Recently Discovered *Scaenae Frons* Decorations." *Journal of the Society of Architectural Historians* 48.2: 172–9.

Ciardiello, R. (2006). "VI 17 Insula Occidentalis 42: Casa del Bracciale d'Oro." In M. Aoyagi and U. Pappalardo, eds., *Pompei (Regiones VI–VII): Insula Occidentalis*. Naples: Valtrend, 69–256.

Clarke, J. R. (1991). *The Houses of Roman Italy, 100 BC–AD 250: Ritual, Space, and Decoration*. Berkeley: University of California Press.

Cohen, A. (1997). *The Alexander Mosaic: Stories of Victory and Defeat*. Cambridge: Cambridge University Press.

(2010). *Art in the Era of Alexander the Great: Paradigms of Manhood and Their Cultural Traditions.* Cambridge: Cambridge University Press.

Conte, G. B. (1994). *Latin Literature: A History.* Trans. J. B. Solodow. Baltimore, MD: Johns Hopkins University Press.

Conze, A. (1882). "Über das Relief bei den Griechen." *Sitzungberichte der königlich Preussischen Akademie der Wissenschaften zu Berlin* 26: 563–77.

Croisille, J.-M. (2005). *La peinture romaine.* Paris: Picard.

(2010). *Paysages dans la peinture romaine: Aux origines d'un genre pictural.* Paris: Picard.

Crowley, P. R. (2016). "Roman Death Masks and the Metaphorics of the Negative." *Grey Room* 64: 64–103.

(2019). *The Phantom Image: Seeing the Dead in Ancient Rome.* Chicago, IL: University of Chicago Press.

Davies, P. J. E. (2004). *Death and the Emperor: Roman Imperial Funerary Monuments from Augustus to Marcus Aurelius.* Austin: University of Texas Press.

Davis, W. (2017). *Visuality and Virtuality: Images and Pictures from Prehistory to Perspective.* Princeton, NJ: Princeton University Press.

de Vos, M. (1980). *L'egittomania in pitture e mosaici romano-campani della prima età imperiale.* Leiden: Brill.

Derrida, J. (1993). *Memoirs of the Blind: The Self-Portrait and Other Ruins.* Trans. P.-A. Brault and M. Naas. Chicago, IL: University of Chicago Press.

Dubel, S. (2009). "Colour in Philostratus' *Imagines.*" In E. Bowie and J. Elsner, eds., *Philostratus.* Cambridge: Cambridge University Press, 309–21.

Elsner, J. (1995). *Art and the Roman Viewer: The Transformation of Art from the Pagan World to Christianity.* Cambridge.

(2006). "Classicism in Roman Art." In J. I. Porter, ed., *Classical Pasts: The Classical Traditions of Greece and Rome.* Princeton, NJ: Princeton University Press, 270–97.

Eristov, H. (2010). "Relief fictif ou genre pictural: Les frises et bandeaux figurés dans la peinture Romano-Campenienne." *Atti del X Congresso internazionale dell'IPMA, Association internationale pour la peinture murale antique, Napoli 17–21 Settembre 2007.* Naples: Università degli studi Napoli "l'orientale," 159–72.

Etlin, R. A. (1998). "Aesthetics and the Spatial Sense of Self." *Journal of Aesthetics and Art Criticism* 56.1: 1–19.

Fairbanks, A., ed. and trans. (1931). *Philostratus the Elder, Imagines; Philostratus the Younger, Imagines; Callistratus, Descriptions.* Loeb Classical Library 256. Cambridge, MA: Harvard University Press.

Freudenburg, K. (2001). *Satires of Rome: Threatening Poses from Lucilius to Juvenal.* Cambridge: Cambridge University Press.

Fried, M. (1980). *Absorption and Theatricality: Painting and Beholder in the Age of Diderot.* Berkeley: University of California Press.

Fuhrmann, H. (1931). *Philoxenos von Eretria: Archäologische Untersuchungen über zwei Alexandermosaike*. Gottingen: Dieterichsche Universitäts-Buchdruckerei Kaestner.

Gazda, E. K., ed. (2000). *The Villa of the Mysteries at Pompeii: Ancient Ritual, Modern Muse*. Ann Arbor: University of Michigan Press.

Gell, A. (1998). *Art and Agency: An Anthropological Theory*. Oxford: Clarendon Press.

Greenberg, C. (1993). "Modernist Painting." In J. O'Brian, ed., *Clement Greenberg: The Collected Essays and Criticism*. Vol. 4, *Modernism with a Vengeance, 1957–1969*. Chicago, IL: Chicago University Press, 85–93.

Gruen, E. (1992). *Culture and National Identity in Republican Rome*. Ithaca, NY: Cornell University Press.

Grüner, A. (2004). *Venus Ordinis: Der Wandel von Malerei und Literatur im Zeitalter der römischen Bürgerkriege*. Paderborn: Schöningh.

Hildebrand, A. (1893). *Das Problem der Form in der Bildenden Kunst*. Strasbourg: Heitz.

Housman, A. E. (1907). "Luciliana." *Classical Quarterly* 1.1–2: 53–74, 148–59.

Iacopi, I. (2008). *The House of Augustus: Wall Paintings*. Milan: Electa.

Jones, N. B. (2019). *Painting, Ethics, and Aesthetics in Rome*. Greek Culture in the Roman World. Cambridge: Cambridge University Press.

Kleiner, D. E. E. (1992). *Roman Sculpture*. New Haven, CT: Yale University Press.

Kleiner, F. S. (1990). "The Arches of Vespasian in Rome." *Mitteilungen des Deutschen Archäologischen Instituts, Römische Abteilung* 97: 127–36.

Koch, N. J. (2013). *Paradeigmata: Die antike Kunstschriftstellerei als Grundlage der frühneuzeitlichen Kunstheorie*. Wiesbaden: Harrassowitz.

Koenderink, J. J., and van Doorn, A. J. (2006). "Pictorial Space: A Modern Reappraisal of Adolf Hildebrand." In L. Albertazzi, ed. *Visual Thought: The Depictive Space of Perception*. Amsterdam: Benjamins, 135–54.

Koortbojian, M. (2023). The Representation of Space in Graeco-Roman Art: Relief Sculpture, Problems of Form, and Modern Historiography. Berlin: De Gruyter.

Kotsidou, H. (2007). *Landschaft im Bild: Naturprojektionen in der antiken Dekorationskunst*. Worms: Wernersche Verlagsgesellschaft.

La Rocca, E. (2008). *Lo spazio negato: La pittura di paesaggio nella cultural artistica greca romana*. Milan: Electa.

Laidlaw, A. (1985). *The First Style in Pompeii: Painting and Architecture*. Rome: Bretschneider.

Lakey, C. (2018). *Sculptural Seeing: Relief, Optics, and the Rise of Perspective in Medieval Italy*. New Haven, CT: Yale University Press.

Lange, H. (2018). "Motion Picture Studies: Relief before and since 1900." Paper presented at "Time, Space, Movement: Art Between Perception, Imagination, and Fiction," College Art Association Annual Meeting, Los Angeles, CA, February 24.

(2020a). "Cimabue's True Crosses in Arezzo and Florence." In S. Elm and C. Ocker, eds., *Material Christianity: Western Religion and the Agency of Things*. Cham: Springer, 29–67.

(2020b). "Relief Effects in Donatello and Mantegna." In A. R. Bloch and D. M. Zolli, eds., *The Art of Sculpture in Fifteenth Century Italy*. Cambridge: Cambridge University Press, 327–43.

(2023). *Giotto's Arena Chapel and the Triumph of Humility*. Cambridge: Cambridge University Press.

Leach, E. W. (1988). *The Rhetoric of Space: Literary and Artistic Representations of Landscape in Republican and Augustan Rome*. Princeton, NJ: Princeton University Press.

(2004). *The Social Life of Painting in Ancient Rome and on the Bay of the Naples*. New York: Cambridge University Press.

Lehmann-Hartleben, K. (1934). "L'arco di Tito." *Bullettino della Commissone archaeologica comunale di Roma* 62: 89–122.

Ling, R. (1977). "Studius and the Beginnings of Roman Landscape Painting." *Journal of Roman Studies* 67: 1–16.

Lipps, J. (2018). *Die Stuckdecke des oecus tetrastylus aus dem sog: Augustushaus auf dem Palatin im Kontext antiker Deckenverzierungen*. Rahden: Leidorf.

Liverani, P. (2010). "New Evidence on the Polychromy of Roman Sculpture." In Brinkmann, Primavesi, and Hollein 2010: 290–302.

Maffei, S. (1991). "La sophia del pittore e del poeta nel proemio delle *Imagines* di Filostrato Maggiore." *Annali della Scuola Normale Superiore di Pisa* 21: 591–621.

Maiuri, A. (1931) *La villa dei misteri*. Rome: Libreria dello Stato.

Marx, F. (1904). *C. Luicilii Carminum Reliquiae*. Leipzig: Teubner.

Mattusch, C. C., ed. (2008). *Pompeii and the Roman Villa: Art and Culture around the Bay of Naples*. Washington, DC: National Gallery of Art.

McLuhan, M. (1964). "The Medium Is the Message." In M. McLuhan, ed., *Understanding Media: The Extensions of Man*. New York: McGraw-Hill, 7–21.

Michelakis, P., ed. (2020). *Classics and Media Theory*. Oxford: Oxford University Press.

Mielsch, H. (1975). *Römische Stuckreliefs*. Heidelberg: Kerle.

Moholt, R. (2011). "Roman Labyrinth Mosaics and the Experience of Motion." *Art Bulletin* 93.3: 287–303.

Moormann, E. (1988). *La pittura parietale romana come fonte di conoscenza per la scultura antica*. Assen: Van Gorcum.

Moreno, P. (1999). "Visita di Dioniso: Rilievo Maffei al British Museum." In P. Morena, ed., *Sabato in museo: Letture di arte ellenistica e romana*. Milan: Electa, 86–94.

Münzer, F. (1895). "Zur Kunstgeschichte des Plinius." *Hermes* 30.4: 499–507.

Naas, V. (2011). "La jeune fille de Corinthe: De l'anecdote à l'invention de l'art." In S. Alexandre, N. Philippe, and C. Ribeyrol, eds., *Inventer la peinture grecque antique*. Paris: ENS, 71–93.

Newby, Z. (2009). "Absorption and Erudition in Philostratus' *Imagines*." In E. Bowie and J. Elsner, eds., *Philostratus*. Cambridge: Cambridge University Press, 322–42.

Nichols, M. (2017). *Author and Audience in Vitruvius'* De architectura. Cambridge: Cambridge University Press.

O'Hara, J. J. (1987). "Somnia Ficta in Lucretius and Lucilius." *Classical Quarterly* 37.2: 517–19.

Panofsky, E. (1991). *Perspective as Symbolic Form*. Trans. C. S. Wood. New York: Zone.

Panzanelli, R., Schmidt, E., and Lapatin, K., eds., 2008. *The Color of Life: Polychromy in Sculpture from Antiquity to the Present*. Los Angeles, CA: J. Paul Getty Museum.

Payne, A. (2008). "Portable Ruins: The Pergamon Altar, Heinrich Wölfflin, and German Art History at the Fin de siècle." *RES: Anthropology and Aesthetics* 53–4: 168–89.

(2011). "On Sculptural Relief, *Malerisch*, the Autonomy of Artistic Media and the Beginnings of Baroque Studies." In H. Hills, ed., *Rethinking the Baroque*. London: Ashgate, 39–64.

Pinotti, A. (2012). "Body-Building: August Schmarsow's *Kunstwissenschaft* between Pscychophysiology and Phenomenology." In M. B. Frank and D. Adler, eds., *German Art History and Scientific Thought: Beyond Formalism*. Farnham: Routledge, 13–31.

Plant, J. (2022). "Hard as a Rock and Light as Air: Stucco Ceilings in Roman Domestic Space." In A. Haug, A. Hielscher, and M. T. Lauritsen, eds., *Materiality in Roman Art and Architecture*. Berlin: De Gruyter, 113–30.

Platt, V. (2011). *Facing the Gods: Epiphany in Graeco-Roman Art, Literature, and Religion*. Cambridge: Cambridge University Press.

Platt, V. (2014). "Agamemnon's Grief: On the Limits of Expression in Roman Rhetoric and Painting." In J. Elsner and M. Meyer, eds., *Art and Rhetoric in Roman Culture*. Cambridge: Cambridge University Press, 211–32.

(in press). *Epistemic Objects: Making and Mediating between Classical Art and Text*. Oxford: Oxford University Press.

Platt, V. J., and Squire, M., eds. (2010). "The Art of Art History in Greco-Roman Antiquity." Special issue, *Arethusa* 43.2: 133–340, 349–69.

Polanyi, M. (2009). *The Tacit Dimension*. Chicago, IL: University of Chicago Press.

Pollini, J. (2007). "Ritualizing Death in Republican Rome: Memory, Religion, Class Struggle, and the Wax Ancestral Mask Tradition's Origin and Influence on Veristic Portraiture." In N. Laneri, ed., *Performing Death: Social Analyses of Funerary Traditions in the Ancient Near East and Mediterranean*. Chicago, IL: Oriental Institute of the University of Chicago, 237–85.

Pfanner, M. (1983). *Der Titusbogen*. Mainz: von Zabern.

Primavesi, O., and Giuliani, L. (2012). "Bild und Rede: Zum Proömium der *Eikones* des zweiten Philostrat." *Poetica* 44: 25–79.

Rackham, H. (2003). *Pliny, Natural History.* Vol. 9, *Books 33–35.* Loeb Classical Library 394. Cambridge, MA: Harvard University Press.

Ridgway, B. S. (2002). *Hellenistic Sculpture.* Vol. 3, *The Styles of ca. 100–31 B.C.* Madison: University of Wisconsin Press.

Riegl, A. (1901) *Die spätrömische Kunstindustrie nach den Funden in Österreich-Ungarn.* Vol. 1, *Im Zusammenhange mit der Gesammtentwicklung der bildenden Künste bei den Mittelmeervölkern.* Vienna: Verlag der Kaiserlich-Königlichen Hof- und Staatsdruckerei.

Rizzo, G. E. (1936a). *Le pitture della "Casa dei Grifi" (Palatino).* Rome: Istituto poligrafico dello stato.

(1936b). *Le pitture della "Casa di Livia" (Palatino).* Rome: Istituto poligrafico dello stato.

Rosenberg, A. (2010). "Taking the First Style Seriously." *Chicago Art Journal* 20: 103–15.

Rostovtzeff, M. (1911). "Die hellenistisch-römische Architekturlandschaft." *Mitteilungen des Deutschen Archäologischen Instituts, Römische Abteilung* 26: 1–185.

Rouveret, A. (1989). *Histoire et imaginaire de la peinture ancienne: Ve siècle av. J.-C.–Ier siècle ap. J.-C.* Rome: École française de Rome.

Sauron, G. (1994). *"Quis deum?" L'expression plastique des idéologies politiques et religieuses à Rome à la fin de la Republique et au début du Principat.* Rome: École française de Rome.

(1998). *La grande fresque de la villa des Mystères à Pompéi: Mémoires d'une dévote de Dionysos.* Paris: Picard.

(2007). *La pittura allegorica a Pompei: Lo sguardo di Cicerone.* Barcelona: Jaca.

Schmarsow, A. (1899). *Plastik, Malerei und Reliefkunst in ihrem gegenseitigen Verhältnis.* Leipzig: Hirzel.

(1905). *Grundbegriffe der Kunstwissenschaft: Am Übergang vom Altertum zum Mittelalter kritisch erörtert und in systematichem Zusammenhange dargestellt.* Leipzig: Teubner.

Semper, G. (2004). *Style in the Technical and Tectonic Arts; or, Practical Aesthetics.* Trans. H. F. Mallgrave. Los Angeles, CA: Getty Research Institute.

Stager, J. M. S. (2022). *Seeing Color in Classical Art: Theory, Practice, and Reception, from Antiquity to the Present.* Cambridge: Cambridge University Press.

Stewart, A. 1993. *Faces of Power: Alexander's Image and Hellenistic Politics.* Berkeley: University of California Press.

Stoichita, V. (1997). *A Short History of the Shadow.* Trans. A. M. Glasheen. London: Reaktion.

Stinson, P. (2011). "Perspective Systems in Roman Second Style Wall Painting." *American Journal of Archaeology* 115.3: 403–26.

Summers, D. (2003). *Real Spaces: World Art History and the Rise of Western Modernism*. New York: Phaidon.

Tanner, J. (2006). *The Invention of Art History in Ancient Greece: Religion, Society and Artistic Rationalisation*. Cambridge: Cambridge University Press.

Tybout, R. A. (1989). *Aedificiorum figurae: Untersuchungen zu den Architekturdarstellungen des frühen zweiten Stils*. Amsterdam: Gieben.

von Graeve, V. (1970). *Der Alexandersarkophag und seine Werkstatt*. Berlin: Mann.

Warmington, E. H. (1938). *Remains of Old Latin*. Vol. 3, *Lucilius, The Twelve Tables*. Loeb Classical Library 329. Cambridge, MA: Harvard University Press.

White, J. (1987). *The Birth and Rebirth of Pictorial Space*. Cambridge, MA: Belknap Press.

Wickhoff, F. (1900). *Roman Art: Some of Its Principles and Their Application to Early Christian Painting*. Trans. E. Strong. London: Heinemann.

Wickhoff, F., and von Hartel, W. (1895). *Die Wiener Genesis*. Vol. 2. *Jahrbuch des kunsthistorischen Sammlungen des allerhöchsten Kaiserhauses 16*. Vienna: Tempsky.

8 Foregrounding the Background in Roman Relief Sculpture

JENNIFER TRIMBLE

Discussions of relief sculpture generally begin with the foreground figures. A relief is characterized as "high" or "low" depending on how deeply those foreground figures are carved, and analysis focuses on their iconography and interactions. This focus is reasonable, since patrons and carvers demonstrably worked to focus the viewer's attention on the foreground. It does, however, raise questions about how to theorize the background surface of a relief, the often flat plane against which the foreground figures are organized and seen. This background is what defines sculptural relief in contrast to sculpture in the round, but it is often treated as unimportant or ignored altogether. Contributing to this dismissal are the standard practices of archaeological photography, including the use of cloth or other neutral backdrops that erase any angles, topography, shadow-casting, or other meaningful space behind the foreground figure, and encouraging an understanding of the background as a kind of immaterial non-space. The background of a sculptural relief is a classic parergon, both essential to the work as a whole and disappearing as a thing in itself.[1]

And yet the background surface on a relief sculpture can have a live and substantive presence – sometimes startlingly so when the three-dimensional object is encountered after much study of two-dimensional photographs. The background can undulate or form a concavity that holds and activates the foreground carving, or otherwise defy and play with two-dimensionality. Above all, an in-person encounter with sculptural relief is a reminder that the background surface is a *thing*, a solid substance, part of the same marble that elsewhere is carved into figures or other details. The background of

I thank the editors of this volume and the participants of the conference on "Relief: Greek/Roman/Late Antique," held May 3–4, 2019, at Yale University, for thought-provoking discussions and helpful feedback. I am grateful also to Annette Haug for the invitation to deliver a version of this chapter in the DÉCOR Lecture Series at the Institut für Klassische Altertumskunde, Christian-Albrechts-Universität zu Kiel, as well as the audience there for their stimulating comments. This article was researched and written during the COVID-19 pandemic, which halted research travel and closed research libraries; online resources and e-publications made this work possible.

[1] A recent consideration of the parergon in ancient art is Platt and Squire 2017: esp. 38–59. On the anachronism of the terminology of "high" vs. "low" relief, see the chapter by Verity Platt (Chapter 1) in this volume. On the background-erasing effects of archaeological photography, see Nikolaus Dietrich's (Chapter 5) contribution in this volume.

a sculptural relief can also play a complex role. For example, on a second century CE funerary relief made of limestone from Palmyra, now in the British Museum, the background surface provides the backdrop for the portrait of a woman carved in high relief; it is also the smoothed surface into which an inscription is incised, identifying the woman as the deceased Aqmat, daughter of Hagagu.[2] In addition, it is a barrier between the living and the dead, since funerary portrait reliefs of this kind were used as *loculus* covers, sealing the burial cavity. And the same background surface connects this woman's grave to a larger kinship group; *loculus* burials at Palmyra were organized within collective tombs that could contain hundreds of burials. On this funerary relief from Palmyra, the relief's flat background surface mediates between image and text, the dead person behind and the living mourners in front, and a single woman's *loculus* and the surrounding tomb and kinship structure.

The background of sculptural relief is thus a complicated place as well as a substantive thing. Existing analyses, however, have focused on the visual operations of the background rather than its material affordances or workings. For example, Alois Riegl's famous discussion of tactile (haptic) versus optical constructions of figures and space in ancient relief sculpture hinges on the way the beholder's eye sees the iconography; deeper relief and the projection of shadows create a more "optical" effect than much flatter relief, which was more visibly grounded in a solid, "tactile," background plane.[3] In a more recent example, in his study of the semantics of style in Roman art, Tonio Hölscher evaluates the disposition of the foreground figures in relation to the background of a relief as part of his arguments about the role of space.[4] In the past two decades, however, a "material turn" in art-historical scholarship suggests taking a different approach to understanding the background of sculptural relief, one that starts from its materiality and substance.[5]

In this chapter, I reconsider the background surface of sculptural relief through the lens of stone-carving processes. These processes offer a material framework for understanding the affordances of the stone and the possibilities and constraints inherent in carving the background. The discussion is organized in two parts. First, I review the processes of carving a relief sculpture and draw out implications for our understanding of the background surface of relief. In part two, I then consider a case study from Oplontis, a marble calyx

[2] London, British Museum, 102612 (registration number 1908,0417.1). Cf. Nicola Barham's (Chapter 9) chapter in this volume. For an overview of funerary art at Palmyra, see Colledge 1976.

[3] Riegl 1985: esp. 51–131 on sculpture. [4] Hölscher 2004.

[5] A notable recent example is Stephanie Langer and Michael Pfanner's study of the Cancelleria Reliefs in Rome, richly integrating material aspects and carving processes (Langer and Pfanner 2018). Beyond ancient Rome, helpful discussions of how the broader "material turn" has shaped art historical work include Rosler et al. 2013; Roberts 2017.

krater used as a garden fountain. Reconstructing the stages by which this krater was carved highlights the skill required and the value of the krater. Considering its making also adds dimensions to the larger play of remediation at Villa A at Oplontis. I close by commenting on differences between the background of a relief sculpture carved in stone and other forms of sculptural relief.

Considering carving processes suggests that we have been thinking about the background of sculptural relief the wrong way around. The background surface is typically seen as a stable plane from which the foreground figures emerge; it seems to anchor them. But this is a viewer's perspective, possible only once the carving is finished. Stone reliefs were carved from the outside in and from front to back. The background was not finalized until quite late in the carving process, often long after the foreground figures were fully carved. This means that the background is not a stable plane for the articulation of the foreground figures; rather, the foreground figures anchor the background. The background surface is a place of potential, instability, and dynamic change; it has a unique status within sculptural relief that has not been fully appreciated. Considering the background of sculptural relief through the lens of carving processes thus highlights rich problems and can help us theorize relief in new ways.

Carving the Background of a Sculptural Relief

Our understanding of how Roman sculptural reliefs were carved is based on the careful study of toolmarks, especially on unfinished pieces that attest to the carving process.[6] An important figure in explaining these processes is Peter Rockwell, a sculptor and the author of numerous works on ancient stone carving. About 2,000 of Rockwell's photographs of toolmarks and other details on ancient sculpture have been made available in an online database, *The Art of Making in Antiquity: Stoneworking in the Roman World* (hereafter, Art of Making, www.artofmaking.ac.uk)[7]. There, each photograph is annotated with

[6] Fundamental in English is Rockwell 1993 (translating and revising Rockwell 1989); see also Rockwell 1990; Dehejia and Rockwell 2016; Wootton, Russell, and Rockwell 2013b, with additional bibliography. In their study of the Cancelleria Reliefs in Rome, Langer and Pfanner (2018: 65–71) further show how specialists interacted with other carvers in the making of a particular relief, and how the many visible mistakes suggest time pressures in the carving.

[7] This database was created at King's College London by Will Wootton, John Bradley, and Ben Russell, with extensive input from Peter Rockwell. In what follows, for the sake of simplicity and stability, I cite individual webpages from the Art of Making website (Wootton et al. 2013) by the photo number rather than the URL. The annotated photo can then be found on the website using the "basic search" tool.

Rockwell's observations about the kind of tool used, including striking angle and force; the site also includes synthetic essays about stone carving processes.[8] My discussion draws extensively on this resource.

Carving in stone generally proceeds from rougher to finer work and from front to back – that is, from the outer surface of the marble inward. A classic demonstration is Nuşin Asgari's 1988 study of the Corinthian column capitals abandoned in various state of unfinish in the ancient marble quarries at Prokonnesos.[9] These capitals were carved in a particular sequence. First, the overall shapes and larger volumes were roughed out with a point chisel or quarry pick, beginning with the overall geometry of the block and then roughing out increasingly smaller shapes. Only then was the more detailed carving begun, using flat chisels and other fine-carving tools. The detailed carving moved from front to back. The outermost, bottom tier of acanthus leaves was carved first, after which the carver cut more deeply into the block to depict the second tier of leaves growing upward and outward from behind that outermost tier.

Within this general framework, Rockwell has described two different methods of carving a relief, each involving the background surface in different ways.[10] One is the "cookie-cutter" method, in which the major outlines were marked, and the surrounding marble was then removed with the point chisel, all the way back to the intended background surface. In this method, the background surface was part of the initial roughing out, though additional carving with finer tools would be required later on to flatten and smooth it. A garland sarcophagus at Aphrodisias was made in this way; we know this because the front half was fully carved, but the back half was left in a roughed-out state.[11] First, the major shapes were outlined on the surface of the block using a point chisel. Then, the marble surrounding those shapes was cut away with the point chisel, leaving larger volumes

[8] For explanations and images of the different tools used, see Wootton, Russell, and Rockwell 2013b. Tool choice and use, though broadly similar in all stone carving, varies depending on the hardness and nature of the stone; e.g. softer limestones are worked somewhat differently from harder marble (Bessac 1986, with Rockwell 1990; cf. Dehejia and Rockwell 2016: 119). These practices also vary culturally and regionally – and even locally and individually (cf. Van Voorhis 2018: 39–40).

[9] Asgari 1988. Asgari's work at Prokonnesos has been important for studies of quarry production and the fabrication of roughed out objects that could then be shipped and finished in workshops elsewhere (Russell 2013). My interest here is instead in the implications of this process for the carving of the background of sculptural relief.

[10] Rockwell 1993: 70–1, 107–11; Dehejia and Rockwell 2016: 183–4. Rockwell sees the cookie-cutter technique primarily in Archaic Greek sculpture, especially metopes, but it also appears in combination with front-to-back carving in Roman sculpture, as on the garland sarcophagus described later in this chapter.

[11] Art of Making, PR305_02_04; Wootton, Russell and Rockwell 2013a.

protruding from a roughed-out background plane. At this stage can be seen a mass of marble swooping across the middle (a future garland); a circular knob above (a future flower), and a roughly triangular lump below (a future bunch of grapes). In the next stages, first the tooth chisel and then the flat chisel were used to shape these larger volumes into detailed forms: the leaves of the garland, the petals of the flower, the individual grapes. Certain details were finished with a drill and a channeling tool. Tooth and flat chisels were also used to flatten and smooth the background surface. In this case, the roughing out followed the cookie-cutter method, while the detailed carving moved from front to back.

Especially interesting here is the second method identified by Rockwell: the "front-plane" technique most frequently used in Roman relief sculpture. In this technique, the carving proceeded entirely from front to back. The initial roughing out was done only on the elements closest to the outermost surface of the marble; these were the figures or details that, ultimately, would be carved in the highest relief. From there, both the roughing out and the fine carving of details moved progressively through deeper planes farther into the surface of the marble. In this technique, the foreground figures were fully carved before any of the deeper imagery was started.[12] The background was the *last* thing carved.

A vivid example of the front-plane technique is an unfinished relief from Aphrodisias depicting a nude male youth (Fig. 8.1).[13] The foreground figure's surface volumes and details have been finely carved, including the pectoral and abdominal muscles, and the gentle swells of the fronts of shoulders and thighs. There are even finishing touches made by the drill in the hair and ear. However, everything else is still only roughly worked with the point chisel. The surface is roughest at the corners of the relief, corresponding to an earlier stage of preparation, while more point chiseling has been done around the figure itself. On this piece, no low-relief elements or any aspects of the background have yet been indicated, not even roughly.[14] This example also shows the unimportance of outlines in the front-plane

[12] Giorgio Vasari described this technique with a vivid analogy; he imagined a sculpture lying flat and submerged in a tub of water, then lifted slowly up so that the receding water level progressively revealed more and more carving, from front to back (Vasari 1907: 151, §48). On the processional reliefs of the Ara Pacis Augustae, Conlin (1997: 86) notes that the foreground and background figures are carved quite differently, with the latter added only after the former were carved.

[13] Art of Making, PR307_02_03, with additional details at PR307_02_07 and PR307_02_09. Cf. Rockwell 1993: 109.

[14] Like reliefs, freestanding sculptures were often carved from front to back; Rockwell comments that it is impossible to say whether this unfinished youth was intended to become a relief

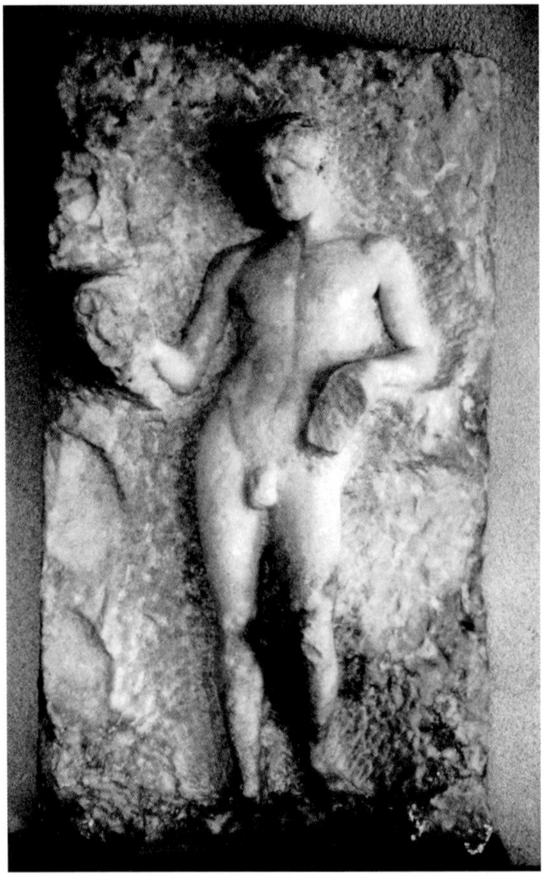

Fig. 8.1 Unfinished relief depicting a nude male youth, imperial period, from Aphrodisias. Marble, Aphrodisias Museum (photograph from Peter Rockwell's collection, available at https://artofmaking.ac.uk/explore/sources/945).

technique. The front surfaces of the youth have been finely carved, but an outline around the figure has not; where the figure and the background meet is still a blur, as, for example, at the back of the head.[15] Again, this is because the carving proceeded from front to back; the sides of the figure and its outline where it met the background surface would not be finely carved until a later stage, as the work cut ever more deeply into the marble.

sculpture (as is more probable) or a freestanding statue, with its background eventually carved away entirely, leaving only the figure in the round (Art of Making, PR307_02_03).

15 Compare Rockwell's comments (1993: 109) on an unfinished sarcophagus in the Capitoline Museums: "The roughing out process does not clarify the outlines of the parts of the composition. The point chisel was used to excavate the spaces around the figures without any strong definition."

These principles of rough-to-fine and front-to-back carving have immediate implications for how we think about the background surface of a stone relief. A first is that the background surface had to be carved, just like any other element of the relief. Whether roughed out at the start (the cookie-cutter method) or not defined until much later (the front-plane method), carving the background required the same general sequence of steps and tools as any other part of the relief, from roughing out to increasingly precise carving. In this sense, the background surface is the result of sculptors' decisions and actions in exactly the same way as any figure or ornamental detail.[16] This suggests that it is productive to assess the background's making, finishing, and visual effects alongside the other elements of a relief.

To illustrate, a background surface can be deliberately textured to create certain visual effects. On a relief panel from the Sebasteion at Aphrodisias, probably depicting Gaius and Lucius, the figures are finely carved and smoothed, but the background surface has been worked only with the tooth chisel.[17] The tooth chisel's characteristic marks roughen the background surface, catching the light in a very different way than the more finely finished figure and thus making the figure stand out more clearly.[18] This is a frequent choice on the Sebasteion reliefs. On other Roman reliefs, a carefully smoothed background surface may have been intended to make the background more unobtrusive, helping focus the viewer's attention on the foreground figures. This kind of background creates an appearance of solidity and inevitability, but it too is the result of decisions and active work during the carving process.

A very different treatment of the background is seen on a second century CE relief from Ostia depicting the expulsion of Vulcan from Olympus (Fig. 8.2).[19] At center left is an olive tree; traces of toolmarks show that the

[16] This raises the question of the semantic meanings of the background surface of a relief. When left plain and unfigured, did this surface always connote "sky" or "air" or simply "functional space" around the figures? Did this vary from one relief to another? Discussing the potential semantic meanings of these relief backgrounds is unfortunately beyond the scope of this chapter. I thank Annette Haug for asking the question, and Jens-Arne Dickmann for a stimulating discussion of the tension between deliberate choices and less conscious preferences for how things should look (pers. comm.).

[17] Art of Making, PR301_04_23. Smith 1987: 123–5, no. 9, pls. 20–1. On the frequent "claw-chisel finish" on the background surfaces of the Sebasteion reliefs, see Smith 1987: 99.

[18] Compare the treatment of the background on the processional reliefs of the Ara Pacis Augustae in Rome (Conlin 1997: 65, 67, figs. 77–81, 95, 96).

[19] Berlin, Staatliche Museen, Antikensammlung, SK 912; Art of Making, PR223_03_09, with additional detail views of the tree at PR223_03_10, PR223_03_11, and PR223_03_12. This relief was part of a longer frieze: Zevi and Micheli 2012.

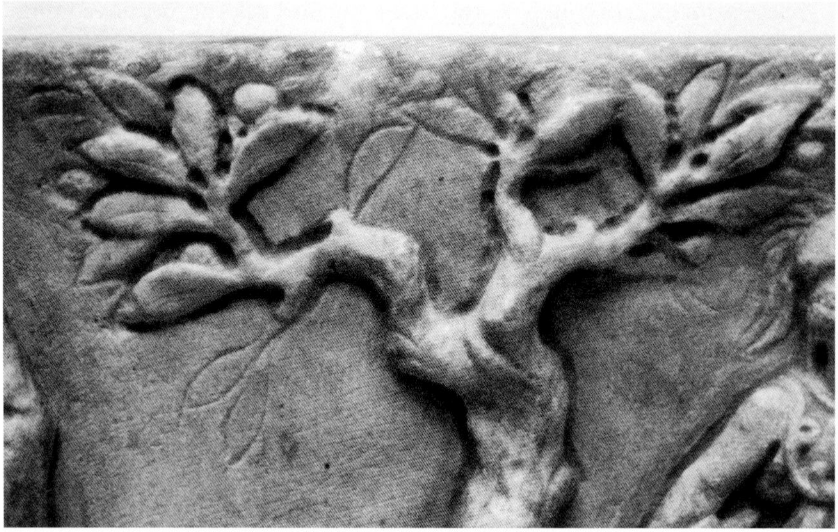

Fig. 8.2 Detail of an olive tree on a relief depicting the expulsion of Vulcan from Olympus, second or third century CE, from Ostia. Marble. Berlin, Staatliche Museen, Antikensammlung, SK 912 (photograph from Peter Rockwell's collection, available at https://artofmaking.ac.uk/explore/sources/1535).

background surface all around the tree was flattened with a fine chisel and then smoothed by a rasp. In this case, additional details were added after this smoothing. The trunk, branches, and leaves were outlined with a channeling tool that cut through the background plane. A flat chisel was then used to incise shallow outlines of additional leaves, depicted as somehow being within that background surface or seen through it. These details invert the ordinary practice of smoothing the background as the final stage; they create additional visual layers and depth; they play with the nature of the background plane as both substance and space. This relief's background is simultaneously a solid surface to be carved into various shapes, an empty space where a tree stands in the open air, and an indeterminate zone where hanging leaves are caught within the stone.

Added color affected these background surfaces and textures, though the poor survival of evidence for color makes it difficult to know exactly how.[20] A thick layer of paint or solid coloring (e.g. gilding or other metalwork) would have covered over and obscured any background texture. A thinner,

[20] Surviving color traces on ancient marble sculptures are normally best preserved inside deep folds and other protected spots – in other words, *not* on the flat, exposed background surface. A useful starting point for recent work on polychromy is Abbe 2015, with bibliography and discussion.

more transparent layer of paint still allowed the texture of the background to catch the light differentially across its many slight surface variations. Recent scholarship has shown that painted color could be extraordinarily sophisticated on Roman sculpture, interacting subtly with the qualities of the marble; sophisticated coloration may have been present on some reliefs, though most background surfaces were no doubt painted more simply than that. Still, plain monochromes could produce very different visual effects: A midnight blue background interacted with the foreground figures in a very different way than a pale blue or a medium red background. Some backgrounds seem to have been deliberately left unpainted, focusing even more attention by contrast on the colorfully painted foreground figures.[21]

A second important implication follows especially from the front-plane method: The background continued to be a place of dynamism and change even after the foreground was finished and set.[22] Here emerges a key difference between foreground and background in relation to carving processes. Earlier in this chapter I stressed that the background had to be carved in the same way as any other element of the relief; here I stress that the background could still be changed well after the foreground elements were already set. The background was the last part of the relief to be carved, but there was no inherent finality or stability to it. As long as any blank surface area remained, more figures or details could potentially be carved into it. In addition, any low-relief elements and background details, like the leaves on the olive tree on the Vulcan Relief from Ostia (see Fig. 8.2), were necessarily carved around and between the already finished foreground figures. For example, on the unfinished relief of a nude youth from Aphrodisias (see Fig. 8.1), it was no longer possible to change or add to the youth without carving away more marble, damaging the existing figure. But the background was not yet shaped; here new figures or additional details could still be carved without destroying any of the work already done. In this sense, the foreground of any relief anchors the background.

A vivid illustration of the way dynamic change is built into the background can be seen in the "vanishing background" that characterizes the making of certain sculptures. Consider a Corinthian capital as it is being

[21] On the uncolored background surfaces of the cuirass of the Augustus of Prima Porta: Liverani 2004: esp. 239–41. On the uncolored background of a colorful relief of Mithras: Magrini et al. 2019: 2168.

[22] "Only after this level of the figures was carved did the sculptor carve the background. The background is not in fact a plane of its own. It is only the space that remains between the details" (Rockwell 1993: 109).

carved.[23] As already noted, the larger volumes are roughed out first, and the detailed carving then proceeds from the outer surface inward. The first acanthus leaves carved are those on the outermost surface; only then are additional leafy details carved around them to indicate the second tier of leaves, growing upward and outward from behind the first. The carver punches ever deeper into the stone until there is no background surface left that has not been transformed into leaves or other decorative flourishes. Throughout this process, the background keeps receding and changing. Something similar happens on densely figured reliefs, such as the Ludovisi battle sarcophagus.[24] Very little background surface can be seen on the front panel of the sarcophagus, partly because soldiers and horses cover almost all the available space, but also because the carvers have progressively carved away any available background. They have transformed all the deeper bits of marble into additional details of the battle: empty spaces between soldiers' and horses' legs, the interior of a shield, the cloak of the general at top center. In these cases, the background surface progressively recedes during the carving; it keeps turning into something else; it eventually disappears. On such a sculpture, the deepest carving ends at a kind of "vanishing point," that moment when the entire surface is now carved into one shape or another, and there is no more uncarved background available.

Another difference between the background plane and everything else on a relief emerges at this point. When the background plane is a more or less smooth surface, it is defined by contrast to all the carved figures and details on the relief; it is defined as the part that is not figured. Consider the role of drawings in making sculptural reliefs. Judging by more recent, better-documented practices, it seems highly likely that the carvers of relief drew volumes, shapes, or details onto the surface of the marble to guide their next stage of work in that immediate zone.[25] These drawings guided the carvers' next strikes of the hammer and chisel, and those strikes quickly carved through the drawings, destroying them. Drawings on the surface of the stone thus had to be continually redrawn, and these drawings changed

23 Asgari 1988. İlhan 2016 shows how a modern sculptor followed these ancient sequences in carving new Corinthian capitals for a reconstruction project at Sagalassos. This same process was demonstrated by the sculptors Matt Auvinen and Nathan Hunt during a workshop on marble carving at Stanford University (Leidwanger and Russell 2019).

24 Rome, Museo Nazionale Romano, Palazzo Altemps.

25 Modern reconstructions of ancient carving processes make extensive use of localized and changing drawings on the marble, as seen in İlhan 2016 or in the live demonstrations at Leidwanger and Russell 2019. A stimulating study of this kind of ephemeral and flexible art used during the making of more durable works, albeit in the very different context of textile production, is Elsner 2020.

in shape and degree of detail as the immediate carving task changed in shape and detail. These drawings were ephemeral but necessary parts of the work. They were made, carved away, redrawn differently as the shape of the work changed, and carved away again, over and over, during the making of the object. But the only element of the carving not drawn on in this way was the plain background surface, since it had no form or detailing of its own.

These carving processes also had implications long after the actual sculpting was finished. Even much later, any change to a relief's background had to engage actively with the materiality of the stone. Similarly, the background surface, as a unique site of potential change, continued to play an important role in any repairs or other updates. For example, a marble altar from the Vicus Statae Matris neighborhood on the Caelian hill was sold with its relief decoration already carved; only then was the personalized inscription carved into the background surface.[26] This sequence matters for the meaning of the object. On the front panel of this altar was carved a *corona civica* (the oak wreath awarded for saving the life of a Roman citizen in battle); on each side panel was a laurel tree; on the back was a *patera* for libations. The *corona civica* and the two laurel trees, as potent political and religious symbols awarded to Augustus, appeared frequently on altars, gravestones, and other objects in this period. In this case, four enslaved men bought the altar already carved with these symbols and then had it inscribed with their names and religious offices. The men were serving as neighborhood officials (*vicoministri*) of Vicus Statae Matris in the year 2 BCE.[27] This information is incised between the raised relief carvings; the potential of the background surface was now activated as a site for an added inscription. The lines of text interact meaningfully with the relief sculpture. The gods to whom the altar is dedicated, the *Lares Augusti*, are written at the top in the largest letters; just below, in smaller letters, is the religious role of these four men as *ministri* in 6 CE after Augustus' urban reforms. Below that, the men's slave names, including their masters' names, are listed inside the oak wreath. The wreath is thus made into a visual frame that simultaneously legitimizes both their enslaved status

[26] Rome, Musei Capitolini, Centrale Montemartini, 2144; *CIL* 6.36809a, b; Hölscher 1988: 392–3, no. 220; Lott 2004: 137–9, 197–8, no. 23; http://arachne.uni-koeln.de/item/objekt/57000.

[27] *Laribus Augustis, ministri anni VI. Felix L(uci) Crautani (servus), Florus Sex(ti) Avieni (servus), Eudoxsus C(ai) Caesi (servus), Polyclitus Sex(ti) Anchari (servus). L(ucio) Caninio Gallo, C(aio) Fufio Gemino co(n)s(ulibus) XIIII k(alendas) Octobr(es)* (To the Lares Augusti, the officials of the year 6. Felix, slave of Lucius Crautanius; Florus, slave of Sextus Avienius; Eudoxsus, slave of Gaius Caesius; Polyclitus, slave of Sextus Ancharius. In the consulship of Lucius Caninius Gallus and Gaius Fufius Geminus, 14 days before the Kalends of October [18 September 2 BCE]); *CIL* 6.36809b (the slightly different inscription on the opposite face is *CIL* 6.36809a).

and their public self-presentation as religious officials. On this altar, the potential inherent in the background surface allowed these men to link themselves to a much larger political and religious framework.

Underscoring the role of the background surface as a place for changes and updates is evidence of repairs or afterthoughts. On the Belvedere Altar in Rome, dated 7–2 BCE, one of the panels depicts the emperor Augustus at right giving two statuettes to three people at left.[28] There is a debate about whether these people are priestesses of Vesta or neighborhood officials; my interest here is in the two statuettes between them. The statuettes depict the *Lares*, twin deities represented as young men dancing, wearing skirted tunics, and holding drinking horns high. A curious detail can be seen from an oblique angle (Fig. 8.3). The statuette on the right is not carved in the standard way, so as to appear to protrude from the background plane. Instead, this *Lar* is carved into the plane of the background surface; a concavity has been carved out in the marble all around him in order to

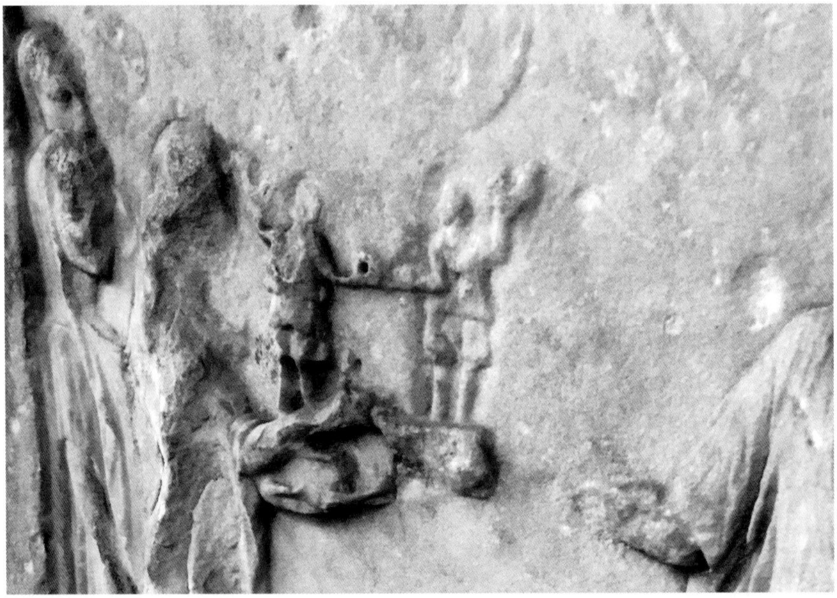

Fig. 8.3 Detail of one face of the Belvedere Altar, depicting two statuettes of dancing *Lares*, 7–2 BCE. Marble. Musei Vaticani, Museo Gregoriano Profano, 1115 (photograph by author).

[28] Musei Vaticani, Museo Gregoriano Profano, 1115. Findspot unknown; may have been reused as building material. Known already in the fifteenth century. Fless 2018 is now the authoritative publication of this altar, with extensive bibliography and discussion. See also Hölscher 1988: 394–6, no. 223; Lott 2004: 104, 217–18, no. 65; Buxton 2014.

allow this figure to appear in relief. This must have been done after the rest of the relief had been carved, and given that the background plane was punctured at this one spot but nowhere else on the altar, this is either the repair of a mistake or a change of plan.[29] Either the carver did not allow enough marble for the depth of carving needed for this second statuette, and so had to dig more deeply into the background surface, or the figure originally carved here had to be replaced for some reason, requiring a much deeper cut into the background surface. We cannot know why this was done, but the role of the background surface as a site of change and potential is clearly demonstrated.

Another way in which carving sequences shape the background surface long after the carving is finished can be seen in certain examples of *damnatio memoriae*. For example, on the Cancelleria Reliefs in Rome, Frieze A famously includes the emperor Domitian's head recarved to portray his successor, Nerva. Because recarving can only be done by cutting marble away, Nerva's portrait head is smaller than expected and the traces of the recarving can still be seen all around the face. Noteworthy here is that the background was not touched. In fact, nothing else in the relief seems to have been changed: not the emperor's body, clothing, or gesture, nor the surrounding deities and personifications. The message is that only the individual fulfilling the role of emperor had to be replaced; once that was accomplished, everything else about the emperor's position, his ritual functions, and the relationship between state and gods remained the same. To put this another way, Cancelleria Relief A visually suggests that the health and functioning of the Roman state remained stable and unthreatened by the *damnatio* of the hated Domitian; his replacement by a better man fully solved the problem of this bad emperor.[30]

On the Arch of the Argentarii in Rome, sculptural *damnatio* was handled very differently (Fig. 8.4).[31] On these reliefs, the emperor Caracalla's brother, wife, and father-in-law did not merely have their portrait heads replaced. Instead, the figures of Geta, Plautilla, and Plautianus were entirely cut away, and those places were leveled and smoothed to match the rest of the background surface. In these locations,

[29] If this were a planning error, it would exemplify Peter Rockwell's (1993: 70) comment about one of the dangers of front-to-back carving: "To rough out details before the whole is clear is to risk not having enough marble for the whole."

[30] Langer and Pfanner 2018: 44–5; on the complex issues surrounding the recarving of this head as Nerva and the emperor's head on Relief B as Vespasian, 71–72.

[31] *LTUR* I, 105–6 (Diebner). The three figures fell from grace at different times, Plautianus in 205 CE, Plautilla in 205 or 211, and Geta in 212, suggesting that there may have been more than one intervention into the reliefs that depicted them on this arch.

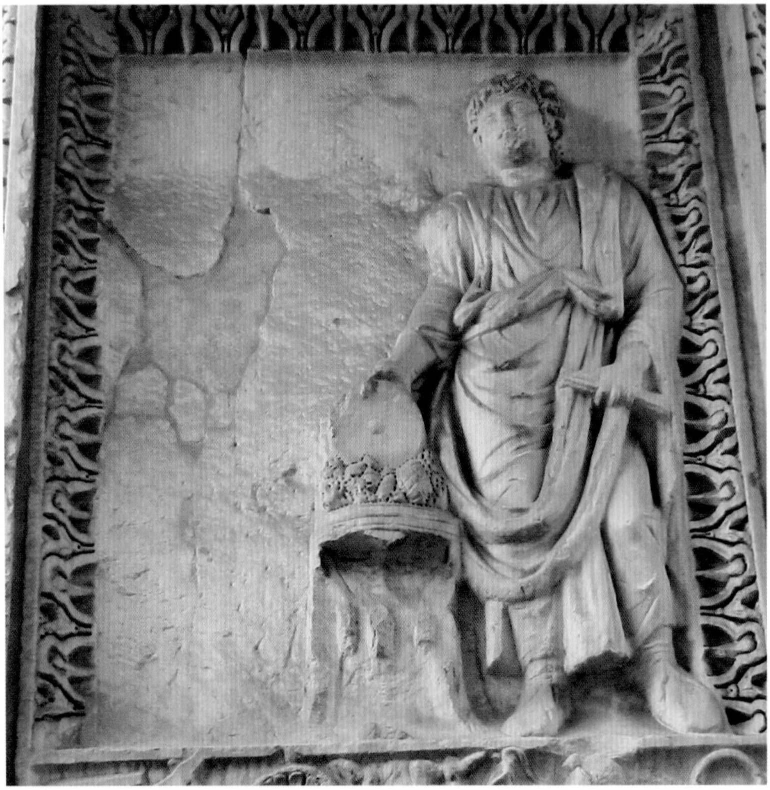

Fig. 8.4 Relief panel from the Arch of the Argentarii, Rome, early third century CE, in situ. Marble. At right, Caracalla pours a libation; at left and center (later carved away), his wife, Plautilla, and father-in-law, Plautianus (photograph by Diletta Menghinello, Wikimedia Commons license CC BY-SA 4.0).

the reliefs were now obviously empty while also appearing finished and unavailable for any further carving. Here, the inherent potential of a large expanse of background keeps the viewer very much aware that figures are missing. The visual message is that these troubles were a much more serious threat than was indicated by the recarving of Domitian's head on Cancelleria Relief A; here there was no straightforward replacement or reuse of the figures. In the case of Caracalla, there had been accusations of treason inside the imperial family itself; apparently, the health of the emperor and Rome required that those individuals be entirely erased and that their erasure remain visible. That was accomplished through the treatment of the background surface.

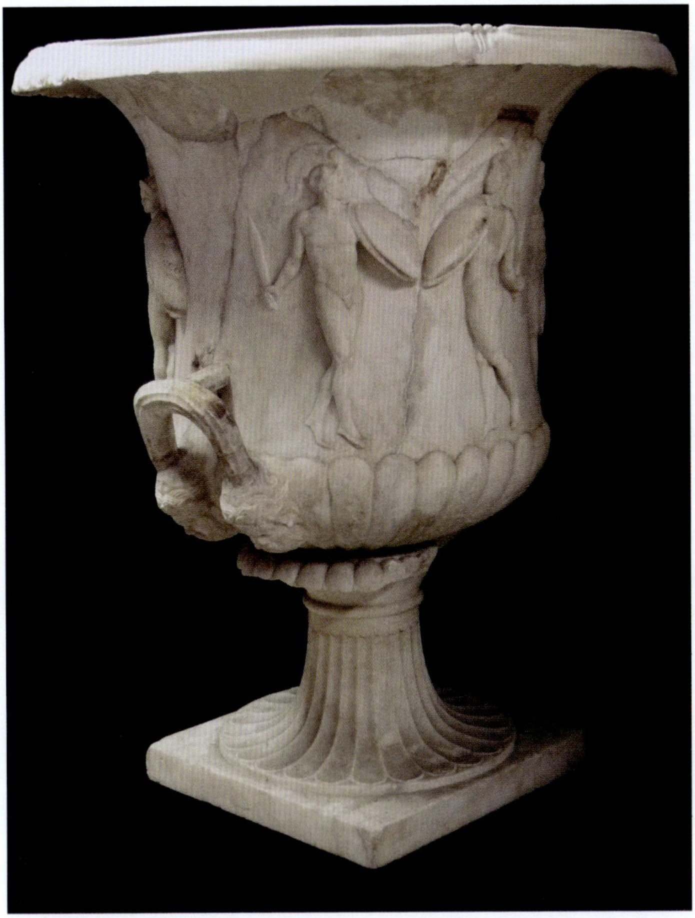

Fig. 8.5 Calyx krater depicting Pyrrhic dancers in relief, used as a garden fountain, before 79 CE, from Villa A at Oplontis. Marble. Oplontis, 70.717, 71.406, 72.724, 72.799 (Photograph by J. R. Clarke, courtesy of the Oplontis Project and by permission of the Ministero della Cultura – Parco Archeologico di Pompei. Further reproduction or duplication by any means is expressly prohibited).

A Case Study from Oplontis

Looking closely at a single example further illuminates the workings and significance of the background surface of relief. My case study is a marble calyx krater from Villa A at Oplontis, just a few kilometers northwest of Pompeii.[32] This krater, used as a garden fountain, depicts armed dancers on the exterior (Fig. 8.5). Reconstructing the stages of carving highlights an

[32] The villa's decorations are now available online in an open access e-publication: Clarke and Muntasser 2019 (reviewed by Lepinski, Bartman, and Herrmann 2021).

intimate relationship between the figures and the vessel wall. In addition, this approach helps explain the value of this object in antiquity and its interactions with the natural, decorative, and social context of the villa.

The calyx krater was made of Pentelic marble.[33] The outward-flaring rim is ornamented with tongues below a line of beads, and the bottom of the vessel has more tongues. The handles are striated and attached to the vessel walls with struts; Silenus heads are carved at the bases of the handles. The fluted pedestal base was made separately. On the exterior wall of the krater are carved six nude male youths wearing plumed helmets and carrying shields and swords, their legs and weapons interacting symmetrically and rhythmically. This is an armed dance, perhaps the Pyrrhic dance attested in Greek writings and vase painting from the sixth and fifth century BCE onward.[34] On this calyx krater, the imagery was Greek and Classicizing, evoking a stylized Other. Once carved, the vessel was colorfully painted; traces of polychromy survive on the surface of at least one shield and in the facial features and hair.

The finished krater served as a garden fountain. Both the base and the vessel had holes in the center to accommodate a water pipe; the water would fill up the vessel and spill over the sides into a basin below. The pedestal base and a lead water pipe were found in situ inside a shallow, rectangular basin in garden 92, at the south end of the large pool (Fig. 8.6). The vessel itself was found on the cocciopesto floor of corridor 53, broken into about sixty fragments.[35] These fragments were reassembled in the 1970s shortly after their excavation, with plain white plaster filling in the gaps. Traces of iron clamps show that the vessel had been broken at least once in antiquity and was considered valuable enough to repair. Interestingly, there was no buildup of waterborne mineral residue on the krater, suggesting that it was either not used as a fountain or not for long.

[33] Oplontis, 70.717, 71.406, 72.724, 72.799. Moormann 2019: paras. 1478–85 (with exhaustive bibliography), no. 62, figs. 16.127–16.133. Total height is 111.5 cm (of which the pedestal base is 48.5 cm); diameter at mouth 94 cm; height of dancers 36 cm. The pedestal base was separately made of a different kind of marble. Grassinger dates the krater to the Julio-Claudian period (Grassinger 1991: 217–18, no. 60).

[34] Goulaki-Voutira 1996.

[35] Moormann 2019 notes that additional fragments were found in garden 56 and in an unrecorded location. It is most likely, though not certain, that this vessel belonged to the pedestal base found in garden 92: the vessel and base fit together; both are perforated to allow passage of a water pipe; no other vessel that might belong to the fountain's pedestal base has been found. A photograph of the reassembled krater standing on this spot in garden 92 is reproduced in Bergmann 2019: fig. 5.8. On the history of the excavations, including scans and transcripts of the excavation notebooks, see Clarke and Muntasser 2014.

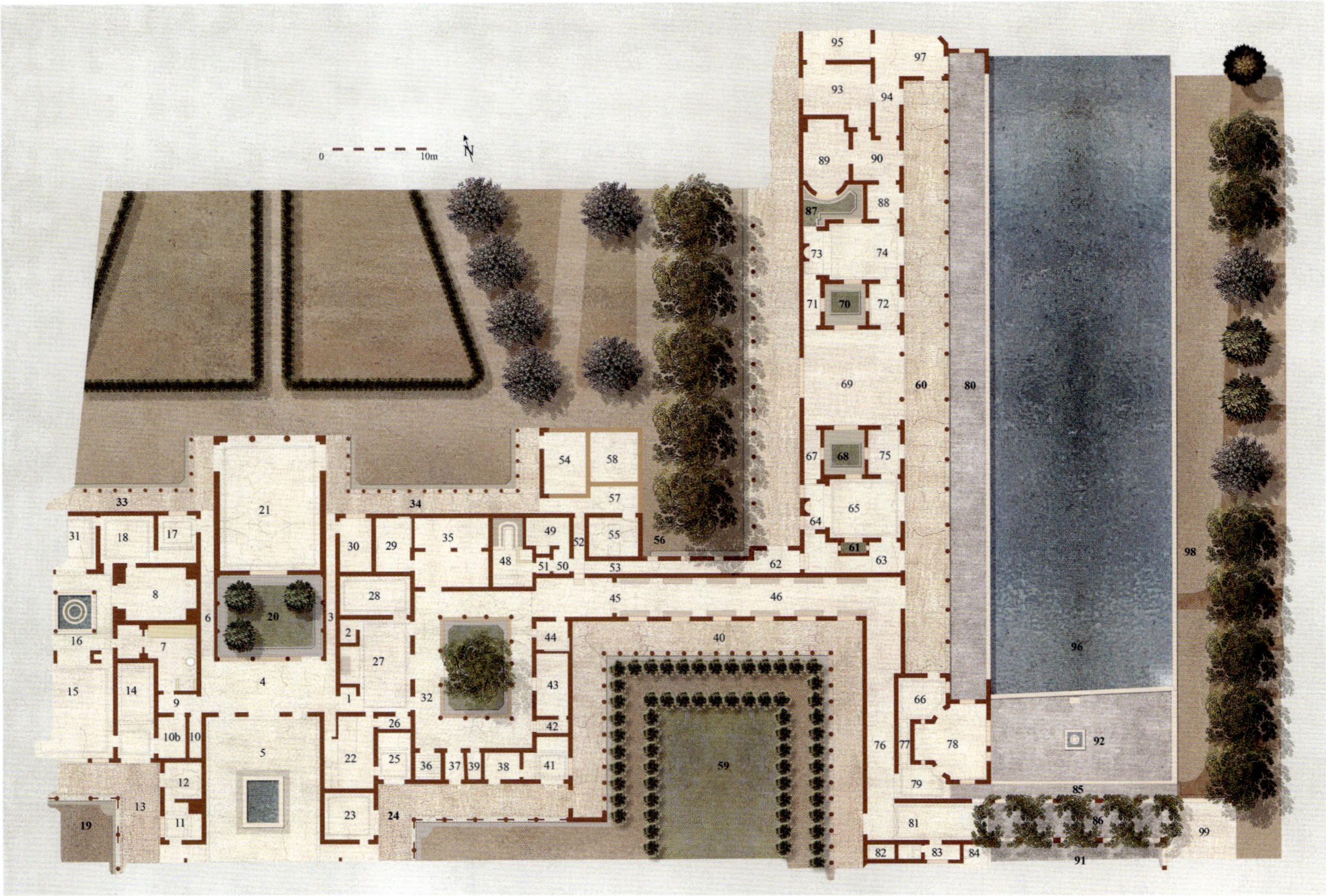

Fig. 8.6 Plan of Villa A at Oplontis. The pedestal base of the calyx krater was found in situ in the square basin (92) at the south end of the pool. The vessel itself was found in ca. 60 fragments in corridor 53. Marble calyx krater fountains were painted on the walls in rooms 68, 70, and 20 (plan by Victoria I and James Stanton-Abbott).

To think about how this object was carved, we first need to mentally disassemble the krater, removing the vessel from the separately made pedestal base. We should also turn it over; practicality and stability dictated that at least the first stages be carved with the widest part down and the narrower portion up. In this chapter, I consider only the carving of the exterior of the vessel, but the hollow interior also had to be roughed out, then chiseled with finer tools, and lastly smoothed with a rasp.[36] The sequence reconstructed below is not necessarily correct in all respects, but for the purposes of my discussion, it matters only that it be approximately right.

1. A solid block of Pentelic marble was chosen for its quality, size, and shape; it had to be large enough to encompass the maximum dimensions of the finished vessel. The first stage was to use a quarry pick or point chisel to shape the block into a cone with evenly sloping sides and flat on the top and bottom (Fig. 8.7a). Overall symmetry was important already at this first stage.

2. The next stage was to rough out the major volumes and remove most of the excess marble, especially from the undercut area just below the rim. The cone-shaped block now became roughly bell-shaped, with two large bosses of marble left on opposite sides of the smaller end, where the handles would later be carved.

3. Stage three saw the smaller volumes roughed out. Most of this work was still done with the point chisel, but a flat chisel may have been used to define the precise location of the edge of the rim and other key lines. The handles were now roughed out, including the struts that connected their upper parts to the vessel wall and the small bosses at the bases, where Silenus heads would later be carved. At this stage or the next, a narrow vertical strip of the vessel wall may already have been finely carved to indicate the desired concave, hour-glass profile, providing a guideline for carvers in the later stages to follow.[37] If so, such a strip had to avoid any area where a dancer was planned; the safest place would be between one of the handles and the rim.

4. Stage four saw a shift to fine carving (Fig. 8.7b). The tooth chisel was probably used first to define the handles, their struts, the Silenus heads at their bases, the ornamental tongues around the bottom of the vessel, and the rim. (Fine-carving the upper rim and its ornament required turning the vessel over, so this would have been done at a different time; it was presumably done in conjunction with carving and finishing the interior, inaccessible while the block was positioned upside down.) Then, flat chisels

[36] It would be useful to measure the thickness of the surviving vessel walls; if they were very thin, this might explain why the vessel broke at least once in antiquity and needed to be repaired.

[37] There is a guideline strip like this on an entablature block from the Temple of Vespasian: Art of Making, PR202_03_01, discussed in Wootton, Russell, and Rockwell 2013a.

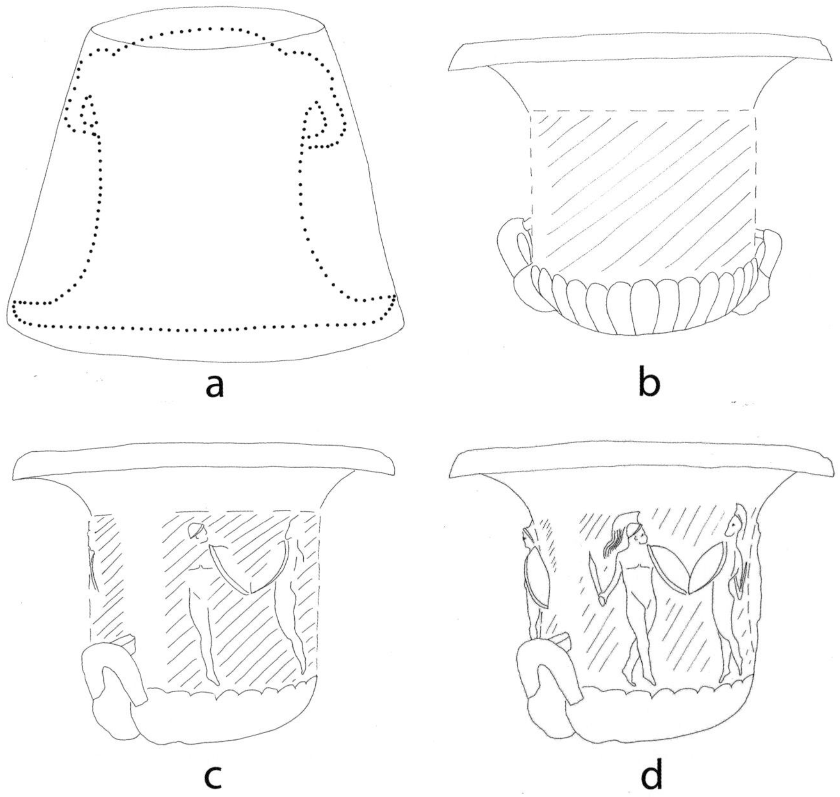

Fig. 8.7 Schematic depiction of four of the stages of carving the Oplontis krater (the base was made separately). (a) Stage one, preparation of a cone-shaped block of Pentelic marble; the dotted line indicates the outlines of the eventual krater. (b) Stage four, after the carving of the rim, the undercut area directly below, the handles, and the base; at this stage, the zone where the dancers would be carved was probably still rough. (c) Stage five, early in the carving of the dancers, illustrating the front-to-back technique in which the outermost elements were carved first; depicted at left is a finished, vertical strip, perhaps carved early on as a guide to carving the rest of the concave vessel wall. (d) Stage six, after the dancers were fully carved, together with the background surface immediately around them; the area between and around the dancers still had to be flattened and smoothed (drawings by author).

and other fine tools were employed to finish shaping and smoothing these elements. Because of the principle of carving from front to back, and because specialized carvers probably carved the Pyrrhic dancers, those figures were not yet carved at this stage. That zone was probably still only roughly defined with the point chisel (i.e. still at stage three), and the walls of the vessel here were still vertical, not yet curving inward (see Fig. 8.7b).

5. The dancers were not carved until these other elements were finished. Their bodies were sculpted from the outside in, cutting from the front plane

ever deeper into the marble. The outermost surface of these figures – that is, the starting plane for their carving – was roughly vertical (see Fig. 8.7b), and the elements closest to the outer surface were the first to be carved: protruding shield edges, outer legs, outer hips, upper backs, and outer parts of the heads (Fig. 8.7c). As the carving proceeded more deeply into the marble, the carver added the inner legs and buttocks, the smalls of the back, and the interior arms. The last elements to be carved were probably the swords in shallow relief and the helmet plumes in even shallower relief, barely emerging from the background surface (cf. Fig. 8.5).

It was only as the carving moved progressively deeper, around the shields, torsos, and hips, that the concave shape of the vessel wall took form around and between the figures. In this zone, carving the vessel wall was part of carving the dancers and vice versa. Indeed, the dancers bend with the vessel wall. The curves of their inner hips follow and complement the inward curve of the background surface (see Fig. 8.5). It was not only the armed men who were dancing: this was also a dance between the figures and the concave vessel wall, a dance dependent on the depth of the carving.

6. The figures of the dancers were now fully carved, together with the immediately adjacent background surface, but everywhere else in this zone, the rough marble of stage three remained (Fig. 8.7d). Now the remainder of the inward-curving vessel wall had to be finalized, which meant carving away any remaining rough patches and regularizing the entire surface. This also meant smoothing out the transition between the previously carved undercut area under the rim and the vessel wall now being finished between and around the dancers. Presumably, the specialists who carved the dancers did not do this simpler work, so a different team may have taken over at this stage.[38] They likely used calipers for reference and comparison. Their challenge was to make the shape of the vessel wall appear symmetrical, graceful, and rhythmic all the way around, like the dance of the armed youths themselves.

7, 8, 9. In stage seven, the background and other surfaces and volumes were smoothed with the rasp. Parts of the vessel may in addition have been polished with abrasives.[39] In stage eight, at least some elements of the vessel were colorfully painted.[40] Stage nine saw the krater installed. Both the vessel and the base were now transported to the site. At the south end of

[38] Compare the evidence for different carvers working on the heads, the feet and shoes, the background, and other details in Roman sculpture in Langer and Pfanner 2018: 65–6.

[39] I have not been able to examine the actual object. The publication does not mention the degree of polishing on the different surfaces of the vessel (Moormann 2019).

[40] Traces of polychromy survive on the shields and the heads (Moormann 2019, with fig. 16.131).

the pool at Villa A at Oplontis, a shallow, rectangular basin had been built and fitted with a lead water pipe. First, the hollowed pedestal base was positioned in the basin so that the water pipe rose up through the base. Then, the heavy vessel was carefully lowered onto the base, again so that the water pipe rose up through the hole in the bottom. Lastly, the water was allowed to fill the krater and spill over the sides into the basin below.

Reconstructing these stages of carving helps explain why it was a valuable piece. The cost reflected the quality of the marble used, the amount of labor involved, and the planning required. Especially striking is the immense skill of the carvers of the armed dancers. There are no visible errors in the depths of the figures or their junctions with the background surface; they interact evenly and gracefully, attesting to tremendous precision and feel in the carving. We also see here the organizational capacity of a first-rate marble workshop. There is a clear division of labor between the superb figure carver(s) and the other individuals or teams who did much of the roughing out at the start and the laborious smoothing at the end. These stages of making attest to a smooth coordination, ensuring that the different stages were carried out in the correct sequence and to the right degree of skill and finish. In a large and busy workshop, this coordination required a very experienced person who knew how long each stage would need and who made sure the right personnel were available for each successive phase.[41]

Considering how the krater was made also highlights its intermedial aspects. For this part of the discussion, Jay Bolter and Richard Grusin's work on remediation is especially helpful.[42] The Oplontis krater signals its remediation – or at least suggests that the viewer think simultaneously about other media – because it includes features such as the Silenus heads at the bases of the handles. Such extra supports for the handles may have been useful on clay or metal versions of this krater, both of which might be picked up by their handles. The Silenus heads are superfluous on a large marble object, which was too heavy to be picked up by the handles. If we now consider the Oplontis krater to be a remediation of similar kraters that were made of metal, we see a fundamental difference in the nature of the background surface. On a similar metal krater, armed dancers in relief could only be added to the vessel's sides as appliqués or by using repoussé technique or alternatively by casting the vessel in a mold. In all these cases, the background surface of the relief would be the starting point from which

[41] Compare Langer and Pfanner 2018: 66.

[42] Bolter and Grusin 1999; cf. the chapter by Nathaniel B. Jones (Chapter 7) in this volume.

the relief was extruded by being hammered out (repoussé) or to which relief figures were attached (appliqué); alternatively, in the case of casting, the background surface and the figures in relief were made simultaneously. Only in stone carving is the background surface of a relief the last thing carved. From the perspective of making, then, these background surfaces are not the same thing at all. Stone carving and metalworking can create very similar forms, but they are achieved in fundamentally different ways.

The plays of remediation continue at multiple scales of viewing, both close up and far away. Bettina Bergmann has illuminated the sophisticated interactions of nature and art at Oplontis and the ways they created visual and sensory experiences for the villa's owners and guests; the following observations build on her work.[43] The Oplontis calyx krater employed Pentelic marble to depict an ancient Greek form of dance in a stylized vision of the Greek past and the Other that was appropriated for a luxurious Roman villa on the Bay of Naples. But this sculpted vessel was also colorfully painted, adding polychrome to its visual effects. And the painted, sculpted krater was also a garden fountain, installed so as to fill up with water and spill it over the rim. This sculpted, painted garden fountain was carefully positioned at the intersection of the long north–south axis of the pool and the east–west axis of view from the adjacent day room, or *diaeta*. That *diaeta* (room 78 on Fig. 8.6) was itself a luxurious, multimedia room that combined marble wall and floor revetments with wood paneling.[44] Decor at Oplontis hinged on these interplays of medium and materiality; thinking about the materiality of the krater and its making allows us to see how this object participated.

Bolter and Grusin describe "hypermediacy" as a particular kind of remediation in which the existence and fragmentation of multiple media are foregrounded so that the beholder is made very aware of the framing and layering of images and other media.[45] Bolter and Grusin cite the contemporary example of someone working in a web browser with multiple open windows, each window presenting multiple images or other elements for the user to resize or click through further. They cite older examples of hypermediacy as well, including medieval cathedrals or the baroque Wunderkammer. The decoration of Villa A at

43 Bergmann 2002, 2019.

44 Published by John R. Clarke and Simon Barker in Clarke and Muntasser 2019: chap. 15. Compare Bergmann 2019: paras. 484–5.

45 In hypermediacy, "representation is conceived of not as a window on to the world, but rather as 'windowed' itself – with windows that open onto other representations or other media" (Bolter and Grusin 1999: 34).

Oplontis is surely another example. There, the layered, framed, and fragmented interplays of nature, wall paintings, objects, and materials constructed a hypermediated environment.

To illustrate, wall paintings of marble garden fountains appear throughout the villa, and at least four of them depict marble calyx krater fountains similar to the three-dimensional one discussed previously. Two such paintings could be seen in the portico complex along the west side of the large pool.[46] A viewer standing in space 69 could look northward and see a marble krater fountain painted on the north wall of room 70; turning 180 degrees meant seeing another painted marble krater fountain symmetrically positioned on the south wall of room 68. The actual marble krater standing at the south end of the pool may have been visible from the same spot. None of these kraters is identical, however; in rooms 68 and 70, the shrubbery behind the painted krater and the birds perching on it are different, and neither is exactly the same as the actual krater fountain. In these paintings of krater fountains, seen in conjunction with an actual krater fountain, remediations activate a play of similarity and difference, actual gardens and painted gardens. Part of this play is that both the painted and the real krater fountains can be part of the foreground or part of the background, depending on where the viewer stands and what the viewer is looking at.

Two more marble krater fountains are painted in *viridarium* 20, a room located along the central axis through the villa from the entrance on the north to a view of the Bay of Naples to the south.[47] In this room, spectacular views of nature (the sea) dominated the distant background, while art and nature filled the foreground inside the room; or we might say that the live trees in the *viridarium*'s central space filled the foreground, while painted art and nature covered the walls in the background; alternatively, the wall paintings foregrounded marble fountains against a garden background, or did the painted columns in the foreground emerge against the background of the painted fountains in gardens? A shifting play of foreground and background is part of the visual and sensory experience of this villa. In *viridarium* 20, the central panel of both the east and west walls depicted a marble krater fountain standing in front of a leafless tree; the fountain was filled with water and had birds perched on the rim. On the west wall (Wall B), the painted krater is depicted with a carved female head between two protomes of sea monsters that emerge in such high relief that they appear to

[46] Bergmann 2019: paras. 471–83, figs. 5.10, 5.14, 5.16, 5.20–5.21.

[47] Bergmann 2019: paras. 461–70, figs. 5.3–5.4, 5.6.

be on the point of escaping the vessel entirely.[48] These protomes blur the boundaries between the living birds painted above, who can approach and leave the fountain under their own power, and carved figures in a relief, permanently attached to a solid background surface. Within the hypermedial space of the villa, these paintings play with medium and possibility – as did the actual marble krater fountain at the south end of the pool in a different medium, in its intimate dance of sculpted figures and vessel wall.

In other words, the kinds of sophisticated intermedial play that Bergmann has so vividly illuminated at Oplontis extended all the way down to individual objects like the marble krater fountain, and we can see some of this at work by tracing the way it was made. The marble krater contributed to this layering of sensory experience at multiple scales, from the sculptural interplay of figures and background on the vessel itself to the remediations of marble garden fountains painted on the walls and the materialities of water between the krater fountain, the adjacent pool, and the distant sea. These interactions were available to beholders whether they looked closely at a three-dimensional object or two-dimensional painting or considered the broader symmetries and sensory echoes of the villa's spaces and walls. At every scale, the marble krater participated; throughout Villa A, foreground and background could trade places, create each other, or dance through the changing focus of the beholder's gaze.

Finally, underpinning these plays of background and foreground in the villa were social hierarchies and their effects on people. Bergmann's analysis of nature and art at Villa A at Oplontis focuses on the visual and sensory experiences of elite owners and guests, who spent time in or strolled through the luxurious rooms and gardens, and who had the leisure and entitlement to look as they wished and to enjoy what they saw. These people populated, so to speak, the social and aesthetic foreground. Offering a contrasting and complementary understanding of lived experience at Oplontis is Sandra Joshel and Lauren Petersen's analysis of the villa's architectural and social background.[49] These authors consider the service corridors and the movements of enslaved servants through them, and how these relate to the pleasurable experiences of owners and guests. Joshel and Petersen argue that the much plainer "zebra stripes" painted on many of the walls of less luxurious corridors and secondary areas helped define these as service spaces. These spaces, and the enslaved people who moved through them, were essential to the functioning of the villa even as the

[48] I am grateful to Annette Haug for pointing this out (pers. comm.).

[49] Joshel 2013: 115–17; Joshel and Petersen 2014: 169–81.

architecture kept them in the background, removed from the foreground vistas of art and nature. The enslaved people working and serving in the background did not see or experience the gardens and rooms in the same way as owners and guests. They did not stroll and enjoy the villa's delights at leisure or as part of their social identity and self-fashioning; instead, they were required to hurry and serve at others' beck and call, focusing on their work and the people they served. In addition, the enslaved staff's encounters with the villa's wall paintings and objects may have included making, installing, moving, maintaining, cleaning, or repairing them. Their background labors permitted the foreground experiences of the villa, in an interlocking and unequal dance between foreground and background, scripted by the hierarchies and practices of the Roman social order.

Conclusions

In this chapter, I have considered the background surface of sculptural relief through the lens of stone-carving processes. In some ways, the background is the same as any other element of the relief, needing to be carved with largely the same sequences and tools and therefore important to assess along with other parts of a relief. The Oplontis krater offered a vivid example in the sculptural interplay of the dancers' bodies and the concave vessel wall. In other ways, the background surface is very different from any other part of the relief. It is the only place where additional carving is still possible without changing or destroying what has already been carved. The background surface represents both the last stage of carving and also an interim point that can potentially be carved more.

This potential was not exploited every time, of course. In most cases, the carving process must have gone according to plan, and finalizing the background meant little more than smoothing the surface. There were also limits on how much more deeply the carving could go, as in the case of a relief carved on a relatively thin slab of stone. But we have also seen that this potential of the background sometimes meant that the background received embellishments and additions (as on the Vulcan relief at Ostia; see Fig. 8.2) or updates or corrections (as on the Belvedere Altar; see Fig. 8.3), or even changed political messages (as on the Arch of the Argentarii; see Fig. 8.4). This potential for change – even if not used – gives the background of sculptural relief a unique and even creative role.

Another implication: because the foreground figures were finished first and carving then moved more deeply into the marble around them, time and sequence are built into any relief sculpture. This sequential nature of the work can express a hierarchy of skill, seen in who carves which elements, or it can have semantic or representational dimensions, depending on how the foreground figures interact with the figures or details carved later on, deeper in the marble. Here again, the dancers on the Oplontis krater offer a vivid example. All around the krater, the outer edges of the shields were among the very first parts of the dancers to be carved, but their swords were all carved at a deeper level, barely protruding from the background surface. This difference in depth between shields and swords contributed to the dancing effect. Shields versus swords, one dancer versus another, foreground versus background – all of these translated the rhythmic movements of a live dance into visual rhythms and oscillations in the unmoving stone.

Lastly, focusing on how the background of stone relief sculpture was carved suggests that any insights gained about stone do not necessarily apply to other media, in which the position and possibilities of the background surface are fundamentally different. In stone carving, the background was typically carved last, an important contrast to processes of punching or incising *into* a surface, as in repoussé metalwork or intaglio. In those cases, the surrounding surface is the starting point rather than the final stage, and the nonfigural surface surrounding the iconography is indeed a stable plane that anchors the figural carving. Interestingly, despite this major difference, the surrounding surface retains a similar potential; it is always a space that remains available to be carved or where additions to the composition can be made. Relief sculpture in stone also differs from clay or wax. In the latter cases, the material can be pinched, modeled, formed, or reformed in its entirety; stone carving is destructive and permanent in a way that clay modeling is not. Stone is shaped entirely by cutting material away, and this can only happen once.

In all these ways, foregrounding the background, and especially the materiality of the background, helps us think in new ways about relief. Focusing on processes of making places the affordances of the material at the center and highlights the constraints and possibilities inherent in working it. These material processes, in turn, help us see how complex and interesting the background of sculptural relief can be and enable us to theorize it in new ways.

References

Abbe, M. B. (2015). "Polychromy." In E. A. Friedland, M. G. Sobocinski, and E. K. Gazda, eds., *The Oxford Handbook of Roman Sculpture*. Oxford: Oxford University Press, 173–88.

Asgari, N. (1988). "The Stages of Workmanship of the Corinthian Capital in Proconnesus and Its Export Form." In N. Herz and M. Waelkens, eds., *Classical Marble: Geochemistry, Technology, Trade*. NATO ASI Series (Series E: Applied Sciences) 153. Dordrecht: Springer, 115–25.

Bergmann, B. (2002). "Art and Nature in the Villa at Oplontis." In J. Humphrey, ed., *Pompeian Brothels, Pompeii's Ancient History, Mirrors and Mysteries, Art and Nature at Oplontis, and the Herculaneum "Basilica". Journal of Roman Archaeology*, supplement 47. Portsmouth, RI: Journal of Roman Archaeology, 87–121.

(2019). "Reading the Garden Paintings in Villa A at Oplontis." In Clarke and Muntasser 2019: chap. 5, paras. 457–517.

Bessac, J.-C. (1986). *L'outillage traditionnel du tailleur de pierre, de l'Antiquité à nos jours. Revue archéologique de Narbonnaise*, supplement 14. Paris: CNRS.

Bolter, J. D., and Grusin, R. (1999). *Remediation: Understanding New Media*. Cambridge, MA: MIT Press.

Buxton, B. A. (2014). "A New Reading of the Belvedere Altar." *American Journal of Archaeology* 118.1: 91–111.

Clarke, J. R., and Muntasser, N. K., eds. (2014). *Oplontis: Villa A ("of Poppaea") at Torre Annunziata, Italy*. Vol. 1, *The Ancient Setting and Modern Rediscovery*. New York: Oplontis Project. ACLS Humanities E-Book. https://hdl.handle.net/2027/heb.90048.0001.001.

(2019). *Oplontis: Villa A ("of Poppaea") at Torre Annunziata, Italy*. Vol. 2, *The Decorations: Painting, Stucco, Pavements, Sculptures*. New York: Oplontis Project. ACLS Humanities E-Book. https://hdl.handle.net/2027/heb90048.0002.001.

Colledge, M. A. R. (1976). *The Art of Palmyra*. Boulder, CO: Westview Press.

Conlin, D. A. (1997). *The Artists of the Ara Pacis: The Process of Hellenization in Roman Relief Sculpture*. Chapel Hill: University of North Carolina Press.

Dehejia, V., and Rockwell, P. (2016). *The Unfinished: Stone Carvers at Work on the Indian Subcontinent*. New Delhi: Roli.

Elsner, J. (2020). "Mutable, Flexible, Fluid: Papyrus Drawings for Textiles and Replication in Roman Art." *Art Bulletin* 102.3: 7–27.

Fless, F. (2018). "Larenaltar (Altar vom Belvedere)." In F. Fless, S. Langer, P. Liverani, and M. Pfanner, eds., *Vatikanische Museen: Museo Gregoriano Profano ex Lateranense; Katalog der Skulpturen*. Vol. 4, *Historische Reliefs*. Monumenta Artis Romanae 40. Wiesbaden: Reichert, 110–24, no. 7, pls. 66.4–67.

Goulaki-Voutira, A. (1996). "Pyrrhic Dance and Female Pyrrhic Dancers." *Répertoire International d'Iconographie Musicale/Research Center for Music Iconography Newsletter* 21.1: 3–12.

Grassinger, D. (1991). *Römische Marmorkratere.* Monumenta Artis Romanae 18. Mainz: von Zabern.

Hölscher, T. (1988). "Historische Reliefs." In M. Hofter, ed., *Kaiser Augustus und die verlorene Republik: Eine Ausstellung im Martin-Gropius-Bau, Berlin, 7. Juni–14. August 1988.* Mainz: von Zabern, 351–400.

(2004). *The Language of Images in Roman Art.* Trans. A. Snodgrass and A. Künzl-Snodgrass. Cambridge: Cambridge University Press.

İlhan, S. (2016). "How to Make Corinthian Capitals for Sagalassos." YouTube video. January 18. www.youtube.com/watch?v=zSC4VKopXC4.

Joshel, S. (2013). "Geographies of Slave Containment and Movement." In M. George, ed., *Roman Slavery and Roman Material Culture.* Toronto: University of Toronto Press, 99–128.

Joshel, S., and Petersen, L. H. (2014). *The Material Life of Roman Slaves.* Cambridge: Cambridge University Press.

Langer, S., and Pfanner, M. (2018). "Cancelleriarelief A und B." In F. Fless et al, eds., *Vatikanische Museen: Museo Gregoriano Profano ex Lateranense. Katalog der Skulpturen.* Vol. 4, *Historische Reliefs.* Monumenta Artis Romanae 40. Wiesbaden: Reichert, 18–90, no. 2.

Leidwanger, J., and Russell, B. (coorganizers). (2019). "From Quarry to Capital: An Experimental Workshop on Ancient Architectural Stone." Workshop organized at Stanford Archaeology Center, Stanford University, 13 April 2019.

Lepinski, S. E., Bartman, E., and Herrmann, J. J., Jr. (2021). "The Born-Digital Publication of Villa A at Oplontis." *Journal of Roman Archaeology* 34.1: 253–74.

Liverani, P. (2004). "L'Augusto di Prima Porta." In P. Liverani, ed., *I colori del bianco: Policromia nella scultura antica.* Musei Vaticani: Collana di studi e documentazione 1. Rome: De Luca, 235–42.

Lott, J. B. (2004). *The Neighborhoods of Augustan Rome.* Cambridge: Cambridge University Press.

Magrini, D., Bracci, S., Bartolozzi, G., et al. (2019). "Revealing Mithras' Color with the ICVBC Mobile Lab in the Museum." *Heritage* 2.3: 2160–70. https://doi.org/10.3390/heritage2030130.

Moormann, E. M. (2019). "Marble Sculpture and Architectural Elements." In Clarke and Muntasser 2019: chap. 16, paras. 1249–1810.

Platt, V. J., and Squire, M. J., eds. (2017). *The Frame in Classical Art: A Cultural History.* Cambridge: Cambridge University Press.

Riegl, A. (1985). *Late Roman Art Industry.* Trans. R. Winkes. Archaeologica 36. Rome: Bretschneider.

Roberts, J. L. (2017). "Things: Material Turn, Transnational Turn." *American Art* 31.2: 64–9.

Rockwell, P. (1989). *Lavorare la pietra: Manuale per l'archeologo, lo storico d'arte e il restauratore*. Beni culturali 7. Rome: Nuova Italia scientifica.

(1990). "Stone-Carving Tools: A Stone-Carver's View." *Journal of Roman Archaeology* 3: 351–7.

(1993). *The Art of Stoneworking: A Reference Guide*. Cambridge: Cambridge University Press.

Rosler, M., et al. (2013). "Notes From the Field: Materiality." *Art Bulletin* 95.1: 10–37.

Russell, B. (2013). *The Economics of the Roman Stone Trade*. Oxford: Oxford University Press.

Smith, R. R. R. (1987). "The Imperial Reliefs from the Sebasteion at Aphrodisias." *Journal of Roman Studies* 77: 88–138.

Van Voorhis, J. (2018). *The Sculptor's Workshop*. Aphrodisias 10. Wiesbaden: Reichert.

Vasari, G. (1907). *Vasari on Technique: Being the Introduction to the Three Arts of Design, Architecture, Sculpture and Painting, Prefixed to the Lives of the Most Excellent Painters, Sculptors and Architects*. Ed. G. B. Brown and trans. L. S. Maclehose. London: Dent.

Wootton, W., Bradley, J., Russell, B., et al. (2013). *The Art of Making in Antiquity: Stoneworking in the Roman World*. www.artofmaking.ac.uk.

Wootton, W., Russell, B., and Rockwell, P. (2013a). "Stoneworking Techniques and Processes (Version 1.0)." *The Art of Making in Antiquity: Stoneworking in the Roman World*. www.artofmaking.ac.uk/content/essays/3-stoneworking-techniques-and-processes-w-wootton-b-russell-p-rockwell.

(2013b). "Stoneworking Tools and Toolmarks (version 1.0)." *The Art of Making in Antiquity: Stoneworking in the Roman World*. www.artofmaking.ac.uk/content/essays/2-stoneworking-tools-and-toolmarks-w-wootton-b-russell-p-rockwell.

Zevi, F., and Micheli, M. E. (2012). "Un fregio tra Ostia e Berlino: Problemi di iconografia e di topografia ostiense." *Mare internum* 4: 41–57

9 | Encrusted in Ancestors

Formal Reflections on the Funerary Reliefs of Palmyra

NICOLA BARHAM

Part 1

The relief funerary portraits from the desert oasis of Palmyra were made during Syria's period of Roman influence (from the first to the third centuries CE) and have long held an iconic status.[1] Popular interest in these works has only become more pronounced following the violent damage done to the many examples still held locally in the Palmyra Museum at the hands of the Islamic State of Iraq and the Levant (ISIL) militants in 2015.[2] The Palmyrene portrait in the collection of the Kelsey Museum of Archaeology, Ann Arbor, Michigan, is representative of the genre (Fig. 9.1).[3] A single figure (in this case a woman) stares resolutely out from a shallow slab of stone, its frontal face measuring 55 by 40 cm at its greatest preserved extent. The majority of Palmyrene portraits are carved on limestone blocks of around this size and portray a single individual or, alternatively, a small family group: a mother with her child, a pair of brothers, or a man accompanied by his wife.[4] In the

Thanks to the American Council of Learned Societies (ACLS) and the Getty Foundation for supporting this project.

[1] For an overview of the genre, classic publications are Ingholt 1928 (for a recent English translation: Ingholt 2021); Colledge 1976: 58–82, 245–64; Böhme-Schönberger and Schottroff 1979; Sadurska and Bounni 1994; see also most recently Raja 2019a and the extensive number of articles and edited volumes produced under the auspices of the Palmyra Portrait Project: https://projects.au.dk/palmyraportrait. The city is known as Tadmur in local languages both in antiquity and now; the name Palmyra was used in Latin and in the Greek spoken in this region from the Hellenistic period. For the long-standing interest in the site and early accounts of these sculptures, see e.g. Wood 1753; Cassas 1799; Shifman 2014: 9–14.

[2] This has been widely reported. See e.g. Curry 2015.

[3] Ann Arbor, Kelsey Museum of Archaeology, 1980.1.1, third century CE; Root 1981; Christie, Manson, and Woods 1980: 39; Colledge female bust subtype III Le: Colledge 1976: 264. This work was purchased by the Kelsey Museum Associates after the UNESCO signing of the Convention on the Means of Prohibiting the Illicit Import, Export and Transfer of Ownership of Cultural Property (https://en.unesco.org/fighttrafficking/1970), but before the convention was officially accepted by the USA in 1983 and the articles of this convention came to be widely recognized by museums in the USA and worldwide. The Kelsey Museum of Archaeology now has a policy of only accessioning objects with a secure provenance: https://lsa.umich.edu/kelsey/collections/collections-policies/acquisitions.html.

[4] For family groups: Krag and Raja 2019; Raja 2019c; for mothers and children in particular: Colledge 1976: pl. 86; Krag and Raja 2016; Krag and Raja 2018; for other (probable) family groups, see also Colledge 1976: pls. 76, 78, 86.

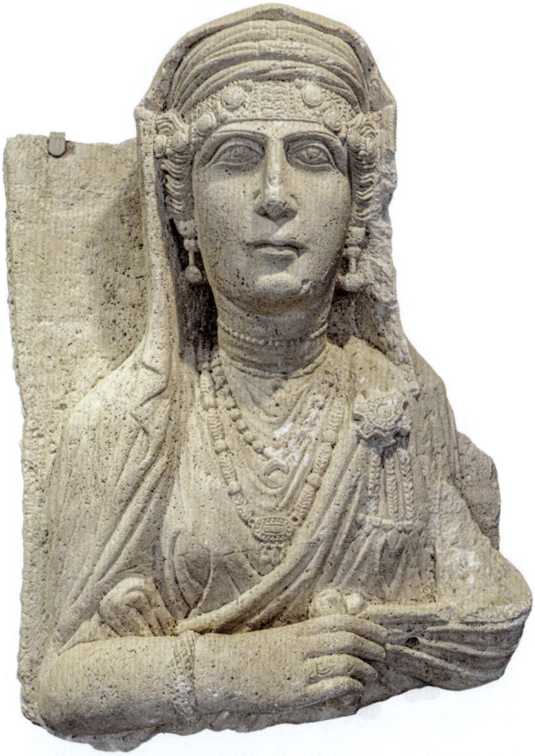

Fig. 9.1 Funerary relief, third century CE, Palmyra, Syria. White limestone. Ann Arbor, Kelsey Museum of Archaeology, University of Michigan, 1980.1.1 (Kelsey Museum of Archaeology).

Kelsey Museum portrait, the woman's head and right forearm are worked in especially deep relief. The fingers of her proper right hand bend slightly as she clutches tentatively at the thick veil that hangs heavily down from her head to envelop her body. The woman draws this covering more closely around her. The squat dimensions and steep angle of the break above the elbow of the woman's proper left arm, by contrast, suggest that this forearm was raised vertically. Her left hand, also carved in deep relief (as is evidenced by the depth and degree of this break), was lifted to her face. In other examples of funerary portraits of women from Palmyra (which copy a motif also used, albeit more sparingly, at Rome), this hand is similarly raised to pull, perhaps coyly, at the veil to the proper left side of the woman's head.[5] The break running vertically

[5] A feature of Colledge's Female Busts Group III: Colledge 1976: 261–4; cf. the earlier preference for the right hand performing the same gesture in Group II: Colledge 1976: 248–51; for a similar gesture from Rome involving the right hand, see e.g. Rome, Centrale Montemartini, 2142; Davies 2018: 161, 163, 167.

down the veil on this side of the Kelsey relief suggests that this was also the case in this example: The deeply carved hand and curve of the veil have broken off as a piece together. The undercutting of this extremely high relief, which is visible on the surviving right arm and is suggested by the break on the left, elegantly articulates these features, even as it leaves them inevitably vulnerable to damage. Yet the result is a striking physical depth of the sculpture in real space. Even the woman's torso is thereby depicted in mid-relief, making room for an abundance of plastically rendered lifelike detail. All these features commonly reoccur within the Palmyrene funerary genre, a kind of vivid embodiment that has given the relief portraits an enduring impact.

The jewelry that adorns the woman is also typical and adds significantly to her splendor. The woman's right arm is bedecked with a thick gold bangle, with fine-grained filigree spiraling across its surface. Her cloak is pinned on the upper-left breast by a similarly handled cogwheel brooch, carved so deeply as to cast a shadow, with three fine-plaited chains hanging from it and splaying delicately across the woman's torso. These are formally matched in the intricacies of the multiple necklaces that encircle the woman's neck and run across her chest. Heavy geometric earrings of the so-called dumbbell type, formed of cuboid blocks, bars, and spheres, hang from each ear under neatly pinned waves of hair, while strings of jewels carved in deep relief, coil out from under the woman's turban and arc across each corner of her brow.[6] Each of these features would have been painted in gold and in bright colors to suggest gems; the embroidered browband on which these jeweled chains rest would originally have been similarly handled, adding to the lively mimetic effect.[7] The medium of relief heightens the drama of the myriad gold ornaments that festoon this female figure and others like her. This once sparkling assemblage insisted upon, even clamored for, the viewer's attention. The embodied physicality of the relief, coupled with its inherent formal strategy of concentrating all this sumptuously colorful sculpted detail upon a single surface, both commands and focuses our gaze.

Meanwhile, distinctive almond eyes appear in the woman's face below fashionably thin, incised, and painted brow lines. A prominent aquiline nose sits above full and gently closed lips, alongside broad and smooth cheeks. Folds of skin, typically known as Venus rings, circle the

6 For the "dumbbell" earring type: Colledge 1976: 255, 262; see further on jewelry: Colledge 1976: 150–3; Krag 2017.

7 For the emerging work on the use of pigments in Palmyra: Østergaard and Sargent 2014; Brøns and Hedegaard 2019; Brøns 2020; Brøns et al. 2020.

woman's neck, implying that she is well fed and therefore from a financially comfortable family. These carefully wrought facial features arguably suggest the specificity of a portrait. Certainly, the variation of features across the Palmyrene funerary corpus would seem to make room for such an interpretation, although stylization remains prominent, and total fidelity to the features of the model was clearly far from the goal.[8] In all of this, the depth of relief is carefully handled to make the plasticity of this nearly life-size figure as impactful as possible. The mid-relief of the woman's torso is still sufficient to mark her corporeality, as her garment gathers over her protruding right breast and bunches in deep folds in the crook of her proper right arm, while the deeply carved jewels gleam on her chest. Yet if it is convincing at first glance, closer reflection reveals that the physicality of the woman's body is, counterintuitively, deliberately under-conceived. The woman's shoulders should be carved in much deeper relief to be naturalistically consistent with her undercut forearm and with her deeply carved head – at least if the stone block from which her form emerges marks a ground, a consistent point in continuous, three-dimensional space. The effect of this self-conscious handling of the depth of relief – the slightly lower-than-realistic rendering of the body by contrast with other elements like the woman's forearms and head – works to focus the attention back onto her face. At nearly life-size, the strongly emphasized physical presence of the woman is only tempered by the mid-relief handling of her torso in order to throw this still greater emphasis upon her portrait. This is a benefit inherent to the medium of relief in particular: neither painting (in its two dimensions) nor fully carved sculpture in the round can reproduce this illusory manipulation of the relative depth of parts of a figure to specific aesthetic ends. The relief art of the Palmyrene tombs, here as in other examples, was clearly designed to make the sense of encounter with a family member who had passed away as arresting as possible. The positioning of the majority of the woman's gold jewelry, set across the brow and encircling her neck, also

[8] Scholars tend to emphasize the idealized schematism of these images. See e.g. Heyn 2010: esp. 634. Montserrat (1993) and Nodelman (1994) also argue for the symbolism of apparent portrait features in Roman period portraiture more broadly. Compare also the observations of Stewart 2003: 79–80. While these elements are certainly often in play, it is important not to overemphasize similarity within the corpus of Palmyrene portraits. Stylized schematism in portraiture need not exclude a commitment to evoking something of the appearance of a given individual. The genre still leaves scope for the representation of individualized face shapes and features.

serves to reemphasize this focal point. In this, as in other respects, the funerary portraits are deft in their handling of relief as a medium.[9]

Questions of Culture

This chapter responds to the challenge raised by this volume: analyzing the aesthetic strategies of relief in the Greco-Roman world, by looking at the case of Palmyrene funerary relief in particular. The status of Palmyra as a desert town at the Eastern fringes of the Rome's sphere of influence makes this case study interestingly distinct in certain respects. In numerous ways, the iconography of the Palmyrene reliefs signals a cultural distance from the wider corpus of Greco-Roman relief sculpture. We experience such distance through the distinctive dress of the figures and the attributes they carry; stylized aspects of the portraits, such as the almond eyes of the figure described earlier in this chapter, are further signifiers of an alternative aesthetic heritage.[10] The installation of the Palmyrene funerary images within the innovative tomb types local to Palmyra also creates a unique application of the medium of relief with specific visual dynamics.[11] This chapter engages each of these aspects of the particular aesthetic strategy of the Palmyrene reliefs – iconography, style, and structural display – in order to demonstrate how Palmyrene funerary sculptures both participate in many of the broader discourses of Greco-Roman artistic production and also create something distinctive. The portraits, like the medium of relief itself, engage liminality on multiple levels: at once concealing and revealing, affectively engaging and emotionally withdrawn, stridently individual and defined by group dynamics.

That traditional considerations of Palmyrene art have often treated the city simply as part of the Roman province of Syria and have therefore viewed these sculptures through an essentialized Roman lens is clearly problematic.[12] Indeed, this problem has often beset scholarship on visual works of the Roman world outside of Italy. The narrative has long framed

9 Such a raked handling of depth would also aid the visibility of portraits positioned further up on the wall. This effect may have been especially accentuated due to the anticipated display location of portraits in some cases, although the dearth of portraits surviving in situ (which I discuss later in this chapter) makes it difficult to say with confidence that such an approach was in fact taken.

10 For the sartorial choices of the Palmyrene portraits: Finlayson 1998: 145–50; Heyn 2012: 439; Krag 2018; Heyn and Raja 2019. For attributes: Colledge 1976: 153–60, 209–11; Heyn and Raja 2021.

11 On these tomb types: Schmidt-Colinet, al-Asʿad, and Müting-Zimmer 1992; Henning 2013a, with bibliography; Henning 2013b; Houman 2019; also classically Gawlikowski 1970.

12 See e.g. Ingholt 1928; Böhme-Schönberger and Schottroff 1979; Parlasca 1990.

such works (particularly in sculpture) as "provincial," contrasting them unfavorably in regard to style with those from the privileged "center."[13] Where attempts have been made to focus on the "local" aspects of these works, elements seen as "Roman" are still often privileged.

The case of Palmyra requires a still more nuanced approach. Though Palmyra came under the influence of Rome from the first century BCE, the city largely maintained its independence into the next century and boasted a proud local culture.[14] It further enjoyed deep-rooted social, political, economic, and cultural connections with Rome's enemy and competitor, the Parthian Empire, which stretched out to Palmyra's East.[15] Any consideration of the visual workings of Palmyrene relief needs to engage this complex identity and cultural heritage.[16] Yet this very complexity and multicultural nuance has contributed to the disciplinary marginalization of these images. Although Palmyra produced the largest surviving collection of ancient portraits from the first three centuries CE besides the city of Rome, until recent years only a handful of studies have engaged this material at any depth.[17] More broadly, the dramatic imbalance in excavated evidence between the Roman world (where so much survives) and the Parthian Empire (where much more must await investigation) has limited the extent to which the subtleties of Parthian influence in Palmyra can be understood. More scholarly research into the regional variations in Parthian art would usefully further our understanding of this imperial visual tradition and clarify its contribution.[18] Meanwhile, the biased preference of previous generations of European and American scholars for the cultures of Greece and Rome has meant that very much more ink has been spilt on the subject of Roman art than on that of Parthia, making the Greco-Roman heritage of certain elements

[13] An early critique of this practice is seen in Scott and Webster 2003.

[14] For an overview, see Smith II 2013, with bibliography.

[15] The past several years have seen a dramatic increase in scholarship on Parthia. See most recently: Overtoom 2020; Schlude 2020; Ellerbrock 2021; Olbrycht 2021; van Wijlick 2021, all with bibliography.

[16] To their credit, several (often more recent) studies of these reliefs have acknowledged (if not always plumbed) this complexity: Krag, Raja, and Yon 2019; Raja 2019a; see also Colledge 1976: 58–82; and the recent thematic edited volumes of the Palmyra Portrait Project: https://projects.au.dk/palmyraportrait.

[17] Colledge 1976: 58–82; Parlasca 1990; Sadurska and Bounni 1994. Since 2012, the Palmyra Portrait Project has been addressing this oversight. See note 1. For an introduction to the Danish scholar H. Ingholt's foundational work on Palmyra and its sculptures, see Raja, Steding, and Yon 2021; Bobou et al. 2022.

[18] Recent important contributions to the field include: Invernizzi 2011; Jacobs 2014. For work of previous decades: Kawami 1987; Brentjes 1990; Mathiesen 1992; Curtis, Hillenbrand, and Rogers 1998; and classically: Rostovtzeff 1935; Schlumberger 1960; Colledge 1977.

of these reliefs (notably the gesture of the raised hand cited previously) significantly easier to identify.

It is also significant that the Parthian Empire was coextensive with much of the region that had once been ruled by Alexander III of Macedon.[19] Following his conquest and (albeit brief) reign over an empire that stretched from Egypt as far as India in the fourth century BCE, Greek remained an important language, and aspects of Greek artistic style served as a key aesthetic touchstone across many of these territories.[20] This cultural history directly affected the Parthian world, with Greek forms embraced for centuries alongside other popular, local styles. Both more and less naturalistic features in the portrait with which I began may thus have seemed equally typical of Parthian art to viewers of the first three centuries CE. Since Greek styles also predominated among the sculptural art of the Roman world, in more or less self-conscious ways sculptors might have equally drawn inspiration for such naturalistic forms from wealthy cultural centers to either the East or to the West. The various naturalistic features of these reliefs therefore resist any reading that seeks to binarize the specific strands of their cultural influence. Styles we may be quick to consider "Greek" had been implicated with those of other cultures in this region for centuries, and so traditional models of stylistic dissemination or influence do not readily apply. While seeking to reconstruct the visual effects of these reliefs and set them within their aesthetic landscape, we need accordingly to be wary of forming neatly divided categories of Eastern and Western influence.

The polyglot heritage of these funerary reliefs, wrought at the nexus of locally Palmyrene, Greek, Roman, Parthian, and other Middle Eastern influences, remains important, even while the identification of many particular features in these terms may be intractable. Here, the challenge set by this volume of engaging the phenomenological characteristics of relief and considering how the medial status of these works, *qua* relief, affects their aesthetic strategies, provides an alternative way into investigating what is specific to the visual dynamics of these images. Attention to the status of these works as relief highlights their double iconographical and structural features. The ability of relief to incorporate imagery into a surface of open-ended, indeterminate, practical function contributed to its popularity across cultures and contexts.[21] In what follows, I address the following

[19] See most recently Heckel 2020, with bibliography.

[20] See recently Dąbrowa 2011; for a significant case study: Menegazzi 2014; for the east of Parthian territory, also significantly: Mairs 2021.

[21] For a very different expression of the medium in this region in antiquity, see e.g. Amrhein, Fitzgerald, and Knott 2019.

questions: How did the status of these works as reliefs enable them to signify in ways that would not have been possible for a sculpture in the round or for a painting with similar iconography? How did the materiality of relief further govern the visual impact of Palmyrene funerary portraits? How did the arrangement of these works operate in conjunction with their physical properties to achieve certain semantic and aesthetic ends? This approach allows for the interrogation of the aesthetic and cultural specificity of the Palmyrene funerary relief tradition – its structural, iconographical, and stylistic choices – in a manner that does not primarily look to other works to provide context, but rather considers the evidence for aesthetic priorities inherent in the works themselves.

Contextualization: The Hypogeum of Yarhai

My first focus in what follows is thus to address the way that the status of these portraits as relief mediates the messages they convey. However, I am also specifically interested – broadening my discussion of this theme from my analysis of the Kelsey Museum portrait – in how these works operate and impact the viewer differently when they are displayed as a group. Viewers in antiquity almost never encountered the Palmyrene tomb reliefs as isolated images in the way that we typically experience and analyze them today. The visual dynamics these sculptures possess when they are juxtaposed are essential to a proper understanding of the way these reliefs were designed to function.

The immediate difficulty we face when considering Palmyrene funerary sculptures in this manner is that the original content of display has been lost for the overwhelming majority of the more than 3,700 relief portraits of this type that are known globally.[22] European explorers, dealers, and looters from the early modern period onward removed these images from the tombs they were made to adorn and typically sold them individually to turn the fastest and greatest profit.[23] As a result, in their presentation

[22] For the size of the corpus of these portraits: Raja 2018a; for the difficulties of preservation of context, see e.g. Kropp and Raja 2014: esp. 397.

[23] For the story of early modern looting at Palmyra, see Baird and Kamash 2019: esp. 14. For a window onto the number of Palmyrene portraits that were available on the art market from the early twentieth century: Ingholt 1928; for context: Raja and Sørensen 2015a; for an account of looting in the early twentieth century, see e.g. Amy and Seyrig 1936: esp. 229; tombs also suffered from the predations of looters who did not always recognize value in the sculptures themselves but removed them from their original loci of display in a search for grave goods that might be concealed behind them. For looting in recent years at Palmyra and other sites, the bibliography is large and growing, but see e.g. Amineddoleh 2015.

in museum collections throughout the world, the Palmyrene funerary reliefs are very commonly displayed as if they were discrete objects, stand-alone works of art.[24] In the tombs, by contrast, these reliefs representing individuals or family pairs formed part of a constellation of similar works that together encrusted the walls of a contained space. Their impact is only truly legible in this original display context.

Yet the objects only rarely survive as groups in this manner.[25] The Hypogeum of Yarhai offers something of an exceptional case (Fig. 9.2).[26] This underground tomb, which an Aramaic inscription on a limestone plaque records as the resting place of Yarhai and his family, was built in 108 CE.[27] Even in this case, when the tomb drew the concentrated attention of archaeologists in 1934, it had been badly looted.[28] The archaeological report describes how the relief portraits had largely been removed from their original place and lay broken in pieces on the ground.[29] As a consequence, scholars have not been able to reconstruct their original arrangement.[30] That the reliefs acted as sealing slabs for the burial plots arranged in grid formation in the tomb walls is clear, but the specific details of this arrangement and their interrelation with one another has been entirely lost. Nonetheless, an extensive collection of portraits was still on site and had not suffered from the attention of iconoclasts, as other works in the

[24] Important exceptions (where an institution happens to hold sufficient examples for something of the original effect to be conveyed and has installed the portraits to showcase this effect) include the Istanbul Archaeological Museum and the Archaeological Museum of the American University of Beirut.

[25] Even the most recently excavated hypogea have few portraits in situ: see al-As῾ad 2013; al-Hariri 2013.

[26] On the Hypogeum of Yarhai: Jong 2017: Online Appendix Palmyra 1, #2 (Hypogeum of Yarhai) 37; Amy and Seyrig 1936; Cantineau 1938; Toynbee 1971: 231–4.

[27] Amy and Seyrig 1936: esp. 242, no. 12; Cantineau 1938: esp. 153–4, no. 36a.

[28] The tomb was brought to the attention of archaeologists by the conservator of the National Museum of Damascus, Emir Djafar Abd el-Kader. Amy and Seyrig 1936: esp. 229.

[29] Amy and Seyrig 1936.

[30] Specifically, the reconstruction drawing in Amy and Seyrig (1936) differs markedly from the arrangement of the portraits in the National Museum of Damascus. Compare Amy and Seyrig 1936: pl. 41, with Fig. 9.6 in this chapter. Amy and Seyrig (1936: 229–30) explain: "In the drawings which accompany our publication, a grey tint has been applied to the stones found in place and on those whose individual location could be determined with certainty. When an element has not been found, neither in place nor among the collapsed stones, and we have deemed it essential to restore it by conjecture; this conjecture is expressly mentioned in the description: you will see, moreover, that the number of these elements is very small" (translation mine). The claim that "the number of these elements is very small" is surprising. Amy and Seyrig are not able to apply their "grey tint" designating a secure find to any of the portrait reliefs in their drawings beyond the banquet scenes from the south exedra and those from the west exedra's recessed central niche. Not one of the rectangular portrait slabs from the tomb walls is assigned to its specific loculus of display.

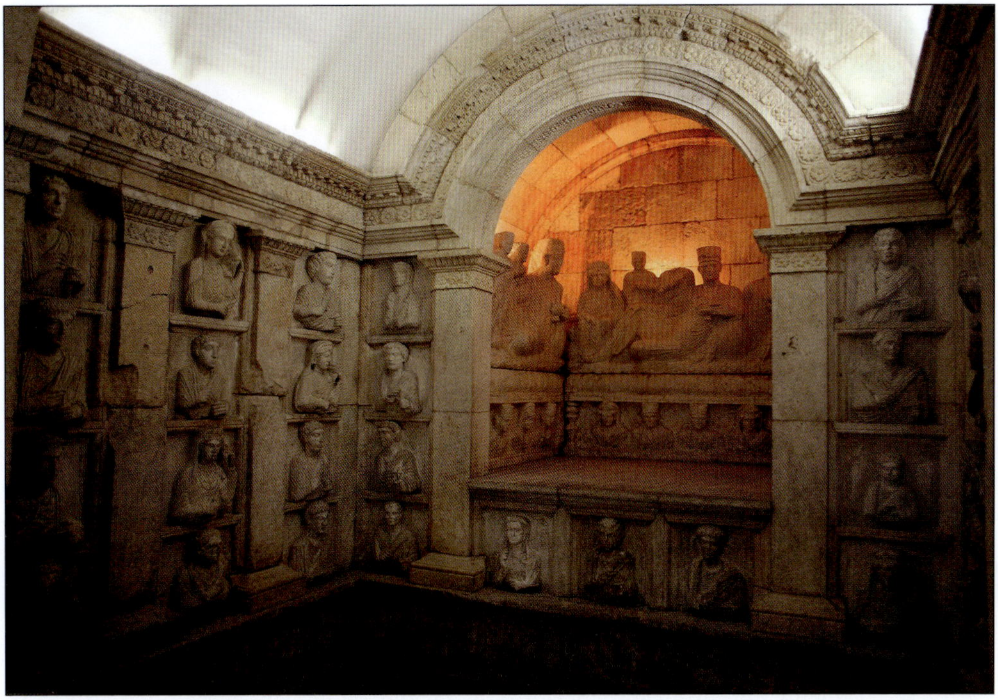

Fig. 9.2 West exedra of the Hypogeum of Yarhai, founded 108 CE. Reconstructed in the National Museum of Damascus, Syria (Getty Images).

region had.[31] The Hypogeum of Yarhai therefore offers an almost unrivaled opportunity for considering the aesthetic effects of an apparently complete set of Palmyrene reliefs, as well as for considering their mediality *qua* relief in context.

The architectural remains of the Palmyrene tombs that survived to the twentieth century, meanwhile, confirm that not only Palmyra's underground hypogea but also the city's iconic tower tombs and the later phase of temple tombs also favored the same general arrangement for display.[32] The portraits were set in sequence, one above the other and side by side in adjacent rows and columns to create a "stacking aesthetic," as Rubina Raja has recently termed the effect (although she does not go on to explore this more formally).[33] Both surviving portraits and the yawning openings of

[31] Amy and Seyrig 1936.

[32] Henning 2013a, 2013b; de Jong 2019; Houman 2019; also classically: Gawlikowski 1970; Schmidt-Colinet, al-As'ad, and Müting-Zimmer 1992. Drawings of early European visitors to the site also bear testimony to the general effect of this display when the reliefs were still in situ (though they can be suspiciously classicizing in the rendering of detail): Cassas 1799: pl. 122.

[33] Raja 2018b.

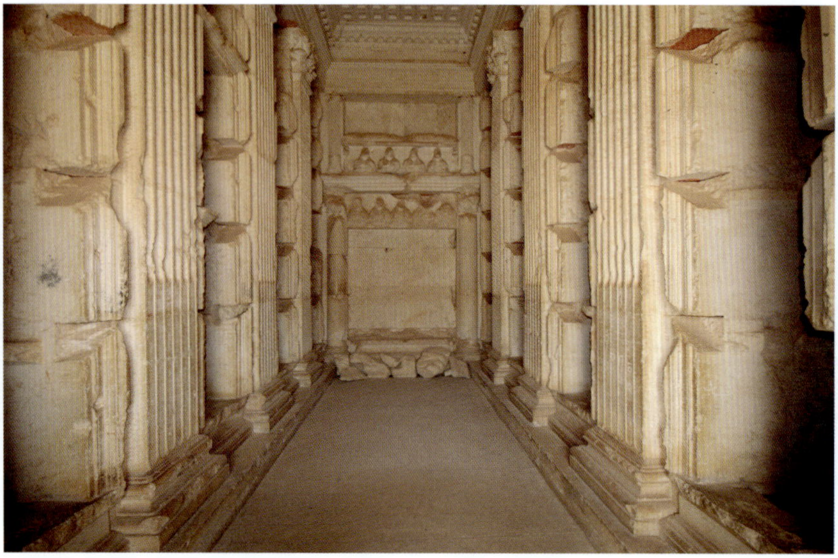

Fig. 9.3 Interior of the Tower Tomb of Elahbel, first century CE, Palmyra, Syria. Destroyed in August 2015 (Getty Images).

loculi now indicate where these stacked relief slabs were once affixed to the walls (Fig. 9.3). The Palmyrene tombs displayed these deep relief portraits of upper bodies covering entire walls around a room. I therefore take the reliefs of the Hypogeum of Yarhai as emblematic of the wider phenomenon.

Part 2

In the second half of this chapter, I consider the consequences of the status of Palmyrene portraits as relief sculptures when operating together formally as a group. I here foreground eight conceptual lenses, or aspects of the way in which these portraits function, that emerge when one considers them as ensembles of relief sculpture acting together in this manner. I think of them, on the one hand, in terms of their fixed figuration as a presence, as marginalia, as a crowd, as a mirror, and as a constellation, and, on the other, in terms of decorated stone slabs that function as seals, labels, and building blocks. The highly varied and impactful purposes of these works cannot be recognized unless their status as a corporate (and indeed slowly, incrementally growing) body of relief sculptures is held firmly in view. Throughout, I meditate on the relationship between the sculpted image and the physicality of the stone slab that supports it. I reflect primarily in the first five cases (presence to constellation) upon the visual dynamics that these portraits create as they protrude from their stone backing. In the remaining cases (seals to building blocks), my focus is on the mediality of the stone slab that backs these portraits and the way in which that, in turn, also directs their meanings.

Modes of Being: Embodied Figures

Presence. The first impression left by the funerary portraits in the Hypogeum of Yarhai is one of collective presence. This is an effect wrought partially through the carving of the figures' eyes. Rows of eyes confront the viewer standing in the reconstructed west exedra of the Hypogeum in the National Museum of Damascus. In the original, dark, lamplit chamber of this underground tomb, a visitor would have encountered these faces as peering out from the gloom. Oversized eyes dominate each of the deeply carved heads, commanding our attention. Incision lines mark large irises once filled with dark pigment, which sometimes survives.[34] These formal features – an exaggerated size, incision, and paint – would have rendered the eyes clear focal points within each face, further enlivened by the light of flickering oil lamps in their original setting, so that the eyes would have seemed to flash and the shadows to dance.[35]

The corporeality of these relief sculptures is also important to this effect. Carved so deeply that the heads are almost rendered in the round, these sculptures protrude markedly into the exedra space. These images are not strictly busts, in fact, but full depictions of the upper body, stretching down to almost the waist. Like the example now in the Kelsey Museum, the torsos are often not carved to quite the same depth as the portrait heads.[36] Multiple figures perform gestures, with hands clutching veils or reaching across the chest. This entails that the figures enter into and occupy the viewer's space in the room still further. The effect is quite different to that of the painted portraits that sometimes appear in Palmyrene tombs, as in the famous case of

[34] See e.g. Copenhagen, Ny Carlsberg Glyptotek, 1146; Brøns and Hedegaard 2019: esp. 258, fig. 4a. More generally for paint on the Palmyra portraits: Østergaard and Sargent 2014; Brøns 2020; Brøns et al. 2020.

[35] For the 259 lamps excavated in the Hypogeum of Yarhai: Amy and Seyrig 1936: esp. 258, 262–4.

[36] See e.g. the figures that appear below the central recessed niche in Fig. 9.2. Others are carved at a more consistent depth, such as the woman who appears in the same figure in the current reconstruction in the middle column on the side wall in the second niche up from the socle base.

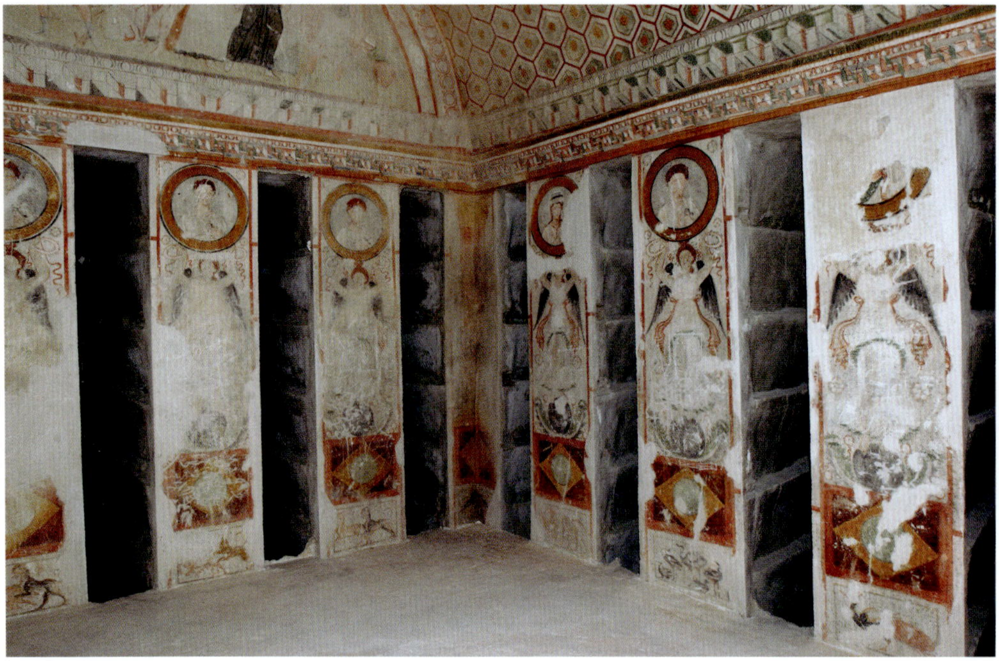

Fig. 9.4 Painted interior wall in the Tower Tomb of the Three Brothers, second century CE, Palmyra, Syria (Getty Images).

the Tomb of the Three Brothers (Figs. 9.4–5).[37] Here, the painted faces likewise capture the features of a missed family member, but the medium ensures that these people are presented at a greater remove from the onlooker in the room.[38] The woman in the west corner of the north wall, for example, is naturalistically portrayed, with highlights on the edges of her turban and shadows falling behind her shoulders and neck suggesting a body in three dimensions. There is even the suggestion of a visual work in relief here: The round frame of the *imago clipeata* (the shield portrait) on which she is depicted is consistently shaded to suggest that its rim actually protrudes from the tomb wall. Yet there is a lack of such overt modeling of a curved surface in the circular space within the portrait roundel.[39] This body is inaccessible: the

[37] Eristov et al. 2019, with bibliography; also on the paintings: Buisson et al. 2014; Sørensen 2014, 2017; cf. also: Sørensen 2016.

[38] For the argument that the Palmyrene portrait reliefs are schematic, see note 8.

[39] Other painted depictions of shield portraits, as at Pompeii, include shading and contort the proportions of the figure presented in an effort to suggest a protruding relief bust. The most famous example is from the wall paintings of Atrium 5 in Villa A at Oplontis. See most recently Moormann 2019: paras. 111–13, with bibliography.

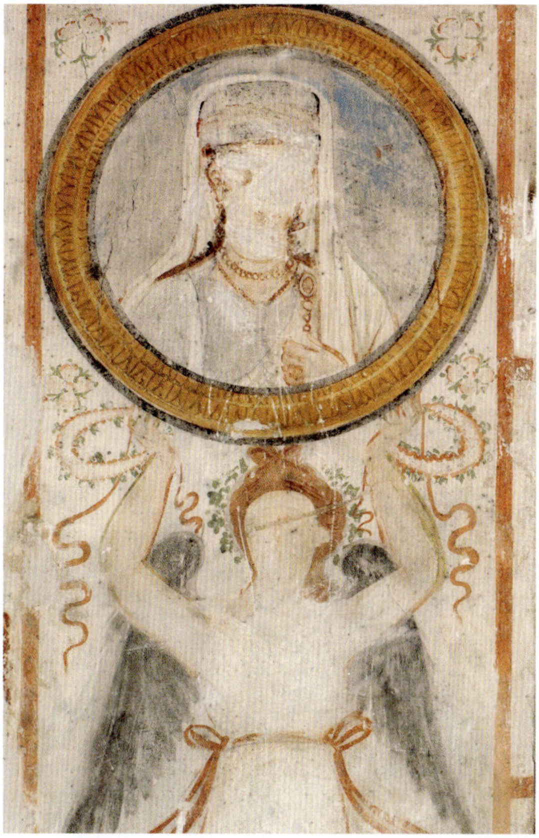

Fig. 9.5 Detail of painted interior wall in the Tower Tomb of the Three Brothers, second century CE, Palmyra, Syria. (Getty Images).

apparently corporeal woman can only exist in an unreachable space beyond the surface of the wall. Indeed, this inaccessibility is doubled as the portraits of the family members in this fresco are further framed and held aloft by flying Victories (*Nikai*), presumably to emphasize something of their altered state after death. It is therefore, in fact, the Victories who are suggested to exist just below the wall surface. For all that the Victory appears to hold the shield portrait that she carries with a slight forward thrust toward the viewer, the figures portrayed in the images they hold aloft are a second-order fiction and so become still more remote. The degree of conceptual and physical remove in these images is thus quite the opposite of what we meet in the Palmyrene relief sculptures, where the physicality of the sculpture allows the figures represented to inescapably enter into the viewers' world. The embodiment effected by the reliefs facilitates a sense of connection, and the representations and the onlooker share a common space.

Marginalia. This bodily presence and eye contact of the relief sculptures in the Hypogeum of Yarhai further combine with two other features: the focused representation of only one individual per stone slab at nearly life-size and the arrangement of these figures in emotive family groups. These features work together to make the hypogeum relief portraits compellingly relatable, further accentuating the viewer's sense of the figures' presence in the room. The Palmyra tomb reliefs thus invite any onlookers to recognize the deceased, and then to imagine themselves as seen by them in turn.

Yet the enduring human immediacy and recognizability of these figures stands in tension with their formulaic austerity. Despite the combined power of these characteristics and the care taken to include particular features that enliven these sculptures – such as dimpled cheeks, full or thin faces, eyebrows of a variety of shapes, and fashionable hairstyles – other aspects of this relief tradition nonetheless serve to mark the distance between the deceased and the family members they have left behind. We should note here in particular the attributes held by the deceased. Though some of these common objects (notably the distaff and key) are more quotidian than others (such as the leafy branch or the frequently seen, curious loop of drapery), their evidently symbolic recurrence across a great corpus of examples renders them indexical of the altered status of the person represented.[40] Clutching his attribute of the loop of fabric in an almost wistful pose, the man in the top right portrait set beneath the cornice on the west wall of the west exedra of Yarhai's hypogeum is typical of the type (see Fig. 9.2).[41] On the west and south walls, meanwhile, several men grasp an angular object, which has been identified as a type of key.[42] In the wider body of Palmyrene portraits, men like priests brandish scrolls, presumably representing literacy or some more specific kind of learning.[43] Many other figures – men, women, and children – hold a leafy branch, which scholars have suggested carried ritual or symbolic significance, perhaps conjuring associations of enduring life or youth.[44] Scalloped curtains hang behind the shoulders of the deceased in numerous images from Palmyrene tombs (as seen on the bottom register of the west wall here),

[40] For the spindle and distaff: Heyn 2010; for keys: Thomsen 2021; for branches: Bobou 2021; for the loops of drapery: Colledge 1976: 155.

[41] The woman displayed diagonally beneath her to the viewer's left, in the central column of that wall, carries the same attribute.

[42] For the angular object, compare the form of the probable keys represented in London, British Museum, 125023; see further Thomsen 2021.

[43] For scrolls: Colledge 1976: 154.

[44] Colledge 1976: 154; Bobou 2021.

possibly suggesting separation and a threshold that the departed must cross.[45] Women hold out the spindle and distaff they once used (or are at least suggested to have busied themselves with) in the daily work of spinning yarn, but here no threads hang down, no action enlivens the image, and the spindle is silent.[46] Meanwhile, the gold chains and bracelets that festoon the arms, necks, and brows of the women depicted in this tomb and others – many worth a year's wages for a laborer or hired hand – would have been of such weight and value that they would surely have hampered a woman's activities if they were continually worn. While it is not impossible that the wives of wealthy Palmyrene merchants were indeed clad in gold in this way, it seems unlikely that they would have been able to busy themselves much with the spinning wheel and distaff in this attire.[47] Inevitably, on some level, these are essentialized, idealized images. Multiple visual markers make clear that we are not to view the people represented as occupying a world contiguous with our own. They are iconographically separated from normal daily life.

The status of these sculptural works as relief is important in this respect too. As I have observed, the depth of the relief carving lends these figures a corporeal presence, enabling them to physically intrude in the space the mourners occupy. Yet conversely, the inherent nature and essence of relief also binds and limits this corporeal intrusion. It constrains these carved personalities to the margins of the room, to the stone blocks that form the very tomb walls. A tension between physical presence and an austere aesthetic of remove is thus inherent to the relief of Palmyrene tomb sculptures. This paradoxical tension between familiarity and the impossibly remote (an effect only further accentuated in their modern reception) ironically serves to intensify the commanding presence of these recognizable, yet distant portraits. More than this, the basic compositional conceit of the portraits is presence, yet the basic iconographic conceit is one of absence, a distance from the world of the living. Within this tension, the Palmyrene portraits effectively diagram the key affective force of all funereal representation. In so doing, they also underline the basic in-betweenness of relief itself.

Crowd. Though liminal in multiple senses, these figural sculptures clearly remain the intended focus for the visitor to the tomb. The status of these works as an ensemble that expands with the passing of time and the appearance of each new generation is centrally important here. When the

[45] Raja 2019b.

[46] On the related soundscape of weaving in classical antiquity, see Öhrman 2020.

[47] On the value of Roman gold jewelry, see Barham 2017.

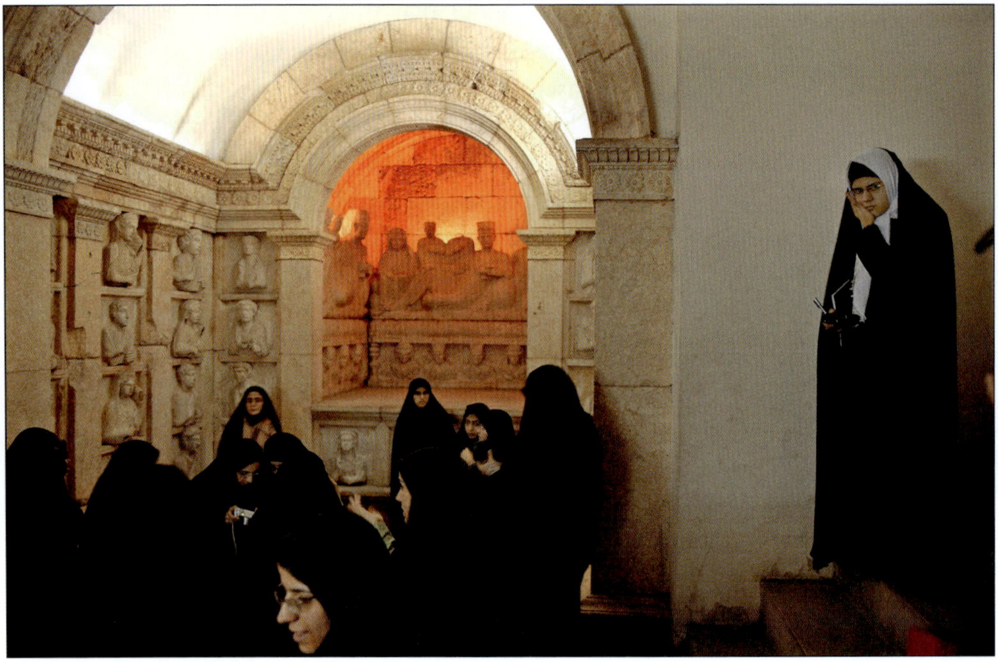

Fig. 9.6 Group of women visiting the National Museum of Damascus, Syria, ca. 2010 (Getty Images).

figures represented on the walls of the Hypogeum of Yarhai intrude upon the space of the viewer, it is fundamental to their visual effect that they do not do so in isolation, nor even in small clusters. Rows upon rows and columns beside columns of portrait torsos carved in similarly deep relief press into the space of the room in concert. As she enters the hypogeum's west chamber, the viewer finds herself confronted with an apparently already occupied – indeed a crowded – space. The impact of this feature of relief's physicality is made clearer still when the room is further occupied by a group of living people, and the two crowds seem to be intertwined (Fig. 9.6). We cannot know precisely what circumstances and rituals filled the tomb with mourners during the years of its active use as a burial site.[48] It is uncertain, for example, whether the visiting family members, and perhaps their wider community, would have gathered in the space in a self-directed and haphazard manner in the way that the women fill the hypogeum exedra reconstructed in the National Museum of Damascus, as seen in Fig. 9.6. Visits to the tomb might alternatively have been more

[48] For the available evidence, see De Jong 2017: 288–91.

regimented, even processional, visually echoing the regular, rhythmic arrangement of the portraits on the tomb walls.[49] These modes also, of course, need not be mutually exclusive. Given the evidently communal orientation of Palmyrene culture, as well as what we know of wider Roman funerary customs, it seems unlikely that mourners would typically have visited the tomb alone.[50] Whatever the case, as the number of burials in the tomb increased over time, mourners would have experienced these images crowding in upon them, even as they themselves crowded into the increasingly tight space of the exedra. The images of ancestors that encrust the tomb walls would, ultimately, threaten to outnumber all but the largest funerary processions.

Mirror. In a manner that may not be obvious to the viewer today, these images also act as a kind of mirror. If we imagine the encounter between these portraits and men and women belonging not only to the same culture, but even to the very same family, and dressed in much the same style as the figures represented, then the near-mirror image that these reliefs would have presented to the onlooker becomes striking. While there is evidence for changes in fashion at Palmyra – women wearing higher or lower turbans beneath their veils, for example, or eschewing these ornaments altogether – the overall bias of the Palmyrene portraits is toward conservatism in representation that preserves key elements over time.[51] Over the decades, the formula broadly remains the same: we see frontal, deep-relief representations of men and of women clad in a Greek chiton with a cloak that is often adapted to be drawn up over the head as a veil for the women and set on top of a twisted column of cloth. Subsequent generations of family members visiting the tomb would typically have been dressed in much the same fashion.[52] Palmyrene men and women visiting the tomb in antiquity would presumably have noted certain differences in dress, style of haircuts, beards, necklaces, or browbands that situated a given portrait in an earlier decade from their own. Still, the overwhelming effect was one of visual continuity, just as the size and dimensions of the reliefs were also standardized by the scale of loculi set into the tomb walls. As women grieved for their lost loved ones and perhaps tugged at their own veil, pulling it close around their body for comfort, they were faced with images of women enacting a broadly similar gesture. Particular family features of

[49] See De Jong 2017 and cf. also broader ritual practice of procession in Palmyra: Finlayson 2013; Le Bihan 2013.

[50] Hope 2009; Borg 2019; see also Draycott and Stamatopoulou 2016.

[51] For such developments, see Colledge 1976: 245–64.

[52] For developments, see Colledge 1976: 245–64; see also note 10.

chin, cheeks, jawline, nose, or brow could even be reflected back at them as they faced this gallery of ancestors in the family tomb. In many respects, the mirror offered by these portrait reliefs could be a nearly literal one. In this dynamic, the physical properties inherent to the medium of relief are significant. The slab of stone from which the image is carved constrains the viewing experience so that the image may not be circumambulated and experienced from a multiplicity of perspectives. The frontal presentation of the deceased selected for the portrait must be accepted and engaged. This confrontation inherent to the ontology of Palmyrene relief creates the mirroring image.

This physical mirroring combines with other details of these reliefs to effect a more symbolic and invitational mirroring in addition. The typical, if not invariable, continuity in bloodline within a tomb is important here.[53] Visitors to this tomb exedra were confronted by a dense crowd of their own forebears (from close family to the generationally removed), who provided a poignant mirror to the living. The medium of relief made this mirror particularly impactful, offering a device that allowed the sheer number of ancestor portraits represented in the hypogeum to be encountered in a single moment, in a manner that could never have been possible on such a scale with sculptures in the round. Nor could painting have offered quite the same embodied challenge. As this mirror in relief also enabled the images to cover a significant proportion of the available space from floor to ceiling – and to do so while protruding into the lived space of the gallery's visitors as I have explored – it must have made all meanings perceived in this array of portraiture particularly insistent. The portraits first operate in a mode similar to the collections of wax portraits – ancestor *imagines* – met in the atrium of a Roman Republican home.[54] Here, however, the ancestor portraits are significantly multiplied in number and made coextensive with the very walls that support the roof of the underground chamber. This body of images crowding in upon the viewer thereby surely served to underline inherited family values. The mirror of figures met here emphasizes and reiterates the enduring nature and power of Yarhai's family in his eponymous hypogeum, as well as the viewer's privileged place within it.

It is notable that the age of the men and women represented at Palmyra hardly varies. With the exception of some children's portraits (which are most frequently added to the relief of a deceased mother), these images

[53] For the sale of part of this very Hypogeum to a new owner – who may have been no relation to the founder Yarhai at all – see Amy and Seyrig 1936: esp. 259–61; see more generally Krag 2019.

[54] For an overview, see Flower 1996.

overwhelmingly depict men and women in their prime.[55] There is evidently more than a degree of idealism here: Whether a person lived to an exalted old age or passed away tragically young, they are inserted into the visual uniformity of the tomb walls at the peak of their adult capacities, still vigorous, but generally mature. The effect of this temporal restriction is to create an aesthetic of strength: Aging is not seen. This effect is also underlined in other ways, not least by the collective presentation of these portraits and the ongoing commemoration of successive generations of family members in the same manner. The continuing power of the family is also formally stressed by the rigidity and regularity of the grid of images that is created by the arrangement of these relief slabs at repeated intervals around the hypogeum walls. Both the individual details and the wider networking of these relief images conspire to make the composition of tomb portraits here one that emphasizes the prowess and status of the family. In so doing, the walls become an invitation (and no doubt also often a burden) to the remaining family members to reflect these same qualities back to the portraits in stone on the wall, behaving like a mirror themselves. The reliefs further challenge the viewer to aspire to uphold this tradition and pass it on when they come to be commemorated in this same fashion in their turn.

Constellation. The social dynamics of these reliefs are not all outward facing, however. The walls of the Hypogeum of Yarhai present the viewer with a gridded constellation of ancestors locked in a common surface. This participation in a shared surface of the room's walls unavoidably entails that there would be both more and less favorable positions of display. The male figure sculpted in the round and reclining on the lid of the central sarcophagus evidently enjoys the most prominent position. Yet it is not simply the case that the reliefs that line the walls are inevitably inferior to such sculptures in the round. The portraits that engage the onlooker from atop the socle directly beneath this niche command attention in much the same way, and are significantly easier to view, than the fully carved figures on the lids of the other two sarcophagi that flank the central chest at ninety degrees.[56] The priority of position and related status of these figures can be difficult to determine. The flanking sarcophagi may have been additions of a later generation once the better spots in the burial chamber walls were filled. What does seem unavoidable is that the central positions on the west exedra's rear wall receive a privileged viewing in comparison with the

55 On children: Krag and Raja 2016, 2018; Krag 2018: 82–5.

56 Amy and Seyrig 1936: esp. 246, pl. 41.

reliefs set in the corners and on the highest and lowest registers of the walls to either side, which we view obliquely upon entrance to the tomb chamber. While it may be that the priority of the elder is the basic principle here, it is not difficult to see how a social hierarchy borne out of family politics might easily take hold and govern decisions of who was commemorated where.

Yet if its medium inevitably allows these negative dynamics, the common surface of the relief remains a leveling factor, emphasizing the participation of all the figures presented in the same family group. The common format and contiguous surface of the reliefs renders them a community. So powerful was the effect of this sumptuously carved, elaborately adorned constellation of ancestors whose portraits literally glittered in the lamplight, that outsiders were awed by the effect and desired the social cachet these tombs communicated. As a result, we have a number of surviving records of the purchase of these tombs by individuals who do not appear to have been related to the tomb's original founder.[57] Outsiders sought to insert themselves into the lofty realm of the people depicted in these tomb reliefs. So great was the social status that people evidently perceived in the ownership of these tomb plots that they would gladly pay a handsome price to gain access for their family to burial in even the presumably less well positioned remaining loculi available. People sought an undying memorial through incorporation into the array of images that bedecked these relief walls.

Modes of Being: Slabs of Stone

The ontology of relief depends upon at least two component parts, as I have observed: the relief figure itself and the material plane against which it is plastically formed. The effects that relief creates, as well as the meanings it communicates as a result, are informed by the interdependent relation of these distinct parts of the medium. In the case of the visual dynamics I have considered, the material physicality of relief governs the phenomenological functioning of the Palmyrene funerary portraits. The material plane here informs and even conditions readings of the image it carries. This relationship, however, can also be inverted. The image constructed in relief will necessarily also dictate and control the ontology and meanings carried by the material picture plane. Indeed, it is the image that renders this surface a relief in the first place. I turn now to this side of this relationship: to

[57] See note 53.

readings of these objects as slabs of stone that are inflected by, and in certain cases even depend upon, the image that they bear.

Typos/Seal. One of the most basic ontological appeals made by the Palmyrene reliefs is to the category of the seal. The technology of the seal stone at the time of Roman influence of Palmyra was already very ancient. Cylinder seals, which can be rolled to impress an image in clay, had been popular in the region for millennia.[58] Iconographic stamp seals (of the kind that were commonly used in the signet rings of the Roman world) had a similarly ancient heritage.[59] In Roman bureaucracy, impressions made by these stones were used to guarantee the authority and confidentiality of missives penned on papyrus or similar materials and sealed with a globule of wax.[60] The image marked into the hot wax by the seal ring would quickly harden, confirming the identity of the owner of the stone impressed in it. It would then ideally remain intact until the intended reader of the document broke the seal. The Parthian world was meanwhile heir to a very ancient tradition of pressing such stones into clay to seal goods in containers and in rooms.[61] The seal image marked the authority of the owner, producer, or official who had sealed a space, dissuading interference from third parties. It stood as a guarantee of the protection of whatever valued commodities lay behind it, until such a time as one should come with authority to break the image and remove them.

The word for "seal" in the Parthian language of Pahlavi (*muhr*) refers directly to the ontology of the seal stone; it thereby also denotes beads and game pieces of a similar form.[62] But in the Greek that had been so influential in the Middle East from the time of Alexander (and which was the dominant language in Rome's eastern provinces), the favored term was *typos*: impression.[63] This term came to be extended from its most literal applications to seal-ring stamps and forms beaten into bronze at an early date and applied to a wide range of visual forms, including carved stone sculptures.[64] Strikingly, this is also the term one consistently encounters in Greek descriptions of relief.[65]

[58] For an introduction to the form, see recently: Ameri et al. 2018: esp. Part I.

[59] Ameri et al. 2018: Parts I–IV. [60] Vandorpe 1995; Andrews 2012. [61] See e.g. Bivar 1982.

[62] MacKenzie 1971, s.v. *muhr*. [63] See Platt's (Chapter 1) contribution to this volume, note 1.

[64] It ultimately encompassed a full range of images, and even text, as Verity Platt has explored, showing that Hellenistic poets self-consciously played with the semantic scope of this terminology, particularly in the epigrammatic responses to sculptural works which were popular at the time: Platt 2018: esp. 507–10.

[65] The Pahlavi categories that might encompass such sculptural works are broader still and equate to the more general term "image": MacKenzie, 1971, s.v. *nigārag*, *pahikar*.

The parallels between the practice of sealing and the use of the stone portrait slabs at Palmyra are compelling. Each stone carries the practical function of sealing the loculus – the burial place – of the individual represented upon its surface. The relief slab is the very literal seal of the grave and its contents, guaranteeing the inviolate preservation of all that lies enclosed behind it. The practice of using a slab of stone (or smaller, cheaper pieces covered in plaster) to close a grave was common in the ancient world.[66] In the exceptionally wealthy desert oasis of Palmyra, however, the Greek semantics of the seal appear to have invited rich patrons to go still further. The Palmyrene funerary slabs take pains to underline and instantiate their status as seals in the fullest form. Not content to merely close the grave loculus with a slab of stone, they draw upon the Eastern tradition of seals in clay to mark the burial with a "seal image," a *typos*, emphasizing the tomb's authoritative closure.[67] Forming the image in the megalographic medium of nearly life-size stone relief, the slabs thereby become *tupoi* in two senses. These slabs play on the double meaning of *typos* to showcase the wealth of their high-status patrons and the spectacular kind of sculptural seal the family can afford. They also draw upon the anthropocentric *apotropaion* of clay seal impressions to close the grave with a similar (if much grander) mark of warning: The grave is to stay shut.

Labels. These image-bearing slabs also function as labels, in some cases literally so. In the Hypogeum of Yarhai, one relief portrait of a bearded man wearing a chiton and cloak, for example, bears an inscription providing his name and lamenting his loss: "Vorod, alas!"[68] In Tyre, tombs with small columbaria-like loculi were reused in the Byzantine period and likewise sealed and labeled.[69] Each loculus was closed with a wall of small stones and plastered over; the epitaph was then applied in paint (Fig. 9.7). Stone plaques bearing a simple epitaph that sealed small loculi in Rome's catacombs functioned in much the same fashion.[70]

Yet the Palmyrene relief slabs overwhelmingly prioritize a different approach: The label is primarily visual. Each relief stone seals the grave

[66] For just a sample of their material variety and temporal scope, see Hizmi et al. 2004; De Jong 2010: esp. 614.

[67] For seals marking tombs, see e.g. Matthew 27.66: "So they went and made the tomb secure by putting a seal on [*σφραγίσαντες*] the stone and posting the guard" (NIV); the NIV captures the meaning of *sphragisantes* better than most other translations. See also Daniel 6:17: "A stone was brought and placed over the mouth of the den, and the king sealed it with his own signet ring and with the rings of his nobles, so that Daniel's situation might not be changed" (NIV).

[68] Amy and Seyrig 1936: esp. 250–1. More generally on these funerary inscriptions: Hillers and Cussini 1996; Yon 2013.

[69] For the general type, see De Jong 2010: esp. 607, 614, figs. 8, 10.

[70] For an overview, see Fiocchi Nicolai, Bisconti, and Mazzoleni 1999.

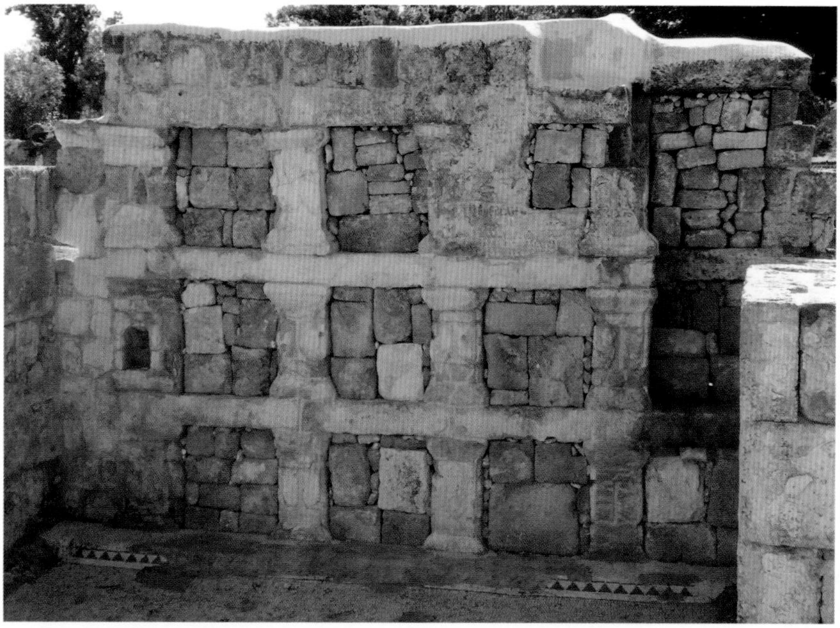

Fig. 9.7 Loculi from Tyre. Painted inscription partially preserved over the top right loculus (photograph by author).

and labels it with the portrait of its owner. These labels overcome the limitations of the textual label where literacy is required for recognition. They further work particularly well in a family setting: the visitor immediately recognizes the portraits of their loved ones in their assigned places within the clan tomb. In their three-dimensionality, these labels also carry a haptic quality, inviting a lingering touch and offering an embodied locus for a simulated connection. Indeed, the relief's status as a label, like its status as a seal, depends upon an invisible, and yet inescapable, point of reference: the body of the deceased. The medium of relief here arguably seeks to deny, distract from, or otherwise attempt to obviate the material loss of the person brought by death. The human body that is buried in the tomb is replaced by its facsimile in stone. Much more effectively than words alone, these three-dimensional, visual labels are designed to transfix the viewer before an individual grave plot and so to trigger the outpouring and subsequent easing of grief.

Building Blocks. Finally, these relief slabs carry the appearance of building blocks: the constituent stones of the tomb wall.[71] This is an important

[71] The hypogea are generally first dug out of the bedrock but can also include elements of masonry construction, as seen in the reconstructed rear wall of this exedra behind the sarcophagi.

effect, which I have touched upon at various points. The impression that the ancestors in their solid, regular arrangement support the exedra in which the viewer stands is a visually insistent effect, as well as a compelling one. Yarhai's family form the very structure of the tomb that commemorates their family line. The kind of wall that ostensibly incorporates these stones is also significant. In a manner somewhat evocative of masonry wall painting of the so-called Roman First Style, these portrait stones are set upon a socle.[72] Like paintings of the so-called Second Style, they further appear between (unusually ornate) Doric columns upholding an ornamental entablature.[73] Hellenistic architecture has long been seen as an important source of inspiration for each of these images.[74] The relief arrangement of the walls of the hypogeum's west exedra resonates formally with the interior incrustation of Palmyra's Temple of Baalshamin, one of the oldest in the city, with earliest phases dating to the second century BCE.[75] The walls of the Hypogeum of Yarhai's west exedra thus insert something of the grandeur and perceived glamor of local edifices of Hellenistic heritage into this personal family memorial.

Of course, the wall, as it appears to the viewer, is a fiction. Like the referents of First and Second Style wall painting, what we see is ornamental stone encrustation, and not the load-bearing arrangement of stones that the socle at ground level, and the columns rising from it, might tempt us to believe. As with the fictive columns and the decorative entablature, the portrait reliefs form part of the ornament of the tomb.[76] The hypogeum is encrusted in ancestors. It is significant that the Palmyrene funerary tradition chose to insert its portraits into a decorative architectural illusion in this way. It would be easy to see the Palmyrene images as framed by the imported architectural elements of Greco-Roman culture. The traditional emphasis on the "classical" cultures of Greece and Rome has entailed that the little attention given to these architectural features has tended to interpret them in this manner.[77] Yet the Hellenistic heritage of this region went back to the time of Alexander, preceding any Roman claim to echo Greek achievements by centuries.[78] When we are mindful of this fact, the architectural arrangement of the Palmyrene exedra begins to look much less like a mere response to Roman fashion. Nor are the portraits simply

[72] See esp. Bruno 1969; Laidlaw 1985.
[73] On the Second Style, see recently Dietrich 2019, with bibliography.
[74] See most recently McKenzie 2007: 80–118, with bibliography.
[75] See Collart 1970; Gawlikowski and Pietrzykowski 1980; Stucky and Aitken 2018.
[76] For this concept in the Roman world, see Barham 2018.
[77] Amy and Seyrig 1936: esp. 244–5. [78] See notes 19–20.

framed by these architectural elements. The portrait blocks rather purport to join the columns in supporting the very entablature that runs over the figures' heads – if we first acknowledge that fiction. If we do not, these slabs are also revealed as forming a continuous surface of ornamental relief with these very architectural elements. In both the illusion and the actuality, the portrait slabs are dignified not by the importation of honorific elements of Greco-Roman culture, but rather as active participants in the edifice – or the adornment – of an ancient Middle Eastern–Hellenistic tradition. The people of Palmyra support that edifice together with the columns. Yarhai's tomb positions his family as upholding the transcontinental tradition of an already ancient past – and having the cultural compass to direct the future.

Coda

The cultural and social ambition of Palmyra's tombs is enormous. It should be little surprise that this milieu produced Zenobia, a self-proclaimed empress who was able to control the eastern Roman Empire from modern Türkiye to Egypt for four years.[79] The fact that the tombs have been read for so long as an idiosyncratic local response to Roman fashion is a bizarre misreading of their visual complexity and proud cultural statement. It is as limiting as the age-old tradition of framing Zenobia as a rebel queen rather than a savvy politician acting on an imperial stage and familiar with Roman symbols of power.[80] The tombs of Palmyra were made to communicate the importance of their families to the empires that lay beyond them. Finally, the medium of relief is revealed as a multivalent tool for delivering both complex symbolic messages and palpable phenomenological effect. Recognizing relief's agency at Palmyra transforms our understanding of these enduringly iconic images.

References

Amrhein, A., Fitzgerald, C., and Knott, E., eds. (2019). *A Wonder to Behold: Craftsmanship and the Creation of Babylon's Ishtar Gate*. New York: Institute for the Study of the Ancient Word, New York University.

Ameri, M., Costello, S. K., Jamison, G., and Scott, S. J., eds. (2018). *Seals and Sealing in the Ancient World: Case Studies from the Near East, Egypt, the Aegean, and South Asia*. Cambridge: Cambridge University Press, 2018.

[79] See most recently Andrade 2018.

[80] For conflicting perspectives in antiquity and beyond: Woltering 2014.

Amineddoleh, L. A. (2015). "Cultural Heritage Vandalism and Looting: The Role of Terrorist Organizations, Public Institutions and Private Collectors," *Santander Art and Culture Law Review* 1.2: 27–62.

Amy, R., and Seyrig, H. (1936). "Recherches dans la nécropole de Palmyre: I. L'hypogée de Iarhai fils de Barikhi, petitfils de Taimarsô." *Syria* 17.3: 229–66.

Andrade, N. (2018). *Zenobia: Shooting Star of Palmyra*. New York: Oxford University Press.

Andrews, C. (2012). *Roman Seal-Boxes in Britain*. British Archaeological Reports, British Series 567. Oxford: Archaeopress.

al-As'ad, W. (2013). "Some Tombs Recently Excavated at Palmyra." *Studia Palmyreńskie* 12: 15–24.

al-Hariri, K. (2013). "The Tomb of 'Aqraban." *Studia Palmyreńskie* 12 (2013): 149–57.

Baird, J. A., and Kamash, Z. (2019). "Remembering Roman Syria: Valuing Tadmor-Palmyra, from 'Discovery' to Destruction." *Bulletin of the Institute of Classical Studies* 62.1: 1–29.

Barham, N. (2017) "Cat. 164 Necklace with Pendant, 2nd/3rd Century AD." In K. Raff, ed., *Roman Art at the Art Institute of Chicago*. Chicago, IL: Art Institute of Chicago. https://publications.artic.edu/roman/reader/romanart/section/1978.

(2018). "Esteemed Ornament: An Overlooked Value for Approaching Roman Visual Culture." in N. Dietrich and M. Squire, eds., *Ornament and Figure in Graeco-Roman Art: Rethinking Visual Ontologies in Classical Antiquity*. Berlin: De Gruyter, 279–98.

Bivar, A. D. H. (1982). "Seal-Impressions of Parthian Qūmis (Qūmis Commentaries 4)." *Iran: Journal of the British Institute of Persian Studies* 20.1: 161–76.

Bobou, O. (2021). "Plants in Palmyrene Funerary Iconography of Adults." In Heyn and Raja 2021: 31–50.

Bobou, O., Miranda, A. C., Raja, R., and Yon, J.-B. (2022). *The Ingholt Archive: The Palmyrene Material*. 4 vols. Turnhout: Brepols.

Böhme-Schönberger, A., and Schottroff, W. (1979). *Palmyrenische Grabreliefs*. Frankfurt: Liebieghaus.

Borg, B. (2019). *Roman Tombs and the Art of Commemoration: Contextual Approaches to Funerary Customs in the Second Century CE*. Cambridge: Cambridge University Press.

Brentjes, B. (1990). *Steppenreiter und Handelsherren: Die Kunst der Partherzeit in Vorderasien*. Leipzig: Seemann.

Brøns, C. (2020). "Reconstructing Ancient Polychromy: The Beauty of Palmyra." *Journal of Eastern Mediterranean Archaeology and Heritage Studies* 8.2: 141–58.

Brøns, C., and Hedegaard, S. B. (2019). "New Research from Ny Carlsberg Glyptotek: Pigments in Ancient Palmyra." In R. Raja and A. Nielsen, eds., *The Road to Palmyra*. Copenhagen: Ny Carlsberg Glyptotek, 252–74.

Brøns, C., Hedegaard, S. B., Bredal-Jorgensen, J., Buti, D., and Pastorelli, G. (2020). "The Rarest Blue: An Exceptional Find of Lapis Lazuli in the Polychromy of a Funerary Portrait from Ancient Palmyra." *Archaeometry* 62.3: 506–20.

Bruno, V. J. (1969). "The Antecedents of the Pompeian First Style." *American Journal of Archaeology* 73.3: 305–17.

Buisson, N., et al. (2014). "The Tomb of the Three Brothers in Palmyra: The Use of Mimetite, a Rare Yellow Pigment in a Rich Decoration." *Archaeometry* 57.6: 1025–44.

Cantineau, J. (1938). "Tadmorea." *Syria* 19.2: 153–71.

Cassas, L.-F. (1799). *Voyage pittoresque de la Syrie, de la Phénicie, de la Palestine, et de la Basse Égypte*. Paris: Imprimerie de la République.

Christie, Manson, and Woods. (1980). *Fine Antiquities, the Properties of Baron Alain De Conde, the Late D. E. Bower, the Pierpont Morgan Library, and from Various Sources*. London: Christie's.

Collart, P. (1970). "Reconstruction du thalamos du temple de Baalshamîn à Palmyre." *Revue archéologique*, n.s., vol. 2: 323–7.

Colledge, M. A. R. (1976). *The Art of Palmyra*. London: Thames and Hudson.

(1977). *Parthian Art*. London: Elek.

Curry, A. (2015). "Here Are the Ancient Sites ISIS Has Damaged and Destroyed." *National Geographic*, September 1. www.nationalgeographic.com/history/article/150901-isis-destruction-looting-ancient-sites-iraq-syria-archaeology.

Curtis, V. S., Hillenbrand, R., and Rogers, J. M. (1998). *The Art and Archaeology of Ancient Persia: New Light on the Parthian and Sasanian Empires*. London: I. B. Tauris.

Davies, G. (2018). *Gender and Body Language in Roman Art*. Cambridge: Cambridge University Press.

Dąbrowa, E. (2011). *Studia graeco-parthica: Political and Cultural Relations between Greeks and Parthians*. Wiesbaden: Harrassowitz.

De Jong, L. (2010). "Performing Death in Tyre: The Life and Afterlife of a Roman Cemetery in the Province of Syria." *American Journal of Archaeology* 114.4: 597–630.

(2017). *The Archaeology of Death in Roman Syria: Burial, Commemoration, and Empire*. Cambridge: Cambridge University Press.

(2019). "Monuments, Landscape, and Memory: The Emergence of Tower-Tombs in Tadmor-Palmyra." *Bulletin of the Institute of Classical Studies* 62.1: 30–52.

Dietrich, N. (2019). "Spatial Dimensions in Roman Wall Painting and the Interplay of Enclosing and Enclosed Space: A New Perspective on Second Style." In R. Gee and V. Rousseau, eds., *Ancient Mediterranean Painting*." Special issue, *Arts* 8.2. www.mdpi.com/2076-0752/8/2/68/pdf.

Draycott, C. M., and Stamatopoulou, M., eds. (2016). *Dining and Death: Interdisciplinary Perspectives on the "Funerary Banquet" in Ancient Art, Burial and Belief*. Leuven: Peeters.

Ellerbrock, U. (2021). *The Parthians: The Forgotten Empire*. London: Routledge.

Eristov, H., Vibert-Guigue, C., al'As'ad, W., and Sarkis, N., eds. (2019). *Le tombeau des trois frères à Palmyre*. Beirut: Institut français du Proche-Orient.

Finlayson, C. (1998). "Veil, Turban and Headpiece: Funerary Portraits and Female Status at Palmyra." PhD dissertation, University of Iowa.

(2013). "New Perspectives on the Ritual and Cultic Importance of Women at Palmyra and Dura Europos: Processions and Temples." *Studia Palmyreńskie* 12: 61–85.

Fiocchi Nicolai, V., Bisconti, F., and Mazzoleni, D. (1999). *The Christian Catacombs of Rome: History, Decoration, Inscriptions*. Regensburg: Schnell and Steiner.

Flower, H. I. (1996). *Ancestor Masks and Aristocratic Power in Roman Culture*. Oxford: Clarendon Press.

Gawlikowski, M. (1970). *Monuments funéraires de Palmyre*. Travaux du Centre d'archéologie méditerranéenne de l'Académie polonaise des sciences 9. Warsaw: PWN – Éditions Scientifiques de Pologne.

Gawlikowski, M., and Pietrzykowski, M. (1980). "Les sculptures du temple de Baalshamîn à Palmyre." *Syria* 57.2–4: 421–52.

Heckel, W. (2020). *In the Path of Conquest: Resistance to Alexander the Great*. New York: Oxford University Press.

Henning, A. (2013a). *Die Turmgräber von Palmyra: Eine lokale Bauform im kaiserzeitlichen Syrien als Ausdruck kultureller Identität*. Rahden: Leidorf.

(2013b). "The Tower Tombs of Palmyra: Chronology, Architecture and Decoration." *Studia Palmyreńskie* 12: 159–76.

Heyn, M. K. (2010). "Gesture and Identity in the Funerary Art of Palmyra." *American Journal of Archaeology* 114.4: 631–61.

(2012). "Female Portraiture in Palmyra." In S. L. James and S. Dillon, eds., *A Companion to Women in the Ancient World*. Chichester: Wiley-Blackwell: 439–41.

Heyn, M. K., and Raja, R. (2019). "Male Dress Habits in Roman Period Palmyra." In M. Cifarelli, ed., *Fashioned Selves: Dress and Identity in Antiquity*. Oxford: Oxbow, 41–53.

(2021). *Individualizing the Dead: Attributes in Palmyrene Funerary Sculpture*. Studies in Palmyrene Archaeology and History 3. Turnhout: Brepols.

Hillers, D. R., and Cussini, E. (1996). *Palmyrene Aramaic Texts*. Baltimore, MD: Johns Hopkins University Press.

Hizmi, H., and De-Groot, A. (2004). *Burial Caves and Sites in Judea and Samaria: From the Bronze and Iron Ages*. Jerusalem: Israel Antiquities Authority.

Hope, V. (2009). *Roman Death: Dying and the Dead in Ancient Rome*. London: Continuum.

Houman, S. (2019). "Sépultures et reliefs sculptés dans le développement de l'architecture funéraire à Palmyre." In Eristov et al. 2019: 153–6.

Ingholt, H. (1928). *Studier over palmyrensk skulpture*. Kobenhavn: Reitzels.

(2021). *Studies on Palmyrene Sculpture: A Translation of Harald Ingholt's Studier over Palmyrensk Skulptur*; Edited and with Commentary. Ed. O. Bobou, J. V. Jensen, N. B. Kristensen, R. Raja, and R. R. Thomsen. Turnhout: Brepols.

Invernizzi, A. (2011). "Parthian Art – Arsacid Art." *Topoi Orient Occident* 17.1: 189–207.

Jacobs, B., ed. (2014). *"Parthische Kunst" – Kunst im Partherreich: Akten des Internationalen Kolloquiums in Basel, 9. Oktober 2010*. Duisburg: Wellem.

Kawami, T. S. (1987). *Monumental Art of the Parthian Period in Iran*. Leiden: Brill.

Krag, S. (2017). "Changing Identities, Changing Positions: Jewellery in Palmyrene Female Portraits." In T. Long and A. H. Sørensen, eds., *Positions and Professions in Palmyra*. Palmyrenske Studier 2. Copenhagen: Det Kongelige Danske Videnskabernes Selskab, 36–51.

(2018). *Funerary Representations of Palmyrene Women: From the First Century BC to the Third Century AD*. Studies in Classical Archaeology 3. Turnhout: Brepols.

(2019). "Palmyrene Funerary Buildings and Family Burial Patterns." In Krag and Raja 2019: 38–66.

Krag, S., and Raja, R. (2016). "Representations of Women and Children in Palmyrene Funerary Loculus Reliefs, Loculus Stelae and Wall Paintings." *Zeitschrift für Orient-Archäologie* 9: 134–78.

(2018). "Representations of Women and Children in Palmyrene Banqueting Reliefs and Sarcophagus Scenes." *Zeitschrift für Orientarchäologie* 10: 196–227.

(2019). *Women, Children and the Family in Palmyra*. Palmyrenske Studier 3. Copenhagen: Royal Danish Academy of Sciences and Letters.

Krag, S., Raja, R., and Yon, J.-B. (2019). *The Collection of Palmyrene Funerary Portraits in the Musei Vaticani: Notes and Observations*. Vatican City: Musei Vaticani.

Kropp, A. J. M., and Raja, R. (2014). "The Palmyra Portrait Project." *Syria* 91: 393–408.

Laidlaw, A. (1985). *The First Style in Pompeii: Painting and Architecture*. Rome: Bretschneider.

Le Bihan, A. (2013). "The Issue of Processional Rites in Palmyra." *Studia Palmyreńskie* 12: 235–50.

MacKenzie, D. N. (1971). *A Concise Pahlavi Dictionary*. Oxford: Oxford University Press.

Mairs, R. (2021). *The Graeco-Bactrian and Indo-Greek World*. London: Routledge.

Mathiesen, H. E. (1992). *Sculpture in the Parthian Empire: A Study in Chronology*. 2 vols. Aarhus: Aarhus University Press.

McKenzie, J. (2007). *The Architecture of Alexandria and Egypt, c. 300 B.C. to A.D. 700*. New Haven, CT: Yale University Press.

Menegazzi, R. (2014). *Seleucia al Tigri*. Vol. 1, *Le terrecotte figurate: Dagli scavi italiani e americani*. Florence: Lettere.

Montserrat, D. (1993). "The Representation of Young Males in 'Fayum Portraits.'" *Journal of Egyptian Archaeology* 79: 215–25.

Moormann, E. (2019). "The Second-Style Paintings at Oplontis." In J. R. Clarke and N. K. Muntasser, eds., *Oplontis: Villa A ("of Poppaea") at Torre Annunziata, Italy*. Vol. 2, *The Decorations: Painting, Stucco, Sculpture, Pavements*. E-book. New York: American Council of Learned Societies, chap. 2, paras. 92–152. https://hdl.handle.net/2027/heb90048.0002.001.

Nodelman, S. (1994). "How to Read a Roman Portrait." In E. D'Ambra, ed., *Roman Art in Context: An Anthology*. London: Pearson, 10–25.

Öhrman, M. (2020). "The Soundscape of Textile Work in the Roman World: Old Sources and New Methods." In K. Cooper, ed., *New Approaches to Ancient Material Culture in the Greek and Roman World*. Leiden: Brill, 183–200.

Olbrycht, M. J. (2021). *Early Arsakid Parthia (ca. 250–165 B.C.): At the Crossroads of Iranian, Hellenistic, and Central Asian History*. Leiden: Brill.

Overtoom, N. L. (2020). *Reign of Arrows: The Rise of the Parthian Empire in the Hellenistic Middle East*. New York: Oxford University Press.

Østergaard, J. S., and Sargent, M. L. (2014). "The Polychromy of a Female Late 2nd Century CE Palmyrene Funerary Portrait." In J. M. Álvarez, T. Nogales, and I. Rodà, eds., *Centro y periferia en el mundo clásico: XVIII Congreso internacional arqueología clásica/Centre and Periphery in the Ancient World: XVIIIth International Congress of Classical Archaeology*. Vol. 2. Mérida: Museo Nacional de Arte Romano, 1231–5.

Parlasca, K. (1990). "Palmyrenische Skulpturen in Museen an der amerikanischen Westküste." In M. True and G. Koch, eds., *Roman Funerary Monuments in the J. Paul Getty Museum*. Vol. 1. Malibu, CA: J. Paul Getty Museum, 133–44.

Platt, V. (2018). "Orphaned Objects: The Phenomenology of the Incomplete in Pliny's Natural History." *Art History* 41.3: 492–517.

Raja, R. (2018a). "Compilation and Digitisation of the Palmyrene Corpus of Funerary Portraits." *Antiquity* 92.365: 1–7.

(2018b). "Stacking Aesthetics in the Syrian Desert: Displaying Palmyrene Sculpture in the Public and Funerary Sphere." In C. M. Draycott, R. Raja, K. Welch, and W. T. Wooten, eds., *Visual Histories of the Classical World: Essays in Honour of R. R. R. Smith*. Turnhout: Brepols, 281–95.

(2019a). *The Palmyra Collection: Ny Carlsberg Glyptotek*. Copenhagen: Ny Carlsberg Glyptotek.

(2019b). "Reconsidering the *Dorsalium* or 'Curtain of Death' in Palmyrene Funerary Sculpture: Significance and Interpretations in Light of the

Palmyra Portrait Project Corpus." In R. Raja, ed., *Revisiting the Religious Life of Palmyra*, Contextualising the Sacred 9. Turnhout: Brepols, 67–151.

(2019c). "Family Matters: Family Constellations in Palmyrene Funerary Sculpture." In K. B. Johannsen and J. H. Petersen, eds., *Family Lives: Aspects of Life and Death in Ancient Families*, Acta Hyperborea 15. Copenhagen: Museum Tusculanum Press, 245–70.

Raja, R., Steding, J., and Yon, J.-B., eds. (2021). *Excavating Palymyra: Harald Ingholt's Excavation Diaries: A Transcript*. 2 vols. Studies in Palmyrene Archaeology and History 4. Turnhout: Brepols.

Raja, R., and Sørensen, A. H. (2015a). *Harald Ingholt & Palmyra*. Aarhus: Fællestrykkeriet Aarhus Universitet.

(2015b). "The 'Beauty of Palmyra' and Qasr Abjad (Palmyra): New Discoveries in the Archive of Harald Ingholt." *Journal of Roman Archaeology* 28.1: 439–50.

Root, M. C. (1981). "A Funerary Relief Bust from Palmyra." *Bulletin: Museums of Art and Archaeology, The University of Michigan* 4: 1–12.

Rostovtzeff, M. I. (1935). *Dura and the Problem of Parthian Art*. New Haven, CT: Yale University Press.

Sadurska, A., and Bounni, A. (1994). *Les sculptures funéraires de Palmyre*. Rome: Bretschneider.

Schlude, J. M. (2020). *Rome, Parthia, and the Politics of Peace: The Origins of War in the Ancient Middle East*. (London: Routledge, 2020.

Schlumberger, D. (1960). *Descendants non-méditerranéens de l'art grec*. Paris: Geuthner.

Schmidt-Colinet, A., al-Asʿad, K., and Müting-Zimmer, C. (1992). *Das Tempelgrab Nr. 36 in Palmyra: Studien zur palmyrenischen Grabarchitektur und ihrer Asstattung*. Mainz: von Zabern.

Scott, S., and Webster, J. (2003). *Roman Imperialism and Provincial Art*. New York: Cambridge University Press.

Shifman, I. S. (2014). *The Palmyrene Tax Tariff*. Oxford: Oxford University Press.

Smith, A. M., II, (2013). *Roman Palmyra: Identity, Community, and State Formation*. New York: Oxford University Press.

Sørensen, A. H. (2014). "Revisiting a Painted Tomb in Palmyra." In J. M. Álvarez, T. Nogales, and I. Rodà, eds., *Centro y periferia en el mundo clásico: XVIII Congreso internacional arqueología clásica / Centre and Periphery in the Ancient World: Proceedings of the XVIIIth International Congress of Classical Archaeology*. Vol. 2. Mérida: Museo Nacional de Arte Romano, 1227–30.

(2016). "Palmyrene Tomb Paintings in Context." In R. Raja and A. Kropp, eds., *The World of Palmyra. Palmyrene Studies 1*. Copenhagen: Royal Danish Academy of Sciences and Letters, 103–17.

(2017). "Palmyra's Colourful Past: Murals for the Dead." In R. Raja, ed., *Palmyra: Pearl of the Desert*. Aarhus: SUN-TRYK, Aarhus Universitet, 87–93.

Stewart, P. (2003). *Statues in Roman Society: Representation and Response*. Oxford: Oxford University Press.

Stucky, R. A., and Aitken, I. (2018). "Fouilles suisses du sanctuaire de Baalshamîn à Palmyre: Le passé confronté au présent et at à l'avenir." *Antike Kunst* 61: 63–72.

Thomsen, R. R. (2021). "Unlocking a Mystery? The Keys in Palmyrene Funerary Portraiture." In Heyn and Raja 2021: 51–62.

Toynbee, J. M. C. (1971). *Death and Burial in the Roman World*. Baltimore, MD: Johns Hopkins University Press.

van Wijlick, H. A. M. (2021). *Rome and the Near Eastern Kingdoms and Principalities, 44–31 BC: A Study of Political Relations during Civil War*. Leiden: Brill.

Vandorpe, K. (1995). *Breaking the Seal of Secrecy: Sealing-Practices in Greco-Roman and Byzantine Egypt Based on Greek, Demotic and Latin Papyrological Evidence*. Leiden: Papyrologisch Instituut.

Woltering, R. A. F. L. (2014). "Zenobia or al-Zabbāʾ: The Modern Arab Literary Reception of the Palmyran Protagonist." *Middle Eastern Literatures* 17.1: 25–42.

Wood, R. (1753). *The Ruins of Palmyra, Otherwise Tedmor, in the Desert*. London: Wood.

Yon, J.-B. (2013). "L'épigraphie palmyrénienne depuis *PAT*, 1996–2011." *Studia Palmyreńskie* 12: 333–79.

10 Relief on and for the Body in Late Antique Numismatic Jewelry

ASHLEY ELIZABETH JONES

Among certain classes and categories of people, the late Roman world was awash in gold.[1] From the fourth century CE, gold coins were minted in extraordinary numbers. They were distributed by the imperial court to civil and military officials on imperial birthdays and anniversaries, at the new year, and on other special occasions.[2] The portrait of the emperor on coins was one of the most widespread and literal images of the power of the Roman state as embodied in the person of the emperor.[3] Belief in the numismatic imperial portrait as not only an image of power but also a powerful image prompted some recipients of the emperor's largesse to memorialize these gifts by mounting them to be worn as jewelry that could act as amulets. Nearly 400 gold and silver coins that have been framed or otherwise set in jewelry survive from the Roman and late antique periods. The majority of such objects consists of gold coins in gold frames, though a few framed silver and bronze coins – sometimes covered with gold foil – exist as well. The coins are almost invariably set so that the obverse, the side containing the imperial portrait, faces out from the body of the wearer. This chapter will argue that the overall relief effect of this ensemble – both the planes of relief of the imperial portrait emerging from the face of a coin and the framed coin projecting from the breast of a wearer – plays a significant role in visually and spatially articulating the intercessory potential of such objects.

A substantial gold breast ornament now in Berlin, one of a matched pair said to come from Egypt and rich with rounded, projecting textures, is a veritable study in relief (Fig. 10.1a–b). A kind of golden cloud, its contours are determined by the rounded edges of framed coins that bubble forth from a semicircular torc. The small gold coins, their settings projecting from a background of granulated rosettes, converge on a larger

[1] See e.g. Brown 2012: 3–30.

[2] The literature on gold and silver coinage and imperial donatives is expansive. Bastien 1988 is the fundamental work. More recently, see Lo Cascio 2008; Carlà 2009.

[3] On the significance of the imperial image see, very selectively, Belting 1994: 102–14; Stewart 2006; Fejfer 2008: 407–26; Elsner 2018: 50–59. In general, on the efficacy of material images in the ancient world, see e.g. Faraone 1992; Bussels 2012.

(a) (b)

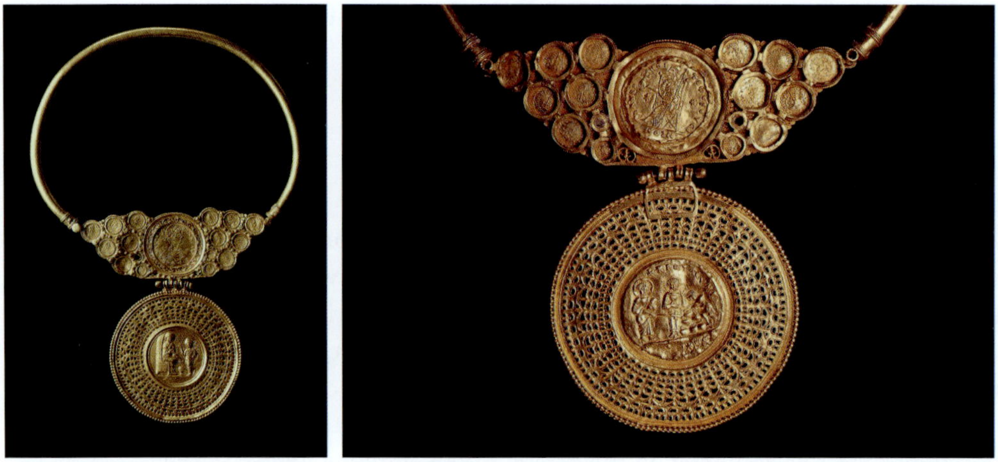

Fig. 10.1a–b Pectoral with coins, pseudomedallion, and pendant with the Annunciation (obverse) and Wedding at Cana (reverse), sixth century CE, said to be from the Assiût Treasure. Gold. Berlin, Antikensammlung, 30219, 506 (Staatliche Museen zu Berlin, Antikensammlung/CC BY-SA 4.0).

central medallion. That medallion, framed with a deep, scrolling filigree border, is anchored by the profile bust of a draped and diademed Roman emperor. The contours of the figure's head, shoulders, and garments follow the circular curve of the medallion. His large eye and aquiline nose, and the flick of his diadem's ribbon draw the viewer's eye to the inscription that also follows the medallion's curves. Prominently framed and emerging in relief out of the textured gold, the imperial medallion portrait and its legend are the central focus of the piece, but they support an even larger element, in turn, a pendant medallion set in a wide, openwork frame. The pendant's image, a scene of the Annunciation, is even more deeply articulated and appeals directly to the Christian divinity. The overall effect of the Berlin pectoral, then, is a literal and metaphorical hierarchy of potent images – small coins, imperial medallion, Marian medallion – that project forward from and indeed shield the breast of a wearer, both visually relieving the plane of the human body and offering metaphysical relief for that body and the soul it housed. Multiple senses of relief, accordingly, are at play in the pectoral's function as a wearable art object. This kind of coin-set jewelry, moreover, was produced and reproduced according to a logic of typology which, as Verity Platt's chapter in this volume (Chapter 1) demonstrates, was central to antiquity's conception of relief as an artistic phenomenon.

The mounting of coins in jewelry attests to enduring belief in the imperial portrait and in the coin form as not just an image of power and a means of exchange but also as beneficial signs that could confer protection on the bodies of their wearers. Patrons and goldsmiths could also copy or mimic coins for jewelry, not as false currency but as efficacious amulets. On some examples of coin-set jewelry the inherent power of the imperial image could be augmented by other religious or magical iconography, as well as by prophylactic inscriptions and signs. Genuine numismatic jewelry, moreover, was often imbricated with other coin-like or medallion-like objects – which not only directly copied coins but also offered a dramatically expanded range of images and texts – as on the pectoral in Berlin (see Fig. 10.1a–b).[4] The central element of the pectoral is set with fourteen genuine gold coins, but the larger imperial image they surround is a pseudomedallion, an imitation produced by a goldsmith and not by the imperial mint.[5] The coins are tremisses, small coins minted at one third of the weight of a standard solidus. The pseudomedallion, in contrast, is constructed to visually imitate a monetary medallion, a larger object struck by the imperial mint in a weight corresponding to a multiple of the solidus.[6] The pseudomedallion is two-sided, in a close formal evocation of a genuine monetary (or "multiple") medallion, but it is made of two thin, embossed gold disks separated and reinforced by a gesso core. It is imperial in style, and both its obverse portrait and its reverse image of an enthroned personification of Roma or Constantinopolis are taken from common coin types, but its "portrait" does not depict an identifiable emperor.[7] The implication is that the imperial image encased in numismatic jewelry could be generic rather than specific, evoking an image of power that may or may not have been understood as congruent with the person of any specific emperor.

[4] Dennison 1918. This and other Christian breast ornaments discussed in this chapter have frequently been referred to in the literature as *enkolpia*. I deliberately avoid the term, which Ivan Drpić (2018) has conclusively demonstrated was not used in the pre-Iconoclastic period.

[5] Ogden 1990: 202–3, fig. 366, describes a third, similar pectoral, unpublished and in a private collection. On the so-called Assiût Treasure, see Williams 2014.

[6] The fundamental work on Roman medallions remains Toynbee 1986 (originally published 1944). More recently, up to the Severan period, see Mittag 2010, 2019; Lorenz 2020.

[7] The combination of profile portrait and profile image of Constantinopolis is unusual. The obverse, diademed profile portrait resembles types of the Valentinianic and Theodosian dynasties that span the mid fourth to mid fifth centuries CE. But the reverse image is most closely related to issues of Theodosius II (r. 408–50), in which a profile, enthroned Constantinopolis holding a cross-surmounted globe is paired with a frontal, helmeted portrait type (cf. *RIC* X, no. 285). Toynbee (1940: 10–13) published a 4 1/2 solidus medallion that she attributed to Theodosius I (r. 379–95) with a similar reverse type but with the more traditional victory-surmounted globe.

The emperor is not the only authority to whom the pectoral appeals, however, as a small inscription decorates one of the gold disks between the coins:

Φ
ΖΩΗ
C

This is an acrostic, the words "life" and "light" arranged in the shape of a cross, referring to the biblical verse John 1:4: "In him was life; and the life was the light of men."[8] And on the pseudomedallion, we find a legend in Greek repeated on both sides: *KY*[*ριε*] *BOHΘ*[*ε*]*I TE ΦOPOYCA*[*ι*], meaning "Lord, aid the [female] wearer."[9] The inscription makes explicit that the layered relief of the ornament is designed to bring relief in the nonartistic sense – relief from pain, illness, misfortune – to the body of the woman who wears it. The "Lord" to whom the inscription addresses itself is surely the Christian God, a point confirmed by the pectoral's final element, its non-monetary medallion-like pendant. This pendant is also two-sided and has been constructed in a similar manner to the pseudomedallion, but its imagery is drawn from the stories of the New Testament rather than from a traditional imperial repertoire. The obverse scene is an Annunciation. Mary sits on a wicker throne on the left, confronted by the angel Gabriel, who approaches from the right, without a legend or inscription. The reverse depicts the miracle at the wedding at Cana: Christ approaches from the left extending a cross-headed staff over six jars, observed by two other figures. A legend reads, *†ΠPΩTA CYMIWN †*, which must mean "first of the signs," referring to Cana as the first of Christ's miracles (John 2:11).[10] The double-sided nature of the pendant suggests that there is something in the medium of the coin or medallion, in its roundness, its goldness, its two-sidedness, that adds to the protective or auspicious character of the texts and images carried on it. The fact that the reverse image of the pendant, the wedding at Cana and its inscription, as well as the reverse images of all the coins and the coin-like pseudomedallion, would have been hidden against breast of the wearer and not in direct communication with any possible viewer suggests that the pectoral also addresses itself to an unseen world.

One of the questions raised by the overall program of the Berlin pectoral, an object designed not just for luxury and display but also for the protection of its

[8] Dennison 1918: 126.

[9] The coins the pseudomedallion imitates would have had Latin legends. On the language of Byzantine coin legends, see Grierson 1999: 38.

[10] Dennison 1918: 127–35.

female wearer, is for what occasion such a large, complex, multilayered ornament might have been commissioned. We know that it was made for a woman. We know that the traditionally powerful image of the imperial portrait was augmented with inscriptions and with Christian images. In such a carefully composed object, the theme(s) of those latter images must have been thoughtfully chosen. Though it may not be immediately obvious, the theme of the Berlin pectoral seems to be marriage. Specifically, the object thematizes a marriage undertaken under the authority and protection of the Christian Lord and in anticipation of a fertile union. The Virgin, here, acts as both intercessor and model for the wearer, and the pectoral may have been a bridal gift, as were more straightforward early Byzantine marriage rings and belts.[11]

A small, round plaque in the Museo Arqueológico Nacional in Madrid depicts a scene that is similar in style, if more crudely done, to the Berlin pendant (Fig. 10.2).[12] The plaque was discovered in Turuñuelo, Medellin, near Badajoz, Spain, and is dated to the late sixth or early seventh century CE.

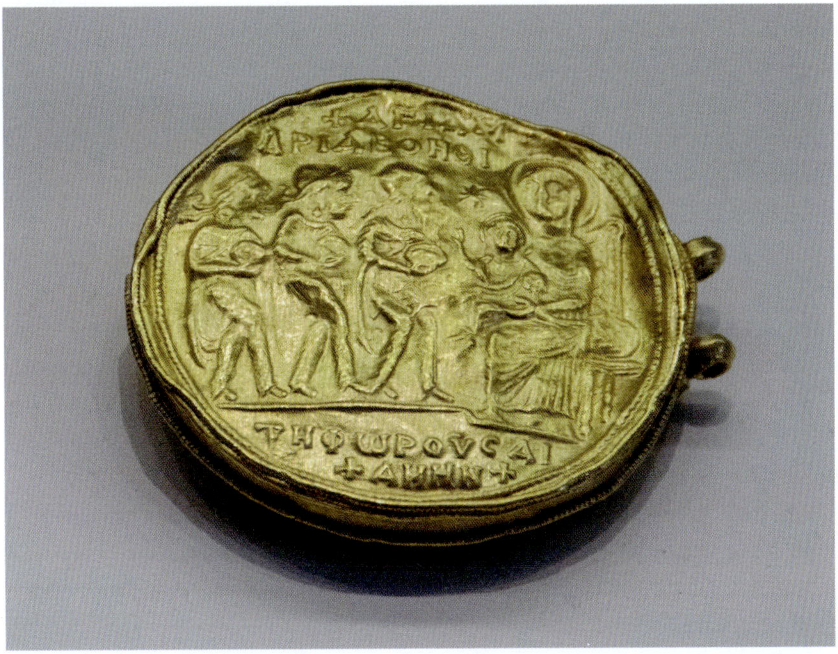

Fig. 10.2 Gold fibula with Adoration of the Magi, sixth century CE, from Turuñuelo. Madrid, Museo Arqueológico, 1963/56/1 (photograph by Ángel M. Felicísimo/CC BY 2.0).

[11] Compare Vikan 1990. [12] Balmaseda Muncharaz 2009: 25–6, with preceding bibliography.

Remains of a catch on the reverse indicate its use as a fibula; its Greek inscriptions suggests that it, or at least its prototype, may have been originally manufactured in the Greek-speaking East. The plaque depicts the Adoration of the Magi. The Virgin is seated on a throne at right – some barely perceptible detail behind her left shoulder suggests that it may be wicker, like the throne in the Berlin Annunciation. She holds on her lap the Child, who sits upright and raises his right hand in blessing. A small, eight-pointed star floats above the child's head. The three magi approach from the left. They wear caps and trousers indicating their origin in the East and carry gifts. An inscription, running above the scene and in the exergue, reads: † *ΑΓΙΑ / ΜΑΡΙΑ ΒΟΗΘΙ-/ ΤΗ ΦΩΡΟΥΣΑΙ /†ΑΜΗΝ†* ("Holy Mary, protect the [female] wearer, Amen"). The Adoration, like the Annunciation, is an easily legible scene that potently symbolizes Mary's role as mother. The inscription makes explicit the plaque's value as an amulet that invokes the protection of the Virgin, protection that would have been especially needed during pregnancy and childbirth. The gold material and round format of the plaque serve to augment its amuletic value, while the physical immediacy of image and inscription, placed in a direct relationship with the wearer's body, can only be understood to increase their potency, directing the object of prayer directly to the petitioning subject. I would like to propose that a similar, though less explicit, mechanism must be at work in the Berlin Annunciation. The Berlin pectoral can be read as simultaneously protective and commemorative, recalling a marriage undertaken according to the Christian rites and invoking the blessings of the Virgin and the protection of God the Father on the wearer. A multilayered object, it also employs with equal deliberateness traditional imperial imagery, its invocation to God the Father wrapping around the image of the emperor. The abstract, which is to say, nonspecific, imperial portrait here becomes just one of a range of protective or beneficial words and images that, arrayed on the pectoral, stand between the wearer and the potentially malevolent seen and unseen forces of the world.

Created by a host of metalworking techniques, including granulation, embossing, repoussé, chasing, and, in the case of the coins, striking from official mint dies, the Berlin pectoral presents a compendium of late antique relief sculpture designed to be worn on the body, which also seeks aid, succor, or indeed relief for that selfsame body. Starting from the issues raised by the object in Berlin, this chapter examines a set of late antique wearable objects that invoke aid for the wearer. These objects include marriage jewelry, religious pendants and plaques, and magical amulets and gems but revolve both thematically and formally around numismatic jewelry – officially issued coins and medallions struck to weights that are multiples of standard coins – set into frames designed to be worn on the body. This chapter expands this volume's discussion of relief temporally and thematically by pushing forward into late antiquity, from the third through seventh centuries CE, and by focusing on a particular typological model of relief: that of struck coins and medals. Authoritative by virtue of its official issue from dies produced by imperial craftsmen, its precious gold materiality, and its close association with the imperial image, the coin or multiple medallion also becomes a model for personal, amuletic objects that evoke protection for their wearers. This act of modeling, as this chapter explores, could be very direct – as some amuletic objects were neither struck nor cast but made either by pressing gold foil into imperial die or by direct or indirect impressions from the medallions themselves. But it was also more broadly typological, and this chapter will conclude by examining some of the semiotic mechanisms by which objects worn or carried on the body could exert a protective force by word, iconography, and materiality.

Protecting the Wearer

The phrase "help/aid/succor/protect the wearer" appears on a wide array of apotropaic and amuletic objects from the late antique Mediterranean meant to be worn or carried on the body. According to Annewies van den Hoeck, Denis Feissel, and John J. Hermann, inscriptions aimed at guarding an often unnamed, but typically masculine gendered wearer first appear in the archaeological record of the ancient Mediterranean in the third century CE, and the formula continues to be used, with variations, on a variety of objects into the seventh century, a period that corresponds exactly with the phenomenon of setting gold coins in jewelry.[13] Particularly in later centuries, a power is directly called upon; often the *kyrie* ("Lord"), a clear reference to the Judeo-Christian God, but also when on coin amulets perhaps a gesture toward the powers of the emperor. Equally or more frequently, however, the *Theotokos* ("God-bearer") is invoked, either explicitly as God-bearer or sometimes as *Hagia Maria* ("Holy Mary"), as on the fibula now in Madrid with the Adoration of the Magi (see Fig 10.2). These objects, found throughout the Mediterranean and Europe, are invariably captioned in Greek, which may imply a material origin in the Eastern Mediterranean but which is also consistent with the use of Greek as the

[13] Van den Hoeck, Feissel, and Herrmann 1994, 2015. Foskolou (2014: 347) also affirms the significance of the anonymity usually afforded to the "wearer" in such inscriptions.

primary language of magical objects.[14] When inscribed on coins and coin-like objects, the invocations of aid or protection lend a degree of explicitness to the objects' function that can otherwise only be inferred and situate coin ornaments within a broad koine of late antique material culture. This chapter will first explore some of the links among these diverse objects, paying attention to their status as relief and the processes by which they were made, before turning to a semiotic reading of their animating underlying principles. An investigation of the ways in which numismatic jewelry parallels and departs from other forms of protective wearables illuminates not only the power imputed to coins but also the mechanisms by which amulets functioned more generally in late antique society.[15]

This chapter considers a variety of strands of a web in which different forms of magical or efficacious material culture were enmeshed across the Mediterranean and Europe and throughout late antiquity. These strands include similarities of language, of iconography, and of materiality.[16] The web itself, I argue, can be understood as the fundamental magical thinking that underlay the construction or, to borrow the phrase of Árpád Nagy, the "*engineering*" of efficacious, wearable objects.[17] Part of that engineering, I will argue, lay in the typological power of the coin or medallion itself, both in instantiating the image of the emperor as type and in the technological chain of the transmission of texts and images in relief. As mentioned, Platt's contribution to this volume demonstrates that the typological language of modeling and molding was crucial to ancient conceptions of what we now call relief. As Platt argues, the idea of the type, or *typos*, is both a product, the raised relief, and a process, the act of stamping or molding. This idea connects relief-work with consistent and authoritative chains of transmission; through the language of *glyptike*, or cutting intaglio gems which were used to impress seals, it is also connected to stone carving. As we will see, the creation of coin and coin-like objects maps quite closely onto the logic of typology. The production of coins and medallions operates according to similar principles of molding

14 See Kotansky 2019: 539, with further bibliography.

15 I am grateful to Ittai Weinryb for pushing me to consider the "wearable" as an ontological category.

16 Text, image, and medium are also identified in Faraone 2012 as the crucial components of magical gems.

17 Nagy 2015: 205 (emphasis mine). Nagy's phrase also felicitously (if perhaps unconsciously) evokes Gell's (1994) "technology of enchantment." This chapter builds on a significant body of recent work on ancient magic, including Collins 2008; Bąkowska-Czerner, Roccati, and Świerzowska 2015; Boschung and Bremmer 2015; Collins 2015; Faraone 2018; Kiyanrad, Theis, and Willer 2018; Parker and McKie 2018; Edmonds 2019; Endreffy, Nagy, and Spier 2019; Frankfurter 2019; Watson 2019; Mastrocinque, Sanzo, and Scapini 2020; Nikki and Valkama 2021.

and stamping, and we may note that the artists responsible for creating the matrices, known as dies, from which coins were struck, may also have been gem carvers. The image on a coin is known in numismatics as a "type," but each type could itself be serially produced, with artists of the mint called upon to carve new dies – which, like gems, were engraved by hand – to replace those broken through the forces of repeated use.[18] A coin or multiple monetary medallion would be created at an imperial mint by sandwiching a metal blank between two dies and striking it with significant force. This act would squeeze the metal of the blank into the negative space of the dies and create a round, two-sided object with raised relief decoration.[19] The use of the die and replicability of the process guaranteed both the officialness of the issue and the consistency of its relief decoration. Gold coinage, in particular, was tightly controlled throughout the late antique period and, from at least the later fourth century CE, produced exclusively in the imperial palace rather than the public mints.[20]

The typology explored here is more than just the literal creation of standardized images, or serial impressions, however; it is also a figurative association between both concepts and forms that permits connections across time and space. This kind of association, on the one hand, has deep roots in Roman practices of exemplary thinking.[21] And the typology of (pre)figuration achieved new prominence and importance in the Christian era, when thinkers sought to establish means of connecting not only Old and New Testament but of putting contemporary, secular time into rhythm with sacred time.[22] While figurative typology had long been a facet of ancient images, it became a particularly important mode of reference for Christian art, which consistently had to navigate anxieties about images and create authoritative connections to a sacred past.[23] The varieties of typology examined here span this spectrum. On the one hand, they are connected to modes of production, as nonofficial versions of coins and medallions could be made by pressing gold onto existing issues or into molds created from those issues, as well as through the adoption of the format, iconography, and language of the mint. But they are also thematic in nature, and, I will argue, the relation between imperial and Christian imagery, written invocations for aid, and the amuletic function of gold worn on the body can also be understood as a kind of typology,

[18] Metcalf 2012: 4–5. [19] For an illustration of the process, Metcalf 2012: 6, fig. 0.1.
[20] Moorhead 2012: 603. [21] See e.g. Langlands 2018; Roller 2018.
[22] Auerbach 1959; cf. Porter 2017.
[23] For the former, see Holliday 1995; for the latter, see Krautheimer 1942; Nagel and Wood 2010: 30, 46–7.

forming a network of words, images, and materialities of objects worn or carried on the body in order exert a protective force. This network of relations, ultimately, connects the objects examined here to a much broader web of relief practices, habits of adornment, and modes of belief.

Apotropaic Words and Images

The explicit amplification of the amuletic power of the numismatic form by epigraphic invocations is highlighted by a humble example. A bronze follis of Justinian I in the collection of Simon Bendall is pierced at twelve o'clock, above the emperor's portrait, presumably to be worn as a pendant, and inscribed by hand around its border: *KE BOEΘI TON ΘOPYNTA* ("Lord, help the [male] wearer").[24] The form of the coin and the head of the emperor are activated by the inscription, which, unusually for a pendant like this, refers to the wearer in the masculine gender.[25] Pierced, mounted, and inscribed coins, many or most of which were probably worn by women, existed among a range of material culture. And such invocations of aid could be found on a wide range of wearable objects, including, for example, early Byzantine marriage rings.[26] The heterogeneous imagery and language of these objects, as well as the sometimes wildly differing media and artisanal skill with which they are composed – and therefore the differing values that have been assigned to them monetarily and art historically – have traditionally impeded their being read alongside one another.[27]

A plea for help, as well as an invocation of peace, can be found on a pendant now in the British Museum (Fig. 10.3a–b). This piece, like the pendant in Berlin, consists of two embossed plaques mounted back to back and fitted with a gold frame and suspension loop. Its obverse depicts the visit of the magi, led

[24] Morisson and Bendall (2012: 221) suggest the coin must have been pierced and inscribed not long after its minting, after 538 CE. They read XE BOETHI TON PHORVNTA. Fulghum (2001: 140) reads KE BOETHI TON PHORINTA. I am inclined to follow Fulghum's reasoning for preferring KE for Kyrie over XE for Christos but read PHORVNTA over PHORINTA.

[25] Most inscriptions referring to wearers are in the masculine gender, but they are found almost exclusively on rings or stones that were likely set in rings, the type of jewelry most commonly worn by men. See van den Hoeck, Feissel, and Herrmann 1994, 2015.

[26] Betrothal or wedding rings may have been more likely to be worn by women than the inscribed rings mentioned earlier in this chapter. See Walker 2002.

[27] This academic siloing has broken down in recent years, with, among others, Entwistle 2005 reading Christian and "pagan" gold, nummiform pendants in parallel; Walker 2010 locating the conventional iconography of marriage jewelry in numismatic sources; and Nesbitt 2016 examining formulae from magical gems on Byzantine lead seals. For a succinct analysis of the socioeconomic diffusion of an "imperial" ornament, the disk fibula, see Corrado and Gentile 2005–6: 19n2.

(a) (b)

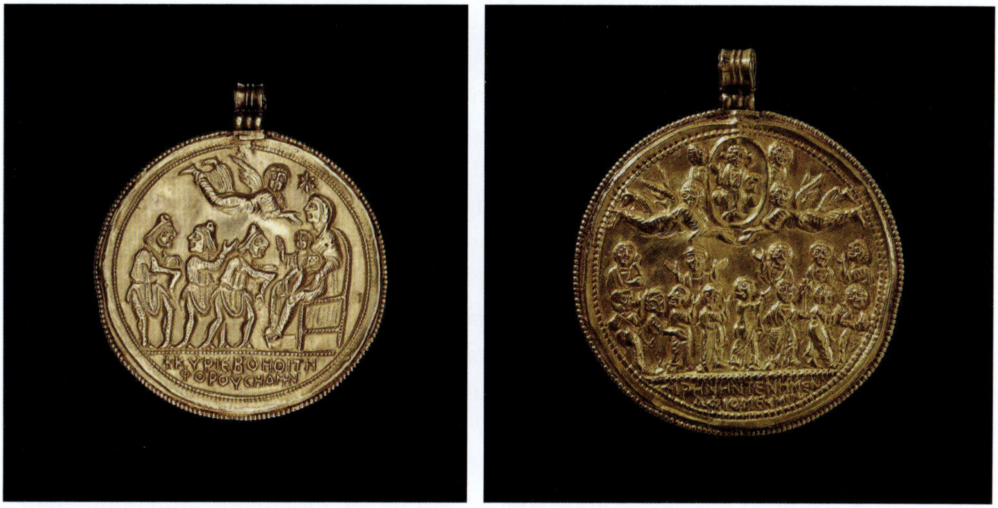

Fig. 10.3a–b Gold medallion formed from two embossed discs, with the Adoration of the Magi (obverse) and the Ascension (reverse), sixth century CE. London, British Museum, 1983,0704.1 (© The Trustees of the British Museum).

by a star and heralded by an angel (see Fig. 10.3a). Bearing gifts, they approach the Virgin and Child from the left, gesturing and seeming to speak to one another. The pendant is reminiscent of but not perfectly matched to the Madrid fibula discussed earlier in this chapter (see Fig. 10.2). The wise men are arrayed in generically Persianizing dress. Mother and child are seated on a high-backed wicker throne that resembles the throne in the Berlin Annunciation scene. The inscription on the obverse reads: *ΚΥΡΙΕ ΒΟΕΘΙ ΤΕ ΦΟΡΟΥϹ ΑΜΗΝ* ("Lord, help the [female] wearer, Amen"). On the reverse, we find a depiction of the Ascension, with Christ in a mandorla borne by angels as his disciples stand in wonder below (see Fig. 10.3b).[28] Its exergue contains a quotation from John 14:27: *ΕΙΡΗΝΗΝ ΤΕΝ ΗΜΕΝ/ΑΦΙΟΜΕ ΥΜΙΝ* ("My peace I leave with you"). Both the thematics of the London pendant and its relation to official imagery are difficult to unpack. The two paired inscriptions parallel those appearing on an early Byzantine marriage ring that also contains miniature scenes from the life of Christ, including the Annunciation and Nativity.[29] On the face of the ring are depicted the bride and groom, Peter and Theodote, crowned by Jesus and Mary. In her work on Byzantine marriage

[28] Kateusz 2015 has persuasively argued that this particular iconography – of orant Mary among the apostles, including Paul – originally represented the Ascension of Mary but was subsequently interpreted as and used for the Ascension of Jesus. Compare Kantorowicz 1944.

[29] Washington, DC, Dumbarton Oaks, BZ.1947.15; Bühl 2008: 124–5.

jewelry, Alicia Walker has argued that images depicting one or both of the couple crowned may well have been produced as *largitio*, in parallel with official coin issues depicting imperial marriages, to be distributed as gifts of slightly lesser quality and value.[30] In the early Byzantine period, the succession was often legitimated through the female line, perhaps prompting the increased prominence of nuptial imagery on official coin issues and a parallel increase in other marriage-themed imperial gifts.[31]

It may be equally plausible, however, that aspects of the Madrid fibula, the London pendant, and the Berlin pectoral are first- or second-degree copies of images produced by the imperial mint, adopted and adapted for private purposes.[32] In 1957, Marvin Ross identified an elaborate medallion with Christological scenes in the Dumbarton Oaks Collection, known as the Epiphany Medallion and said to have been found in Cyprus, as an official issue of the imperial mint (Fig. 10.4a–b).[33]A few years later, Philip Grierson solidified this assertion by contextualizing the medallion and pinpointing its production to mark the occasion of the baptism of Theodosius, son of Maurice, the first *porphyrogenitos* in more than a century, on the Feast of the Epiphany in 584.[34] The work of Ross and Grierson lifted the Dumbarton Oaks Epiphany Medallion from the realm of pre-Iconoclastic, private devotional objects and transported it to the realm of imperial coins and gifts. Grierson argued, in effect, that the tradition of large format medallions created for presentation on significant imperial occasions and found most frequently in gold in the third and fourth centuries continued into the later sixth century but was transformed via a new metaphorical language of Christian imagery.[35] The medallion commemorates the imperial birth and baptism through an image of the enthroned Virgin and Child between two angels on its obverse, underpinned by miniature scenes of the Nativity and Adoration, and that of the Baptism of Jesus on its reverse.

The only other officially minted, struck medallion with Christian imagery to survive depicts the Annunciation on its obverse, above smaller scenes of the Visitation and the Nativity, and the Ascension on its reverse (hereafter referred to as the Annunciation Medallion). Not illustrated here but known from the art

[30] Walker 2010. On crowning in early Byzantine marriage rites, see Radle 2012; Biliarsky 2015.

[31] Brubaker and Tobler 2002; Biliarsky 2014.

[32] This is the conclusion largely reached by Stolz (2009), although the piece she discusses may be a prominent exception (see discussion of the "Munich medallion" later in this chapter).

[33] It had previously been believed to be cast rather than struck, and therefore not a product of the imperial mint. See Ross 1957.

[34] Grierson 1961.

[35] A parallel to this use of biblical stories as imperial metaphor is the David Plates. Compare Leader-Newby 2000.

(a) (b)

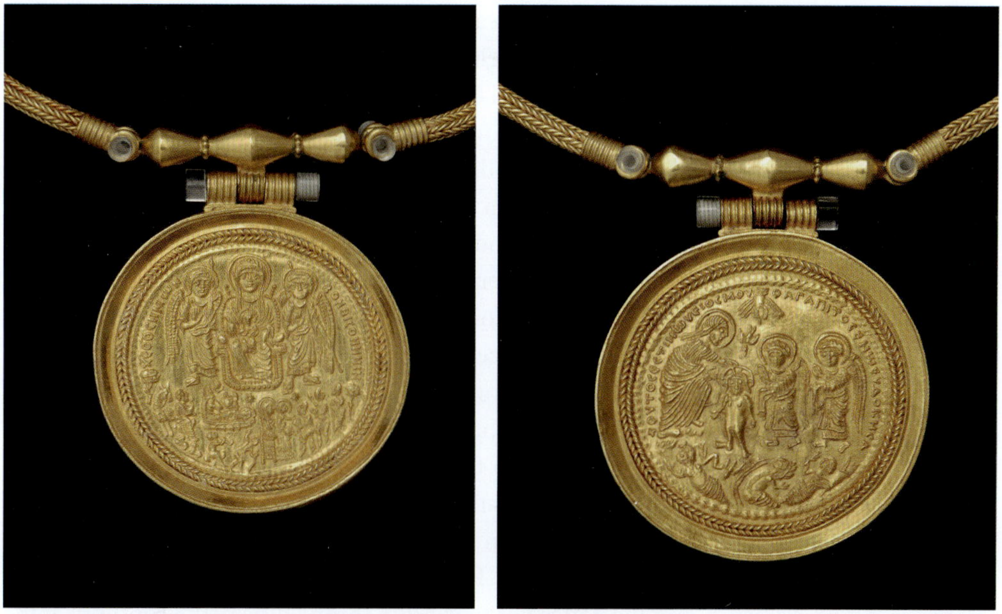

Fig. 10.4a–b Pendant gold medallion, known as the Epiphany Medallion, with the Baptism of Christ (reverse) and the Enthroned Virgin, Nativity, and Adoration (obverse), sixth century CE. Washington, DC, Dumbarton Oaks, Byzantine Collection, BZ.1955.10.1 (© Dumbarton Oaks, Byzantine Collection, Washington, DC).

market, it has previously been published and discussed in relation to the examples just provided.[36] Michael Metlich organized this struck medallion into a hypothetical series with the Dumbarton Oaks Epiphany Medallion, together with the London and Berlin pendants, of commemorative imperial issues that follow a Christological logic and span the sixth century. His series proceeds from Annunciation to Visitation, Nativity, Epiphany, Baptism of Jesus, Miracle at Cana, and finally Ascension. The theological organization is clear, but Metlich's seriation not only mingles the two struck medallic examples with copies or echoes produced with other techniques; it also regularly separates obverse type from reverse, which defies the existing material record and the established logic of die links. But in its complexity, Metlich's scheme reveals the entangledness of the web of objects, which are tightly related in their iconography and inscriptions but divided by geography and the technique and quality of their production.

[36] Metlich 2003; Gemini Numismatic Auctions 2009, 2011; Roma Numismatics Auction 2014; Iannascoli 2021. Metlich's description of it as two struck, uniface medallions joined together is not supported by the auction listings.

The corpus of late Roman and early Byzantine cast, embossed, and repoussé medallions and bracteates with Christian images is implicated in the history of numismatic jewelry not just by their round and sometimes biface form and their occasional direct association with coin and pseudocoin ornaments but also as pseudomedallic objects in their own right. The invocations of protection we find on the Berlin, Madrid, and London objects, however, distinguish them from the legends on struck examples, which are limited to liturgical phrases and biblical quotations – themselves distinct from standard numismatic legends and inscribed in the Greek of the New Testament rather than the Latin of the imperial mint – although these too could carry an apotropaic force. The amuletic inscriptions on the Berlin pectoral and related objects amplify the already potent amalgamation of imperial and Christian power that the officially minted objects possess.

Accordingly, we might see in the London pendant (see Fig. 10.3a) not the ghost of a missing piece in a putative imperial series, but rather a fairly close, if enlarged, copy of the Adoration scene from the exergue of the Dumbarton Oaks Epiphany Medallion (see Fig. 10.4a). While it lacks the nimbi of the official issue, and the pattern of the wicker throne differs, the contours of the faces of the magi, their gestures, and the lines of their drapery map closely onto that element of the official issue. The Madrid fibula, with the magi in different proportions and postures, may be a more distant echo (see Fig. 10.2). Similarly, the Ascension on the reverse of the London pendant (see Fig. 10.3b) copies closely but not perfectly the reverse of the Annunciation Medallion. An even closer connection can be observed, however, between the same scene and a now lost medallion. Seventeenth-century drawings of what are presumed to be the two faces of the lost medallion, depicting the Flight into Egypt and the Ascension, were preserved in the so-called Paper Museum of Cassiano del Pozzo and are now in the British Royal Collection. No legends are recorded in the drawings, though the space where they would appear is blank, and it is impossible to say whether the two depictions represent a multiple medallion struck at the imperial mint, or whether they represent a direct copy in thinner gold.[37] Apart from a few missing or misunderstood details – Peter's cross, Mary's veil, Paul's beard – the reverse of the lost medallion appears to have been identical to the reverse of the Annunciation Medallion. That the drawing may represent something other than another medallion struck from the same die is attested by a frequently published pendant now in the Diözesanmuseum Freising in Munich (Fig. 10.5a–b). The latter, at less than half the weight of the

[37] Osborne and Claridge 1998: 258–9, no. 284. The inventory seems to record that the original object was gold and possibly found in the vicinity of Rome. See Entwistle 2005: 270n8.

(a)

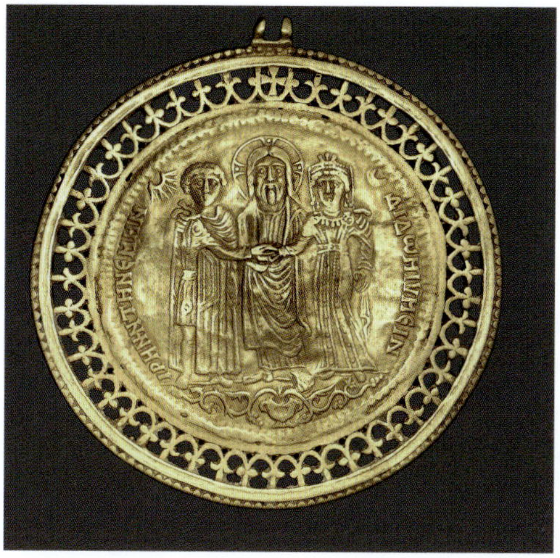

(b)

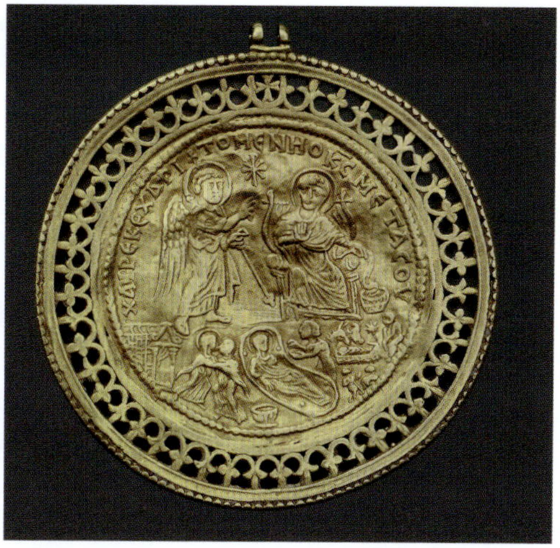

Fig. 10.5a–b Pressed gold medallion, with the Annunciation (obverse) and the Imperial Marriage (reverse), fifth–sixth century CE (© Diözesanmuseum Freising. Photograph by highresobjects).

struck examples, consists of two thin, embossed gold disks. The obverse of the Munich medallion (see Fig. 10.5a) seems to have been made by pressing gold foil directly into the very same die that created the struck obverse of the Annunciation Medallion.[38] Its reverse, a corresponding die for which is not known from any surviving struck examples, depicts a scene of the *dextrarum iunctio* that may commemorate an imperial marriage: of Ariadne to Zeno (466/7 CE) or to Anastasius I (491); or of one of the daughters of Tiberius II Constantine, Constantina and Charito, to Maurice and Germanus, respectively, in 582 (see Fig. 10.5b).[39]

The Munich medallion is said to have been found in northern Sardinia.[40] It may represent an example of a mass-produced, less-valuable imperial gift, as per Walker, created in tandem with heavier, struck examples at the imperial mint; a specially commissioned gift for a high-ranking official; or perhaps an unofficial facsimile created directly or via a mold from a struck example rather than from the die at the mint.[41] We might describe it, die-matched as it is to

38 Iacobini 1991; Deckers 1998; Radnoti-Alföldi 2006; Stolz 2009. For a discussion of pressing gold sheets over struck coins and medals versus molds in a different context, see Jones 2019: 345n41. The Munich medallion can now be found in the collection of the Diözesan Museum Freising.

39 The exact rank and identity of the bridal couple have been a subject of fierce debate in the literature, effectively summarized in Stolz 2009: 115–16.

40 Atzori et al. 1999: 132; Sedda 2013, with preceding bibliography.

41 The Epiphany and Annunciation Medallions are among the largest struck medallions known, probably twenty solidi. Compare Grierson 1961: 221; Roma Numismatics Auction 2014: 281. Even at just under half the weight of the struck examples (Deckers 1998: 207), and allowing for

a struck example, as a first-degree copy, where the London pendant is a second-degree copy of (elements of) official issues, and the Madrid fibula and Berlin pendant third-degree (or more) copies, distant enough to perhaps be only loosely "inspired by." The drawings of the lost medallion, while themselves materially and temporally even more distant replicas, may represent a struck medallion or another first-degree copy.[42] I would suggest that each of these chains of replication, whether created through literal techniques of molding or not, was in some sense typological, an extension of the power of the imperial prototype, albeit with further amuletic invocations enacted through text and image. This kind of typological association could be very broad, indeed, and to the group of looser, more distant copies we can also add two identical medallions with narrative scenes now in the Istanbul Archaeological Museum, which are referred to as the Adana Medallions because they were said to come from Adana in southern Türkiye (Fig. 10.6).[43]

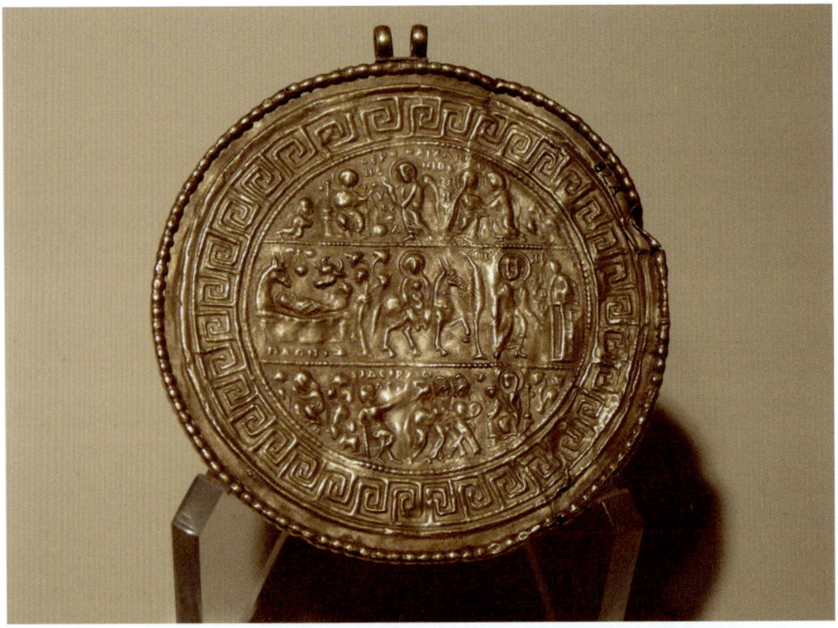

Fig. 10.6 Medallion with scenes from the life of Christ, sixth–seventh century CE, said to be from Adana (Türkiye). Istanbul Archaeological Museum (photograph by author).

some of that to lie in the frame and the gesso core, the Munich medallion is probably equivalent in weight to at least two solidi.

42 Both Smith (1914–19), who first published the drawings, and Entwistle (2005: 269–70) assume them to represent pressed gold disks rather than a monetary medallion, but neither was aware of the Annunciation Medallion.

43 Olsen Lam 2019: 46–50, with earlier bibliography.

Like the Berlin or London pendants, the Adana Medallions were made by mounting two pressed-gold disks back to back, probably with some filler in between. They include ornamental borders, loosely reminiscent of openwork frames, on the flanges of the disks themselves – a Greek key pattern on the obverse and a scroll pattern with busts of the apostles on the reverse – and their simple mounts are beaded. Like the struck Annunciation and Epiphany Medallions, they incorporate multiple scenes, creating a narrative. Unlike in the former examples, however, no one scene dominates. This format, which emphasizes narrative over iconic aspects, in some ways relates them more closely to objects like the lead pilgrims' ampullae preserved in Monza and Bobio than to known issues of the imperial mint.[44] Despite the relatively humble metal from which they were constructed, in comparison with precious metal coins, the ampullae drew their material power and efficacy from their holy contents. The ampullae of Monza and Bobio may themselves have been a royal gift to those monasteries.[45] In addition to such ampullae, which were also made in clay and contained oil from lamps burned at holy sites, many other forms of Holy Land relics and pilgrims' souvenirs circulated in the sixth-century CE Mediterranean. Another prominent category are clay *eulogia*, or blessings, made from the earth at or around sacred places. Though materially very different, these clay tokens are rather coin-like in their form. And like coins, their valuable matter is affirmed by the images stamped on them, which recall their sites of origin. As with coins converted to amulets, this process could also be inverted, as Vicky Foskolou has observed, such that through long association with holy matter, certain images could come to function autonomously: The power of the relic was transferred to the icon.[46] In addition to recalling pilgrimage art, the iconography of the obverse(s) of the Adana Medallions also tracks closely with the nativity cycle on the imperial medals. The postures of Mary and Gabriel and the curve of her throne in the upper register are mirror images of the larger examples (see Figs. 10.5a, 10.6). The swaddled child overlooked by ox and ass similarly repeats the iconography of the nativity on struck examples (see Figs. 10.4a, 10.5a, 10.6). The poses of Mary, Jesus, and the ass map perfectly on to the Flight into Egypt on the lost medallion (see Fig. 10.6). Variations in the inscriptions of these overlapping classes of objects (imperial medallions, amuletic medallions, pilgrimage art), however, may hint at subtle variations in their origins and functions.

[44] Another set of objects, also known in duplicate, that may be rarer and more costly pilgrim's tokens are two uniface pressed gold disks depicting the Incredulity of Thomas, which closely parallel flasks from Monza (Cotsonis and Nesbitt 2011).

[45] Grabar 1958; Filipová 2015. [46] Foskolou 2012: 58–9, with further bibliography.

The imperial medallions deploy biblical and liturgical quotations that are appropriate to the content of their iconography and that may also allude to the occasions of their creation and liturgies celebrated for those occasions. The shared obverse of the Annunciation Medallion and the sheet metal Munich medallion is inscribed with Gabriel's greeting to Mary: "Hail, most-favored/graceful one, the Lord is with you" (Luke 1.28), which in the liturgy of Mark became the first line of a well-known Marian prayer (see Fig. 10.5a).[47] André Grabar attributed the amuletic power of the Annunciation as an image to the layers of meaning inherent in the first word given to Gabriel by the gospel writer, Χαῖρε. His gloss of the word is more straightforward in the French (*Salut*) or Italian (*Salve*) editions of his text.[48] In both languages, the word can be used as a greeting but also implies health, well-being, and salvation, all of which the angel wishes to Mary and, through her as intercessor, to the faithful. Even the common English translation, however, "Hail," carries the implication of a wish for (hale) good health.

The reverse of the Annunciation Medallion, depicting the Ascension, borrows a line from Thessalonians 3:18 that also had a liturgical use: "The Grace of our Lord Jesus Christ be with you all."[49] The Munich medallion's nuptial reverse bears the same line from John as the marriage ring discussed earlier (14:27): "Peace I leave with you, my peace I give to you" (see Fig. 10.5b). The reverse of the Dumbarton Oaks Epiphany Medallion, with the Baptism of Jesus, quotes Matthew 3:17, "This is my beloved son in whom I am well pleased," a sentiment that resonates with the proposed occasion of its minting, the birth of an imperial heir (see Fig. 10.4b). The obverse of the Epiphany Medallion entreats divine aid. But unlike the other objects we have examined, its invocation is formulated in the plural and makes no mention of a wearer, thus gesturing not to an individual but to a community of believers: "Christ, our God, help us" (see Fig. 10.4a). This latter phrase echoes a refrain from the divine liturgies of Saint Basil and Saint John that were sung in Hagia Sophia. The official imperial issues are all therefore inscribed with formal language that carries liturgical and occasional resonance.

The inscriptions on the indirect copies of these imperial issues, such as the pendants in London and Berlin and the fibula in Madrid, sometimes reflect their sources directly, as on the reverse of the London pendant (see Fig. 10.3b),

[47] Olsen Lam 2019: 49.

[48] Indeed, I long overlooked this passage's significance in the original English text of Grabar's 1961 A. W. Mellon Lectures (Grabar 1968: 97–8). For the French, see Grabar 1979. In Italian translation, see Grabar 2021.

[49] Metlich 2003: 110.

perhaps modeled directly on the Ascension on the reverse of the Annunciation Medallion. More frequently, however, they deploy a different strategy.[50] Their straightforward pleas for aid from holy figures can also be found on a wide variety of other objects intended to be worn or carried on the body. The Adana Medallions do not fit neatly into either of these categories: official/liturgical or apotropaic/magical. They seem at first to be closest to the imperial models; they carry Gabriel's greeting on their obverse in the upper register (see Fig. 10.6). Andrea Olsen Lam has suggested that this caption, evoking a Marian prayer, could prompt viewers in their devotional practice, which would then be guided by the abbreviated labels, such as "in the manger," that punctuate other scenes.[51] The inscription that captions the Adoration is unusual, however. It reads: "Here is the *Basileus*," which Grabar understood to be both prophylactic and a direct reference to imperial power.[52] In Olsen Lam's view, by contrast, epigraphic and iconographic cues – including miniature kneeling figures – demand the viewer's attention to the holy figures.[53] The inscriptions of the London and Berlin pendants and the Madrid fibula, in contrast, ask for the holy figures' attention to be turned to the wearer.

Even more difficult to interpret but undoubtedly related are ten uniface, or one-sided, gold discs, often described as bracteates, from Basilicata and the Ionian coast of Calabria in southern Italy,[54] which include at least two examples with the Adoration of the Magi (Fig. 10.7) and one of Christ in Majesty with Angels that could be excerpted from a more elaborate image of the Ascension.[55] They also include images of mounted warrior saints. The bracteates differ from the other gold, numiform ornaments with Christian imagery in several respects. To begin with, at least as currently preserved, they are chiefly uniface. While the Madrid fibula, unlike the pendants, is also only figured on one side, it has

50 To these examples, we can add two fibulae, cited by Entwistle (2005: 272), in the Demirjian Collection and the Fribourg Museum.

51 Olsen Lam (2019: 49–50) also points to small kneeling figures that might also act as devotional cues.

52 Grabar 2021: 129; Entwistle 2005: 273.

53 Olsen Lam 2019: 48–50.

54 The connection among (then known examples of) this diverse group of objects was previously made by Volbach (1943–4, with preceding bibliography). For the Italian bracteates, Pannuti 2011 collects six examples with reasonably well-attested provenance. To these, we can add a further three catalogued by Baldini Lippolis (1999: 172), who omits the six discussed by Pannuti because they cannot be securely identified as jewelry.

55 Some of the bracteates may have been cut down. Baum 1934 collects further examples of the Adoration, including (possibly gilded) bronzes in the Vatican and pieces that are now lost. Both Smith (1914–19) and Volbach (1943–4) class the medallion from the Paper Museum with the south Italian bracteates, further demonstrating the fungibility of these categories.

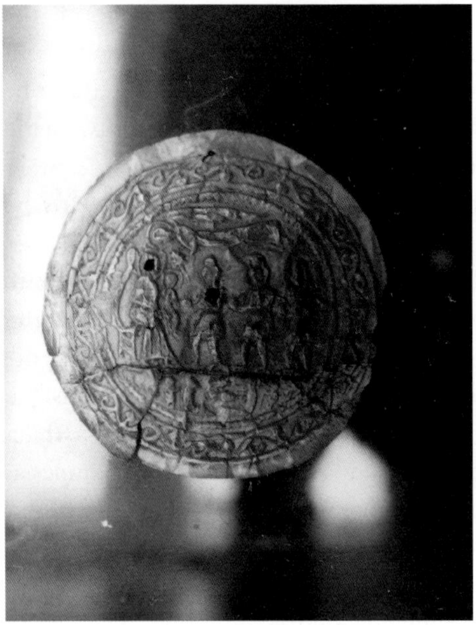

Fig. 10.7 The Adoration of the Magi (medallion, isolated work) – south Italian workshop (late sixth–early seventh century) Sopratindenza per i Beni Storici Artistici ed Etnoantropologici della Calabria

a second piece that forms the back, to which the findings for its pin were soldered. In contrast, the bracteates are not "finished" as jewelry objects in the same way: They have no backs, no frames, and no suspension loops or other jewelry findings. They have sometimes been interpreted as funerary ornaments that might have been sewn to fabric, though that argument has been refuted by Isabella Baldini.[56] Their status as wearables has been uncertain. Reports from the discovery of the Siderno bracteate with the Adoration of the Magi, now in the Museo Archeologico Nazionale di Locri (see Fig. 10.7), suggest that it was originally affixed by resin to a wooden box that disintegrated upon exposure to air.[57] Nonetheless, it retains certain formal resonances with more elaborate pendants. Like the Adana Medallions and a southern Italian bracteate of two warrior saints now in Berlin, it incorporates ornamental borders that mimic the openwork frames of richer pendant medallions.[58] Those

[56] Baldini Lippolis 1999: 167; Pannuti 2011: 343. [57] Di Lorenzo 1886.

[58] The Siderno bracteate was for many years in the Museo Archeologico Nazionale di Reggio Calabria (now reorganized as the Museo Nazionale della Magna Grecia). I am grateful to the staff of the Museo Archeologico Nazionale di Locri for going out of their way to provide me access to the bracteate.

ornamental borders, as well as the ways in which the images of the Adoration and of Christ in Majesty loosely mimic the struck medallions and their closer copies, suggest that these disks participate in the same visual and social economy of protective images, derived not only from biblical stories but also from imperial, numismatic prototypes.[59]

Margherita Corrado has connected the southern Italian bracteates to finds of box fibulae in the Balkans and further afield, raising the possibility that in many cases they may have been encased in silver frames that were damaged or discarded.[60] This supposition is confirmed in part by an early illustration of a Virgin and Child bracteate now in Berlin, which Raffaele Garrucci claimed in the nineteenth century to have purchased in Naples.[61] Its silver frame appears simpler than some of the more elaborate versions, such as a repoussé Adoration in the British Museum (1987,0101.1), but it accords well with the fibula with the Adoration of the Magi from Attalens, Switzerland, found in the grave of a child (Fig. 10.8). The latter is, to my knowledge, the only example of a bracteate or box fibula with a protective inscription, an abbreviated *KE BOETHI* ("Lord, Help!").[62] Sheet metal ornaments found from the Alps to the Balkans to the Danube were not only made of pressed gold but also of gilded silver, bronze, and copper alloys. They were cast, hammered into molds, and worked in freehand repoussé. Their iconographic repertoire is limited and repetitive, overlapping substantially with pilgrimage artifacts, the southern Italian bracteates, and the imperial medallions and their copies. Images range from the mythological to the imperial to the Christian, many of which resonate with images from coins and from magical gems. Most have been found in the graves of women and children.[63]

A (slightly) wider corpus of Byzantine embossed gold pendants, which feature mythological characters and images of imperial apotheosis drawn from a pagan world, also overlaps with the repertoire of the box fibulae.[64] Some figures, such as Herakles and Omphale or Dionysos and his entourage, may have maintained an association with marriage celebrations well

[59] It is hard to discern, given the state of preservation, but tiny images of the Nativity appear in the exergue of the Siderno bracteate, an unmistakable parallel with the imperial Annunciation and Epiphany Medallions.

[60] Corrado 2003, 2004, 2011; Corrado and Gentile 2005–6. On connections between the Keszthely Culture and Italy, the Eastern Roman Empire, and the Merovingians, see Vida 2008.

[61] The early illustration is in Forrer 1893: pl. 13. For the account of its acquisition, Garrucci 1877: 122, where the hand-drawn illustration (pl. 479, no. 16) does not include the silver frame.

[62] Martiniani-Reber 2015: 366, no. 396, with earlier bibliography.

[63] Daim 2002; Toth 2005; Pannuti 2011.

[64] For the former, Daim 2002. For the latter, see e.g. Grabar 1951; Entwistle 2005: 273–5; Ross 2005: 135–9, no. 179A, pls. 92–3.

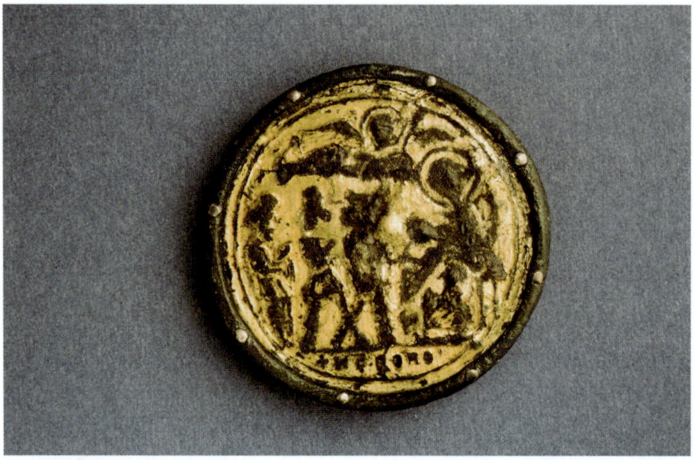

Fig. 10.8 Fibula with the Adoration of the Magi, sixth–seventh century CE, from Attalens. Gilded bronze. Fribourg, Musée d'art et d'histoire, MAHF 5823 (Musée d'art et d'histoire Fribourg).

into the early Middle Ages. One of the most recognizable and most amorphous images of power is a figure on horseback, often spearing an animal, monster, or demon. Frequently called the "Holy Rider," the mounted warrior defeating evil is identified on the box fibulae as Bellerophon, on the bracteates as one or more warrior saints, and on overtly magical amulets as King Solomon. The conqueror on horseback is also, of course, an eternal image of the ruler. One example in the Kelsey Museum of Archaeology, in Ann Arbor, Michigan, a bronze amulet with King Solomon spearing a demon and greeted by an archangel, illustrates the collapse of these identities into a singular type with its inscription: "One God who conquers evil" (Fig. 10.9a–b). The reverse depicts Christ enthroned in a mandorla surrounded by the symbols of the Evangelists/Beasts of the Apocalypse, with the notation "Holy, Holy, Holy, Lord Sabaôth," underlined by magical *charakteres*, and in the margin: "The seal of the Living God guard from Evil him who carries this."[65]

Another amulet preserved in an electrotype copy at the British Museum (Fig. 10.10a–b) pairs a bust of Christ in a mandorla lifted up by four angels in the distinctive pose of the imperial medallions (and the Monza ampullae) in an abbreviated scene of the Ascension with a winged, Horus-like figure. The former overlooks three registers of miniature narrative scenes,

[65] Ann Arbor, Michigan, Kelsey Museum of Archaeology, 26119. Bonner 1946: 307, pl. 27, no. 324.

(a) (b)

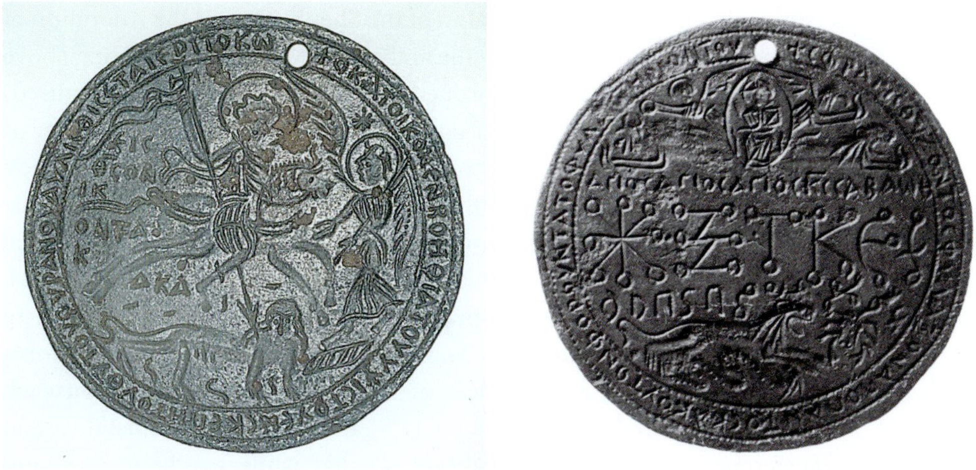

Fig. 10.9a–b Amulet with the Holy Rider (obverse) and Christ enthroned in a mandorla (reverse). Bronze. Ann Arbor, Michigan, Kelsey Museum of Archaeology, KM 0000.02.6119 (Kelsey Museum of Archaeology, University of Michigan).

(a) (b)

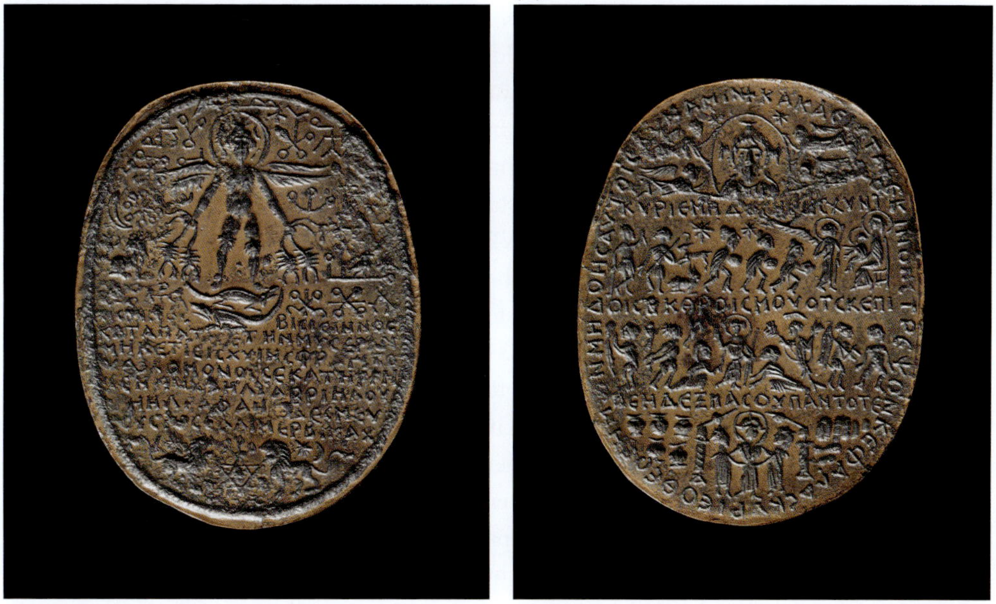

Fig. 10.10a–b Magical amulet with a bust of Christ in a mandorla and scenes from the life of Christ (reverse), twentieth-century electrotype of a sixth-century bronze (?) original. London, British Museum, 1938,1010.1 (© The Trustees of the British Museum).

not unlike those of the Adana Medallions, including, in the upper register, a composite image of the Adoration of the Shepherds and the Adoration of the Magi, all of whom are led by the archangel, who instead of flying above stands poised in front of an enthroned Mary in an echo of the (unpictured) Annunciation. The central vertical axis passes through a standing figure of Jesus healing the Woman with the Issue of Blood, among other miracles, and concludes at the bottom with a pronubial Christ, joining together the bride and groom, flanked by wine jugs, at Cana. These overtly magical objects employ different materials and words but nonetheless use a round, coin-like form and simple, adaptable iconography to offer protection to their wearers in much the same way as the numismatic and nummiform jewelry. The tight interwovenness of text, image, and material on such objects – like on Holy Land eulogia – allows for the meldability and transference of their various powers, so that while words, images, and matter can amplify each other, all three are not required.

The Materiality and Semiotics of Magical Relief

Despite a general ambivalence, if not outright distaste, for the luxury represented by the materiality of gold in Republican and Imperial Rome, there are some uses of the substance toward which Pliny the Elder, still widely read in late antiquity, is neutral or approving: the ancient tradition of gold bullae – round, convex, usually undecorated pendants – as amulets for young boys, the limited use of gold as a status symbol, and the limited use of gold as a symbol of divine honors (*HN* 33.10, 29, 39). Pliny also details the beneficial medicinal uses that were ascribed to gold. It is useful not only for children's amulets, guarding them against "poisonous charms," but can also serve as an amulet for the wounded (*HN* 33.84). In addition, the physical application of gold to sick persons can lead to a cure, and if specially prepared with salt, copper, and other ingredients, it makes a poultice to draw poisons out of the body. If it is burned with other substances, the ash that remains after the (incorruptible) gold has been removed can also be used as a poultice for acne, fistulas, and hemorrhoids. Prepared in other ways, it is appropriate for other ailments (*HN* 33.84–5). The ash preparation detailed by Pliny may be related to the "goldsmith's ash" that appears repeatedly in spells in the Greek Magical Papyri.[66] All these charms and cures have in common the fact that they are either worn on or applied to the body of the afflicted person. The

[66] E.g. *PGM* 4.2005, 2105, 3202, translated in Betz 1992: 73, 75, 100.

application of gold to the body worked to transfer its quality of incorruptibility to the flesh through the direct medium of physical contact.[67] The contagious power of touch allows the incorruptible gold to produce its like-from-like healing effect.

Amulets and talismans have traditionally been defined as objects or charms worn on the body that are believed to avert evil and draw good, respectively. Modern scholarship has come to accept that the aversion of evil and the attraction of good fortune are rarely mutually exclusive, and the two terms are today used almost interchangeably.[68] In the premodern Mediterranean, an amulet could consist of an object made from a material believed to have beneficial properties and/or an object inscribed with protective or beneficial symbols. Examples of amulets range from simple knotted cords to the kinds of spells, charms, or incantations written on papyrus or metal sheets, rolled up, and worn as described in the Greek Magical Papyri, a set of heterogeneous documents produced from the second century BCE to the fifth century CE and probably largely compiled by a single collector in late antique Egypt. Plain or inscribed stones could also serve as amulets. As Pliny attests, in the Roman world, simple gold ornaments, such as bullae, could also be considered amulets. Amulets could, in theory, be worn by both men and women and by all social classes. Many of the surviving depictions of amulets, like those of the mummy portraits, show them worn by children, who were seen as particularly vulnerable.[69]

The kind of amulets described and depicted in the Greek Magical Papyri or represented by the objects known as magical gems – with their syncretism, long strings of magical names and unpronounceable characters, and sometimes crude artistic depictions – seem far removed from refined opulence of gold numismatic jewelry.[70] But on the level of their components and how they function, there are deep parallels. At their most sophisticated, Greco-Roman and late antique amulets are composed of a material that is believed to be inherently beneficial, and which may or may not be precious or semiprecious, a visual representation of a divine figure and magical words, including especially the name(s) of the deity invoked. The centrality of images, sacred names, and magical invocations on amulets was recognized by John

67 "Sympathetic magic" is most frequently associated with Frazer, but the principle of sympathy was well known to the ancients. See Frazer 1925: 11; Barasch 1992: 77. For an excellent overview of anthropological theories of magic since Frazer, see Collins 2008: 1–26.

68 Bonner 1946: 26. I use both terms interchangeably and in the broader sense of "talisman" defined by Dureau (2002: 23) as "an object or a parchment bearing a text or image meant to either protect the bearer, or endow him with precise powers."

69 E.g. Walker and Bierbrier 2000: 108, no. 94. On children's amulets, see Dasen 2003: 275–89.

70 For magical gems, see Bonner 1946; Michel 2004. For magic and money, see Maguire 1997.

Chrysostom (ca. 347–407 CE), who wrote: "Each of you knows that those who trust in incantations are introduced in that way to amulets and the spells of witches; and the image of the cross is surely then covered in shame, since the letters (that cover it) are held in even greater honor" (*Ep. ad Col. Hom.* 8.5).[71] The image evoked by Chrysostom is illustrated almost perfectly by a surviving gem in the British Museum (Fig. 10.11), of uncertain date, but probably the third or fourth century CE, which depicts the crucified Christ surrounded by text, which reads "Lord, Father, Jesus Christ," followed by a string of magical symbols and bracketed with the magical name IAO, generally understood as the Greek transliteration of the Hebrew YAHWEH, but also recognized as standing, on gems and in the magical papyri, as a generic icon of power not unlike the imperial portrait.

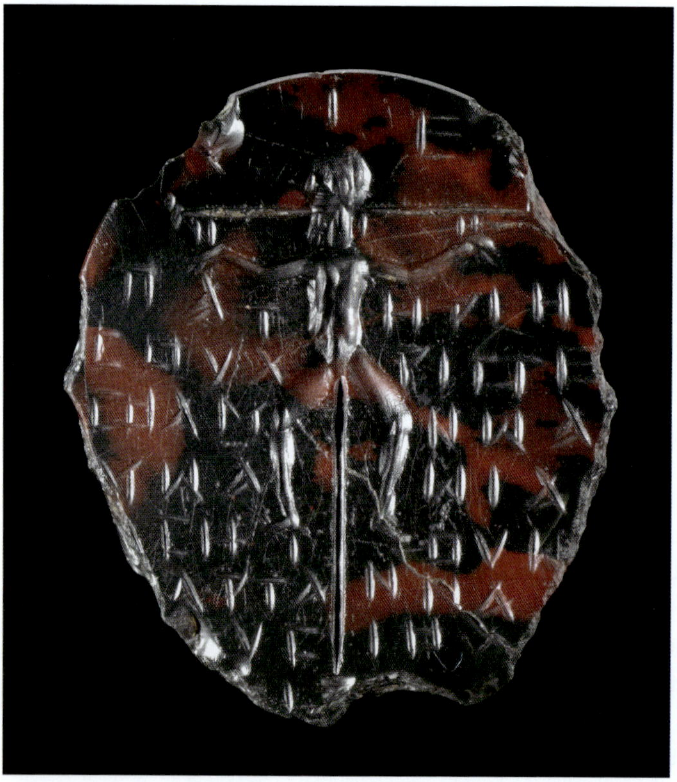

Fig. 10.11 Magical gem with crucified figure. Jasper. London, British Museum, 1986,0501.1 (© The Trustees of the British Museum).

[71] Janowitz 2002: 15.

In numismatic jewelry, the relationship observed by Chrysostom between text and image is reversed. Where the avoidance of images or the drawing or engraving of unsophisticated stick figures may perhaps have made most phylacteries and amulets more accessible, since they did not require a skilled craftsman to instill them with efficacy, coins came pre-stamped with an identifying legend (although in coin-set jewelry that was often obscured), and an official, visual icon – the coin type. The coins' origin at the imperial court, from which they passed directly or indirectly into the hands of those who commissioned the jewelry in which they were set, no doubt added to the authority of their iconic images. Both the iconic and material portions of the amulet worked to protect the wearer by transmitting their positive properties through the sympathetic magic of touch. In the case of numismatic jewelry, gold thus transmitted its incorruptibility, while the icon of the emperor allowed access to his power and protection, which could also be transmitted via touch. In the sixth-century medallions, which code Christian figures as imperial figures or imperial figures as Christian figures, that transmission of authority is sustained through the medium of relief. As discussed earlier in this chapter, direct and indirect copies of the official issues were also produced via molds or impressions, and while our surviving examples are rare in the material record, they were almost certainly produced in multiples.[72] The modality of replication preserved the authoritative images and enabled their diffusion.

Ancient amulets and talismans could be multilayered objects consisting of a potent icon in words or images inscribed on a beneficial material. Worn on the body, they could transmit the power of the icon and the beneficial qualities of the material to the wearer via touch, while simultaneously repelling evil forces. Unlike magical gems that relied on the divine names and magical incantations, the authoritative imperial – and later Christological and Marian – image type on gold coins and struck medallions served as a ready-made icon stamped on a health-bringing material characterized by its incorruptibility. The characteristics of coin-set jewelry used as amulets – image, gold, touch – illuminate the mechanisms by which amulets and talismans could function more generally. Medallic amulets, molded in relief and modeled on direct and indirect imperial prototypes, engaged a range of magical, imperial, and religious iconography. By the sixth century CE, the Eastern Roman Empire began issuing gold multiple

[72] On impression, replication, and tactility, see Jones 2019. Surviving jewelry molds are rare in the archaeological record, but for a steatite mold for casting (probably bronze) medallions of the Virgin and Child and of the Holy Rider, see Israeli and Mevorah 2000: 158; Spier 2007:120, pl. 139, fig. 13; Foskolou 2012: 65, fig. 12.

medallions on significant imperial occasions that used a new metaphorical language of religious imagery, overlaying and eliding the roles and powers of the Holy Family and the imperial *domus*. Where official issues deployed scriptural citations to both code metaphors and commemorate liturgies, copies of those issues, deploying the amuletic language of protection for a wearer, make explicit the use to which the imperial models could themselves be put.

Conclusion

We return, then, to the multiplicity of relief, its capacity not only to cross traditional artistic boundaries but indeed to mediate among the material, the metaphorical, and the metaphysical. The objects discussed here are reliefs in many senses of the term. They are visual reliefs, which play with the very idea of a figure–ground relationship by virtue of a set of nested dynamics: The Christian narrative scene or portrait of the emperors emerges in relief from the ground of the surface of the coin or medallion, which emerges from the ground of the framework linking the nummiform objects together. That framework, in turn, is articulated by and through relief effects of goldworking, such as granulation, embossing, repoussé, and chasing, and a physical surface that at one point functions as ground might at another appear as figure. And when worn, the ensemble emerges as figure from a most unlikely visual ground: the human body. Hanging from the neck and set on the chest of a living, breathing human wearer, the work of numismatic jewelry is enlivened by the movement of the body, but it, in turn, fixes the body into the blank background from which it can offer visual relief.

Other relief logics are equally in play in this dynamic. As this chapter has discussed at length, the coins and medallions that form the backbone of numismatic jewelry are typologically produced. Squeezed into molds by the force of a single blow, these official issues are given shape through a process that dominated ancient thinking on relief in relation to perception and cognition. But they, in turn, become authoritative types for other, less mechanical means of image production and reproduction, including pressed gold foil and freehand repoussé. What the shared chain of amuletic invocations among all these objects reveals, then, is the common authority of the image type, regardless of the mechanicity of its circulation and dissemination. The logic of the relief, in other words, is the driving force behind the efficacy of the numismatic and nummiform jewelry discussed here.

This brings us back, finally, to the sense of relief as alleviation: from physical pain, from psychic distress, from metaphysical threat, and indeed from damnation. The verb most commonly employed on these objects, βοηθέω, is often rendered as "come to aid," "assist," or "aid," but it can have the medicinal sense of "to be an antidote to,"[73] and the noun βοήθεια can explicitly mean "cure."[74] The help that these objects request, accordingly, can at least partially be understood as relief – as a lightening or lifting away of afflictions. Whether these afflictions are corporeal, spiritual, or both may be left unresolved, but the metaphor of the relief from distress is clear enough. What is most striking is that these objects combine so many layers of relief in the modern English senses of the word – the visual, the typological, the phenomenological, and the corporeal.

References

Atzori, M., Acquaro, E., Mariani, V., Pirozzi, G., and Flore, S. (1999). *Gli ornamenti preziosi dei sardi: Dai Fenicio-Punica al primo Novecento*. Sassari: Delfino.

Auerbach, E. (1959). "Figura" in *Scenes from the Drama of European Literature: Six Essays*. New York: Meridion Books. 11–76.

Baldini Lippolis, I. (1999). *L'oreficeria nell'impero di Costantinopoli tra IV e VII secolo*. Bari: Edipuglia.

Balmaseda Muncharaz, L. J. (2009). "Orfebrería epigrafada de época Visigoda en el Museo Arqueológico Nacional." In J. C. Galende Díaz and J. de Santiago Fernández, eds., *VIII Jornadas Científicas sobre documentación de la Hispania altomedieval (siglos VI–X)*. Madrid: Universidad Complutense de Madrid, 11–42.

Barasch, M. (1992). *Icon: Studies in the History of an Idea*. New York: New York University Press.

Bastien, P. (1988). *Monnaie et donativa au Bas-Empire*. Numismatique romaine 17. Wetteren: Numismatique Romaine.

Baum, J. (1934). "Die Goldbrakteaten von Attalens und La Coppelenanz." *Schwizerische numismatische Rundschau = Revue suisse de numismatique = Rivista svizzera di numismatica* 26.4: 394–404.

Bąkowska-Czerner, G., Roccati, A., and Świerzowska, A., eds. (2015). *The Wisdom of Thoth: Magical Texts in Ancient Mediterranean Civilisations*. Oxford: Archaeopress.

Belting, H. (1994). *Likeness and Presence: A History of the Image before the Era of Art*. Trans. E. Jephcott. Chicago. IL: University of Chicago Press.

[73] *LSJ*, s.v. βοηθέω, 2. [74] *LSJ*, s.v. βοήθεια, 2.

Betz, H. D. (1992). *The Greek Magical Papyri in Translation, Including the Demotic Spells*. Vol. 1, *Texts*. 2nd ed. Chicago, IL: University of Chicago Press.
Biliarsky, I. (2014). "Legitimating Figure: Women, Marriage and Power." Centre for Advanced Study Sofia Working Papers 6: 1–23.
(2015). "Marriage and Power (Images of Authority)." *Studia Ceranea* 5: 9–32.
Bonner, C. (1946). *Studies in Magical Amulets, Chiefly Graeco-Egyptian*. Ann Arbor: University of Michigan Press.
Boschung, D., and Bremmer, J. N., eds. (2015). *The Materiality of Magic*. Morphomata 20. Leiden: Brill.
Brown, P. (2012). *Through the Eye of a Needle: Wealth, the Fall of Rome, and the Making of Christianity in the West, 350–550 AD*. Princeton, NJ: Princeton University Press.
Brubaker, L., and Tobler, H. (2002). "The Gender of Money: Byzantine Empresses on Coins (324–802)." In P. Stafford and A. B. Mulder-Bakker, eds., *Gendering the Middle Ages*. Oxford: Blackwell, 42–64.
Bühl, G., ed. (2008). *Dumbarton Oaks: The Collections*. Washington, DC: Dumbarton Oaks Research Library and Collection.
Bussels, S. (2012). *The Animated Image: Roman Theory on Naturalism, Vividness and Divine Power*. Leiden: Leiden University Press.
Carlà, F. (2009). *L'oro nella tarda antichità: Aspetti economici e sociali*. Turin: Zamorani.
Collins, D. (2008). *Magic in the Ancient Greek World*. Malden, MA: Blackwell.
(2015). *Magic and Demons: Antiquity and Its Legacy*. London: Bloomsbury.
Corrado, M. (2003). "Note sul problema della lamine bratteate altomedievali dal Sud Italia." In P. Peduto and R. Fiorillo, eds., *Atti del III Congresso nazionale di archeologia medievale (Salerno, 2–5 ottobre 2003)*. Florence: Giglio, 110–14.
(2004). "Tarda antichità e alto medioevo nell'odierna calabria centro-orientale: Il terriorio di Crotone nei reperti della raccolta Attianese." *Archivio storico per la Calabria e la Lucania* 71: 5–34.
(2011). "I Magi 'di Siderno' dal XIX al XXI secolo: Resistenze antiquarie nell'era di internet." Paper presented at the conference Aspetti e problemi del Tardo-Antico nella Calabria Jonica: Territorio, materiali, iconografie, organized by the Circolo di Studi Storici "Le Calabrie" in the ex-Convento dei Minimi di Gioiosa Ionica, 15 April.
Corrado, M., and Gentile, A. M. (2005–6). "Fortune calabresi di San Teodoro di Amasea: Dalle fibule altomedievali con lamine bratteate agli stemmi civici di età moderna." *Studi Calabresi* 5–6.6–7: 19–38.
Cotsonis, J. and Nesbitt, J. (2011). "An Early Byzantine Lead Seal with an Image of the Incredulity of Thomas." *Byzantion* 81: 127–37.
Daim, F. (2002). "Pilgeramulette und Frauenschmuck? Zu den Scheibenfibeln der frühen Keszthelly-Kultur." *Zalai Múzeum* 11: 113–32.
Dasen, V. (2003). "Les amulettes d'enfants dans le monde gréco-romain." *Latomus* 62.2: 275–89.

Deckers, J. (1998). "Medaillon (enkolpion)," In L. Wamser and G. Zahlhaas, eds., *Rom und Byzanz: Archälogische Kostbarkeiten aus Bayern*. Munich: Hirmer, 207–11, no. 308.

Dennison, W. (1918). *A Gold Treasure of the Late Roman Period from Egypt*. Studies in East Christian and Roman Art 2. New York: Macmillan.

Di Lorenzo, R. (1886). "Regione III (Lucania et Brutii) XXV: Siderno; Lamina d'oro istoriata trovata in una tomba cristiana a Siderno." In *Notizie degli scavi di antichità*. Rome: R. Accademia dei Lincei, 137–8.

Drpić, I. (2018). "The Enkolpion: Object, Agency, Self." *Gesta* 57.2: 197–224.

Dureau, Y. (2002). "The Talisman or the Word as an Object and as an Image-Signifier." *Semiotica* 139: 23–62.

Edmonds, R. G. (2019). *Drawing Down the Moon: Magic in the Greco-Roman World*. Princeton, NJ: Princeton University Press.

Elsner, J. (2018). *Art of the Roman Empire: 100–450 AD*. 2nd ed. Oxford: Oxford University Press.

Endreffy, K., Nagy, Á. M., and Spier, J., eds. (2019). *Magical Gems in Their Contexts: Proceedings of the International Workshop Held in the Museum of Fine Arts, Budapest, 16–18 February 2012*. Rome: Bretschneider.

Entwistle, C. (2005). "Some Notes on Two Late-Antique Gold Pendants in the British Museum." In N. Crummy, ed., *Image, Craft and the Classical World: Essays in Honour of Donald Bailey and Catherine Johns*. Montagnac: Mergoil, 267–76.

Faraone, C. A. (1992). *Talismans and Trojan Horses: Guardian Statues in Ancient Greek Myth and Ritual*. Oxford: Oxford University Press.

(2012). "Text, Image and Medium: The Evolution of Graeco-Roman Magical Gemstones." In C. Entwistle and N. Adams, eds., *Gems of Heaven: Recent Research on Engraved Gemstones in Late Antiquity, AD 200–600*. London: British Museum, 50–61.

(2018). *The Transformation of Greek Amulets in Roman Imperial Times*. Philadelphia: University of Pennsylvania Press.

Fejfer, J. (2008). *Roman Portraits in Context*. Berlin: De Gruyter.

Filipová, A. (2015). "On the Origins of the Monza Collection of Holy Land *Ampullae*: The Legend of Gregory the Great's Gift of Relics to Theodolina Reconsidered." *Arte Lombarda*, n.s., vol. 173–4.1–2: 5–16.

Forrer, R. (1893). *Die frühchristlichen Alterthümer aus dem Gräberfelde von Achmim-Panopolis*. Strasbourg: Lohbauer.

Foskolou, V. (2012). "Blessings for Sale? On the Production and Distribution of Pilgrim Mementos in Byzantium." *Byzantinische Zeitschrift* 105.1: 53–84.

(2014). "The Magic of the Written Word: The Evidence of Inscriptions on Byzantine Magical Amulets." *Δελτίον της χριστιανικής αρχαιολογικής εταιρείας* 35: 329–48.

Frankfurter, D., ed. (2019). *Guide to the Study of Ancient Magic*. Leiden: Brill.

Frazer, J. G. (1925). *The Golden Bough: A Study in Magic and Religion*. London: Macmillan.

Fulghum, M. M. (2001). "Coins Used as Amulets in Late Antiquity." In S. R. Asirvatham, C. O. Pache, and J. Watrous, eds., *Between Magic and Religion*. Lanham, MD: Rowman and Littlefield, 139–47.

Garrucci, R. (1877). *Storia dell'arte cristiana nei primi otto secoli della chiesa*. Vol. 4, *Musaici cimiteriali e non cimiteriali*. Prato: Guasti.

Gell, A. (1994). "The Technology of Enchantment and the Enchantment of Technology." In J. Coote and A. Shelton, eds., *Anthropology, Art and Aesthetics*. Oxford: Clarendon Press, 40–63.

Gemini Numismatic Auctions. (2009). "Unique Byzantine Presentation Medallion." Lot 593, Gemini Numismatic Auctions VI, Sunday, January 10, 2010, Chicago, 102–3.

(2011). "Unique Byzantine Marriage Medallion." Lot 928, Gemini Numismatic Auctions VII, Sunday, 9 January 2011, Chicago, 165–6.

Grabar, A. (1951). "Un Médaillon en or provenant de Mersine en Cilicie." *Dumbarton Oaks Papers* 6: 25, 27–49.

(1958). *Les ampoules de Terre Sainte*. Paris: Klincksieck.

(1968). *Christian Iconography: A Study of Its Origins*. The A. W. Mellon Lectures in the Fine Arts, 1961, National Gallery of Art, Washington, DC. Princeton, NJ: Princeton University Press.

(1979). *Les voies de la création en iconographie chrétienne, Antiquité et Moyen Âge*. Paris: Flammarion.

(2021). *Le vie dell'iconografia cristiana, Antichità e Medioevo*. 6th ed. Trans. R. Della Torre and M. Colombo and rev. M. della Valle. Milan: Jaca.

Grierson, P. (1961). "The Date of the Dumbarton Oaks Epiphany Medallion." *Dumbarton Oaks Papers* 15: 221–4.

(1999). *Byzantine Coinage*. 2nd ed. Washington, DC: Dumbarton Oaks Research Library and Collection.

Holliday, P. J. (1995). "Narrative Structures in the Francois Tomb." In P. J. Holliday, ed., *Narrative and Event in Ancient Art*. Cambridge: Cambridge University Press, 175–97.

Iacobini, A. (1991). "'Dextrarum Iunctio': Appunti su un medaglione aureo protobizantino." In *Studi in onore di Carlo Bo*. Notizie da Palazzo Albani: Rivista di storia e teoria delle arti 20. Urbino: Argalìa, 49–66.

Iannascoli, L. (2021). "Medaglione aureo." Pensiero in immagini: Taccuino di note degli studenti di storia dell'arte medievale della Università di Verona e Trento, April 4. https://pensieroimma.hypotheses.org/tag/annunciazione.

Israeli, Y. and Mevorah, D., eds. (2000). *Cradle of Christianity*. Jerusalem: The Israel Museum.

Janowitz, N. (2002). *Icons of Power: Ritual Practices in Late Antiquity*. University Park: Pennsylvania State University Press.

Jones, A. E. (2019). "Coins as Seals in Lombard Italy." In L. Whatley, ed., *A Companion to Seals in the Middle Ages*. Leiden: Brill, 333–54.

Kantorowicz, E. (1944). "The 'King's Advent' and the Enigmatic Panels in the Doors of Santa Sabina." *Art Bulletin* 26.4: 207–31.

Kateusz, A. (2015). "Ascension of Christ or Ascension of Mary? Reconsidering a Popular Early Iconography." *Journal of Early Christian Studies* 23.2: 273–303.

Kiyanrad, S., Theis, C., and Willer, L., eds. (2018). *Bild und Schrift auf "magischen" Artefakten*. Berlin: De Gruyter.

Kotansky, R. D. (2019). "Textual Amulets and Writing Traditions in the Ancient World." In Frankfurter 2019: 507–54.

Krautheimer, R. (1942). "Introduction to an 'Iconography of Mediaeval Architecture.'" *Journal of the Warburg and Courtauld Institutes* 5.1: 1–33.

Langlands, R. (2018). *Exemplary Ethics in Ancient Rome*. Cambridge: Cambridge University Press.

Leader-Newby, R. (2000). "The David Plates Revisited: Transforming the Secular in Early Byzantium." *Art Bulletin* 82.3: 407–27.

Lo Cascio, E. (2008). "The Function of Gold Coinage in the Monetary Economy of the Roman Empire." In W. V. Harris, ed., *The Monetary Systems of the Greeks and Romans*. Oxford: Oxford University Press, 160–73.

Lorenz, J. (2020). *Römische Medaillons der Severerzeit: Julia Domna, Caracalla und Geta*. Schriften zur Klassischen Archäologie 6. Hamburg: Kovač.

Maguire, H. (1997). "Magic and Money in the Early Middle Ages." *Speculum* 72.4: 1037–54.

Martiniani-Reber, M. (2015). *Donation Janet Zakos: De Rome à Byzanze*. Geneva: Musée d'art et d'histoire.

Mastrocinque, A., Sanzo, J. E., and Scapini, M., eds. (2020). *Ancient Magic Then and Now*. Stuttgart: Steiner.

Metcalf, W. E., ed. (2012). *The Oxford Handbook of Greek and Roman Coinage*. Oxford: Oxford University Press.

Metlich, M. (2003). "Religious Byzantine Medallions and Plaques Struck in Gold." *Israel Numismatic Journal* 15: 107–11.

Michel, S. (2004). *Die Magischen Gemmen: Zu Bildern und Zauberformeln auf geschnittenen Steinen der Antike und Neuzeit*. Berlin: Akademie.

Mittag, P. F. (2010). *Römische Medaillons*. Vol. 1, *Caesar bis Hadrian*. Stuttgart: Steiner.

(2019). *Römische Medaillons*. Vol. 2, *Antoninus Pius*. Stuttgart: Steiner.

Moorhead, S. (2012). "Coinage of the Later Roman Empire, 364–498." In Metcalf 2012: 601–32.

Morisson, C., and Bendall, S. (2012). "Byzantine 'Medals': Coins, Amulets and Piety." In D. Sullivan, E. Fisher, and S. Pappaioannou, eds., *Byzantine Religious Culture: Studies in Honor of Alice Mary Talbot*. Leiden: Brill, 217–38.

Nagel, A., and Wood, C. S. (2010). *Anachronic Renaissance*. New York: Zone.

Nagy, Á. M. (2012). "Magical Gems and Classical Archaeology." In C. Entwistle and N. Adams, eds., *Gems of Heaven: Recent Research on Engraved Gemstones in Late Antiquity, AD 200–600*. London: British Museum, 75–81.

(2015). "Engineering Ancient Amulets: Magical Gems of the Roman Imperial Period." In D. Boschung and J. N. Bremmer, eds., *The Materiality of Magic*. Paderborn: Wilhelm Fink, 205–40.

Nesbitt, J. (2016). "Apotropaic Devices on Byzantine Lead Seals and Tokens in the Collections of Dumbarton Oaks and the Fogg Museum of Art." In C. Entwistle, ed., *Through a Glass Brightly: Studies in Byzantine and Medieval Art and Archaeology Presented to David Buckton*. Oxford: Oxbow, 107–13.

Nikki, N., and Valkama, K. M. J., eds. (2021). *Magic in the Eastern Mediterranean: Cognitive, Historical, and Material Perspectives on the Bible and Its Contexts*. Gottingen: Vandenhoeck and Ruprecht.

Ogden, J. M. (1990). "Gold Jewellery in Ptolemaic, Roman and Byzantine Egypt." PhD dissertation, Durham University.

Olsen Lam, A. (2019). "Female Devotion and Mary's Motherhood before Iconoclasm." In T. Arentzen and M. B. Cunningham, eds., *The Reception of the Virgin in Byzantium: Marian Narratives in Texts and Images*. Cambridge: Cambridge University Press, 44–61.

Osborne, J., and Claridge, A. (1998). *Early Christian and Medieval Antiquities*. Vol. 2, *Other Mosaics, Paintings, Sarcophagi and Small Objects*. Paper Museum of Cassiano dal Pozzo, series A: Antiquities and Architecture 2. London: Harvey Miller.

Pannuti, F. (2011). "Lamine auree bizantine dalla Calabria." In I. Baldini Lippolis and A. L. Morelli, eds., *Oggetti-simbolo: Produzione, uso e significato nel mondo antico*. Ornamenta 3. Bologna: Ante Quem, 337–51.

Parker, A., and McKie, S., eds. (2018). *Material Approaches to Roman Magic: Occult Objects and Supernatural Substances*. Oxford: Oxbow.

Porter. J. I. (2017). "Disfigurations: Erich Auerbach's Theory of Figura." *Critical Inquiry* 44: 80–113.

Radle, G. (2012). "The Development of Byzantine Marriage Rites as Evidenced by *Sinai Gr. 957*." *Orientalia christiana periodica* 78: 133–48.

Radnoti-Alföldi, M. (2006). "Ein rechgläubiger Christ, ein Römer, einer mit allen herrscherlichen Tugenden soll gewählt warden." In G. Seitz, ed., *Im Dienste Roms: Festschrift für Hans Ulrich Nuber*. Remshalden: Greiner, 27–33.

Roller, M. B. (2018). *Models from the Past in Roman Culture: A World of Exempla*. Cambridge: Cambridge University Press.

Roma Numismatics Auction. (2014). "Gold Medallion or Enkolpion." Lot 1144, Roma Numismatics Auction VIII, September 28. London, 281–9.

Ross, M. C. (1957). "A Byzantine Gold Medallion at Dumbarton Oaks." *Dumbarton Oaks Papers* 11: 247–61.

(2005). *Catalogue of the Byzantine and Early Medieval Antiquities in the Dumbarton Oaks Collection*. Vol. 2, *Jewelry, Enamels, and Art of the*

Migration Period. 2nd ed., with an addendum by S. A. Boyd and S. R. Zwirn. Washington, DC: Dumbarton Oaks Research Library and Collection.

Sedda, S. (2013). "Sulla Medaglia Aurea della Collezione Christian Schmidt di Monaco di Bavaria." *Theologia & Historica: Annali della Pontificia Facoltà Teologica della Sardegna* 22: 417–46.

Smith, E. B. (1914–19). "A Lost Encolpium and Some Notes on Early Christian Iconography." *Byzantinische Zeitschrift* 23: 217–25.

Spier, J. (2007). *Late Antique and Early Christian Gems*. Wiesbaden: Reichert.

Stewart, P. (2006). "The Image of the Roman Emperor." In R. Shepherd and R. Maniura, eds., *Presence: The Inherence of the Prototype within Images and Other Objects*. Aldershot: Ashgate, 243–58.

Stolz, Y. (2009). "Kaiserlich oder bürgerlich? Ein Anhänger in München, frühbyzantinische Diademe und anderer Hochzeitsschmuck." *Mitteilungen zur spätantiken Archäologie und byzantinischen Kunstgeschichte* 6: 115–35.

Tóth, E. (2005). "Zur Herkunft und Ikonographie der Scheibenfibeln der Keszthely-Kultur." *Zalai Mùzeum* 14: 183–202.

Toynbee, J. M. C. (1940). "Two New Gold Medallions of the Later Roman Empire." *Numismatic Chronicle and Journal of the Royal Numismatic Society*, 5th ser., vol. 20.77: 9–23.

(1986). *Roman Medallions*. Reprint ed. New York: American Numismatic Society.

van den Hoeck, A., Feissel, D., and Herrmann, J. T. (1994). "Lucky Wearers: A Ring in Boston and a Greek Epigraphic Tradition of Late Roman and Byzantine Times." *Journal of the Museum of Fine Arts Boston* 6: 41–62.

(2015). "More Lucky Wearers: The Magic of Portable Inscriptions." In Boschung and Bremmer 2015: 309–56.

Vida, T. (2008). "Conflict and Coexistence: The Local Population of the Carpathian Basin under Avar Rule (Sixth to Seventh Century)." In F. Curta and R. Kovalev, eds., *The Other Europe in the Middle Ages: Avars, Bulgars, Khazars, and Cumans. Vol. 2, East Central and Eastern Europe in the Middle Ages, 450–1450*. Leiden: Brill, 13–46.

Vikan, G. (1990). "Art and Marriage in Early Byzantium." *Dumbarton Oaks Papers* 44: 145–63.

Volbach, W. F. (1943–4). "Un medaglione d'oro con l'immagine di San Teodoro nel museo Reggio Calabria." *Archivio storico per la Calabria e la Lucania* 13: 65–72.

Walker, A. (2002). "Myth and Magic in Early Byzantine Marriage Jewelry: The Persistence of Pre-Christian Traditions." In A. L. McClanan and K. R. Encarnación, eds., *The Material Culture of Sex, Procreation, and Marriage in Premodern Europe*. New York: Palgrave, 59–78.

(2010). "Numismatic and Metrological Parallels for the Iconography of Early Byzantine Marriage Jewelry: The Question of the Crowned Bride." In C. Morrisson, ed., *Mélanges Cécile Morrisson*. Trauvaus et mémoires 16.

Paris: Association des amis du Centre d'histoire et civilisation de Byzance, 849–63.

Walker, S., and Bierbrier, M., eds. (2000). *Ancient Faces: Mummy Portraits from Roman Egypt*. New York: Routledge.

Watson, L. (2019). *Magic in Ancient Greece and Rome*. London: Bloomsbury.

Williams, E. D. (2014). "'Into the Hands of a Well-Known Antiquary of Cairo': The Assiut Treasure and the Making of an Archaeological Hoard." *West 86th: A Journal of Decorative Arts, Design History, and Material Culture* 21.2: 251–72.

Index